D0224325

The Urban Lifeworld

Formation, Perception, Representation

Urban conditions are crucial to our experience of modernity. Art and literature, as well as popular culture, have captured a variety of aspects of city-life and thus contributed to current attitudes toward urbanization.

The Urban Lifeworld investigates how perceptions and representations of the urban experience interact with the formation and transformation of cities. Two exceptional cities, New York and Copenhagen, are the focus of this exploration of urban fabric and urban culture.

Integrating sociological, anthropological and aesthetic, as well as architecural and urbanistic, approaches, this collection of essays presents a comprehensive approach to urban and cultural studies, which will enrich both academic studies and public debate about the future of cities.

This volume includes contributions by:

Christine Boyer • Peder Boas Jensen • Helle Bøgelund-Hansen • Birgitte Darger • Michael Eigtved • Andrea Kahn • Hans Ovesen • Jens Kvorning • Peter Madsen • Peter Marcuse • Joan Ockman • Anne Ring Petersen • Richard Plunz • Henrik Reeh • Grahame Shane • Robert W. Snyder • Gwendolyn Wright • Martin Zerlang

The Urban Lifeworld

Formation, Perception,
Representation

Edited by
Peter Madsen
and
Richard Plunz

London and New York

First published 2002
by Routledge
11 New Fetter Lane, London EC4P 4EE

Simultaneously published in the USA and Canada
by Routledge
29 West 35th Street, New York, NY 10001

Routledge is an imprint of the Taylor & Francis Group

Typeset in Sabon and Akzidenz Grotesk
by Florence Production Ltd, Stoodleigh, Devon

Printed and bound in Great Britain
by TJ International Ltd, Padstow, Cornwall

British Library Cataloguing in Publication Data
A catalogue record for this book is available from the British Library

Library of Congress Cataloging in Publication Data
The urban lifeworld / edited by Peter Madsen and Richard Plunz
    p. cm.
  Includes index.
    1. City and town life. 2. City and town life in art. 3. City and town life in
    literature. 4. Intellectual life. 5. Popular culture. 6. New York (NY).
    7. Copenhagen (Denmark) I. Title: Urban life world. II. Madsen, Peter
    III. Plunz, Richard.
HT119 .U693 2001
307.76–dc21   2001019575

ISBN 0–415–23403–4 (hbk)
ISBN 0–415–23177–9 (pbk)

Contents

Contributors

Peder Boas Jensen: Architect, Professor of Architecture at the School of Architecture, Royal Danish Academy of Fine Arts, Copenhagen.

Helle Bøgelund-Hansen: M.A. in Comparative Literature and Modern Culture; Ph.D. student, School of Architecture, Royal Danish Academy of Fine Arts, Copenhagen.

M. Christine Boyer: Ph.D. in Urban Planning; Professor of Urban Planning at the School of Architecture, Princeton University.

Birgitte Darger: M.A. in Comparative Literature and Modern Culture; faculty of the Free High School, Copenhagen.

Michael Eigtved: M.A. and Ph.D. in Music and Modern Culture; Assistant Professor, Department of Theatre History, University of Copenhagen.

Andrea Kahn: M.Arch; Adjunct Associate Professor of Architecture, Graduate School of Architecture, Planning and Preservation, Columbia University.

Jens Kvorning: Architect and Senior Lecturer, School of Architecture, Royal Danish Academy of Fine Arts, Copenhagen.

Peter Madsen: M.A. in Comparative Literature; Professor and Chair, Department of Comparative Literature, University of Copenhagen.

Peter Marcuse: Ph.D. in Urban Planning; Professor of Urban Planning, Graduate School of Architecture, Planning and Preservation, Columbia University.

Joan Ockman: B. Arch; Adjunct Associate Professor of Architecture and Director of the Temple Hoyne Buell Center for the Study of American Architecture, Graduate School of Architecture, Planning and Preservation, Columbia University.

Hans Ovesen: Architect and Senior Lecturer, School of Architecture, Royal Danish Academy of Fine Arts, Copenhagen.

Anne Ring Petersen: M.A. in Art History; Ph.D. from the Center for Urbanity and Aesthetics, Department of Comparative Literature, University of Copenhagen.

Richard Plunz: M.Arch; Professor of Architecture and Director of Urban Design Program, Graduate School of Architecture, Planning and Preservation, Columbia University.

Henrik Reeh: M.A. in History and Literature; Senior Lecturer, Department of Comparative Literature, University of Copenhagen.

Grahame Shane: Ph.D. in Architecture; Adjunct Professor of Architecture, Graduate School of Architecture, Planning and Preservation, Columbia University.

Robert W. Snyder: Ph.D. in American History; Associate Professor and Director of the Journalism and Media Studies Program, Visual and Performing Arts Department, Rutgers University, Newark.

Gwendolyn Wright: Ph.D. in Architectural History; Professor of Architecture, Graduate School of Architecture, Planning and Preservation, Columbia University.

Martin Zerlang: M.A. in Comparative Literature, Senior Lecturer, Department of Comparative Literature; 1993–1998 Head of Center for Urbanity and Aesthetics, University of Copenhagen.

Acknowledgements

Most of the essays in this collection have their origins in the conference on "The Urban Life World. Formation, Perception, Representation. Copenhagen and New York Compared," held at the University of Copenhagen in November 1977 and organized by the Editors in collaboration with the University of Copenhagen Center for Urbanity and Aesthetics and the Columbia University Urban Design Program. The conference and publication of this book were possible only through the generous support of the Faculty of Humanities of the University of Copenhagen.

For assistance with the conference and the preparation of this manuscript the Editors are especially indebted to Maiken Derno, Pernille Feldt, Annette Jallberg, Agus Soweto at the University of Copenhagen; and Akiko Kyei-Aboagye, Stephen Lynch, Sara Moss, and Melanie Taylor at Columbia University. We also wish to thank the archive staffs of the following institutions who have assisted in locating much of the visual material for this book: City Museum of Copenhagen (Bymuseet); Town Hall of Copenhagen (Stadsarkivet); Avery Architectural and Fine Arts Library; New York Public Library; Brooklyn Museum; National Gallery of Art; Smithsonian; Adirondack Museum; Keene Valley Library Assocation.

Finally we must mention the events of September 11, 2001 and the likelihood of their profound impact on life in New York City and cities elsewhere. We hope that this work contributes a vital discourse at this defining moment for the future of urban life.

Peter Madsen and Richard Plunz

Introduction

Peter Madsen

I CITY, DESIRE, KNOWLEDGE

In his "satire" *Rameau's Nephew*, Diderot starts out presenting himself sitting on a bench in the Garden of the *Palais Royal*: "I hold discussions with myself on politics, love, taste or philosophy, and let my thoughts wander in complete abandon, leaving them free to follow the first wise or foolish idea that comes along, like those young rakes we see in the Allée de Foy who run after a giddy-looking little piece with a laughing face, sparkling eye and tip-tilted nose, only to leave her for another, accosting them all, but sticking to none." [1]

This way of relating the movement of thought to the city (as a young lad following attractive girls) is radically different from Plato's treatment of the question of the ideal *polis* – except for the thinking in analogies. In Plato, reason, will, and desire are the modes of the human soul, and the just human being is he who lets reason govern desire with the help of will. The city should be justice writ large and thus easier to read than the soul of man. [2]

On the one hand, the city as manifestation of justice, on the other hand, the city as playground for desire and philosophical questioning; on the one hand, thought as search for insight in justice, on the other hand, thinking as joyful experiment. "In my case my thoughts are my wenches" – nothing could be farther away from the austere Platonic attitude than Diderot's mode of thinking, his *Gedankengang* – the German word indicates the *steps of thought*, the philosophical itinerary.

Yet the desire involved in Diderot's analogy is desire for insight, for knowledge. According to Freud the ground of all desire for knowledge is desire as such, i.e. of sexual nature. In the great *Encyclopedie* Diderot describes the reading of an encyclopedia as a stroll in a city, with references bringing one from one entry to another in an endless and lustful pursuit of knowledge, just as one moves from one point in the city to another, without any preconceived itinerary. *Thinking*, *desiring*, *learning* – the city is the world where these activities are intermingled.

What is hinted at in Diderot is the decisive principle in Walter Benjamin's later work. His book of memories, *Childhood in Berlin around 1900*, is an attempt to "secure the images sedimented by the experience of the metropol in a child of the bourgeoisie" as it is stated in the Preface. [3] *History*, rather than individual experience, is at stake, yet it is only through individual experience that Benjamin is able to grasp that which is historically significant:

> I inhabited the nineteenth century like a mollusc in the shell, that is lying in front of me now like a hollow conch. I lift it to the ear. What do I hear? I do not hear the noise of field artillery or Offenbach's ball music, nor the wailing of factory sirens or the shouts echoing

at noon in the halls of stock exchanges, not even the fidgeting of horses on the pavement or the flourish of the changing of the guard. No, what I hear is the brief rattling of the anthracite coal falling from the tin pail into the iron oven, it is the muffled crack at the ignition of the gas lamp, and the chinking of the lamp globe in the brass sleeve when a vehicle passes by in the street. (IV.1, 261–2)

This passage is typical both thematically and in the mode of expression. The vulnerable mollusc is protected, but also enclosed – in the interior. Elsewhere Benjamin describes how the child moves away from home and family. Simultaneously the image of the conch – a seaman's favorite souvenir – relates to the well-known phenomenon of empty shells seeming to contain sounds from their locus of origin, like whispering from the seven seas.

Here the image changes from space to time: the empty shell seems to preserve the sounds of the past. The medium of Benjamin's research is the image. The empty conch is one such image, but so are images brought forth through the act of memory, paired images of the past century: battlefield and operetta, i.e. death versus hectic joy – the German–French war and *la belle époque*; the pipe of the industrial plant and the shouting in the stock exchange: two aspects of *Gründerzeit* in the image of finance capital; and finally the noise of horses and flourish, i.e. emblems of the empire, Wilhemine masquerade, modernity's old-fashioned disguise about to be destroyed by the world war and the breakdown of the *German Reich*. Battlefield and operetta, industrial plant and stock exchange, parade and flourish: the late nineteenth century in one constellation of images. This was not what Benjamin's personal memory provided, but the mature Benjamin's reconstruction of the historical situation. His own memories have to do with the *interior*. But the universe of the interior is no less historical: before the advent of the automobile and electric lightbulbs, before central heating. His interest in the book of memories is often concentrated on interiors, the inner side of the historical process. The telephone represents the intrusion of technological change in the interior, personal universe: "Not many of those who use it today do still realize what uproar its appearance in the bosom of the family engendered. The sound it produced between two and four in the afternoon, when yet another friend from school wanted to talk to me was an alarm signal that not only disturbed my parents' afternoon nap, but the entire world historical epoch in which they indulged in it" (VII.1, 391).

The topography of the city is in Benjamin's account not only a question of streets, squares and buildings, but also of functions. In "*Krumme Strasse*," i.e. Twisted Street, the child should have payed his regular visit to the bathhouse, but finds it closed and turns his attention to a stationery shop instead. "Uninitiated gazes were caught by cheap Nick-Carter-booklets in the window. But I knew where to find the dubious publications in the back . . . I could by staring through the window for a long time use passbooks, compasses and scraps as an alibi, and then suddenly push forward into the bosom of this paper-creature. *Desire guesses what will turn out to be the most persistent in us*" (415, my italics). Without any explanation the municipal reading room is then introduced, for Benjamin it is his "essential area." Having turned away from *the cleaning bath* he is led by desire into the bosom (*in den Schoss*) of *the dirty shop* and from there to *the reading room – reading and desire are intertwined* whether the reading is concerned with texts or with cities. The last of Benjamin's short memory sketches is about the awakening of sexuality. This time the synagogue is the institution, which is avoided by young Benjamin. He is simultaneously overwhelmed both by a wave of anxiety for having broken the religious norm and by a wave of total recklessness, lack of bad conscience: "And both waves ceaselessly clashed in my first feeling of lust, in which the offense against the holy day was mixed with *the procuring air of the street* that at this occasion for the first time gave me a hint of *the services it would later grant the emerging desire*" (432, my italics).

New electronic devices, official spectacle and family interior, dubious side streets, religious and public institutions: the range of urban phenomena linked by personal involvement in the historical process is vast. No less complex are Benjamin's unfinished ruminations on Paris as the Capital of the Nineteenth Century, the "Arcades-Project," his attempt to "read" the city within a historical perspective. This is one of the most inspiring contributions to an understanding of the cultural role of cities, but also one of the most epistemologically complex.[4]

II SIGNIFYING BUILDINGS

In more than one sense, Martin Heidegger's peasants' farmhouse in *Schwarzwald* is far from Benjamin's Berlin or Paris. Its prominent place in his essay "Building Dwelling Thinking,"[5] which has attracted much attention in architectural theory, may motivate a consideration of the implications of Heidegger's approach. Although the essay has no immediate bearing on questions of urban analysis, it does indirectly shed some light on the question of the urban lifeworld.

In Aristotle, man is essentially a *polis*-being, Heidegger's approach is entirely different, his horizon is agrarian: "To be a human being means to be on the earth as a mortal" (349), since the German "bin" (meaning: are, is) is related to "the old word" "bauen," "which says that man *is* in so far as he *dwells*, this word *bauen*, however, *also* means at the same time to cherish and protect, to preserve and care for, specifically to till the soil, to cultivate the vine" (ibid.). "To build," "to dwell," "to cultivate," and "to be" belong to the same agrarian horizon. It is no wonder that the supposed Indo-European roots of the words, and thereby language, "the master of man" (348), would rather be related to the typical activities of ancient times than to modern ways and manners.

Heidegger's indifference, if not hostility to democratic politics, his identification of the entire system of communication with alienation (neglecting that the public sphere and the means of communication are essential to democratic politics and an enlightened horizon), his permanent anti-modern position in general, has made his analysis difficult for many readers to accept. There are, nevertheless, aspects of his texts which it would be foolish to reject altogether. Neither sheer exegesis or amplification of the text, nor a simple critique of his "ideology of authenticity" would be to the point. What would be gained from a critical reading of Heidegger's essay? A closer look at his more concrete analysis may provide some hints.

Here is his farmhouse in Schwarzwald, "which was build some two hundred years ago by the dwelling of peasants (*den vor zwei Jahrhunderten noch bäuerliches Wohnen baute*)" (361). First, then, the fully fledged metaphysics: "Here the self-sufficiency of the power (*die Inständigkeit des Vermögens*) to let earth and sky, divinities and mortals enter in simple oneness into things ordered the house" (362). It is remarkable that this sentence not only restates the general frame of the essay ("the fourfold" – earth, sky, divinities and mortals – as essential elements), but also provides a non-personal agent (parallel to language) as grammatical subject for the following description:

> It [i.e. "the self-sufficiency of the power"] placed the farm on the wind-sheltered mountain slope, looking south, among the meadows close to the spring [it is difficult not to take this spring as more than a source of water, and not also a kind of metaphor for "Ursprung,"[6] further: the source is so to speak the essential *earth*, emerging from the depths of the ground]. It gave it the wide overhanging shingle roof whose proper slope bears up under the burden of the snow, and that, reaching deeper down, shields the chambers against the storms of the long winter nights [and is thus in accordance with the *sky*]. It did not forget the altar corner behind the community table [representing the relation to the *divinities*]; it made room in its chamber for the hallowed places of childbed and the "tree of the dead" – for that is what they called the coffin there: the *Totenbaum* – and in this way it designed for the different generations under one roof the character of their journey through time [and thus the fourth aspect of the fourfold: *mortality*, is in place]. (ibid.)

And then Heidegger adds a sentence which further explains this "power": "A craft that itself sprung from the dwelling, still uses its tools and its gear as things [and not objects], built the farmhouse" (ibid.). The tradition, in other words, of craftsmanship, whomever the bearer of the specific activities, is the origin. The farmhouse thus emerges in the natural setting, under the sky, incorporating death and divinities – *Totenbaum* and altar, created by an anonymous essential power. In the center: the community table. *No human beings are present in the text*, only the essential features of their dwelling, their house and their life (this is, of course, consistent with Heidegger's anti-humanism).[7]

The farmhouse is the final example in the essay, with the first examples being "Bridges and hangars, stadiums and power stations . . . railway stations and highways, dams and market halls" (347). These are all modern constructs and edifices, none of which is intended for residential use. Nonetheless "residential buildings" do appear a few lines later, "but – do the houses in themselves hold any guaranty that *dwelling* occurs in them?" (348). This remains the question. From this modern world, with its idle communication and strife for "maximum yield" (354), the focus shifts by way of the example of the bridge (354–56). Its basic characteristic and task is simple: crossing a stream: "It brings stream and bank and land into each other's neighborhood. The bridge gathers the earth as landscape around the stream" (354). Yet it does also lead from one place to another, and it does so "in many ways" (ibid.): "The city bridge leads from the precincts of the castle to the cathedral square; the river bridge near the country town brings wagons and horse teams to the surrounding villages. The old stone bridge's humble brook crossing gives the harvest wagon its passage from the fields into the village and carries the lumber cart from the field path to the road" (ibid.). This is obviously an image of bygone days, the mention of the horses stressing the pre-modern context. Moreover it is worth noting that the movements lead to *the Cathedral* and *the village* respectively – not from the village to the town and the boisterous commerce at the marketplace, but in the other direction. The religious and the agrarian come together in the image of the bridge with "the figure of the saint of the bridge" (355), and this leads to Heidegger's conclusions concerning the "gathering" of "the fourfold." But in between there are some last reminiscences of the modern world, before everything retreats into the provinces and the road to death: "The highway bridge is tied into the network of long-distance traffic, paced and calculated for maximum yield" (354). The formulation, seen in contrast to the formulations related to the pre-modern, seems to suggest that these bridges and highways do not lead anywhere, that they simply set the scene for "the lingering and hastening ways of men to and fro" (ibid.). *The final image of the farmhouse is thus the culmination of the rejection of the modern world*, a rejection that simultaneously is "cleaning" the pre-modern world from features that would contaminate it and potentially highlight similarities with the modern world (like the activities at, and related to, the marketplace). It is further a world of preparation for death and the retreat of man in favor of tradition, craft, and language.

But what would happen if these two historical pictures were superimposed? What would occur if, that is, the features highlighted by Heidegger in the pre-modern context were taken into consideration in the modern context, preferably in a secularized form? The reception of Heidegger's essay has usually stressed his concern with the situation of the house in the natural surroundings (or the entirely abstract question of "the fourfold"), including climatic conditions. One line of argument based on Heidegger's essay has thus stimulated ideas about *genius loci*. However, in relation to the question of urban conditions there is another interesting aspect: Heidegger's concentration on crucial aspects of the human condition, *and* the way in which his essay provides an image of *situation* as *locus*, in a pattern of production and communication (not the least of goods).

It is illuminating to compare Heidegger's farmhouse to the Berber-house no less famously analyzed by Pierre Bourdieu.[8] The rectangular house is divided into two parts, one for the animals, and one – larger – for the family. A door in the middle of the longer eastern wall faces the rising sun and opens towards the outer world, the realm of the activities of the men. Opposite the door is the site of the weaving-loom, the woman's space and the source of protection, and in a sense the light of the house. Entering the main door and facing the weaving-loom, you'll have the fireplace to the right, again the woman's sphere. Between the main room and the stable there is a dividing wall and over the stable there is a loft. This is the "dark part" of the house:

> The dark, nocturnal, lower part of the house, the place for things that are damp, green or raw – jars of water placed on the benches on either side of the stable entrance or next to the wall of darkness [i.e. the dividing wall], wood, green fodder – and also the place for natural beings – oxen and cows, donkeys and mules – natural activities – sleep, sexual intercourse, childbirth, and also death – is opposed to the light-filled, noble, upper part. This is the place for human beings and especially the guest, for fire and things made with fire, such as the lamp, kitchen utensils, the rifle – the attribute of the male point of honor (*nif*) which protects female honor (*h'urma*) – and the loom, the symbol of all protection. It is also the site of the two specifically cultural activities performed within the house: weaving and cooking. (272–73)

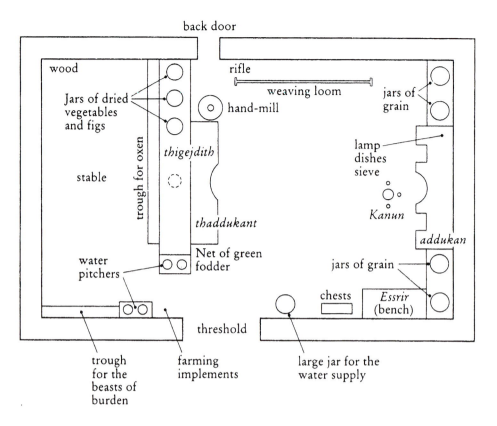

I.1 Plan of the Berber-house. From Pierre Bourdieu, *The Logic of Practice*, p. 272. Courtesy of Blackwell Publishers Ltd.

The organization of the house is based on a specific interrelationship between the sphere of humans, the sphere of animals, the sphere of the agrarian activity and the sphere of nature. Bourdieu's analysis clearly demonstrates, *that the organization of the house is not only based on technical considerations, but depends on patterns of imagination*: e.g. on the one hand, the position of the weaving-loom is technically motivated by the influx of light, but on the other hand the position also enters the pattern of interrelated oppositions. Bourdieu's analysis is vintage structuralism. Although in a way his object of analysis has features comparable to those analyzed by Heidegger, the approach is fundamentally different: in Heidegger's phenomenological analysis everything is referred back to essentials, in Bourdieu (as in Lévi-Strauss) everything is inserted within a structural pattern that is simultaneously material, practical, and symbolic.

The central part of the construction of the house is also at the center of the symbolic and ritual patterns:

> At the center of the dividing wall, between "the house of the humans" and "the house of the animals," stands the main pillar, supporting the "master beam" and the whole framework of the house. The master beam (*asalas alemmas*, a masculine term) which extends the

protection of the male part of the house to the female part, is explicitly identified with the master of the house, whereas the main pillar, a forked tree trunk (*thigejdith*, a female term), on which it rests, is identified with the wife . . ., and their interlocking symbolizes the sexual union. . . . (274–75)

"Thus," says Bourdieu, "this symbolic summary of the house, the union of *asalas* and *thigejdith*, which extends its fertilizing protection over all human marriage, is, like ploughing, a marriage of heaven and earth" (275).

These patterns are not only *symbolic*, they are also *ritual*. The word designating the transport of the master beam is the same as the word used to designate the loft (which belongs to the dark part of the house, the realm of death), and the "stretcher used to carry a corpse," and this transport "gives rise to a social ceremony, the meaning of which is exactly similar to that of burial" (note 4, 317). Marriage, childbirth, and death are symbolically and ritualistically related to the symbolic space of the house – or, to put it otherwise, the symbolic structure of the house is interrelated to the cycles of life as well as the cosmic space and the ancestors. These patterns, on the other hand, also govern everyday life. The man has to leave the house at daybreak (280), and in general be seen in the "male world of public life and farming work" (275). His life is a life among men in the open and in search of honor, whereas the woman stays hidden in the interior, which is conversely her privileged and, in some sense, secret space (ibid.). Just like the man leaves the house facing east – "towards the high, the bright, the good and the prosperous" (281), he "starts his ploughing from west to east" (ibid.). One word indicates the interrelatedness of these various levels of life: "It will suffice to note that the verb *qabel* means not only to face, to affront with honor and to receive in a worthy manner, but also to face the east (*lqibla*) and the future (*qabel*)."[9]

These are but a few of the intricacies of Bourdieu's immensely rich and fascinating analysis. But they suffice to give an idea of the way in which it demonstrates how the physical structure of the house is interrelated with the memory of ancestors, the overall interpretation of existence (the cosmological aspect), the rituals and symbolizations of the major phases and thresholds of life as well as with everyday life. The symbolic and ritual structure does not only concern the house and its interior, but also its relation to the exterior – most especially the limit between interior and exterior: the threshold, which is particularly rich in symbolic meaning and ritual prescriptions. The clues to the symbolic and ritual structures are not only physical (like the distribution of things, animals and humans in the space of the house) or derived from behavior, but also dependent upon language (as in the case of the transportation of the governing beam, or in the case of the verb *qabel*), and on more specific linguistic evidence like sayings, proverbs or adages.

III ANTHROPOLOGY OF THE URBAN LIFEWORLD

Appropriating the anthropological gaze in Bourdieu's study of the Berber-house for a renewed consideration of Heidegger's peasant house could have an estranging effect. The analysis could proceed as follows. based on a specific collection of linguistic material, the

Bible, the significance of which was maintained and transformed during the centuries, and the location of the cross with a dead male figure (and other well-known characteristics) in the house must clearly be interpreted as indicating that the activities in the house are understood with a view of a transcendental sphere. The stress on the cyclical revealed through the location of the cradle and the coffin – a specific ritual feature that becomes obvious through repeated observation – is superimposed by the transcendental perspective of redemption (as we know from the basic written tradition), which implies an ambiguity in the evaluation of the existence, its provisional character, etc.

How could Heidegger's myth relate to the urban lifeworld? Let us consider three aspects of the lifeworld: (1) the immediate *horizon of perception*, the material frame of life in its aesthetic aspects ("aesthetic" meaning: perceptual); (2) the practical organization of the everyday as meaningful activity, the *practical horizon*; (3) the general frame of interpretation, the *cultural horizon*. Why "horizon"?[10] The phenomenological tradition has stressed the relation between, on the one hand the general horizon, and on the other hand what is "thematic," what is in focus. These concepts were developed in an investigation of philosophical questions related to theories of knowledge, but in a more general usage they are useful for the analysis of the question of the urban lifeworld. Everyday life is for immediate consideration a heterogeneous sequence of activities. Each of them, more or less, at the center of our attention at certain moments. Most of these activities are routine, and thus not thematic, but both routine, and what becomes thematic, take place in the frame of a broader context, the horizon. The means of transportation are most often chosen routinely, but at certain moments the choice becomes thematic: would one use the bike when it rains heavily? Certain meals tend to provide one with the necessary nutrition, but the display at a street corner of fresh vegetables makes one want to make something special for dinner. The idea of the autonomy of teenage kids is challenged when one of them strays dangerously close to drug communities, bringing the general frame of reference for socialization into focus. A controversial friend's suicidal jump from the 16th floor makes one focus on one's own major choices and life perspectives. Anything could become thematic, and an experimental survey demonstrates how much is provided or taken for granted as horizon.

Heidegger's *Schwarzwald* farmhouse provides, according to his analysis, an entire frame of life, a horizon reaching from the immediate to the general understanding of life – and death. One interesting aspect of his text is that it is all *material* – from roof to *Totenbaum*. If one generalizes, the text may make more sense. What would be the equivalents to the altar and the *Totenbaum* in modern housing? Bookshelves and paintings? The television set? Major aspects of life have been thematized in other ways than those Heidegger refers to or relies upon. Their presence or absence in the interpretative horizon of entirely different contexts does not invalidate Heidegger's insistence on their relation to the ways in which daily life is organized and framed. Nor do the speculative aspects of the description of the location and construction of the house invalidate the more general points: the relation between location and building.[11]

What is striking in Bourdieu's analysis is the embeddedness of the organization of daily life in a framework that is related not only to the immediate surroundings but also to the larger interpretation of the existential situation, as well as the intertwinement of technical and symbolic organizations (just as the practical source of water is simultaneously a kind of "bringing forth of the ground" in Heidegger's account). Although Bourdieu's structural-semiotic analysis is obviously quite distinct from Heidegger's hermeneutic analysis, similarities should not be overlooked. Yet, even if in both cases an entire life-horizon is implied, a comparison brings forth what is out of focus in Heidegger's case: the actual work activities and human relations (the bed is curiously absent from the farmhouse in Heidegger's description, only a deathbed and a cradle are implied). Another difference should be stressed, namely that whereas Bourdieu clearly aims at an explicitation of the inherent pattern of interpretation in the Berber culture *from the outside*, it is not at all clear what the status of Heidegger's interpretation is, although he probably would regard his implication of the fourfold as actually brought forward in the craft and life of the peasants, taking the horizon of the analysis and of what is analyzed as compatible.

What is gathered in the farmhouse and its "locale"[12] would first of all be *spread out* in the urban context. The dinner table might still be the center of the modern house or apartment, but just about everything else would be more or less distant and transformed, or have its more important equivalents elsewhere. The altar would be in the church or in whatever institution may substitute for the religious one. The realm of death would be constituted, on the one extreme, by hospitals and similar institutions, and, on the other, by churches and cemeteries.[13] Water would pour out of the faucet as a result of complicated technological constructions, etc.

The immediate lifeworld would, in other words, be entirely different, but it would still be a lifeworld. The built structures and the organization of space would still contribute to the horizon of interpretation for the citizens – together with all the other factors involved in socialization, formation, and orientation. Everyday life in a modern city has its rituals, its linguistic, visual, and auditive media, and its prominent institutions – the city thus provides a frame for a way of life, or rather: a multitude of ways of living.

IV THE PHENOMENOLOGICAL CONCEPT OF LIFEWORLD AND URBAN ANALYSIS

> The concept of "life-world" has found an astounding resonance in the contemporary mind. A word is always an answer. What does this new word, "life-world," answer? What is the question to which this word presents an answer that has been accepted by the general consciousness of language ... An objective concern, persistently pursued and shared by many persons, which has not yet been expressed but has nevertheless long sought proper expression, is what alone permits an individual person's arbitrary conceptual coinage to become a word.[14]

Gadamer answers his own question pointing out that the counter-concept to the concept of lifeworld "is without doubt the 'world of science'."

The concept of *Lebenswelt*, or lifeworld, became prominent in the philosophy of Edmund Husserl towards the end of his life, particularly in *The Crisis of European Sciences and Transcendental Phenomenology*. His concern is double, one aspect is a critique of the role of natural sciences and the technological attitude, another aspect concerns the question of the foundation of an alternative knowledge. The two questions are interrelated: "*the crisis of the European sciences* is none other than *the crisis of the modern technological world*."[15] In a double lecture in Vienna in May 1935 entitled "Philosophy and the Crisis of European Humanity,"[16] Husserl argued that the humanities (*Geisteswissenschaften*) should not give up the field to the natural sciences. "The result of the consistent development of the exact sciences in the modern period was a true revolution in the technical control of nature" (271). The humanities do not have confidence in a similar elaboration of its own field. "But what if the whole way of thinking that manifests itself in the foregoing presentation [i.e. Husserl's own lecture] rested on portentous prejudices and, in its effects, itself shared in the responsibility for the European sickness?" (272). Towards the end of the first part of his lecture, Husserl formulates his vision of the impact of a renewed philosophy on "*die geistige Gestallt Europas*" (Europe's spiritual situation): ". . . a new spirit, stemming from philosophy and its particular sciences, a spirit of free critique and norm-giving aimed at infinite tasks, dominates humanity through and through, creating new, infinite ideals" (289).

Husserl was not alone in his rejection of the ideal of the natural sciences and technology as models for philosophical investigation, he took part in a broader movement which included Heidegger and numerous other anti-modern intellectuals. Like Heidegger, he saw the European philosophical tradition as being permeated by a fundamental misunderstanding which stemmed from as far back as Parmenides: "Science, from its origin at the beginning of the modern era, is derived from the presupposition that it can know the world in a manner which supersedes the relativity of sensuous experience and the opinions (that is, the *doxa*) grounded in it. Nature understood in this way requires, in addition, the hypothesis of being-in-itself" (Landgrebe). But this hypothesis – i.e. Kant's hypothesis – is, says Husserl, only "*one* among many practical hypotheses and projects which make up the life of human beings in this life-world."[17] By absolutizing this hypothesis, sciences and philosophy fell – in Landgrebe's formulation –

> under the spell of a metaphysical concept of true being, an inversion of true being, one which took it to be a persisting and permanent being-in-itself behind the changing and fluctuating world of belief (*doxa*) and of perceptual illusion and prejudice. The modern sciences were convinced that the scientifically explicated world was the true world . . . This presupposition of an eternal and unchanging Being, situated behind the world experienced as moving, changing, and continually in flux, forms the foundation for the development of Western metaphysics in all of its varieties.

It is precisely in opposition to that point that Husserl directs his critique, in order to articulate his contribution to the solution of the crisis of the technologically determined modern world. The crucial move, then, is to focus precisely on the world of immediate perception, the world of preconceived ideas, the world of *doxa*.

> Under the heading of the *Lebenswelt*, *the world of common experience is rehabilitated by phenomenology* [my italics] as *the* reality from which all conceptions and constructions of

other domains of existence [among them the sciences] start and to which these domains essentially refer. Accordingly, the *doxa* is reinstated in its right. Moreover, defined in a broad and all-inclusive sense, the Lebenswelt comprises the products and accomplishments of all cultural activities, hence also the sciences, their results, and theories.[18]

In Husserl's own words: "Now the scientific world . . . itself belongs to the life-world, just as all men and all human communities in general, and their human ends both individual and communal, with all their corresponding working structures, belong to it."

In contrast to the theoretical construct, which is in principle not immediately perceivable, actual immediate experience takes place in the lifeworld. Husserl's project is, then, to analyze the experience of the lifeworld, which is ultimately also the condition of the possibility of scientific knowledge. The lifeworld is – in contrast to the world constructed in the natural sciences – a *historical* world. The subject is situated in a specific historical moment, with a past and a possible future. That means that the lifeworld is ever-changing, and thus the horizon of the subject is also constantly changing. *At this point, the analysis of the lifeworld can go in two directions.* One direction would be the analysis of the *structure* of the lifeworld beyond the *historical* change, and this is Husserl's primary concern. The other direction would be the analysis of particular lifeworlds, or types of lifeworlds. This is the direction taken by *historical, sociological, and anthropological analysis,* and obviously the direction that might lead to questions concerning the urban lifeworld. "In other words, the life-world is nothing other than the concrete historical world with its traditions and its changing 'images' of nature. The question of the constitution of the life-world, therefore, is conceived, in its full range, to be nothing other than the question of the constitution of the world as a historical world" (Landgrebe). To the extent that the analysis of the lifeworld is governed by the question of natural sciences, the images of *nature* must be of central concern, but in so far as the focus is on matters of cultural history, this is – as understood by Gurwitsch – not necessarily so:

> To be sure, the world includes nature. The nature here in question is obviously nature as given in direct and immediate experience, and not the idealized nature of physics. However, the world comprises more than mere nature. Among the existents[19] by which we find ourselves surrounded, there are not only natural things, i.e., objects which may exhaustively be described by indicating their color, shape, size, weight, etc., but also instruments, books, objects of art, and so on, briefly *objects which have human significance, serve human ends and purposes, satisfy human desires and needs* [my italics]. Because the world contains objects of this kind and, therefore, proves the frame within which we lead our human existence, we speak of it as our *Lebenswelt.*

From the point of view of urban studies, this could be turned around: in fact, *very few of the phenomena surrounding us are natural* in the sense indicated by Gurwitsch: "Human beings concern themselves, through their conscious acts, with mundane realities like animals, houses, fields, etc." It is as if the urban context is in some sense repressed, what comes to mind immediately is either the interior: "instruments, books, objects of art, and so on," or a landscape: "animals, houses, fields, etc." With the concept of "horizon" itself borrowed from the perceptual experience of a landscape, what kind of "horizon" would Times Square or similar urban "landscapes" then provide? What would "horizon" mean in the context of cityscapes? Merleau-Ponty addressed this question in his *Phenomenology of Perception*:

> In the natural attitude, I do not have *perceptions*, I do not posit this object as beside that one, along with their objective relationships, I have a flow of experiences which imply and explain each other simultaneously and successively. Paris for me is not an object of many facets, a collection of perceptions, nor is it the law governing all these perceptions. Just as a person gives evidence of the same emotional essence in his gestures with his hands, in his way of walking and in the sound of his voice, each express perception occurring in my journey through Paris – the cafés, people's faces, the poplars along the quays, the bends of the Seine – stands out against *the city's whole being* ['*l'être total de Paris*], and merely confirms that there is a certain *style* or a certain *significance* which Paris possesses. And when I arrived there for the first time, the first roads that I saw as I left the station were, like the first words spoken by a stranger, simply manifestations of *a still ambiguous essence, but one already unlike any other*. Just as we do not see the eyes of a familiar face, but simply its look and its expression, so we perceive hardly any object. There is present *a latent significance*, diffused throughout the landscape or the city, which we find in something specific and self-evident which we feel no need to define.[20] (my italics, except the first)

As a description of urban perception, though, these lines raise a multitude of questions. To what extent could the cityscape be compared to, in one regard, a landscape and in another an individual human being, except at the very high level of abstraction where Merleau-Ponty is concerned with fundamental aspects of human perception? And in the case of Paris itself: in what sense do social gathering places (cafés), human beings, trees, and the river participate in the same *essence*, "*l'être total de Paris*," endowed with "*un style*" or "*un sens*"? Yet, what is closer at hand, as an example of "a flow of experiences which imply and explain each other simultaneously and successively," than the stream of consciousness as developed by James Joyce in *Ulysses*? What is at stake in this novel, though, is not the "essence" of Dublin, but rather the interaction of mind and urban space. Franco Moretti has analyzed Joyce's stream of consciousness as a literary form that is appropriate for urban experience,[21] stressing its base as the stock of "*idées recues*," a "bricolage"[22] of commonplaces, that are available to the city dweller as a means of interpretation of the heterogeneous experience, thus linking *Ulysses* to Flaubert's *Bouvard et Pécuchet* rather than canonic contemporary novels like Proust's *À la recherche du temps perdu*, or Musil's *The Man Without Qualities*. The concept of the *doxa* is similar to the concept of the commonplace. "*Ulysses* is a polycentric urban universe where the objective culture is divided between a multitudinous variety of situations and discourses none of which is dominating the others or substituting them and thereby making them superfluous" (186). The stream of consciousness is thus polyphonic, "the new polyphony. The polyphony of the metropolis and of the division of labor making its way there" (198). But what is the source of the commonplaces interwoven into the stream of consciousness? "If the multitude of languages of the Joycean polyphony seem to 'speak by themselves' without any longer being supported by concrete subjects, it is because they have all been transformed into institutionalized languages and now follow the 'entirely objective norms' of the Church, of Education, of Journalism, of the Nation, of Advertizing ..." (184). These are essential institutions of the *urban mental map*. The interesting aspect of Joyce's achievement is not that he is "making it new," *tout court*, as the received idea of the avant-garde would have it, but rather that the *innovation corresponds to a new experience*, "the innovation *that manages to solve problems*": "The *construction of a new perspective and symbolic horizon*: this is what is a sensible project and a project that has an obvious social value" (166).

"A new perceptual and symbolic horizon – this formulation corresponds to the concerns of a phenomenological analysis of the life-world in a changing world.[23]

> Even the typifications and symbolizations in terms of which we distinguish the several strata of our social world, construe and interpret their contents, determine our action in it and upon it and its action upon us according to all degrees of ability, are predefined as unquestionably given by virtue of the socially conditioned schemata of expression and interpretation prevailing in the group to which we belong and which we used to call the "culture" of our group. It too, above all, is part of our life-world which we take for granted. (260)

Alfred Schütz's approach to the lifeworld is that of a sociologist, his concern is the way in which members of a society rely on and relate to the horizon of interpretative "schemata" provided by socialization and other culturally formative instances. The point of departure is the Husserlian "natural attitude" (as opposed to the scientific attitude) towards the life-world. This attitude implies a variety of "certainties": "Therefore we can speak of fundamental assumptions characteristic of the natural attitude to the life-world, which themselves are accepted as unquestionably given; namely the assumption of the constancy of the structure of the world, of the constancy of our experience of the world, and of the constancy of our ability to act upon the world and within the world" (257). The world is within our "reach," either immediately or as a reminiscence or prospectively, one structure of the lifeworld is therefore the *temporal* differentiation: "The stratification of the world into zones of actual, restorable and obtainable reach already refers to the structure of the life-world according to dimensions of objective temporality and their subjective correlates, the phenomena of retention and protention, recall and expectancy, and to the peculiar differentiations of the experience of time which correspond to the manifold dimensions of reality" (259). This is *one* example of the *structures* involved in the *experience* of the *situation* of which the *schemata* provide the *horizon*. All these concepts belong to the analysis of the lifeworld. The origins of the schemata are manifold, but all belong to the socialization process and thus stem from the surroundings of the individual: "The overwhelming bulk of this knowledge is socially derived and transmitted to the individual in the long process of education by parents, teachers, teachers of teachers, by relations of all kinds, involving fellow-men, contemporaries and predecessors. It is transmitted in the form of insight, beliefs, more or less well founded or blind, maxims, instructions for use, recipes for the solution of typical problems, i.e. for the attainment of typical results by the typical application of typical means" (261). All this "socially derived knowledge" in its turn "forms both a common schema of interpretation of the common world and a means of mutual agreement and understanding" (261).

It is a characteristic feature of this way of looking at the lifeworld, that it tends to refer exclusively to *linguistic* phenomena and thus to remain in the realm of verbal hermeneutics. But the discursive patterns that are involved are intertwined with social institutions (like Church, Education, Journalism, Nation, Advertizing . . ., as Moretti underlines), institutions that are centers of power, Michel Foucault would add.[24] And that means that they are transmitted not only by means of verbal instruction, but also by regulation of behavior. These institutions are, furthermore, not just loci of discourses and action, they operate in physical structures, buildings and built spaces. It is illuminating to recall Bourdieu's analysis of the Berber-house and the rituals related to the organization of the house. Bourdieu's analysis clearly demonstrates how the regulation and the interpretation of daily life as well as major events are *embedded in the physical structure of the house and its location* as well as *discursively transmitted*. An application in the context of urban studies of the concept of lifeworld and the elements of the analysis of its structures developed in the phenomenological tradition must take this aspect into consideration. In the case of the Berber-house *regulating institution* and *sphere of daily life* are to a certain extent identical: the house – although the male sphere outside the house should not be forgotten. *In the urban context the spheres of life as well as the institutions are increasingly spread out in various locales.* An anthropology of the urban lifeworld encounters a series of questions that are different from the example studied by Bourdieu, as well as from the articulation of the questions in the phenomenological tradition. The experiencing, interpreting and acting subject is always in a specific situation:

> To the experiencing subject's mind, the elements singled out of the pre-given structure of the world always stand in sense-connections, connections of orientation, as well as of mastery of thought or action. The causal relations of the objective world are subjectively experienced as means and ends, as hindrances or aids, of the spontaneous activity of thought or action. They manifest themselves as complexes of interest, complexes of problems, as systems of projects, and feasabilities inherent in the systems of projects. (Schütz, 263)

The focus determines what is relevant in relation to the intentions of the subject. When this takes place in a horizon that is not contested, but taken for granted, Schütz will talk about "*motivational relevancy*," but the horizon can become contested for whatever reason, which means that specific aspects of the horizon become *thematized* (or "become thematic"). "The actual stock of knowledge is nothing but the sedimentation of all our experiences of former definitions of former situations," says Schütz (264), new situations are thus approached with a certain "foreknowledge."[25] *We apply previously appropriated schemata to the new situation.* "However, it may happen that not all motivationally relevant elements foreknown in sufficient degrees of familiarity are adequate, or that the situation proves to be one which cannot be referred by synthesis of recognition to a previous situation typically alike, similar, etc. because it is radically new" (265).

This is, of course, a crucial point in the urban context, since it is permanently undergoing changes, and since the demographic fluctuations constantly confront people with unknown or only partially known types of situations. This engenders what Schütz calls *"thematic relevancy,"* because the relevant element enters the conscious focus and thus no longer is a horizon that is taken for granted. Now the element can be negotiated, discussed, modified, rejected, and substituted by consciously elaborated solutions, etc. It will then have a third kind of relevancy: *"interpretational relevancy"* (268).

> As long as in the natural attitude man experiences his life-world and unreflectingly directs himself to it in his actions, thoughts and feelings, the differentiation into several systems of relevancy does not come within his view at all . . . Every consequential decision in the life-world brings man face to face with a series of thematic relevancies of hypothetical nature, which have to be interpreted and questioned as to their motivational insertion into the life-plan. (272)

As soon as the role of the horizon of the lifeworld is articulated in this manner, it becomes obvious that the various discourses and institutions that provide schemata for identification and interpretation in relation to new situations must be at the center of attention for the sociological analysis (sociology was, after all, basically developed as a means of interpreting the formation of modernity – Tönnies, Weber, Simmel, and Durkheim were all concerned with this question). So much more, when it comes to the analysis of the *urban* lifeworld, the scene of – and the source of means for the mastering of – the experience of modernity. The cultural framework not only provides the horizon taken for granted, *it is also the source of alternative patterns of interpretation.* In a lifeworld that permanently challenges human expectations, is characterized by perpetual change, and is permeated by conflicts,[26] the ways in which the various situations are defined by inner and outer horizons, by discourses and institutions, as well as by interpersonal relationships becomes a crucial subject. The particular challenge for urban studies derives from all those factors which are *not* merely discursive or institutional in the narrow sense of being derived from a specific organization: the urban space, organization and fabric – as lifeworld, that is intertwined with and permeated by discourses, symbolic systems, structures of power, socio-economic organization, and institutions.[27]

V THE FRANKFURT SCHOOL: *VERDINGLICHUNG*, NATURE AND LIFEWORLD

To the extent that the concept of lifeworld is taken as including all the features just enumerated, it may tend to encompass too much, and thus become insignificant, something like an alternative denomination of society. But that is a problem built into the concept by its history and background in the phenomenological-hermeneutic tradition. Its very origin as a counter-concept to the world of sciences inscribes the concept in the tradition of *Geistesgeschichte* from Dilthey onwards. Dilthey's effort to define a specific realm for the humanities (*Geisteswissenschaften*) engendered a sharp distinction between what belonged to the material realm and what was spiritual, what could be handled in terms of cause and effect, of *explanation*, and what should be treated according to *understanding* and meaning, i.e. interpreted. A prison is, he says, a physical structure, and as such an object for natural science, for *explanation*, but it also takes part in the socially meaningful activities of the juridical institution, and as such it has to be *understood* – in accordance with the intention of laws and juridical institutions. *This approach falls short of social phenomena, that cannot be taken as the expression of intention, nor as just physical matter*, i.e. exactly the phenomena the particularity of which called forth the creation of sociology: *quasi-natural, but nevertheless human phenomena* – like economic market relations or what Max Weber termed the "iron cage" of bureaucracy. What is beyond control can only indirectly be analyzed in terms of intention, even if it may be the outcome of a multitude of intentional acts over time. *The privileging of the linguistically articulated aspect of the lifeworld limits the concept to the hermeneutically informed understanding of the humanities.* Urban studies, to the contrary, must include all the phenomena that are "in between," all the non-natural, but nevertheless physical structures, all the objective features that are the outcome of human activity, etc. In a radical way, Michel Foucault stressed one aspect of this problem, when he insisted on a concept of power without center, i.e. power that does not "emanate" from a center (a highly controversial idea, particularly in France with its obvious concentration of power in Paris). This kind of power "happens" through institutional praxis that is local, a kind of *tactics* of power. There may be attempts to concentrate this power and create a central *strategy* of power, but that would then be *après coup*, not an initiation of power as the result of an intentional act.[28] Whatever the shortcomings of Foucault's radicalism, his approach does demonstrate the limitations, in particular for urban studies, of a concept of lifeworld that does not incorporate crucial aspects of the regulating functions of modern society.[29]

In the context of the Frankfurt School the introduction of the concept of lifeworld represented an important change of problematic compared to the general frame of the first generation of the School. The inspiration from Georg Lukács' *History and Class Consciousness* (1923) was of great importance to Adorno and Horkheimer, i.e. the main representatives of the first generation. The crucial concept in Lukács' book was *Verdinglichung*, reification. The concept, of course, was out of Marx, but in Lukács it was merged with inspirations from classical German sociology, first and foremost Max Weber and Georg Simmel. In Marx, *Verdinglichung* is analyzed as an effect of the relations involved in production and circulation of commodities. The word means "making into a thing," and this can be deceptive. *Veräusserung*, objectivation or exteriorization, is the word Marx uses in his early writings as the denomination of the fact that the act of producing, in a sense, brings human potentials out in the exterior world. The use of generic powers (*Wesenskräfte*), as he has it in his early writings, results in products that are present as objects. This is the case in all kinds of society. The specific feature of societies based on commodity production is, that the products in a sense take on a power of their own, just like the fetishes of primitive society – that is why Marx uses the term commodity fetishism referring to the same phenomenon. Relations between human beings take on the character of relations between things in the sense that the "social" relations between things, i.e. the relations between their values, exchange values, dominate the social relations between human beings. Georg Simmel's philosophy of culture had as a central theme the idea that the cultural objectifications accumulated and thus increasingly established a force outside the culturally committed individuals. This theme is easy to associate with the idea of *Verdinglichung*. Simmel also stressed the abstract character of modern society, again an obvious parallel to the effect of the governing role of value relations: the abstract general as opposed to the particularity of the use value. For Max Weber *rationalization* was the crucial feature of Western society, imposing itself at all levels and creating modern bureaucracy. *Verdinglichung*, objectification, abstraction, and rationalization – the unification of these themes provided an unusually powerful diagnosis of modern society in the period of transition to modern capitalism, a process that made itself felt, not least, in Germany.

Theodor W. Adorno, the most influential representative of the early Frankfurt School, was deeply inspired by this analytical construct and *Verdinglichung* became the central category in his entire *œuvre*, although in a different conceptual framework: namely in opposition to *nature*. Two themes are interwoven here. First the fact that work not only can be identified as exteriorization of generic powers, it is as much domination of *exterior nature*, *Naturbeherrschung*. Second, that rationalization, coping with the reality principle, as well as the effects of the super-ego, represents domination of *inner nature*. In both cases nature turns into forces that confront the subject: quasi-autonomous social forces of commodity relations, and quasi-autonomous forces of hidden psychic factors. Human spiritual forces are furthermore in themselves turned into autonomous forces of calculation, instead of being a medium for reflection and ultimately the locus of *Geist* in the Hegelian sense. *Myth* is the word for this *quid pro quo*, this turning around of "nature" and "spirit." In as few words as possible – and that also means too few words: in Adorno the working class is substituted by nature as oppositional force, and that implies that the inner dialectic of capitalism is substituted by the dialectic of the domination of (inner and outer) nature and the dialectic of enlightenment in their mutual interrelation.[30] As sources of opposition to the logic of capitalism only nature, spirit, and the aesthetic sphere seem to be left. Whatever the incomparable merits of Adorno's work, the conceptual framework does not seem to be well suited to application in concrete analysis outside the aesthetic and philosophical sphere.

In his *Theory of Communicative Action*, Habermas then suggested "that we conceive of society simultaneously as a system and a lifeworld."[31] This theoretical move is crucial, it integrates two traditions: what was covered by the Lukácsian version of the concept of *Verdinglichung*, but also later attempts to develop sociology in terms of system theory, and the tradition of hermeneutic sociology, Schütz being a central representative of this tradition. The lifeworld is in modern society characterized by an increasing differentiation of its various spheres and functions. This is a process that, according to Habermas, implies an increasing autonomization of the individual subject and rationalization of interaction. "Rationalization" should here be understood not as instrumental rationality, but in terms of "*Vernunft*" (autonomous self-reflexive consideration) "consensus formation that rests *in the end* on the authority of the better argument" (415). Weber used the term "*Entzauberung*," disenchantment, to indicate the eclipse of the domination of religious interpretation, the process of secularization, that liberated

A

Reproduction processes \ Structural components	Culture	Society	Personality
Cultural reproduction	Interpretive schemes fit for consensus ("valid knowledge")	Legitimations	Socialization patterns Educational goals
Social integration	Obligations	Legitimately ordered interpersonal relations	Social memberships
Socialization	Interpretive accomplishments	Motivations for actions that conform to norms	Interactive capabilities ("personal identity")

I.2 Three schemata from Jürgen Habermas, *The Theory of Communicative Action*, vol. 2, Boston, 1989, pp. 142–44. Courtesy of Surhkamp Verlag. A: Contributions of reproduction processes to maintaining the structural components of the lifeworld.

sciences, ethics and (aesthetic) culture from institutional dependence on the church, a process that was parallel to the emancipation from dependence on central political power. This historical process is more or less characteristic of societies of "Western" type and engenders structural changes in the lifeworld.[32] "The vanishing point of these evolutionary trends are: for *culture*, a state in which traditions that have become reflective and then set aflow undergo continuous revision; for *society*, a state in which legitimate orders are dependent upon formal procedures for positing and justifying norms; and for *personality*, a state in which a highly abstract ego-identity is continuously stabilized through self-steering" (146, my italics). These are the three aspects of the lifeworld stressed by Habermas: *Culture*, the resources for interpretation (the main focus on the lifeworld of phenomenological sociology); *Society*, the sphere of interaction and consensus building; and *Personality*, the formation of the individual. These three aspects are obviously inter-woven, but it is Habermas' concern to stress the mutual relative autonomy that is also the precondition for the reflexive, critical attitude. Only to the extent that the individual personality is autonomous will it be able to take a critical stance towards the system of norms implied in the cultural system. The implication at the political level is obviously crucial – and ultimately Habermas' major concern:

B

Structural components Distur- bances in the domain of	Culture	Society	Person	Dimension of evaluation
Cultural reproduction	Loss of meaning	Withdrawl of legitimation	Crisis in orientation and education	Rationality of knowledge
Social integration	Unsettling of collective identity	Anomie	Alienation	Solidarity of members
Socialization	Rupture of tradition	Withdrawl of motivation	Psychopath-ologies	Personal responsibility

I.2 *(cont.)* B: Manifestations of crisis when reproduction processes are disturbed (pathologies).

> Mead and Durkheim further stress the evolutionary significance of democracy: democratic forms of political will-formation are not only the result of a power shift in favor of the carrier strata of the capitalist economic system; *forms of discursive will-formation* are established in them. And these affect the quasi naturalness of traditionally legitimated domination in a similar way, even as modern natural science, jurisprudence with specialized training, and autonomous art break down the quasi naturalness of ecclesiastic tradition. (146–47)

The functions and interactions of the various spheres of the modern lifeworld as Habermas conceives it are brought together in a diagram (Figure I.2A), even without an explanation of all the features it demonstrates the complexity of the analysis. It should be stressed how the various instances interact. In the actual society, though, all kinds of conflicts and disturbances influence the process of social reproduction, as it is demonstrated by a second diagram (Figure I.2B). A third diagram, then, brings together the potential effects of communicative action (Figure I.2C). The conceptual framework that includes social integration as formation of the individual is presented by Habermas as a critical broadening of the horizon of phenomenological sociology and its "culturalistically abridged concept of the lifeworld."[33] In this context it should be stressed that it is one of

C

Reproduction processes \ Structural components	Culture	Society	Person
Cultural reproduction	Transmission, critique, acquisition of cultural knowledge	Renewal of knowledge effective for legitimation	Reproduction of knowledge relevant to child rearing, education
Social integration	Immunization of a central stock of value orientations	Coordination of actions via intersubjectively recognized validity claims	Reproduction of patterns of social membership
Socialization	Enculturation	Internalization of values	Formation of identity

I.2 *(cont.)* C: Reproductive functions of action oriented to mutual understanding.

Habermas' major concerns to displace the focus from the individual subject towards the collectively experienced process of communication, i.e. towards society, human interaction, and that also implies that society should not be conceived in the image of the individual.[34]

Habermas broadens the horizon in another respect as well. He points to the fact that "processes of system differentiation [like division of labour as it is analyzed by Durkheim] affect the lifeworld and possibly cause disturbances of its symbolic representation" (147). He proceeds further in a direction that opens a variety of perspectives in the context of an analysis of the modern urban lifeworld and thus motivates a relatively long quotation:

> In this way, phenomena of reification can also be analyzed along the lines of lifeworld deformations. The counter-Enlightenment that set in immediately after the French Revolution founded a critique of modernity that has since branched off in different directions.[35] Their common denominator is the conviction that loss of meaning, anomie, and alienation – the pathologies of bourgeois society, indeed of posttraditional society generally – can be traced back to the rationalization of the lifeworld itself. This backward-looking critique is in essence a critique of bourgeois culture. By contrast, the Marxist critique of bourgeois society is aimed first at the relations of production, for it accepts the

rationalization of the lifeworld and explains its deformation by the conditions of material reproduction. This materialist approach to disturbances in the symbolic reproduction of the lifeworld requires a theory that operates on a broader conceptual basis than that of the "lifeworld." It has to opt for a theoretical strategy that neither identifies the lifeworld with society as a whole, nor reduces it to a systemic nexus. (147–48)

Society is thus defined by the interaction between system and lifeworld, and that brings the analysis far away from a "culturalistic" concept of lifeworld as well as from an idea of modern society as permeated through and through by Verdinglichung – *or power.*

This shift of ground in relation to Adorno is crucial. But what happened to "nature"? Or in other terms, what happened to perception, to the aesthetic realm in terms of sense-experience (rather than what Habermas conceives as the autonomous realm of art)? "Nature," of course, became during the historical process more or less socialized in the case of inner nature,[36] and transformed into artifacts and various kinds of products aiming at the fulfillment of human needs in the case of outer nature – if it was not just polluted or downright destroyed. But that does not mean that sense-experience disappears, nor do questions like those raised by Adorno, or for that matter by his source for some of these questions: Sigmund Freud. Habermas has in several respects contributed to a decisive change of ground in relation to a variety of traditions, but from the point of view of urban studies, again, important questions are left out of the argument.[37] An important question is touched upon, though, in Habermas' laudatory discourse for Hans-Georg Gardamer from 1979. He characterizes Gadamer's intellectual achievement as "Urbanization of the Heideggerian province." Heidegger's "turning his back on all articulated representatives of the tradition" is contrasted with Gadamer's attempt to renew the tradition through actualization of basic humanistic concepts like "Formation," "Consensus," "Judgement" and "Taste." Habermas' interpretation is, that these ideas belong to an urban and urbane context – in contrast to Heidegger's anti-humanist cult of pre-modern (and thus anti-urban) conditions: "A humanism that emerges from the horizon of experience of city dwellers and always is threatened by the decline of urbanity."[38]

VI ARCHITECTURE AS (RE)PRESENTATION OF HUMAN *PRAXIS*

In a complex discussion of "Architecture and the Poetics of Representation,"[39] Dalibor Vesely has pointed to the relation between architecture and *praxis* in a way that can illuminate some of the questions raised above. Vesely is looking for "the more authentic tradition of representation" (25) before the modern period, a tradition in which concepts like *convenance* and *bienséance* represented a "tendency to move into the depths of architectural reality, towards an order still understood in terms of *ethos*" (28). "The shift towards *ethos* brings architecture into the realm of a humanistic culture, of which it was until the seventeenth century an indivisible part" (ibid.). A reference to Cicero brings the perspective back to ancient Greece: "What in Latin is called decorum (propriety), in Greek is called *prepon*. Such is its essential nature, that it is inseparable from moral goodness, for what is proper is morally right, and what is morally right is proper."[40] What for an immediate appreciation might be taken as a purely superficial correspondence with some established rules, *tout court*, is thus rooted in the relation to the good:

> In the primary sense *prepon* belongs to the domain of appearances and means simply "to be seen clearly, to be conspicuous." In its fully articulated sense, it means an harmonious participation in the order of reality and the outward expression of that order. The outward expression does not refer to mere imitation or representation of order which is already familiar to us. It implies rather that order is represented in such a way that it becomes conspicuous and actually present in sensuous abundance. (29)

What emerges from Vesely's discussion of the ancient philosophical terms and concepts is a nexus between the good, human acts, presentation and creation. A concept of *situation*, then, becomes crucial – like in Schütz. "For a more specific understanding it is better to see praxis as a situation, where people are not only doing or experiencing something, but which also includes things that contribute to the fulfillment of human life" (31–32). But even more central to Vesely's argument is *myth* understood as "the dimension of our culture which opens the way to a unity of our experience and to a unity of our world" (32). This is a tricky argument for more than one reason. First, the identification of myth in the sense of tragic narrative with myth as uncontested frame of interpretation stumbles at the fact that Greek tragedy rather questions the stories about the heroes than accepts them *tout court*. Second, the argument would only hold in some kind of a "primitive" society. But it makes sense as an alternative articulation of the features of the Berber-house analyzed by Bourdieu. Vesely now argues that myths essentially are interpretations of "primary symbols which are spontaneously formed and which preserve the memory of our first encounters with the cosmic conditions or our existence" (ibid.). If that is so, architecture can be brought into the discussion in so far as the "persistence of primary symbols . . . contributes decisively to secondary symbols and finally to the formation of *paradigmatic situations*." What are paradigmatic situations? Their nature "is similar to the nature of the phenomena described in different terminology as institutions, deep structures or archetypes" (ibid.). It lies at hand to remember the concept of *schemata* in Schütz's discussion of the lifeworld, but Vesely is aiming at more than the ritualistic or interpretative aspects, and here a lengthy quote brings out some major features:

> What then is the ground on which architecture, art and practical life can meet in a way that they constitute a meaningful unity? In our earlier discussion of the nature of situations, we have emphasized their synthetic role and their capacity to structure our experience, but situations act also as receptacles of experience and of those events which sediment a meaning in them, a meaning not just as survivals and residues, but as the invitation to a sequel of future experiences. *This receptive aspect of situations is mostly pre-reflective and synaesthetic.* There is no clear distinction between visual, auditive or tactile phenomena, and this constitutes an important condition for the life of metaphors. It is mostly due to the metaphorical structure of situations and more specifically due to the mimetic nature of metaphor, that paradigms are formed; paradigms which play a not only synthetic but also receptive role. (Ibid., my italics)

Here, again, it makes sense to remember the Berber-house and the intertwinement of cosmic patterns, patterns of ritual, patterns of building, patterns of everyday life, and linguistic patterns. But what would be left of all this, when we are not living in those blissful days

> when the starry sky is the map of all possible paths   ages whose paths are illuminated by the light of the stars. Everything in such an age is new and yet familiar, full of adventure and yet their own. The world is wide and yet like a home, for the fire that burns in the soul is of the same essential nature as the stars; the world and the self, the light and the fire, are sharply distinct, yet they never become permanent strangers to one another, for fire is the soul of all light and all fire clothes itself in light. Thus each action of the soul becomes meaningful and rounded in this duality: complete in meaning – in *sense* – and complete for the senses; rounded because the soul rests within itself even while it acts; rounded because action separates itself from it and, having become itself, finds a centre of its own and draws a closed circumference around itself.

This description (from the first page of Georg Lukács' *Theory of the Novel*) could perhaps be taken as the *locus classicus* of dreaming nostalgia for a supposedly lost, but never existing, harmonious world.[41] Something of the kind seems to be lurking behind Vesely's account of the tradition that was gradually lost in the course of history since Greek antiquity. What, again, would be left, when the mythical realm is not a primary reference (nor is substituted by Jungian ideas of archetypes), when symbols and metaphors consequently are constituted by specific social and cultural processes without reference to myth? A lot, it seems to me.

What is a metaphor? A multitude of approaches are trying to cope with this question, among them the cognitive approach. A basic component in this kind of account of metaphoric phenomena is the stress on immediate bodily experience and various basic, typical situations, particularly of a narrative character. To put it very briefly: if metaphors based on the bodily experience (and that implies immediate sensuous experience) are substituted for what Vesely calls symbols and metaphors, and if basic narrative situations are substituted for what Vesely calls myth, then his entire approach might be carried over to the present debate. A similar approach would provide basic patterns for the integration of perceptional aspects of the experience of architectural and (by extension) urban situations and a way of grasping the sequential, temporal aspect of all situations: paradigmatic situations and paradigmatic narratives, *schemata* in Schütz's sense, but in this context related to the dimension of *aisthesis*, sensorial perception, as well as to the constitution of "meaning."

VII THE SIGNIFICANCE OF INSTITUTIONS

Like in Schütz's sociology, the concept of situation is crucial in Sartre's social philosophy, yet there is in his work a shift in attention towards the question of the individual. In his early philosophy the question of freedom is at the center of attention, whereas his later work stresses the constraints on the individual, although still with a view of the way in which the individual copes with the constraints – what the individual does with what has been done to him, as Sartre formulates the question in his Flaubert biography. The focus on the individual provides a dynamic feature in the image of the urban lifeworld that is similar to, but not identical with, Benjamin's. Phenomenological sociology is concerned with the acquired *doxa*, the result of the process of socialization, the "horizon" of the grown-up individual, Sartre and Benjamin are looking for the process of acquiring and coping with this knowledge, from the point of view of both child and adolescent – for the sake of clarity, at least, this contrast might have some validity.

Growing up in a city does involve more than words and gestures of the parents and other people around the child. It also involves an experience of social institutions, of material structures, of means of transportation, means of communication, etc. Significance and meaning are derived from the interaction between these rather variegated phenomena.

The acquisition of different abilities to move around in this world and to cope with conflicts rapidly becomes increasingly conscious as a child grows, yet much only becomes understandable later in life, if ever. Mass communication, television, and movies interact with stores and advertizing in the introduction to the world of consumption and the need for money, while parents and schools try to develop a sense of obligation in relation to relatives, fellow citizens, and the future. Social structures are inscribed in the urban fabric in many ways, and this inscription is readable for future generations; it becomes part of their horizon, their lifeworld.

Schools provide one example of institutional structures of both social and material character. Not only the adult, but also the child and the adolescent meet several other such institutions which contribute to their understanding of their situation, their past and their future. Heidegger's peasant's farmhouse is in his account inscribed with elementary aspects of human existence from birth to death.

The old rural community could relate to the village church and other significant buildings in the landscape. Isak Dinesen (Karen Blixen) has eminently reconstructed a similar reading of a Danish landscape towards the end of the eighteenth century:

> A child of the country would read this open landscape like a book. The irregular mosaic of meadows and cornlands was a picture, in timid green and yellow, of the people's struggle for its daily bread . . . On a distant hill the immovable wings of a windmill, in a small blue cross against the sky delineated a later stage in the career of the bread. The blurred outline of thatched roofs, – a low brown growth of the earth, – where the huts of the village thronged together, told the history, from his cradle to his grave, of the peasant, the creature nearest to the soil and dependent on it, prospering in a fertile year and dying in years of drought and pests.
>
> A little higher up, in the faint horizontal line of the white cemetery wall around it, and the vertical contour of tall poplars by its side, the red-tiled church bore witness, as far as the eye reached, that this was a christian country . . . a plain, square embodiment of the nation's trust in the justice and mercy of heaven. But where, amongst cupolar woods and groves, the lordly, pyramidal silhouette of the cut lime avenues rose in the air, there a big country house lay.
>
> The child of the land would read much within these elegant, geometrical ciphers on the hazy blue. They spoke of power; . . . Up here was decided the destiny of the surrounding

land and of the men and beasts upon it, and the peasant lifted his eyes to the green pyramids with awe. They spoke of dignity, decorum and taste. Danish soil grew no finer flowers
than the mansion to which the long avenue led. The country house did not gaze upward,
like the church, nor down to the ground like the huts: it had a wider earthly horizon than
they, and was related to much noble architecture all over Europe . . .

    The big house stood as firmly rooted in the soil of Denmark as the peasants' huts . . .[42]

Dinesen's account of the landscape shows not only how it is possible to read it, but also
how her reading is an interpretation, and by implication how this reading – in combination with the narrative – may influence her readers, take part in the shaping of their horizon. Both of these perspectives are relevant to the question of the urban lifeworld. What is
involved in Dinesen's description is – apart from the landscape in the narrow sense – a combination of *questions of work*, *questions of power*, and *aethetic questions*. Four architectural forms are mentioned: peasant *dwellings*, a *work building* (the mill), a house of
transcendental *interpretation* (the church) and a house of social *power*. In Heidegger's and
Bourdieu's essays the three first of these forms are combined in one, whereas the question
of power remains implicit or merely hinted at. In the urban context, the various types of
buildings are even more manifold, educational institutions being one obvious addition. But
from the point of view of the individual as well as from the point of view of a comprehensive urban analysis, the overall pattern of, and the interaction between, the various types
of buildings and ways of distributing and ordering must be taken into consideration, as
well as the ways in which artistic and other representations are formative in the perceptions and interpretations of the urban lifeworld, not the least those provided by television.
These perceptions and interpretations have their role to play in future urban development,
in at least two ways: individual choices are influenced by perceptions and interpretations
– the flight to the suburbs is the most obvious example; public – or autocratic, depending
on the situation – decisions and planning are influenced by perceptions and interpretations.

VIII THE HEARTBEAT OF MANHATTAN

What would a Dinesen-like depiction of a modern city read like? Let me take first
Manhattan around 1930 and then the development of Copenhagen as examples.

    What were the defining aspects of Manhattan from the point of view of the approach
sketched here? What would, for example, a snapshot of New York City in the 1930s highlight? Two highly significant features in the structure of Manhattan are its traffic structure
and the sites of popular culture. Both are concentrated in Midtown. Grand Central Station
(completed 1913) can be seen as an immense machine for the distribution of working
power or "an urban dynamo" powering the Midtown area which it transformed into the
"unchallengeable centre of Manhattan" (Kenneth Powell),[43] it might even be regarded as
a cathedral for working power, since the central hall was one of the largest and loftiest
everyday interior spaces in the city. It was not only originally conceived as a concentration of long distance and suburban connections linked with subways, elevated trains and
trams, and taxis as well, but by subterranean passages it also became connected with, for

example, the Chanin Building (10,000 employees) and the Chrysler Building (25,000 employees) nearby around 1930. This complex did thus form a new type of combination between traffic and work – not only, as the building magnate Chanin coined the expression, a city within the city, but a city connected to the suburbs.

> Not only long-distance travelers use the terminal; many of the more than five hundred trains that enter and leave daily carry commuters who live north and northeast of the city, while on an average of every four seconds during the day three IRT subway lines . . . discharge and receive passengers in stations connected with the terminal. The number of people who pass through Grand Central in a year approximates the total population of the United States.[44]

As an urban construction Grand Central Terminal thus ultimately defined the commuters first and foremost as working power. "Here you see the highest and most modern high risers, here traffic becomes ever more intense, here is the heartbeat of New York . . ." – according to a German guide from 1931. *The pulse of traffic is the heartbeat*.[45]

A few blocks away the definition was different. Times Square was also a traffic center: "Every twenty-four hours, two hundred thousand passengers emerge from the IRT and BMT subways to the cement passageways of the underground stations extending from Fortieth to Forty-third Street."[46] However, it was first and foremost an entertainment district: "This is the Great White Way, theatrical center of America and wonder of the out-of-towner. Here midnight streets are more brilliant than noon" (167). The German guide has this description of "The Great White Way": "In the evening hours the impression of this confusing multitude of light and colors is fantastic in its endless change between lightening up and dying away, and then the witch's broom of mass traffic and its immeasurable rows of cars among the crammed crowd of people longing for entertainment" (131).

Work and *entertainment* thus seem to be the defining ways of life in this city for the masses, ways of life defined by the city, laid out by the structure of the city.

A third example introduces an integration of corporate administration, new technology, and high art. The Rockefeller Center was planned as one such integration, although the result differs from the original plans. At the outset a new building for the Metropolitan Opera was considered, which was at one point located at Park Avenue at 96th Street: the architect's idea was to locate the opera as a cultural counterpoint to precisely Grand Central Terminal.[47] Later the site of what became the Rockefeller Center was chosen. The opera house would – it was suggested – raise the value of the location – as John D. Rockefeller's public relations representative wrote to his boss, who lived a few blocks north of the suggested site, after a presentation of the project: it would "make the square and the immediate surroundings the most valuable shopping area in the world" (cit. 630). In 1929 the opera project withdrew from the Rockefeller project (633), to the delight of the man Rockefeller had put in charge of the project – he did not share the belief in the value of an opera house for a shopping area (638). General Electric (GE), including Radio Corporation of America (RCA), became a new ally and the cultural role of the center was conceived from the point of view of broadcasting, as the chairman of GE expressed the idea: "the time has come when an organization that serves the country as completely and effectively as the Radio

Corporation does can no longer be considered apart from opera, from symphony, and education . . ." (cit. 639). "Radio City" was under way; what had started out as an opera project conceived mainly in terms of high society audiences had now developed into a project for mass audiences – in combination with the main aspect of the project: space for retail shops and offices. The era of electronic media had made its impact. Two massive theaters were built, Radio City Music Hall and the RCA Roxy, both larger than the earlier opera projects, but neither of them dedicated to opera; the first was meant for "supervaudeville," and the second for a mixture of movies and live musical entertainment (652). Initially the theaters proved no great success and subsequently the center's name was changed to Rockefeller Center. However, plans for cultural institutions at the site were not given up. A "Municipal Art Center" was suggested to the north of the center, including among other institutions an opera house and a symphony hall. In addition, in the original plan for the Museum of Modern Art it was located on the southern side of 53rd Street, closing the view from Rockefeller Plaza and thus participating in the center's overall pattern. None of this was realized. The Museum of Modern Art was built on the north side of 53rd Street without any connection to the Rockefeller Center, and after the war Lincoln Center's huge complex of musical and theatrical institutions was created elsewhere.

The concentration of retail shops, office buildings, public spaces, rooftop gardens, opera house, concert hall and museum of modern art on one site was not realized, but as a concept it did represent an attempt to create a city in the city, that should signal a nexus between the arts and corporate capital, a philanthropic concern for the beautification of the city combined with an interest in developments that could generate profit. Instead, the result brought together corporate capital, business administration, new media, and popular culture, appropriately signaled by the spectacular mass ornament of the Rockettes in Radio City Music Hall, rather than by the select few producing themselves in their opera boxes in the style of the old Metropolitan Opera. But both the enormous Rockefeller Center and the small Museum of Modern Art celebrate in their own manner the new style, progress, and eye for the future. About the MoMA the *WPA Guide* remarks that "the strikingly modern building . . . has become a symbol of those technical and imaginative innovations that have transformed the character of art during the past seventy years" (347). With regard to the center the guide writes: "In its architecture Rockefeller Center *stands as distinctively for New York as the Louvre stands for Paris . . .*" (334, my italics). Here, everything is gigantic: "the largest office building in the world" (336), "the largest broadcasting company in the world" (337), "the largest indoor theater in the world, Radio City Music Hall" (ibid.), "a six ton chandelier . . . that is reputed to be the largest in the world" (339), in sum: "Nearly everything about the Music Hall is tremendous" (338).

In a striking comment on the *Chicago Tribune* competition in the 1920s a German writer gives an interpretation of the significance of the skyscraper in his own country that brings Isak Dinesen's reading of the buildings in the Danish landscape to mind:

> The German skyscraper is assigned a definite role within the urban context: it is the expression of forces concentrated in a single point, and thus its value lies not in itself but in its relation to the comprehensive image of the city. What is revitalized here is the medieval idea of the cathedral. The function of the cathedral, which dominates the urban image with its

mass and is the symbol of metaphysical aspiration and spiritual comportment, was to be assumed by the skyscraper, its translation in modern terms, since in a certain sense the skyscraper represents the exaltation of work.[48]

Manfredo Tafuri takes this interpretation as "an attempt to counter the reality of the metropolis with the regressive utopia of the village" (405), i.e. an interpretation of the skyscraper in terms of *Gemeinschaft*, community, a "reenchantment" of the urban *Gesellschaft*, modern society. Yet the idea of the skyscraper as a modern cathedral, a "cathedral of work" (Tafuri), provides an apt approach to the Rockefeller Center as a dominating structure in the mental cityscape of Manhattan. A cathedral of work, business, and entertainment in terms of modern mass society. All of this based on an imaginative appropriation of technological innovations. In Giulio Carlo Argan's words "the skyscraper as a symbolic form, image of the spatial infiniteness in which we are enabled to live by virtue of an architecture that has completely absorbed the means, procedures, and very rhythm of industrial production,"[49] in other words, a symbolic form which is in accordance with modern society rather than a reemergence of the symbolic function of medieval cathedrals. Even if the symbolic dimension of the skyscraper is vertical, transcendence is not spiritual or transcendental in any religious sense, the spirit of modernity is temporally oriented, towards progress. In this sense, however, an ideological reenchantment is at work: the spirit of progress is not a neutral phenomenon. In a public relations pamphlet the official presentation of the center stressed how it was "designed to satisfy . . . the many-sided spirit of our civilization" and how it should bring "beauty and business into closer companionship."[50]

Together Grand Central Terminal and its surroundings, "Terminal City" (as *New York 1930* has it), Rockefeller Center, and Times Square area represent a social order based on mass scale distribution of working power, high concentration of masses, whether of people or of building material, collective mass entertainment, mass communication, mass consumption, and huge corporate capital concentration as the organizing factor behind the spectacle. There is more to Midtown than this, of course, but these are three significant factors that contribute to the definition of the horizon of the lifeworld. Robert Musil provided an apocalyptic vision of a similar American urban context in *The Man Without Qualities*:

> Overhead-trains, overground-trains, underground-trains, pneumatic express-mails carrying consignments of human beings, chains of motor-vehicles all racing along horizontally, express lifts vertically pumping crowds from one traffic-level to another . . . At the junctions one leaps from one means of transport to another, is instantly sucked in and snatched away by the rhythm of it, which makes a syncope, a pause, a little gap of twenty seconds between two roaring outbursts of speed, and in these intervals in the general rhythm one hastely exchanges a few words with others. Questions and answers click into each other like cogs of a machine. Each person has nothing but quite definite tasks. The various professions are concentrated at definite places. One eats in motion. Amusements are concentrated in other parts of the city. And elsewhere again are the towers to which one returns to find a wife, family, gramophone, and soul.[51]

The urban structure predetermines our behavior in many ways, the relation between home and work, the traffic structure, location of sources for daily necessities, institutions for activities in our free time, sports, entertainment, etc. Our understanding of these various factors is not given *a priori*, even if the surroundings are signifying. We have to "learn to read" what they have to tell, we have to learn to do our own reading. The ability to read is acquired through socialization, through situations and sequences of events in their intertwinement with verbal, visual, and other sensual representations. Popular songs and music are perhaps the most obvious examples of a more general fact. They endlessly articulate the same fundamental stories about, and reactions to, hope, fulfillment, and loss. In Kenneth T. Jackson's *Encyclopedia of New York*[52] the entry "*songs*" has no less than 500 numbers in a selective list of songs about New York. Literary critic Kenneth Burke once suggested an understanding of literature as "equipment for life,"[53] this point of view is relevant to an understanding of more than just literature: the various art forms, popular and high forms, all have a similar role to play, in a more or less complicated manner – for good or for bad, that depends. Popular songs, electronic media, movies, and the city belong together. Many standards were first presented in musicals, a quintessential urban form of popular art, or they were hits in successful movies, another popular art form that belongs to the city. Crime novels are yet another medium for addressing urban experience, often becoming material for movies. But visual media, including photography, movies, television, as well as variety shows and musicals are probably most important as "equipment" for the broader audience's adaptation to, or appropriation of, urban life. In these media, bodily experience can be articulated, reactions displayed, and ways of coping demonstrated. Early silent movies abound with instructive situations, whether the hero succumbs or succeeds is not as important as the recognition of reactions, the formation of a set of "schemata," in Schütz's terms. You have to learn to shake hands at the right moment and with the appropriate pressure of the hand according to the situation. This is only an obvious example from an immense field of bodily behavior that is so much more important as the proximity between different people increases. Movies demonstrate typical situations again and again in all kinds of variations, and they single out aspects of urban surroundings, exterior and interior. They "thematize" specific aspects of the urban situation. The setting of a narrative is not just background, it is a specific reading of the context – or, in most cases, a reconstruction of typical, and thus *thematized*, surroundings in cinema studios. The narrative, then, represents a sequence of events in interaction with the surroundings, and the urban context is thus integrated into an ordered version of possible human actions – in relation to a specific set of conditions and a specific point of view. This is also what takes place in television series and news reports – possibly the most important media-transferred cultural factor in the formation of mindsets and behavior in the present. Here both the image of the city and life in the city are organized, reproduced, and occasionally challenged. Personal experience is surely an important element, but it is organized, interpreted, and consolidated by the various forms of art and information. There is no such thing as "pure" personal experience. The interaction of lived experience and mediated interpretations and reorganizations thus provides a basis for individual and collective behavior in relation to the city. Individual choices concerning home and work accumulate and have their effects on the city – the escape to the suburbs is, again, the most obvious and probably also the most important example;

gentrification another. But the *image* of the city and its life also influences decision-makers, investors, planners, politicians – as well as grass roots activists. The formation of the city is, of course, the result of the interaction of an infinite number of factors – among them representations of the city, and the perception and understanding of the city which is influenced by representations, as well as the actual urban context itself, are not the least important. The lifeworld is involved in, and determined by, this triangulated reciprocity between formation, perception, and representation.

IX THE SIGNIFICANCE OF COPENHAGEN'S CITYSCAPE

Copenhagen began as a harbor, just as New Amsterdam did when the Dutch settled on Manhattan. At the time of Hans Christian Andersen and Søren Kierkegaard the city was still essentially defined by the sea. It was only in the second half of the nineteenth century that this changed – and then the changes increased rapidly.

A *bird's eye view* of Andersen's and Kierkegaard's Copenhagen reveals an urban structure that is enclosed by old fortifications. It was thus defined in terms of military and naval defense, yet simultaneously in terms of trade: the harbor defended by the navy was

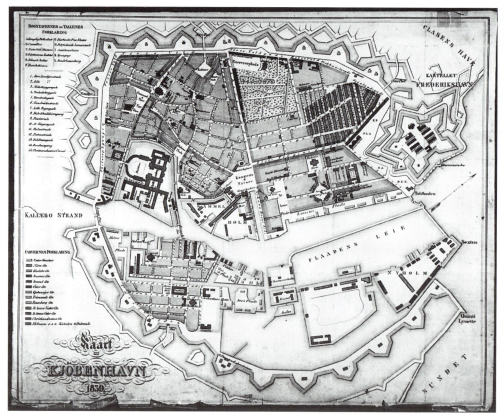

I.3 Map of Copenhagen from 1839. Courtesy of Copenhagen City Museum. NB: To the right, an arrow indicates north–south direction.

used by the merchant marine. Together with the agrarian sector the marine was the most important economic factor, and thus a defining factor, for the city. It was not only a city of administration, but also a city of commerce. Like the city, the harbor is closed in between the city proper to the west, and to the east the new city area built in the seventeenth century (Christianshavn) and several islands occupied by the navy. The medieval city, with its irregular streets, stands out not only against the regularity of the new city across the harbor, but also against the similarly regular part of the city towards the northeast (Frederiksstaden), which was constructed in the eighteenth century in a layout that is distinguished by large city blocks: an aristocratic extension of the medieval city. The narrow rows in the northern sector consist of a series of low rowhouses built in the seventeenth century as housing for mariners. The center of the city, with the Royal Castle (Slotsholmen), stands as an island because it is separated from the rest of the city by canals. North of the medieval city lies an extensive formal garden with a Royal Summer Castle (Rosenborg). The island northeast of the Royal Castle also belongs to the navy.

A horizontal view reveals another aspect of the city, the skyline. The most obvious features are the churches and their spires, and the castle, not to mention the city's windmills. The rest of the skyline is comprised of low buildings. How does this define the city? Whether one approached the city from land or from sea, the fortifications, the castle, and the churches would remain the most striking features, i.e. religion, central power, and the role of military force. And this was in fact the situation at one level. The bird's eye view confirms the role of the navy and the centrality of royal power. However, it also brings the opposition between aristocracy and general population into view, at least from the historical point of view, since the bourgeoisie – which means first and foremost the merchants – have increasingly made their mark upon the city, and have moved into the aristocratic areas. Once inside the fortifications, it is obvious how important the harbor and the merchant marine are.

It was only from *the point of view of the person in the street* that it was possible to reach a more detailed insight into the social and cultural structure of the city. One square on the map might already have attracted the visitor's attention, the rectangular square towards the western corner of the city, originally two squares separated by a small town hall building. The large building indicated on the map is the new combined Town Hall and Court House, which also included a prison. Walking in the streets, and across the square, one would notice this building as a remarkable neoclassical construction unto itself, yet also as an edifice which imposes itself with importance. The inscription in the tympanum quotes one of the oldest Danish medieval laws, insisting that "The country shall be built on law." For the pedestrian strolling through the square, this is a reminder that something other than law may govern: power. In 1848, the conflict between law and power was solved by preparations for a democratic constitution, which became what in Danish is called fundamental law (*Grundlov*, i.e. constitution) in 1849. Within a distance of a few hundred meters, two institutions (the castle and the town hall/court house) thus represented two conflicting principles, although the civil servants in charge of the application of law were at that point probably mostly leaning in favor of the Royal Castle. Civil servants, i.e. servants of the king, were an important part of the social structure, and in general were a conservative factor. Around the corner from this square, the walker would encounter the university, the institution primarily educating civil servants, priests, teachers, law specialists, doctors, etc. Stemming from the late fifteenth century this institution is amongst the oldest universities in Europe. Its location should be taken into account, since the university is situated opposite to the cathedral and next to the house of the bishop. This is due to the fact that in its early years, the university was predominantly educating inside the framework of Christian faith. In 1871, when the literary critic Georg Brandes inaugurated his ground-breaking lectures on *Main Trends in Nineteenth Century Literature* at the university, it was a scandal. His guiding line was the fate of the idea of freedom, and his attitude towards church and family was not reassuring for the Establishment. In the meantime, however, a modern intelligentsia was on its way to making its mark on Danish society. Brandes had his followers – the least amongst engineers, doctors and scientists. Industrialization was in the making. Copenhagen had abolished the fortifications which enclosed the medieval city. New areas rapidly developed. An immense movement from the countryside to the city was changing the composition of the urban population.

Turning away from the institutions, the stroller of the streets in pre-1848 Copenhagen would soon realize that the city was characterized by the close proximity of a variety of social classes. Splendid aristocratic and high bourgeois buildings stood side by side with humble buildings. The city was overbuilt, and backyard houses abounded. Yet the immediate impression of the exterior remained in a way remarkably homogeneous, due in part to the fact that large parts of the city were rebuilt after two huge fires, in 1728 and 1795, and after the English bombardment in 1807. The majority of the houses remain relatively narrow four-story buildings, while the larger buildings are of approximately the same height, but wider. Upper level housing thus fits in without standing out spectacularly at first glance – their extensions behind the front building are not visible from the street. Certain areas, of course, obviously stood out as better than others for the more attentive gaze, and some – now slum-cleared – blocks and areas were horrible and remained so well into the twentieth century.

At another level, the new housing areas built during the *Gründerzeit* outside the old city also developed into a relatively homogeneous type of *quartier*. That is primarily an effect of standardization of this mass scale building activity, public regulations were only concerned with the width of the streets. "Even if there was plenty of space," writes Steen Eiler Rasmussen in his book about Copenhagen,

> high and densely located buildings became the characteristic structure of the bridge-areas [i.e. the new working class areas beyond the lakes]. The streets became as broad as the laws demanded, and corresponding to the heights of the buildings ... Entire areas were now constructed for the poor. In London slums gradually developed, when old distinguished houses were allowed to degenerate and became occupied by lower strata than what they were built for. But in Copenhagen slum areas were built systematically. I shall not elaborate on how problematic it is to bring the stepchildren of society together in such areas.[54]

The result was five-story buildings with regularized fenestration and few variations in the roof profiles. This does not exclude considerable differences in the quality and size of the apartments. Generally speaking, the larger apartments faced the main thoroughfares, whereas the smaller apartments usually occupied the side streets and parallel streets. Spaces for the larger shops were also provided along the main streets, while the side streets had numerous small shops, most of which disappeared during the 1960s when supermarkets took over much of the distribution of everyday commodities. In the backyards a certain number of trades and small industries settled. Horse-drawn trams, and from around 1900 electric trams, provided the primary means of public transportation, becoming one of the determining factors shaping the development of the city. The impact of bikes should also be mentioned. Around the beginning of the twentieth century there were forty-five bicycle shops in Copenhagen – a hundred years later, about one-third of the people living and working in Copenhagen commute via bicycles. In the 'bridge areas' a huge number of ale houses and saloons provided public gathering space outside the cramped apartments, while also creating social problems. Entertainment establishments with dancing and variety performances developed quickly. Later on movie theaters proliferated in these areas; only a few of them were built in the old city.

At the beginning of the twentieth century, the structure of the city had thus changed almost entirely. The old city was now surrounded by a new inner periphery that expanded gradually towards the south, west and north. The character of the new parts of the city engendered a reaction, and already around the turn of the century private associations developed plans for areas with relatively cheap, more or less standardized villas with small gardens outside the new housing areas and intended for two or more families. Such initiatives, in fact, were already enacted before, or simultaneously with, the construction of the inner *Gründerzeit* periphery. The first example was the result of the 1853 cholera epidemic. At the initiative of a doctors' association, a series of two-story rowhouses, with green spaces in between them, were constructed not far from the city center. Various workers' associations followed this initiative, again building rowhouses as the typical structure, yet with very little outdoor green space. The rowhouse development closest to the center has, since the 1960s, developed into a very fashionable area for "baby

I.4 Photo of model illustrating the ground prices in Copenhagen – and thus what the skyline would look like, if ground prices determined building heights. From *København – skitse til en generalplan*, Stadsingeniørens Direktorat, 1954. Courtesy of Copenhagen City Hall.

boomers": houses originally consisting of two two-room apartments and a roof level with two small rooms, have been turned into upscale, single-family housing.

Expansions of the city during the twentieth century have produced a mixture of apartment buildings, rowhouses, and villas. Part of the lifestyle of the inhabitants of the new Copenhagen from the lower classes was also, it should be mentioned, spending free time during the warmer seasons in Schreber Gardens, which are spread around in the city outside the immediate center. It is worth mentioning that by the end of the 1920s one out of every forty-five inhabitants had such a garden.

In a book on Copenhagen dating from 1928, i.e. the period when the Rockefeller Center was planned, the city is introduced in this manner: "One fine day we will approach Copenhagen by train from the West. Already at a distance we have been busy looking for the city with the many towers; the capital, where 700.000 people are teeming (. . .)."[55] The city is approached by train not by sea, yet the profile is still characterized by the towers, although it has become a teeming city. The word "teeming" was used by Baudelaire in relation to Paris: "*fourmillante cité*," and Eliot quoted Baudelaire in *The Waste Land* in his attempt to characterize London. Copenhagen is conceived as a metropol. The Central Station is the gate to the city – and the connection to foreign countries: on his way our author gets a glimpse of the Berlin-Express. Close to the Central Station is the new Town Hall Square; here, as Nygaard explains, we are in the center of Copenhagen – we are "in the midst of the anthill." Here is the town hall building, which was inaugurated in 1905, and here stands a junction of numerous tramlines. The square itself is located next to the old city, on the site of the old ramparts and the town gate that once opened towards the west. What was formerly the boundary between the city and the open landscape had at this time, i.e. around 1930, become the center of the new metropolis. This is modern Copenhagen. An advertisement (for chocolate) inserted in this book praises "the new beauty the city has acquired by the electric advertising signs on the roofs."

The attitudes towards modern Copenhagen were diverse. To one of the characters in Henrik Pontoppidan's novel *The Reign of the Dead*, from the first decades of the twentieth century, the area around the new Central Station with crowds, cars, and electric advertising signs appeared as "Hell." For the protagonist in the classic novel about *Gründerzeit* Copenhagen, Herman Bang's *Stucco* from the 1880s, the new city, on the contrary, is life itself. In a retrospective summary of his life before he became a student he recalls: "Now *he* began to live – together with the new Copenhagen."

"This city is like a work in many chapters, written by various alternating authors" – thus another Danish writer (Johannes Jørgensen writing in the 1880s) indicated how the city isn't merely one entity for its inhabitants. Instead it is defined by representations, each of which may appeal to different readers or spectators, but nevertheless together interpret the city. The area between the old city and the new housing districts, including the Town Hall Square, Central Station, and various entertainment establishments, has in particular been a center of attention and thus a defining factor in the formation of Copenhagen's significance.[56]

Towards the end of the nineteenth century, Copenhagen had thus undergone a radical transformation. The decisive factor was industrial dynamics, similar to the *Gründerzeit* in

Germany. The fortifications were torn down, and working class housing areas were erected outside the military areas, just as in Vienna. Clearly defined social differentiations became part of the *doxa*, the generally accepted understanding of the social situation. There are many stories to tell about the early periods of these areas, but the most interesting comparison between Copenhagen and New York may perhaps be how they developed since the late 1960s, i.e. the period when gentrification became widespread.

The *Gründerzeit* areas of European cities were to a large extent working class areas. Over the last couple of decades the building stock in these areas has turned out to be eminently adjustable to changing social conditions. The inner part of the northern periphery in Copenhagen may be taken as an example.[57] It was one of the first peripheral areas to be developed. During the 1950s and in particular the 1960s, the social composition of the population changed radically, as the majority of the stable, working class families moved out of the city and into the suburbs. What remained were predominantly singles, outcasts, the unemployed, etc. The majority of the apartments comprised, as in most of the inner periphery, two rooms and toilet, but no bath, nor central heating. Students moved in. The municipality wanted to get rid of the old buildings in order to create an area of clean, new, modern housing. In the meantime, however, an activist movement had begun sketching an alternative development of this and similar areas.[58] Working class, *Gründerzeit* housing in this area meant several rows of courtyard buildings, very little light and generally unhealthy conditions. These areas were, as Steen Eiler Rasmussen wrote, built as slums in the first place. The municipality wanted these buildings destroyed, *tout court*. It was a historical issue: the generation in charge at the municipality still remembered the social misery of the areas that for younger generations represented a welcome chance to establish one's own home. Activists thus had different ideas: the backyard buildings should be torn down and the yard spaces developed into green areas; the front buildings should be redeveloped and central heating and bathrooms should be installed, etc. This conflict of visions, which was

I.5 Photos from 1953 and 1961 showing the same inner periphery block at Vesterbro before and after the clearing of the back yard. From Helge Nielsen, *En by i forandring – byfornyelse gennem 50 år*, København, 1987, pp. 110–11. Courtesy of Byfornyelsesselskaberne København og Danmark.

also a generational conflict, was played out at various levels, some more violent than others. At one point, barricades were even erected on the main thoroughfare of this area (in 1981). However, the end result was that the authorities, the municipality and the state, initiated a redevelopment plan that completely transformed this and similar areas, a plan still being realized under the heading "Urban Renewal." The basic idea was – as the activists had suggested – to get rid of the backyard buildings while maintaining the street line buildings. Today the inner periphery of Copenhagen is full of green spaces situated behind the buildings facing the streets. The result, in fact, is similar to a building type that had been realized in other areas since the time between the two world wars as an alternative to the congested inner periphery areas. The general idea which came to the forefront in the 1970s, somewhat like the breakthrough of ideas like Jane Jacob's in the American context, was concerned with city-renewal in lieu of slum-clearing, i.e. clearing of entire blocks and areas before the construction of new buildings.

A similar conflict came to the forefront in relation to traffic planning. The most prominent example is a plan for a new City West.[59] In its earliest and most radical form from 1959, a huge area west of the Central Station should have been developed into a spectacular new area with high-rises and buildings of a size that would have been entirely out of scale with the rest of the city, including even Arne Jacobsen's SAS hotel. The plan included subterranean parking levels and elaborated motorway systems that would be reached by a huge motorway along the lakes (similar to developments along the Seine in Paris), and connected to a north–south-bound motorway under construction at that point. In view of these plans, Robert Moses might appear as an early, sensitive contextualist. After about 10 years and a few somewhat less dramatic plans, public opinion and economic considerations had turned around, and the critics of similar plans had won the upper hand. Nothing ever came of it.

Nevertheless, another plan conceived in the same period is being realized today as part of a vision that includes the entire area around the Øresund. The bridge across the Sound was completed in 2000, and an entire new city area, the Ørestad ('stad' means city) is under construction, including sections of the University of Copenhagen, an institution for education and research in information technology, and new headquarters for the Danish public radio and television.

If one pays attention to the ornamentation and detailing of the Central Station[60] one will discover a pilot among the many reliefs. At the time when the building was inaugurated (1912), J.C.H. Ellehammer had already, as the first in Europe, demonstrated the potentials of motorized airplanes (in 1906); and thus inaugurated the development that, towards the end of the century, was one of the main factors in the planning of the Ørestad, i.e. the airport. The center of Ørestaden is located at the junction of a new highway and railroad between Denmark and Sweden across the bridge, and a new mini-metro line from the center of the city. Both the highway and the railroad pass by the airport. The idea is that the proximity to the airport will make this new urban area attractive for businesses that are frequently dependent on foreign connections. From the point of view of traffic the development of Copenhagen has, after the impact of the railroads (and before that the harbor), first and foremost been determined by automobiles. Since their conception both the Ørestad project and the bridge to Sweden have generated heated debates. Yet, regard-

I.6 Model photo of City West plan; in the upper right corner the Central Station and Arne Jacobsen's SAS hotel. From *City Plan West, prepared 1958 by the Development Plan Section of the Town Planning Office, Chief Engineer's Department*, City of Copenhagen (text in Danish and English), København, 1958. Courtesy of Copenhagen City Hall.

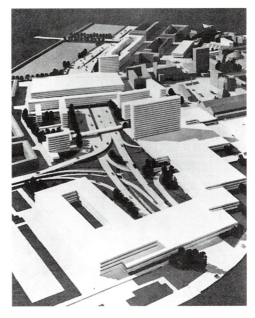

less of the evaluation of the projects, they do represent a new type of development and a new definition of the city, this time in terms of air traffic and of a reevaluation of railroads, although the bridge also will generate an increase in truck transportation and automobile driving in general.

In a few years there will be a twin-city structure, with Malmö in Sweden as a sister city. About 15 kilometers east of Malmö is the home of Lund University, an institution of approximately the same age and size as the University of Copenhagen. The link across the Sound will thus engender – or strengthen the potential of – a new development of the area that has a major airport as its nucleus. It has been pointed out, for example, that from the viewpoint of scientific output the area ranks as number six in Europe; a surprisingly high level when considering the size of Copenhagen, Malmö and Lund. Critics spurn the entire project as a late output of the kind of blind belief in growth and economic development that engendered projects like the City West plan. Since the days of Hans Christian Andersen and Søren Kierkegaard, when the city was enclosed behind the fortifications and the harbor represented the main link to foreign countries, technological developments have integrated the city in a larger context in many ways. In our age of airports and internet, new definitions of life in Copenhagen are added to those accumulated over the centuries, the lifeworld has changed not only in terms of the immediate urban situation, but also in terms of external relations.

X SYSTEM AND LIFEWORLD IN AN URBAN PERSPECTIVE

If "lifeworld" is understood as a concept developed in order to grasp the horizon of understanding of the everyday, as well as life's threshold events, and thus also life's different perspectives, and "system" is taken as the denomination of alienating factors that intervene in the organization and understanding of everyday life, then it becomes obvious that the issue is not a clearcut separation, but rather an identification of the various factors that govern our way of life, and our understanding of it. The example of Grand Central Station as the heartbeat of New York is illuminating. As a physical structure and in its connectedness to surrounding physical structures, this urban construct is not only organizing the everyday, but it is also organizing the understanding of the everyday. It is *making sense of being a commuting working power*, so to speak. And that means that it represents the intrusion of system and rationality of work into the lifeworld. It is defining the lifeworld in terms of rationality of work. In Habermas' terms: systemic relations are "colonization" of the life-world. With its echoes of the relation between empire and colony the term may sound somewhat awkward, but what it does point to is the fact that the understanding of situations is generated by a complex of, say, partial horizons that are not necessarily in mutual harmony. On the other hand, the concept of lifeworld may display a certain *a priori* positive air, since it is the lifeworld that is supposed to provide the ground for opposition to systemic factors. There is no guarantee here, though. It is a matter of controversy, a matter of questioning, debating, discussing, what the relevant criteria for an evaluation of defining factors of the lifeworld should be. In other words, what a good life and a just life in the city could look like, what positive conditions for cohabitation of desire and justice could look like in urban contexts as they are . . . or could become.

Notes

1   Denis Diderot: *Rameau's Nephew* and *D'Alembert's Dream*, translated with Introductions by Leonard Tancock, London: Penguin Books, 1966, p.30.
2   *Republic*, II.368D-E. Claudia Brodsky Lacour stressed this point in Plato in a lecture in Copenhagen, Spring 1999: "Architecture in the Discourse of Modern Philosophy: Descartes to Nietzsche."
3   *Berliner Kindheit um Neunzehnhundert*, in: *Gesammelte Schriften*, VII.1, Frankfurt: Suhrkamp, 1989, p. 385.
4   It would lead too far in this context to sketch the content of the *Arcades Project*, although it would fit into the argument of this introduction (cf. Christine Boyer's contribution to this volume). The best extensive account and analysis of the Arcades Project is Susan Buck-Morss: *The Dialectics of Seeing*, Cambridge, Mass.: MIT Press, 1989. *The Arcades Project* was published in a two-volume English version in 1999 by Harvard University Press.
5   In Martin Heidegger *Basic Writings* (edited by David Farrell Krell), 1993 (1977) – the German original, "Bauen Wohnen Denken," was published in Heidegger *Vorträge und Aufsätze*, Pfullingen 1954. Some of the following remarks are inspired by a lecture given by Jacques l'Homme in Copenhagen, Fall 1994: "Heidegger ou l'oubli de la ville."
6   Cf. Claudio Magris in *Donau*, where he is critically elaborating on the myth of origin in the German tradition, referring also to Hölderlin, one of Heidegger's absolute favorites.
7   A striking manifestation of his attitude appears in "The Thing": "Science's knowledge, which is compelling within its own sphere, the sphere of objects, already had annihilated things as things long before the atom bomb exploded. The bomb's explosion is only the grossest of all gross confirmations of the long-since-accomplished annihilation of the thing: the confirmation that the thing as a thing remains nil." (In: *Poetry, Language, Thought*, New York: Harper & Row, 1971, p. 170.) There is a certain stubbornness involved in insisting on referring to the annihilation of things in a lecture given in the summer of 1950 at the Bayrische Akademie der Schönen Kunste. This is not the place to elaborate on Heidegger's peculiar discussion of the relation between homelessness as "housing shortage" (the essay is from 1951, just a few years after the end of the

war with all its destructive effects for Germany's cities), and the supposedly deeper question: "What if man's homelessness (*Heimatlosigkeit*) consisted in this, that man still does not even think of the *proper* (eigentliche) plight of dwelling (*Wohnungsnot*) as *the* plight (*Not*)." (363 – in the English version "plight" seems to be used both in the sense of "suffering" and in the sense of "obligation" or "pledge," the German word *Not*, one of Heidegger's favorite terms, has similar semantic aspects): not the circumstances, but the attitude to the circumstances matters.

8   Pierre Bourdieu "The Kabyle House or the World Reversed," appendix in *The Logic of Practice*, Cambridge: Polity Press, 1990 and later (the original essay was printed with the title "The Berber House or the world reversed" in *Social Science Information*, April 1970 (IX–2), pp. 151–70 and in a Festschrift for Claude Lévi-Strauss in 1968). Cf. the Introduction in Kenneth Frampton: *Studies in Tectonic Culture: The Poetics of Construction in Nineteenth and Twentieth Century Architecture*, Cambridge, Mass.: MIT Press, 1995.

9   This quote is from the version in *Social Science Information*, p. 167. It is omitted in *The Logic of Practice*, but integrated in a more extensive discussion of the word "qabel" elsewhere in the book, cf. pp. 268–69 *et passim*.

10   Hans Georg Gadamer used the concept of horizon prominently in his *Truth and Method*, London, 1993 (published in German in 1960 as *Wahrheit und Methode: Grundzüge einer philosophischen Hermeneutik*).

11   Cf. Christian Norberg-Schultz's insistence on *genius loci*, (cf. his *Genius loci. Towards a Phenomenology of Architecture*, New York, 1984, and elsewhere), and Kenneth Frampton's arguments for a "critical regionalism," (in: Hal Foster (ed.): *The Anti-Aesthetic*, 1987). Both are inspired by the phenomenological tradition.

12   Cf. 359: "To say that mortals are is to say that in dwelling they persist through spaces by virtue of their stay among things and locales."

13   Cf. Foucault: "Of Other Spaces: Utopias and Heterotopias," in: Joan Ockman (ed.): *Architecture Culture 1943–1968*, New York: Rizzoli, 1993.

14   Hans-Georg Gadamer: "The Phenomenological Movement," in: *Philosophical Hermeneutics*, Berkeley: University of California Press, 1976.

15   Ludwig Landgrebe: "The Problem of a Transcendental Science of the A Priori of the Life-World," in: *The Phenomenology of Edmund Husserl. Six Essays*, London: Ithaca, 1981.

16   *The Crisis of European Sciences and Transcendental Phenomenology*, Evanston, 1970, pp. 269–99. German original: "Die Krisis des europäischen Menschentums und die Philosophie," in: *Die Krisis der europäischen Wissenschaften und die transzendentale Phenomenologie* (Husserliana Band VI), Haag, 1962, pp. 314–48.

17   Quoted by Landgrebe.

18   Aron Gurwitsch: "The Last Work of Edmund Husserl," in: *Philosophy and Phenomenological Research*, Vol. XVII, September 1956–June 1957, Buffalo, pp. 397–98. Gurwitsch's essay, which is about the concept of "life-world," is the second part of an essay on *Crisis*.

19   In phenomenological parlance "existent" means phenomenon in the experienced world.

20   Maurice Merleau-Ponty: *Phenomenology of Perception*, translated from the French by Colin Smith, New York: Routledge & Kegan Paul, 1962 and later, p. 281; *Phénoménologie de la perception*, Paris 1945 and later, p. 325.

21   *Modern Epic. The World System from Goethe to Gárcia Márquez*, London and New York: Verso, 1996.

22   The Lévi-Straussean concept from *La pensée sauvage* is central to Moretti's argument.

23   Alfred Schütz: "Some Structures of the Life-World," in: Thomas Luckmann (ed.): *Phenomenology and Sociology. Selected Readings*, Harmondsworth: Penguin, 1978. Also in: A. Schütz: *Collected Papers*, vol. 3, The Hague: Nijhoff, 1966, pp. 118–39.

24   In Foucault's œuvre the classic analysis of the intertwinement of power, institution and building concerns is, of course, Bentham's prison plan, the panopticon (in: *Discipline and Punish*, London: Penguin, 1991). Inspired by Foucault, John Bender has proposed an intricate connection between prison reform – including the organization of prison buildings and their relation to the world

outside, the early English novel in the eighteenth century, and the formation of the modern (idea of the) subject, in: *Imagining the Penitentiary. Fiction and the Architecture of Mind in Eighteenth Century England,* Chicago and London: University of Chicago Press, 1987.

25   Schütz's term in the English translation of his essay, the concept corresponds to what Gadamer calls *Vorverständsniss*, and actually defends in the form of *Vorurteil* (prejudice) against the critique directed against preconceived understanding by the Enlightenment (in: *Truth and Method*).

26   The idea of "the socially derived knowledge" as providing "a common schema of interpretation of the common world and a means of mutual agreement and understanding" (Schütz, 262) can only be taken as a provisional step in the direction of a more concrete analysis of situations that are conflictual and occasionally traumatizing in their unexpected character.

27   The rapidly expanding cities in the second part of the nineteenth century and the first decades of the twentieth century witnessed immense immigration (as in the case of New York) and inmigration (in the case of most European cities – in London this happened earlier). From the subjective point of view that meant that millions and millions encountered a lifeworld that was radically different from their background, a discrepancy, if you like, between their interiorized horizon and the horizon of their new habitat, their new situation. By what means did they handle this upsetting conflict? The question is, of course, very broad, but it brings forward a series of particular questions that are related to urban studies in the broader sense: the role of popular literature, crime fiction, the role of movies (the silent movies being accessible to a linguistically challenged audience), the role of popular songs, of vaudevilles, of musicals, etc., as well as the role of unionizing and political organizations in general, the role of religious institutions, etc., the role of specific parts of the city (e.g. ethnic concentration), the role of the press (among immigrants in New York also the press in their own language, Yiddish, Italian, Swedish, etc.) and radio, etc. Cf. below.

28   The distinction between local tactics and central strategy is discussed, evidently in a rather sketchy manner, in Foucault's *History of Sexuality*, vol. 1, New York: Vintage Books, 1988. For a – sympathetic, but sharp and relevant – critique of Foucault's concept of power and a discussion of its background in Nietzsche, cf. Jürgen Habermas: *The Philosophical Discourse of Modernity: Twelve Lectures*, Cambridge: Polity Press, 1987.

29   What is, of course, at stake here is the entire epistemology of sociology, and this is not the place, nor am I the writer, to provide a solution. The intention of this essay is more limited: to point out a series of questions, it seems relevant to raise, and perspectives, it seems relevant to indicate, in relation to a variety of theoretical approaches and examples of analysis, with a view to articulating an approach to urban studies.

30   This is not to say that the structure and dynamic of capitalism is absent from Adorno's analysis; it is permanently implied. Jürgen Habermas seems to underestimate this historical materialist aspect of Horkheimer and Adorno's *The dialectic of Enlightenment* (The Continuum Publishing Company, 1990) in his critique in *The Philosophical Discourse of Modernity*.

31   *Theory of Communicative Action*, Volume Two "Lifeworld and System: A Critique of Functionalist Reason," Boston, 1987, p. 120. In general, the section VI "Intermediate Reflections: System and Lifeworld," Part I: "The Concept of Lifeworld and the Hermeneutic Idealism of Sociology" provides a detailed critical discussion of the concept of lifeworld. The two volumes of Habermas' *chef-d'œuvre* comprise more than 1,200 pages of densely conceptualized prose. In this context no more than a few points can be discussed.

32   Just like the *Structural Transformations of the Public Sphere*, the subject of Habermas' first book (Cambridge: Polity Press, 1996).

33   Page 139, "*kulturalistisch verkürztes* Lebensweltkonzept" (210). The presentation of Schütz in this paper suggests, however, that his concept actually has broader implications, even if it is true, that it is primarily concerned with the perspective of the individual intentional subject.

34   This is also the direction of Habermas' critique of the early Marxian concept of society as a kind of macro-subject in exchange-relation to nature in *Philosophical Discourse of Modernity*.

35 In a note Habermas here refers to Heidegger among others, and points out that the tradition "is continued at a comparable level only in French poststructuralism." This is a theme that can only be hinted at here, but it is important to keep in mind how the various theoretical and analytical contributions discussed or mentioned in this essay are all deeply involved in this debate. Richard Wolin. *The Terms of Cultural Criticism: The Frankfurt School, Existentialism, Poststructuralism* (1992) provides several discussions of these questions in a perspective close to Habermas'. His *The Philosophical Discourse of Modernity* is a major, at some points fiercely polemical, contribution to this debate.

36 If we follow Norbert Elias: *The Civilizing Process: The History of Manners, State Formation, and Civilization*, Oxford: Blackwell, 1994.

37 This is not meant as a critique, but rather as an indication of the extent to which the urban experience is a challenge to social theory.

38 Jürgen Habermas and Hans-Georg Gadamer: *Das Erbe Hegels*, Frankfurt am Main: Suhrkamp, 1979, p. 23.

39 In *Daidalos*, 15. September 1987, pp. 24–36.

40 Cicero, quoted p. 29.

41 Georg Lukács: *The Theory of the Novel*, translated from the German by Anna Bostock, London: Merlin Press, 1971, p. 29.

42 *Winter Tales*, Harmondsworth: Penguin, 1983, pp. 172–73.

43 *Grand Central Terminal*, London: Phaidon, 1996, p. 4.

44 *The WPA Guide to New York City. The Federal Writer's Project Guide to 1930s New York*, New York: The New Press, 1992 (original edition 1939), p. 222.

45 Grieben Reiseführer: *New York*, Berlin, 1931, p. 122.

46 *WPA Guide*, p. 171.

47 Stern, Gilmartin, Mellins: *New York 1930*, p. 628.

48 Gerhard Wohler, p. 404 in Manfredo Tafuri's contribution, "The Disenchanted Mountain: The Skyscraper and the City," to Giorgio Ciucci *et al.*: *The American City. From the Civil War to the New Deal*, Cambridge, Mass.: MIT Press, 1983.

49 Cit. in Tafuri, op. cit., p. 405.

50 Cit. in Tafuri, op cit., p. 469.

51 *The Man Without Qualities*, vol. 1, translated by Eithne Wilkins and Ernst Kaiser, London: Secker & Warburg, 1961, p. 30.

52 Yale University Press, 1995.

53 In Kenneth Burke: *The Philosophy of Literary Form. Studies in Symbolic Action*, 3rd edition, Berkeley and London, 1973.

54 *København*, 1969, p. 106.

55 Fredrik Nygaard: *Kend København*, p. 11.

56 Cf. the contributions by Kvorning, Bøgelund-Hansen, Zerlang and Madsen below.

57 As it happens, this is where the author of this introduction lives.

58 Similar plans had, in fact, been proposed *as an intermediate stage* in a development towards total clearing and renewal of entire areas by prominent planners in the 1950s. Cf. *København – skitse til en generalplan*, Stadsingeniørens Direktorat, København 1954. "In the long run it should be taken into account, that very large parts of the buildings from before the turn of the century will have to be substituted, even if backyards have been cleared and the building stock has been thinned out during a first phase" (p. 85). Most of the inner periphery was built before the turn of the twentieth century. By the turn of the twenty-first century this was no longer official politics.

59 Cf. Arne Gaardmand: *Dansk Byplanlægning 1938–1992*, Arkitektens forlag, København, 1993, pp. 169–71. Gaardmand's book is the most recent comprehensive account of planning in Denmark with a rich visual documentation.

60 As Jørgen Bonde Jensen has done in an essay about the Central Station, in: *Mit navn er hare og andre essays: Modernitetens æstetik i praksis*, København: Gyldendal, 1984.

Part I

Formation

Chapter 1

City: Culture: Nature
The New York Wilderness and the Urban Sublime
Richard Plunz

In their new Foreword to the 1977 edition of *The Intellectual Versus the City* (1962), Morton and Lucia White point to the deepening crisis of the American city as further evidence of the "ambivalence or antagonism" toward the city that their research had attempted to demonstrate had always existed in American arts and letters. But a re-reading of the Whites' text today does not necessarily have to lead to the same conclusion that they reached in 1962, when the process of American post-war de-urbanization was still being expedited with maximum dispatch, and with the resultant urban degradation and suburban dispersal still fresh in people's eyes and minds. Indeed, as we move into another era it is possible to see the Whites' exercise in a somewhat different light, cast by a new historiographic understanding of the enormous scale and intensity of the de-urbanization strategy from the New Deal onward, tempered by our having moved from this first post-industrial crisis to a second or even third today. Now we can more clearly see that by the end of the 1950s, de-urbanist revisionism had penetrated the academic world, such that urban historiography began to devalue the role of the city in the development of our national culture.

The 1930s' post-industrial economic remedies entailed invention of a culture of consumption on an unprecedented scale, linked inextricably to urban dispersal through suburbanization. Within this reconfiguration, which was highly motivated by political ideology, the old city of density and propinquity could not function as the incubator for the new society. A new historiography had to be found which redefined American culture as anti-urban to validate the new ideology. In particular, works like *The Intellectual Versus the City* consciously or unconsciously served such purposes. Now it is important to reconsider this period, to reassert that cities large and small served as the crucial incubators of American culture; and to verify that historical discourse relative to the virtues of city and country was far more complex than the post-war revisionists would lead us to believe. In this regard, a re-reading of the texts of many of the Whites' urban "protagonists" provides us with a complex intellectual reflection on the nature of American culture in the nineteenth and early twentieth centuries. Given that American cities were growing exponentially like everywhere in the industrializing world, one would expect this process to raise doubts about the course of urban events, producing an important debate about the viability of the city. Notably, however, there was little by way of urban rejection until well into the twentieth century.

An important ingredient for this re-reading is the relation between city, culture, and nature. It is true, perhaps, that a big difference between the European and American approaches to the idea of the industrial city had to do with the conception of nature. One line of reasoning allowed that if Europeans had "culture," Americans had "nature," presenting a very real psychological divide. But even this is not exactly true: more precisely, the Americans had "wilderness." And in the formative period of nineteenth-century American urban culture, this wilderness was seen as a symbiotic force in urban development. American nature was not placed in a confrontational stance to urbanization. It was not the antidote to the American city deployed by the early European modern movement, just as it was not the antithesis of urbanity as deployed by the post-moderns.

This chapter will focus on the relationship between New York City and the spectacular wilderness of the Adirondack region of New York State. It was there, and especially in the Keene Valley, where between 1868 and World War I a formidable concentration of urban intellectuals congregated. This was a phenomenon unique for its scale and diversity in the American experience. The evolution of the Keene Valley intellectual community over those six decades followed closely the evolution of intellectual sensibilities regarding nature and the city during the same period; and more precisely, the changing self-image of urban intellectuals during the formative years of New York's development as the North American metropolis.

By 1810, New York City had definitively moved to its position as the largest city in North America having by then exceeded Philadelphia in population. More than Philadelphia, New York City took on certain aspects of what one might call a "city-state;" and indeed the State of New York had also exceeded the State of Pennsylvania in population.[1] The aphorism "Empire State" became popular. It had to do with the fact that New York City lay at the head of a 350 mile long metropolitan corridor, to the contemporary mind very much an "Empire." Stretching up the Hudson River to Troy, which was as far as the ocean-going ships could reach, it then turned westward along the Mohawk River to Buffalo and the Great Lakes. This natural watershed corridor was reinforced by construction of the Erie Canal completed in 1825; later by the railroad completed in 1842; and then by telegraph completed in 1846.[2] Thus the first North American "megalopolis" developed along this route, comprising a series of cities that were large by early nineteenth-century standards. Such was the growth of the corridor that by 1875 it contained one-half of the State's population; by 1920 over 80% in spite of the fact that it represented only 20% of the State's geographic area.[3] The cities of the corridor were wealthy and culturally sophisticated industrial centers, very much interconnected along the transportation and communication spine with New York City, which of course remained a primary catalyst for this configuration. New York City's commercial preeminence was also reinforced by the Champlain Canal, which connected northward from Albany to Lake Champlain in 1823 and extended to the Saint Lawrence by 1843. Thus by the mid-nineteenth century the Port of New York had been connected strategically with the Saint Lawrence basin, Montréal, and the North Atlantic via this inland route.

Incredibly, however, as late as the 1850s, within this same territory of the "Empire State" lay the largest unexplored region within the eastern United States, whose natural environment, while differing from the far western wilderness, easily rivaled it in terms of spectacular landscape. So remote was the region that it was not until 1838 that it acquired a Euro-American name, the "Adirondack Group." This was based on a Native American appellation transliterated by the state geologist Ebenezer Emmons (1800–1863), who

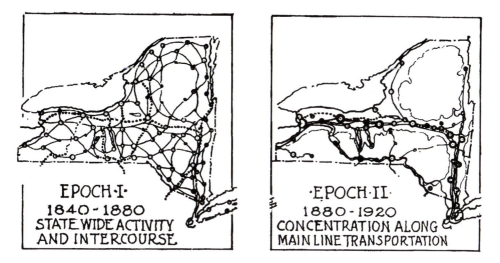

1.1 Two stages of the urbanization of New York State published in *Report of the Commission of Housing and Regional Planning*, 1926.

made the first geological survey in 1836.[4] Indeed, until the second half of the nineteenth century the area might as well have been in the far west as far as New York City was concerned. This situation changed quickly with improved transportation along the metropolitan corridor. Soon thereafter, the intellectual "discovery" of the Adirondack region followed, consequent to the emergence of the new urban culture. Today the region is the Adirondack Preserve, a state park that comprises more than six million acres and which, if taken alone, would equal or exceed the area of six of the original thirteen English colonies, or for that matter, well over half the area of Denmark.

Although the Adirondacks were isolated there was subsistence settlement in the early nineteenth century, much of it hidden away in remote valleys and totally dependent on local agriculture, lumbering and mining. This early population came primarily from New England in the early nineteenth century during the so-called "Yankee Invasion."[5] By mid-century this Yankee culture was marginalized and isolated relative to the culture of the new metropolitan Hudson-Mohawk corridor. After one or two generations, the sparse Yankee population lost contact with the urbanizing state and, more importantly, with the cultural changes that were being wrought by the industrial revolution and urbanization. In 1837 the *New York Mirror* summarized this phenomenon succinctly:

> It seems strange to find so wild a district in "one of the old thirteeners," the "empire state of New-York." But the Erie canal, in carrying emigration westward, has retarded the improvement of this region at least thirty years; by not only diverting the tide of new settlers, but preventing the increase of population among the old ones, by luring off the young men as fast as they become old enough to choose a home for themselves. Some, however, seem so attached to the woods and streams of their native mountains, that no inducement could lure them to the prairies.[6]

Thus the remnants of the Yankee Invasion came to represent an archaic human landscape as important to the intellectual "discovery" of the Adirondacks as the natural landscape.

Indeed, not all of the original Yankees stayed. By the mid-nineteenth century, the Adirondack region had lost population to the urbanizing areas. New York City was growing phenomenally, not only from foreign immigration but also from internal reset-tlement as rural areas declined.[7] The culture of those left behind fascinated the new urbanites who began to rediscover the rural regions. The human and natural landscape that the urban intellectuals discovered was more wild than several decades earlier, as the early settlement and exploitation of the natural resources was abated.

I THE "CENTRAL PARK OF THE WORLD," 1837–1875

The intellectual discovery of the Adirondacks can be traced to 1835, when the painter Thomas Cole (1801–1848) began to visit the area around Schroon Lake. His painting *Schroon Mountain* was shown at the National Academy of Design in New York City in 1838,[8] setting a precedent for many artists over the next decade who drew attention to the existence of an extraordinary eastern wilderness largely unknown. In 1837, the painter Charles Cromwell Ingham (1796–1863) accompanied geologists on the first recorded ascent of Mount Marcy, painting on site his depiction of Indian Pass called *The Great Adirondack Pass, Painted on the Spot*. It was shown at the National Academy in 1839.[9] Interest in such landscapes went beyond romanticism or nostalgia for a pre-urban society. The new painting was intertwined with developments in the natural and social sciences such that old boundaries were being transgressed so that geology, landscape painting, and morals could be part of one and the same investigation.[10] And this speculation could come only from the new urban culture that was evolving. When confronted with the Adirondack "discovery," the urbanites were incredulous. In the case of the Ingham painting, the writer Charles Fenno Hoffman (1806–1884) went to Indian Pass later on in 1837, to verify if indeed such a landscape existed. This he confirmed in his series of articles for the *New York Daily Mirror* in which the natural phenomenon is presented as follows:

> I must adopt a homely resemblence to give you an idea of the size of the rocks and their confused appearance in this part of the defile; you may imagine, though, loose boulders of solid rock, the size of your tall city dwelling-houses, hurled from a mountain summit into a chasm a thousand feet in depth, lying upon each other as if they had fallen but yesterday.[11]

Thus, in this first journalistic account, the Adirondack "discovery" is related to an urban metaphor so that urban readers could comprehend the remarkable landscape: in the same way that the geologist could appropriate the depiction as scientific knowledge; or the theologian as moral representation. With this precedent began the evolution of a complex interchangeability between urban and wilderness metaphors within nineteenth-century cultural paradigms. Eventually the city itself would come to represent a natural sublime.[12]

The relationship between the "second discovery" and the city was highly dependent

1.2 Charles Cromwell Ingham, "The Great Adirondack Pass, Painted on the Spot," 1837. 48″ × 40″. Courtesy of the Adirondack Museum, Blue Mountain Lake, New York.

on emerging urban cultural institutions that could commodify nature for the new urban population. Both Cole's and Ingham's "discoveries" were immediately shown at the National Academy of Design. Hoffman's journalistic account was immediately published in the *Daily Mirror*. There was the tendency to possess or even colonize the new nature, rather than to act simply as voyeur. The most famous early Adirondack intellectual encounter was known as the "Philosophers' Camp," organized at Follensby Pond near Saranac Lake in August 1858, with several members of the Saturday Club from Boston.[13] Included were Ralph Waldo Emerson (1807–1873), by then the principal American man of letters; Louis Agassiz (1803–1882), the famous Swiss naturalist who was based in the United States since 1846; Professor Jeffries Wyman (1814–1874), an American naturalist; John Holmes (1812–1899), brother of the famous justice Oliver Wendel Holmes; Dr. Estes Howe (1814–1887), a prominent physician; Judge Ebenezer Rockwood Hoar (1816–1895); James Russell Lowell (1819–1891), the poet laureate of the eastern intellectual establishment; and William J. Stillman (1828–1901), the artist and journalist whose famous painting documented the event.

The Saturday Club group entered the Adirondack region from Lake Champlain via the Ausable River to Ausable Forks and then traversed the Wilmington Pass westward to the Lower Saranac Lake. From there it took two days by canoe with portage to reach the Follensby campsite that had been prepared in advance by Stillman. Another party happened by in the following days and described what they found: Lowell rowing a boat with Agassiz at the stern and Emerson at the prow; Wyman attempting to dry the stomach of a buck to take as a specimen; Emerson ecstatic about virgin trees; a discussion between Agassiz and Wyman about maternal habits of snakes; and a disagreement between one of the guides and Agassiz about the copulation of trout.[14] Stillman's painting of the group on site depicted a typical morning later described by Edward Waldo Emerson (1844–1905), Ralph Waldo Emerson's son, who revisited the site in the following year:

> Stillman painted on the spot an admirable picture of the morning hours' work or diversions, before the excursions by boat or on foot began, the sun filtering down between the foliage of the vast, columnar trunks of pine, maple, and hemlock. There are two groups; on one side, Agassiz and Dr. Jeffries Wyman disecting a fish on a stump, with John Holmes, doubtless with humorous comment, and Dr. Estes Howe, as spectators; on the other, Lowell, Judge Hoar, Dr. Amos Binney, and Woodman trying their marksmanship with rifles, under the instruction of the tall Don Quixote-like Stillman; between the groups, interested, but apart, stands Emerson, pleased with the gifts of all. Prolonging the shooting party towards the edge of the picture two or three guides are gathered, silent critics.[15]

The iconography of Stillman's painting is significant, especially the categorical groupings and Emerson's relation to the others. Emerson in his isolation becomes the poetic voyeur rather than primitive woodsman or engaged naturalist. In this sense his relationship to nature is something new in the American context and anticipatory of the evolution of intellectual discourse of the following decades.[16] Emerson's experience at Follensby Pond was conditioned by his urban formation; the New England nature that he knew was highly gentrified. While he had previously written of the wilderness experience, until his visit to Follensby Pond, he had never experienced true wilderness. He framed his wilderness fantasies and his urban fantasies as a dialectic.[17] Emerson's view of nature tended toward the romantic, using such terms as "idealistic," "graceful," "mediate." Nature was seen as the "perfection of creation," and the "apparition of god."[18] In the primeval woods of the Saranacs, however, Emerson saw another nature far different from the manicured woods of suburban Boston. Emerson's rapture with this new world of "sacred mountains" is evident in his account of the trip. Indeed it is likely that Emerson had never before seen the virgin white pine of "fifteen feet in girth" or "Maple eight" he mentions and Stillman's painting depicts.[19]

Leo Marx has provided the useful distinction between the "primitive" and "pastoral" natures in the American experience.[20] By the time of Emerson, the "primitive" wilderness landscape known to the New England Pilgrims had all but disappeared in the east, making the Adirondacks appear as an archaic "apparition" on the one hand; on the other, they provided dramatic proof of the continuing existence of the "primitive" for consumption by the new urban culture. In America, as in Europe, industrialization was transforming the city. As numerous scholars have observed, if America could not exactly claim to have "history," it did possess "nature," which became a kind of surrogate "history" in this period.[21] The political dimension of this sensibility is worth noting. Lacking history, the Americans also lacked historical nobility. Therefore such historical reassurances present in the European nineteenth-century urban industrial culture were supplanted in America by the natural environment. For Americans, instead of nobility there was God. And it was argued that there was no need for "history" given the perfection of God's hand in nature.

For Emerson, the experience at Follensby Pond only seemed to expose the contradictions of an idealism inseparable from his urban experience. Toward the end of *The Adirondacks* he asks the obvious:

> We flee from cities, but we bring
> The best of cities with us, these learned classifiers,
> Men knowing what they seek, armed eyes of experts.
> We praise the guide, we praise the forest life:
> But will we sacrifice our dear-bought lore
> Of books and arts and trained experiment . . .[22]

Stillman, who was the influential founder of the journal *The Crayon*, had organized the 1858 trip to Follensby Pond after a previous visit to the Adirondacks.[23] In 1859 he organized the short-lived "Adirondack Club," which included most of the "Philosophers' Camp" group. At the time the notoriety of the experiment remained pretty limited to the Boston intellectual community, but over time much was made of the "Philosophers' Camp" as interest in the Adirondacks intensified. In 1867 Emerson published his first extensive description of the experience: an epic poem called "The Adirondacks." This recollection, undoubtedly embellished in Emerson's mind over the years, coincided with the growing body of Adirondack literature.

The earliest popular account of Adirondack travels was published in 1849, before the Philosophers' Camp experience. It was John Tyler Headley's *The Adirondack; or Life in the Woods*. This account probably inspired Stillman's interest, as well as the interest of many of the early generation of artists. In 1860 came Alfred Billings Street's *Woods and Waters: or, The Saranacs and Racket*, followed in 1869 by the Reverend William H.H. Murray's *Adventures in the Wilderness or Camp-Life in the Adirondacks*. This latter book became immensely popular, launching the first wave of Adirondack mass tourism. The urban migration to Keene Valley in the 1870s was reinforced directly by Murray's book. Prior to 1869, urban vacationers had long frequented the Catskills and the White Mountains because of their accessibility. The Adirondacks opened in part because of improvements in accessibility, but beyond this factor, the new generation of "Murray's Fools" represented an escalation of the consumption of nature related to the development of leisure in the new urban age. This new era of massive summer migration established "nature" as an extension of the city.[24]

By the 1860s, the Adirondack region, the most spectacular of the remaining eastern wilderness, had become reasonably accessible for summer migration because of improved water and rail transportation. An 1864 editorial in the *New York Times* foresaw the day when, with completion of better rail connections ". . . the Adirondack region will become a suburb of New York," a suburb, however, to be preserved as a park. In great part justified by the nostalgic intention of rediscovering "the old passion for nature which is never permitted to die out;" this preserve was to provide a "solitude almost as complete as when the 'Deerslayer' stalked his game in its vastness, and unconsciously founded a school of romance equally true to sentiment with that of feudal ages."[25]

In the soliloquy of the *New York Times*, the vast scale of the Adirondacks was to be measured against the ambitions of empire. New York was seen as a global city and the Adirondacks were not just to be suburban. They were to be the ultimate urban park: the "Central Park for the World," offering amenities which were unknown to the great European cities:

> . . . a variety of mountain scenery unsurpassed, if even equaled by any region of similar size in the world . . . lakes count[ed] by the hundreds, fed by cool springs, and connected mainly by waters threads, which make them a network such as Switzerland might strive in vain to match, and . . . hunting and fishing which our democratic sovereign-citizen could not afford to exchange for the preserves of the mightiest crowned monarch of Christendom.

It should be noted that the *Times* did not see the beneficiaries of this paradise to be particularly plebeian, but instead the province of the surrogate American nobility: of "merchant, or financier, or *letterateur*, or politician . . . .." And in reality only this elite could reach the region, which is why Frederick Law Olmsted in the real Central Park attempted to bring the Adirondacks to the city, rather than the opposite:

> It is the one great purpose of the Park to supply the hundreds of thousands of tired workers, who have no opportunity to spend their summers in the country, a specimen of God's handiwork that shall be to them, inexpensively, what a month or two in the White Mountains or the Adirondacks is, at great cost, to those in easier circumstances.[26]

Olmsted did incorporate many features of the Adirondack landscape into his park design: the Ramble in Central Park, for example, or the Ravine in Prospect Park.

During the period between 1837 and 1869, the experiences of Ingham, Hoffman, or Emerson were repeated many times over by the numerous artists and writers who made their reportage back to the cities from numerous locations in the Adirondacks, most notably from the eastern and central regions that were more accessible to the urban areas (still a trip of several days' duration, however). By the 1860s, intellectual interest in the Adirondacks gravitated to the Keene Valley in the eastern High Peaks region. Its natural situation was found by many to be the most spectacular in the Adirondacks: a secluded mountain valley cleared for subsistence farms, surrounded by mountains, and dominated by the East Branch of the Ausable River and its tributaries which were rushing streams descending with waterfalls from the surrounding plateaus. In the highlands of the far southern end of the Keene Valley lay the Ausable Lakes. In this setting, a phalanx of prominent artists, writers, theologians, and philosophers arrived from the cities. There has been no such concentration since in an equivalent context. They began to appear in the Keene Valley after the Civil War, the first wave notably related to New York and Hartford. In 1869, *Putnam's Magazine* published "Keene Delights" by New York writer and French and Italian scholar Kate Hillard (1840–1915) which for the first time for a popular readership described the attractions of "the lovliest valley in the world."[27] Hillard early on had adopted Keene Valley as a summer place. Her article, especially in the wake of Murray's *Adventures in the Wilderness*, was important in augmenting the numbers of "city enthusiasts." Her connections in New York helped bring others, including her cousin Seth Low (1850–1916), then Mayor of Brooklyn and later President of Columbia University. She was also the sister-in-law of William A. White (1843–1927), the prominent Brooklyn businessman and civic leader who eventually built a house in St. Huberts at the southern end of the Valley.

The artists were the first urban visitors to arrive in Keene Valley, following in the footsteps of Ingham and Cole in search of ever more spectacular landscape, and of possi-

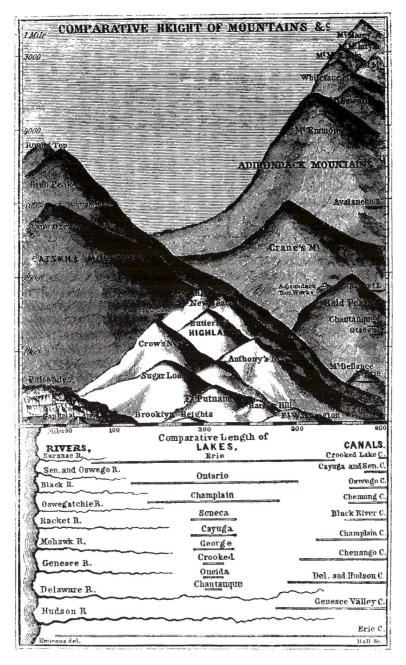

1.3 Longitudinal section through New York State, from J. Disturnell, *A Gazetteer of New York State*, 1842. Courtesy of New York State Library.

1.4 Globalized panorama of "New York & Environs" published by Bachman in 1859. Courtesy of Eno Collection, New York Public Library.

bilities which could go beyond the limitations of the "Hudson River School."[28] By the end of the 1860s, the nation's prominent landscape painters had produced a large body of work in Keene Valley which made its way back to the New York art market. These included in roughly chronological order: Asher B. Durand (1796–1886), William Trost Richards (1833–1905), William Hart (1823–1894), Horace Wolcott Robbins (1842–1904), Homer Martin (1836–1897), William Tyler (1825–1896), John Lee Fitch (1836–1910), John Henry Dolph (1835–1903), Alexander Lawrie (1828–1917), Roswell Shurtleff (1838–1915), Samuel Colman (1832–1920), and James Smillie (1833–1909). Others included, especially in the following decades: John Kensett (1816–1872), John Casilear (1811–1893), Alexander Wynant (1836–1892), J. Alden Weir (1852–1919), Robert Minor (1839–1904), George Inness (1825–1894), and Winslow Homer (1836–1910).[29] There were also many lesser artists, attracted by the big names and the growing fame of the place.

Some artists returned to the Keene Valley for years while others moved on to new discoveries in the west; or to new representation altogether. A significant number stayed, however, such that Keene Valley became one of the best-known American artist colonies until well into the twentieth century. Those who stayed included Shurtleff, Wynant, Minor, William Hart, Robbins, and Weir, who all built summer houses and studios. On the surface, at least, what the artists were after seems obvious. The burgeoning art market required perennially new material and technique for success, and for a short period Keene Valley supplied the fodder for changes in American landscape painting. The sudden accessibility of the most remote of eastern wilderness made this landscape "new" to urban audiences. The urban cultural institutions were crucial to its promotion, especially those in New York City: principally the National Academy of Design; the Century Association; and the Tenth Street Studio.[30]

The artists led the way for a rapid succession of urban intellectuals who established themselves in the Keene Valley, the next group being the theologian-philosophers. They were the leaders among the new generation of urban clerics who were ideologically united in their anti-Calvinism, and driven, at least in part, by the practical realities of having to address the large urban congregations of the industrial northeast. They especially included those theologians who were promoting an elixir of "play, repose, and plenty" to their urban constituencies, partly as a foil to the regime of the industrial society.[31] With this new outlook came a changing perspective on the natural environment relative to the conception of God. God was no longer seen as presiding over nature, but rather as existing within nature.[32] This fundamental deviation suited the practical realities of urban life which required the reassurances of a more approachable, engaged deity: "one of us" rather than an inaccessible dogmatist. While Emerson saw nature as the balanced and hermetic realm of the "wood-god murmer[ing] through the leaves,"[33] for some of the new generation theologians, the relation between God, nature, and the city was considerably more complex.

Several of the principal figures in this new period of theology gravitated to the Keene Valley, around the figure of Horace Bushnell (1802–1876)[34] Bushnell's famous essay, "An Argument for Discourses on Christian Nurture," was greatly admired by many including Emerson.[35] Bushnell was a part of the intellectual circle in Hartford, dominated by Mark Twain and his Nook Farm contemporaries. Within this milieu, in the 1860s, Bushnell had founded the "Monday Evening Club" as a forum for the exchange of ideas reminiscent of Emerson and the "Saturday Club" in Boston.[36] Toward the end of his life, beginning in 1868, Bushnell spent summers in Keene Valley after having consummated his ideas during the two decades (1833–1853) of his urban pastorate of the North Church in Hartford. Bushnell was joined in Keene Valley by his somewhat younger fellow Connecticut theologian, Noah John Porter (1811–1892), who was Professor of Moral Philosophy and then President of Yale University. His widely used text *The Human Intellect* (1868) was a pioneering work in the American development of psychology. The national prominence of Bushnell and Porter brought many other younger theologians who, like the artists, built early Keene Valley summer houses.[37]

Compared with the artists, whose interests led them primarily to the wilderness landscape, the theologians focused equally on the natural and human environments. Bushnell best articulated the relationship between nature and the city. Rather than Emerson's ideal of a harmonious balance, Bushnell saw in nature a prevalent condition of "deformity." Thus for Bushnell, nature was a realm of "disorder, jargon and death," a dystopic cathedral with an organ of "badly voiced pipes." Dominated by the same scourges, nature and city were one, both suffused with the "mysterious transcendent hymn" of "sin."[38] The "perfection" of nature was not to be polarized against the "dysfunction" of cities; nature was also dystopic. This conceptual interchangeability of the urban and wilderness environments reflected changing perceptions of both. Responding to the needs of their urban constituencies, liberal urban theologians had to reinterpret previous notions of God and nature, expanding the concept of "nature" to include "human nature." As Max Eastman underlined much later, it was these theologians who originated American philosophical studies: "Professors of philosophy were ministers of the gospel, who . . . had found it easier to teach than to preach. They were a sort of plain-clothes chaplain employed by the colleges to see that science did not run away with the pupils' minds."[39]

It was logical that Bushnell, Porter, and the others found equal beauty in Keene Valley between the natural landscape and the "human landscape," with its way of life so intimately connected to the vagaries of the harsh local wilderness. It was via these theologian-philosophers that this landscape became integral to the development of philosophical discourse within the American urban experience by the twentieth century. Bushnell's daughter, Mary Bushnell Cheney, later described her father's attachment to the Keene Valley population:

> . . . his thoughts often adverted with a peculiar tenderness to the lowly Christian souls there, having an experience that differed so widely from his own, sustaining in those quiet recesses of the mountains an inward life with God which was almost unrecognizable by man. Of one household, beneath whose roof he found a peaceful shelter, he said, "How beautiful are such lives, growing in obscurity, hidden away here like the mosses in the forest!"[40]

This same sentiment was expressed early on by others. Kate Hillard in her 1869 description of "Keene Delights" volunteered that "the inhabitants of this secluded spot are no less worthy of study than their mountains and streams." One inhabitant in particular caught the attention of Hillard whom she described as:

> a man of about fifty-five, small and wizened as a winter pear, but, to use his own words, "as tough as a b'iled owl." His little keen eyes are half lost in a forest of tangled and rusty hair and beard, which "he doesn't calk'late to comb out more'n twice a-year," and from whence issues a singularly small and squeaky voice.[41]

Hillard goes on to describe reciting Tennyson to this guide who, of course, was Keene Valley resident Orson Schofield Phelps (1817–1905), popularly known as "Old Mountain Phelps." He could be considered the perfect character study for theorizing the interconnectivity between the natural and human environments. Early on, the intellectuals, and especially Bushnell, developed a particular intimacy with him. An extraordinary figure, Phelps was intelligent and highly articulate, providing a bridge with the archaic beyond the capacity of other local citizenry.

Phelps, who emigrated from New England toward the end of the "Yankee Invasion," was emblematic of the local pre-industrial culture. His idiosyncratic ways and flair for publicity made for his great notoriety among the urban visitors. He cultivated relationships with the most interesting of the early intellectuals. Mary Bushnell Cheney described the relationship between Phelps and her father:

> He made, or rather found, some true friends in that beautiful valley. He honored the manly qualities of some of the guides, enjoyed the ruminations and piquencies of "Old Phelps," and all the meandering walks and talks they had together.[42]

Phelps fascinated numerous of the early visitors, not the least of which was Winslow Homer, who in 1877 included Phelps as one of the two heroic figures in his famous painting, "The Two Guides." Phelps appears in several later Homer paintings as well, underscoring the fact that, like the theologians in Keene Valley, Homer was interested in the "human landscape" as much as the natural, an interest which escaped his other artist contemporaries, at least in their Keene Valley work.[43]

In 1874, Seneca Ray Stoddard featured Phelps in his definitive *The Adirondacks Illustrated*, which, unlike previous guidebooks, gave Keene Valley ample urban coverage.[44] Thus, as much as the scenery, it was Phelps' fame which helped to project Keene Valley to its prominence beyond the province of the artists and the theologian-philosophers. This escalation was also fueled by the writings of Charles Dudley Warner (1829–1900) about the Keene Valley, especially his essay on Phelps first published in the *Atlantic Monthly* in May 1878.[45] Early on Warner had built a summer cottage in Keene Valley. He was an important member of the New York-Hartford literary circle. Warner was co-author with Twain of *The Guilded Age*, and by the time of his Phelps piece he had reached national prominence as a writer. The question of who invented "Old Mountain Phelps" is a difficult one in that it is not entirely clear how much of his persona can be attributed to Phelps himself and how much was simply what urban visitors hoped to find in him. Warner's essay is instructive in that he heightens Phelps' idiosyncrasies, promoting him as a "discovery" of sorts; as a "primitive man" dislocated from contemporary life. Warner tailors the concept of the "primitive" to his urban audience. For example, he distinguishes Phelps' primitivism from the "primeval," instead seeing him as a "survivor," or one of those who are "left here and there in our era."[46] This reading of Phelps fulfilled a populist need to recapture the quickly vanishing pre-urban and pre-industrial past. Yet in reality Phelps was a modern urban invention: he religiously read Horace Greeley's *Tribune* along with tens of thousands of urbanites. Warner was forced to admit that such contradictions "complicate the problem" such that:

> . . . no scientific observer, so far as we know, has ever been able to watch the development of the primitive man, played upon and fashioned by the hebdomadal iteration of "Greeley's Weekly Tri-bune." Old Phelps educated by the woods is a fascinating study; educated by the woods *and* the Tri-bune, he is a phenomenon.[47]

As for his own role in the "urbanization" of Phelps, Warner also admitted that "when the primitive man comes into literature, he is no longer primitive."[48] The ambiguities in the character of Phelps, real or imagined, represent the dialogue between city and nature and the condition of intellectual existence during this crucial moment of the emerging metropolis in the cultural life of the nation.

II WILLIAM JAMES AND KINDRED SPIRITS, 1875–1910

The informal reign of the theologian-philosophers in the Keene Valley moved to a period of more institutionalized communal socialization related to the new urban intellectual activity. Beginning in the 1870s, intellectual "institutions" sprang up throughout the Valley. These ranged from informal places of exchange to formal educational programs. The first was "Putnam Camp," best known as the retreat of the philosopher William James (1842–1910). In 1874 James passed through Keene Valley on a hiking trip with three former Harvard Medical School classmates. They were two brothers, James Jackson Putnam (1846–1918) and Charles Pickering Putnam (1844–1914); and Henry Pickering Bowditch (1840–1911). They boarded at a farmhouse at the southeastern end of the valley, and were so taken with the place that they returned the following summer and purchased a small plot of land from the owner, constructing a camp shelter called "The Shanty." In the following year they purchased more land including the old farmhouse, which became the core of what is still known as Putnam Camp.[49] Over the years an eclectic admixture of rustic buildings evolved: the "Coop" for the Bowditch family; the nursery and "Parents Assistant" for the Putnams; the "Chatterbox," a one-room cabin; and the "Stoop," a common room with walls that opened to the outdoors.[50]

Putnam Camp was conceived very much in the spirit of the Philosophers' Camp at Follensby Pond. In effect it realized the project that Stillman had attempted but never materialized with his "Adirondack Club." To be sure, the four Harvard classmates knew of the Philosophers' Camp from Emerson's publication of "The Adirondacks" in 1867. James no doubt had heard of the experience firsthand from Emerson since the two families were close.[51] Indeed, Edward Waldo Emerson (1844–1905), physician and son of Ralph Waldo and James' contemporary and friend, had visited the Follensby Pond site in the year following the "Philosophers' Camp" experience. In addition, Louis Agassiz and Jeffries Wyman, who were both present at Follensby Pond, were the Harvard faculty who had most influenced all four.[52] In any event, Putnam Camp became the logical successor to the ideals that Emerson and Stillman had imbued in the Philosophers' Camp experience, tempered of course by the intervening decades of enormous change in both the cities and the Adirondacks alike.

At Harvard, James, Bowditch, and the Putnams all shared an interest in the connection of the embryonic science of neurology to other areas of knowledge. By the 1890s Putnam Camp became a catalytic force among the principal actors in what one scholar has called "the Boston 'School' . . . , notable for the informal cooperation of psychologists, philosophers, neurologists and psychiatrists," and the center of "the most sophisticated and scientific psychotherapy in the English-speaking world."[53] These were the sciences of the new urban age, cultivated not just by advances in medicine but also in social science.[54] Of particular importance to the "Boston School" was the philosophical work of William James and the psychological work of James Jackson Putnam. During the summer Putnam

1.5 Putnam Camp group photo detail with William James. September, 1896. Courtesy of Keene Valley Library Association.

Camp became a center in its own right for exchange between James, Putnam, and other major personalities in the emerging sciences. For example, regulars at Putnam Camp also included Josiah Royce (1855–1930), the philosopher who taught with James at Harvard and was a close friend who admired and wrote about James. Another was Richard Hodgson (1855–1905), physician and Secretary of the American branch of the Society for Psychical Research.[55]

With this initial circle as catalyst, a stream of visitors to Putnam Camp ensued including many of those who were active in developing the new discourse on physiology, psychology, and philosophy. Among them were Sir James Bryce (1838–1922), British politician and historian; Sir William Osler (1850–1919), Chief Physician at Johns Hopkins and later Oxford; Sir Lauder Brunton (1844–1916), the widely known consulting physician in London and pioneer in physiology; Angelo Mosso (1846–1910), Professor of Physiology at the University of Torino; Sir Michael Foster (1836–1907), British physiologist; Karl Hugo Kronecker (1839–1914), German Physiologist; and Thomas Davidson (1840–1900), Scottish philosopher who had emigrated to the United States. Among other intellectuals who frequented Putnam Camp were the well-known British playwright Edward Knoblock (1874–1945); the zoologist Edward Sylvester Morse (1838–1925), founder of the collection of Japanese art at the Museum of Fine Arts in Boston; and Hendrick van Loon (1882–1944), the prolific writer who married Bowditch's daughter.[56]

What the visitors found at Putnam Camp was exotic, having evolved over the years to a considerable state of eccentricity. Sigmund Freud (1856–1936) visited for five days in 1909 together with Swiss psychologist Carl Jung (1875–1961) and Sandor Ferenczi

(1873–1933), the Hungarian psychoanalyst. Freud wrote an account of his experience to his family in Vienna:

> Of everything I have experienced in America this here is probably the strangest: a camp, you must imagine, in a wilderness in the woods, situated like on a mountain-meadow, like on the "Loser" where the Inn stands. Stones, moss, groups of trees, uneven ground which on three sides merge into densely wooded hills. There is a group of roughly made log cabins with a name to each as one discovers. One is called the "Stoob" (sic.), that is the parlour where library, piano, desks and card-tables are, another the "Hall of Knights" with amusing old objects, with a fire-place in the centre and benches along the wall as in a peasant's dining-room. The rest are living quarters. Ours with just three rooms is called "Chatterbox." Everything is rough and natural in character, seems artificial, but it comes off somehow. Mixing-bowls due for wash-basins, mugs for drinking-glasses, etc, because naturally nothing is lacking, in one form or another everything is available. We discovered the existence of special books on camping with detailed instructions about all these primitive appliances.
>
> The reception at 2.30 consisted in an invitation to go for a walk to the next mountain, where we had a chance to know the utter wilderness of such an American countryside. We went along rough tracks and down slopes for which even my antlers and hooves were insufficient.
>
> Fortunately it is raining today. In the woods there are numbers of squirrels and porcupines, but the latter have not put in an appearance so far. In winter black bears can be seen as well. Supper afterwards with ladies present. One of the hostesses a lady from Leipzig, extremely affected. The unmarried sister of the Putnams, a well preserved middle-aged lady accompanies first a young English girl who sings in English, then Jung who sings in German.
>
> The Putnams understand German, have often been to Germany, also to Vienna. They made me learn a very funny game, played on a board together with two other girls and Ferenczi. Amazing!
>
> This morning I sorely miss the barber to trim my hair. Fortunately people dress quite unconventionally, but perhaps this is the wrong impression. Breakfast very unusual and plentiful. There will be a lot to tell you when I return.[57]

Freud did not join a strenuous climb, as he was suffering appendicitis.[58] Instead he was determined to see a porcupine, given his interest in the fact that unlike other mammals, their quills prevented them from crowding together in the nest. He did not find a live specimen, but apparently a guide did manage to locate a dead one for him along a trail.[59]

William James sold his partnership in Putnam Camp early on to James Jackson Putnam, and built a summer house instead at Chocorua in New Hampshire. Still he returned regularly to Putnam Camp throughout his life. The Keene Valley wilderness played a singular role in the development of his thinking. In 1909, toward the end of his life, he wrote of Keene Valley to the Harvard philosopher Ralph Barton Perry (1876–1957) who had just returned from a stay at Putnam Camp: "I love it like a person, and if Calais was engraved on the heart of Mary Tudor, surely Keene Valley will be engraved on mine when I die."[60] Throughout his lifetime, Keene Valley was consummate with his greatest pleasures and most powerful personal experiences. From his earliest visits, what he found in Keene Valley reinforced the "rugged individualism" which lay at the epicenter of his spirituality and his work.[61] Already by 1876, the year when the Beede Farm was purchased, James writes that he had:

> . . . never before (at least not in so many years) so deeply and thoroughly enjoyed Nature. I actually feel that as if I should like to buy some land there and become a sort of hermit, winter and summer, leading a natural animal life & throwing all the vanities of learning to the dogs.[62]

Throughout his life James' fantasies of the "animal life" were integrated with his intellectual production in Keene Valley. The place stimulated him enormously. He was capable of jumping headlong into both the natural and intellectual milieu without distinguishing between them. In 1877, Sarah Goell Putnam (1851–1912), the artist and grandmother of the Putnams, described what was likely to have been a typical Jamesian scene as he arrived at Putnam Camp, heading immediately to the Upper Ausable Lake where:

> We were reclining in the shade of the trees on the Lake banks and after enjoying our lunch, Dr. James entered into the argument about a man's right to commit suicide if he considered himself of no use in the world. I got very provoked not knowing whether he spoke in earnest or not.[63]

Very important to the evolution of James' work was the summer of 1878 at Putnam Camp where he spent his honeymoon and began work on his *Principles of Psychology* (1880). He wrote of spending "a ballad-like summer in this delicious cot among the hills . . . I need not say that our psychic reaction has been one of content – perhaps as great as ever enjoyed by man."[64]

Keene Valley became a crucial extension of James' workplace, not only for writing but for teaching and socializing as well. His intellectual production required the interludes given by this wilderness experience. In 1885 he wrote to the French philosopher Charles Renouvier (1815–1903) of Putnam Camp and its importance to his psyche: "I need to lead a purely animal life for at least two months to carry me through the teaching year." In the same letter he strikes another theme which recurs often – the differences between the nature of Keene Valley and what is to be found in Europe:

> The virgin forest comes close to our house, and the diversity of walks through it, the brooks and the ascentions of hilltops are infinite. I doubt if there be anything like it in europe. Your mountains are grander, but you have nowhere this carpet of absolutely primitive forest, with its indescribably sweet exhalations, spreading in every direction unbroken.[65]

Henry James (1843–1916) who chose to spend much of his life in Europe, was frequently reminded by his brother of Keene Valley and its importance to him. In 1895 William writes to Henry of a "fine 10 days in Keene Valley, quite renewing my youth,"[66] to which Henry responds, "'Keene Valley' (where in the world is it?);"[67] probably facetiously, undoubtedly having heard much of the place for the previous fifteen years. By

1907, however, in response to William's reference to "3 weeks of Sept – warm ones – in my beloved & exquisite Keene Valley,"[68] Henry concedes that:

> your annual go at Keene Valley (wh[ich]: I'm never to have so much as beheld) & the nature of your references to it – as this one tonight – fill me with pangs & yearnings, I mean the bitterness, almost, of envy: there is so little of the Keene Valley side of things in my life.[69]

James frequently wrote of a special relation of American culture to American nature, although the exact cause and effect for him seemed to remain inexplicable. In 1898, he wrote to his wife after spending a night camping at Panther Gorge near Mount Marcy:

> . . . it became a regular Walpurgis Nacht. I spent a good deal of it in the woods, where the streaming moonlight lit up things in a magical checkered play, and it seemed as if the Gods of all the nature-mythologies were holding an indescribable meeting in my breast with the moral Gods of inner life. The two kinds of gods have nothing in common . . . The intense significance of some sort, of the whole scene, if one could only *tell* the significance; the intense inhuman remoteness of its inner life, and yet the intense *appeal* of it; its everlasting freshness and its immemorial antiquity and decay; its utter Americanism, and every sort of patriotic suggestiveness.[70]

His frequent sojourns to Europe only seem to have heightened such emotions, especially in later years. In 1901 from Nauheim in Germany he wrote:

> What I *crave* most is some wild American country. It is curious organic-feeling need. One's social relations with European landscape are entirely different, everything being so fenced or planted that you can't lie down and sprawl. Kipling, alluding to the "bleeding raw" appearance of some of our outskirt settlements, says, "Americans don't mix much with their landscape yet." But we mix a darned sight more than Europeans, so far as our individual organisms go, with our camping and general wild-animal personal relations. Thank Heaven that our Nature is so much less redeemed![71]

James and Bushnell shared many emotions regarding their Keene Valley experience, but for James, who was of the next generation, the experience translated to a more self-conscious articulation. James, like Bushnell, saw a disjunction between modern urban life and nature, but James had more difficulty than Bushnell to negotiate this divide, which became more and more a preoccupation in his later life, especially when his health seemed more and more to limit his activity in Keene Valley.[72] Perhaps against his will, and in the Bushnellian sense, James became a modern "primitive savage," sharing the same disjunction and the same unaccountability as his pre-modern forebears. James follows Bushnell in arguing that nature is multifarious. And so is the city. James is annoyed with the romanticism of Whitman's naturalistic analogs for urban culture, for example in his commentary on "Crossing Brooklyn Ferry":

> When your ordinary Brooklynite or New Yorker, leading a life replete with too much luxury, or tired and careworn about his personal affairs, crosses the ferry or goes up

Broadway, his fancy does not thus "soar away into the colors of the sunset" as did
Whitman's . . . There is life; and there, a step away, is death.[73]

Yet unlike Bushnell, James appears little interested in anything but the natural
environment in Keene Valley, apart from the immediate circle of intellectuals at Putnam
Camp. Certainly he shared none of Bushnell's intimate interest in the local social environment. James' somewhat vicarious relationship to the social environment in Keene Valley
was emblematic of the shift by the 1880s, as the second generation intellectual community became more introverted than those who had come before. Indeed, one of the real
attractions of the place was its relative isolation in nature, which in fact made hermetic
socialization among intellectuals easier than in the urban milieus from which they came.
In the increasingly complicated cities, the demands of work and other daily obligations
meant that colleagues did not necessarily meet; even that important persons from diverse
disciplines did not meet at all. In this regard, Joseph Twichell recounted how Noah John
Porter and William James first met; not at an academic conference or social gathering in
New Haven or Cambridge, but by accident on the road south of Putnam Camp, apparently a more likely happenstance than in New Haven or Cambridge. Years later Twichell
recalled that "How quickly, as by common impulse, the two fell into psycho-physical
discourse."[74]

In the case of William James, there were a number of people who were of profound
importance to his intellectual and personal life and at the nexus of his Keene Valley experience. One can cite, for example, his acquaintance with Felix Adler (1851–1933), whom
he first met in Keene Valley in August 1883 when both joined a week-long camping party
in the High Peaks. Adler had founded the Ethical Culture Movement in New York and
was already prominent in social reform causes in the city.[75] That Adler was Jewish was
underscored in a letter from William to Henry James describing the event as including the
"company of several first-class Hebrews of N.Y."[76] This meeting was also a likely
anomaly in the Brahmin atmosphere of Harvard and Cambridge, and at odds with the
markedly anti-semitic sensibilities of James' earlier years.[77] James and Adler soon became
intertwined through shared beliefs and organizations. The Keene Valley wilderness had a
way of leveling distinctions, witnessed in emphatic terms by James' great infatuation with
Pauline Goldmark (1874–1962) during his later years.[78] Goldmark was one of the five
daughters of Joseph Goldmark, a Viennese émigré physician turned industrialist. Pauline's
sister, Helen, was the wife of Felix Adler and convinced the Goldmarks to build their
house down the road from Putnam Camp in 1889. Adler constructed his house at St.
Huberts in 1883.[79] Through Adler, James would find himself in the midst of several prominent Jewish families at the southern end of the Valley, including the intermarried families
of Marcus Goldman (1853–1938) and Samuel Sachs (1851–1935), founders of the New
York banking establishment. In all probability they were introduced to Keene Valley by
Marcus Goldman's son, Julius Goldman, who married Adler's daughter, Sarah.

Like those intellectuals before him, and William James in particular, Adler assigned
to the natural landscape of Keene Valley a spirituality conducive to personal renewal.
Passages from an 1882 letter written by Adler to his wife from Beede's reveal his awe in
returning to the Valley after three years:

So I am here once more in these beautiful mountains! and every breath of air imports new vigor and joy to the body and soul. How I delight in the sense of being here, in the glorious freedom of the hills, and what a satisfaction it has been this afternoon to go over the same ground that is familiar to me from three years ago, and to find how vividly it had all remained portrayed in my memory.[80]

James' letters from Keene Valley written to his wife would express a similar experience. In 1885 he wrote:

I have been here 30 hours and the beauty and old associations have melted me almost to tears. It never was so touchingly penetratingly beautiful. The sleeping circle of hills with their solemn green carpets, the everlasting voices of the brooks, now very full with the rain, the magical crimson topping of individual trees that promise to be something the like of which I never saw before, like strong wine for its moist cool potency – and yet it all makes me feel so utterly sad![81]

Much of the development of the intellectual community at the southern end of the valley can be traced to the presence of William James and Felix Adler. In the outside world, their activities interlocked sufficiently to form a single informal circle. For example, James' interest in psychic phenomena led to his role in the founding of the American Society for Psychical Research in 1884, whose roster included Adler as well as Putnam, Bowditch, Royce, and others associated with Putnam Camp.[82] James followed closely the development of Adler's Ethical Culture Movement, and in fact joined the fledgling Philadelphia Society organized in 1885. Felix Adler's prominence as the founder of the Ethical Culture Movement made him an important catalyst for broadening the Keene Valley intellectual community beyond the scope of Bushnell and James by the mid-1880s. Adler was directly or indirectly responsible for another cluster of "campers" in addition to the Putnam Camp group, who were related to philosophy and theology, but with origins more in urban activism than in medical science and psychology. These figures of the Ethical Culture Movement spent many weeks at Beede's, strategizing their urban initiatives for the exploding metropolises of New York, Philadephia, Chicago, St. Louis, and elsewhere.

Highly charged politically, the Ethical Societies were focused on the problems associated with the social assimilation and poverty emerging from new urban economies and massive immigration. Of particular importance in Keene Valley was Sammuel Burns Weston (1855–1936), a graduate of the Harvard Divinity School who had gravitated toward Adler and in 1885 was made leader of the Philadelphia Society for Ethical Culture. Another of the early Ethical Culture "campers" was William M. Salter (1853–1931), a graduate of the Harvard Divinity School and the Leader of the Chicago Society for Ethical Culture founded in 1882. In 1885 Salter became William James' brother-in-law, having married Mary Gibbons, the sister of James' wife. Walter Sheldon (1858–1907) was another "camper;" a Princeton graduate who first met Adler in Berlin in 1881. Adler helped sustain Sheldon's interest in religion without theology, especially in relation to childhood education. He was also the brother-in-law of S. Burns Weston. By 1886 Sheldon had become leader of the newly founded St. Louis Society for Ethical Culture. S. Burns Weston's twin brother, Stephen F. Weston (1855–1935), also was a "camper." He directed the Workingmen's School begun by the Philadelphia Society; later he became the Dean of Antioch College.[83]

Finally, apart from James and Adler, a third figure was an essential catalyst in the Keene intellectual activity. He was Thomas Davidson (1840–1900), the Scottish émigré classics scholar who was as important as James or Adler in attracting the intellectual community that had assembled by the 1890s. He coalesced the group of intellectuals at the northern end of the valley. Davidson and James had become intimate friends by 1874 when Davidson moved to Boston and was embraced by James' circle from the "Metaphysical Club" and the "Radical Club." Such was the intimacy of their relationship that in 1876 Davidson introduced James to his future wife, Alice Howe Gibbons (1849–1922).[84] Davidson was by all accounts one of the most erudite scholars of his generation and perhaps the foremost classicist. Gregarious and peripatetic, never attaching himself to an established academic institution, he nonetheless wielded considerable influence over many within the academy. James, in his famous memorial essay of 1903, called Davidson the "knight-errant of the intellectual life."[85]

By the 1880s, Davidson was pursuing his own approach to urban activism. He was, however, a supreme individualist.[86] In London in 1881 he organized a group, "Fellowship of the New Life," to consider the reorganization of individual life with the goal of pushing the evolution of collective society toward a higher plane. Davidson soon implemented a "New York Fellowship" along similar lines.[87] After several years, however, a faction within the London Fellowship began to pursue more collectivist political ideas whose sentiments, Davidson felt, were coming too close to accepting the "morbid *idée fixe* of state socialism." By 1884 the faction had evolved to become the "Fabian Society" which played a crucial role in English political life for the best part of the next century.[88] Although Davidson's importance in the evolution of late nineteenth-century ethical socialism in England and his role in the founding of Fabian socialism was frequently evoked, he adamantly denied any connection. Certain of his ideas related to the London and New York Fellowships, however, were maintained in his vision for the Glenmore School of Culture Sciences, which he founded on East Hill at the northern end of the Keene Valley in 1890. Concurrent with the development of Glenmore for academics was the Breadwinners College for workers, founded on the Lower East Side in 1898, as an educational institution for the working poor to augment their social and political power through self-motivated education.[89] Thus, Davidson's vision of social evolution engaged diverse social strata.

The precedents for Glenmore were several, beginning with Emersonian ideals associated with the Philosophers' Camp, or with George Ripley's Brook Farm where Emerson was active. More contemporary to Glenmore, however, was the Concord Summer School of Philosophy founded in 1879 by A. Bronson Alcott, Emerson's closest friend. Alcott was a key figure in New England literary circles. He helped Davidson when he moved to the United States and invited him to lecture at the Concord Summer School. When Concord closed in 1888, Davidson founded a similar school devoted to philosophy and ethics at Farmington, Massachusetts.[90] Early on, Davidson's urban activism crossed paths with

1.6 Glenmore School for the Culture Sciences faculty posing at Hilltop Cottage in 1892. Courtesy of Keene Valley Library Association.

Adler's almost as soon as the Ethical Culture Movement had emerged.[91] The Ethical Culture Movement emphasized alternative modes of education. By then the idea of the summer cloister for academics had developed within American urban culture,[92] with the changing character of the city making this "urban naturalism" an obvious option for the academy.

It made sense that when Davidson wanted to move his school to a location that would not suffer "too many distractions, too many nearby cities, too many frivolous people . . ."[93] he looked toward Keene Valley, undoubtedly familiar with the enthusiasm of both James and Adler for the place. Adler's follower, Stephen F. Weston, then living in New York as a doctoral student at Columbia and sharing quarters with Davidson, accompanied him to Keene Valley in March 1889. Weston showed Davidson the Cox farm on East Hill at the northern end of the valley. As one of Adler's "campers," Weston knew the location,[94] in that they had already explored the idea of an alternative school on East Hill in 1885, but they decided instead to pitch their tents close to Adler where the camping was easier.[95] Davidson found the isolation and rugged primitivism to his liking and immediately bought the farm and improved it using funds secured from Joseph Pulitzer, a close lifelong friend and supporter whom Davidson had met in St. Louis when Pulitzer was a young immigrant there.[96] By the following year, in the summer of 1890, the first classes were held at the Glenmore School for the Culture Sciences, so named after his place of birth in Scotland.[97]

Davidson quickly evolved Glenmore to a more organized institution than Putnam Camp, replete with an elaborate rustic campus. By the opening of the school in 1890, the old log farmhouse and its barn were complemented with a new refectory with four guest rooms above. Surrounding this core were numerous buildings added by 1893. Largest was "Hilltop Cottage," a structure that combined a lecture hall with Davidson's private rooms, seven more guest rooms, and elaborate porches. Here Davidson had his library, which James apparently used extensively in completing his *The Variety of Religious Experience* (1902). Nearby was the small two-room cottage where Davidson had first lived with Percival Chubb (1860–1959), one of those who originated the Fabian faction in London, and had remained a close associate of Davidson, having also participated at Farmington. There were also several cottages, and a tent pitched by Stephen Weston. Gulf Brook and a tributary ran through the complex with an island which was cleared and seats installed for outdoor gathering. Upstream were pools convenient for bathing.[98] The primitivism of Glenmore was remarked upon by many visitors, and especially by James, who found Glenmore exotic, even by Putnam Camp standards. James once remarked:

> Twice I went up with Davidson to open the place in April. I well remember leaving his fireside one night with three ladies who were also early comers, and finding the thermometer at 8° Fahrenheit and a tremendous gale blowing about. Davidson loved these blustering vicissitudes of climate. In the early years the brook was never too cold for him to bath in, and he spent hours in rambling over the hills and through the forest.[99]

Glenmore quickly became a major force among the circle of intellectuals whose sensibilities followed in one way or another James, Adler, and Davidson. By the time of Glenmore, the base group of intellectuals in Keene Valley had grown in both numbers and prominence. Geographically, the newcomers were far more diverse than before, though New York figured more importantly, and there was a shift in critical mass from Harvard to Columbia. James and Adler lectured on a limited basis almost every year. Other regulars included Stephen Weston who ran the school after Davidson's death in 1900. Also a frequent later visitor was Charles M. Bakewell (1867–1957), Professor of Philosophy at Yale to whom Davidson left the property; and Frederick J. Woodbridge (1887–1940), Professor of Philosophy at Columbia and Dean of Graduate Faculties. Glenmore had greatly broadened the cast of intellectuals in the Valley. The 1892 *Prospectus* gives an indication of the range of faculty. There was Royce of Harvard who was already a regular at Putnam Camp and lectured on "Some Recent Tendencies in Ethical Doctrine." William Torrey Harris, US Commissioner of Education[100] who was for decades in the vanguard of American developments in philosophy, spoke on "The Philosophy of A. Bronson Alcott, R.W. Emerson, and the New England Transcendentalists." Also included was the philosopher John Dewey, then of the University of Michigan, and who was becoming the single most influential person in modern theories of cognition and education, discussing "Tendencies in English Thought During the Nineteenth Century." There was Ibn Ali Suleiman (Albert J. Léon) of Beirut who had just received a Ph.D. from Johns Hopkins and presented such topics as "The Quoran," "Development of Islam," and "The Modern East." John Clark Murray, Professor of Mental and Moral Philosophy at McGill University discussed "Philosophy of Kant," "Evolution of Knowledge," and "Social Morality." Max Margolis, the philologist and editor-in-chief of the English translation of the Hebrew Bible, spoke on "Jewish Literature." Poet and playwright Louis J. Block lectured on "The Philosophy of Literature," and Thomas Davidson himself on "Greek Philosophy," "Aeschylus," "Shakespeare," and "Christianity and its Relation to Judaism."

Like Adler and James, Dewey, Harris and Murray returned to Glenmore year after year until the school ceased in 1910. John Dewey was of a younger generation, but he also was very interested in Glenmore's pedagogic lineage: his lectures on nineteenth-century

English thought notably ended with Emerson as "The Hope." Dewey's textbook, *Psychology* (1891) established a continuity with Noah John Porter's *The Human Intellect* (1868), which he intended to augment with newer ideas.[101] Long-time acquaintances, both Harris and Davidson were mentors of Dewey, Harris having published Dewey's first scholarly essays in 1882 in the *Journal of Speculative Philosophy*,[102] and Davidson having asked him to teach at Farmington.[103] By the mid-1890s Davidson was reading Dewey's work and advising him. By the early 1890s Dewey had become acquainted with William James, who supported his work. James appreciated Dewey's *Outlines of Ethics* (1891). In turn, Dewey was discovering James' *Principles of Psychology* (1890) written in Keene Valley a decade earlier.[104] Dewey's intellectual development owed a large debt to James. And for Dewey, the opportunities for informal contact provided by Glenmore were important. Like Harris, Dewey built a house at Glenmore, along Gulf Brook but slightly downstream from the "campus."[105]

Of the triad, it was Dewey whose early formation placed him closest to the Glenmore setting. Unlike Harris and Davidson, Dewey was a native to the region, born and raised across Lake Champlain in Burlington, Vermont, where he also attended the University of Vermont. He taught nearby at Charlotte, where the profile of the Adirondacks, including Hurricane Mountain behind Glenmore, was a powerful presence in the natural landscape. At Charlotte the ferry left on its routine runs to Essex and the Adirondack interior across the lake. It is important to note that as Dewey's prominence and his urban engagements increased, he returned to a nature that was familiar. In this, he was undoubtedly attracted to the same "landscape" as were the theologians before him, and with whom his work represented a historical continuity: especially Bushnell and Porter and even Phelps.

Dewey and Harris were quite possibly the two most important pioneers in the development of twentieth-century cognitive science and certainly the two most influential figures in applied education in the United States in the first half of the twentieth century. Their many years together along Gulf Brook within the intellectual milieu created by Davidson undoubtedly reinforced their production of ideas and their activism. Davidson, although less recognized today, was perhaps more known in his period than either Harris or Dewey. He died early, in 1900. His importance was recounted by Felix Adler at his burial at Glenmore: "But even from us who survive him he can not entirely vanish. He has sown thought seeds that will flourish in many hearts. He has helped shape lives that will never entirely lose the nobler imprint he has given them."[106] One of those lives was that of William James, who on Davidson's death wrote of his profound personal influence: "Fortunately this type of man is recurrent, and from generation to generation literary history preserves examples. But it is infrequent enough for few of us to have known personally more than one example. I count myself happy in having known two. The memory of Davidson will always strengthen my faith in personal freedom and its spontaneities, and make me less unqualifiedly respectful than ever of 'civilization'."[107]

Of the many persons who passed through Glenmore and who took much from Davidson, one stands out in continuing the tradition of the alternative social community. She was Prestonia Mann Martin, the daughter of John Preston Martin, a New York City physician, and a cousin of the educator Horace Mann. She had attended Alcott's Concord

Summer School of Philosophy and then Davidson's Glenmore School for the Culture Sciences.[108] Around 1895, she bought some of the land near Glenmore from John Dewey's brother, Davis R. Dewey, which one or the other had recently purchased.[109] Mann had been so impressed with Glenmore that she began her own experiment. She built a "camp" that became the nexus of an informal summer colony for a group of social reformers distinct from the roster of participants already involved at Glenmore. Apparently early in her effort she was visited on East Hill by Sophia Dana Ripley, sister of Charles Dana, owner of the *New York Sun*, and wife of George Ripley (1802–1880), founder of Brook Farm. Based on discussions with Ripley, Brook Farm became an important precedent for Mann's thinking such that she even named her experiment "Summer Brook Farm." "Farm" was later dropped, and the name evolved to "Summerbrook."[110]

In 1899 at Glenmore, Mann met Dr. John Martin (1864–1956), the political scientist who had just come from England to the United States where he was teaching at Columbia. Martin had been active in London with Davidson's efforts to found the "New Fellowship," and he became a leader of the Fabian Society in the United States. He was also a member of the Executive Committee of the London Fabian Society.[111] He remained active in social causes in the United States; notably he would join Felix Adler as a founding Director of the City Housing Corporation in the 1920s. Prestonia Mann married John Martin in 1900, the year that Davidson died. Given both of their connections, Summerbrook quickly became the second catalyst for urban intellectuals and activists on East Hill. Mann created a "social camp" for urban activists of their liking. Many were personal friends. In contrast to Glenmore, Summerbrook more closely resembled the Brook Farm precedent, conceived of not so much as a formal academic institution but as an informal collective engaged in discussion and recreation. The only systematic activities were related to chores such as woodcutting and laundry, made in lieu of payment for room and board.[112]

While Summerbrook never published curricular or programmatic materials, some record exists of visitors and activities. In attendance were Edward A. Markham, the American poet who followed issues of social justice; Upton Sinclair, the author and crusader for social justice whose most famous book *The Jungle* (1906) spawned a generation of urban reform; Henry D. Lloyd, the New York lawyer and well-known writer on issues of labor and political economy; Clarence Darrow, the renowned criminal lawyer who by the time of Summerbrook was identified with labor causes; Jane Addams, the Nobel Laureate welfare worker and social advocate who had founded Hull House in Chicago in 1889; Lillian Wald, also famed for her social work, especially in the Lower East Side where she founded the Henry Street Settlement in 1895; James Graham Phelps Stokes, known as the "millionaire socialist" whose philanthropic activities fostered a broad range of causes; W.D.P. Bliss, another socialist who had authored the massive *Encyclopedia of Social Reform* (1897); Ray Stannard Baker, the journalist (using the pseudonym David Grayson), who championed social causes; and Charlotte Perkins Gilman, the writer and poet who was an important advocate for feminist and other social movements.[113] Among the most notable visitors to Summerbrook was Maxim Gorky, the Russian writer and a leader against the Czarist regime who, after the unsuccessful revolution of 1905, came to New York to raise funds for Russian revolutionary activities.[114]

III THE URBAN SUBLIME AFTER 1910

Both ends of the Keene Valley continued to attract well-known intellectuals until well into the twentieth century. James died in 1910; Bowditch in 1911; and Putnam in 1914: but Putnam Camp lived on, with the next generation of family members and others continuing each summer. Putnam Camp remains today, although in an altered state.[115] Davidson died in 1900, but Glenmore continued as a formal school under the directorship of Stephen Weston until 1910. Then it was used as an informal camp by some of the remaining families.[116] Prestonia Mann lived until 1945, and for many years she continued her ad hoc educational activities at Summerbrook.[117] Felix Adler remained as an important presence in Keene Valley almost to his death in 1933; and some offspring of the Ethical Culture leadership remain today.

In general, generations stayed and the extraordinary physical beauty of the Valley continued to extend the coterie. For example, in 1908, Harmony Twichell, the daughter of the Reverend Joseph H. Twichell, married the composer Charles Ives (1874–1954) who could subsequently be found in the Valley in the summers. The St. Huberts community was reinvigorated when Henry Sloan Coffin (1874–1954), President of the Union Theological Seminary, bought Stephen Weston's house at St. Huberts. As a prominent liberal theologian Coffin continued the lineage of urban clergy following Porter and Bushnell. Paul J. Sachs (1878–1965), who pioneered critical acceptance of modern art, was a founder of the Museum of Modern Art in New York and Director of the Fogg Art Museum at Harvard, was a life-long summer resident of St. Huberts, where his parents, Samuel Sachs and Louisa Goldman had a house and were related by marriage to the Adlers. Of course there were many other academics who had settled into the Valley in the early twentieth century. The representation from the Columbia philosophy faculty was reinforced by Frederick J. Woodbridge who was first introduced to the area through Glenmore and subsequently built a house in St. Huberts. Among the others was Alan P. Marquand (1853–1924), the head of the department of Art and Archeology at Princeton University who bought Shurtleff's house at St. Huberts. James Conant (1893–1978), the President of Harvard was a dominant personality in St. Huberts, especially during the period when he was President of the Ausable Club. Also of note was Henry Barrett Learned (1868–1931), the historian and authority on US government who had taught at Yale and elsewhere. He came to the Valley through his marriage to Emily Cheney, the granddaughter of Horace Bushnell. There was also the critical mass of wealthy businessmen who were serving as the patrons of the new urban culture: for example, Robert DeForest, a key figure in New York philanthropy best known as the long-term President of the Metropolitan Museum of Art. He was an early investor in Adirondack land and a dominant figure in the St. Huberts summer community.

By the 1920s and 1930s, a picture developed of genteel relations between the second and third generations in a domesticated landscape, now no longer urban wilderness but suburban idyll, accessible by private automobile within an easy day's drive from New York, Philadelphia, or Boston. In one sense, the collegiality of the urban intellectuals was as it always was. But there was also something new. In the social setting of 1930s St. Huberts, the distinctiveness of the wilderness social landscape far more easily transmuted

THE

CLIFF-

DWELLERS

OF

NEW

YORK.

1.7 "The Cliffdwellers of New York," *The Cosmopolitan*, 15, July 1893. Courtesy of New York State Library.

into the urban social landscape than fifty years earlier in the social setting of Putnam Camp. The old local culture had all but disappeared. And the latest generation of summer colonizers were celebrants of the metropolis rather than the skeptics of the Bushnellian era. The conception of wilderness evolved to an urban construct. Robert DeForest was said to have once proclaimed to the effect that in his philanthropic activities he did not distinguish between "preserving the masterpieces of art for the public good" and preserving "the masterpieces of nature."[118] Very much intertwined in this mentality was the question of power in the sense of the ease with which urban power games could be transliterated to the wilderness context.

It is significant that by the 1920s at the southern end of the Valley, for example, Felix Adler, Henry Sloan Coffin, Robert DeForest, Henry Barrett Learned, Allan Marquand, Julius and Paul Sachs, Alfred T. White, William A. White, and Frederick Woodbridge were all members of the Century Association in New York,[119] indicating that a power elite had developed such that the urban and wilderness settings were interchangeable. Its extent can be open only to speculation, but the same social entitlement now could exist anywhere, even in Emerson's formerly sacrosanct "apparition of God." And in terms of intellectual ideas, the balance in American culture had tipped toward the city. By this time, American culture and creativity was the province of the city: an evolution from the "call of the wild" to the "call of the city," as Charles Mulford Robinson so

1.8 "Roof atop the RCA building, with clouds," photo circa 1935. Courtesy of the Museum of the City of New York.

aptly framed it.[120] With the death of Adler in 1933, the last of the older generation that included James and Davidson was gone. The intellectual uses of the wilderness passed to a new era more and more identified with urban real-politik and power.

By the beginning of the twentieth century, the intellectual response to the metropolis was changing, as was the response to wilderness. The reaction to the city was filled with the same sense of wonder and awe as was the reaction to nature of one or two generations before. Interestingly, the emotive models for describing the metropolis of the early twentieth century were frequently borrowed from the naturalist vocabularies of the early nineteenth century: the sublimity of nature now was replaced by an urban sublime.[121] The New York skyscraper especially became the source of such depiction. Visitors, for example, would describe "forests of skyscrapers" with their peaks "lifted up to match the Himalayas."[122] Of course New Yorkers were engaged in such hyperbole, but interestingly, so were the European observers. If they could not exactly find "culture" in New York (and some could), they at least could find a metaphoric "nature" in the new urban technology of the city – a new ecology of the artificial. In a sense, "city" and "nature" and "culture" became interchangeable. Within the Keene intellectual community, this new sensibility was reflected in many ways as the third generation came into its own. And more than before New York City was dominant relative to the redefinition of the place as both natural and urban environment.

Unlike their successors, the power in the older generation lay in the realm of ideas. And among the coterie of Valley intellectuals no ideas were more powerful or more lasting relative to the new metropolis than those of William James, more so perhaps than he ever could have imagined. Upon James' death, Josiah Royce, his Harvard colleague who was frequently in attendance at Putnam Camp, wrote that James could be "viewed as a prophet of the nation that is to be"[123] And that was true, at least for the first half of the twentieth century. George Santayana (1863–1952), James' student at Harvard and also said to have attended Glenmore, wrote lucidly about James' importance not long after he died. James was, in Santayana's estimation, the new spiritual master to the twentieth-century American urban population. Recently Ann Douglas has written much along the same lines: for Manhattan culture especially, it was James and his two students, Gertrude Stein and W.E.B. DuBois, together with Sigmund Freud, who "debated and determined the chances of psychological and cultural survival and gave the metropolitan moderns weapons for the struggle." Douglas presses the point even further: "If Freud was willy-nilly the European founding father, or, rather, stepfather of urban American modernism, James and Stein were its very American biological parents."[124]

James provided the operational mechanism of thought in the void left by a Calvinism fading from American life, especially as cities gained cultural dominance. James' definition of pragmatism, in his own words, "derived from the Greek word, meaning action, from which our words 'practice' and 'practical' come," could give the "concrete consequence" that was essential to the realization of modern urban culture. "Theories thus become instruments, not answers to enigmas, in which we can rest."[125] Early on, Santayana found that "his [James'] way of thinking and feeling represented the true America and represented in a measure the whole ultra-modern, radical world." It was an intelligence with "its roots and its issue in the context of events;" with the profound understanding that "ideas are not mirrors; they are weapons; their function is to prepare us to meet events, as future experience may unroll them." For Santayana, James' thinking was inclusive and embodied the new urban culture:

> William James became the friend and helper of those groping, nervous, half-educated, spiritually disinherited, passionately hungry individuals of which America is full. He became, at the same time, their spokesman and representative before the learned world; and he made it a chief part of his vocation to recast what the learned world has to offer, so that as far as possible it might serve the needs of these people.[126]

In this assessment, Santayana is insightful about the relevance of James' conception of nature to his pragmatism: "the more materialistic the pragmatist's theory of the mind is, the more vitalistic his theory of nature will have to become." He argues that for James:

> . . . nature must be conceived anthropomorphically and in psychological terms. Its purposes are not to be static harmonies, self-unfolding densities, the logic of spirit, the spirit of logic, or any other formal method and abstract law; its purposes are to be concrete endeavors, finite efforts of souls living in an environment which they transform and by which they, too, are affected.[127]

It would be hard to overestimate the importance of the Keene Valley wilderness to James' sensibility: of his almost four decades of highly emotive response to that nature and the very particular social exchanges which it fostered. James was always quick to admit its effect on his own psychological state. In his most widely influential work, *Pragmatism* (1907), he opens the seminal essay on "What Pragmatism Means" with the phrase, "Some years ago, being with a camping party in the mountains . . ."[128] It is in the Keene Valley wilderness that James begins this odyssey in representation of what Santayana called the "whole ultra-modern, radical world;" and it is also there that, by inference, he interprets the urban life which it nurtured.

Notes

1   Ira Rosenwaike: *Population History of New York City*, Syracuse: Syracuse University Press, 1972, p. 16.
2   The development of the Mohawk corridor westward was crucial to enhancing New York's strategic geographic position. See Carol Sheriff *The Artificial River. The Erie Canal and the Paradox of Progress, 1817–1862*, New York: Hill and Wang, 1996.
3   An excellent history of the Hudson-Mohawk megalopolis is given in: *State of New York, Report of the Commission of Housing and Regional Planning, May 7, 1926*, Albany: J.B. Lyon, Printers, 1926. This commission was chaired by Clarence Stein with considerable input from Henry Wright and Benton Mackaye.
4   The importance of Emmons in the appellation is cited by Alfred L. Donaldson: *A History of the Adirondacks*. 2 vols, New York: The Century Company, 1921, vol. 1, p. 36.
5   On this phenomenon, see David Maldwyn Ellis: "The Yankee Invasion of New York, 1783–1850," *New York History*, vol. 32 (1951), pp. 1–17. A good general source on early Adirondack land development is Brenda Parnes: "A History of Land-Use Policy in the Adirondack Forest Region of Northern new York State, 1789–1905" (Ph.D. thesis), Graduate School of Arts and Sciences, New York University, May 1989.
6   Charles Fenno Hoffman: "Scenes at the Source of the Hudson," *New York Mirror* (October 14, 1837), p. 124.
7   Rosenswaike, op. cit., Table 9; David M. Ellis *et. al.*: *A History of New York State*, Ithaca, New York: Cornell University Press, 1967, p. 278; Report of the Commission of Housing and Regional Planning, op.cit.
8   Patricia C.F. Mandel: *Fair Wilderness. American Paintings in the Collection of the Adirondack Museum*, Blue Mountain Lake, New York: The Adirondack Museum, 1990, p. 44.
9   Mandel, op. cit., p. 73.
10 Barbara Novak: *Nature and Culture. American Landscape Painting 1825–1875*, New York: Oxford University Press, 1980, p. 58.
11 Hoffman, op. cit.
12 For an excellent study of the development of the urban sublime within American literature see Christopher Den Tandt: *The Urban Sublime in American Literary Naturalism*, Chicago: University of Chicago Press, 1998.
13 A contemporary description of the Philosophers' Camp was given by passers-by who themselves camped nearby. See F.S. Stallknecht: "Sporting Tour in August, 1858," *Frank Leslie's Illustrated Newspaper* (November 13, 1858), pp. 379–80. Most accounts came much later, however. Emerson wrote the first popular account in the form of an epic poem, "The Adirondacks," in: *May-Day and Other Pieces*, Boston: Ticknor and Fields, 1867, pp. 41–66. Stillman later wrote extensive accounts of the Philosophers' Camp and his subsequent Adirondack activities on behalf of the Saturday Club. See William J. Stillman: "The Philosophers Camp," in: *The Old Rome and the New and Other Studies*, London: Grant Richards, 1897, pp. 265–96. In this Stillman quotes extensively from Emerson's account. Slightly later he also includes a detailed account in William J. Stillman: *The Autobiography of a Journalist*, 2 vols. London: Grant Richards, 1901, vol. 1, pp. 200–39, 242–46. Edward Waldo Emerson, who accompanied Stillman to the site in the second year of the Adirondack Club, also wrote an account. See Edward Waldo Emerson: *The Early Years of the Saturday Club 1855–1870*, Boston: Houghton, 1918, pp. 169–79. Many interpretations have since been written. In particular see Paul F. Jamieson: "Emerson in the Adirondacks," *New York History*, vol. 39 (July 1958), pp. 215–37.
14 Stallknecht, op. cit. pp. 379–80.
15 Edward Waldo Emerson, op. cit., pp. 170–71.

16   Jamieson, op. cit.

17   In his famous 1836 study, *Nature*, Emerson could proclaim that "In the wilderness I find some-thing more dear and connate than in streets or villages." Ralph Waldo Emerson: *Nature*, Boston: James Munroe & Company, 1836. Reprint, New York: Scholars' Facsimiles & Reprints, 1940, p. 13.

18   Ibid. For example, see lines 78.9, 6.6, 25.4, 50.20, 77.12.

19   Ralph Waldo Emerson: "The Adirondacks," p. 45. This point is well made by Paul F. Jamieson: "Emerson in the Adirondacks," *New York History*, XXXIX (July 1958), pp. 214–37.

20   Leo Marx: *The Machine in the Garden. Technology and the Pastoral Ideal in America*, New York: Oxford University Press, 1964.

21   Novak, op. cit., p. 59.

22   Emerson: "The Adirondacks," pp. 60–61.

23   For a general monograph on Stillman see Anne Ehrenkranz *et al.*: *Poetic Localities. William J. Stillman. Photographs of Adirondacks, Cambridge, Crete, Italy, Athens*, New York: Aperture Books, 1988.

24   On this subject see Hans Nuth: *Nature and the American. Three Centuries of Changing Attitudes*, Lincoln, Nebraska: University of Nebraska Press, 1957, Ch. 7; also David Strauss: "Toward a Consumer Culture: 'Adirondack Murray' and the Wilderness Vacation," *American Quarterly*, 39 (Summer, 1987), pp. 270–86.

25   "Adirondack," *New York Times* (August 9, 1864), p. 4.

26   Frederick Law Olmsted, Jr. and Theodora Kimball (eds): *Forty Years of Landscape Architecture: Central Park. Frederick Law Olmsted Sr.*, Cambridge, Mass.: The MIT Press, 1973, p. 46.

27   Lucy Fountain (pseudonym for Kate Hillard): "Keene Delights," *Putnam's Magazine*, XIV (December 1869), pp. 669–74.

28   Novak, op. cit., p. 96; John I.H. Baur: "American Luminism," *Perspectives*, no. 9 (1954), pp. 90–98.

29   Most of the notable Keene Valley artists are mentioned in Mandel, op. cit. Any study of the subject must begin with the research of Margaret Goodwin O'Brien. In recent years her work has been enhanced by Robin Pell. In particular see "Durand in the Adirondacks," *Adirondack Life*, 2 (Summer 1971), pp. 36–39; "Capturing the Great North Woods: Alexander Wyant, 1836–1892," *Adirondack Life*, 3 (Spring 1972), pp. 38–41; "Shurtleff," *Adirondack Life*, 10 (November/December, 1979), pp. 40–43; "Artists in the Valley," in Byrne (ed.), op.cit. pp. 116–26. Robin Pell has continued O'Brien's work. See "Drawn to the Valley," *Adirondack Life*, 27 (July/August, 1996), pp. 44–51; *Keene Valley. The Landscape and Its Artists*, exhibition catalog, New York: Gerald Peters Gallery, 1994. For Shurtleff's involvement in Keene Valley also see Alfred L. Donaldson: *A History of the Adirondacks*, 2 vols, New York: The Century Company, 1921, pp. 40–43; Roswell M. Shurtleff: "Recollections of Keene Valley," manuscript, n.d., Keene Valley Library Association.

30   The politics of the emerging New York art market were very much intertwined with these insti-tutions. See Elliot Candee Clark: *History of the National Academy of Design: 1825–1953*, New York: Columbia University Press, 1954; A. Hyatt Mayor and Mark Davis: *American Art at the Century*, New York: Century Association, 1977; and Annette Blaugrund: *The Tenth Street Studio Building. Artist-Entrepreneurs from the Hudson River School to the American Impres-sionists*, Southhampton, New York: Parrish Art Museum, 1977.

31   See Daniel T. Rodgers: *The Work Ethic in Industrial America, 1850–1920*, Chicago: University of Chicago Press, 1974, Ch. 4. Also see Strauss, op. cit.

32   This change is highlighted in William G. McLoughlin: *The Meaning of Henry Ward Beecher. An Essay on the Shifting Values of Mid-Victorian America, 1840–1870*, New York: Alfred A. Knopf, 1970, Prologue and p. 5.

33   Ralph Waldo Emerson, op. cit.

34   For Bushnell's work and significance see Mary Bushnell Cheney: *Life and Letters of Horace Bushnell*, New York: Harper and Brothers, 1880; also Barbara M. Cross: *Horace Bushnell:*

Minister to a Changing America, Chicago: University of Chicago Press, 1958; Ann Douglas: *The Feminization of American Culture*, New York: Alfred A. Knopf, 1977; David W. Haddorf: *Dependence and Freedom. The Moral Thought of Horace Busnell*, Lanham, Maryland: The University Press of America, 1994.

35 Robert D. Richardson, Jr.: *Emerson. The Mind on Fire*, Berkeley: University of California Press, 1995, p. 467. This essay accompanied Bushnell's 1860 republication of his earlier work, *Views of Christian Nurture and Subjects Adjacent Thereto* (1847).

36 The Nook Farm circle included Mark Twain (1835–1910), Harriet Beecher Stowe (1811–1896), daughter of Henry Ward Beecher, and William Dean Howells (1837–1920) who was editor of the *Atlantic Monthly*. For Bushnell's role see Kenneth R. Andrews: *Nook Farm. Mark Twain's Hartford Circle*, Cambridge, Mass.: Harvard University Press, 1950, pp. 102–3. Monday Evening Club members included William H. Hammersly (1838–1920), Hartford lawyer and judge, and more peripherally, Austin C. Dunham (1833–1917), Hartford industrialist. Daughters from both families were among the first summer residents in Keene Valley, having arrived in the early 1860s. See Donaldson, vol. 2, p. 44. The Reverend Joseph H. Twichell (1838–1918), another club member, also appears to have arrived early on. Along with John Lee Fitch, these people appear to have paved the way for Bushnell and the lineage of intellectuals who followed him.

37 The first appears to have been William H. Hodge (1838–1919) of the Columbia Avenue Presbyterian Church in Philadelphia, who designed and built a rustic "camp" in 1873–1874. Hodge was followed by a succession of well-known theologians including: Joseph H. Twichell (1838–1918) of the Asylum Congregational Church in Hartford; Frederick Baylies Allen (1840–1919) of the Trinity Church and later the Episcopal City Mission in Boston; George Washington Dubois (1822–1909) of the Calvary Episcopal Church in Wilmington, Delaware; Wilton Merle-Smith (1856–1923) of the Central Presbyterian Church in New York City and founder of the Hwai Yuen Mission in China; John Balcom Shaw (1860–1935) of the West End Church in New York City; William Rivers Taylor (1856–1941) of the First Church in Philadelphia and later the Brick Presbyterian Church in Rochester. Finally, there was Walter Lowrie (1868–1959) of Saint Paul's American Church in Rome and an expert on Kierkegaard who also taught at Princeton; and Henry Sloan Coffin (1877–1954) of the Madison Avenue Presbyterian Church in New York City and later President of the Union Theological Seminary.

38 Horace Bushnell: *Nature and the Supernatural, as Together Constituting the One System of God*, New York: Charles Scribner's Sons, 1858, pp. 192–93. The implications of Bushnell's ideas for urbanism are discussed in David W. Haddorff, op. cit., pp. 72–77; also Cross, op. cit., pp. xiii, 127–129.

39 Max Eastman: *Great Companions. Critical Memoirs of Some Famous Friends*, New York: Farrar, Straus and Cudahy, 1959, p. 258.

40 Cheney, op. cit., p. 498.

41 Fountain, op cit.

42 Cheney, op. cit., p. 497.

43 For a useful study of Homer's Adirondack experience see David Tatham: *Winslow Homer in the Adirondacks*, Syracuse, New York: Syracuse University Press, 1996.

44 Seneca Ray Stoddard: *The Adirondacks Illustrated*, Albany and Glens Falls, New York: Published by the author, 1874.

45 Charles Dudley Warner: "The Adirondacks Verified. V. A Character Study," *The Atlantic Monthly*, XLI (May 1878), pp. 636–46. Later in the same year the essay was published in Warner's book, *In the Wilderness*, Boston: Houghton, 1878, Ch. 5.

46 Warner: "The Adirondacks Verified," p. 636.

47 Warner, op. cit., p. 639.

48 Warner, op. cit., p. 646.

49 The farmer Smith Beede moved to the south-western side of the Keene Valley where he constructed a new hotel. See Edith Pilcher: *Up the Lake Road. The First Hundred Years of the*

Adirondack Mountain Reserve, Keene Valley, New York: The Adirondack Mountain Reserve, 1987, pp. 20–22.

50 The evolution of the physical setting of Putnam Camp is documented in Richard Upjohn: "Putnam Camp. The first 100 Years," in: Margaret M. Byrne (ed.): *The History of Keene Valley. A Bicentennial Lectures Series, Keene Valley, New York. July and August, 1975 and 1976 under the auspices of the Keene Valley Library Association*, Keene Valley: Keene Valley Library Association, 1978, pp. 154–55.

51 The families' friendship dated from 1842 when the Jameses lived in New York City. Moreover, Emerson's son Edward Jr., who chronicled the Philosophers' Camp, was William James' close friend at Harvard Medical School and a frequent visitor to Putnam Camp. See Ralph Barton Perry: *The Thought and Character of William James*, Cambridge, Mass.: Harvard University Press, 1948, Ch. 2.

52 Perry, op. cit., pp. 67–68.

53 Nathan G. Hale, Jr.: *James Jackson Putnam and Psychoanalysis*, Cambridge, Mass.: Harvard University Press, 1971, pp. 6–12.

54 This is a question thoroughly explored in Ann Douglas: *Terrible Honesty. Mongrel Manhattan in the 1920s*, New York: Farrar, Straus, and Giroux, 1995.

55 These are persons described as "regulars" by Charles W. Putnam: "Sketch of Putnam Camp," manuscript, n.d., KVL Archive.

56 This group is singled out by Elizabeth Putnam McIver, the daughter of James Jackson Putnam. See "Early Days at Putnam Camp," manuscript of talk given to Keene Valley Historical Society, September 1941. KVL Archive. Photographic documentation exists in the Putnam Camp Albums, KVL Archive.

57 Sigmund Freud to his family, dated Putnam's Camp, September 16, 1909. Translation typescript, Adirondack Museum, Blue Mountain Lake, New York.

58 Jung, who did participate, complained of the "crazy American desire to set a record." Harold Bowditch to Wardner Cadbury, dated March 23, 1962. Adirondack Museum, Blue Mountain Lake, New York.

59 Saul Rosenzweig: *Freud, Jung, and Hall the Kingmaker. The Historic Expedition to America (1909)*, Seattle: Hogrete & Huber Publishers, 1992, pp. 202–3, 322; George E. Gifford, Jr.: "Freud and the Porcupine," *Harvard Medical School Bulletin* (March–April 1972), pp. 28–32.

60 William James to Ralph Barton Perry, dated January 2, 1900, in: Frederick J. Down Scott (ed.): *William James. Selected Unpublished Correspondence 1885–1910*, Columbus, Ohio: Ohio State University Press, 1986, pp. 213–14.

61 See Kim Townsend: "William James Rugged Individualism," in: Austin Satat and Dana R. Villa: *Liberal Modernism and Democratic Individuality*, Princeton, NJ: Princeton University Press, 1996, Ch. 12.

62 William James to Catherine Elizabeth Havens, dated December 25, 1876, in: Ignas K. Skrupskelis and Elizabeth M. Berkeley (eds): *The Correspondence of William James. Volume 4 1856–1877*, Charlottesville, Va.: University Press of Virginia, 1995, p. 550.

63 Putnam's Diaries, 28 volumes, 1860–1912, are at the Massachusetts Historical society. A copy of excerpts, transcribed by Robin Pell and dated March 1997, is at the Keene Valley Library archive.

64 William James to Francis J. Child, dated August 16, 1878, in: Henry James (ed.): *The Letters of William James*, 2 vols, Boston: The Atlantic Monthly Press, 1920, vol. 1, p. 197.

65 William James to Charles Renouvier, dated August 5, 1883, in: Henry James (ed.), op. cit., vol. 1, p. 232.

66 William James to Henry James, dated September 19, 1895, in: Ignas K. Skrupskelis and Elizabeth M. Berkeley (eds): *The Correspondence of William James. Volume 2 William and Henry 1885–1896*, Charlottesville, Va: University Press of Virginia, 1992, p. 377.

67 Henry James to William James, dated September 30, 1895, in: Skrupskelis and Berkeley (eds), op. cit., vol. 2, p. 379.

68   William James to Henry James, dated October 6, 1907, in: Ignas K. Skrupskelis and Elizabeth M. Berkeley (eds): *The Correspondence of William James. Volume 3 William and Henry 1897–1910*, Charlottesville, Va.: University Press of Virginia, 1994, p. 345.

69   Henry James to William James, dated October 17, 1907, in: Skrupskelis and Berkeley (eds), op. cit., vol. 3, p. 347.

70   William James to Alice Gibbens James, dated July 9, 1898, in: Henry James (ed.), op. cit., vol. 2, pp. 76–77. James' *Walpurgis Nacht* refers to the eve of May 1, in which according to an old German folk legend, witches gather on the Bloxberg, the highest peak of the Harz Mountains.

71   William James to Frances R. Morse, dated July 10, 1901, in: Henry James (ed.), op. cit., vol. 2, p. 158.

72   James' long correspondence with Pauline Goldmark gives a far-reaching view of his thinking about the importance of nature especially in his later years. Goldmark was a summer resident in Keene Valley; the Goldmark family house was near Putnam camp. See Josephine Goldmark, "An Adirondack Friendship. Letters of William James," *The Atlantic Monthly*, 154 (September and October 1934), pp. 265–72, 440–47.

73   William James: "On a Certain Blindness in Human Beings," in: *Talks to Teachers on Psychology: and to Students on Some of Life's Ideals*, New York: Henry Holt and Company, 1899, pp. 252–53, 257.

74   Joseph H. Twichell: "In the Adirondacks," in: George S. Merriam (ed.): *Noah Porter. A Memorial by Friends*, New York: Charles Scribner's Sons, 1893, p. 159.

75   For an overview of how Adler defined the ethical Culture Movement, see Felix Adler, "The Ethical Culture Movement," in: Horace L. Friess (ed.): *Our Part in this World*, New York: Kings Crown Press, 1946, p. 57. Also see Felix Adler: *An Ethical Philosophy of Life, Presented in its Main Outlines*, New York: D. Appleton and Company, 1918.

76   William James to Henry James, dated August 12, 1883; Henry James to William James dated August 17, 1883, in: Skrupskelis and Berkeley (eds), op. cit., vol. 1, pp. 368–70.

77   On James' anti-semitism, see: Skrupskelis and Berkeley (eds), op. cit., vol. 4, pp. xli–xlii; and correspondence noted therein.

78   Excerpts from their correspondence are given in Josephine Goldmark: "An Adirondack Friendship," *Atlantic Monthly*, vol. 154 (September 1934), pp. 265–72; (October 1934), pp. 440–47. Also see Rosenzweig, op. cit., pp. 182–95.

79   Background on Adler's relationship to Keene valley is given in Helen Goldmark Adler: "Dr. Felix Adler. One of the Early Pioneers in Keene Valley," typescript, n.d.

80   Felix Adler to Helen Goldmark Adler, August 18, 1882, Adler Papers, Columbia University Rare Books Library, Box 1.

81   William James to Alice Howe James (Gibbens), September 10, 1885, William James Papers, Houghton Library, Harvard University, #1418.

82   On James and the ASPR, see Linda Simon: *Genuine Reality. A Life of William James*, New York: Harcourt Brace & Company, 1998, pp. 190–95.

83   Howard B. Radest: *Toward Common Ground. The Story of the Ethical Societies in the United States*, New York: Frederick Ungar Publishing Company, 1969, pp. 62–72, 69, 99, 100, 159–60, 166.

84   These early days are summarized in Linda Simon: *Genuine Reality. A Life of William James*, New York: Harcourt Brace & Company, 1998, pp. 149–55.

85   William James: "A Knight-Errant of the Intellectual Life," *McClure's Magazine*, XXV (May 1905), pp. 3–11. Another version was published in William Knight (ed.): *Memorials of Thomas Davidson. The Wandering Scholar*, Boston: Ginn and Company, 1907, Ch. 15. The same essay was republished in William James (Henry James Jr., ed.): *Memories and Studies*, New York: David McKay Company, 1941, Ch. 5.

86   In this he was considerably influenced by the Italian Antonio Rosmini-Serbatini (1797–1855) on whose work he had completed a book in 1882, *The Philosophical System of Antonio Rosmini-Serbati, translated with a sketch of the author's life, bibliography, introduction and notes by Thomas Davidson*, London: K. Paul, Trench & Co., 1882.

87 Much information on the London and New York Fellowships is given in Knight (ed.), op. cit., Chs 3, 4, 8, 9.

88 For the origins of the Fabian Society in London, see Edward R. Pease: *The History of the Fabian Society*, New York: Barnes & Noble, Inc., 1963. This account generally plays down the role of Davidson relative to the accounts published in the United States. For example, see Knight (ed.), op. cit.

89 Knight (ed.), op. cit., Ch. 13; Appendix A.

90 It appears that Davidson knew Adler and the Westons as well as Sheldon and Salter by the mid-1880s when they were camping out at Beede's. Davidson's faculty at Farmington represented people from the Ethical Societies including William M. Salter, Stephen F. Weston, and Percival Chubb, who had helped to organize the London Ethical Society. It was at Glenmore that Adler first met Chubb, whom he subsequently invited to join the faculty of the Ethical Culture School in New York.

91 Concord is described in Ledleicker, op. cit., Ch. 18. The Farmington School is described in some detail in Knight, op. cit. pp. 55–59.

92 J. Clarke Murray in his account of Glenmore provides an interesting perspective on the invention of the alternative summer academy in America. See "A Summer School of Philosophy," *Scottish Review*, 19 (January 1892), pp. 98–113. In 1889 the Ethical Culture annual convention proposed to begin a "school of applied philosophy and ethics." It was never realized. Mentioned in Radest, p. 100.

93 This connection is given by Mildred Bakewell Hooker, "Excerpts from article by Mildred Bakewell Hooker on Thomas Davidson and the Glenmore Summer School of the Culture Sciences," transcribed by Margaret Emmett O'Brien, September 1967, p. 3, Adirondack Museum, Blue Mountain Lake, New York.

94 Weston's role is credited in S. Burns Weston Jr., "A Modern Socrates and the Challenge to Individualism," paper read to the Philosophical Club (no location), dated April 6, 1947. KVL Archive, VF "Glenmore."

95 Helen Goldmark Adler, op. cit., pp. 6–7.

96 Pulitzer's support is mentioned in a local newspaper article, "The Colony at Glenmore," *The Evening Post* (August 10, 1906). KVL Archive, Loomis Scrapbook, vol. 3, p. 35. For various references to Pulitzer's relationship to Davidson, see: W.A. Swanberg, *Pulitzer*, New York: Charles Scribner's Sons, 1967.

97 The *Prospectus* of 1890 is excerpted in Knight, op. cit., pp. 55–58. The archive of the Keene Valley Library is in possession of the *Prospectus* for the years 1892, 1902–1906, 1908–1909. See KVL Archive, VF "Weston," S. Burns, Jr. The McGill University Archives has copies of 1893 and 1908. The author has not been successful in locating the other years.

98 A good description of the physical setting is given by a Glenmore student, Mary Foster, in: Knight, op. cit. Ch. XI.

99 James, in: Knight, op. cit. pp. 113–14.

100 The best account of Harris's involvement in Glenmore is given in Kurt F. Leidecker *Yankee Teacher: The Life of William Torrey Harris*, New York: The Philosophical Library, 1946. Harris was a powerful figure at Glenmore. He had become the United States Commissioner of Education in 1889, a post he held for 17 years. He was a long-time Davidson acquaintance, dating from St. Louis where both taught in public schools. In 1866, Harris was an organizer of the St. Louis Philosophical Society, the beachhead of Hegelianism in North America. Davidson was a member. Perry, pp. 166–67. Harris was also founder of the *Journal of Speculative Philosophy*, which was widely influential. Harris participated in Glenmore for many years, having owned a house within the complex. Harris was a crucial figure in the success of Glenmore, in that he had the experience of assisting Alcott with the Concord Summer School of Philosophy between 1879 and 1888, and where Davidson had also regularly taught before beginning his own school at Farmington. The Concord programs were published each year in *The Journal of Speculative Philosophy*. In particular, see "The Concord Summer School of Philosophy,

1879–1880," *Journal of Speculative Philosophy*, 14 (January 1880), pp. 135–38. Harris wrote the definitive early biography of Alcott: Franklin B. Sanborn and William T. Harris: *A. Bronson Alcott: His Life and Philosophy*, 2 vols, Boston: Roberts Brothers, 1893. Also see: Leidecker, Ch. 18. Davidson and Harris evolved Alcott's precedent from Concord to Farmington to Glenmore with Harris providing continuity. It was Harris who most effectively articulated the relationship between Glenmore and the American tradition of the alternative academy and its relation to naturalism.

101   See Andrew J. Reck: "The Influence of William James on John Dewey in Psychology," *Transactions of the Charles S. Pierce Society*, 20 (Spring 1984), p. 91.

102   This correlation is mentioned by Max Eastman, op. cit., p. 258. The articles were: "The Metaphysical Assumption of Materialism," *Journal of Speculative Philosophy*, 16 (1882), pp. 208–13; "The Pantheism of Spinoza," 16 (1882); "Knowledge and Relativity of Feeling," 17 (1883), pp. 56–70.

103   The participation of Harris and Dewey at Farmington is documented in Knight, op. cit.; also mentioned by S. Burns Weston: "A Modern Socrates and the Challenge to Individualism," manuscript dated April 6, 1947. KVL Archive, vertical file "Glenmore," p. 6.

104   This relationship of Dewey to Davidson and James is noted in Steven C. Rockefeller: *John Dewey. Religious Faith and Democratic Humanism*, 1991, pp. 182–83. Also see Michael Buxton: "The Influence of William James on John Dewey's Early Work," *History of Ideas*, 45 (July–September 1984): pp. 451–63.

105   While Dewey used the house for many years, very little biographic material exists regarding this aspect of his life and work. Mention is made in Jane M. Dewey (ed.): "Biography of John Dewey," in: Paul Arthur Schilpp, *The Philosophy of John Dewey*, New York: Tudor Publishing Company, 1939, pp. 30–31.

106   Knight, op. cit., p. 36.

107   Knight, op. cit., p. 261.

108   "Mrs. John Martin," Obituary, *New York Times* (April 3, 1945). For general accounts of Prestonia Mann's activities on East Hill, see: Martin, op. cit.; Hale, op. cit.; Robert J.A. Irwin: "Ad Majorem Amicitiae Gloriam," transcript of talk given to the Pundit Club, Buffalo, New York, October 12, 1987. KVL Archive, VF "Summerbrook."

109   For the beginnings of Summerbrook, see Martin, op. cit., pp. 2–3; Hale, op. cit., pp. 12–13; Irwin, op. cit., pp. 4–5.

110   Martin, op. cit.

111   Pease, op. cit., p. 158. Martin was active in liberal causes in New York City for decades.

112   Martin, pp. 3–4, gives a detailed description of the ritual laundry.

113   Martin, pp. 3–4; Hale, p. 13.

114   Gorky's difficult American experience is recounted in L. Jay Olivia: "Maxim Gorky Discovers America," *The New York Historical Society Quarterly*, LI (January 1967), pp. 45–60. For aspects related to Summerbrook, see: Martin, op. cit.; Hale, op. cit.; Irwin, op. cit.; Spargo, op. cit. Also see Steve Barnett: "The Summer Maxim Gorky, Russian Writer, Spent at Keene;" "Experimental Living at Keene in Days of Gorky's Stay There;" Barnett Describes the Summer House Where Gorky Stayed;" *Adirondack Daily Enterprise* (September 9, 10, 11, 1958). Adirondack Museum, Summerbrook file.

115   For an account of the more recent Putnam Camp activities, see Upjohn, op. cit.

116   For an account of the final demise of Glenmore, see S. Burns Weston: "Glenmore," op. cit.

117   Martin, op. cit.

118   Harold Weston: *Freedom in the Wilds. A Saga of the Adirondacks*, St. Huberts, New York: Adirondack Trail Improvement Society, 1971, p. 103.

119   There have been a number of other Century Association members within the Keene Valley summer community. See *The Century, 1847–1946*, New York: Century Association, 1947.

120   Robinson was an important spokesman for urban values at the turn of the century and an advocate for the "City Beautiful" movement. His play on Jack London's *Call of the Wild* was the

basis for one of Robinson's books. See Charles Mulford Robinson: *The Call of the City*, New York: Paul Elder & Company, 1908.

121   Den Tandt, op. cit.

122   For an overview of how New York was viewed in literature during the period 1900–1930 see Bayrd Still: *Mirror for Gotham as Seen by Contemporaries from Dutch Days to the Present*, New York: New York University Press, 1956, Ch. 9.

123   Josiah Royce: *William James and Other Essays on the Philosophy of Life*, New York: Macmillan Company, 1911, p. 45.

124   Ann Douglas, op. cit. p. 129.

125   William James: *Pragmatism. A New Name for Some Old Ways of Thinking*, New York: Longmans, Green, and Company, 1907, p. 28.

126   George Santayana: *Winds of Doctrine. Studies in Contemporary Opinion*, New York: Charles Scribner's Sons, 1913, pp. 204–7.

127   Santayana, p. 207.

128   William James: *Pragmatism*, p. 27.

Chapter 2

Framing the Urban Development
Choices: Policies, Planners, Market, Participation
Peder Boas Jensen

Copenhagen appears as a city of two combined structures: a structure of central Copenhagen, with the suburbs radiating from the city center to the northwest and south-west, and a linear structure extending 80–100 km along the coast of the Øresund, located at the crossroads of vehicular traffic and railway lines running from Scandinavia to Central Europe and shipping from the West to Russia and the other nations around the Baltic Sea.

The population of Copenhagen numbers around 1.7–1.8 million, or about one-third of the total Danish population, approximately 5.5 million. There are about 850,000 residential entities, including 220,000 single-family houses or villas, 100,000 terraced houses or similar low-density types of settlements, and 530,000 units in apartment blocks of three to five stories, seldom higher.

I THE RICH, THE POOR AND THE IMMIGRANT WORKERS

Between 20 and 25% of all flats are owned by social, non-profit housing organizations. Between 10 and 15% are cooperative houses or flats, i.e. privately owned but explicitly excluded from being bought and sold in speculative transactions. Between 60 and 70% are private, i.e. to be bought and sold in the free market without restrictions. The construction of social housing and cooperatives is subsidized by national and local government whereas private single-family houses and condominiums are partly financed by favorable tax regulations.

The Danish population is a fairly homogeneous population, a population without substantial differences in cultural and ethnic background or household incomes. There is, however, a marked tendency for the most well-to-do to gather in the northern parts of the region, in the most beautiful, undulating and forested landscapes along the Øresund coast.

The less fortunate or the indigent live in the central parts of the city, in the worn-out substandard housing areas close to the city center and now undergoing urban renewal, or else they live in the monotonous suburbs situated southwest of the city center. The following statistical information illustrates the housing conditions in central Copenhagen in comparison with those of the surrounding municipalities:

- 70% of all flats in central Copenhagen were constructed before 1940, in the suburbs only 25%;
- 85% of all flats in central Copenhagen are small one to three room flats, in the suburbs 50%.

The social housing system is in crisis. A number of social housing estates are dominated by guest workers, immigrants and refugees, social-security recipients or mentally disabled tenants. They move in according to local government directives, the rent being paid through public welfare programs. This engenders a vicious circle.

The more fortunate (and thus more powerful) tenants move out to escape the inconveniences of facing a neighborhood experiencing social collapse. The flats remain empty until more tenants, even less powerful than the preceding ones, move in with the aid of municipal assistance.

II A CAPITAL WITHOUT OVERALL GOVERNANCE

Danish public administration is organized on a three-level system: the national government and the local government, divided once again into counties – or regions – and municipalities. In Copenhagen, there are five county units and fifty-two municipalities. Local government plays a strong political role. Thus the local government budgets comprise 25–30% of the gross national product, an impressive share compared to that of other countries.

This strong role of local government was further enhanced by local government reforms at the beginning of the 1970s. Regional planning became mandatory for all counties. A Metropolitan Council was established as a fourth level in the governance of Metropolitan Copenhagen. Its tasks were to conduct regional planning for the entire region, i.e. all five county units, to plan for and operate public transportation in the area, to plan for the hospitals and the health services and to decide on certain environmental issues. Unfortunately, the Metropolitan Council became a weak organization what with the councilors being indirectly elected and without being furnished with any economy of its own with which to operate as either partner or opponent to the counties and the municipalities.

Accordingly, by the New Year 1990, the Metropolitan Council was dissolved, as an allegedly superfluous and toothless organization, although paradoxically enough, it did indeed constitute an annoyance to the counties and municipalities during its lifetime, and also as a sacrifice to what was at the time the ruling ideology of de-regulation. The tasks were then transferred to the five historic county units under the guidance and control of the national government, including the Ministry of Environment's National Spatial Planning Department.

A new proposal for overall governance in Metropolitan Copenhagen was presented in 1995 by the Minister of Domestic Affairs but was immediately dropped as it ran up against heavy political opposition. However, the issue remains continuously subject to heated debate.

III THE CONFLICT, CENTRAL COPENHAGEN VS. THE SUBURBS

Regional plan no. 1, the so-called "Fingerplan" (see Figure 2.1) was the very first attempt to frame the city's urban growth. The plan was based on the assumptions of limited

(a)   (b)   (c)

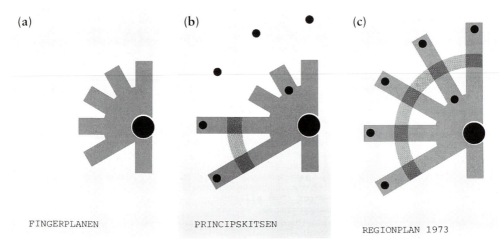

FINGERPLANEN   PRINCIPSKITSEN

REGIONPLAN 1973

2.1 Three stages of the regional plan ("Fingerplan"), schemata.

increase in the number of inhabitants, the housing stock and the consumption of land for urban purposes, all based on the experiences of pre-war demographic development in the European cities.

The goals for such a plan accommodating limited growth were naturally to complete and refine the existing city structure. The result was a plan for a city shaped like a hand, with fingers of urban expansion drawn around the S-train lines (the suburban train and metro lines) running from the suburbs to the city center, from home to work.

Ironically, the decades of the 1950s and 1960s became a period of accelerating urban growth, in Copenhagen as in many other European cities. The consumption of land for urban purposes exceeded by far the assumptions foreseen in the Fingerplan. A regional plan no. 2 (See Figure 2.1b) was therefore prepared at the beginning of the 1960s in order to face this new challenge. The planners proposed a basic break in the existing city structure. They proposed a conurbation of the future, vigorously growing suburbs around a new regional center in Høje-Taastrup, situated on the most important railway line connecting Copenhagen to the southwest and the rest of Denmark.

The aim was to protect the most valuable landscapes in the northern parts of the region against urban sprawl, to protect the inner, historical parts of the city against high-rise office development, to protect the city center and the immediate surrounding districts (brokvartererne) against increased car traffic and to provide the growing population in the southwestern suburbs with jobs and urban services near their homes; in the terminology of that time, to avoid dormitory town districts.

Thus, these proposals of regional plan no. 2 implied radical changes in the existing city structure and stirred up a heated debate. The conflict between the developing municipalities in the southwest, the affluent municipalities in the north and the municipalities in central Copenhagen became apparent. The municipalities in the north and in central Copenhagen wanted their share in the urban growth, or their share in the increased number of taxpayers.

Accordingly, regional plan no. 2 was modified in order to accommodate a compromise acceptable to all parties. This was also delayed, however, due to incessant political and professional disagreements and due to delayed grants for public capital investments. To cite just one example: as early as 1963, it was resolved that a new railway station be built in Høje-Taastrup for international, national and local public transportation, amounting to a second main railway station for the Copenhagen area. But the station was first inaugurated in 1998, 25 years later.

IV CENTRAL COPENHAGEN IN A STATE OF SOCIAL COLLAPSE

Already in the 1960s, the large, and centrally located, Copenhagen municipality was facing serious financial and social problems. And this is still the case. The population peaked at 750,000 in 1950 but has since decreased to less than 500,000 today. More prosperous groups of families have moved out to better, more up-to-date apartments, terraced houses or family houses in open, green surroundings, and to what are quite possibly better conditions for their children in the suburbs. The weak, the sick and the unemployed have been left behind in an old and worn-out housing stock.

This decrease in population in the central municipality and the parallel increase in the suburbs are, first of all, a direct result of the demand for consumption of much more urban area per capita, all as foreseen in the regional plan no. 2. The extraordinary growth in the number of cars and the favorable tax regulations provoked an extraordinary urban sprawl inasmuch as low-rise/low-density housing, i.e. dispersed single-family houses were mushrooming in layers around the Fingerplan city.

Public institutions such as the Technical University (Danmarks Tekniske Universitet), Roskilde University Center (RUC), national government departments and national research activities were also moved out into the suburbs which offered sufficient indoor and outdoor space. Enormous shopping centers and large-scale service sector estates were located in the outer municipalities for the very same reasons.

V NOW, WHAT ARE THE RESPONSES TO SUCH A COLLAPSE?

There are, at least, the following:

- to change the national government system of block grants meant for local government so as to transfer more financial means from funds not already earmarked to the poor municipalities, including the central municipality of Copenhagen;
- to establish a new metropolitan county for metropolitan Copenhagen as one financial unit so as to transfer financial means from the affluent municipalities predominantly in the north of the region to the less fortunate municipalities in the southwest and the center of the region;
- to invest in new large-scale commercial estates, in large-scale housing development and to support large-scale infrastructure systems so as to boost the economic development.

The central municipality preferred the last of the aforementioned responses. During the 1960s and 1970s a number of plans and projects were prepared for shopping centers, convention centers, hotels and office premises immediately adjacent to the city center. Among these was the so-called City Plan West, entailing the destruction of extensive sections of the urban fabric.

Plans and projects were prepared for new, large-scale housing schemes on the reclaimed land on Vestamager, an island in the southern part of Copenhagen, on areas in co-ownership of the national government and the municipality, foreshadowing what was later to be called the Ørestad. The slogan of the Lord Mayor in his first election campaign was "housing, housing and still more housing."

Plans and projects were prepared for new capital investments in the infrastructure in central Copenhagen, a new system of urban expressways including, for example, the much disputed penetration road from the north to City Plan West (the conduit access from the Lyngbyvejen and the ring road around the Lakes) and a new extensive system of metro lines, which, in accordance with the legislation of that time, was supposed to be financed by national government funds.

Implementation of these plans and projects would most certainly have resulted in the accumulation of more traffic, generating large-scale commercial activities close to the city center and quite possibly the destruction of the historic urban environment, with more cars in the narrow streets, as one experiences, with horror, in other European cities like Stockholm.

The aforementioned plans and projects were not implemented, however. They were presented for a first reading in the City Council, then referred to readings in the pertinent City Council Committees, and that is where they have remained until this very day, without having been endowed with any ultimate political resolution, for or against.

VI GRASSROOTS AND A STAGNANT ECONOMY

The preferred municipal strategy ran into resistance from a motley crew of political opponents: parties from the new left movement (not the communists, at least not whole-heartedly), active residents in various housing areas, young people from the flower-power generation, politicians from other parts of the country, the so-called green front in the parliament, who will most likely oppose almost any development programs for the capital, and even people from labor party or conservative party circles.

It was, however, the stagnant economy that became the most decisive factor. There were simply insufficient funds for investment in the proposed large-scale projects, and if such funds were found, they would most likely rather be spent in the periphery of Denmark than in the capital. The many plans and projects for central Copenhagen were shipwrecked. But some of the fundamental games of the stakeholders in the planning process were disguised:

- counties and municipalities are, of course, acting to the greatest possible extent in a way that satisfies their own demands for a sound economy, so as to attract more and wealthier taxpayers and, above all, in a way that avoids taking in those who might prove to be a burden on the social welfare programs. It is not their immediate responsibility to be concerned about the well-being of the total conurbation;

- the City Council of central Copenhagen will, for the very same reasons, often *take opposition to* what are otherwise perfectly sensible development plans and projects for the entire region and also will often *work against* the suburban municipalities and their planning efforts;

- national line ministries, e.g. the Ministry for Public Works, are involved in regional and local development with the dispersal of substantial grants to infrastructure systems such as the major road network, but in many cases they tend to pursue their own objectives rather than the overall objectives for the total development of the city;

- counties and municipalities will do whatever is necessary to obtain a maximum share of the national grants thus risking a distortion in the balance of capital investments in the city as a whole or in the various parts of the city;

- local government politicians are elected for a period of four years in office, and they want to produce conspicuous here-and-now results visible before the next election, whereas planners, by vocation, are supposed to contemplate the long-term goals of proposed developments;

- local government politicians tend to care for economic growth, whereas a growing number of the citizens care for the preservation of existing city structures and for the environment.

In short, the stakeholders in planning for Copenhagen are all acting naturally and in sound accordance with their own roles in the game, whether these be inside the national government, the counties, the municipalities or out there in the housing districts. But stakeholders who are motivated to act on behalf of the entire conurbation are missing.

VII THE CAPITAL AND THE PERIPHERY

The first two of the aforementioned regional plans from the 1940s and 1960s had no formal or legal status. In contradistinction to this, regional plan no. 3 from the mid-1970s (see Figure 2.1c) was prepared by the planners of the Metropolitan Council and adopted by a majority in the same council by authority of the new planning legislation following the local government reforms.

The plan anticipated further urban growth and further radical changes in the city structure. The main idea was to locate a number of centers for commercial activities, public and private services in a semicircle transverse to the fingers of the Fingerplan. New housing areas were grouped along this development corridor.

But, once again, the winds shifted immediately after adoption and suddenly the expected urban growth was virtually halted by economic recession and the energy crisis. The expected urban development did not materialize in Copenhagen whereas there was flourishing growth in the little towns in the western provinces of Denmark, an astounding situation when compared to what was the development in other European countries, and presumably the result of many factors, such as:

- the fundamental changes in the Danish community from being an industrial- and even more correctly, a mainly agro-industrial-based economy to being a post-industrial society of communication and services;
- the very special structure of the Danish business community with many little business units and very few large-scale companies, where small-scale commercial activities perhaps feel more comfortable in little towns in the provinces, while the large-scale industrial complexes in Copenhagen were dismantled;
- the goals for Danish national planning policy, as formulated in the regular planning reports prepared for the parliament, have for many years been the promotion of an even development of the country, e.g. to promote economic growth in the periphery as opposed to a development of the "one-sided Denmark" with Copenhagen as a dominating capital;
- the local government reforms of the early 1970s implied decentralization of government works and services, i.e. decentralization from national government to the counties and from the counties to the municipalities, resulting in a better staffing of the municipalities and the creation of a number of municipal, well-paid, secure jobs throughout the nation;
- Danish entry into the Common Market at the beginning of the 1970s, with large areas of the western provinces becoming more integrated in the hinterland of Hamburg and less integrated in the hinterland of Copenhagen.

VIII URBAN RENEWAL AND PARTICIPATING CITIZENS

Also in the 1970s, the municipality of central Copenhagen altered its strategies, as a response to the aforementioned economic recession and energy crisis. The enumerated large-scale plans and projects for commercial activities, housing and infrastructure systems were abandoned. New strategies were formulated for the same purpose as before, i.e. to reverse the economic and social developments of the municipality:

- a new system of non-earmarked national government block grants was negotiated in order to improve the financial conditions for the disadvantaged municipalities in central Copenhagen, but in vain;
- large-scale urban development plans and projects in virgin land became less interesting for the politicians, who turned their attention instead towards the reuse of former industrial areas and buildings of now vacant, former seaport areas situated in the inner parts of the city;
- urban development plans and projects became, on the whole, less interesting as politicians and planners began to spend much more time working with the urban renewal of worn-out housing districts adjacent to the city center, e.g. the urban renewal projects for Nørrebro and Vesterbro.

The course of urban renewal in the *Sorte Firkant* (Black Rectangle) in Nørrebro turned out to be a drama, in fact, a real war, almost, between the tenants on the one side and the municipality, assisted by the police, on the other. The renewal projects entailed radical, and for a number of tenants unacceptable, changes in the existing urban fabric, transformations which were inclined toward a monotonous suburban-like settlement in the middle of central Copenhagen. But for many elderly politicians and civil servants in the municipality, these changes were perceived as the quintessence of a welfare city with light, fresh air and contemporary sanitary installations.

All plans in Denmark, including plans for urban renewal, are subject to community approval according to the terms of the planning legislation. But many citizens consider public participation a mock trial or mere lip service partly due to the experiences surrounding the drama at the Sorte Firkant and other urban renewal projects.

Mutual mistrust prevails, despite subsequently implemented tenant-friendly and participation-oriented changes in the urban renewal legislation and in the management of another large-scale urban renewal project in Vesterbro.

IX THE WILL OF GREATER COPENHAGEN METROPOLITAN COUNCIL

The regional plan no. 4 (see Figure 2.2) was prepared at the end of the 1980s, constituting a sort of last will and testament of the Greater Copenhagen Metropolitan Council, which was abolished by the New Year of 1990.[1] The preconditions of the plan were a slight decline in the population, a limited increase in housing constructions and a limited but somewhat stronger growth in the provision of office premises as an indication of the changes from an industrial or agro-industrial economy to a communications and service-based community. Politicians and planners in the capital expressed their very pessimistic views:

- Greater Copenhagen is no longer among the most wealthy urban societies in Denmark inasmuch as the standard of living has fallen to a level below the average of the rest of the country, the higher costs of living in Copenhagen being taken into consideration;
- five billion Danish crowns (800 million US$), a small amount in terms of the US economy, but a considerable sum in the Danish context, is annually transferred out from the capital and into other regions, and national government investments in the Copenhagen region are far below the national average, e.g. investments in main road systems;
- the growth of the Danish population stagnated at the beginning of the 1980s and was actually decreasing in metropolitan Copenhagen;
- half the worn-out Danish housing stock is located in Copenhagen.

The strategic conclusions to such limited growth were much like the conclusions of the Fingerplan. Like the Fingerplan, the aim was to cultivate and refine the original city structure by using the means of localization policies and land use planning as implements

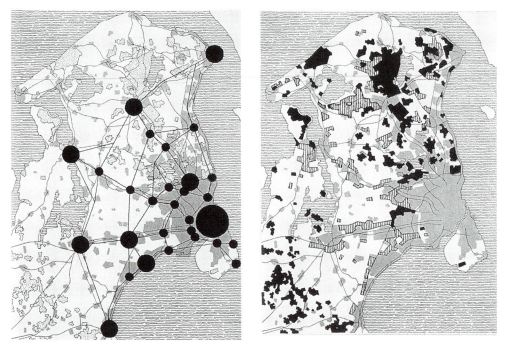

2.2 Two maps from regional plan no. 4.

for reducing travel time for the inhabitants of the city and to favor mass transportation in competition with car traffic. However, the regional plan no. 4 is much more complex than the Fingerplan, as it introduces a number of other issues, such as planning for non-urban land and planning for the environment.

For example, the regional plan no. 4 recommends well-located large-scale afforestation, since this can contribute to the European Community's policy of reducing surplus agricultural production and simultaneously provide special recreational opportunities for the inhabitants of Copenhagen.

X NEW SIGNALS IN NATIONAL AND REGIONAL PLANNING

As a consequence of the abolishment of the Metropolitan Council, the tasks of regional planning were taken over by the five county units, under the guidance and control of the national government, especially the National Spatial Planning Department. The first results of this transfer of responsibility can be seen on the map (Figure 2.3), where the recent regional plans are presented together.

In the northern county, Frederiksborg Amt, the town of Hillerød appears to be the center of development, or the spider in the center of the web. The outer parts of the little finger and the middle finger are somehow chopped off and live a life of their own in the periphery of the county. The plan for the western county, Roskilde Amt, presents the same picture, but with two spiders, the towns of Roskilde and Køge. And in the middle,

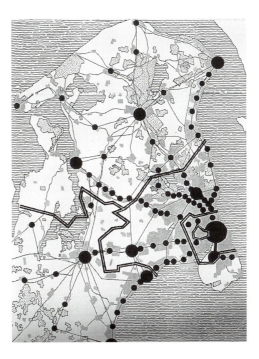

2.3 Copresentation of recent regional plans for Northern Zealand.

in Københavns Amt (Copenhagen County), the middle parts of all the fingers are chopped off at the palm of the hand.

A number of innovative methods concerning the organization of planning, urban development and urban renewal were introduced almost simultaneously. The intention was to include investors and real estate owners in the planning and implementation process, on an equal footing with local government agencies. New cooperations have been created to initiate development. Ørestadsselskabet, a sort of a development corporation set up to initiate, plan and promote the development of a new town in the island of Amager, is a good example.

And the government changed national and regional planning policies. Previous goals aimed toward a more even development of the country, aimed directly in opposition to the "one-sided Denmark," were abandoned. The goals are now to strengthen the urban structures facing competition from other European cities, primarily the fortification of the urban structures of Copenhagen and Malmö around the strait of Øresund.

XI A NEW ØRESUND CITY OF 2.5 MILLION INHABITANTS

The fixed link (bridge and tunnel) between Denmark and Sweden, with Copenhagen on the Danish side and Malmö on the Swedish side of Øresund, has been subject to public debate for many years, but is now under construction. A new Øresund City comprising Copenhagen, Malmö and other urban settlements has similarly been subject to public debate as a Nordic growth axis in competition with Berlin and Hamburg. The proponents argue:

- a new coherent city will appear after completion of the fixed link, being a city of 2.5 million inhabitants, with a population of 1.7 million in metropolitan Copenhagen and 0.8 million in southern Sweden;
- this growth axis is geopolitically located at the crossroads of vehicle and train traffic from Scandinavia on its way towards central Europe and of shipping from the Western world to the Baltic countries, and near to one of the most important airports in Europe;
- the potentials of commercial activities in the region will be substantially strengthened in the context of the European competition and additional urban services, in terms of cultural, educational and research centers, will be made accessible to the same population.

The skeptics, among these being the environmentalists, are going for other goals: a friendly, open, and green city, a clean environment, smoothly running car traffic and public transportation without delay, and low real estate prices. And they question whether a single fixed link is sufficient, after all, for the creation of this new and bigger city of 2.5 million inhabitants.

Can this still very open composition be compared in any way to a compact metropolis like Hamburg?

XII THE CITY TURNED UPSIDE DOWN

In any event, the fixed link (bridge and tunnel) now under construction will certainly turn the present city structure of Copenhagen upside down. The major thrust of the international traffic on roads or railways today penetrates the city from the north, either from the town of Elsinore (Helsingør) or the northern part of the seaport, toward the south and west, as it moves through some of the most densely populated urban areas.

This picture will be reversed after the completion of the fixed link, with the major bulk of future international traffic moving south of and around the outskirts of the city.

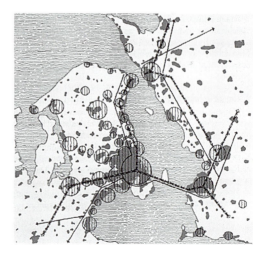

2.4 Urban settlements and plans for development in the Øresund region.

The present linear city structure, as described at the beginning of this section, may be replaced by a triangular structure of development corridors running from north to southwest – as is the case today, from east to west – south of the city – and from north to southeast – along the coast of Øresund. The accessibility of new extensive areas for urban development will be increased markedly.

- there are plans for a new city, Ørestad (a city which is designed to attract international investors), which will be situated on the reclaimed land of Vestamager, totally vacant land owned by the Danish state and the municipality of Copenhagen, very close to the city center and to the airport. The city is to be developed according to special legislation and partly undisturbed by normal planning procedures as prescribed in the general planning legislation. A special development corporation has been established as in the British tradition for new towns. An architects' competition has been held and a final master plan was presented in the mid-1990s;
- almost all of the former seaport area is ready for redevelopment. This water front extends approximately 10 km traversing central Copenhagen. The potentials for urban development are unique, integrating the city and the possible recreational values of the former seaport;
- in addition a number of former industrial areas are becoming vacant for redevelopment, e.g. along the coast of Øresund from the city center and down to the airport.

XIII URBAN SPRAWL, ONCE AGAIN?

Such potential changes in the city structure will naturally influence the entire development of Greater Copenhagen and not only the redevelopment of the central districts. The goals for this development of the entire region, however, have not yet been clarified. The urban development projects mentioned have not been evaluated and assessed in regional planning for the entire metropolitan area, giving rise to a number of questions.

Is there at all a demand for such a massive supply of new urban areas? Is there a need for such extensive areas for location of large-scale communication and service activities as some politicians and planners apparently dream of? And is it possible, as in the past, to build cities in appropriate stages of smaller, complete city units, *cities in the city* for attracting foreign and Danish investors?

Or is it more likely that these central and attractive areas in question shall be subject to haphazard and dispersed urban sprawl as in the suburban municipalities in the hectic years of the 1960s and 1970s?

Note

A new Greater Copenhagen Metropolitan Development Council was established by July 2000, after this chapter was written. The new council is supposed to take care of regional planning for the same planning area.

Chapter 3

The Layered City

Peter Marcuse

Engels . . . points out the differences between the urban vision of the working class, the middle class and the upper class. The "members of the money aristocracy," confining themselves to their "business or pleasure walks," may never know the working-people's quarters and never "see . . . that they are in the midst of the grimy misery that lurks to the right and the left," and the facades of the shops along the thoroughfares "suffice to conceal from the eyes of the wealthy men and women of strong stomachs and weak nerves the misery and grime which form the complement of their wealth."[1]

I THE QUARTERED CITY

The quarters of the city today result, in several meanings of the term, in a truly *quartered* city. It is hardly possible to speak accurately of "the" city any longer, when speaking of any of the major cities of the world; certainly not when speaking of a city like New York. What is seen, felt, experienced of New York City, or of any other major city, by one will be very different from what another sees or feels.

The quartering of the city runs along a number of dimensions, however: for a city like New York, the key ones that may be experienced run according to lines of race, of class, of occupation, of ethnicity. While these are correlated among themselves, they are also overlapping in their spatial configuration. The result is not only a quartered city but a layered city, in which one line of division overlaps another, sometimes creating congruent quarters, sometimes not. The quartering will further vary by time: the occupancy of a given space in the morning may be very different from the occupancy of that same space at night, certainly in those quarters where people work. When the white male yuppie accountants leave the downtown office building in the late afternoon, the black female elderly cleaning crews come in to start their work. Adding together the multiple spatial divisions and superimposing the time dimension, we may well have to speak not only of a quartered but also of a *layered* city.

Let us begin with the conception of a quartered city. It may be seen both in the spatial arrangement of residential life and in the spatial arrangement of business activities.

One may speak of separate *residential* cities . . .

The *luxury areas of the city*, the residences of the wealthy, while located in clearly defined residential areas, are at the same time non-spatially bound. The very rich, in terms of residential location, are not tied to any quarter of the city, just as the men that whipped the horses that pulled apart the quartered prisoner are not linked to any one of the resulting quarters. For the wealthy, the city is less important as a residential location than as a location of power and profit. The restructuring of cities has led to an increased profitability of real estate, from which the already wealthy disproportionately benefit. Joel Blau cites figures that indicate from 1973 to 1987 additional revenue from property constituted 45% of the income growth among the top 1% of the population.[2] It is for them first and foremost a profit-making machine. They profit from the activities conducted in the city, or (increasingly) from the real estate values created by those activities; they may enjoy living in the city also, but have many other options. If they reside in the city, it is in a world insulated from contact with non-members of the class, with leisure time and satisfactions carefully placed and protected. If the city no longer offers profit or pleasure, they can abandon it; 75% of the chief executives of corporations having their headquarters in New York City lived outside the city in 1975.[3] It is a disposable city for them. Many years ago they were concerned to protect their separate space in the city by public instrumentalities such as zoning;[4] Seymour Toll vividly describes the interests of the wealthy residents of Fifth Avenue to protect their mansions from "inconsistent neighboring uses" through the adoption of New York City's first zoning law in 1916. Today, each private high-rise condominium has its own security, and elsewhere walls protect the enclaves of the rich from intrusion. The new architecture of shopping malls, skywalks, and policed pedestrian malls is a striking physical mirror of the social separation. Downtown skywalks, for instance, both symbolically and physically, permit the men and women of business to walk over the heads of the poor and the menial.[5]

The clarity of the separation of the luxury areas of the city from the rest is startlingly evident in the obsequiousness with which a city like New York rushes to evict the homeless from the streets or transportation centers that serve the wealthy, removing the homeless from the sight and sensibility of the rich to the distant ghettos of the poor – even to the point of putting up the "occupied look decals," posters of plants and venetian blinds pasted on the boarded-up windows of abandoned houses to create a Potemkin village for the rich to look at on their drive to work. Engels would have found the pattern familiar. While the luxury areas depend on other quarters of the city for their services and support, they exist spatially apart from them.

The *gentrified city*[6] serves the professionals, managers, technicians, yuppies in their 20s and college professors in their 60s: those who may be doing well themselves, yet work for and are ultimately at the mercy of others. The frustrated pseudo-creativity[7] of their actions leads to a quest for other satisfactions, found in consumption, in specific forms of culture, in "urbanity" devoid of its original historical content, more related to consumption than to intellectual productivity or political freedom.[8] The residential areas they occupy are chosen for environmental or social amenities, for their quiet or bustle, their history or fashion; gentrified working class neighborhoods, older middle class areas, new developments with modern and well-furnished apartments, all serve their needs. Locations close to work are important, because of long and unpredictable work schedules, the density of contacts, and the availability of services and contacts they permit.

The *suburban city* of the traditional family, suburban in tone if not in structures or location, is sought out by better paid workers, blue and white collar employees, the "lower middle class," the petit bourgeoisie. It provides stability, security, the comfortable world

3.1 Abandoned tenements in Brooklyn with World Trade Center, then extant, behind. Photo by Dan Wiley.

of consumption. Owner-occupancy of a single family house is preferred (depending on age, gender, household composition), but cooperative or condominium or rental apartments can be adequate, particularly if subsidized and/or located close to transportation. The home as symbol of self, exclusion of those of lower status, physical security against intrusion, political conservatism, comfort and escape from the work-a-day world (thus often substantial spatial separation from work) are characteristic. The protection of residential property values (the home functioning as financial security and inheritance as well as residence) are important. Archie Bunker is the pejorative stereotype; the proud and independent worker/citizen is the other side of the coin.[9]

The *tenement city* must do for lower paid workers, workers earning the minimum wage or little more, often with irregular employment, few benefits, little job security, no chance of advancement. Their city is much less protective or insular. In earlier days their neighborhoods were called slums; when their residents were perceived as unruly and undisciplined, they were the victims of slum clearance and "upgrading" efforts; today they are shown their place by abandonment and/or by displacement, by service cuts, deterioration of public facilities, political neglect.

Because they are needed for the functioning of the city as a whole, however, they have the ability to exert political pressure, to get public protections: rent regulation, public housing, were passed largely because of their activities, although often siphoned up to higher groups after the pressure went off. When their quarters were wanted for "higher uses," they were moved out, by urban renewal or by gentrification. The fight against displacement, under the banner of protecting their neighborhoods, has given rise to some

3.2 Charlotte Gardens in the Bronx. Photo by Richard Plunz.

of the most militant social movements of our time, particularly when coupled with the defense of the homes of their better off neighbors.

The *abandoned city*, economic and, in the United States, racial, is the place for the very poor, the excluded, the never employed and permanently unemployed, the homeless and the shelter residents. A crumbling infrastructure, deteriorating housing, the domination of outside impersonal forces, direct street-level exploitation, racial and ethnic discrimination and segregation, the stereotyping of women, are everyday reality. The spatial concentration of the poor is reinforced by public policy; public (social, council) housing becomes more and more ghettoized housing of last resort (its better units being privatized as far as possible), drugs and crime are concentrated here, education and public services neglected.

II THE MULTIPLE CITIES OF BUSINESS

In similar fashion, one may speak of different *cities of business and work*. The city of business and its divisions is not congruent in space with the residential city and its divisions. The dividing lines in the spatial patterns of economic activity define areas in which people of many occupations, classes, status, work in close proximity. Yet, if we define economic divisions by the primary activity taking place within them, one may again get a four- or five-part division.

The *controlling city*, the city of big decisions, includes a network of high-rise offices, brownstones or older mansions in prestigious locations, that is less and less locationally circumscribed. It includes yachts for some, the back seats of stretch limousines for others, airplanes and scattered residences for still others. But it is not spatially rooted. The controlling city is not spatially bounded, although the places where its activities at various times take place are of course located somewhere, and more secured by walls, barriers, conditions to entry, than any other part of the city.

Yet the controlling city tends to be located in (at the top of, physically and symbolically) the high-rise centers of advanced services, because those at the top of the chain of command wish to have at least those below them close at hand and responsive, and so it goes down the line. Our interviews with those responsible for planning the then new high-rise office tower for the Bank für Gemeinwirtschaft in Frankfurt revealed professionals who had concluded that a separation of functions, with top executives downtown but all others in back office locations, was the most efficient pattern for the bank, but were over-ruled by their superiors, with only the advantage cited above as their reasoning. By the same token, Citibank in New York City wants its next level of professionals directly accessible to its top decision-makers; credit card data entry operations may move to South Dakota, but not banking activities that require the exercise of discretion. Those locations, wherever they may be, are crucially tied together by communication and transportation channels which permit an existence insulated from all other parts of the city, if dependent on them.

The controlling city parallels in its occupancy and character, but is not congruent in time or space, with the luxury areas of the residential city.

The *city of advanced services*, of professional offices tightly clustered in downtowns, with many ancillary services internalized in high-rise office towers, heavily enmeshed in a wide and technologically advanced communicative network. The skyscraper center is the stereotypical pattern, but not the only possibility. Locations at the edge of the center of the city, as in Frankfurt/Main, outside it, as in Paris at La Defense or outside Rome or what investors hope will be the Docklands at London; or scattered around both inside and outside a city with good transportation and communications, as in Amsterdam. Social, "image," factors will also play a role; the "address" as well as the location is important for business. Whether in only one location or in several in a given city, however, there will be strong clustering, and the city of advanced services will be recognizable at a glance.

The city of advanced services parallels in the economic city the characteristics of the gentrified residential city.

The *city of direct production*, including not only manufacturing but also the production aspect of advanced services, in Saskia Sassen's phrase, government offices, the back offices of major firms, whether adjacent to their front offices or not, located in clusters and with significant agglomerations but in varied locations within a metropolitan area. Varied, indeed, but not arbitrary or chaotic: where customers/clients (itself an interesting dichotomy!) wish to be in quick and easy contact, inner city locations are preferred (as in the industrial valley between midtown Manhattan and the Financial District for the printing industry, or Chinatown and the garment district for textile production, in New York City).

For mass production, locations will be different. Here the pattern has changed dramatically since the beginning of the industrial revolution. At first factories were near the center of the city; indeed, to a large extent they led to the growth of the city around them, as in the manufacturing cities of New England or the mid-west or the industrial cities of England. But more modern manufacturing methods require more single-story space, vastly more, with parking for automotive access rather than paths for workers coming on foot, and many more operations are internalized; so land costs become more important than local agglomeration economies, and suburban or rural locations are preferred.

The city of direct production parallels but is clearly not congruent with, in either space or time, the residential suburban city.

The *city of unskilled work* and the informal economy, small-scale manufacturing, warehousing, sweatshops, technically unskilled consumer services, immigrant industries, closely intertwined with the cities of production and advanced services and thus located near them, but separately and in scattered clusters,[10] locations often determined in part by economic relations, in part by the patterns of the residential city. Because the nature of the labor supply determines the profitability of these activities, the residential location of workers willing to do low-paid and/or unskilled work has a major influence. Thus in New York City sweatshops locate in Chinatown or the Dominican areas of Washington Heights, in Miami in the Cuban enclave, or in the slums of cities throughout the world.

The economic city of unskilled work parallels the tenement city, although again in different times and places.

The *residual city*, the city of the less legal portions of the informal economy, the city of storage where otherwise undesired (NIMBY – Not In My Back Yard) facilities are located, the location of abandoned manufacturing buildings, generally also congruent with the abandoned residential city. But for political protest many of the most polluting and environmentally detrimental components of the urban infrastructure, necessary for its economic survival but not directly tied to any one economic activity, are located here: sewage disposal plants, incinerators, bus garages, AIDS residences, housing for the homeless, juvenile detention centers, jails. New York City's recently adopted Fair Share regulations, aimed at distributing NIMBY facilities (undesired facilities like jails or waste treatment facilities, evoking a response of Not In My Back Yard) "equitably" among districts, are a reflection both of the extent of the problem and its political volatility.

The residual city parallels but is, in this case, likely to be congruent with the abandoned residential city.

Putting these lines of residential and business division together, a general pattern emerges, in which the lines of separation are more or less congruent, and the social, economic, political, and cultural divisions largely (but not completely) overlap. One may thus speak of five distinct cities coexisting within the single "city" of municipal boundaries and popular reference. But the lines of separation are more complex than this five-part division suggests. As one progresses down the scale both in the quarters of the residential city and of the economic city, in the United States the proportion of black and Hispanic and immigrant households increases and the proportion of women heading households increases. Race, class, ethnicity and gender create overlapping patterns of differentiation – invidious differentiation, for there is no doubt that the differences are not simply of "lifestyles" or

Location of Asian Persons in Poverty
1 dot = 5, Total = 80,497

3.3 Map: Asian persons in poverty.

Asian Households Earning $75,000 or more
1 dot = 1, Total = 17,504

3.4 Map: Asian households earning $75,000 or more.

Location of Persons of English Ancestry
1 dot = 3, Total = 103,942

3.5 Map: Persons with English ancestry.

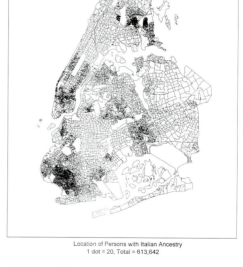

Location of Persons with Italian Ancestry
1 dot = 20, Total = 613,642

3.6 Map: Persons with Italian ancestry.

Location of Black Persons in Poverty
1 dot = 20, Total = 513,168

3.7 Map: Black persons in poverty.

Location of White Persons in Poverty
1 dot = 20, Total = 455,199

3.8 Map: White persons in poverty.

Location of Manufacturing Workers
1 dot = 20, Total = 590,443

3.9 Map: Manufacturing workers.

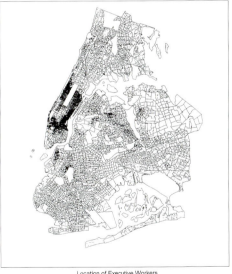

Location of Executive Workers
1 dot = 20, Total = 414,303

3.10 Map: Executive workers.

"special needs," but reflect positions in a hierarchy of power and wealth in which some decide and others are decided for.

One way to provide a visual representation of the complex divisions referred to above is to map residential locations. For New York City, four pairs of maps reflect the major types of division: by race, by ethnicity, by income, by occupation.

III THE FORMS OF CLUSTERING

A complex pattern of clustering thus characterizes the city, clustering along a number of dimensions, some related to and congruent with others, other lines independent of all others. Nor does the intensity of clustering itself provide a homogeneous description of the character of those found together and divided from others. To begin with, in each case all those within the group are not clustered together; the extent of clustering varies greatly from group to group, being greatest by race, black and white on our maps, least by ethnicity for some of those groups present for a long time in the city and well integrated towards the middle of the spectrum of its economic life, as Italians are. Further, the patterns of clustering vary; all clusters are not alike. One may distinguish at least five different patterns, ranging from the forms of the poverty-stricken and excluded ghetto to the classic integrated but spatially separated ghetto through the different types of enclave, immigrant, cultural, or exclusive, to the citadels of the rich. Chart A shows the key characteristics of each form; I have tried to define each in more detail elsewhere.[11]

Each of the five characteristics listed requires definition.

1   Spatial formation: "Separated" is of course a characteristic of all enclaves and ghettos, by definition; we are simply taking separation as the defining characteristic of the object of study of this paper. But the physical form the separation takes, reflective of its economic and social characteristics, will vary widely. "Insular" is here used to mean sharply separated by well-known, generally visible, boundaries: they may either be actual walls, as was the case with many medieval ghettos, or physical demarcations such as highways, rivers, steep slopes, blocks of buildings, or legal boundaries, such as group area boundaries in apartheid South Africa.[13]

Each of the spatial formations here listed is consistent with a variety of different overall spatial patterns for the cities/metropolitan areas in which they are located, the variety of which is vast, dependent on scale, internal boundaries, likelihood of social integration, etc. A gastronomic metaphor may be appropriate: mixing can occur as in a melting-pot, where no separate identities can any longer be discerned; or as in a stew or a salad, where the different ingredients can still be detected but affect each other, producing a composite that is none of them; or as a fruit bowl, each item preserving its own skin, touching each other but not affecting how any of the separate objects tastes.

2   Voluntariness is a matter of degree. There may be some who obtain pleasure in living in a fortified enclave that gives them a commanding position over their surroundings, who enjoy the status of a citadel; but there may be many more who would, given their first

Chart A Ghettos, enclaves, and citadels: a preliminary taxonomy

	Example	1 Spatial formation	2 Voluntary or not	3 Economic relationships	4 Social relationships	5 Identifying characteristics
Ghettos						
Classic ghetto	Jewish ghettos: Harlem, 1920	Insular, walled in	No	Separated but linked, exploited	Discriminated against	Race, color, religion
Outcast ghetto	South Bronx today	Insular, walled in	No	Excluded	Discriminated against	Race, color, class (bottom)
Enclaves						
Immigrant enclave	Chinatown Cuban Miami	Concentrated but mixed	Yes, seen as transitional	Separated but linked	Open	Nationalist, ethnicity
Cultural enclave[12]	Williamsburg, Soho	Concentrated but mixed	Yes, seen as permanent	Various: generally integral	Not hierarchically discriminating	Culture, language, religion, lifestyle
Exclusionary enclave	Beverly Hills	Insular, physically protected	Yes	Integral, exploitative	Discriminating	Class (upper), status
Citadel						
Imperial citadel	Canton, Trump Tower	Insular, physically dominant	Yes	Integral, exploitative	Discriminating	Class (upper), political, military power

preferences, rather live more freely and less surrounded by walls. Likewise, some residents of a ghetto may find their inability to move out in fact a blessing, removing challenges and creating an inescapable solidarity. But in most cases voluntariness will be a matter of degree; both enclaves and ghettos have some advantages and some disadvantages. At the extremes, however, the distinctions are clear.

3   A crude measure of the economic relations of those within the area and those without is in the location of employment: are residents primarily or exclusively employed within the area, or do they use their residence within it to increase their opportunities without? The Venetian Jewish ghetto or Hasidic Williamsburg are examples of outward linked areas; Cuban Miami is largely inwardly oriented, and current Empowerment Zone legislation[14] clearly contemplates inward linkages.

4   Social relationships are meant to cover the more or less hierarchical, more or less oppressive relationships between those within the area and those outside it. A wall may somewhat similarly surround an enclave of luxury garden apartments and a public housing project; the decisive difference is in the difference in the social (and economic and political) relationships between those on different sides of the wall.

"Minority" and "majority" might seem a first approximation to the central distinction here, but only if the terms are not quantitatively but qualitatively defined. In general, those ghettoized will also be a numerical minority, those forming exclusionary enclaves parts of a numerical majority. But the key question is relationship; if Yinger's definition is used, that "a minority is defined as a group which, regardless of where it is on the class ladder, faces barriers to the pursuit of life's values that are greater than the barriers faced by persons otherwise equally qualified," then the minority/majority distinction becomes directly useful here.[15]

Cultural differences of course do not have to be connected to hierarchical social differences – but it may be doubted if the two are ever really separable. Thus, Louis Wirth, in speaking of the Jewish ghettos of the middle ages, says "the geographically separated and socially isolated community seemed to offer the best opportunity for following their religious precepts."[16] It may be questioned whether such an "opportunity" was freely chosen, or whether it does not rather represent an adaptation to an (undesired) hierarchical relationship with the non-Jewish surrounding power. See the discussion of "voluntariness" and its ambiguity, above. On the other hand, many well-established and economically integrated groups use "residential clustering as an aid to the conservation of ethnic characteristics;"[17] the examples are too numerous to require repetition.

5   Contrary to what may be intuitively concluded, I do not believe there is a systematic relationship between the identifying characteristics of a group and the nature of any separated area they may occupy. It may seem, in the United States, that "race" or color, black, correlates completely with the excluded ghetto; but, as I have argued earlier, I believe this is true only when combined with income or economic position, and is not a function of color alone. There are religious ghettos and religious enclaves; Chinese people may live in separated areas with quite different relationships to the outside in Hanoi or

Jakarta than they have in New York City or San Francisco. Indeed, fundamentally to argue otherwise would be taking seriously distinctions based on race or ethnicity or origin as related to position in the world; a racist form of blaming the victim.

Poverty or power, on the other hand, are socially created distinctions,[18] and correlate directly with the form of separateness of a particular space occupied by those thus characterized.

IV THE LAYERED CITY OF EXPERIENCE

The metaphor of the quartered city with walls between the quarters describes key aspects of the divisions I have tried to illustrate above, but it does not adequately capture the lifeworld experience of the residents and users of these separate quarters. This is so for three reasons.

The first is that individuals experience the city both as part of their lifeworlds and as part of their integration into its economic world. The residents and users of the city are not necessarily the same people, and even when they are, they experience the city in quite different capacities. We have a striking example of the difference in some of the political conflicts we see in the planning of New York City in recent years, in which individuals who are in the real estate business and act as developers of property in Manhattan, and thus in their economic activities strongly support the loosening of zoning restrictions, the building to high densities, the gentrification of neighborhoods, who benefit from increases in property values, at the same time, as residents of the city, oppose building in the immediate vicinity of their homes, oppose higher appraisals of their residences that would increase their taxes, fight development proposals that would impact their personal lives outside of work. They use the city in one way, experience it as residents in another. This contradiction is also captured in the lack of congruence between the quarters of the city viewed as a residential city and the quarters of the city viewed as a site of economic activity.

The metaphor of the walled and quartered city further implies, incorrectly, that individuals are confined within their quarters for all of their activities and at all times. But, precisely because the residential and the economic quarters of the city are not congruent, there is passage from one to the other, by most people and generally every day. The conception of the ideal city (in the past often espoused by planners) as one where one lives and works in the same place – minimizing the travel time to work, is the standard formulation – hardly has substance today. Commuting is taken for granted; making it short and comfortable is the goal, not eliminating it. Only in odd and questionable circumstances is the approach to provide employment where a person lives. The two examples that spring to mind for New York City are the Empowerment Zone plans, in which poor African-Americans are to be supplied with jobs within the zones where they already live, and the so-called "edge cities," in which a deliberate attempt is made to provide work space, overwhelmingly offices, in suburban communities also being developed for housing. Race, in the United States context, plays a major role in both conceptions: in the one case, to keep blacks in the ghettos, in the other, to prevent middle class whites from having contact with them. Otherwise, even where communities are developed with both economic and residential opportunities, the two are kept spatially separate. Working at home remains the exception rather than the rule. One has only to look at Tokyo Central Station at rush hour to realize this.

Thus a given individual occupies different spaces for different activities, and the metaphor of the quartered city must reflect the movement among them.

And that brings me to the third dimension as to which the static metaphor of walling and quartering is inadequate: the time dimension. Not only do people occupy their homes and go to work in different places, they also do so at different times. In the rich white suburbs of Johannesburg the white home owners go to work in the morning, and the black servants come in as they leave; the residential area changes from white to black at eight in the morning. In the downtown skyscrapers in New York City, the lawyers leave their offices at five or six in the evening; the cleaning crews, earning one one-hundredth of what the lawyers make, come in after they go, and are gone when the lawyers return the next morning. Recent studies both of Tokyo and of Manhattan show that the daytime population of key locations is vastly greater than the night-time population, and the composition is quite different. The same space is occupied by very different people at the different times. In the recent rediscovery of the importance of space, the time nexus is often overlooked.

So the image of the walled and quartered city must take into account the different spatial structure of residential as against economic activities; must take into account the movement of individuals between one and the other; and must reflect the temporal aspect, in which different spaces are occupied by different persons as different times for different purposes.

I suggest the metaphor of a *layered city* as one that begins to capture these complex dimensions of division. The maps presented here, if thought of as transparencies that can be overlaid one on the other, might concretize such an image. The separation into different layers reflects an actual separation in lifeworlds; the level of segregation in New York City, as in most United States cities, is quite remarkable. One may even further split each layer by race, so that one can see clearly that black and white professionals live at different locations, in different layers. But a map of their workplaces will show much less difference; it operates at a different layer, and at different times. Thus on another layer of transparency one could visualize the division of that same space by use, as represented by the zoning code. On a third, one could visualize transportation patterns, with usage at each hour of the day. A different layer may show where children go to school; another, where the recreational facilities or the commercial facilities used by each group are located. Each layer shows the entire space of the city, but no one layer shows the complete city. Each one reflects the quartering and the walls of which I have spoken, but most in different spatial configurations from the others.

V GLOBALIZATION AND THE DETERMINANTS OF SPATIAL PATTERNS

The forces that produce the internal structure of cities may be divided into two categories: (1) those derived from a supra-city level (global, national, regional), beyond the control of individual cities and present, as common tendencies, in all of them, and (2) those particular to specific cities, based on their particular histories, the particular shape of their own built environment and natural setting, the balance of forces within them, their particular form of past economic, social, and political development. I want to focus here on the more general patterns, for I believe that developments in New York City, global city that it is, are not dissimilar from those in other cities throughout the world.[19]

The causes of changes within cities can for an important part be traced back to developments that take place on higher spatial levels, at least regionally[20] but even more critically the nation and the world. The latter, with their concomitant national and regional implications, is today generally subsumed under the concept of globalization, a term that is often used, but not always well defined. Globalization can comprise many processes, such as the changing spatial structure of economic activities, migration of capital, migration of people, and values and norms that spread along various parts of the world. We take it here to mean globalization in its present configuration,[21] that is, a combination of (1) new technology, (2) increased trade and mobility, (3) increased concentration of control, and (4) reduced welfare-oriented regulatory power of nation-states. [At least this is my meaning; we shouldn't complain about others not defining if we're not defining.] Globalization has clearly much to do with mobility of goods, of capital, of persons. The globalization of production has for instance led to the movement of shipyards and textile production from Western European countries to countries on the Pacific Rim. Effects of this process may influence the labor market position of people in both areas. Effects of migration are also on both sides, of course. Sending countries, which are often poor countries or countries with oppression, are losing people, while other areas, mainly the more wealthy countries, receive people who have to find a home. The influx of people into a country may change the character of cities and neighborhoods, because these areas become inhabited by new kinds of people. One of the principal points in discussing the new partitioned city is the question why some areas do receive people from other countries, while others do not. The local consequences of an influx of immigrants is often (but not always; see, e.g., White, 1998), tied to the influx of poor households, who more often than not belong to a different culture or "race." Hundreds of studies address these topics.

How can globalization influence social inequality? And, more specifically, how can it influence the division within cities and life within neighborhoods, as we have described them for New York City in this chapter? Basically, two lines of reasoning can be discerned (see Burgers *et al.*, 1997). The first follows Robert Reich's "The Work of Nations" (1991). He argues that local forms of social solidarity become less important as a consequence of the ever increasing process of globalization. Elites are becoming less dependent on the services of the lower status groups in neighborhoods. People are living increasingly independent of each other. The lifeworld of the wealthy is clearly larger than their living neighborhood. Melvin Webber's old idea of "communities without propinquity" seems to become more important for those at the upper end of the economic spectrum today; the "urban realm" becomes "non-spatial." For the very poor, by the same token, their spatially defined neighborhoods become more and more irrelevant to the functioning of the mainstream economy. The location of either with relation to the other recedes dramatically in importance.

The second line of reasoning focuses on globalization as leading to a kind of socio-economic symbiosis within an increasingly polarized society, which can be seen in a growing number of highly educated, wealthy persons and households, but also in an increasing number of people in lower segments. The crux in this second line of reasoning is that they are dependent on each other. One group has the money for products and services that the other group can provide (see, e.g., Sassen, 1988, 1991). The effects of the two lines of reasoning on the spatial divisions of the cities, and on life within specific areas, can be very different. The emphasis on non-spatial developments could lead to a society that is increasingly socially and spatially disconnected, fragmented and polarized. The emphasis on symbiotic relationships might (but not necessarily will) end up with a society that is both more polarized and more interdependent. Urban areas might therefore include neighborhoods where people with different incomes, ethnicities, skills, and education all live (Sassen is in fact very ambiguous and/or unclear in whether the interdependence is of ALL people, and what intra-urban spatial consequences it has) together. Or, the polarization can have very different consequences for different groups, leading some to form enclaves, others to be confined to ghettos.

Globalization could thus lead to the declining importance of neighborhoods, integrated neighborhoods, or segregated ones – or some combination of all three. The answer, for the United States at least, is discernible, and so are its reasons.

The increasingly hour-glass (more realistically, bowling-pin) shaped configuration of the income distribution produced by globalization is by now well known,[22] whatever the theory of its ultimate consequences may be. Recent studies of the results of the 1990 census in the United States reflect it, as does the discussion of the "two-thirds society" in Germany.[23] The cause is in some part a change in the job requirements derived from changes in technological methods of production: a greater need for higher skills and a lesser need for lower skills. But that is only part of the picture, for there is no inherent reason why those with lower skills cannot be upgraded, and those at the top do not possess skills as much higher than those of the unskilled as their incomes are to the incomes of the unskilled. The increasing differentiation comes as much from the increasing concentration of control, and of wealth that goes with it, as from the increasing bargaining power given those who control capital by the possibilities for the mobility of capital derived from its internationalization. The movement of jobs from high-wage to low-wage countries, after all, has nothing to do with higher physical productivity, but only greater economic profit: transportation costs plus lower skills make third world production technically less efficient, but such movement both increases profits where it takes place and constitutes a potent threat even where it does not. The Australian pattern has been described in detail.[24] Concentration, internationalization, and technological progress, the first element in our model, have thus led to a drastic change in the balance of power between capital and labor, leading to the further enrichment of the former and the increased impoverishment of the latter, the second element in our model.

"Two-thirds society" hardly grasps the nature of that change, however, because it suggests a two-way division, lumping everyone in either one or the other of two extremes. That is not the case. I have suggested above a five-way division. Others have other, more complex, categorizations. The important point for present purposes is not just what the range of divisions in society is, but rather that there is an increasing division at the bottom, between what used to be called the "working class" and those poorer than they, largely excluded at least from the formal economy, more and more often impoverished and even homeless. I desist from using the term "underclass," for reasons eloquently argued elsewhere[25]; but the intuitive resonance the term has found suggests it refers to a widely perceived new reality. Let me substitute the term "excluded;" I would then argue that the new changes in wealth and poverty have had different effects in at least five categories of people: for the owners of wealth and the decision-makers of power, increases in wealth and power; for professionals, technicians, managers, the winners (together with most owners) in the process of economic change, a large increase in numbers, and often in income and privilege, but accompanied by some insecurity as to status[26]; for the old middle class, civil servants, skilled workers, semi-professionals, a decline in numbers and a loss in status and security; for the old working class, a continuing erosion of their standard of living and decline both in their economic and their political bargaining power; and, most important for our purposes: for the excluded and the marginalized, the victims of economic change, the very poor, squeezed more and more out of the mainstream of economic activity, presumptively no longer needed even as a "reserve army of the unemployed," with no perceptible long-term prospects of improving their situation through normal economic channels, and used despite themselves as a threat to those better off. Just how and to what extent each group will be affected in these ways depends on the relationships of power and the related distribution of wealth among them and the manner in which each deals with the inevitable conflicts involved. In those conflicts, both space and race have played key roles in the United States.

Victims are inevitably produced by the processes of economic change that lead from Fordism to post-Fordism. How those victims are treated, including, among other things, where they will live and how the government will deal with them, depends on who they are and how they react.

The selection of victims then becomes a central determinant of the policies a state will follow in deciding how to treat victims. There are two polar choices, and reality will include some mixture of the two, in varying proportions, in any given society. Sometimes victims appear to be selected *at random*, regardless of group identifying characteristics, on the basis of their particular economic location. They may be those who happened to work in one industry rather than another; they may be those who entered the job market at a particular time, and have less seniority or work experience; they may be those in one particular part of a country instead of another. They may thus appear to be people just like all other people, and the majority may identify fully with them, sympathize with them, feel that, when they see them on the street, there but for the grace of God, go I. That was, for instance, the situation in the United States during the Great Depression.

It is the situation that leads to a welfare state type of response. Such welfare state legislation as we have in the United States was in fact largely passed during the Great Depression. Middle class homeless families with children evoke much greater sympathy, and charitable contributions for them flow much more freely than for single unemployed young black men. Unemployment benefits are much more easily passed in Congress than welfare benefits, for working and facing unemployment is a fear most people have to one degree or another, regardless of who they are. The more like the majority of the population the victims are, the better the treatment they are likely to receive.

If victims can be *cast out as a group*, e.g. by race, however, the situation is quite different. African-Americans in the United States, Turks in Germany, Algerians in France, Pakistanis in England, have all been stigmatized in the past; in the United States, certainly, there is a long tradition of oppression and racism from which African-Americans have suffered more than any other group, and have suffered regardless of their actual status in the workforce, in formal law, or in contribution. It is a stigmatization in this sense unconnected with class, although it increases the vulnerability to victimization by economic change particularly of working class and young African-Americans, and of African-American women.[27]

Where such a stigmatized group exists, repression and segregation are a much more readily available alternative to those in power for the treatment of the new victims than were the victims to appear to be arbitrarily selected and "just like everyone else." The tendency to stigmatize victims is a general one – to differentiate between the deserving and the undeserving poor. The welfare state is an expensive and unpopular approach with many. If increasing stigmatization can save money by justifying repression without risking loss of social control, then it is an alternative likely to be chosen.

The possibility of *spatial separation*, i.e. ghettoization, increases the likelihood of repressive treatment of the victims of change dramatically. Gunnar Myrdal, remarkably, laid out the scenario succinctly 50 years ago: "[Racial segregation creates] an artificial city . . . that permits any prejudice on the part of public officials to be freely vented on Negroes without hurting whites".[28] The ultimate point is arrived at when victimized and segregated become identical. Is that not the ultimate implication of William Wilson's shift from "underclass" to "ghetto poor" – by equating the two, spatial location becomes the defining characteristic by which the victims can be identified (it being remembered that, in the United States context, "race" and "ghetto" are also inseparable concepts). But a non-ghetto or a non-racial underclass is not considered important for discussion.[29] The outcast is defined by his/her connection with the outcast ghetto. It is the history of racism [i.e. if racism is discounted] that makes this extreme form of spatial ghettoization possible in the United States. Yet the tendency towards spatial segregation exists even absent racism [i.e. if racism is discounted], if in significantly attenuated form. Wacquant speaks of "territorial fixation and stigmatization" of the marginal, of a "stigma of place," of "penalized spaces."[30] Marginalization and then exclusion, created as a result of economic relationships, become transmuted into spatial ones: "social polarization through the field of collective consumption."[31]

The selection of the victims of the particular form of economic change now taking place will help determine how those victims are treated by government. There are two possible ways a society – more specifically, a state – can deal with the victims of such changes: through welfare benefits distributed by the state, or through repression and rigid external control. While both can and generally are used together, they are conceptually and politically very different.

Welfare state benefits are expensive. They are paid for by taxes, taxes which those in the upper echelons of the economic hierarchy would always rather minimize, and which those in the lower echelons can generally be counted on to resist as well. One might well argue that welfare state benefits are today simply a means to deal with the problems of the victims of economic change, in somewhat parallel fashion to the forces creating its origins in rapidly industrializing states in the nineteenth century.

Exclusion and repression, however, provide an alternative to the welfare state. Segregation is a form of exclusion and repression; ghetto walls function much like prison walls as a restraint on a population. Segregation, as I am using the term here, is involuntary, forced on a population by those having more power; it is a form of confinement, a form of repression. It is another possible answer to the problem of what to do with the victims of economic change: segregate them, confine them, repress any danger they may cause to others.

The repressive approach to the victims of economic change has ramifications up and down the line of the economic and the spatial hierarchy. For the line between the working class and the excluded is a fluid one; if the segregation of the excluded is to be legitimated by reference to their own weaknesses and evils, as it is, the working class will seek to separate itself from them. But so will the middle class; and seeing the fluidity of the line separating common workers from the excluded, the middle class will seek to separate itself from both. Both those at the top of the hierarchy and the professionals, technicians, managers, directly responsible to them, will also be concerned about their separation from those below; in seeking their own security, they will, and do, attempt to differentiate themselves and separate themselves from all below. The pattern of a quartered city is a result. That, at least in the context of the history and prevailing social relationships of the United States, is the result in that country. It is a tendency to be dealt with, I believe, in countries throughout the globe.

VI CONCLUSION

To return to the point with which this chapter began: the danger of speaking of "the city" as if it were a whole, and organic, entity. The organic metaphor for the city stems from the Chicago school of sociology in the 1920s, which envisaged cities as growing and/or declining organically, with a life cycle that could be described as that of any organism could be. But this is simply wrong. "The city" is not an actor; it is a place occupied and used by many actors. A city does not prosper or decline, particular groups in it do, and generally in a very different fashion. In New York City, the gap between rich and poor is growing. What is a crisis for one group may be prosperity for the other. Development may mean profits for one, displacement for the other. A corporate headquarters moving out of town may be a disaster for its local employees, but bring a surge in the price of its stock for its owners. Gentrification is a move up for some, a burden for others. A "city" is not global; some of those doing business in it are, but others very like them will do very similar business in other "non-global" cities. Those doing business on a global scale will have a similar impact on the spaces of the cities in which they do business, wherever they are. That impact may be concentrated in some cities, but that is because of what those actors do in them, not because that "city" has done something. At best, the city as actor is the municipal government of a city; and I think the evidence shows that municipal governments have at best marginal impact on the extent to which businesses ultimately locate within their boundaries.

So, the picture is of New York City as a city divided into quarters spatially, residentially, and economically; in which quite different spaces are occupied by different groups at different times, and often, and increasingly, with walls between them. In short, a quartered, walled and layered city.

Notes

1   Martin Zerlang from "The City Spectacular of the Nineteenth Century," Center for Urbanitet og Aestetik, Copenhagen, p. 8.
2   Blau, p. 85.
3   Steven Brint, in Mollenkopf and Castells, p. 155.
4   *Zoned American*, Grossman: New York, 1969.
5   See Peter Marcuse: "Stadt – Ort der Entwicklung," in: *Demokratische Gemeinde*, November 1988, pp. 115–22, and Jonathan Barnett: "Redesigning the Metropolis: The Case for a New Approach," *Journal of the American Planning Association*, vol. 55, No. 2, Spring 1989, pp. 131–35.
6   I use the term here, not in its narrower sense, as a portion of the city in which higher class groups have displaced lower class (see definitions in Peter Marcuse: "Gentrification, Abandonment, and Displacement: Connections, Causes, and Policy Responses in New York City," *Journal of Urban and Contemporary Law*, vol. 28, St. Louis: Washington University, pp. 195–240), but in the broader sense of areas occupied by, or intended for, professionals, managers, technicians, which may include newly constructed housing as well as housing "gentrified" in the narrower sense of the word.
7   The reference here is not to creative artists, to what in earlier days would have been called Bohemians, who cannot generally afford the prices of the gentrified city, and are more likely to live somewhere between the abandoned and the tenement city. To the extent that they tend to congregate in specific neighborhoods, they may serve as precursors of gentrification (see Rose Damaris: "Rethinking gentrification," *Environment and Planning D: Society and Space*, vol. 2, 1984, pp. 47–74, who differentiates sharply among different categories of gentrifiers).
8   Hartmut Häusermann and Walter Siebel: *Neue Urbanität*, Frankfurt am Main: Suhrkamp, 1987. See also Peter Marcuse: "Housing Markets and Labour Markets in the Quartered City," in: John Allen and Chris Hamnett: *Housing and Labour Markets: Building the Connections*, London: Unwin Hyman, 1991, pp. 118–35.
9   I still find Damaris Rose's "Toward a Re-evaluation of the Political Significance of Home-Ownership in Britain," Political Economy of Housing Workshop, Conference of Socialist Economists, March 1980, *Housing Construction and the State*, London, pp. 71–76, one of the best pieces dealing with the very ambiguous relationships of home ownership to political position.
10   See, for instance Saskia Sassen: "New Trends in the Sociospatial Organization of the New York City Economy," in: Robert A. Beauregard (ed.): *Economic Restructuring and Political Response*, Newbury Park, Ca.: Sage, 1989, with brief but provocative comments on the intra-city spatial aspects of the trends she describes.
11   See "The Ghetto, the Enclave, and the Citadel," in the *Urban Affairs Review*, forthcoming.
12   Peter Marcuse: "Walls as Metaphor and Reality" in, Seamus Dunn (ed.): *Managing Divided Cities*, Keele, Staffordshire: Ryburn Publishing, 1994, in association with the Fulbright Commission, London.
13   *Every* enclave and *every* ghetto has aspects of cultural identity; what is meant here are those enclaves that are *primarily* cultural. The distinction is often neglected. See the discussion of voluntariness and social characteristics below.

14 Peter Marcuse: "What's Wrong with Empowerment Zones?" *City Limits*, May 1994.

15 Boal, p. 43, quoted from Yinger. So, defined by position rather than numbers, blacks in South Africa are a minority. Anglo-Saxons aren't. "Minority" in this sense in effect means an oppressed group.

16 Louis Wirth: *The Ghetto*, Chicago: University of Chicago Press, 1928, p. 19.

17 Boal, p. 49.

18 So, of course, are the meanings of race and ethnicity, but in a different sense from that relevant here. If "race" is interpreted as socially defined superiority or inferiority, then the text comment does not apply. I wish simply to say that no physical characteristic is as such a "cause" of any particular spatial treatment or choice.

19 In a forthcoming book, *The Partitioned City*, London: Blackwell, with Ronald van Kempen, the contributions from cities around the globe support (although with modifications) this general thesis. See also the special issue of *The American Behavioural Scientist: A New Spatial Order of Cities?* edited by Ronald van Kempen and Peter Marcuse, Fall 1997, from which part of this discussion is extracted.

20 There is a growing body of literature calling attention to the importance of regional structures and linkages in the explanation of contemporary spatial process, sometimes suggesting that, economically, regions have become a more appropriate unit of analysis than either cities or nations; the "archipelago Europe" metaphor illustrates the concept. Its impact on city spatial structure is not explored in detail in this issue, although the separate issues of metro-politanization recur frequently. The megalopolis concept first suggested by Jean Gottman does not seem to us to have developed as a significant determinant of city spatial structure, i.e. the development of Washington, DC, Baltimore, Philadelphia, Trenton, Newark, and New York City still seem to us to be each on their own trajectory, if subject to similar regional and national forces.

21 See, for a general discussion, Peter Marcuse: Is Australia Different? Globalization and the New Urban Poverty, Australian Housing and Urban Research Institute, Melbourne, Occasional Paper #3, December 1995, and Peter Marcuse: "Glossy Globalization," in: Peter Droege (ed.): *Intelligent Environments*, Amsterdam: Elsevier Science Publishers, 1997. The definition is consistent with (although neither disaggregate as is suggested here) those used by, e.g., Saskia Sassen and Manuel Castells, although the latter tends to stress the role of informational technologies as the critical motor of globalization.

22 See, for instance, Jencks, op. cit., pp. 7 and 254; Sassen, 1990, op. cit., p. 477.

23 See Hauserman and Siebel.

24 A. David and T. Wheelwright: *The Third Wage: Australia and Asian Capitalism*, Sydney: Left Book Club, 1989.

25 Most notably by Herbert Gans: "From 'Underclass' to 'Undercaste:' Some Observations about the Future of the Postindustrial Economy and its Major Victims," *International Journal of Urban and Regional Research*, vol. 17, no. 3, 1993, who recognizes the need for a structural definition but rejects "underclass" as being increasingly linked to a behavioral one.

26 The most recent account of the increase in income and wealth for this group – although blurring it with the next – is Derek Bok: *The Cost of Talent: How Executives and Professionals Are Paid and How It Affects America*, New York: The Free Press, 1993. He points out that J.P. Morgan "considered it a matter of principle that no C.E.O. in his companies earned more than twenty times the lowest-paid worker – compared to 200 times or more today." See review by Richard Parker in *The Nation*, January 3, 1994, p. 28.

27 Norman Fainstein, in several recent articles, has gone further than most in disentangling the racist elements in the present urban context in the United States.

28 Gunnar Myrdal: *American Dilemma: The Negro Problem and Modern Democracy*, New York: Harper and Brothers, 1944, p. 618. Logan and Molotch make the same point eloquently and in detail in John Logan and Harvey Molotch: *Urban Fortunes: The Political Economy of Place*, Berkeley: University of California Press, 1987.

29 See Gans' comment on the use of the term, going back to Myrdal, defining underclass by structural economic position, rather than by race or space.

30 Loic Wacquant: "Advanced Marginality in the City: Notes on its Naure and Policy Implications," Notes for Experts Meeting, OECD, Paris, March 1994, p. 8.

31 Christian Kesteloot: "Three Levels of Socio-spatial Polarization in Brussels," paper presented at the ISA International Congress, Bielefeld, Germany, 1994, p. 2.

Chapter 4

Copenhagen
Formation, Change and Urban Life

Jens Kvorning

I BETWEEN PERMANENCE AND CHANGE

The dynamic of the city is to be seen in the tension between the already formed structures and the demands of later periods for change. It is in the struggle with the landscape and later in the front zones between landscape and city, between natural place and man-made place that the city arises and develops. It is in the struggle between tradition and renewal, between permanence and change that the city matures, gathers and incorporates the many cultural statements and experiences, and achieves its complexity. And it is through this process that each city achieves its individuality.

Modernism saw this process of change, this accumulation of layer upon layer, as a process of decay. Today it is generally regarded as a process of improvement.

Our period is characterized by a deep concern for history and the historical urban settings. The modernist urban manifesto with its simple ideal pictures and unlimited belief in progress wiped out history or reset it to zero.

Our present concern for history tends to freeze or trivialize the history of the city by not permitting additions to the city that are fully valid statements about our own time.

For this reason to focus on the battle zone between landscape and city, between permanence and change, and to attempt to understand and grasp the friction between tradition and renewal seem to me to be an important way of approaching the current urban discussion – but also an important place to start if one wishes to say something about the special qualities of a city.

So in my account of Copenhagen I shall be looking at the formation of the city, at the processes of change and at the ways in which different parts of the city set the conditions for the everyday lives of their inhabitants.

II FORMATION

City and landscape enter into a dialectic. The city subjects the landscape, eradicates it as natural place, but at the same time absorbs it in built-up form.

The balance in this dialectic is determined by place and time: a strong landscape dictates the form of the city high-handedly and unmistakably. A weak landscape infiltrates the city in an almost indefinable fashion. A city that is built slowly reacts to many aspects of the landscape. Rapid urbanization suppresses most of the features of the landscape.

Copenhagen is built in a weak landscape – a gentle and compliant landscape. The landscape where the central parts of Copenhagen were built was a kind of hybrid of land and water, a landscape that could be built on and formed together with the formation of the city. It is a constructed or built landscape. But even though the original landscape cannot be traced in conspicuous forms or divisions within the body of the city, it is there nonetheless by not being there in any, so to speak, immediately visible way, but as mood, light, horizon, as tradition – and as the undramatic, as an easiness.

Copenhagen developed in the course of its first 450 years as a city by the open sea, protected against sea attack by the castle on the island in front of the city. In 1617 Christianshavn was established as a new district, built on reclaimed land opposite the medieval city, thereby creating the basis for the double city with its inner, protected harbor as we know it today.

Both in its original single form and later in its double form Copenhagen's structural layout and its relation to the sea resembled those of a large number of other contemporary European towns and cities.

The extension of its fortifications during the second half of the seventeenth century gave the city a new geometry and a new logic. This new figure can also be said to have been almost prototypical of European cities of the period and, furthermore, exhibited a kind of pragmatic concurrence with the ideal urban diagram of the Renaissance.

A special feature of Copenhagen's ring of fortifications was that it included a very large body of water, which constituted almost a quarter of the encircled area. This set up new conditions and possibilities for the city, both for its relation to the sea and for what we might call the logic of its growth.

The functional contact with the sea – concretely expressed in the unloading and loading of ships' cargoes – had hitherto taken place by the castle – at Nybrogade and at the street appositely called Ved Stranden (At The Shore). The coast outside was used for a number of secondary functions, for which there was insufficient room inside the ramparts, and it was not considered a particularly attractive piece of landscape.

The encircled and controlled surface of water that appeared with the construction of the extended fortifications changed the city's relation to the water and also the way it was perceived both architectonically and with regard to defense: the water inside was secure and as a result of its encirclement it presented other possibilities than the open Sound.

The second consequence of the encirclement had to do with the growth of the city. Because the areas enclosed were so large there arose a duality in the way the city reacted to the new situation.

Every fortified city is subject to a logic of growth that is connected with a gradual increase in density within the line of fortifications. What distinguished Copenhagen as a fortified city was that the very large area available for development came to include its own contradiction – the sparseness of the buildings in the new area. For long periods this area remained unbuilt on with the large body of water as a protected anchorage – a mixture of natural harbor and a regulated and constructed port. Slowness became a characteristic feature in the process of Copenhagen's growth.

The logic of increasing density means that in the process of its development the city reconsidered and invented new ways of structuring its buildings in order to create room for a constantly increasing number of people and activities within the designated area.

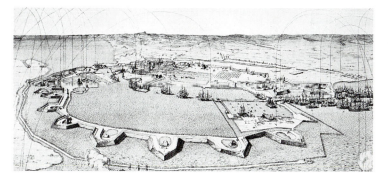

4.1 Old depiction of the extended fortifications. Courtesy of the Royal Library, Copenhagen.

At different phases during this process a set of typologies emerged: urban structural typologies as well as building typologies.

The encircled city filled up its area so slowly that besides the medieval city it came to contain a Renaissance city, a baroque city and, as a late addition, a historicist early industrial city.

The medieval city found its form by reacting directly to differences in the land-scape, allowing the system of streets and buildings to give way to even minor differences or difficulties in the terrain. There was an immediate relation between natural place and man-made place. In the medieval city the cohabitation of a civic structure and a monumental structure is not hierarchical in a geometrical sense. Instead the monumental emerges from an organic connection to the civic structure.

The Renaissance city interposed between the landscape and the physical form of the buildings an abstract, preconceived ideal based on straight streets and a simple geometrical order. This is to be found in its pure form in Christianshavn, but it also underlies large parts of Nykøbenhavn (New Copenhagen) and the Bremerholm district.

To the geometric system of the Renaissance city the baroque city added a highly developed hierarchization, ordered systems based on great organizing axes culminating at their point of intersection. It is to be found in its purest form in Frederiksstaden with the Amalienborg Palaces and Frederikskirken at the center of the composition.

The city squares derive their basic meaning and form types by virtue of their placing within or in relation to these structural types.

Kongens Nytorv (The King's New Square) occupies a special position by being the intermediary of all three types of structure, as a meeting point for and deriving energy from the medieval, Renaissance and baroque cities. At the same time it is connected through Nyhavn (New Harbor) with the harbor, the constitutive element of the city.

Amalienborg Slotsplads (Amalienborg Palace Square) is also in contact with the sea, and it too creates a great culmination. But it is internal, surrounded by the same type of urban structure – the grandly staged baroque city – on all sides, and thereby acquires a different role and character.

Christiansborg also occupies a special position and demonstrates a fixed or inlaid boundary in the city. Despite all the changes in their buildings both the castle and Slotsholmen still bear witness to their original function as protection of the city behind them, preserving at the same time the special symbolic value that the castle had. The civic

4.2 Two early stages of development of Copenhagen. The medieval city and the extended city, including the Renaissance and baroque quarters. Courtesy of Copenhagen Municipality.

structure extends as far as it can go, meeting the castle along Nyborggade and Ved Stranden in as elegant an architectonic shape as possible. When one reaches the castle, one still has the sense that it is here the city culminates. The original shoreline and the original relation between city and castle are manifestly inscribed in the place.

The houses of the city form correspondingly clear typologies. Clear because the great fires have left behind far fewer types than the city originally consisted of and have thereby disciplined the typologies of the city's buildings.

After the fire in 1728 Copenhagen was rebuilt on the basis of a set of model plans that presented a moderate baroque house designed to be placed on the narrow building sites, and which is characterized by the heavy cornices around the triangular gables.

After the next great fire in 1795 the city was again rebuilt on the basis of a set of model plans and some building examples and now formed a classicist type – just as moderate as the baroque house, but clearly influenced by neoclassicism with its horizontal string courses and the prominence given to parts of the facade. In addition there were the cut-off corners, which were required by law after the fire of 1795 in order to ensure an easier flow of traffic. However, these cut-off corners often came to carry special style-specific decorations, thereby displacing the balance of the house. At each street intersection in the rebuilt city this resulted in four cut-off, finely decorated bays in a diagonal dialog with each other.

It is these types of building that administer, so to speak, the final phase of the process by which the rebuilt Copenhagen reached maximum density so as to be able to receive the very considerable growth in population experienced by the city in the first half of the nineteenth century.

This process took place both horizontally and vertically. The houses were made higher and often an extra building was attached to the house facing the street, thus forming small, very constricted yards, for which both the Borgergade district and Christianshavn were notorious. It reached its limit with the outbreak of a cholera epidemic

4.3 Urban expansion and landscapes 1870–1950. Courtesy of Copenhagen Municipality.

in 1853. The city council had already determined to permit building outside the ramparts, but the decision did not come into force until after the epidemic had begun.

This inaugurated a new phase in the city's logic of development. Condensation within the fixed defense line is substituted by expansion. The city spreads like a stream of lava over the surrounding landscape, but yields when it meets locations which represent obstacles – physical or in terms of significance. The landscape surrounding the fortified city is by and large undeveloped, but it is loaded with significance.

The coastline towards the north was distinguished by summer residences, mainly for the wealthy, or by the presence of the king's summer palaces. The coast and the North Zealand landscape were described and illuminated in painting and literature, which saw these landscapes in a romantic perspective, linking them with the idea of national identity.

However, other places were also assigned special importance. Frederiksberg Bakke (Frederiksberg Hill), with the royal summer palace, had attracted both the summer residences of the rich and also the gardens for popular entertainment outside the royal park.

In the seventeenth and eighteenth centuries the water supply to the moats of the fortifications had been ensured through the re-routing of a number of water courses, so that they supplied a large reservoir outside the ramparts with sufficient water. In this way the beginnings of one of the most important architectonic features of the future city had already been established in the landscape.

Around the places that had been assigned a special importance beforehand the city formed itself in particularly exclusive districts. In between, in the landscapes that did not contain so many significant sites, new districts for the working and lower-middle classes arose. This was a simple matter of overlaying the landscape. All the divisions already present in the landscape made themselves felt in the structure of the new suburbs. The pattern of streets in Vesterbro repeated the oblong farming lots that stretched from the present Vesterbrogade down to the coast. Nørrebro was given a different street system that reflected the different pattern of land ownership in this district.

Tent camps were established on the terrain of the fortifications during the cholera epidemic. Looking at pictures of them, one can read them as predictions of the biggest innovation in the coming city outside the ramparts – the detached house. In the wealthy districts – especially along the coast but also in Frederiksberg – colonies of one-family villas were built. The villa and the residential neighborhood made their entry as a new type in the city's typological register. The working class districts outside the ramparts also formed new types, which though different from the types inside the ramparts were a development of the same kind of organization and social interaction.

The sort of model homes sponsored by the Medical Association were built as an attempt to intervene in the discussion by putting forward a model for the new working class districts. But the ideal of low density and plenty of open spaces that was presented here did not have much influence on urban planning and building legislation until around the beginning of the twentieth century, and it was not until after World War I that its impact really made itself felt.

In Rådhuspladsen (City Hall Square) the expansion phase, and with it the transition to a new logic in the formation of the city, received its own great monument. Like Kongens Nytorv it is situated at the meeting place of different urban types – the medieval city and the new suburbs. But it is also connected through what were originally broad boulevards – today Copenhagen's busiest road sequences – with the harbor and also, one senses, with all the new suburbs. With its size and its contact with the city's most important lines of communication it became a monument to Copenhagen's opening towards a new era and towards the surrounding world and the great arteries of communication – and in many ways it has retained this role.

In a certain sense, the way in which Vesterbro faithfully repeated the divisions of the landscape that had previously existed was a revival of the logic by which the medieval city was formed. But now this logic was attached to a new liberal doctrine that rejected any form of regulation as a reminiscence from the absolute monarchy. As had been the case when the Renaissance city replaced the medieval city, an ever stronger ideal picture was again interposed between the landscape and the built-up structure. The town plan was to become a decisive element in the formative process of the city and an important arena for the discussion and mediation of different views and interests.

The first extension of Copenhagen took place on the far side of the ramparts and the Lakes. The earthworks themselves remained in place and retained their recreational functions. When it was the turn of the fortified terrain to be built on, it was planning experience from Vienna and Paris and the first town planning ideas from Germany that provided a model and ended by producing a new district, which like Ringstrasse in Vienna contained all the facilities that supported the social and cultural development of the new middle class: the exclusive homes near the parks. The parks, which were created on parts of the terrain occupied by the old earthworks, served as areas in which the new bourgeoisie could promenade; close by and in the parks supporting points were built for the edification and education of the new era – museums for cultural education and institutes for technical education; also the Botanic Gardens – a combination of promenade and education – were moved out to the new park terrain.

The rampart districts, as they were called in reference to the landscape they had supplanted, became an example of a compromise between different ways of viewing the landscape – both the natural and the urban landscape. On the one hand, the landscape was seen as a recreational asset that should be incorporated into the new urban landscape, but at the same time it was also seen as potential building land that could yield considerable profits and should therefore be exploited as intensively as possible – an economic and a social landscape. The rampart districts became a compromise between these two views – an alternation between built-up area and park.

The further the present century advanced, the weaker became the claims of the natural landscape and the more and more dominant the logic of the built-up landscape.

Ironically this weakening of the structural influence of the landscape took place at the same time as the great modernist campaign to create the modern city as a new union of culture and nature constituted the dominant ideological manifesto. But the other great modernist lode-star, the invocation of the rational – rational building processes, and a rational administration capable of organizing the economic and political processes – became stronger and stronger and gradually succeeded in overcoming the resistance of the landscape and its ability to penetrate the urbanized structure.

From the last years of World War I the city council increasingly intervened in the formation of the new districts by drawing up local plans and through the requirement of large inner courtyards within the blocks of apartments. As in Vienna some of the housing blocks of this period contained almost park-like inner courtyards. In the course of the 1920s a very fruitful collaboration arose between a city council in which the young Social-Democratic Party had acquired a significant influence, and the new social housing associations formed by other parts of the Social-Democratic movement. The outer districts of Vesterbro, Nørrebro and Østerbro stand as monuments to this period. These districts, consisting of large well-constructed four-sided blocks, with park-like courtyards and many small squares to create space and variety in the street scene, reflect the same ideals as those to be found in many other large European cities of this period – perhaps especially Berlin and Hamburg.

The 1930s introduced what in Denmark is called "park developments." The park was seen as an outer landscape, in which the houses stood as free elements – oriented optimally in relation to the sunlight. The street became an access road winding through the park. The park development emerged in its pure form at the conclusion of a transitional period around 1930, in which experiments were made first with opening one side of the block and later with replacing it with detached blocks of apartments, but still subordinated to the organizational and directional influence of the street.

At the same time as Danish architects and parts of the political and administrative system were occupied by the organizational and architectonic innovations taking place in German building, the great modernist doctrines from Germany, and later from France, were subjected to a clearly independent and somewhat skeptical reworking in these park developments, which makes the best of the building projects from the 1930s uniquely Danish statements.

The developments at Ryparken and Blida reflect very directly the ideals that had evolved with their starting-point in the Bauhaus School. But the buildings retain the Danish brick and the classicist perception of the body of the house.

The Bispebjerg development – and other big developments from the latter half of the 1930s – departed from the strict principle of orientation towards the sun in favor of a development organized around a large green area.

These developments continued the tradition of building on the given landscape in a moderate interpretation of both the architectonic and town planning manifestos that modernism had provided. It is the housing district that is at the center of the town planning debate in the period between the two world wars. The good home with easy access to green spaces, with good new schools for the children, with the first crèches, kindergartens and after-school institutions, with common facilities for residents and with small local shops placed in various apartment buildings or in small local shopping centers formulated what is still today the immediately appealing Social-Democratic vision of a new future for the Danish worker – on the way to the welfare state. But also on the way to a sharper functional and social division of the city as a possibly unrecognized consequence.

In the post-war interpretation and use of the ideas of modernism it is the emphasis on the rational translated into huge plans for industrialized construction using prefabricated elements that initially set the agenda. The natural landscape was eradicated and a new form of built-up or constructed landscape arose. The landscape's ability to resist, to deform and to lend special features to building projects was eliminated.

The new districts of post-war Copenhagen were a kind of delayed realization of the CIAM Manifesto: a city divided into large housing districts, specialized industrial areas, great shopping centers and sports centers, connected and made functional by broad new highways and a well-developed system of local trains – realized by the welfare state that saw it as part of its social and political program to intervene in the building sector in order to modernize its production plant and thereby achieve the construction of a large number of homes. The wish to eliminate the housing problem – the great social and political trauma of the 1930s – occupied a very central place in post-war policy.

But the growing prosperity challenged the ideas of the CIAM Manifesto concerning the modern rational city and Corbusier's later visions of the vertical city. Throughout the

4.4 Three types of urban structure: *right*: the fortified city and part of the first suburban ring composed of dense urban blocks; *lower left*: urban structures from the 1920s and 1930s, characterized by open block structures and villa areas; *lower right*: urban structures from the 1960s and 1970s – huge industrially produced housing schemes and vast villa areas. Courtesy of Matrikelstyrelsen, Copenhagen.

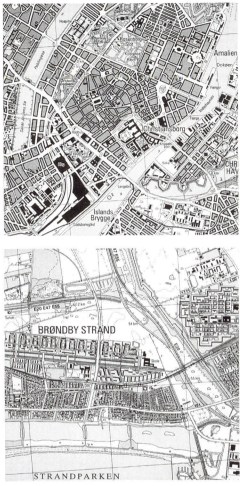

second half of the 1960s and the first half of the 1970s it became increasingly possible for working class families to buy their own homes – to achieve the individual house and garden that had hitherto been the preserve of wealthier groups. The building industry succeeded in creating a high degree of standardized elements for this form of housing, and the mushrooming suburban developments with their one-family homes – based on this production – constituted the most important component in the dramatic expansion of Danish towns and cities. The consumption of urban land per inhabitant in the new post-war Copenhagen suburbs is among the highest in Europe.

The standardized production methods and the functional specialization of the city meant that these new districts came to formulate a very simple, introverted and vulnerable logic that lacked the potential to meet the needs and interests of a new era.

It was ironical that in its implicit faith in its own ideological manifesto the period that experienced a hitherto unparalleled urban dynamism produced the most static new urban districts, the greatest permanence, the greatest resistance to amendments of or additions to the philosophy that had created these districts.

The huge post-war building boom was made possible by a real increase in prosperity and a marked industrialization of construction processes, but it was also directed by an extended form of planning: the regional plan.

The "Fingerplan" from 1947 introduced the discussion of the relation between the natural landscape and the urban landscape on a megascale with its proposed concentration of all building in urban fingers organized around the local railway system and with easy access to the open landscape.

When the private car eliminated the necessity of placing housing near the railways, the regional plans had to react by becoming more strategic in their attempts at structuring and controlling, and planning legislation had to be tightened up in order to regulate the establishment of new suburbs that were no longer tied to rail transport. The pressure on the historic city center was relieved through the introduction of a number of easily accessible peripheral centers that could be organized to meet the requirements of the private motorist.

Planning processes were streamlined, and a special state planning office was established to look after the development of one of the urban fingers – the Køge Bugt finger.

Ironically one of the centers of gravity in the post-war regional strategy is Høje Tåstrup, a suburb that today both short-circuits and continues this historical evolution. Architectonically Høje Tåstrup with its obvious Leon Krier inspiration points back to the classical city, the city formed of streets and squares. But this is only appearance. The stores that ought to be giving life to the streets are placed elsewhere, in a vast shopping mall. The streets are lined not by apartment blocks but by office blocks, in such large units that the internal communication arteries of the buildings are far stronger than the streets. In appearance Høje Tåstrup points back to the city center, but the specialization of its parts and spaces still corresponds to the modernist urban project. In its ambivalence Høje Tåstrup is the final monument to a long and one-sided period of expansion. Ideologically the city had looked outward ever since the fall of the ramparts, out towards the new territory that could be colonized, out towards the limits of the city, where the new was taking shape.

In the 1980s the picture changed. Now the ideological focus returned to the city center, to the classical city and classical urban life. Economic stagnation led to stagnation in the dynamic building activity that had driven the borders of the city further and further into the countryside. Structurally the old industrial districts and the other central areas were calling for a new interpretation that could enable the city to meet the demands posed by internationalization and inter-city competition and had become key points on the urban agenda of the decade. From expansion and the outer limits of the city the focus now moved to the processes of change in the already formed urban landscape.

III CHANGE

The city has always changed and is in a state of permanent change. It changes through additions that place the existing components in a new context. And it changes by virtue of new departures in existing structures.

The second part of this history of Copenhagen will attempt to describe and give examples of the process of urban change in Copenhagen as an ongoing parallel to the processes of its formation.

The city can be seen as a field of manifestos preserved from different periods. The various parts were built on and for the ideas and needs of different epochs. For a period after its formation a district functions and develops in accordance with the ideas and needs on which it was based – it is inhabited by people who have the same ideas as those inscribed in the structure and expression of the district. But at some point the tension between the original needs and new needs becomes so great that the district breaks up. Its original order is recast in a new mould.

The break-up may take the form of a physical restructuring, but it can also be seen in the structures and spaces of the district being used in ways that differ from the original intentions.

The processes of change are impelled by an economic and social dialectic, the tension between places that contain the new and prestigious and places that fail to live up to current demands.

Ever since the fall of the ramparts there has been a constant stream of the wealthy to the new suburbs, leaving the old districts with an increasing share of impoverished inhabitants.

With the creation of the welfare city after World War II moving out was no longer something that only the wealthiest groups could do. It now became a possibility for all the groups that participated in the welfare state. Only those who could not live up to the demands of the labor market were left behind in the least prestigious parts of the old city. In the post-war period these exchanges ceased to be a matter of the relation between the old center and the suburbs. The new suburbs formed a clear segregation between areas for workers, areas for the middle class and areas for the wealthy. And these areas also began their own form of segregation as, soon after their construction, some of the big industrialized apartment blocks began to collect the weakest members of society.

The changes were often triggered by – or explained in reference to – changes of an economic or technological nature. But the economic or technological cannot manifest itself in the city as economy or technology. It manifests itself as an expression of economic power, as an expression of technological rationality. The city is the pre-condition for economic activity to take place, but it also assigns a language to economic activity. For this reason economically motivated change is continually obliged to fight for its cause in the cultural spaces of the city in order to conquer a position in a space that has already been expressionally structured by other actors and other periods.

In Copenhagen, as everywhere else, one can identify periods dominated by trade capital, by industrial capital, and most recently by the post-industrial complex, a specially information-dependent and service-dominated economy. And one can see how these epochs manifest themselves in a particular urban-structural logic, but also that as a rule they interact, as layer upon layer, as injections, as processes of change in which one major form is about to be replaced or obscured by another.

Depending on their character, changes can be described as the establishment of a new layer, as injections, as eradications, as tabulae rasae. Changes that add new layers to the city and increase its complexity – or changes that wipe out existing layers and reset the complexity to zero.

Trade with the Danish colonies produced, during the eighteenth century, large concentrations of capital and correspondingly large buildings to store the companies' goods, and these changes initiated one of the first layering processes that can still be clearly seen in the city's structure. In Christianshavn, which will be described in more detail in a case study below, and in front of Frederiksstad land was reclaimed to create room for the big warehouses that corresponded to this new economic organization of trade. This placed the existing parts of the city in a new relation to the sea. The harbor was narrowed, and the remains of the original coastline disappeared to be covered by large docks.

Later industry came on the scene and repeated this layering process in its own way. Industry brought a turbulent energy to the city and introduced new types of dynamic change, adding a new layer to the already existing city.

Industry drove a wedge into the existing urban structure or placed itself at the periphery of the built-up areas. It took over the role as the creator of the city's new land-scape. Industries were placed down by the docks, where they formed their own landscape through land reclamation, thereby producing a new and more constricted harbor, but also a new relation to the hinterland. The industries formed colonies in the body of the city, and these grew large, forming points of resistance that the civic structure of the city found difficult to link up with and incorporate. In a formal perspective these industrial colonies can be seen as points of resistance of the same order as the monuments in the medieval city. Industry changed the trading district of Christianshavn into an industrial district, and with the formation of Islands Brygge to the south of Christianshavn it initiated a land reclamation project just as comprehensive and with just as large an effect on the geography and geometry of the city as the establishment of Christianshavn. Where Christianshavn had made the city two-sided, bringing it to a meeting point around a narrow harbor entrance, land reclamations continued this building up of a river port by adding to both sides of the coast south of Christianshavn, a project that culminated with the establishment of Sydhavn in the 1930s. On Amager and in, for example, Valby the implanting of large industrial colonies in the body of the city can still be clearly experienced. The street system of the civic city suddenly loses its coherence or is brutally deformed. Here we have arrived at one of those points of otherness that constitute the new type of monument.

The railways influenced and changed the city in a different way. Traditionally the traveler would have encountered the city after having covered a long stretch of an approach road, where stabling facilities, inns and lodging-houses were the physical expression of this encounter. The railway connected the city with a far larger surrounding area, but at the same time the concentrated energy that this connection brought was deposited at a single point, the station, which was placed within the city limits and thereby injected energy into the already built-up urban district and forced it into a redefinition that assigned it a new role and a new significance within the city.

The railway tracks in Copenhagen were relaid three times in the period from 1847 to the turn of the century and thereby activated different parts of the city at short intervals. Some of the places died down again or were left open for new interpretations outside the chronological logic of the city's development. The Main Station and the stations along the boulevard still bear witness to this powerful injection of energy, which was repeated daily by the commuters streaming into the city and also preserved in the range of modernist buildings opposite the present Main Station and in the Nyropsgade district. The sequence of buildings which encapsulates and embraces the historicizing building of the Main Station is the largest parade of modernist office buildings in central Copenhagen, and the closest we can approach to an international ambience. In their breach of chronology, Vesterport, Buen (The Arch), Hotel Royal and the Panoptikon building are partly a product of this injection, which for a long time kept the area outside the continued development of the city. It was therefore activated and formed by the needs and ideals of another epoch than those that have formed their surroundings. But the manifest acceptance of modernism here can scarcely be understood without taking into account the injection of energy and new meaning that the stations brought to the place. One might say that its opening to the surrounding world made it more receptive to modern architecture than other, more conservative parts of the city.

The great urban manifestos of modernism, whether they were formulated by Ernst May, by Corbusier or CIAM, emphasized rational construction processes and logical zone-divided urban structures as the only way of creating a healthy and modern city. With its narrow streets and enclosed blocks the classical city was both unhealthy and suppressive. The process of liberation that the modern project had set as its goal could not take place within the framework of the classical city. A complete tabula rasa was legitimized and even illuminated in these manifestos. This was simply the way – and indeed the only correct way – to create the modern city. The districts within the ramparts which had gathered the poorest section of the population were exposed to this tabula rasa renewal. But it did not take place in accordance with the modernist idea that the modern city should consist of detached buildings placed on a park-like surface. Instead the renovated districts were given a classicizing form in which buildings that Danish modernism, with its somewhat skeptical attitude to the great manifestos, considered to be modern were placed in a newly designed four-sided block structure. Dogmatically, this was a betrayal of the modernist urban project and in reality something that could be seen as a continuation of the Haussmann era's way of incorporating the modern street into the city.

A complete erasure of the existing structure was carried out in the Borgergade district and in Christianshavn, the poorest districts with the oldest and most run-down buildings. But in the debate of the 1930s Vesterbro and Nørrebro were also singled out for demolition. For the progressive political forces the strategy appeared to be the only way to create healthy and modern working class districts. Tabula rasa renewal was also on its way into the medieval city, where the big newspaper publishers and printers began to build huge new office and production buildings. At first within the existing layout of streets, but soon attempts were made to dissolve this system in order to be able to create sufficiently large building sites, as was the case at the upper end of Pilestræde and around Landemærket. This renewal corresponded with the prevailing view of the medieval city as structurally outdated, physically run down and devoid of architectonic value in the ordinary residential buildings.

At the end of the 1960s the city council decided to stop this style of modernization of the city center. It is ironic that high modernism has subsequently succeeded in pushing its renovations into the city in an apparently more discreet and sensitive way, through commercial and social gentrification. The most interesting parts of the classical districts have been given prominence and vitalized through the implantation of new energy in a reinterpretation of the districts' representative and narrative qualities. In the course of the 1980s the medieval city underwent a complete change in content and character. Through extensive renewal it has been adapted to the great ideological shift of the decade and become the laboratory for modern urban life in a Copenhagen variant constituted by a mixture of cafés, special shops and galleries merging with the great established art institutions.

As late as in the middle of the 1970s it was only Strøget and Købmagergade that contained the special shops and the other functions that mark the core center of the city. All the side streets and back streets were characterized by dilapidated buildings, poor living conditions and marginal commercial activities.

Tabula rasa renewal was practiced for the last time around 1980: inner Nørrebro – one of the first working class districts to be built outside the ramparts – was subjected to very comprehensive urban renewal that virtually replaced all the existing houses with a single type of building, which with only slight variations in materials reoccupied the district. This operation led to some violent confrontations, which in turn led to the government intervening with a new Urban Renewal Act dictating that future renewal must pay greater attention to the possibilities of restoring existing buildings.

The urban renewal policy that emerged as a reaction to this heavy-handed experiment can be studied in Vesterbro and also in a different part of Nørrebro, around Skt. Hans Torv. In the course of the 1970s Vesterbro was gradually emptied of its traditional inhabitants, whose presence made it reasonable to call this part of Copenhagen a working class district. The well-functioning working class families moved out to the new suburbs, and in their place the district was gradually populated by members of the weakest social groups, by immigrant families and students. This development was accompanied by a considerable decline in population, which led to a collapse of the retail structure. The traditional stores along the shopping street were replaced by a new structure of immigrant stores as the visible expression of an epoch in the history of the district. In the middle of the 1990s a comprehensive, publicly supported project of urban renewal was initiated with the existing buildings being restored to a standard – and a price – close to the standard and cost of new construction. In the shape of small colonies of alternative cafés one can already see expectations that as a result of the renewal process youth cultures and a socially more viable population will come to set their mark on the district.

This has already happened around Skt. Hans Torv, where the combination of many young people, sensitive restoration of the old buildings mixed with a certain amount of new construction, and public investment in the renewal of the square has created a very active district, dominated by the youth cultures but in uncomplicated coexistence with immigrant shops and restaurants.

During the 1970s Christianshavn was one of the first districts in the inner city to experience an overlaying that did not change the physical structure of the district, but gave it a new social structure in which the well-educated middle class became the most conspicuous element. When the ideological climate changed around 1980, similar gentrification processes began in several of the other attractively situated districts in the center.

Nyhavn with its harbor dives had long maintained a reference to the original structure and function of the city, but now it underwent a rapid commercial gentrification that reflected both the renewed interest of the middle classes in the classical city and also a significant increase in urban tourism. In the course of a single season all the joints and dives with their accordion music and brawls were replaced by restaurants serving pâté and baguettes.

As already mentioned, the "Bro" districts also experienced changes that contained a form of gentrification, with the youth cultures and the middle class moving in at the expense of the weakest social groups, which had long been concentrated there.

In contrast to these developments some of the programmatic modernist districts, with their huge prefabricated buildings, now fell out of favor and were criticized as being unable to create contact with the cultural realities of the city or to create a framework for a meaningful and modern daily life.

Although these buildings also underwent restoration in this period, they seemed incapable of receiving modern statements. In a desperate attempt at making them popular they were given a post-modern or merely a totally characterless popularity-seeking architectonic garb. But they continued to contain only one history. And today they still appear to be socially vulnerable, unable to indicate to their residents a possibility of meaningful activity.

Only the residential neighborhood, for which none of the recent ideologies have wished to take a responsibility, and which resources-oriented analysis must reject, lives on without particular problems. The residential neighborhood is the logical response to mass consumption, to the individualization brought about by the culture of modern communications. But it also contains an attempt at a protest against the standardization and trivialization to which apartment blocks were subjected during the 1960s and 1970s.

In the post-industrial reality of today the industrialized monumentalization points that formed the intractable and impenetrable fortresses of resistance in the industrial city now constitute the city's potential for new interpretation, the most vital points for a possible adaptation to new conditions. But they are also favored targets for big investors, whose concepts of privatized urban space and one-dimensional architecture dissolve the syntax of the city while seeming to conform to its basic grammar.

Copenhagen is today in a unique situation because these former industrial areas, which as in all European cities present the greatest potential for renewal, are in Copenhagen situated close to the docks. This affords the city the possibility of reinterpreting its origins, the harbor as an intrinsic and central part of its identity.

There is one area of Copenhagen, namely Christianshavn, that has undergone all the types of change described in this section. In conclusion I shall therefore retell the history of the city as it has been enacted within the framework of Christianshavn.

Christianshavn, the Renaissance township that doubled Copenhagen's size and formed an inner harbor in its port was, early on, subjected to the process of change that I have called overlaying. The township was based on the idea of the merchant's house with its four-sided yard as its economic foundation, the houses being built on narrow sites that stretched from the street along the quay to a back street. The buildings housed the merchant, his wares and his employees – they expressed both the economic and the social

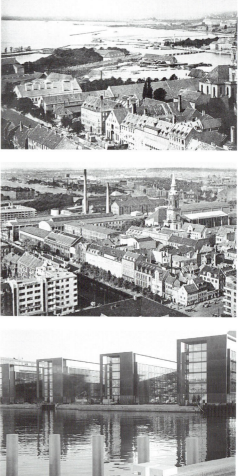

4.5 Christianshavn, four stages of urban change. *Above*: courtesy of Matrikelstyrelsen; *middle right*: courtesy of Burmeister & Wain Museum, Copenhagen.

structure of the township. The sites were functionally planned to permit the access of goods through the gateway opening onto the canal and their further transport through the gateway opening onto the back street.

One hundred years after the founding of Christianshavn world trade was being restructured. The trade with the new colonies was no longer carried out by individual merchants but by trading companies that operated with more capital, bigger ships and greater quantities of goods. Christianshavn was rebuilt to make room for these functions. This made itself felt in the urban structure in the shape of large detached warehouses. Strandgade (Beach Street) no longer ran along the waterside, since the warehouses were built on reclaimed land, which formed a new quayside.

So far we have looked only at the economic motives behind this overlaying. At the same time, however, a new architectonic ideal was imposed on the existing Christianshavn. In the process of adaptation to the new economic reality the township was subjected to the baroque view of architecture.

New meanings were read into some of the township's spaces. The first church in Christianshavn – the Church of Our Savior – was placed on a square site, thereby emphasizing that the streets in the original plan were seen as neutral zones between the built-up areas. When Christianskirke was erected in connection with the expansion of Christianshavn, it was placed to be visible standing at a distance from the end of Strandgade. From being a neutral zone, the street became imbued with meaning, became part of a new architectonic staging of the township. Corresponding installations of distant points took place through other eighteenth-century additions to Christianshavn. The rebuilding of the district to contain the facilities needed for the new international trade was at the same time the beginning of the district's social déroute. Although the wealth brought to Copenhagen by this trade was stored in Christianshavn, the elegant houses into which it was channeled were built in the new baroque district of Frederiksstaden on the other side of the harbor. Through a slow process the social structure of Christianshavn changed from being dominated by wealthy merchants and by craftsmen to containing the poorest section of the population. The segregation of the city had begun – or had become visible as it assumed a different scale and form.

When industrialism reached Denmark, it brought about new types of dynamic change in the existing city, by gradually taking over and rebuilding individual buildings and districts and by the railway's injection of energy into the city.

Christianshavn had not yet been involved in a radical process of change when in 1850 the company later to be called Burmeister & Wain built the first factory building by Christianshavns Kanal and from this starting-point gradually rebuilt almost a quarter of Christianshavn as a huge industrial complex that totally surrounded Christianskirke, thereby imposing a new economic meaning and a new architectonic order on the district.

In the middle of the eighteenth century this district, which had been created on the basis of a Renaissance ideal diagram, was subjected to a baroque view of urban space, only to have a new logic imposed on it a century later. This time the change was not accompanied by an architectonic program, but nevertheless in its pragmatism and economic logic it contained clear architectonic ambitions in respect of the individual buildings.

After another hundred years or so the order superimposed on Christianshavn melted down once again. Burmeister & Wain's motor factories ceased operating, and the district was facing a new start. Its structure and potentialities were faced by a new interpretation, seen in the light of the needs and ideas of the next millennium.

But another type of change had taken place during the previous 20 years. At the end of the 1930s attempts had been made to change the trend by clearing the old buildings along the district's central street, Torvegade, and to build new apartments in harmony with the ideals of the period. In spite of this the district continued to became more impoverished, and by the end of the 1960s a large number of the houses had been condemned and emptied of their original residents. In their place young people had moved in – with temporary contracts or illegally. This gave rise to two important developments. First came the Squatters Movement, which fought to preserve the houses as cheap accommodation, and this made Christianshavn one of the centers for strong youth cultures in the turbulent years around 1970. And it was from these youth cultures that Christiania arose – the illegal occupation of an empty barracks complex at the periphery of the district and the establishment of the Free City of Christiania. Thus, at the beginning of the 1970s

Christiania had become a compression chamber for alternative lifestyles in Copenhagen. But the alternative by its very nature is impermanent, and this status became the springboard for the special form of gentrification that now began in Christianshavn. Many of the people who had lived there as students returned once they had completed their degrees and bought apartments in a Christianshavn that was undergoing radical change. The houses were restored, but with great attention being paid to their original and historical qualities. The district was moving upwards socially, though with an unmistakably alternative profile. The district became an experimental laboratory for the demand that Copenhagen's old buildings should be restored rather than replaced by new buildings. This in turn made Christianshavn interesting for the so-called creative professions, for advertizing bureaus, architectural firms, for those who wished to be a little different from the suit-and-tie brigade on the other side of the bridge.

This development, which combined what was a actually a typical gentrification process with the establishment of an alternative cultural profile, had a significant role to play when the time came to formulate a program for the new interpretation of the Burmeister & Wain site.

Through some speculative purchases land prices had reached a very high level that could only be recouped if it proved possible to erect very prestigious commercial buildings on the site. But the demand of the local community, which met with considerable understanding in the city council, was that the special character of Christianshavn should be preserved through a large number of apartment buildings, and this demand was presented so insistently that the series of speculative land deals was followed by a series of spectacular bankruptcies until prices had come down to a level at which this program could be realized.

The plan that Henning Larsen's drawing office has formulated for the area can be seen as an exemplary conclusion to the many economic, social and cultural overlayings that have taken place in Christianshavn. Industrial capital, which took over the area from trade capital, has been replaced by finance capital in the form of the head office of a bank. The bank has been allowed to occupy the representative site facing the port. But the alternative cultures that have evolved as the product of a long process of social development have gained control of the canal side with a demand for small-scale housing designed in a dialog with the original architectural structure. And the alternative professions, which are perhaps no longer so very alternative – the architects, management consultants, advertizing bureaus – have pushed their way into the remains of the fine industrial buildings still standing on the site.

In terms of urban architecture the solution has been found by identifying and reinterpreting the architectonic ideals that have successively been imposed on Christianshavn. The church, which represents permanence both culturally and architecturally, has been made the center. It is the church that makes the link with history, but by virtue of the role it was given in the baroque overlaying of the district, it is also the church that is able to link the new development with the rest of Christianshavn. By its position beyond the end of Strandgade it leads the movement from the surrounding district into the new area. By allowing the church to occupy a more significant role on a larger central site than is the case today, it will be possible for it to organize the new functions surrounding it in accordance with the original architectonic principles. The large office buildings facing the harbor stand, like the warehouses from the era of colonial trade, with their gables facing the water. The apartment houses along the canal follow the tradition by being built together with the long side facing the water. And the new center is a historical center with the church as its visual focus. It is a quiet and dignified space, creating through its stillness a unity among the activities that surround it. None of these activities will be able to take over this space and make it their own. It belongs to the church and thereby to history, to all of us.

IV URBAN STRUCTURE AND EVERYDAY LIFE

Modernism described the city as a conjunction of specialized areas for residence, work, consumption and for physical and intellectual culture – with circulation as the decisive liberating factor that both made possible and realized this project.

Circulation, accessibility, communication are the basic preconditions for the life of the city. Futurism and, later, Modernism ideologized movement, seeing it not only as the necessary precondition for the functioning of the city, but also as a phenomenon that made man free. In the 1980s came the reaction to the modernist manifesto and to the modern city. The reconstruction of the European city – understood as the classical city of streets and squares, with its various functions closely interwoven – was placed once more on the agenda. And the new cultural programs were massively oriented towards urban density.

Like all other Western cities Copenhagen reflects these great manifestos and the ideological trends and ideas upon which they rest.

The city's communication systems have become increasingly specialized, and the various spaces of the city are becoming more and more specialized functionally, socially and culturally, almost privatized.

In the traditional street one can just stop if one sees something interesting, and one can meet many different activities. Modern communication is effective, but narrowly goal-oriented. One decides where one wants to go on the big roads or the local rail system, but one cannot stop on one's way, and one is limited to a handful of destinations. One moves towards a certain goal, and by virtue of this fact the goal is already specialized and commercially exploited to the utmost. The modern city has become a city of stations or terminals – places where energy is injected, but from which it is not disseminated. The structure of a modern city is so specialized beforehand that it cannot receive a spreading of the already established.

The vast shopping malls are terminals for modern life in the suburbs. In Høje Tåstrup, the relief shopping center to the west of Copenhagen and the great monument to post-war regional planning strategy, there is a mall called City 2. As a type it is also an example of another kind of city, the modernist city. Through the super-highway system Høje Tåstrup services large parts of the residential neighborhoods in the western suburbs, which are inhabited by well-paid workers and the lower-middle class. But there are also large apartment blocks in this sea of one-family homes. These prefabricated buildings are very largely inhabited by immigrants. One will also meet many immigrants in the mall, but none of the stores are owned by immigrants. The shopping center is the modern center in the sense that it is created in the image of high modernism and created for the consumer society. But it is

4.6 Daily life spaces: *left*: the traditional street; *right*: the pedestrian street ("Strøget").

very difficult for it to adapt to and reflect new conditions. It is a centrally controlled space, the space of normality. In this context the modern stands for a norm-governed, carefully controlled environment with wares designed for a controlled and tested public.

The other is possible only on the screens inside the cinema center. Outside, the otherness and the energy that accompany the immigrants have no way of expressing themselves. We might say that we don't know how to calculate with cultural fractions.

Daily life is organized and structured by a simple goal-oriented logic. Home, institution, work, consumption, leisure have been assigned their defined and fixed worlds. And these worlds find it very difficult to react to new conditions that involve an increase in complexity. They can be taken over entirely by new groups, but they cannot grow in complexity. The shopping streets further within the body of the city – Vesterbrogade and Nørrebrogade – are still expressions of the city's original form of communication. They contain both the local and the regional, the goal-oriented, but also the possibility of stopping and contacting the local, which through contact becomes regional.

The surrounding district projects its structure and its life onto the shopping street. Immigrants, students, the outcast, and the alternative move side by side without any particular conflicts. The city is capable of absorbing new social conditions and making room for them. The immigrant is not merely present in the street, he is also a businessman with his own travel bureau. Even though the district – assessed in relation to ideological models – is unmodern and anti-modern, it is capable of reacting quickly to and absorbing new conditions, allowing new groupings to gain a foothold and set their mark on the spaces of the city, because these are not centrally controlled spaces like the suburban centers.

The city within the ramparts is historically the most original part of Copenhagen, but it does not contain the immediate coupling of the local and the regional to be found in

Vesterbro, Nørrebro, and Østerbro. It contains a number of specialized urban spaces – not specialized as a result of their architectural structure, like the suburban center, but through their function.

The two old main streets, Strøget and Købmagergade, are the spaces of mainstream culture – focusing on popular culture at one end and upper-middle class culture at the other.

Around them lie streets that specialize either in the alternative youth cultures or the well-educated middle class's special version of mainstream culture.

The spaces at the center of Copenhagen have become excursion spaces forming an art event city. One goes to town on a Saturday to experience, to be a part of city life, to stage one's consumerism by exploiting the overlap between the commercial and the cultural spaces and to move about in the spaces and pass by the monuments that are bearers of our collective symbols.

Only a very limited part of the population visits the center of Copenhagen daily. Many know it only as tourists know it, stimulated by the main streets and the focal points of popular culture. It is not a framework around the kind of everyday life that is an authentic expression of the region or of our time. For most of the population it is a cultural compression chamber that one visits in the same way that the middle class visit the central parts of Paris, London, Barcelona, etc., for a weekend ministay.

But although the suburbs constitute the experiential world of most Copenhageners, the centre of the city retains its position for their identity – and perhaps also culturally – not only because it houses the central monuments but also because it has proved capable of adapting to new conditions, of containing and reflecting the present.

The suburbs are the present for most of the region's inhabitants, but the suburbs have difficulty forming understandable symbols and have no possibility of placing the present in a perspective by confronting it with history.

This schism is repeated in the treatment of the great potential for renewal that lies in the former industrial areas down by the docks.

Høje Tåstrup is split between its architectonic image, which points back to the center, the classical city of streets and squares, and its specialization, which places it in modernist suburbia.

But the fact that the image points inwards into the history of the city can be seen as a monument to the death of the expansionist era. Current renewal of the city is taking place not at the periphery but from inside – from many points in the body of the city. History has short-circuited or returned to its point of departure because the city's meeting with the sea, its birth at the water's edge have to be rethought. But this rethinking is influenced by the fact that Copenhagen has lost its historical orientation. It is no longer the city that one arrives at from Zealand and the city one sails to from across the Sound. It is the city at the crossroads between Scandinavia and the continent.

The harbor area is once again at the center. But it is no longer where it was when we first mentioned it. The harbor has become an example and a symbol for our discussion of Copenhagen today because it was formed by the industry that has had to leave the social agenda in the hands of a post-industrial concept. That this concept lacks any real content is a clear statement of the fact that we know what we have left behind, but we do not know where we are going.

Chapter 5

Spotting Modern Copenhagen

Helle Bøgelund-Hansen, Birgitte Darger, and Hans Ovesen[1]

I ARRIVAL – THE VISITOR'S COPENHAGEN

When you arrive in Copenhagen by train and make your entry into the city via the main entrance of the Central Station, you begin your relationship with the city at Banegårds-pladsen, the square in front of the Central Station – the best imaginable spot for a visitor who is interested in urban and cultural history. This is not at first glance the most exciting square in the city, but you find here a multiplicity of references to central chapters of the history of Copenhagen. The square's placing in the context of the city, the adjacent streets and urban space, its buildings and monuments tell the story of Copenhagen's evolution into a modern city. This is the story of the city's development from "Kongens København" (The King's Copenhagen) surrounded by ramparts and fortifications to a modern metro-polis governed by its citizens and without any clearly marked limits – a development that is linked to the story of Denmark's transition from agricultural to industrial nation. Thus, the station square is a meeting place for the historical and the modern, for the national and the international – and for many people.

If you look straight across the square, your eye will be caught by an obelisk, which is the central figure in a monument of national significance: the Liberty Memorial. It was erected in 1792–1797 (somewhat less than 100 years before the USA's Statue of Liberty) to commemorate the abolition of adscription in 1788. Adscription was introduced by a law of 1733, tying the peasants to a kind of villeinage in order to secure cheap labor, and the repeal of the law can be considered as a step in the direction of the mobility that was to become the dominant characteristic of modern society. The Liberty Memorial stands in the middle of Vesterbrogade which was once called Vesterbros Passage (Vesterbro Passage) because it was the link between the still fortified city and the surrounding coun-tryside with the early suburban development.

Going to the right from the station square you arrive at the place where one of the original city gates, Vesterport (Westgate), once stood. Here you will find Rådhuspladsen (City Hall Square), where Martin Nyrop's towering city hall from 1905 stands as the proud symbol of the civic administration of Copenhagen. If you venture into the building, you will find the words "Saa er By som Borger" (Like Town Like Citizen) inscribed above the huge door in the vestibule.

If, on the other hand, you look towards the northwest from the Liberty Memorial, you will see Skt. Jørgens Quarter (St. George's District), which with the modernity of its architecture and the layout of the buildings must be said to constitute the first modernist urban district in Copenhagen. The earliest specific plans for the district emerged from

5.1 Copenhagen's Central Station calmly resting on the busy traffic underneath. Opposite Central Station, the Liberty Memorial and the unequal assembly of buildings from the modernist era. Drawings by Hans Ovesen.

discussions about moving the Liberty Memorial in 1910 and were followed by a long series of proposals up to the end of the 1920s. In this way the station square is connected with Skt. Jørgens Quarter, which is the first modernist and most detailedly planned district in inner Copenhagen. Perhaps the closest Copenhagen comes to Manhattan's grid and mid-town modernism though on a much more modest scale.

II THE INTERVAL – THE COPENHAGEN OF TRANSITION

Thus modernity found its first expression in Copenhagen in a strange interval between medieval Copenhagen and the earliest suburban development (from the 1860s to the 1890s) in an area that had been reserved for military purposes and could not be built on until the last years of the nineteenth century. Only a row of facades forms a hairline boundary between the Copenhagen that arose in the twelth and thirteenth centuries and whose cramped buildings and narrow, winding streets still bear the stamp of the city's origins, and the modern Copenhagen that was formed in less than 100 years from the 1890s to the 1970s.

Here by the side of medieval Copenhagen stands the City Hall from 1905. At the southern end of the modern district the Main Station from 1911 marks its boundary with the suburb of Vesterbro. Between the City Hall and Central Station lies Tivoli, which was established in 1843. Before the city burst its boundaries and began to grow outwards the famous pleasure gardens were situated outside the city. Tivoli was actually created to earn money for its founder's newspaper, which was one of the city's first modern popular papers and contained a mixture of cultural material and sensationalism.

One of inner Copenhagen's more recent and busiest roads cuts between Rådhuspladsen and Tivoli, while a little further north it marks the boundary of the modern city. Even though the trees with which it was originally lined have been sacrificed for the sake of the traffic, the road is still called a boulevard, and it even bears the name of the great Danish fairytale writer H.C. Andersen. In reality it is an unromantic thoroughfare connecting the northwestern districts of the town with the island of Amager.

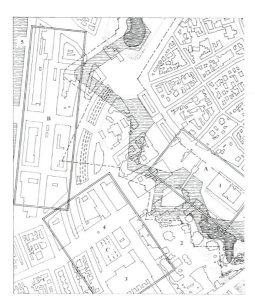

5.2 The three districts and the urban features of 2001 as discussed in the chapter. The West Gate and the moat and rampart system in the middle of the nineteenth century are marked on the map. A: City Hall Square District. B: Skt. Jørgens District. C: Central Station Square District. 1: City Hall. 2: Tivoli Gardens. 3: Central Station. 4: Liberty Memorial. 5: The Lakes. Map drawing by Hans Ovesen.

To the west the district is bounded by the Lakes. Thanks to an enormous effort in the sixteenth and seventeenth centuries the watercourses around Copenhagen were redirected to provide water for the city's mills, wells and moats. The Lakes are actually artifical basins made by dams blocking the natural flow of the streams. In the course of the eighteenth and nineteenth centuries their shores were straightened out and lined with promenades on the model of the Seine in Paris. However, up to the end of the nineteenth century this Copenhagen "river" ran a good way outside the city.

In comparison with other major European cities like Paris, Frankfurt, Rotterdam or Stockholm, the modernist part of Copenhagen is very small. All in all it constitutes a triangle of about 500,000 square meters. On the other hand, this district contains in compressed form a number of the characteristic features of the modern city and both as a district and in its individual buildings it can be seen as a monument to its epoch.

Its buildings, which were all erected at brief intervals over a period of 70 to 80 years, represent the best in recent Danish architecture, and each of them is a statement about the period in which it was born, and – in many cases – about the special form of Danish modernism that never voluntarily lost touch with common sense or the classical virtues.

The district contains a number of the modern city's activities and institutions. In its spatial form and structure and as urban architecture it presents a half-hearted and incoherent appearance. The lack of coherence has arisen both in spite of and because of the fact that in recent times probably no other part of Copenhagen has received so frequent and so intense attention from politicians and town planners, has been exposed to such heroic plans or has so frequently been the place where ambitious plans have been so dramatically shipwrecked by the tides of modern liberalism. Modernity has manifested itself in this district both in the form of grand visions of order, control and rational organization of the life of the city and its inhabitants and as the free expression of every conceivable form of entrepreneurial initiative.

III HISTORY – COPENHAGEN AS A ROYAL AND MILITARY CITY

Two historical factors must be highlighted as the background for the district's special status with its merging of varied and distinct identities and its far from immediately obvious spatial and architectonic articulation.

One of the factors is the restrictions imposed on the areas outside the city ramparts for defense reasons. The terrain had to be kept open up to a certain distance from the ring of fortifications. It was only permitted to erect small buildings, which could be quickly torched in case of war. The idea was that there should be nowhere for an enemy to seek shelter during a siege of, or an attack on, the city.

The decision to establish this safety zone was taken after an attack on Copenhagen by Denmark's arch-enemy, the Swedes, in 1658, a fateful and ironic chapter in the competition between the development of arms technology and defensive works. As an extra protection for the city and the little western suburb outside the ramparts an advanced system of earthworks had been established just under a kilometer to the west of the existing defense system in the 1620s. But when the Swedish army attacked Copenhagen, it settled down comfortably in the shelter provided by the new earthworks. From this position the Swedes could easily bombard the city with their new long-range canons, while the defenders of Copenhagen ensconced behind the old ring of fortifications did not possess weapons that could reach the Swedes.

As the buildings of the suburb had also provided shelter for the attackers, it was decided to establish a vacant safety zone around the city. In the course of time its outer limits were repeatedly moved closer to, or further from, the city in accordance with the range of weapons at the time and assessments of the risk of war. The risk of war and the extent of the safety zone were especially liable to be reconsidered when either the king or the city administration was short of money. The financial situation could be quickly and simply improved by reducing the safety zone and leasing or selling the building sites that were thereby freed from the restrictions on building.

Towards the middle of the nineteenth century it was finally accepted that ramparts and moats in a ring around the city no longer constituted an adequate defense. This realization took place at the same time all over Europe, building restrictions were abolished and all at once the cities began to spread endlessly over the open countryside. The last area in Copenhagen from which the restrictions were lifted and which could now be built on was a narrow belt close to the city. The new suburbs had shot up outside this belt, which is the reason for the unusual fact that the districts closest to the oldest part of Copenhagen are *younger* than more distant parts of the city. The land west of the center thus made available for building had long been surrounded by the city, and it became the place in Copenhagen where a new era would manifest itself.

The second historical factor of importance for the character of the district is also connected with the city ramparts and access to the city through its three city gates. The names of the three gates were, as it happens, misleading and more an attempt at creating a somewhat strained logic than at describing things as they were. Vesterport (West Gate) faced southwest and not west, Nørreport (North Gate) almost west, and Østerport (East Gate) almost due north. Because of the extensive agricultural hinterland to the west of the

5.3 Traffic jam at the West Gate, the busiest of the Copenhagen gates. A few years after the drawing was made the gate was demolished. Drawing by Klæstrup, *c.* 1850. Courtesy of Copenhagen City Museum.

city Vesterport was especially busy. From here farmers arrived with fruit and vegetables, corn and straw, cattle and milk to sell their produce in the markets of the city. The city gates were closed at night, and most farmers had so far to travel that they only arrived late in the day and could therefore only make use of the last hours of the markets. In addition, they had to pay a charge to be allowed to sell their produce in the city, so it was customary for them to spend the night outside the ramparts in order to enter early the next day and have a full market day at their disposal.

Because of the stench, noise and flies the cattle market, slaughtering and butcher's stalls had already been banished from the city within the ramparts by the end of the sixteenth century. These activities also established themselves along the road leading to Vesterport, and that is where the capital's meat distribution center has been situated ever since.

In course of time the area developed into an informal meeting place for farmers and traders, butchers and slaughterers, and innkeepers. As the Danish saying has it: "where good folks are, good folks come," and except for the trade in cattle and beef the major part of the activities in the area were connected with the needs of people who had to pass the night waiting and who had plenty of spare time. From the inns, pubs and hostels, brothels, pleasure gardens, theater troupes, and from the conjurors, street entertainers, brawlers, swindlers and confidence men there arose outside the city a town that quite literally represented the night side of the city, a place where urban order and control did not apply.

When the ramparts and the building restrictions were abolished, when farmers, smallholders and agricultural laborers in their thousands abandoned the countryside, which had been hit by a depression, and moved to the towns, and when building speculators initiated a massive construction of tenements containing wretched little apartments on the released areas along the approach roads to the city, Vesterbro's more or less shady activities were absorbed into the new, densely built-up and densely populated suburb.

The district that soon after would become the modern district of inner Copenhagen still lay as relatively virginal land between the old Copenhagen and the young and hectic suburb. The place was actually called Passagen (The Passage), a place of movement, of transit between more stable and well-defined points in the city. This character of always being on the way towards other goals was incorporated into the transformation of the area into a modern district.

IV THE CITY HALL AND THE BOULEVARDS – THE COPENHAGEN OF MIDDLE CLASS FREE ENTERPRISE

In his very personal guidebook "Gennem det gamle og det nye København" (Through Old and New Copenhagen) from 1948, the writer and art critic Rudolf Broby-Johansen has this to say about Rådhuspladsen: "A tour of Rådhuspladsen produces a rather villainous portrait of the time of our forefathers. That is what the architecture of Liberalism looked like. Every houseowner his castle. There are many kinds of freedom, and it can be used in many ways."[2]

There has always been much controversy about Rådhuspladsen and Copenhagen's City Hall (1892–1905) designed by the architect Martin Nyrop. The place is inhomogeneous and cut off by H.C. Andersen's Boulevard, which is today as broad as a freeway. Behind its physical appearance are hidden the ideals of the bourgeoisie concerning free enterprise and a passionate resistance to the constricting ties of town planning. But the square is also an expression of attempts at rationalizing and making more efficient the rapidly growing city of the last decades of the nineteenth century.

V THE TOWN HALL SQUARE – A CENTER FOR TRAFFIC, ENTERTAINMENT AND NEON SIGNS

Copenhagen's present Town Hall Square (Rådhuspladsen) was not planned as the site of its City Hall but as a central traffic junction in a busy modern metropolis. The few plans that were ever made for the area did not aim to deal with buildings but to improve the distribution of the traffic along the roads leading to and from the city. In accordance with the ideas of the time concerning the most effective circulation of traffic an ingenious system was devised. It was made up of radial and ring roads with special lanes for the trams at the intersections of these roads.[3] In the first overall plan for trams from 1886 it was decided to have as many tramlines as possible intersect at what would one day be Rådhuspladsen. The effects of this decision can be felt to this very day in the just completed central bus terminal erected at the north end of the square.

Several of the street names bear witness to this traffic-oriented aspect of the square's history. Traffic of all speeds has filled and still fills the area: here lies Jernbanegade (Railway Street), which led travelers to and from the station; here lies the street which after the removal of the ramparts was called Vesterbros Passage and which constitutes the link between the old city and the new suburbs. As the city's first boulevard of European dimensions Vesterbros Passage gave the promenading citizenry the sense of being in a metropolis. The present H.C. Andersen's Boulevard was projected as Vestre Boulevard just before it was decided to place the city hall here. According to plans from 1872 and 1885 it ended as a cul-de-sac in a little park north of Rådhuspladsen. The street seems to have been primarily conceived as a promenade.[4] Vesterbros Passage and Vestre Boulevard could function as an extension of the area's many pavement cafés and of Tivoli's semi-public space. The plans were later changed, and Vestre Boulevard became part of the belt of boulevards. From the middle of the twentieth century it became the main artery of the city carrying motorists both in and out of the center.

Rådhuspladsen is encircled by boulevards that follow the curving lines of the old ramparts. The square is irregular, curving to the right and narrowing towards the northeast. Standing with your back to the City Hall, you have the boundary of the oldest part of Copenhagen on your right. The original buildings, inns and hostelries are long gone, replaced by hotels from the beginning of the twentieth century.

Throughout the twentieth century the big national newspapers have been housed on this side of the square. In 1912 the liberal newspaper *Politiken* moved here from its original offices by Kongens Nytorv (King's Square) close to what was then the center and has dominated one corner of Rådhuspladsen ever since. Soon after its competitor, *Berlingske Tidende*, moved into a disused hotel with its advertising department and an electric newspaper. Its tabloid edition, *BT*, had offices at Rådhuspladsen until the 1970s.

The winding sequence of medieval streets, now called Strøget (The Stroll), emerges here into the open spaces of the new city. In 1918 the poet Emil Bønnelycke published a collection of poems entitled "Asfaltens Sange" (Songs of the Asphalt) about life in the modern metropolis. In his poem "Rådhuspladsen" he describes his arrival from Strøget at the bustling square: "Welcome to the open City Hall Square, to the newspapers, the trams, the cabs, to the Umbrella [a popular café], the Industrial Café, Bodega, the Dagmar Café, the Palace Hotel. Welcome to the beloved spot where we live, feel that we are active, and where our way passes. Welcome to this July day in the middle of our young and smiling city."[5] Emil Bønnelycke gives a cute and syrupy impression of metropolitan life, which in its Copenhagen version is resonant with bicycle bells and the squeal of tires on the asphalt: "Do you see in this mighty arena of shining asphalt how the trams turn, the cars maneuver in the stream, the harness of the carriages rings, and the national procession of bicycles sings sweetly and harmoniously?"[6] From the beginning of the century bicycles were already a modern feature of the city that Copenhageners were proud of. Copenhagen has been called "The City of Bicycles," the name signaling a modern culture of the body, freedom and youth.

For good reason there were no buildings on the side of the square opposite Strøget before the ramparts had been removed. The first building to be erected was that of the Confederation of Danish Industries, which housed a number of Nordic industrial exhibitions during the 1870s. The great Copenhagen exhibitions were held on the terrain of the former ramparts with Tivoli as an important backdrop. Later hotels, concert halls and variety theaters were also built on this side of the square. These have now been demolished and replaced by banks, insurance companies and one large cinema, all in modern buildings from the twentieth century.

From the middle of the nineteenth century the area between the station and Rådhuspladsen took shape as the new entertainment center of the city. In the 1870s enter-

5.4 Vesterbros Passage around 1880. From *Illustreret Tidende*. Courtesy of Royal Library, Copenhagen.

prising craftsmen and merchants envisaged stores and places of entertainment here in competition with the elegant shopping neighborhood near Kongens Nytorv.[7] It was the places of entertainment that won. Naturally Tivoli set its mark on the place and it was joined by several other forms of popular entertainment. The city's first permanent circus was built here, and from 1881 to 1890 it had as its neighbor one of the great attractions of the day: the Panorama Building, where panoramas of Constantinople, the destruction of Pompeii and the like were shown. Next door Master Builder Hans Hansen built his Dagmar Theater on the model of the Vaudeville Theater on Boulevard des Italiens in Paris.[8] This was not an attempt by Hans Hansen at outdoing the elite culture presented at Kongens Nytorv, where the Royal Theater stood and still stands. It was perfectly well understood by everyone that here by the station, Tivoli and Vesterbros Passage a different kind of culture was being offered.

And the Copenhageners came in crowds. From the top of a concert hall called National the writer Herman Bang observed this, the busiest spot in the city. In a reportage he writes that "on a summer afternoon when the incoming and outgoing currents along Vesterbros Passage conjoin with the crowds wandering into Tivoli or leaving via the station or on a summer evening when the gaslights and the illuminations are sparkling everywhere, when the tones of orchestras can be heard from different sides and the shrill of the railway signals can be heard, [the place] gives a picture of the bustle and life of a metropolis."[9]

In the 1920s the neon signs became a striking feature of the square during the hours of darkness.[10] Ever since the first lamp advertisements were set up in 1907 the names of the leading firms of the day have flashed from Vesterport to Rådhuspladsen. In the 1920s and 1930s the former Vesterbros Passage, which sounded and looked so exciting in Herman Bang's description from the end of the nineteenth century, became the city's center for the newest and most impressive neon advertisements. Their dominance strengthened people's sense of Rådhuspladsen as a place where one could at any moment measure the city's throbbing pulse.[11]

The Copenhagen evening and the area around Vesterbrogade and Rådhuspladsen constitute the enticing, dizzying universe of Tom Kristensen's "Hærværk" (Havoc) from

1930, which has the main character's work place "The Daily News" at the corner of Rådhuspladsen as its both attractive and repellent pivotal point. The neon lights have become the demonic omens of the place and the night.

> Fiery red and gaseously blue neon tubes blazed out signatures written in a single flaming line: Scala. Blue electric bulbs shone mysteriously like Chinese lanterns in foliage: The Marble Garden. Names in yellow. An electric newspaper flashed across a roof with a glowing veil of mist trailing after each letter. And before and behind the megaphones of the various newspaper offices blared the election results out over the streets, filling the air with voices. It sounded as though invisible giants, tall as houses, were walking about shouting among the facades of the buildings. The square [Rådhuspladsen] was black with people, and the cars that got through the dense masses revved their motors and with a sudden jerk increased speed, out along Vesterbrogade as if they had just crossed a miry stretch. The cones of their lights swept over the tarmac, which shone with gasoline. It was one of Copenhagen's brilliant evenings.[12]

VI THE CITY HALL

Opposite the City Hall stands Helmerhus, a long brick building with a narrow facade fronting the square. It stood there before the City Hall was built and it has irritated all right-minded people ever since. It bothered Martin Nyrop, the architect who built the City Hall, who wanted to have a square that would express concentration and calm as a contrast to the hectic modern life in the streets of the city.[13] His ideals harmonized poorly with the premises on which the square had come into being and been formed. In accordance with Martin Nyrop's instructions the area in front of the City Hall was established as a depression in the ground in the shape of a scallop shell. His model was Piazza del Campo in Sienna, but the effect was wrong, and the scallop shell in front of Copenhagen City Hall was removed after World War II. In 1996 the square was restructured and a new large depression was established in front of the City Hall in memory of the architect's original intention. For the first time radical changes have been made to the street system. The connection between Strøget and Vesterbrogade has been closed to create a large coherent traffic-free area surrounded by heavily trafficked streets.

The City Hall makes a heavy and somber impression. It is built in a national-romantic style, the mixture of the Danish medieval and Italian inspiration that had influenced a special "down-to-earth" school of Danish architects.[14] Nyrop had been inspired by the Gothic town hall in Sienna and by traditional Danish architecture. The face is of "honest Danish brick," as it was spoken of at the time, and the building is full of references to the Danish landscape and the common people. Both on the facade and inside the building there is an abundance of decoration. Besides brick the dominant materials are wood and granite. Everything bears the mark of careful craftsmanship.

Generations of architects have mocked the City Hall for its reactionary predilection for detail, for the embrasures on the roof, for the polar bears and walruses and for the heavy castle-like exterior. Nevertheless the building seems to contain a forewarning of modernism. At its inauguration the daily press and the professional journals were filled with discussions of its unusual exterior. It was important that Copenhagen should have received a building worthy of the city, one that was both functional and sent out the right signals at the start of a new century. Later Danish modernist architects would draw upon monumental buildings like the City Hall, in which the treatment of the materials and the rational use of space gave inspiration for a continuation of the special Danish tradition for brick.

Copenhagen's City Hall is open to more than one reading. In his very central critical essay directed against the cultural consensus of the period "Hva' mæ kulturen" (Wot about culture) from 1933, the critic and architect Poul Henningsen wrote of the City Hall that: "despite all the folk high school foolery there was a rationale in its plate-glass windows, asymmetry, planning from within and so on that was the precursor of Functionalism."

With its placing, the program behind it, and its architecture, the City Hall tells the story of a new and modern Copenhagen from the middle of the nineteenth century up to the first decade of the twentieth.

VII THE CITY COUNCIL AS A BOURGEOIS VISION

At a council meeting in June 1887 there was a long and stormy discussion of the placing of Copenhagen's new City Hall. The meeting took place in the City Council and Court House at Nytorv, which had been designed by C.F. Hansen and in use since 1816. Here in the center of the medieval city, the city administration shared rooms with the state. The council had established a committee, which in 1886 had found two suitable places for the erection of the City Hall. The committee had looked at the areas just outside the medieval city, the terrain formerly occupied by the ramparts, where a new town was being built. Here the City Hall could be placed by Ørstedsparken, where the streets had already been established and a number of buildings put up, or it could be built on what was Halmtorvet (Haymarket) at that time, by Vesterbros Passage, at the interval between the old town and the suburbs of Vesterbro.

Since the 1870s the council had been discussing the necessity of the city having its own building instead of, as was the case at that time, sharing a building with the police and the judiciary. For centuries Copenhagen had been governed and formed by the kings, who had residences in the city. During the absolute monarchy it was the king who appointed the council, but gradually the citizens achieved more and more liberty as part of the constitutional struggle that in 1849 led to Denmark receiving a constitution, which is still in force. In 1840 Copenhagen acquired its first city council directly elected by the citizens (an exclusive group, restricted to property owners and people with a certain income), but the administration and the mayors were still appointed by the king. In 1857 this council was given real influence over the administration and the selection of mayors. It was after this that the reshaping of the rapidly growing capital was begun; the administration was rationalized, and a mass of new construction projects from schools to sewers was initiated.[15] In the 1880s the council was in no doubt that a new city hall was necessary and that it should be placed outside the medieval city. The city had moved its

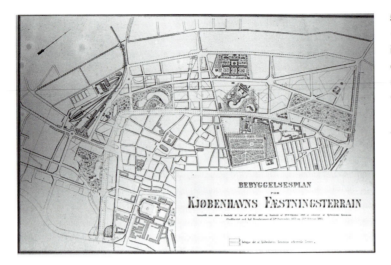

5.5 Plan for Parkring (1885) (Ringstrasse-inspired plan for development of the rampart area.) Courtesy of Copenhagen Municipality Archive.

boundaries and its center. Now it needed a chance to show what it could do – the civic municipal administration wanted to go where its citizens already were.[16]

In the 1872 plan (revised in 1885) for the development of the terrain of the former fortifications, it had been decided in principle that all public buildings should be built there. Under the leadership of the highly influential, internationally oriented architect Ferdinand Meldahl a proposal was presented in 1866 for turning the terrain into a park inspired by Ringstrasse in Vienna and with boulevards of Parisian dimensions. Because of financial speculation and a liberal policy that opposed a general plan for the area the result was a more modest and not particularly homogeneous green belt around the old part of Copenhagen. Much of the land was left to private developers rather than being subjected to municipal planning.[17] The municipality got some cash, the citizens got Aborreparken, Ørstedsparken, Botanisk Have (The Botanical Gardens), Østre Anlæg (East Park) and Kastellet (The Citadel). Meldahl succeeded in realizing his broad, tree-lined boulevards, and, following examples from abroad, many municipal and state buildings received a monumental placing along these boulevards with the parks as an attractive green background. Here stand the National Art Gallery, the Geological Museum, the Technical University of Denmark, where engineers were educated, the Central Fire Station as well as art collections financed by enterprising industrial magnates of the period: Glyptoteket, the Hirschsprung Collection and the building which once housed the Museum of Decorative Art but now contains the Tivoli Museum and a branch of Madame Tussaud's. It was therefore natural in 1888 to consider placing the new City Hall in this belt of parks.

What, then, separated the two possible sites for a new City Hall that were discussed in such detail at the meeting in 1887?[18] By Ørstedsparken the development of the terrain formerly occupied by the ramparts had proceeded a long way. In the area around Nørrevold a new, internationally inspired district with parks, exclusive apartment buildings with a Parisian look, monumental buildings and broad streets had taken shape. Ferdinand Meldahl had been chief architect of the street grid and the central square, Søtorvet, which functioned as a gateway to the center when one arrived along Nørrebrogade. There was an empty site available in this district, and if the City Hall were placed on it, it would have the attractive Ørstedsparken as its neighbor. The place had the qualities of a center, as several of the councilors pointed out.

Matters were very different with respect to the square by Halmtorvet, Tivoli and the road leading to the suburbs of Vesterbro and Frederiksberg. Here plans had only been made for the traffic, and the broad new Vestre Boulevard had been projected, but there were no plans for the erection of monumental buildings. Along Vesterbros Passage and Jernbanegade places of entertainment and hotels arose and disappeared according to the caprices of the financial winds. A few new buildings had been erected on the square, but without creating any kind of whole. There was no connection between the dense maze of houses in the medieval city and the long straight lines of the new districts with Vesterbros Passage as their central axis. The placing of the new City Hall on this site would make it possible to establish that connection. Old streets could be extended to link up with the new streets, with the City Hall as their pivotal point.

The committee gave preference to the square by Vesterbros Passage. The advantages of the site were emphasized at the council meeting in June 1887. It seemed that a new and much more lively center had already appeared without any intervention from the planners. This part of the city was enterprising and quick to act. The councilors noted that Halmtorvet was situated close to the part of the city that housed the business sector. This is where one found the people who one had to assume would be dealing with the City Hall, it was argued with considerable commercial flair, as if the city administration was a store that should be situated where the customers were.

The place was dynamic, dominated by the traffic arteries to the hinterland and abroad. This was where new arrivals met the city, as they had always done. This was where the station was, and a new station should be built in the same area. "By placing a monumental building here with its front facade facing Vesterbro, one would embellish the main entrance to the city," Meldahl pointed out in his speech at the council meeting of 6 June, 1887.

It was also an advantage that the placing on almost virgin land made it possible to give the building prominence as a monumental symbol of the new Copenhagen. It played a role that the area had previously been, and would again in 1888 be, the framework for a great Nordic agricultural and industrial exhibition, and it is very probable that the area already contained a selection of foreign guests. At the council meetings Halmtorvet came across very strongly as the place where the city presented its potential in the service of progress and development.

But there was more. It was argued that from a placing by Vesterbros Passage it would be easy to move to and from the nearby parliament building (burned down in 1884 and rebuilt and inaugurated in 1918). The City Court House, which was to be left to the judicial system and the police, was also within easy reach. These were factors worth taking into account in a city that was rapidly expanding. In this way the site possessed not only a practical but also a symbolic connection between the city administration and the national judiciary, legislative and executive organs.

Furthermore, there was the question of space. It had taken several years to work out how much space the administration of the rapidly growing city would require. The administrative departments and their mayors had calculated and calculated while the tasks facing the city administration had grown and grown, rendering their calculations outdated with a corresponding speed. In 1887 it was feared that there was not enough space at Ørstedsparken.

It had been realized by this time that it would be necessary to build a new City Hall. Now the council needed to define what kind of hall it wanted, one that could manifest the growing municipal self-esteem. It was important not to be limited by miserliness or mediocrity.

It was necessary to think big, beautiful and of posterity. Carl E. Schorske has pointed out in "Fin-de-Siècle Vienna" that Ringstrasse was a manifestation of the new bourgeoisie's world picture. The magnificent buildings reflect the self-view and values of the class that had the money and the power to reshape Vienna in the middle of the nineteenth century. Ringstrasse was the expression of new ideas for a rationally structured city, but the representative was given priority over the practical elements of this reorganization.[19]

Something similar was about to happen in Copenhagen. True, the new City Hall was to be a practical building for an ever bigger administration necessitated by the rapid growth in municipal services. But as the discussion of the new city hall proceeded, the symbolic meaning of the building took on a central importance. On the one hand, the municipal administration was beginning to intervene formatively into all areas of the citizens' lives. Schools, swimming halls, playgrounds and hospitals were being built and administered by the municipality. The water supply was re-routed and a plan for a new sewer system and modern hygienic measures was discussed for years and adopted for implementation towards the end of the century. But, on the other hand, it was perhaps not essential that the ever-increasing rationalization of the city should be made visible in the new City Hall. At council meetings it was discussed whether it was really necessary to find space for the gas company boards. Or whether the offices of the poor relief system should be situated next door to the mayor's meeting rooms. "Could it really be necessary that there should be a daily parade at the City Hall of individuals who are to be sent to the workhouse [where people on relief had to report daily in order to carry out forced labor]?" asked a councilor at the meeting in June 1887.

It appears that the new City Hall would be a unifying representation of all the ugly inequality contained in the metropolis. It was to bear witness to progress and the rational administration of the city but signal this through beauty and monumentality. There seemed to be an emotional need for this among the citizenry. There was "a general feeling that it is a serious lack and sorely missed that we do not have a city hall . . . In relation to the numerous foreigners who visit Copenhagen it is almost a cause for shame that in so large and prosperous a city one has to conduct them to the present home of the Council with its extraordinarily confused interior when one wants to show them the City Hall," said Councilor Knudsen, a Supreme Court judge, at a meeting on 11 May, 1885. One of the criticisms was that the City Court House was open to the tumultuous life of the metropolis, where one was confronted with high and low in society, a shameful lack of order. Instead one should erect a building that would fully "correspond to the new Copenhagen," Knudsen argued at the same meeting. It was not only the useful and practical that should be taken into consideration, but also "the demands of beauty." He continued: "If we are unable to build a memorial that with due regard for existing conditions and our economic

5.6 The Copenhagen City Hall shortly after construction. Courtesy of Copenhagen City Museum.

capability is worthy of the city and the era, it would be better to leave to the future a task that the present is unable to manage."

In 1888 the council decided to place the future City Hall on the square by Vesterbros Passage. Sufficient funds and land were voted to ensure Copenhagen a worthy City Hall, one that could enter into the system of magnificent buildings along the boulevards. This placing signaled that the center of the city was located at the entry road from the west, the impressively busy Vesterbros Passage. Here the large scale and the small scale were connected, the outside world to the medieval city, the financial world to the world of entertainment. In "Scenes of the Street" Anthony Vidler points out that Hausmann's boulevards satisfied the new commercial order in Paris as well as meeting strategic needs.[20] The boulevard is a work of art built for a city that has to be open inwards and outwards towards the world.[21] In Copenhagen Vesterbros Passage and the surrounding streets seemed to be the quintessence of this metropolitan openness.[22] Copenhagen's new City Hall contains the idea of participating in the new center of a new and modern city.

The Copenhagen bourgeoisie created the boulevards in their own image. However, the City Hall that was chosen later turned out to be an entirely autonomous building that both pointed forward to the twentieth century and also manifested ideals dating back to the founding of the city.

VIII NYROP'S CITY HALL – A GESAMTKUNSTWERK

In 1889, following modern democratic and international practice, the council arranged an open architectural competition for the new City Hall. The program was influenced by old models and new requirements. The project was to be made up of one or more adjoining buildings and contain a vestibule and a roofed courtyard. In addition, there was to be a "beletage" for the rooms that would show the city's face to the world: a ceremonial hall, the chambers of the council, and the assembly hall for the mayors. The administrative departments were to be split up: the technical departments and the poor relief administration were to be placed in the rear building with its own entrance. The dream of a new City Hall as the citizens' visiting card when receiving foreigners made the council formulate a program which, like their own houses, had a front and a back entrance.

In a beautiful publication from 1908, which documents all the details of the new City Hall, the art critic Francis Beckett writes that with this program Copenhagen has frankly declared its pretensions to being a metropolis.[23] It regards itself as such and feels that it is on a level with the other European capitals.

It was the relatively young architect Martin Nyrop who won the competition. In 1888 he had enjoyed great success with his main building for a very ambitious Nordic industrial and agricultural exhibition, which had been held on the very site where the City Hall was to be placed. His project won in competition with buildings in, for example, "German Gothic" style, "Rosenborg" style, "French Renaissance" style and "Classical Renaissance" style. Nyrop's proposal, which was realized in a revised version, was more difficult to place stylistically and encountered a fair amount of criticism. Powerful objections were voiced by Ferdinand Meldahl, who claimed that the plan would never have been approved at the Academy. Here, as a professor, he had defined the requirements for a correct imitation of "great" European architecture.

The council did not agree with Meldahl. An incipient dislike of historicism was expressed and Nyrop's project was well received because it pointed forward, broke with the established rules and was new. Nyrop had shown independence in the treatment of his models. The asymmetrical and effective placing of the tower corresponds to that of his model in Sienna. This breach of the symmetry that was a characteristic of the city's historical buildings was something new. In Sienna the tower stands on a line with the facade and makes the building look flat and two-dimensional. Nyrop gave more emphasis to the central axis of the building, where the council would meet. The placing of the tower made his City Hall three-dimensional, and gave it depth and volume. The building was not to be a historicizing backdrop intended to put the viewer in the right mood with reminiscences of world culture and Parisian charm. On the contrary, one was to be drawn into the center of the building and its life. The building was to have a weight that announced that this was where weighty decisions were taken.

The City Hall is formed as a square with two courtyards. The council chamber is placed in the middle and constitutes the dividing line between the two parts of the building. Facing Rådhuspladsen we have the mayors' offices and reception rooms. Here we find the ceremonial hall with its windows facing the square and here too the beautiful roofed hall, about which it was remarked at the time that the building's facade seemed to look inwards. The other part of the building is its working part, where the offices are arranged like cells in the long corridors. Circulation in the building is mediated by a beautiful panoptic galleried lobby with a stairway that connects all the floors. The building seems to be centered in these two spaces, which not only permit circulation between the parts of the building but also invite one to linger for a while and take in one's surroundings.

The decoration ranges from gilding, mosaics and polished granite through toads and frogs to abstract frescos painted on the raw walls above the doors of the offices and on the ceilings of the side stairs. On the roof there are polar bears and at the rear entrance walruses, which provoked ridicule from critics but were defended by Nyrop as being just as good as lions and sphinxes. They are a reminder of Denmark's trade with Greenland and the increased interest in the polar regions. The polar bears were not an empty sign but a reference to Denmark's expansionist ambitions and overseas territories. The many symbols in the City Hall seem to be centered around the idea of a castle, the original form of the city, placed by the seashore. Similarly, the quotations from the town hall of Sienna are also loaded with meaning, since they appear to establish a link between the free city states of the Renaissance and a municipality governed by its own citizens.

Nyrop's City Hall can be seen as an example of *Gesamtkunstwerk*. Everything is decorated according to an overall scheme that draws on motifs from the sea, the seashore and the city. A multiplicity of figures inhabit the building, and no corner or border seems to have been omitted. At the same time there seems to be a less symbolic aesthetic at work: a cultivation of flat ornamentation appears in the frescos that Nyrop had applied to the surfaces in the more modest sections of the building. The frescos move away from realistic representation to depict seaweed and algae as twining forms in an interaction with the white walls.

Nyrop saw handicrafts as the point of departure for architecture. Openly stating his debt to William Morris, he regarded the Middle Ages as a period in which art and handicrafts formed a synthesis,[24] while he found Henry van der Velde decadent in his use of handicrafts and in his symbolism. Nevertheless Nyrop's City Hall presaged the aesthetics of the coming decades. The division into rooms, the treatment of materials, the use of handicrafts and the interest in all details from washbasins to lamps show that Nyrop was trying to find answers to questions that would later become central to, among other things, the so-called Skønvirke style. This style derived its name from an association of artists that was formed at the beginning of the twentieth century as a Danish counterpart to the European Jugend and art nouveau movements and was, like them, originally inspired by the English Arts and Crafts movement.

What did Nyrop's contemporaries think of their new City Hall? Had the council hit the bull's-eye when they selected Nyrop's project to be the expression of the government of Copenhagen by its own citizens?

IX THE CITY HALL AS A SYMBOL

"Like town, like citizen" promised the City Hall's motto above the entrance to the vestibule. Despite criticism from adherents of historical eclecticism the City Hall was generally praised. Reading the reactions in the daily newspapers and the professional journals of the day, one finds a widespread feeling of solidarity with Copenhagen's monumental new City Hall.

Now the city had been given a uniting symbol. With the City Hall the citizens of Copenhagen could confidently meet the twentieth century, it was said. The spirit of

Denmark had at last become master of its own house, and the citizens masters of their own city, wrote Vilhelm Andersen, the most important literary historian of the era. In 1905 he described in an article in the daily newspaper *Politiken* what he had experienced walking from the old to the new City Hall. As one approached the new City Hall from the Court House, one encountered the tower as if it had suddenly shot up out of the earth. It encouraged Copenhageners to straighten their backs and to meet the future with self-assurance, bringing their history with them.

P.V. Jensen-Klint, the architect and later representative of Skønvirke, praised the City Hall for its practical design with the council chamber as its symbolic center. He also pointed out that though Nyrop's major work was not particularly innovative, it nevertheless contained the advice to all to seek their own true forms of expression. P.V. Jensen-Klint did not find it justified to call the building "the people's house," since in his view it was not the people that set their stamp on the council's decisions and the public face of the city. It was better to call it "the citizens' house." The struggle for a more extended democracy can be felt in the various reactions. Even though it is the middle class that has found its expression in the building as a whole, Nyrop's decorations point in the direction of the broadly popular. One critic draws attention to the fact that popular artists have been made to interact with more elitist artists from the capital. The chief artist, who was responsible for all the carvings, came originally from a small farm in Jutland, and one critic interpreted this as a radical and oppositional gesture, as a parallel in art to the constitutional struggle proceeding in that period.[25]

The building corresponds to various trends around the beginning of the twentieth century and seems to embody the self-view of the citizens of Copenhagen. In describing the building the writers see it as either Danish or popular or as a personal artistic statement. The City Hall connects the traditional with the new, the modern metropolis with the countryside and the people with their elected representatives. In the many subtle details contained by the building a bourgeoisie that is rapidly growing in strength finds the very elements that characterize the era: nationalism, democratization and a focus on individual freedom.

With the twentieth century came the Social-Democrats' accession to power in the municipality of Copenhagen, initiating an era that has lasted for almost 100 years. And with the Social-Democrats came new ideals for art and architecture.

X SKT. JØRGENS QUARTER – THE CITY OF MODERNITY

Rådhuspladsen marks the opening of the city towards a new era and can be seen as a monument to the liberal bourgeoisie's view of the city, of culture and of history. The crystallization of ideas concerning the new era took place in Skt. Jørgens Quarter with its colonialization of the open spaces outside the ramparts during the city's expansion phase, with its carefully planned system of streets and buildings and with its inherent vision of motor traffic, dynamism, prosperity and progress. The district is also a monument to a new era in the history of Copenhagen city council, in which the Social-Democrats obtained a political majority and thereby a majority influence on decisions concerning Copenhagen's development in the twentieth century.[26]

Skt. Jørgens Quarter is the history in compressed form of modernist Copenhagen with buildings mainly erected in the period from the 1930s to the 1970s, in which Denmark consolidated itself as a democratic, industrialized welfare society with all the new types of social tasks and changed commercial functions this involved.

As a classical paradox in twentieth-century urban development this district ended in a shape very different from the original conception. This is due partly to the length of the period in which it was built, 1910–1974, and partly to economic considerations that had to be given priority over political decisions. The contradictions between political control and freewheeling capitalism have had a decisive influence on the formation of the district.

As a monument to how not to build, the area is a miniature Brasilia, built on a tabula rasa (after the closing of the earlier Central Station), a strangely isolated enclave with few pedestrians and many cars. No framework has been created for the kind of dynamic city life for which Rådhuspladsen is a place of transit between Strøget's consumer pleasures and the entertainments on offer in the adjacent streets. Skt. Jørgens Quarter consists mainly of hotels, educational institutions and office buildings, but there are hardly any stores, cafés or recreational spaces. It is an area one visits only for a specific purpose and not just to stroll around and pass the time. Because of this lack of atmosphere Skt. Jørgens Quarter is probably the least noticed district in Copenhagen, but architectonically it contains many interesting Danish functionalist or modernist buildings. Many of the great modernist Danish architects are represented here: Kai Gottlob, Vilhelm Lauritzen, Arne Jacobsen, Frits Schlegel, Mogens Lassen and others. If one asks Copenhageners, they will describe it as anonymous and boring. It does not even have an official name, being merely designated as "the old station terrain." We have assigned it the name of Skt. Jørgens Quarter after the nearby lake.

XI CHANGING PLANNING IDEALS

The history of the many plans drawn up for the area gives a picture of how rapidly ideals changed in the first decades of the twentieth century, ending with the choice of a modern urban plan based on motor traffic and a zone-divided city with trade and commerce in the center and housing outside. Over this period eight projects were produced, in which ideas about how the district should be structured change from systems of romantic, crooked streets with heterogeneous buildings over a neoclassicist system of geometrically straight streets and severely designed identical blocks to a modernist preference for broad streets with ample space for traffic and a block structure characterized by a certain homogeneity.

The experience gained from Copenhagen's explosive growth in the second half of the nineteenth century with a large amount of speculative building and very little general planning had led to a greater focus on urban planning both in the council and among architects. The council's competition for "the old station terrain" in 1910 therefore evoked considerable interest. First prize went to a plan, which according to the journal *Arkitekten* (The Architect) ". . . creates a calm and attractive background to the [Liberty] Memorial, while a superb architectural solution has been found for the rear of the project."[27]

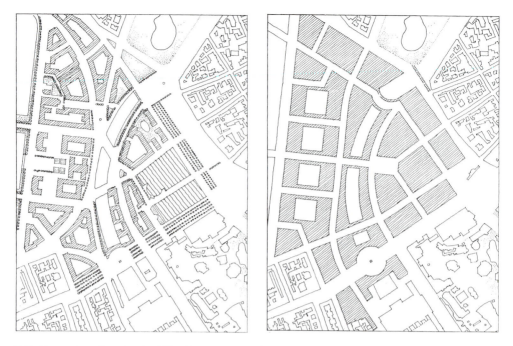

5.7 Alternative plans for the "Skt. Jørgens" area (Fischer 1910 and Schou 1915). Map drawings by Hans Ovesen.

The two winning architects had been strongly inspired by the urban planning theoretician Camillo Sitte and his book from 1889 *Der Städtebau nach seinen künstlerischen Grundsätzen*, in which he criticizes urban planning projects like Vienna's Ringstrasse and points out how the rational thinking of modern engineers had created inhuman urban spaces. According to Sitte, it was not rational and economic, but solely aesthetic intentions that should shape the town, and the model was to be found in the naturally occurring streets and squares of the Middle Ages.[28] One of the winning architects, Egil Fischer, had argued for an artistically composed townscape with picturesque irregularities and squares that would give identity to the different parts of the town and create a setting that was favorable to the outdoor life of the town.

The winning project therefore had curving streets, many diagonal links, rows of trees in a number of streets, blocks in various irregular forms and small recesses and prominences in the line of the buildings along the street, all intended to create life and variety in the urban scene. The proximity to the lake was to be exploited with great effect in the form of a large symmetrical park with a central square that included both sides of the lake through two dikes that would connect the districts on the east and west sides of the lake. The project not only connected the city across the lake but also at Rådhuspladsen which thus became the top of the triangle comprised by the district (see Fig. 5.7).

However, the plan gave rise to traffic problems, and in the course of the next couple of years it underwent some revision. In 1912 the council adopted a final plan for the area, which retained the influence of Sitte's ideas.

5.8 Wild West bazaars on the old station terrain in the 1940s. Drawing from a photo by Hans Ovesen.

In the following years this plan was subjected to severe criticism, and especially the irregular shapes of the blocks were criticized because they made it difficult to carry out a profitable division into sites and to erect buildings that harmonized with one another. The town planning pioneer Charles I. Schou[29] was one of the sharpest critics of the council's plan, and in 1915 he submitted his ideas for a suitable plan for the area. Anticipating the modernist endeavor to create order and rationality, his plan aimed at the abstract spaces of neoclassicism, with simple lines and the elimination of unnecessary nooks and corners in the blocks and haphazardly formed squares. The plan linked up with Rådhuspladsen by leading Gammel Kongevej through Jernbanegade from the southwest into the north-west end of the square (see Fig. 5.7).

The proposal was rejected by the municipality and the sale of building sites in the ensuing years followed the 1912 plan. It was mainly the area to the east of the railway tracks and thus closest to Rådhuspladsen that was built on in these years, which meant that Sitte's ideas came to expression in this part of Copenhagen.

While plans were being drawn up and decisions made regarding a more monumental use of the area, a disordered townscape – a wild west – had grown up on the unused land of "the old station terrain." For while waiting for the great sale of sites to take place, the municipality leased sites for temporary building in order to get at least some income from the area. Along the stretch towards the Liberty Memorial, which was to have been so dignified and elegant, there arose a line of small stores, popularly called "Flies' eyes," because of their protruding, convex and many-sided show windows, which were designed to make room for as many of the cheap goods as possible. One could also find obscure pubs and coffee bars. Workshops and engine sheds remaining from the railway were leased out as stables, garages, to plasterers, mechanics, haulage contractors and small industries. The northeast end towards Gyldenløvesgade was leased to traveling circuses and as an exhibition area. In summer a motley street life unfolded itself here, as when the open-mouthed Copenhageners went to see plate-lipped Negroes at the Dutch Exhibition in 1913.

In 1918 only a few plots had been sold in the area to the west of the railway cutting. The Association of Free Architects blamed the Sitte plan's irregularly shaped plots, which according to the Association constituted a practical and artistic impediment to an

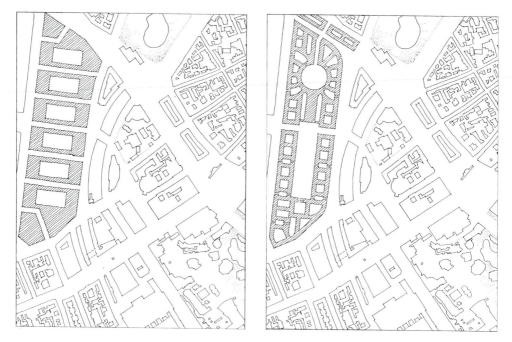

5.9 Alternative plans for the "Skt. Jørgens" area (Schou 1918 and Rafn 1918). Map drawings by Hans Ovesen.

economically viable and aesthetically satisfying development of the district.[30] At the insistence of the Association Charles I. Schou submitted yet another proposal, which this time concerned only the area to the west of the railway cutting. Hereby the part of the area that could have linked the whole district to Rådhuspladsen was cut out of the plan. The city architect rejected Schou's plan as impractical and immature, and the city council stuck to the 1912 plan (see Fig. 5.9).

Shortly after, Aage Rafn presented a proposal for the development of the area which, in complete opposition to Schou's, consisted of coherent building projects and the formation of two squares. Together with Hack Kampmann and others, Rafn had the opportunity of working further on a similar neoclassicist courtyard at Politigården (The Police Headquarters), 1918–1924.

The proposal was regarded as impressive, but incomplete, problematic and, according to Mayor Jensen, not in keeping with the times. In Jensen's opinion the plan "... is far from the *clarity and simplicity* in its organization that should be the distinguishing feature of future developments."[31] It did, however, lead to the question of "the old station terrain" being reopened, and the city architect drew up a new proposal containing reminiscences of all the previous plans (see Fig. 5.10). A committee appointed by the city council recommended this, for the time being, last proposal, because it "... contains the opportunity of creating a district that could become an adornment to our city and a *testimony for posterity to the architectonic ability and sense of beauty that our era has at its disposal.*"[32] This assessment underscores the monumental ambitions that the decision-makers attached to this district. King Christian IV had built Christianshavn and Ny København (New

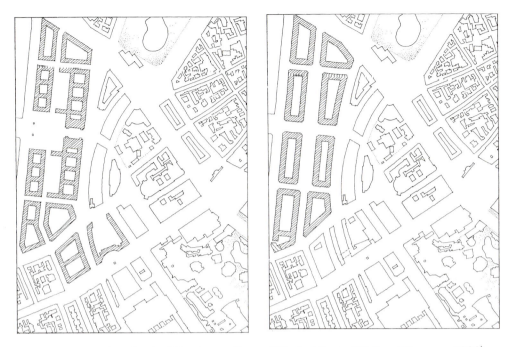

5.10 Alternative plans for the "Skt. Jørgens" area (City Architects 1918 and Thomsen 1928).
Map drawings by Hans Ovesen.

Copenhagen) in the Renaissance – now the Social-Democrat civic administration would show how to build in modern times.

The proposal was adopted and the mayor invited three architects to submit draft plans to a competition for the forming of the facades. In 1920 the city council adopted Edvard Thomsen's proposal, which contained a central eight-sided square like that at the Royal Palace of Amalienborg. The proposal required strict adherence to aesthetic guidelines to secure the desired order and harmony. Mayor Jensen pointed out that future developers should have a reasonable latitude with respect to the insides of the buildings, but that aesthetic considerations made it necessary to attach strict easements to the sites. He was in no doubt that it would be necessary to require that the buildings had the same number of stories, the same windows, and for the sake of the architectonic effect it would also be necessary to require a degree of harmony which precluded one building having a different character from the next.[33] The city council imagined that the sites would mainly be sold to private and public institutions rather than for apartment buildings, as the rent would be very high.[34]

In a mere 10 years the city council had fundamentally changed its view on how a satisfactory district should be formed. The ideal had shifted from Egil Fischer's "unruly" medievally inspired planning ideal of variation, multiplicity and picturesque irregularity to an ideal of rationality and uniformity partly based on the idealistic attitude that the appearance and placing of the buildings should imbue the urban scene with calm and harmony and partly on a financial strategy to make it easier to sell the sites.

However, the new plan made the sale of building sites more difficult precisely because it demanded so much uniformity, and in 1927 the municipal administration had to call upon Edvard Thomsen once again and ask him for yet another street plan which permitted dispensation from the restrictive easements. This plan consisted of eight big north–south oriented rectangular blocks. Like Manhattan's grid, the street system had a long central street cutting through the district from north to south, and cross-streets running east–west. In 1928 the city council was then able to adopt this plan which was to form the final basis for the development of the station terrain (see Fig 5.10).

The idea of an ideal urban plan had moved from an aesthetically conceived district linked up with the existing city to an ideal of a rationally conceived enclave in the enterprising commercial life of the modern metropolis. From the romantic plan in 1910 with its focus on the formation of squares, picturesque variety and irregularity to the severe neoclassicist plan in 1918 the ideal had shifted to a requirement for calm and harmony achieved through uniformity and a coherent urban architecture. But the modernist view of space is also displayed in broad, straight streets: "What a release there is in the experience of the refreshing effect of being able to see far. It was the desire to liberate the eyes that brought the straight street into existence."[35] It was the broad vista and overview that was needed in a city of cosmopolitans.

As mentioned above, the only square that remained in the final plan was the long parking area down the middle of the central street. No public squares where the people might gather or just linger to absorb the atmosphere of the city. The promenading street life of the boulevards had been swept away by the century of the motor car. With its many parking lots – multi-storied inside, outside in a number of rows and underground – gas stations and car hire firms the district has become a machine for producing traffic,[36] fully living up to the modern urban ideal as expressed by Le Corbusier and the CIAM's Athens Charter "The functional city".

XII MODERN ARCHITECTURAL IDEALS

The 1930s was the decade in which the architectural profession happily turned its back on centuries of architectural traditions and aesthetic principles for the idioms of architectural form. There was great optimism regarding the profession's possibilities in those years, and the most important standard-bearer of *the new* was the architect, designer and critic Poul Henningsen. From the 1920s onwards he was a central figure in the Danish Cultural-Radical Movement, and through his newspaper criticism and his journal *Kritisk Revy* (Critical Review) he exerted considerable influence on modernist Danish architecture. He was deeply engaged in everything going on in society around him. Among other things, in his role as architecture critic on the leading daily newspaper of the day, *Politiken*, he initiated the discussion of what should be done with the station terrain, "where the future of architecture in Copenhagen lies" (1932). He was to be proved right. The aesthetic principles displayed in the best of the buildings in the area express the ideas of the functionalist movement concerning social commitment, informality and democratic

5.11 Photos of Nyropsgade and Fisker and Møller: "Vestersøhus". Parking lots and modernism. Courtesy of Copenhagen City Museum.

solidarity regarding social issues. And they express a will to internationalization through the inspiration from foreign sources like Le Corbusier and Mies van der Rohe.

In this district there unfolded a chapter of Danish cultural history concerning the entry of functionalism into Copenhagen and the entry of cubism into the formal idioms of architecture with sharp contours and concise block-like forms. It is also a piece of cultural history that has to do with cultural radicalism with its provocative challenges to the philistine values of the bourgeoisie and the fake facade architecture with which it was so prone to stage itself. Against all this, cultural radicalism fought for freedom, democracy, solidarity and an honest and unpretentious architecture.

The 1930s was also the decade in which the sale of building sites finally got going in Skt. Jørgens Quarter, and a strange urban landscape developed in the form of a judicious mixture of large-scale office buildings among many small wooden barracks and old engine sheds, where small firms had been doing business undisturbed during the almost 20 years that planning for the area had been in progress. The step-by-step winding-up of these small firms lasted right into the 1950s.

In the course of time considerations of salability meant that the municipality became increasingly cautious about attaching easements to the sites. The few easements that were enforced were inspired by the first building in the area to the west of the railway cutting, Teknologisk Institut (Technological Institute): maximum six stories, a tiled pitched roof with a slope of 45 degrees and a height from street level to roof ridge of 20.5 meters. In this way it was ensured that the many developers who would be building a block together would harmonize their buildings sufficiently to give the blocks a uniform profile.

Modern-thinking architects found these demands from the municipal authorities quite fatal for the development of an architecture that was interesting and in keeping with the times. Poul Henningsen raged in *Politiken* at the politicians' unwillingness to create opportunities for the new architecture. He wrote that "the municipal authorities are still messing around with Thomsen's uniform plans, which are now thoroughly out of date. It appears that the area is to have the old red tiled roofs because Teknologisk Institut is situated there."[37] The worst thing for him, however, was that the municipal authorities were hindering the development of an architecture that could live up to the requirements of the day and of the future: "In other words, this means, that new ways of building, new materials and constructions will not be allowed to penetrate the station terrain, where lies the future of architecture in Copenhagen."[38] Where Meldahl had found the city council rather too modern in its choice of Nyrop's City Hall, Poul Henningsen now judged it to be too conservative.

The same year as this polemic battle was being fought in the press, two buildings were erected on the terrain: on Gyldenløvesgade Købstadsforeningen (The Association of Provincial Towns) erected a building in conformity with the easements and in the same style as Teknologisk Institut. The other building was Shell's head office in Denmark. The building had contributed to the polemic, because the easements had led to radical changes in the architect's original concept. The building had been planned with a flat roof and the top floor set back from the line of the facade, but it ended with a red pitched roof and became therefore, according to Poul Henningsen, "a building in a worried Thomsenish Empire style of the worst and most godforsaken kind."[39]

Shellhuset (Shell House) was completed in 1934, but was bombed in 1945 by British planes as the Gestapo had requisitioned the building and stored their archives on the Danish Resistance there. In 1950 Shell erected a new building designed by Vilhelm Lauritzen on top of the old foundations, but by then the easements had been relaxed considerably and the new building was given seven stories and a flat roof. The shortage of materials after the war made it difficult to procure slate for the panels, but with a little ingenuity Carlsberg Brewery's old fermenting vat ended up on the facade of the monumental building. The building is a major example of a functionalist office building, cubist in expression with a displacement between the big cube facing Kampmannsgade and the smaller and lower outbuilding facing Vesterfarimagsgade. This shift between the two bodies of the building strengthens the impression of a focus on geometric forms and rational, mathematical order in the same way that the operation of a multinational company must be based on hard-nosed, "sharp-edged" economic calculations in order for it to be successful. The ground floor housed the most up-to-date gas station in the country. "Rationalization sets its stamp on the building in many ways," commented a special edition of *Shell Magasinet* (Shell Magazine) in 1950, thereby describing the essence of this ultramodern office building.

Paradoxically, it was in the decade of the Depression, the 1930s with an economic recession and increasing unemployment, that the development of the station terrain really got going. For architecture the economic crisis meant that modern labor-saving building techniques soon began to meet resistance, and towards the end of the decade there was a reversion to Danish building traditions. At the same time there was a good deal of discussion in the press for and against modern architecture, in which nationalists and traditionalists maintained that the proper Danish building material was "the earth-born tile," which together with the red and white brick-and-mortar facades almost constituted a national symbol.[10] In 1936, when the municipality built a large building in Gyldenløvesgade, it did so as a "traditionalist." The building was Hans Nansen's Gård, popularly dubbed Skattepalæet (The Tax Palace).

The building was designed by Poul Holsøe, who was the city architect from 1925 to 1943, and thereby exerted considerable influence on Copenhagen's appearance. He could build in a modern, international style as is evidenced by his Bauhaus-inspired Kødbyen (Meat Town) southwest of Central Station, but the Tax Palace was built in red brick with a pitched roof. Its functionalist element was constituted by the fact that it was based on modern planning from the inside, and its form resulted from its function. The building was intended to provide an efficient framework for a modern bureaucracy, for which there was no longer enough space within the walls of the City Hall.

The only residential building in the district was also of red brick. A large consortium was behind the erection of "Vestersøhus," which was built on the lake front in two stages in 1937 and 1939. The building contained various kinds of what at that time were considered to be luxury apartments. In democratic fashion all residents had access to the roof terraces on the top floor, which was set back from the line of the facade. The special corner window-balcony system, with a corner window half out onto the balcony, became a common feature of Copenhagen's new apartment buildings in the 1930s, primarily for fire safety reasons and also to ensure air and light for the residents.

With Vestersøhus its architects, Kay Fisker and C.F. Møller, had created a regular and uniform building facing the lake in accordance with the ideals of the earlier plans. Kay Fisker shared Mayor Jensen's view, namely that uniformity equals harmony, which is what architecture is about.

Kay Fisker became one of the most important and influential figures in twentieth-century Danish architecture, especially with respect to residential building, the general standard of which he contributed to raising through his own works and his teaching as a professor at the School of Architecture of the Royal Academy of Fine Arts. In his view of what constitutes good architecture we may find the explanation why Skt. Jørgens Quarter has received so little attention: "It is the neutral, anonymous architecture that must set its stamp on our environment. Such an architecture cannot be subjected to the winds of fashion, and it cannot be inspired by great individual achievements. Ordinary architecture must be anonymous and timeless."[41]

In the 1940s the war put a stop to the further development of the station terrain, but in the 1950s it started again with a vengeance. A building worth noting is the long administration building belonging to Statsanstalten for Livsforsikring (The State Life Insurance Institute) in Kampmannsgade and Nyropsgade. The building was designed by Frits Schlegel, who introduced a Perret-inspired use of concrete into Denmark,[42] and Mogens Lassen, who built talented Le Corbusier-inspired villas in the beginning of the 1930s.[43] The main block of the building was intended for Statsanstalten's own offices, while the rest of the building was to be leased out as was often the case for the big administration buildings from the 1930s onwards.

The building is noteworthy because in direct opposition to traditional functionalist principles it has decorated facades. Perhaps Schlegel also derived inspiration in this respect from Auguste Perret, especially his building from 1903 in Rue Franklin in Paris, where the fields created by the skeleton of the facade are filled with windows and decorated panels.[44] In close collaboration with the modernist multi-artist Axel Salto (a close friend of Poul Henningsen's) Schlegel has created a striking interaction between windows and panels with decorative reliefs. The decoration, which consists of four basic figures, repeated in the total of 327 panel reliefs, signals not pomp and circumstance but, rather, industrialized mass production, as if the building had passed through an enormous printing press.

The international style received its first clear expression in Danish architecture in Skt. Jørgens Quarter. In 1955 the district was once again the setting for something new and never previously seen in Denmark: a building with a curtain wall, raised on two piles so the traffic could stream unimpeded beneath the building, as Le Corbusier had done with Unité d'Habitation. Arne Jacobsen, who was famous for his sensitivity to the international trends of the day, was the architect behind this Danish version of the international style.

The continued development of new materials and constructions, which from the very beginning had made modern building techniques possible, now began to make the actual construction process easier because more and more elements could be prefabricated, and putting them in place on the building site required fewer and fewer man-hours. While earlier materials were of mineral origin, from the 1950s they were increasingly produced at factories, where their chemical composition, size and durability were determined. Functionalist rationalism was in practice linked to capitalist methods of production and was soon adopted by the entire construction industry.

One of the ways of making the production of building materials more efficient was to increase the information available concerning the new industrially produced building materials and elements, and for that purpose a group of architects founded the association Byggecentrum (Building Center) in 1956. There was a need for a centrally situated showroom, and the choice fell on an address at the corner of Nyropsgade and Gyldenløvesgade, where Niels and Eva Koppel – who have designed a number of educational and research institutions in Copenhagen – created a building that stands as an example of industrialized construction with its repetition of the same element with narrow oblong windows and panels tied together by vertical bars just like its contemporary, the Imperial Hotel, at the other end of the district.

Internationalization also made itself felt in the form of an increased need for hotel and congress facilities, where meetings between innovative and multinational enterprises could take place in a professional framework. Because of its position close to the Central Station, Skt. Jørgens Quarter was a central area for visitors to the city, and in 1959 the Imperial Hotel was erected as one large complex covering an entire block of streets, with parking spaces on the first floor, meeting rooms, a conference hall and the like. Otto Frankil had designed the complex, but it was Jørgen Buschardt who completed it. And he was also responsible for the next hotel to be built in the district, the 20-story Sheraton, now called the Scandic Hotel. It was built by an American consortium in 1968–1971 on the basis of expectations of a City Vest [City West] that would undergo a dynamic development after the City Council's approval of City Plan West and Søringen (The Lake Ring Road) in 1968 (see p. 169).

In order to ensure an optimal construction rhythm, time schedule, economy and flexibility the hotel complex was constructed of prefabricated modules, and the process was computer-controlled, so that all deviations from the construction plan could be quickly corrected without unnecessary loss of time or money, and in 1971 the completed building was launched in the daily paper *Politiken* as follows: "A well-greased machine is starting up, a gathering place for luxury-lovers from all over the world."[45]

The hotel consists of different buildings linked to form a whole and can be described with Siegfried Giedion's definition of the cubist structure of the Bauhaus complex in Dessau: "It is impossible to get an overview of this complex in one glance; you have to go all the way round it, see it both from above and below: This means new dimensions for the artistic imagination, a hitherto unseen many-facetedness."[46]

By 1974 Skt. Jørgens Quarter was fully developed, not in as uniform a manner as had originally been intended, but its functionalist character with severe geometric facades, its unpretentious aesthetic ambitions and its cubist plasticity executed in a number of variations nevertheless give a total impression of great homogeneity.

XIII A MONUMENT TO THE MODERN EPOCH

With its street grid, its buildings and their owners and its aesthetic principles Skt. Jørgens Quarter stands as a monument to the impact of modernity in Copenhagen. The district was formed by three aspects of modernity: a political aspect in the shape of a democratically elected city council, a developmental aspect in the shape of the needs of an industrialized welfare society for new traffic conditions and new types of office building, for local government and the business sector, and, finally, the architectonic aspect manifested in endeavors at creating adequate forms for the modern city.

The Social-Democratic self-view that is expressed in Skt. Jørgens Quarter is based on a cult of the future and of progress. Just as the Social-Democrats had won a majority in the city council, so with the establishment of the new district they wished to conquer new territory in the city and to form it on the basis of quite different values from those favored by the right wing in its historicist and national-romantic buildings and Vienna-inspired boulevards.

Social-Democratic mayor for finance Jensen's statements from the beginning of the century to the effect that one must strive for "uniformity and harmony" in the development of the district contain echoes of the party's entire political program for the leveling out of social differences and the provision of social security for all. The Social-Democratic endeavor to distribute the goods of society equally harmonized with the functionalist wish to remove all decoration from architecture in order to make it as cheap as possible and thereby accessible to as many people as possible. The Social-Democrats wanted to look forward and build a society that was quite different from the existing society. There was the same impetus in Le Corbusier's and Poul Henningsen's writings from the 1920s and throughout the modernist movement: to clear the decks and start all over again "towards a new architecture." Both endeavors wanted a tabula rasa situation, and it was at hand on "the terrain of the old station." "It was to the colonization of new territory and the structuring of empty space that thinking about the modern city was attached."[47]

The people who commissioned the new buildings in Skt. Jørgens Quarter are not striking individual profiles as in the time of the building of the old city but anonymous institutions like the State and the municipality, trade unions, insurance companies and multinationals, and their need was for big, well-functioning office blocks inside which aesthetic considerations were subordinated to practical and rational requirements. One element that characterizes many of the facades is, as already mentioned, repetition: a corner window balcony system, vertical ribbons of windows, a panel relief, etc. The repetition signals both assembly-line effectiveness and that everyone inside behind the facades has the same conditions. The dominant impression in the district is of a machine aesthetic, both the individual building as a well-greased machine and the whole district as "a machine for producing traffic."

The city council's original intention that the district should be an "adornment to our city and a testimony for posterity to the architectonic ability and sense of beauty that our era has at its disposal" was fulfilled with respect only to "testimony;" it never became an adornment. The contradictions between public planning and private capitalist economics and between modernist architecture and the block structure of the classical city would seem to explain the district's "neither-nor" character and its lack of outstanding features. It did, however, become an interesting testimony to its epoch.

The especially Danish quality of the district consists of the restraint with which the trends of international modernism have been reinterpreted for a Danish context. There is little pathos to be found here, but a quietness of expression as a result of which the district does not claim much attention despite the intentions of the original plans. The homogeneity of the buildings speaks of the Social-Democratic ideal of equality and solidarity, and perhaps this kind of urban district has already become a rarity in an age of globalization in which the rivalry among the major cities calls for spectacular architecture in the competition to attract attention.

XIV AT THE CENTRAL STATION – THE COPENHAGEN OF NEW DEPARTURES

The square of Central Station lies at the intersection of the central north–south axis of Skt. Jørgens Quarter with Vesterbrogade, the east–west link between Rådhuspladsen and Vesterbro. It marks the meeting-place among different periods of Copenhagen's recent history as it has been expressed in different perceptions of architecture and space, a cross between planned and market-determined urban development, between firmness and indecision, between stability and dynamism, between visions and cold calculation. It is a place where neither spaces nor functions are strongly rooted, it is a place of new departures.

Coming out of the main entrance to Copenhagen's Central Station one sees immediately to the right a hotel of rather indeterminate age and architecture. There is no doubt that it was built in the twentieth century, but the external wooden panels on the ground floor and the smooth, sooty-gray plaster and machine-produced curlicues on the other stories point without much conviction to baroque, an early modernist sobriety – or perhaps merely parsimony – or an English country squire's smoking-room turned inside out. Unless, of course, the panels are meant to be a reference to the wood-clad railway coaches of a now vanished era.

The hotel, which dates from the beginning of the twentieth century, was originally called the Terminus, but now bears the proud name of the Plaza. However, guests of the hotel will seek in vain for the *plaza* that the name so deceptively promises. What they find instead is a gigantic hole, a two-story deep railway cutting with constantly passing trains.

Since the building of Copenhagen's original Central Station in connection with the establishment of Denmark's first railway line in 1847, the management of the railway traffic at this very point has been a recurrent problem. The rapidity with which the city expanded meant that the tracks had to be moved and widened time after time, and each time Central Station had to be pulled down and erected somewhere else. The present Central Station is the third to be built within a period of little over 50 years, and paradoxically it occupies almost the same site as the first.

For centuries this area, just outside the former Vesterport, had been one of the city's busiest spots, and during the creation of the modern part of the city it also proved to be a focal point. Vesterport was the most used connecting link between the city and the surrounding countryside, and while other early development outside Copenhagen was kept at a distance by the belt of lakes, there was on this axis an uninterrupted connection between Vesterbro and the heart of the old city.

But the instability of the new times brought with it an unbroken succession of unforeseen conflicts between railway traffic and other traffic, where the steam engine cut straight through the street system in the new districts, between and through cattle markets, workshops, trading stalls, places of entertainment, great water purification plants, and property and other economic interests. This meant that the area was subjected to a multitude of plans, projects and decisions, all of which had to undergo constant change. Of all the urban districts immediately around the center, this, the most highly charged focal point in the city's development, was the district which – with the ironic logic of history – was the last to be fully developed.

The present siting of the rail tracks at Central Station was determined after a public competition in 1899. Reiterating a proposal from 1885, the project on which the future organization of rail traffic was based proposed a return to the original track to the south of the new suburbs and with a continuation towards the north under ground. At the same time Copenhagen's second Central Station from 1864 was to be closed. The moving of the track and station meant that the large and valuable area to the north of Vesterbrogade became vacant. Nevertheless 50 years would pass before the area had been developed as a modern district for commerce and administration.

After the already mentioned competition in 1910 there followed at intervals of only a few years a succession of revised and new projects for the development of the area. However, they all had one common characteristic, namely the retention of the great curve of the underground rail track from the new Central Station northwards. The way in which this siting of the track divided the district into sharply angled and curved triangles clearly created problems for all the planners, and a distinctive feature of the district in its present form is to be found in the dynamically parallel curves of the streets, which to the west of the track and without any real practical reason continue as weaker and weaker echoes of the original curve.

The new and third Central Station stood completed in 1911. It was designed in accordance with the period's National-Romantic architectural ideals, which had various specific stylistic expressions for churches, town halls and other public buildings. But not for buildings that had to do with the new form of public transport. The noise and steam, the bustle of arrival and departure cannot be read out of the station's architecture, which, on the contrary, expresses an imperturbable calm. Even the station clock on the under-sized central tower is so modest that it later had to be supplemented with shining neon numbers.

Just as the small size of the old clock would not whip up an atmosphere of unnec-essarily hectic urgency, so the building itself rests in a state of restrained monumentality. The outer monumentality is not of mass and height but of horizontal extent embracing the entire breadth of the many tracks below. The interior, however, is of a monumentality that must have had an overwhelming effect, not least for the passengers of that time. The huge vaults of the central hall are like those of a cathedral dedicated to travel, and the sacral atmosphere is repeated in the no less impressive vaults above the platforms – they are even more impressive considering the fact that the construction is of wood. Where the main stations of other cities had iron constructions, Copenhagen's was built in accordance with national-romantic principles in brick and wood. True, the roof construction is prosaically visible, but the new era's speed and dynamism had not yet entered into its architecture.

But the station's architect, Heinrich Wench, had premonitions. Representatives of power and speed are depicted: the inventor of the steam engine and an engine driver, and

5.12 Like a runaway train, the Astoria Hotel seems to rush forward, tearing apart the traditional architecture's intentions of calm and stable harmony. Drawing by Hans Ovesen.

on the facade a line of statues of men and women in folk costumes from the provinces, a reference to the building as a terminus where journeys to and from the rest of the country begin and end.

A similarly anecdotal reminder of the station as a point of departure towards new destinations is to be seen in the double reliefs on each side of the entry hall with a hedgehog and a hare on one side and a lobster and a fish on the other: speed contrasted with slowness. As was typical of the period the building contains many rounded relieving arches, and with a little goodwill the special forms that some of them have can be seen as symbols of railway bridges and rails weaving in and out. Even so, these are very subdued symbols since it is against the nature of relieving arches to set forth on journeys, and the building itself is quite unaffected by all these asides.

Only 20 years after the inauguration of Central Station a building of a quite opposite character was erected on the other side of the railway cutting to the Plaza. The building site was squeezed in between the cutting and a side street and with its mere 6-meter breadth it would probably have been considered as quite impossible to build on by the national-romantic school of architects. But also in Denmark modernism was beginning to make itself felt in the possibilities of expression available to architecture as well as in its materials and principles of construction. The oblong site was used by the architect Ole Falkentorp to express the dynamism of the era and of the locality in the actual form of his railway hotel: the Astoria. Because of the limited space the building's form would have to reach out beyond itself, the static becomes an image of speed, in a radical breach with the architectonic ideals that, as in Central Station, had aspired to a calm and serene consummation.

The dynamic element is of course underscored by the long form of the four-story building, but it is also emphasized by the fact that on both sides the two middle stories are pushed out over the edge of the site in a teasing game of intrusion and withdrawal with the surrounding space. The traditional building line, in which the facade rises straight up from street level, has become ambivalent. The delimitation of the building by the space of the city is no longer a given quantity, their interface is now a matter of mutual intervention. Furthermore, the stairway gable closest to Central Station is formed as a cylinder with the windows following the spiral of the stairs, while the pointed corbie-step front gable bears the logo of the Danish State Railways – a wheel with wings. Like a runaway railway carriage the hotel has not allowed itself to be stopped by the station building, but passes it in full career along the line of the cutting towards the place which was to become the new Copenhagen in the course of the following decades.

Inside, the long building consists of a central corridor with hotel rooms on either side, as in a sleeping car. Hearing the rumble of the passing trains, the screeching of their brakes, the hotel guest feels as if he is still traveling.

XV BUILDINGS FOR A MODERN CITY

The Astoria, which is built of reinforced concrete, was completed in 1935. The railway cutting had long been established to link up with the excavation of the "boulevard line," which was inaugurated in 1917 – Copenhagen's 2-kilometer-long answer to the Underground in London and the Metro in Paris. On the other hand, the area in front of Central Station still consisted of small buildings, barracks, hoardings and unbuilt-on sites and the Liberty Memorial. The area had not yet become a part of the city – it was still a diffuse transitional zone between the medieval center and the working class suburb of Vesterbro.

The district did, however, already contain one building representative of the new era. A few years earlier, in partnership with Povl Baumann, another prominent architect of the period, Ole Falkentorp had built "Vesterport," the large complex of shops and offices on the other side of Vesterbrogade. Anticipating future developments in urban life the building was designed to contain office space for various firms, each of which could announce its presence in neon advertisements on the roofs and facades of the buildings – a fascinating new and modern phenomenon – space to rent for showrooms and stores in indoor shopping arcades on the lower floor of the building, which was intersected by a lane for cars. There was underground parking in the basement and a restaurant on the roof. In addition, "Vesterport" was built as a "skyscraper," in which the prevalent construction method of bearing outer walls was replaced by a steel skeleton. And, as an epoch-making feature, the outside of the building was clad in copper.

The new building made an impression. On the occasion of its inauguration the daily newspaper *Politiken* brought out a special issue, in which the writer Tom Kristensen published a poetic tribute to the building. The last verse of the poems runs:

> To me a house, which bears the sign of
> a beauty, made by many a mile,
> by luxury train, by luxury liner,
> a beauty of speed, now buildings' style.
> A house for people. But not for gods.
> Simple features. Big as a fort.
> With neon signs. Big window panes.
> A house of our time: Vesterport.

The bearing construction of rolled steel sections made it possible for the facades of the stores throughout the ground floor of the building, both inside and outside, to be of glass. This was another factor that turned the traditional concept of a house upside down, the concept that one needed massive weight in the foundation and ground floor and increasing lightness the higher the house rose. With the glass facades of its ground floor the enormous copper block initiated the subtle games played by modernism with the force of gravity.

Even though the building was innovative in its functions, arrangement and construction, it had not freed itself from the Danish classicist tradition, as can be seen from its internal central axis and the symmetrical division of its main facade on both sides of the entrance. The undecorated regularity of the window ribbons meets the modernist requirement of anonymity in architecture, but in its monumentally classicist main form and its copper sheathing it is an extremely attention-claiming anonymity. The building is probably the most beautiful and illustrative architectural example of breach, transition – and coherence – between the time-honored principles of the tradition and the new orientation towards modernity, so definitively manifested in the onward-rushing impetus of the railway hotel.

The Depression in the 1930s, World War II and the German occupation of Denmark were accompanied by a loss of optimism about future developments and a standstill in building activities. Immediately after the war planning for the Copenhagen area was resumed, the first result being the "Fingerplan" from 1947. As its nickname suggests the plan proposed that the future development of the capital should take place in a radial system of urban fingers built up around private and collective traffic routes with shopping centers, institutions, residential and commercial buildings around the railway stations as nodal points. The open countryside between the fingers would be kept free of urban development and become extensive, easily accessible recreational areas reaching close into the center.

The Fingerplan attracted international attention, not least thanks to the brilliant simplicity of the concept. It would be largely capable of absorbing the dynamic forces of urban development, and at the same time it would have ideational and functional coherence irrespective of the speed at which the city grew. The plan rested on the assumption that the growth of the city would take place in an organic succession, and that the city's traffic arteries would form the skeleton for this growth. The historic center of Copenhagen would continue to constitute the core of the future metropolis. It was there that the future growth had its roots and from there that it would spread.

In 1954 the Fingerplan was followed up by a more detailed plan for central Copenhagen. Among other things, this "Draft Overall Plan" contained proposals that part of the city's commercial development should take place in a ring around the core, in the belt between the former terrain of the ramparts and the Lakes. And once again the focus was placed on the district that is the theme of this article. It was especially the traffic conditions that made the district interesting. Central Station was already in place, and both the Fingerplan and the Draft Overall Plan suggested the meeting here of a western approach road and an internal ring road from which motor traffic to the center could be distributed.

The Draft Overall Plan was as such never adopted for Copenhagen, but as early as in 1958 the municipality of Copenhagen published its "City Plan West", which carried the ideas behind the draft plan to their logical conclusion. City Plan West focused entirely on the district to the west of Central Station and proposed that it should be transformed into a commercial, traffic and parking center of colossal dimensions. Once again it was here that the future of the city was to be cast.

In other European cities, such as Paris, Hamburg, and Stockholm, the planning and development of corresponding commercial areas had already begun. These initiatives were signals of fundamental changes in the occupational structure of the big cities. Industry was being replaced by office operations, and blue collar workers by white collar employees.

At the end of the 1960s City Plan West was further concretized, among other things with a proposal for a gigantic freeway along the Lakes. Other European cities like Madrid, Paris and Hamburg had already been "modernized" with this kind of freeway route cutting through the city above or below street level, but in relation to Danish conditions this was a far too radical project. Nobody – neither public authorities nor private investors

– dared undertake the gigantic clover-leaf intersections in central parts of the city that the plan envisaged, quite irrespective of the fact that the plan was very far from being favorably received by the inhabitants of the city.

An additional discouraging factor may have been the district's *location*. It is true that on one side the area bordered on Copenhagen's historical and economic center, but it was neighbored on the other side by the extensive slums of Vesterbro, a proximity that rarely has an incentive effect on venture capital. Even though there was renewed optimism regarding the future, the economic, physical and political costs might well prove to be too great.

In the meantime some fairly large projects had been realized in the area. Between the railway cutting and the copper building and on each side of Vester Farimagsgade, one of the inner ring roads of the city, two long office and shopping complexes had been built in the middle of the 1950s. The two buildings were connected by a third, which forms a ten-story bridge building across the street. The complex, whose individual buildings were designed by different architects, Ib Lunding, Thomas Dreyer, Ole Hagen and Allan Christensen, on the basis of a revision of a development project by architect Ib Lunding, is called "Buen" (The Arch) after the arched roof of the bridge building.

Ib Lunding's first draft project continued the complex across the railway cutting and included the site on which the SAS Royal Hotel was later erected. The building across the cutting was kept low in relation to the rest of the complex so as not to distract attention from the Liberty Memorial. Furthermore, the building curved away from the Liberty Memorial and the cutting, which was expected to be covered and transformed into a proper square. Despite the modernism of "The Arch," the intention was to create in the best Classicist tradition a place of calm in the midst of the district's architectonic unrest.

But the development plan was changed a number of times, and in opposition to Lunding's original intention the result was a very dynamic development, in which the "unrest" was further increased when Arne Jacobsen twisted the high-rise of the SAS Royal Hotel away from the lines and directions in "The Arch" that Lunding had proposed.

Together with the vertical lines of small balconies in each of the gables of the bridge building, which seem more like naval lookout posts, the light yellow color of "The Arch" gives the complex lightness and associations with the sea. In addition, the gable facing Central Station on one of the long buildings has been cut off at an angle and closed in with plate glass with zigzag edges. The effect is of the bow wave of a ship cutting through the urban sea in the opposite direction to the railway hotel's sleeping car obliquely across the square.

The "maritime" element in Nordic architecture can be traced back to Scandinavia's first modernist exhibition of architecture in Stockholm in 1930, where much in the form and details of the buildings derived its inspiration from the beauty in the extremely simplified, economical and functional design of ship construction.

In 1950 the so-called "Panopticon Building" burned down next door to the already mentioned Plaza Hotel – the Panopticon Building's misleading name derives from the fact that at the beginning of the century there had been an exhibition of wax figures on its ground floor. It was replaced by an office building, which was designed by the architects Alex Poulsen and Mogens Jacobsen, and which still bears the name of its predecessor. It was commissioned by "Arbejdernes Landsbank" (The Workers' National Bank) under the Danish Trade Unions Congress and stands obliquely across the street from "Axelborg" (Axel Castle), the headquarters of the Danish agricultural organizations. Workers and farmers, formerly the two most powerful political factors in the country, are thus symbolically represented in the melting pot of modernist Copenhagen on opposite sides of the street.

Like "The Arch" the Panopticon Building exceeds the general building height in Copenhagen of five or six stories. Both are part of the city's first experiments with high-rise building as a challenge to Copenhagen's historical skyline.

The Panopticon Building is also ambivalent towards the tradition of building along the street line. The building is folded into two wings of six and 12 stories respectively in an inverted L-shape which draws away from the corner of the street block, while the lower part of two to three stories fills the space inside the L-shape and follows the corner angle of the street line. Like "The Arch" this building also bears maritime associations. On top of the low corner building there is a small glass pavilion, which stands there like the bridge of a huge ship. The pavilion breaks the lines and right-angles of the high building and the street corner. Without any apparent practical reason the walls of the pavilion point in other directions as if this pigmy was in the process of maneuvering the big building onto a quite new course.

With the Panopticon Building's tall main wing the international style in architecture had made a resolute entry onto the Copenhagen scene. The building was, however, soon to be overshadowed. When it was decided to build Arne Jacobsen's 21-story SAS Royal Hotel on the corner opposite the Panopticon Building, its architects are reported to have said with barely concealed distress to Jacobsen: "You're going to make our Panopticon look like a dog's kennel," to which Jacobsen replied: "That's precisely my intention!"

The SAS Royal Hotel from 1961 was one of Denmark's first "proper skyscrapers," and there are still very few in the country – probably less than half a dozen in the Copenhagen area. The hotel, which, both in Denmark and abroad, has been accused of plagiarizing New York's Lever House, consists of a low flat block, from which the skyscraper rises vertically. Between the low and the high buildings the architect has placed an intervening glass-covered story that appears to separate the skyscraper from its basis, so that it almost seems to be hovering freely.

Although the "inspiration" from Lever House is thus obvious in the external forms of the building, there are nevertheless important differences. In relation to the urban context the most significant is that in the open ground floor of Lever House the street space continues in among the pillars, while the horizontal part of the SAS Royal Hotel is closed off, keeping the life of the street as a movement *around* the building. By abolishing the boundary between street and building Lever House dissolves the tension of the contrapuntal interaction with the surrounding urban space.

Just as in the Astoria Hotel, the lowest glass-covered story of the SAS Royal Hotel is drawn back from the line of the facade, from which the skyscraper has removed itself completely. The skyscraper stands far back from the street line in majestic self-sufficiency, an arrogance of pose that expresses no desire whatsoever to enter into a dialog with the dwarf Panopticon Building opposite. On another side, however, the skyscraper protrudes over the edge of the low part of the hotel and even a little over the edge of the low building next door. Together both parts of the hotel create a vertical and horizontal interplay with the street space and the facade lines, a challenge to the otherwise unambiguous relation between the building and the surrounding space.

In its spatial form, delicate coloring and the smoothness of the facades with the cobweb thinness of the bars in the vertical building's body, the SAS Royal Hotel is both playful and unapproachable. It is a *cool* building and with its unmistakable reference to Lever House an *international* building. In its original version everything in the building – curtains, furniture, door fittings, even the cutlery in the restaurant – was designed by the architect. A work of total art, which thanks to its smooth, highly finished aesthetic gives the impression that with this late version of modernism things are really under control. Here at the border of a Vesterbro which was at that time a crumbling slum and even poorer than today, the hotel's elevated aestheticism seems almost an idiosyncratic shield against the trials and tribulations of daily life.

The advancing ship's prow of "The Arch," the low building across the railway cutting and the SAS Royal Hotel, with the extremity and confidence of its challenge to spatial restrictions, make up the set of buildings that meet the traveler's eyes as he or she emerges from Central Station. On the other side of the space that is not a *plaza* these three buildings stand in a flow that is not merely indeterminable but also indecisive. Besides offices and special stores these buildings contain hotel rooms, banks, air companies and travel bureaus. Everything, both indoors and outdoors, has an air of being on its way: a modern rootlessness that is reflected in the ephemerality of the space and the buildings. In no way does the locality invite one to linger. The old Vesterbros Passage and its continuation across the station square is still a place of passage.

The expectations formerly attached to this area of its becoming a dynamic center in the city's economic development have now been moved to other parts of the region. Perhaps it is to those parts of Copenhagen that all the passers-by are hurrying.

XVI EXIT COPENHAGEN

The history of the district spans more than a century, two world wars and a development that contains all the drama and dynamism brought about by the impact of the modern era: industrialization, urbanization, rationalization, anonymization, fragmentation, fluctuation and strivings towards democracy, solidarity, education, social security, welfare and equality. This is a development full of inner contradictions between planned and market-determined urban development, between the wish for stability and the wish for dynamic change, between, on the one hand, social and aesthetic visions and, on the other hand, cold economic calculation.

From a town planning perspective the district contains some enormous fluctuations between various ideals. A common factor is that all the major steps in the development of the district have been influenced by the ideal of being modern. In Copenhagen the ideals and the concept of what being modern means have shifted from Paris to Manhattan, as can be seen if you walk from Rådhuspladsen to the station square. The first plans were drawn when the city was given the entire terrain of the fortifications in which to expand.

Centuries of confinement within the overbuilt medieval and Renaissance center, contained by ramparts since the seventeenth century, found release in the plans for great boulevards with oceans of space for the life of the city, monumental squares and the long vistas from the city out towards the suburbs and the surrounding countryside. This was the view that the philosopher Søren Kierkegaard (1813–1855) so passionately longed for, and when he felt too physically and mentally confined by Copenhagen, he would go up on Nørrevold (North Rampart) and let his eyes wander freely in the distance. With the fall of the ramparts the distant became directly accessible, and the border areas of the city were treated differently in each of the three urban spaces that we have presented here.

Rådhuspladsen cultivated the link between the old city and the open country, with the City Hall placed as a hinge and at the same time a gateway to the city and thereby connecting itself to the traffic of visitors to the city. By way of contrast Skt. Jørgens Quarter became a modernist enclave, oriented towards the edge of the city and what lay beyond while "turning its back on the old city." The station square retained its original function as a place of passage, which gives it its character as an intermediate space.

It is a characteristic of the three areas described here that politicians and planners have taken note of their intrinsic dynamism and have wished to exploit it as a basis for the future development of the city. Today all three areas appear as places of transit, though in different ways. Both the station square and Skt. Jørgens Quarter have been the objects of a series of grandiose plans, but economic factors have led to the majority of them being rejected, as was the case with City Plan West and the Lake Ring project, or radically revised, as was the case with the plans for Skt. Jørgens Quarter. Thus, the present form of these areas is a result of the interplay of, on the one hand, the endeavours of the public authorities to create order, control and rationality and, on the other hand, the unleashing of private capitalist initiatives.

Neither the Liberal nor the Social-Democratic city council succeeded in binding the old and the new cities together. Along the line where the old moat separated the city from its hinterland a river of cars now streams on H.C. Andersen's Boulevard. The former passage between the hinterland and the city still bears the character of an intermediate space between two clearly defined urban areas: the working class district of Vesterbro and the medieval city, but the area itself is indeterminate with its character of a place of transit and fragmented space. If the space of the Central Station square is fragmented, this also applies to the whole district, which has disintegrated into fragments: Vesterbrogade between the station square and the City Hall as a place of transit, Rådhuspladsen and the boulevard as part of a large, monumentally conceived park, then the area that was built up on the basis of the 1912 Sitte-inspired plan with its curved streets and widely different buildings, which are especially places of entertainment: the music house Pumpehuset, the circus building, the Palace Theatre, Vægtergården with its night club, discotheque and so on. This area is intersected by the railway cutting, and on the other side a modernist urban plan has been realized in Skt. Jørgens Quarter with great homogeneity in the buildings and the broad, straight streets, which are devoid of any kind of recreational activities – these take place on the roof terraces and balconies of the buildings or elsewhere in the city in accordance with the modern town planning idea of dividing the city into function-determined zones.

The station square, Rådhuspladsen and Skt. Jørgens Quarter are characterized by passage, fluctuation and speed. They are places of transit for travelers, for the city's pedestrians, for the employees in the many office buildings and the many customers to the area's numerous travel bureaus. The area is also an example of the city formation that is typical of the modern metropolis with its concentration of public and private administration buildings, service and information undertakings, cultural offers and popular entertainment in the center, while the residential areas are placed at the periphery. With its rapid pulse and the confusion signaled by its architecture and the street scene the area is possibly the part of Copenhagen that will seem least foreign to a visitor from New York, and yet it will seem very different thanks to its special history and its Nordic version of modernist urban building.

Notes

1   This chapter is a result of a collaboration between the three authors. However Helle Bøgelund-Hansen is responsible for the part concerning Skt. Jørgens Quarter, Birgitte Darger for the part on the City Hall, and Hans Ovesen for the part concerning the Central Station square. The article is based on further studies published in books and papers and on Bøgelund-Hansen's and Birgitte Darger's unpublished MA theses.
2   Broby-Johansen, p. 49.
3   Bramsen, pp. 150 and 198.
4   Ibid., pp. 163 and 458–59.
5   Bønnelycke.
6   Ibid.
7   Bramsen, pp. 102 ff.
8   Ibid, p. 112.
9   Ibid, p. 127.
10 Ibid., p. 246.
11 Nielsen.
12 Kristensen, p. 70.
13 Beckett.
14 Millech.
15 Bech and Knudsen.
16 In the first years of the council its members did not represent particular political groupings nor were they divided into parties. Nor were there big ideological, economic or social differences among the councilors. The council was concerned with, on the one hand, establishing its power vis-à-vis the State and, on the other hand, in relation to the growing demand from the citizens for greater influence on municipal matters (Poul Møller, *Københavns bystyre gennem 300 år* [Copenhagen City Council through 300 years], vol. 2, 1858–1940, p. 20, Copenhagen 1967). As a whole the council was influenced by the National-Liberals, who were absorbed into the Højre (today Conservative) Party in 1870. In 1884 four representatives of the Venstre (Left) Party and two Social-Democrats ran for election, and they were elected to the council in 1893 on the common Liberal-Socialist list. In 1898 this list achieved a majority in the Council.
17 Knudsen.
18 Schorske, pp. 24–26.
19 Minutes.
20 Vidler.
21 Ibid., p. 70.
22 In Copenhagen there were no strategic or military considerations behind the establishment of the boulevards – the social "battles" were fought elsewhere in the city, on its commons.
23 Beckett.

24 Funder.
25 Mylius Erichsen, in *Vagten*.
26 The Social-Democratic Party was founded in 1871 on the model of the German Social-Democrats as a working class party. It went in for socialist ideas, including public ownership, and worked to strengthen the interest of the workers. The Social-Democrats obtained a majority in the city council in 1898. In 1903 the party newspaper rejoiced at the changed composition of the Council: "What an improvement in the level of the Council over the last 10 years! Only a few titles and only fewer gongs on the breasts of the Councillors. But this very 'shortage' is an advantage. What cultural progress there is in, for example, the fact that among the 39 councillors there are two working men." 1903 was also the year in which Jens Jensen became mayor for finance. *Københavns bystyre gennem 300 år* (Copenhagen City Council through 300 Years), vol. II, 1858–1940, Poul Møller, p. 331.
27 Stadsing. Dir., p. 3. Quote from the journal *Arkitekten* 1910–1911. This journal has been the architectural profession's central forum for debate in the twentieth century.
28 Schorske, p. 63.
29 Schou was inspired by both Ebenezer Howard and German town planning. He followed the German discussion closely and due to his solid knowledge of the field he exercised a great influence on Danish town planners in the 1920s and 1930s, among other things through Danske Byplan Laboratorium (The Danish Town Planning Laboratory). Gaardmand, p. 22.
30 Stadsing. Dir., p. 7.
31 Ibid., p. 8.
32 Ibid., p. 8.
33 Ibid., p. 10.
34 Ibid., p. 12.
35 Oxvig, p. 216.
36 Ibid., p. 167.
37 *Politiken*, October 1932.
38 Ibid.
39 Ibid.
40 Finsen, p. 114.
41 Ibid., p. 93. Kay Fisker's view, formulated in 1964, concurs with Mayor Jensen's attitude in 1918 when he criticized the population for having an enormous need for self-assertion: "When someone builds a house, the main thing is that it should not resemble the others, and the architects have been willing to play along, so to speak, and give the buildings faces even though this means that they fit in very badly with their surroundings" (Stadsing. Dir., p. 9).
42 Faber, p. 148.
43 Ibid., p. 148.
44 Ibid., pp. 61–62.
45 *Politiken*, 1971.
46 Oxvig, p. 270.
47 Jens Kvorning in Kural.

References

Arkitekten (1956): Månedshæfte.
Articles and readers' letters in: *Arkitekten, Politiken, Berlingske Tidende et al.* 1890–1905.
Bech, Cedergreen *et al.*: *Københavns Historie*, vol. 4.
Beckett, Francis: *Københavns Rådhus*, Copenhagen 1908.
Berman, Marshall (1988): All That Is Solid Melts Into Air. The Experience of Modernity, Penguin, New York (1st edn 1982).
Bramsen, Bo and Palle Fogtdal (eds.): *København før nu og aldrig*, vol. 9, Caspar Jørgensen, *Vestervold Falder*.

Bøgelund-Hansen, Helle (1993): *At tænke sig en by*. University of Copenhagen, Department of Comparative Literature, MA Thesis, (manuscript).

Bønnelycke, Emil: *Asfaltens Sange*, 1918.

Broby-Johansen, R. (1948): *Gennem det gamle København*, Copenhagen.

Darger, Birgitte: *København omkring 1900*, University of Copenhagen, Department of Comparative Literature, MA Thesis, 1992 (manuscript).

Faber, Tobias (1962): *Rum, form og funktion*, Berlingske Leksikon Bibliotek, Berlingske Forlag, Copenhagen.

Finsen, Helge (1947): *Ung dansk arkitectur*, Copenhagen.

Funder, Lise (1979): *Arkitekten Martin Nyrop*, Copenhagen.

Gaardmand, Arne (1992): *Dansk byplanlægning 1938–1992*.

Henningsen, Poul: Kommunen og det gamle banegårdsterræn, *Politiken* (1932) October 8.

Holm, Axel and Kjeld Johansen: *København 1840–1940*.

Knudsen, Tim (1988): *Storbyen støbes, København mellem kaos og byplan 1890–1917*, Akademisk Forlag.

Københavns Bystyre gennem 300 Aar, vol. II, 1858–1940, Copenhagen, 1967.

Kristensen, Tom (1968): *Havoc*, Madison.

Kural, R. (ed.) (1997): *Antydninger af nye byscener*, Copenhagen.

Lind, Olaf and Annemarie Lund: Arkitektur Guide København/Architectural Guide to Copenhagen, Arkitektens Forlag.

Millech, Knud (1951): *Danske arkitekturstrømninger 1850–1950*, Copenhagen.

Minutes from the Meetings of the City Council 1885, 1887 and 1888.

Nielsen, Anker Jesper (1994): *Lysene over København. Hovedstadens lysreklamer 1898–1994*, Borgen.

Ovesen, Hans (1996): Den samspilsramte arkitektur (Architecture Caught in the Poverty Trap), in: *Har de en æstetik?* SBI.

Ovesen, Hans (1998): Det for(t)satte rum – en arkitektonisk analyse af Københavns Rådhusplads (The [dis-]continued space – architectural analysis of Copenhagen City Hall Square), KAKTUS.

Ovesen, Hans (1999): I mellemtiden – en arkitektonisk analyse af Kobenhavns Banegårdsplads (Meanwhile – an architectural analysis of Copenhagen Central Station Square), KAKTUS.

Oxvig, Henrik and Lise Beck (eds.) (1998): *Rumanalyser*, Fonden til udgivelse af arkitekturtidsskriftet B.

Politiken (1932): Special issue about Vesterport.

Politiken (1971): *Stor luxus fra stor højde*. April 16, p. 1.

Rasmussen, S.E. (1994): *København. Et bysamfunds særpræg og udvikling gennem tiderne*, Gads Forlag.

Schorske, Carl E. (1981): *Fin-de-siècle Vienna. Politics and culture*. New York: Vintage Books.

Skall, Eigil (1980): *Københavns Rådhus 75 år.*, Historiske Meddelelser om København.

Stadsingeniørens Direktorat: *København under borgerstyre og de indlemmede distrikter*, 1975 (manuscript).

Turell, Dan (1977): *Storby Blues*.

Vagten. Tidsskrift for Litteratur, Kunst, Videnskab og Politik 1899–1900.

Vesterbro – en forstadsbebyggelse i København (Vesterbro – a Suburban Development in Copenhagen), Miljøministeriet (Ministry for the Environment), 1986.

Vidler, Anthony (1991): "Scenes of the Street" in: Standford Anders (ed.): *On Streets*.

Chapter 6

Midtown Manhattan at Midcentury
Lever House and the International Style in the City[1]
Joan Ockman

I THE CURTAIN WALL RISES

In the concluding scene of Busby Berkeley's Hollywood fantasia *42nd Street* (1933), the sky-scrapers of Manhattan literally dance in the streets. The Chrysler, the McGraw-Hill, the *Daily News*, and the Empire State buildings engage in a free-wheeling revel that defies the statics of architecture. In the depths of the Depression, the flamboyant embodiments of American laissez-faire capitalism enact a delirious dream of liberation from the ground plane.

A quarter century later, a dramatic reversal has taken place. The economy is booming, and there is frenzied real estate development. The grand old apartment houses on Park Avenue in midtown can hardly be torn down fast enough to make way for a generation of glass-faced office towers. Lever House, the first of the new kids on the block, has opened to much fanfare. But the high-rise now speaks a different language. Corporate capitalism has been stripped bare, making an exhibition of high technology. The orna-mental individualism of the earlier buildings has given way to the aesthetics of rationalism. The syncopation between plan and elevation, the counterpoint between Manhattan's retic-ulated street grid and its exorbitant facades, has been disciplined. Architecture and urbanism are becoming almost one. The skyscraper has become an extrusion from the ground plane, the single building a metonym of the city. Midtown Manhattan is being transformed into a continuous monument.[2]

So too the urban imaginary is populated by a new cast of characters. Broadway's high-stepping girls with their fixed smiles and collective legs have exited the scene. Enter Business Man, a seemingly one-dimensional type whose attributes are conformism and alienation. The *flâneur* – protagonist of the pre-World War II city novel, personification of the metropolis – has all but disappeared. The man in the gray flannel suit, his successor, comes from greener pastures. "The gray flannel suit is the uniform of the man with a brief-case who leaves his home each morning to make his living as an executive in the near-by city."[3] If the noir films of the 1940s and 1950s obsessively retread the city's darker recesses in pursuit of its unreconstructed low-life, on the part of many writers and artists there is a turning inward, an "abandonment of the public world," of "politics, class, manners and mores, even the very feel of the streets."[4]

The proliferating glass blocks have their symbolic counterpart in the fast-rising developments in the suburbs. Lever House stands on one side of the schism that has opened between – literally – high and low architecture; on the other sprawls Levittown. In the first, triumphalism reigns. The "American Century" has dawned, and the standard bearer of the global ambitions of the United States is the International Style skyscraper.

In the second, in the white middle class households to whom the new suburban settlements are consecrated, the nesting instinct flourishes. Returning from battlefront to homefront, G.I. Joe resumes his anointed role as patriarch. "The fifties [are] a great period for home and family, for getting and spending, for cultivating one's garden." But the escape is illusory. "Behind [the suburb's] material growth hovers a quiet despair, whose symbols are the Bomb and the still-vivid death camps . . ."[5] Gathered around a new kind of hearth, the Cold War family internalizes its fears of annihilation, watching reports on the evening news of arms build-ups and communist subversion of "the American way of life." Consolation comes in the form of cheery political slogans and advertising messages. Eisenhower, personification of "determined optimism," runs his 1956 presidential campaign on the bromide, "Don't underestimate the value of a grin."[6] The sellers of consumer goods also know the power of positive thinking: "Confidence and spending are the handmaidens of an expanding economy."[7]

At first glance, the mass-produced suburban house with its picket fence, manicured lawn, and family car appears the antithesis of the strong silent types that are being erected in the city. But the "happy housewife" is as "upwardly mobile" as her husband; she aspires someday to be a "wife of management."[8] The facade of stability barely conceals the dynamic of development. The skyscraper and the suburb are opposite sides of the same coin – or the daily commute – indissolubly bound. "Both bear the stigmata of capitalism, both contain elements of change," Adorno wrote of the relationship between high modernism and mass culture. "They are torn halves of an integral freedom to which, however, they do not add up."[9]

Lever House, highwater mark of sophisticated midcentury urbanism, is the corporate headquarters of a company selling soap to the mass consumers forging a new life in post-war America.

II SOAP OPERA

Affixed to one of the stainless steel-clad columns in the ground-level plaza of Lever House is a plaque bearing the following statement:

> The mission of our company
> as William Hesketh Lever saw it
> is to make cleanliness commonplace
> to lessen work for women
> to foster health and
> contribute to personal attractiveness
> that life may be more enjoyable
> and rewarding for the people
> who use our products.

Designed in 1949–1952 by the firm of Skidmore, Owings & Merrill (S.O.M.) under the direction of Gordon Bunshaft, Lever House presented itself in its day as a monument

6.1 Lever House, 390 Park Avenue, New York City. Skidmore, Owings & Merrill, 1952. View from southeast side of Park Avenue. Photo: Ezra Stoller, © ESTO.

to benevolent corporate capitalism and post-war American modernism. Located on the west side of Park Avenue between 53rd and 54th Streets, it was built to house 1,200 company employees at a cost of six million dollars. The Italian architectural historian Manfredo Tafuri once extravagantly called it "the virtual manifesto of that impersonal and illusionless purism which makes the curtain wall the sole and silent element of the language." Standing in midtown Manhattan today, however, it does not immediately strike one as a polemical work.[10] Only twenty-four stories high and dwarfed by a later generation of megaliths, it appears something of a period piece. Amid the myriad imitations and variations up and down Park Avenue, three blocks west on Sixth Avenue, in Manhattan's financial district, in downtowns across the nation, and around the world, it hardly possesses the singularity and charm it had when once, as the first building on the avenue to turn its shoulder to the street wall, it appeared "a bright young child in a room full of dowagers."[11] The proportion of the building's two-story horizontal base to its vertical slab feels paltry (it does not benefit in this respect from comparisons to one of its far-flung progeny, the SAS Building in Copenhagen), and its shiny green-blue skin – the first heat- and glare-resistant tinted glazing to become available after the war (transparent glass having proved intolerable in buildings like Mies van der Rohe's Lake Shore Drive apartments in Chicago) – streaks and ripples in Manhattan's sunlight. The city fire code at the time prescribed that brick walls be built behind the glass to parapet height, a requirement that gives the building its striated appearance. Thus the actual amount of "vision glass" or transparency on Lever House's facades is not significantly greater than that on a standard masonry-clad building with punched-out windows. It has therefore been observed that the effect of the facades "is not [due to] structural honesty at all, but merely a modernist brand of ornament."[12] Because of extensive water infiltration and corrosion over the years, the curtain wall is today undergoing a costly twelve-million-dollar replacement.[13] The theory of the "remediation," under the direction of the current New York office of S.O.M., is replacement in kind – the building is to be restored to exactly its original appearance. The task is complicated by the obsolescence of the original technology. Yet as the public debates that took place over the authenticity of the restoration made clear, this once pioneering building has by now acquired an affectionate place in the collective memory. A decade after it was built, when the dreaded Pan Am Building was going up ten blocks south on Park Avenue, a cartoon appeared in the *New Yorker* with the caption, "It's a sad state of affairs when Lever House begins to seem like a warm old friend." Two decades later, Lever House was one of the first International Style buildings to be granted landmark status in Manhattan – ironically, the beneficiary of legislation enacted precisely to preserve the older buildings from the onslaught of modernist development.[14] No more a radical manifesto in the urban landscape, it has become a moment in the city's history.

Actually, what was most radical about Lever House in its day, at least from the local point of view, was not its curtain wall, but the decision to fill the site with less than one-third the allowable coverage. Whereas most office buildings were built as far out to property lines as the zoning regulations permitted – usually resulting in a stacked floor area about twenty times the area of the site – Lever House occupied only one-sixth. (Had it filled the whole site, it would have been only eight stories high.) The decision to sacrifice usable office area to other considerations was unprecedented in a city where "form follows finance" is axiomatic.[15] Lever House was virtually the first building to take advantage of a special provision in the ordinance that allowed an office tower that had a small footprint – 25 percent of the site or less – to rise from its base with no setbacks. The slim slab "floating" asymmetrically above the elevated horizontal pedestal gave the office floors maximum access to sunlight and views. Although the windows were inoperable because of air conditioning, Lever House conformed to office planning standards developed in the era of the Rockefeller Center, before the advent of sophisticated climate control systems and fluorescent lighting, when every desk had to be located within 25 feet of a window.

It was by virtue of its generous amenities rather than its glass rhetoric that the new building won over many of those who might have cried heresy. At street level, the roughly square horizontal pedestal, raised on *pilotis* and hollowed out in the center like a doughnut, cleared the ground plane for a skylit public court inset from the hubbub of the avenue and cross-streets, and a glazed lobby containing public exhibition space. The raised base also afforded a roof terrace at third-story level, which served as an outdoor recreational area for the company's employees, complete with shuffleboard court. Inside were an employees' lounge and an elegantly appointed cafeteria. The office floors, designed by Raymond Loewy for the building's mostly female workers, were notable for their variation in color from level to level, shading from "brisk yellows" and "delicate blues" to pink and lavender. While Lewis Mumford found the color scheme charming, the female critic for the *New York Times*, Aline Louchheim, found Loewy's decoration fussy and "chichi."[16] Both critics strongly objected to the executive suite, located on the top floor, which violated the building's otherwise modern and "democratic" atmosphere with its stuffy and pretentious furnishings. Yet overall the building was viewed as a stunning success. As Mumford noted, "Even the least-favored worker on the premises may enjoy the psychological lift of raising her eyes to the clouds or the skyscape of not too near-at-

6.2 Lever House. Office "landscape" by Raymond Loewy. Photo: Ezra Stoller, © ESTO.

hand adjoining buildings. I know of no other private or public edifice in the city that provides space of such quality for every worker."[17]

The owner of the building was Lever Brothers, a large international "fats and oils" cartel based in Great Britain and the Netherlands, founded in the 1880s by William Hesketh Lever. Lever had pioneered the idea of precutting bars of soap so that they could be packaged and sold individually. He had also built a company town, Port Sunlight, on the Mersey River in northwest England near Liverpool, begun in 1888, which combined model housing for his Sunlight soap factory workers with healthful and pleasant surroundings.[18] By midcentury, Lever Brothers was the purveyor of American household products like Lux, Lifebuoy, Surf, Rinso, Pepsodent toothpaste, and Good Luck margarine, and one of the largest corporations doing business in the United States. In 1946, 37-year-old Charles Luckman made the cover of *Time* magazine when the company named him head of their American operations. A Horatio Alger born in Kansas City, Missouri, Luckman was known as the "boy wonder." He not only had a sixth sense for advertising and publicity but also a degree in architecture from the University of Illinois. He had never practiced, however, having been diverted after graduation into a business career by the Depression. It was he who made the decision to relocate the company from its staid headquarters in Cambridge, Massachusetts, to Park Avenue, Manhattan. "New York is the inevitable answer to our major problem – selling," explained Luckman. "All advertising centers in New York, all show business except the movies. The platform from which to sell goods to America is New York."[19] Luckman also claimed credit for selecting the architects and for coming up with the bold concept of a glass slab inset from the site boundaries.[20] In 1950, however, a disagreement with the American subsidiary's parent company forced him to resign his position, so he did not get to see the building through. That job fell to his successor, Jervis J. Babb, who before coming to Lever Brothers had served as vice-president at the S.C. Johnson Company in Racine, Wisconsin. There Babb had been party to the building of another masterwork of modern architecture, the company's headquarters by Frank Lloyd Wright. Luckman, for his part, embarked on a new career after leaving Lever Brothers – as an architect. This had some further consequences for Manhattan's development, as will be seen presently.

A generation earlier, Wright had realized an office headquarters for yet another company in the soap business, the Larkin Building in Buffalo, which, with its sculptural massing, monumental skylit atrium, and totally designed interior furnishings, offered itself as a paragon of the enlightened white collar work place. Lever House now did the same, but in the vocabulary of light rather than heavy construction. As in the case of its predecessors, the generous amenities at Lever House were strongly motivated by the company's desire to fulfill its liberal mission. At the same time, the building's spectacularly modern image was not merely altruism. For one thing, as sole tenant, Lever Brothers did not have to be concerned with profits from rent. For another, Charles Luckman shrewdly appreciated the symbolic value of a high-profile headquarters on Park Avenue. The price of soap was 89 percent advertising. The advertising benefit to accrue from an all-glazed facade that could be publicly sudsed with the company's own detergent by a crew of window washers riding along the building in a specially designed gondola was inestimable. One thinks of a remark once made by the German philosopher Ernst Bloch, who decried the demise of the utopian and expressive impulse in post-war glass architecture. In the end, said Bloch, the major achievement of functionalist architecture was to give washability a face.[21] This Lever House literally did. As a latter-day link in the Glass Chain, it was a long way from the visionary dream that had animated the visionary schemes of early modernism. Yet its innovative solution to providing light, air, views, and public space in the midst of Manhattan's overwhelming urban congestion had indisputable virtue and practicality, vividly embodying the company's desire for an "American" building that was "clean, bright, colorful throughout."[22] The exploitation of the publicity value of glass architecture by the client and architect – a potential that avant-garde precursors like Erich Mendelsohn and Oscar Nitschke had certainly recognized earlier – in no way discounts an authentic civic gesture on the part of a powerful corporation.

How, then, did the strategy used at Lever House became a blueprint for so many poor and mean-spirited imitations? Mumford presciently anticipated this devolution in his otherwise laudatory review of the building, which appeared in his "Sky Line" column in the *New Yorker* at the time Lever House opened:

> Standing by itself, reflecting the nearby buildings in its mirror surface, Lever House presents a startling contrast to the old-fashioned buildings of Park Avenue. But if its planning innovations prove sound, it may become just one unit in a repeating pattern of buildings and open spaces.[23]

Paradoxically, the excellence of Lever House depended on its singularity rather than its implicit reproducibility. The "new doges of Park Avenue" that marked the street's passage from social aristocracy to "soap aristocracy" did not benefit by multiplication and could not sustain the original building's quality.[24] Lever House's reputation is owed precisely to its atypical circumstances – its historical priority, its owner's special program and enlightened aspirations, and not least the design talents of Bunshaft and his team. Once adapted from the meticulously planned headquarters for an owner occupant to the bottom-line economics of the speculative office tower, the universal language of the gridded glass frame and the bartering of civic amenity for verticality tended to degenerate into empty repetition and greedy skyscraping, banishing lingering traces of idealism. For the historian Vincent Scully, writing a decade later, Lever House's brilliant and brazen gesture was a misguided application of Le Corbusier's utopian planning theory to one of the few great avenues in America, and it ominously spelled "the death of the street."[25] In the wake of the post-modernist backlash, another critic would confirm this judgement:

> Lever House, erected in 1952, has to be considered the most *imitable*, if not the most influential post-war commercial building. But it is important to separate Lever House from its flush-glass progeny . . . The planning legacy of Lever House . . . is the now discredited tower-in-a-plaza building type that was incorporated into zoning codes throughout the country during the 1960s. As an interruption of a continuous street wall, Bunshaft's plaza seemed elegant when built. As a patchwork solution mindlessly applied anywhere, Modernist plazas now often read as chaotic urban intrusions.[26]

On the one hand, Lever House is a spectacular crystallization of the functionalist aesthetic into the exceptional, totally designed building. On the other, it represents a premonitory fragment of the city to come. The conflict that it embodies, however, is not so much between architecture and urbanism as between opposite visions of the city, and the gap between good intentions and the realities of capitalist development.

III THE ARCHITECTURE OF THE LIBERAL CONSENSUS

From the moment it was completed Lever House became one of the defining monuments of the post-war International Style. The latter appellation had been coined two decades earlier by Philip Johnson, Henry-Russell Hitchcock, and Alfred Barr, Jr., on the occasion of an exhibition of modern architecture at the Museum of Modern Art in New York. The European modern movement had not yet made deep inroads in the United States in the early 1930s, and the museum's initiative was both an introductory package designed to educate the taste of the American public and profession to the new European aesthetics, and at the same time a revisionist strategy intended to make an architecture rooted in the social ideologies of Europe "safe for capitalism," as Colin Rowe later put it (Catherine Bauer said at the time, "safe for millionaires").[27] Among the array of building types presented at the 1932 exhibition, the four masters who were featured in the main gallery – Le Corbusier, Ludwig Mies van der Rohe, J.J.P. Oud, and Frank Lloyd Wright – were all represented by luxury villas rather than by the more utilitarian and collective type of housing with which the modern movement had been previously more identified. The curators harbored an ambivalent attitude toward the skyscraper, and had doubts with respect to the one New York architect included in the show, Raymond Hood. Skyscrapers like Hood's McGraw-Hill Building, a hybrid of Art Deco and functionalist impulses, verged on being "modernistic" rather than modern – not altogether pure enough for the brahmin taste of Johnson (at least at this time) and his colleagues.

The aesthetic tenets proselytized by the exhibition and disseminated by its accompanying publications were soon reinforced by the prominent European architects who streamed into the United States throughout the 1930s and early 1940s in flight from European fascism. Among the most influential were the Bauhaus masters Walter Gropius and Mies van der Rohe. Welcomed by the American professional and academic establishment, they set up shop at Harvard University and Illinois Institute of Technology in Chicago respectively. But if the International Style was a European import to the United States in the 1930s, within little more than a decade it became an American export with major new dimensions and features.

Emerging victorious from World War II, the United States was now in a position to shore up its military and political triumph with a bid for cultural hegemony as well. Popular taste, which had clung to more traditional imagery through the late 1930s (not precluding, however, romantic visions of a futuristic "world of tomorrow"), converted virtually overnight to modernism as functionalist aesthetics became associated with the rational planning and technology that had won the war. "Mechanization took command" of the imagination, to evoke the title of a book published in 1948 by the Swiss architectural historian Siegfried Giedion.[28] A decade earlier Giedion had described modern architecture as an embodiment of the *Zeitgeist* of Einsteinian space-time; now, sitting out the war years in the United States, he discovered an alternative genealogy for architectural modernity in the anonymous history of American technological ingenuity and invention. The war years also elicited a new polemic by Giedion. Together with two other wartime refugees in New York, the Spanish architect-planner José Luis Sert and the French painter Fernand Léger, he called for a "new monumentality" in architecture and the plastic arts.[29] Modern buildings, they argued, needed to be infused with a new civic and structural grandeur, transforming the earlier European mindset of rationally planned minimums into a more expressive Esperanto, one that emblematized the spirit of the incipient *pax Americana*. Such a symbiosis between European aesthetics and American triumphalist culture was heralded by wartime exhibitions like *Road to Victory* (1942) and *Airways to Peace* (1943), both held at the Museum of Modern Art in cooperation with the US Office of War Information and designed by another Bauhaus emigré, Herbert Bayer.

The decision immediately after the war to locate the United Nations headquarters in New York City, a result of John D. Rockefeller, Jr.'s largesse in donating to the world's new flagship institution a 17-acre site along Manhattan's East River between 42nd and 48th Street, bolstered New York's ambitions as the political, financial, and cultural capital of the post-war world. The Swiss-French architect Le Corbusier, who had harbored a love-hate relationship with New York City since his first visit in 1935 when he famously pronounced its skyscrapers "too small," and who longed to implant a piece of his Ville Radieuse on the North American continent, proclaimed, "A Cartesian hour has struck."[30] Despite his unquestionably greater talents, however, Le Corbusier was passed over in favor of the American architect Wallace Harrison. Harrison was purportedly chosen to head the international design team entrusted with the commission because he had technical "know-how" with respect to large-scale construction in New York City, having previously worked on the design of the Rockefeller Center. He also had diplomatic skills that Le Corbusier sorely lacked, and happened to be related by marriage to the Rockefellers (a nepotism Le Corbusier did not fail to denounce bitterly). But above all it was clear that the architect of a symbolic building like the United Nations had, at this stage of history, to be an American.

It was also clear that the choice signaled the ascendancy of a new type of architectural production. In an article entitled "The Architecture of Bureaucracy and the

Architecture of Genius," published in 1947, Henry-Russell Hitchcock identified two opposite categories of architecture that he saw as coexisting in the United States at mid-century.[31] One was bureaucratic architecture, which he defined as "all building that is the product of large-scale architectural organizations, from which personal expression is absent." He specifically noted that he was using the term *bureaucratic* "without the pejorative connotation." Indeed, Hitchcock stated, "Bureaucratic architecture can achieve in experienced hands a high level of amenity." As an example he cited the firm of Albert Kahn in Detroit, architects of factory buildings like the world-renowned Ford plant at River Rouge, which depended "not on the genius of one man . . . but in the organizational genius which can establish a fool-proof system of rapid and complete plan production."

Hitchcock's second category, on the other hand, referred to "a particular psychological approach and way of working at architecture which may or may not produce masterpieces." The qualities of genius architecture "depend on overall impact, just as the qualities of the more intensely expressive types of art such as poetry or painting or music do." Hitchcock viewed this type of architecture as an "artistic gamble," as likely to fail as to succeed. Although he acknowledged that "the world of the mid-twentieth century will need some buildings by architects of genius, for only thus can the necessary monotony and the low level of plastic interest of bureaucratic architecture be balanced and relieved" – in particular when it came to "focal structures" like public monuments – he also warned that, in the hands of lesser architects or applied to large and complex projects, the architecture of genius could easily lead to "pretentious absurdity." Predicting that in the foreseeable future the emphasis would more likely be on the anonymous architecture of bureaucracy than on genius, he cited as the two supreme and exceptional figures epitomizing the latter tendency Le Corbusier and Frank Lloyd Wright, whose *Unité d'Habitation* in Marseilles and the Guggenheim museum respectively (neither yet realized at this date) provided ample evidence of the fertility of the modern architectural imagination in the hands of masters. Significantly, Hitchcock did not mention Mies van der Rohe in his article, a point to which we shall return.

Not surprisingly, Hitchcock's argument elicited strong antagonism from Wright. Wright's antipathy toward both the capitalist metropolis and the standard skyscraper did not endear him to New York's "boxment" establishment, nor they to him. His own relatively rare high-rise projects – like his cantilevered St. Marks tower (1929) – represent a conscious critique of the normative frame structure. In his book *Genius and the Mobocracy*, published in 1949, a belated tribute to his *lieber Meister* Louis Sullivan, Wright ranted, "The great master? Well, by now he is done. He is dead . . . Nevertheless we are not through with him. Mobocratic 'art' having a chronic bad conscience, if any, is more than ever likely to join the popular tendency to mob the tribe up by mobbing the master down." In a chapter entitled "Incapable of Conception They Are Masters of Appropriation," he branded the standardized architecture of the "code-made and code-making expert" an inauthentic "technical makeshift."[32] In 1952, in a lecture before the American Institute of Architects, he disparaged Lever House as a "box on sticks."[33]

Despite the fulminations of two of modern architecture's still active masters, though, the Americanized image of the International Style that became dominant both in the United States and abroad by the early 1950s with the completion of the United Nations and Lever House was that of the tall glass office building, emblem of a powerful bureaucratic and technical rationalism. Mumford, watching the United Nations going up on the urban sky-line, acknowledged that the complex indeed had a new monumentality, but all the wrong symbolism:

> [I]t was a mistake to make the Secretariat Building the monumental, dominant structure instead of the General Assembly Hall and the Conference Building, which should be the focus of visual interest as well as the symbol of political authority. If the Secretariat Building will have anything to say as a symbol, it will be, I fear, that the managerial revolution has taken place and that bureaucracy rules the world.[34]

It is illuminating to compare the triumph of this form of American architectural culture to the contemporaneous success in the art world of Abstract Expressionist painting. In a revisionist account of the ascent of the "New York School" after World War II, the Canadian art historian Serge Guilbaut has argued that the epicenter of the art world shifted from Paris to Manhattan during the late 1940s and 1950s not solely because American painting was inherently superior in quality to what was being produced in Europe at this date – as American art critics like Clement Greenberg and others claimed at the time – but also because the style's non-representational and bravura aesthetic, exemplified by the drip paintings of Jackson Pollock and the gestural calligraphy of Franz Kline, was consonant with the ideology of American Cold War culture.[35] No longer inflected by the explicit social commentary that had characterized American art in the 1930s, and antithetical to the socialist realism being promulgated as the style of state in the Soviet bloc in the 1940s and early 1950s, the expansive painterly surfaces seemingly stood only for the art and act of painting itself. They thus served to project an image that was "powerful, abstract, modernist, and American."[36] As such, Abstract Expressionism succeeded in attracting the institutional backing of the Museum of Modern Art as well as, eventually, those in the American government seeking a cultural expression that could be aligned with the "vital center" of American political life.

In a broader context, as the historian Godfrey Hodgson has suggested, what the American government required of its professional elites after World War II was "a maximum of technical ingenuity with a minimum of dissent."[37] In an essay entitled "The Ideology of the Liberal Consensus," Hodgson characterizes the mentality that prevailed among American intellectuals during this period as a new "conservative liberalism":

> The Left, in short, had by the late 1950s virtually ceased to count in American political life. But this fateful eclipse was masked by the triumph of the liberals.
>
> To draw a distinction between the Left and the liberals may sound sectarian or obscure. It is not. It is vital to understanding American politics in the age of the consensus . . . What I mean by the "Left" is any broad, organized political force holding as a principle the need for far-reaching social and institutional change and consistently upholding the interests of the disadvantaged against the most powerful groups in the society. The liberals were never such a force.
>
> What I mean by the liberals is those who subscribed to the ideology . . . that American capitalism was a revolutionary force for social change, that economic growth was supremely good because it obviated the need for redistribution and social conflict, that class

had no place in American politics. Not only are those not the ideas of the Left; at the theoretical level, they provide a sophisticated rationale for avoiding fundamental change . . .

[I]n the very parts of American society that might have been expected to hold out as the bastions of the Left, the liberals had triumphed. Organized labor, the intelligentsia, and the universities had become the citadels of what was in effect a conservative liberalism.[38]

This description may be applied to the architecture of the post-war International Style as well. Having been "safely" depoliticized by the Museum of Modern Art in 1932, modern architecture was now poised to become a product of the American conservative-liberal establishment. Like the contemporary tendency in painting, it largely relinquished its earlier reformist aspirations for a new technical and aesthetic competence. It is hardly surprising that its defining program was no longer social housing or the factory, as in the earlier phase of modernism, but the commercial office tower, beacon and bulwark of American big business. Closely related was the embassy building, flagstaff of United States ideology abroad, likewise acquiring its definitive architectural expression during the 1950s. "If we consider at random some of our most successful American buildings," as one critic of the period wrote with regard to Lever House and other exemplars of the new glass architecture, "we are confronted with compositions with which the cultivated taste cannot quarrel. But . . . [t]hese buildings must constitute, short of the pyramids, the most noncommittal body of architecture in history."[39] Although the point cannot be further elaborated here, it may be suggested that the New York "schools" of painting and architecture were parallel phenomena. Notwithstanding their temperamental extremes – one associated with "hot" strokes of individual artistic genius, the other with the coldly calculated grids of the bureaucratic design firm – both were virile, non-representational aesthetics that fit the bill of *technical virtuosity with a minimum of dissent*. They represented alternative answers to the post-war demand for a distinctively American modernism.

Thus, while ostensibly inspired by European aesthetic conceptions of the interwar period, the suavely sophisticated architecture built in post-war America became an exposition of structural mastery pushed to the point of exhibitionism. The new economic realities of post-war technology offered architects a kit of parts capable of endless variations, the basis of a new, universalizable language. As early as 1950, the Museum of Modern Art staged an exhibition of recent buildings by Skidmore, Owings & Merrill. Lever House, still on the drafting table at the time, was displayed in model form. The museum stated its rationale for the exhibition:

When a museum exhibits a painting, a piece of sculpture, an architectural drawing or model, the first question in the minds of both the staff and the public is "who is the painter, the sculptor, or the architect who designed it?" In the past, all of the architectural shows the Museum of Modern Art has exhibited have been designer's shows – the work of individuals like Le Corbusier, Ludwig Mies van der Rohe, Frank Lloyd Wright . . .

When the Museum invited Skidmore, Owings and Merrill to exhibit its recent buildings, it did so because this firm, composed of a group of single designers working exclusively in the modern idiom, produces imaginative, serviceable and sophisticated architecture deserving of special attention. The single designers who function within this organization have no fear of a loss of individuality. They are able to work within their corporate framework because they understand and employ the vocabulary and grammar which developed from the esthetic conceptions of the twenties. They work together animated by two disciplines which they all share – the discipline of modern architecture and the discipline of American organizational methods.[40]

Thus, however syllogistically, the museum linked the formal rationalism of the modern movement with the bureaucratic rationalism of American big business. While in the 1932 exhibition modernism had been conjoined with American capitalism only by a negative logic – that is, by being disembarrassed of its ideological origins in European economy and politics – now the two were brought together in a positive new relationship, once again authorized by America's most powerful modern art institution and arbiter of taste.

A rather precise gauge of the changing international reception of the new American architecture is afforded by two special issues of the leading British architectural magazine of the day, the *Architectural Review*. Ever since the war years, Britain's foremost journal of architectural tendency had been proselytizing an empirical, picturesque, and domesticated version of modernism modeled on Scandinavian architecture – in particular, that of Sweden, which, having remained neutral during the war, had been building in a non-doctrinaire modern idiom since the 1930s. In 1950, the same year as the S.O.M. exhibition at the Museum of Modern Art, the *Architectural Review* published a special issue devoted to "the mess that is man made America." In it, the editors vigorously condemned the products of American technocracy and consumerism, then finding their way to the Western bloc countries under the auspices of the Marshall Plan, as deadly materialistic threats to Western humanist culture.[41]

Within seven years, however, the journal would completely reverse its position. In an issue of 1957 entitled "Machine Made America," it celebrated American technical achievement as an object of desire and emulation. An Arcimboldo-like robot head by the Independent Group artist John McHale appeared on the cover – a proto-Pop photomontage of spark plugs, cake mixes, parkways, and television sets – while inside, extensive coverage was given to an up-and-coming generation of American architects from S.O.M. to I.M. Pei. Above all, the 1957*Review* attached importance to the curtain wall in architecture's future development. The editors suggested that the replicative glass facades had the potential to act as a "new vernacular," a universal language that could bring aesthetic discipline to an eclectic building practice and chaotic landscape. The editors noted that the curtain wall had achieved a separate category in *Sweet's Catalogue* for the first time in 1956. "An age or a nation may or may not produce its geniuses," they stated, "there is nothing you can do about it, but if the average man is left without terms of reference, codes of practice, vocabulary or pattern book, he flounders . . . The curtain wall is the first sign of such a discipline presenting itself to modern architecture and being generally accepted."[42] The next forty pages of the journal contained a detailed album of American curtain wall construction, surveyed historically, syntactically, and typologically.

If for the "man in the street" – a mythic figure who still preoccupied the liberal imagination (more in the spirit of the "century of the common man" than that of the "American century," however[43]) – the proliferation of an architecture without qualities augmented the perception in the 1950s of an alienating and one-dimensional environment, for many architects the notion of the curtain wall as a common coin, a "discipline" that would make it harder to build bad buildings, was persuasive. Beyond this, for some, the glass and steel city was tantamount to a new urban sublime, a magical, almost science-fiction embodiment of late-capitalist production and society. In their "Letter to America," written after a first trip to New York, the British architects Alison and Peter Smithson quibbled with the use of the term *vernacular,* but they embraced the idea:

> . . . although the application of curtain-walls cannot be called a vernacular (as that implies a language), buildings which use them are undoubtedly better than they would have been if their architects had had to develop a brick and stone facade of their own. Glass and metal faced buildings give the maximum light reflection into the street and this in itself is a contribution to the city. And there are, moreover, magical distortions when two straight-up-and-down buildings are opposite one another. A blue glass city, no matter how organisationally banal, is never optically boring.[44]

By 1958, when the Smithsons wrote this, Lever House had spawned more than half a dozen variations up and down Park Avenue. These ranged from the undistinguished 25-story Colgate-Palmolive Building three blocks south, built by the firm of Emery Roth & Sons for

6.3 Cover of *Astounding Science Fiction*, November 1953, with view of United Nations.

6.4 View up east side of Park Avenue from 47th Street, 1971. *Right to left*: 245 Park Avenue, Shreve, Lamb & Harmon, 1967; 277 Park Avenue, Emery Roth & Sons, 1958–1964; 299 Park Avenue, Emery Roth & Sons, 1965–1967. Photo: Office for Metropolitan History, New York.

one of Lever Brothers' major competitors, to the equally undistinguished 32-story Davies Building at 57th Street, by the same firm. The major innovation that the latter building could claim was that its prefabricated aluminum-panel curtain wall had been erected in fourteen hours. While S.O.M. catered to the most prestigious clients in town, Roth was the firm that increasingly built the "bread and butter vernacular" skyscrapers that would ultimately transform the look of midcentury Manhattan. As the critic Ada Louise Huxtable put it in 1967, the Roths' ubiquitous glass-and-metal boxes made them "as responsible for the face of modern New York as Sixtus V was for baroque Rome."[45]

As such, the Smithsons' enthusiastic response to an architecture of "organizational banality" is somewhat paradoxical, especially in light of the fact that the staunch commitment to modern architecture of these two architects was matched only by their passionate championing of the values of "urban reidentification," cohesive "patterns of human association," and a vital, communal street life. Yet the contradiction goes to show the disparities of reception that could exist among different taste cultures with respect to the aesthetics of the new architecture. Or perhaps it was the exotic allure of midtown Manhattan to a first foreign view. Clearly the "blue glass city" took on different coloration when seen from the perspective of an airplane arriving from abroad, an executive suite atop a skyscraper, or the subway stops delivering up their daily load of commuters at Grand Central Station and along 53rd Street.[46]

There was, however, one new building, completed in 1958, that added a different, more poetic dimension to the International Style city. As the Smithsons themselves noted,

Seagram, in cool bronze, makes everything else look like a jumped-up supermart.[47]

IV HIGH MODERNISM ALONG THE 53rd STREET CORRIDOR

It is more than a matter of good camera angles that the classic photographs of Lever House are taken from the Seagram Building, and those of Seagram are taken from Lever House. For the urban conversation between these two monuments diagonally opposite each other on Park Avenue and built a few years apart is as articulate as that which takes place between, say, the Doges Palace and the Procuratie Vecchie on the Piazza San Marco in Venice. Designed by Mies van der Rohe with the collaboration of Philip Johnson and the firm of Kahn and Jacobs and completed in 1958, Seagram stands on the east side of the avenue between 52nd and 53rd Streets. The circumstances of the commission were well publicized. Samuel Bronfman, a Canadian distiller who acquired Joseph E. Seagram & Sons in 1927, having made his fortune during Prohibition, did not necessarily set out to beautify New York, as one writer has put it, when in 1954 he announced plans to build a corporate headquarters on the blockfront site. But he apparently did have it in mind that the new "Seagram House" should give Lever House a run for its money. Accordingly, he hired Charles Luckman – who by this time had reconstituted himself as a principal of the architecture firm of Pereira and Luckman – to design the building. When Luckman produced a model for a vertically accented shaft of dark glass and marble sitting symmetrically atop a heavy four-story base – resembling more than anything else the

6.5 Seagram Building, 375 Park Avenue, New York City. Ludwig Mies van der Rohe, Philip Johnson, and Kahn & Jacobs. 1958. View looking southeast from Lever House. Photo: Ezra Stoller, © ESTO.

6.6 Seagram Building. View looking west to Racquet and Tennis Club by McKim, Mead & White, 1916. Photo: Ezra Stoller, © ESTO.

packaging for a whiskey bottle – Bronfman's daughter, Phyllis Lambert, trained in art history at Vassar, interceded. After consulting Philip Johnson in the architecture department of the Museum of Modern Art, she prevailed on her father to engage Mies van der Rohe to redesign the building.[48] Thirty-six million dollars later, the German architect's first major office building was completed. While Lever House would have been unthinkable without the precedent of Mies's post-war glass buildings in Chicago, from Illinois Institute of Technology to the Lake Shore Drive apartments, Seagram is a very different type of urban conception from Lever House, an observation that becomes all the more striking when one studies the two together.

Indeed, the 35-story Seagram has no real precursors except in Mies's own œuvre. And if we go back to his visionary projects of 1921–1922 for glass skyscrapers, we become aware of important similarities and differences. Separated in his career by more than three decades, the respective skyscrapers share an aspiration to the sublime, polemically asserting the transcendent role of architecture in the city. At the same time, the crystalline openness and expressionist lyricism of the earlier projects are superseded by Seagram's austere decorum. Urbanistically, in fact, Seagram is pure classicism, and the point is the more apparent relative to Lever House. The relationship Seagram establishes with McKim, Mead & White's 1916 Beaux-Arts Racquet and Tennis Club directly across the avenue could hardly be more dignified and urbane. Mies painstakingly reclaims the horizontality of the plaza on the building's sloping site, making it function as a classical plinth, and centering his noble glass portal axially on that of the racquet club for an extended dialog. Lever House, on the other hand, barely acknowledges its classical neighbor or any other aspect of the surrounding context, except in the sense of offering a maximum contrast. Unlike Seagram, the ground plane at Lever House ramps awkwardly in tandem with the avenue, and the entrance to the lobby, despite its function as a public exhibition space, is minimally expressed.

If Lever House is only inadvertently monumental, every element of Seagram is deliberately put in the service of classical grandeur. Seagram's vertically striated – as if "fluted" – square columns are set out almost to the edges of the slab, further stabilizing the building against the flux of the city. At Lever House, the columns are thinner and inset, allowing the street to flow through. At Seagram, the vertically attenuated I-beam profiles welded to the curtain wall are spaced at narrow intervals, lending the facade something of the depth and scale of a pilaster wall. At Lever House, the metal frame is almost flush with the glass, and the vertical rectangles of the windows are "democratically" balanced by the horizontal striation created by the internal parapets. If Lever House projects a clean and shiny image of advertising, Seagram's rich, dark, and expensive palette – the materials are bronze, travertine marble, and topaz-tinted glass – exudes patrician exclusivity. Tafuri famously characterized Seagram as glacially "aloof" and "tragically" "self-aware" of its own separateness from the city.[49] In my view, this interpretation is excessive, more a reflection of the Italian critic's politics than those of Mies. While the building steps back from the avenue almost 90 feet to the eastern half of its formal plaza to maintain its distance, it does so more as a gesture of noblesse oblige with respect to the unruly element of the street than as an act of "critical resistance." The effect is more Medici than Marxian.

Indeed, for all the vaunted minimalism of its architect, Seagram is an extravagant building, down to its custom-designed mail chutes, fire alarms, and bathroom fittings. As Hitchcock quipped, there never was more of less.[50] Mumford called it the "Rolls Royce" of contemporary buildings.[51] With Seagram, Mies not only gave the *Zeitgeist* of modern technology an ahistorical timelessness, but "improved" upon it with his choice of materials and treatment of details. Even while insisting on speaking of *Baukunst* rather than architecture, he thus preserved an elite role for the discipline. Significantly, Seagram's magisterial discourse of "quality" is analogous to the one that was at this very same time being enshrined three blocks west in the galleries of the Museum of Modern Art. Nor is it an accident that Philip Johnson – who also designed the *luxe* Four Seasons restaurant in the building – played an instrumental role on both ends of the 53rd Street corridor.[52]

Hitchcock, as noted earlier, omitted Mies from his article on bureaucracy and genius. I would suggest that this was because he didn't fit either category. Unlike Wright, Mies willingly took the new vernacular of the standard curtain wall as a given, or at least a point of departure. However, he pushed it to such a point of rarefaction that it exceeded its banal origins to become high art. In this sense, Mies may be said to be the high priest, the genius, of bureaucracy.

V BRAVE NEW LIFEWORLD

At the time Seagram opened not many people knew that it was one of the few buildings in New York City to incorporate a bomb shelter. The following year, designs were submitted to the city by a New York engineering firm for twenty-five fallout "shelter groups" around Manhattan to house the city's four million daily residents, workers, and visitors. Each group of shelters was designed to accommodate 160,000 people for up to 90 days. The facilities, like the one designed for Bryant Park behind the New York Public Library, would have been sunk 800 feet below street level and reached by steel ramps, chutes, and elevators or rock conveyors.[53] Seven years earlier Mumford had concluded his review of Lever House on a determinedly upbeat (or wishful) note: "Fragile, exquisite, undaunted by the threat of being melted into a puddle by an atomic bomb, this building is a laughing refutation of 'imperialist warmongering,' and so becomes an implicit symbol of hope for a peaceful world."[54] Undeniably there was an Orwellian dimension to the new glass architecture, rising in defiance of a Cold War apocalypse.

Less apocalyptic, perhaps, but more immediate was the impact of the new urban landscape on everyday life. Sociologists and popular writers wrung their hands about the gray-flannel culture of the organization man.[55] Philosopher Herbert Marcuse diagnosed the pathology of "institutionalized desublimation" that was engendering this new "one-dimensional" personality. Instead of encouraging the liberating forms of resistance or opposition by which individuals counteract a repressive reality – a role historically played by both avant-garde art and eroticism, for example – the highly technological and administered environment embodied in the new corporate urbanism diminished the need for such sublimation. According to the emigré Frankfurt School thinker, it did so by providing conveniences and freedoms that "satisfied" individuals' desires at a much lower level, thereby weakening their appetite for protest and seducing them into submission and compliance:

> The new technological work-world thus enforces a weakening of the negative position of the working class: the latter no longer appears to be the living contradiction to the established society. This trend is strengthened by the effect of the technological organization of production on the other side of the fence: on management and direction. Domination is transfigured into administration. The capitalist bosses and owners are losing their identity as responsible agents; they are assuming the function of bureaucrats in a corporate machine. Within the vast hierarchy of executive and managerial boards extending far beyond the individual establishment into the scientific laboratory and research institute, the national government and national purpose, the tangible source of exploitation disappears behind the facade of objective rationality. Hatred and frustration are deprived of their specific target, and the technological veil conceals the reproduction of inequality and enslavement. With technical progress as its instrument, unfreedom – in the sense of man's subjection to his productive apparatus – is perpetuated and intensified in the form of many liberties and comforts. The novel feature is the overwhelming rationality in this irrational enterprise . . . [But nothing changes] the fact that the decisions over life and death, over personal and national security are made at places over which the individuals have no control.[56]

6.7 Manufacturers' Trust Company (now Chase) Fifth Avenue Branch Bank, New York City. Skidmore, Owings & Merrill, 1954. View of vault door through facade. Photo: Ezra Stoller, © ESTO.

According to this theory, an architecture of extreme technical rationalism, however benevolent its intentions, only intensified the individual's loss of agency and free will. To trade the possibility of dissent for a merely technical improvement in the quality of the work environment was thus to enter a Faustian bargain. As Peter Madsen has written, citing Hans-Georg Gadamer, "The counterconcept to the concept of the lifeworld 'is without doubt the world of science'."[57]

Yet it was a book published in 1961 by Jane Jacobs, *The Death and Life of Great American Cities*, that most concretely and persuasively connected the critique of a technocratic society to the malaise of everyday urban life as perceived from the perspective of the man and woman on the street. Pointing to the stretch of new office buildings along Park Avenue between Grand Central Station and 59th Street, she noted that, despite their intensive daytime use, they went "ominously dead at night." This was a result of the rapacious redevelopment that had made commercial real estate on Park Avenue far more valuable than any other kind, driving out residential tenants and mixed uses. Moreover, from a psychological and aesthetic point of view, the effect of such de facto zoning was not coherence, in Jacobs' opinion, but a deadly and disorienting uniformity. Rather than making the city more rational, such architecture only accentuated its overall lack of intentionality:

> The new office stretch of New York's Park Avenue is far more standardized in content than Fifth Avenue. Park Avenue has the advantage of containing among its new office buildings several which, in themselves, are masterpieces of modern design (Lever House, Seagram, Pepsi-Cola, Union Carbide). But does homogeneity of use or homogeneity of age help Park Avenue esthetically? On the contrary, the office blocks of Park Avenue are wretchedly disorganized in appearance, and far more given than Fifth Avenue to a total effect of chaotic architectural willfulness, overlaid on boredom.[58]

The seeds sown on Park Avenue would soon be reaped on Sixth Avenue. Here Manhattan's "culture of congestion" would reach such a point of banality that even its later celebrant, Rem Koolhaas, would acknowledge that here "Manhattanism" had been "unlearned."[59]

VI APOLLONIAN MELTDOWN

But let us return to Park Avenue for the dénouement of the present story. If Mies succeeded at Seagram in transforming the commercial glass skyscraper back into an auratic artwork, the Pan Am Building, designed by Walter Gropius in association with Pietro Belluschi and Emery Roth & Sons and completed in 1963, represents a complete inversion, as it were, of Seagram's transcendence. It may thus serve as the third variation on our theme of the International Style city and the final act in a historically definitive *pas de trois* on Park Avenue. While both Lever House and Seagram effectively negotiated new and – in their different ways – radical relationships with the preexisting urban context,

6.8 Pan Am (now MetLife) Building, 200 Park Avenue, New York City. Walter Gropius, Pietro Belluschi, and Emery Roth & Sons, 1963. Photo: Joseph Molitor. Courtesy of Avery Architectural and Fine Arts Library, Columbia University in the City of New York.

6.9 *Proposed Colossal Monument for Park Avenue, New York City: Good Humor Bar.* Claes Oldenburg, 1965. Collection Donna and Carroll Janis.

the building by Gropius and his collaborators succeeded primarily in blocking the axis of the avenue visually, creating a building that functions urbanistically as a giant obstacle. Striving to dominate its site, it is unable to liberate itself from the urban fabric. The sculptor Claes Oldenburg travestied the building as a melting Good Humor ice cream bar.[60] It is not necessary to repeat here the reasons for the decision to erect a gigantic building straddling Park Avenue just north of Grand Central Terminal, at the heart of one of the most congested four-block areas anywhere in the world, except to say that the air rights were very valuable, that they were owned by railroads in desperate need of income at a moment when train travel in the United States had been dealt a fatal blow by the automobile, and that the site was extremely tricky as a result of layers of underground trackage and infrastructure.[61] In the end, the utopia of modern architecture met the reality of urban development. Development won.

That Gropius, for over four decades the preeminent spokesman on behalf of the heroic mythos of modern architecture, completed a kind of epic degeneration with this building was evident in the early 1960s to most New Yorkers and even the most stalwart modernists. At fifty-nine stories and a cost of a hundred million dollars, it contained over two million square feet of office space, making it the largest commercial office building in the world at the time. Bearing the name of the airline company that was its major tenant in supergraphics at the cornice line, it also romanced the sky with its rooftop heliport (which subsequently was taken out of service after a fatal accident). But only the most perverse tastes – *pace* Koolhaas – would persist in celebrating it for its bigness. The flattened octagonal slab represents a thorough misappropriation of Le Corbusier's Algiers skyscraper, the principal prototype on which it is based. Amputating the Corbusian slab at kneecap, turning it north-south while making the fenestration pattern uniform (in contrast to Le Corbusier's highly modulated brise-soleil), hanging heavy concrete panels on what ought to be a buoyant and dematerialized volume, and wedging it into an impossibly dense site – all this exposed the colossal hubris of latter-day modernism and the tiredness of Gropius's pieties, which he would rehearse one last time in his book *Apollo in the Democracy: The Cultural Obligations of the Architect* (1968).

Nor was this the end of brutal International Style assaults on the same site. The ultimate morphing of Apollonian rationality into Dionysian delirium threatened to occur five years later, in 1968, when Marcel Breuer, Gropius's former collaborator and Bauhaus compatriot, was retained to design a building filling the air space directly above Grand Central Station, just south of the Pan Am Building and parallel to it in orientation. Breuer proposed to erect a 55-story concrete-and-granite slab that would "float" atop the terminal, now asked to do double duty as a skyscraper podium. The pastiche quality of Breuer's project was so strong that it could easily have been a work of Pop art – especially given the date – were it not that the architect was dead serious. The *New York Times* said the project "had the bizarre quality of a nightmare." The public outcry against what it perceived as a mortal threat to Grand Central's Beaux-Arts integrity was quick, galvanized not only by loathing for Pan Am but by a new preservation movement that had coalesced in Manhattan in belated response to the demolition of the city's other beloved monumental rail terminal, Pennsylvania Station. The latter was knocked down to build yet another behemoth of overwhelming mediocrity, Madison Square Garden and Two Penn

6.10 Proposal for 175 Park Avenue, above Grand Central Terminal. Marcel Breuer, 1968.

Plaza, completed in 1963, the same year as Pan Am. The architect of the complex was none other than the boy wonder of Lever Brothers, Charles Luckman. Among those who emerged as leaders in the nascent preservation movement rallying around Grand Central Station were such prominent New Yorkers as Philip Johnson and Jacqueline Kennedy Onassis. Incredibly, however, it was not until 1978 that plans to build Breuer's slab were finally scrapped after the railroad exhausted its appeals against the New York City Landmarks Preservation Commission in a battle fought all the way up to the United States Supreme Court.

By this time, of course, much water had flowed over the dam, and a different style was beginning to leave its mark on the city. A new urbanism paying lip service to history and context, strongly inspired by Jane Jacobs's passionate polemic, was in the ascendant, eclipsing the impositions of a now discredited International Style. It would be epitomized by Johnson's Chippendale-roofed AT&T Building one block west on Madison Avenue. In retrospect, Pan Am seems as much to herald the post-modern phase of "collage city" as to mark the end of the generation of Lever House.

VII EPILOGUE: INSTANT CITIES

The powerful, even sublime experience of the late capitalist city and the International Style ideology that underwrote it exerted a major influence around the world, even in places where local development and technology still lagged well behind. The adoption of the

6.11 SAS Building, Hammerichsgade 1–5, Copenhagen. Arne Jacobsen, 1961. Photo: Bruno Balestrini, Milan.

International Style not on the basis of similar technological and economic preconditions but rather as a cultural phenomenon and showpiece caused American-looking buildings to crop up in places as remote geographically and culturally as Caracas and Copenhagen.[62] This "groundless" process of dissemination and transfer was accelerated by the proliferation of architectural journals and publications, international exhibitions, travel, and educational exchanges. In the case of the "Caracas Lever House," for example – the Polar Building (1952–1954), by Vegas and Galia – one of the architects, Martin Vegas, had been a student of Mies van der Rohe at Illinois Institute of Technology. In view of these dynamics, it is hardly surprising that some of these recyclings had a certain "strangeness," even when based on firsthand knowledge. The phenomenon of a reproduction that precedes production – of an architecture that appears to be the product of a new mode of construction, but is more a symbolic token of that construction – is symptomatic of the economics of uneven development. As such it is increasingly familiar in the global context of today's "generic" cities (as witness the Southeast Asian cities where American-style skyscrapers cropped up virtually overnight in the 1980s and early 1990s). The complex questions raised by this phenomenon with regard to notions of authenticity, community, and lived experience inevitably go to the very heart of any discussion of the urban life-world.[63]

In the case of Copenhagen, the SAS Building, designed by the Danish architect Arne Jacobsen in 1958–1961 as an air terminal and hotel, represents one of the most sophisticated yet decontextualized reproductions of the style of New York ever built on foreign soil. It seems rather appropriate that Scandinavia's national airline should have been the client for Jacobsen's first high-rise project in the International Style.[64] Located diagonally across from Tivoli Gardens and set back on its podium from the high-traffic thoroughfare of Vesterbrogade, SAS is a highly original – in many respects more elegant – variation on the base-and-tower *parti* of Lever House. Yet even today the metallic gray-green 22-story building, which fades into the clouds on overcast days, retains a certain hallucinatory presence on the low-rise skyline of the Danish city. This is so even if a number of other modern office buildings are also to be found in this sector of town.[65] In Jacobsen's hands, the International Style becomes a kind of commentary on itself. Inside, the glamorous, almost Hollywood interiors, designed by the architect down to the glassware and hanging orchid holders (today only preserved in photographs), suggested a tongue-in-cheek, almost serio-comic attitude toward Americanization as the historical destiny of the European city – especially a city like Copenhagen, so long sustained by its arts and crafts tradition. In an urban fabric that, 50 years later, is still dominated by its pre-industrial features, SAS remains singular, a figure in the urbanscape marked by difference. It is a monument in which the ideology of the International Style may be experienced today as a past vision of the future, a somewhat surreal reflection on the "new vernacular" of midcentury New York.[66]

Notes

1   Parts of this chapter have been adapted from two earlier essays of mine, "Between the Glass Curtain and the Iron Curtain: Reflections on Architecture during the Cold War" in: Mary McLeod (ed.): *Modernity, Tradition, and Historical Change: Essays on Architecture and Theory in Honor of Alan Colquhoun*, New York: Princeton Architectural Press, forthcoming, and "Toward a Theory of Normative Architecture," in: Steven Harris and Deborah Berke (eds): *Architecture of the Everyday*, New York: Princeton Architectural Press, 1997, pp. 122–52.

2   The "continuous monument" is a reference to a project of 1969 by the radical Italian group Superstudio, which envisioned a series of sites around the world, and eventually the entire globe, being subsumed by an infinite, tentacular grid.

3   Sloan Wilson: *The Man in the Gray Flannel Suit*, New York: Simon and Schuster, 1955, jacket copy.

4   Morris Dickstein: "Cold War Blues: Politics and Culture in the Fifties," in: *Gates of Eden: American Culture in the Sixties*, New York: Basic Books, 1977, p. 38.

5   Ibid., p. 50. The literature on both everyday life during the Cold War and the post-war American suburb is vast at this point. But for an engaged and still persuasive discussion of the ethos (and mythos), see Marty Jezer: *The Dark Ages: Life in the United States 1945–1960*, Boston: South End Press, 1982.

6   Vance Packard: *The Hidden Persuaders*, New York: Pocket Books, Inc., 1958, p. 199.

7   Ibid., p. 195. Cited from an article on "psychological marketing" published in 1956 in *Tide*, a trade magazine of marketing and management.

8   The term "happy housewife" was coined by Betty Friedan in her book *The Feminine Mystique* (1963). "The Wives of Management" is the title of a widely read article by William H. Whyte, Jr., published in *Fortune*, October 1951: "Resolutely antifeminist, [the corporate wife] conceives her role to be that of a 'stabilizer' – the keeper of the retreat, the one who rests and rejuvenates the man for the next day's battle" (p. 86).

9   Theodor Adorno, letter of 1936 to Walter Benjamin. Cited by Thomas Crow: "Modernism and Mass Culture in the Visual Arts," in: Francis Frascina (ed.): *Pollock and After: The Critical Debate*, New York: Harper & Row, 1985, p. 263.

10 Manfredo Tafuri and Francesco Dal Co: *Modern Architecture*, New York: Harry N. Abrams, Inc., 1979, p. 366.

11   Henry S. Churchill: "New York Re-Zoned," *Magazine of Art*, 44, December 1951. Cited in Christopher Gray: "Park Avenue's First Glass House to Get a Face-Lift: $7 Million Project Will Replace the Facade on the 1952 Landmark," *New York Times*, July 28, 1996, sect. X, p. 7.

12   Comment by Paul Goldberger, cited in James Trager: *Park Avenue: Street of Dreams*, New York: Atheneum, 1990, p. 190.

13   On the restoration and the building's recent change in ownership, see David W. Dunlap: "Designing a Restoration, and Words to Describe It," *New York Times*, December 29, 1999, sect. B, p. 7.

14   Cartoon by Weber, published in the *New Yorker*, March 23, 1963. Lever House was designated a landmark in 1982. For a building in New York City to be considered for landmark status, it has to be at least 30 years old.

15   On the economic imperatives of skyscraper building in Manhattan up to World War II, see Carol Willis: *Form Follows Finance: Skyscrapers and Skylines in New York and Chicago*, New York: Princeton Architectural Press, 1995. In her book, Willis also coins the concept of "vernaculars of capitalism" to characterize the different development of the skyscraper in New York and Chicago, a suggestive idea to which we shall return below.

16   Lewis Mumford: "The Sky Line: House of Glass," *New Yorker*, August 8, 1952, p. 49; Aline B. Louchheim: "Newest Building in the New Style," *New York Times*, April 27, 1952, sect. II, p. 9. Louchheim cited in Robert A.M. Stern, Thomas Mellins, and David Fishman: *New York 1960: Architecture and Urbanism between the Second World War and the Bicentennial*, New York: Monacelli Press, 1995, which contains extensive background and bibliography on Lever House, pp. 50–53, 338–42, 1246–47.

17   Mumford: "The Sky Line: House of Glass," p. 48.

18   On Port Sunlight, see *Heritage Outlook*, July–August 1985, p. 81. The village, built over several decades and well preserved today, also contains generous public facilities – church, school, library, hotel, theater, gymnasium, art gallery, social and educational institutions, and gardens – and remains a pre-Garden City model of enlightened community planning. Instead of forty housing units to an acre, the standard for industrial housing at the time, Port Sunlight was built at the density of seven to an acre. Working conditions in the soap factory were also exemplary. Lever was one of the first employers to introduce an 8-hour workday, and he strongly promoted a 6-hour day.

19   *Saturday Evening Post*, February 11, 1950, p. 27; cited in Stern *et al.*, *New York 1960*, p. 61.

20   Charles Luckman's autobiography is *Twice in a Lifetime: From Soap to Skyscrapers*, New York: W.W. Norton & Company, 1988, chapter on Lever House, pp. 230–48. Luckman died in 1999 at age 89.

21   I have not been able to retrace the exact source of this memorable statement by Bloch, but for the general idea, see "The Creation of the Ornament" (1973) and "Building in Empty Spaces" (1959), in: Ernst Bloch: *The Utopian Function of Art and Literature: Selected Essays*, trans. Jack Zipes and Frank Mecklenburg, Cambridge, Mass.: MIT Press, 1988, pp. 78–102, 186–99.

22   As stated in a promotional brochure issued at the time of the building's opening. S.O.M. Clippings File.

23   Lewis Mumford: "The Sky Line: House of Glass," p. 49.

24   First phrase quoted from Daniel Bell: "The Three Faces of New York," *Dissent*, Summer 1961, p. 227; second phrase from Ada Louise Huxtable: "Park Avenue School of Architecture," *New York Times*, December 15, 1957, sect. VI, pp. 30–31; cited in Stern *et al.*: *New York 1960*, pp. 62, 330.

25   Vincent Scully, Jr. "The Death of the Street," *Perspecta*, 8 1963, pp. 91–96.

26   James S. Russell: "Icons of Modernism or Machine-Age Dinosaurs?" *Architectural Record*, June 1989, p. 142.

27   Colin Rowe, introduction to *Five Architects: Eisenman, Graves, Gwathmey, Hejduk, Meier*, New York: Wittenborn, 1972, p. 4; Catherine Bauer to Lewis Mumford, January 29, 1932, cited

in: Terence Riley (ed.) *The International Style: Exhibition 15 and the Museum of Modern Art*, New York: Rizzoli, 1992, p. 209.

28   I refer to Giedion's important book *Mechanization Takes Command*.

29   J.L. Sert, F. Léger, and S. Giedion: "Nine Points on Monumentality" (1943), in: S. Giedion: *Architecture, You and Me*, Cambridge, Mass · Harvard University Press, 1958, pp. 48–52.

30   Le Corbusier: *U.N. Headquarters*, New York: Reinhold, 1947, p. 13.

31   *Architectural Review*, January 1947, pp. 3–6.

32   Frank Lloyd Wright: *Genius and the Mobocracy*, New York: Duell, Sloan and Pearce, 1949, pp. 16, 89.

33   "Frank Lloyd Wright Ridicules Architectural Schools as Waste," *New York Times*, June 26, 1952, p. 47; cited in Stern *et al.*, *New York 1960*, p. 340.

34   Lewis Mumford: "The Sky Line. United Nations Headquarters: Buildings as Symbols," *New Yorker*, November 15, 1947, p. 104.

35   Serge Guilbaut: *How New York Stole the Idea of Modern Art: Abstract Expressionism, Freedom, and the Cold War*, Chicago: University of Chicago Press, 1983. Guilbaut's argument has provoked considerable debate from both the left and the right. For a different assessment, crediting Guilbaut's insights although faulting him for fusing the promotion of Abstract Expressionism with its formation, see Michael Leja: *Reframing Abstract Expressionism: Subjectivity and Painting in the 1940s*, New Haven: Yale University Press, 1993.

36   Ibid., p. 184.

37   Godfrey Hodgson: *America in Our Time*, Garden City, New York: Doubleday & Company, 1976, p. 97.

38   Ibid., pp. 89–90.

39   James Marston Fitch: *Architecture and the Esthetics of Plenty*, New York: Columbia University Press, 1961, p. 27.

40   "Skidmore, Owings & Merrill, Architects, U.S.A.," *Museum of Modern Art Bulletin*, Fall 1950, p. 5.

41   "Man Made America," *Architectural Review*, December 1950, pp. 339 ff.

42   "Machine Made America," *Architectural Review*, May 1957, p. 308.

43   The slogan "American century" was coined in 1941 by archcapitalist Henry Luce, publisher of *Time*, *Fortune*, and *Life* magazines, to herald a new consciousness of the period of American world leadership and domination that was already under way. In opposition to this world view, New Dealer Henry Wallace, Franklin Delano Roosevelt's third-term vice-president (subsequently to be an unsuccessful candidate for the American presidency on a third-party ticket against Harry S. Truman), proposed a vision of American democracy based on a "people's revolution" in which the "common man" would be the protagonist.

44   Peter and Alison Smithson: "Letter to America," in: *Ordinariness and Light: Urban Theories 1952–1960*, Cambridge, Mass.: MIT Press, 1970, p. 141.

45   Huxtable: "The Skyline Factory," *Newsweek*, September 18, 1967, p. 98; cited in Stern *et al.*, *New York 1960*, p. 51. Within two decades, from 1950 to 1970, Emery Roth & Sons constructed some seventy office buildings in New York City, amounting to half the total office space built during the period. In general on Manhattan's "Rothscrapers," see Stern *et al.*, op. cit., pp. 50–51 and passim. Richard Roth, one of the firm's principals, defended the work of the firm against charges of aesthetic banality, saying in 1963, "we are sometimes criticized unfairly, because of the way in which we are judged: ours is not a field of architecture in which we create or try to create masterpieces. The entire endeavor in our office is to create the best that can be produced within the restrictions that are placed upon us; and these restrictions are seldom those of our client, but rather of lending institutions, economics and municipal authorities' laws" (Stern *et al.*, p. 51). See also Richard Roth: "The Forces That Shaped Park Avenue," *Perspecta* 8, 1963, pp. 97–101.

46   See the Smithsons' other writings in *Ordinariness and Light*. Their attraction to the optical titillations of an American architecture "uncomplicated by doubt and uncorrupted by concept"

(p. 137) may be compared to the celebration by a later European observer, Rem Koolhaas, of a "delirious New York" and its "culture of congestion." Clearly the charm of the latter may differ from the standpoint of the tourist and the resident (see below).

47 Peter and Alison Smithson: *Ordinariness and Light*, p. 141.

48 Luckman predictably gives a more self-serving explanation of Lambert's role and the rejection of his scheme in his autobiography *Twice in a Lifetime*, pp. 323–25. For background on the Seagram Building, its reception, and comprehensive bibliography, see Stern *et al.*: *New York 1960*, pp. 342–52, 1247–48. The best architectural analysis of Seagram and its relationship to Lever House remains, in my view, William Jordy's chapter "The Laconic Splendor of the Metal Frame: Mies van der Rohe's 860 Lake Shore Apartments and His Seagram Building," in his book *American Buildings and Their Architects*, volume 5, *The Impact of European Modernism in the Mid-Twentieth Century*, New York: Oxford University Press, 1972, pp. 221–77, to which the following discussion is indebted.

49 Manfredo Tafuri: *Architecture and Utopia: Design and Capitalist Development*, Cambridge, Mass.: MIT Press, 1976, p. 45; Tafuri and Dal Co: *Modern Architecture*, pp. 340–41.

50 See "Monument in Bronze," *Time*, March 3, 1958, p. 55; cited in Stern *et al.*: *New York 1960*, p. 346.

51 Lewis Mumford: "The Sky Line: The Lesson of the Master," *New Yorker*, September 13, 1958, p. 19.

52 On the development of 53rd Street during this period as a crosstown cultural strip, see: Stern *et al.*: *New York 1960*, pp. 473 ff.

53 Ibid., pp. 97–99.

54 Mumford: "The Sky Line: House of Glass," p. 50.

55 Cf. William H. Whyte, Jr.: *The Organization Man*, New York: Simon and Schuster, 1956.

56 Herbert Marcuse: *One-Dimensional Man*, Boston: Beacon Press, 1964, pp. 31–32.

57 Peter Madsen: "The Urban Lifeworld: Approaches to the Analysis of Urban Experience," unpubl. ms. 1996, p. 13.

58 Jane Jacobs: *The Death and Life of Great American Cities*, New York: Vintage Books, 1961, pp. 168, 227.

59 Rem Koolhaas: *Delirious New York: A Retroactive Manifesto for New York*, rev. edn, New York: Monacelli Press, 1994, pp. 290–91.

60 Together with a big banana for Times Square, Oldenburg's drawing of the ice cream popsicle was one of a series of "Proposed Colossal Monuments for New York City" executed in 1965. Interestingly, Herbert Marcuse appreciated the radical surrealism of the artist's Pop gesture. In an interview in 1968 – clearly reflecting the emancipatory euphoria of the moment – he stated, "Strangely enough I think that would indeed be subversive . . . you would have the revolution. If you could really envisage a situation where at the end of Park Avenue there would be a huge Good Humor ice cream bar and in the middle of Times Square a huge banana I would say – and I think safely say – this society has come to an end. Because then people cannot take anything seriously: neither their president, nor the cabinet, nor the corporation executives. There is a way in which this kind of satire, of humor, can indeed kill. I think it would be one of the most blood-less means to achieve a radical change. But the trouble is you must already have the radical change in order to get it built, and I don't see any evidence of that. And the mere drawing wouldn't hurt, and that makes it harmless. But just imagine that overnight it would suddenly be there." Cited in *Perspecta*, 12, 1969, p. 75.

61 On Pan Am (now MetLife), see Stern *et al.*: *New York 1960*, pp. 357–69; and Trager: *Park Avenue: Street of Dreams*, pp. 219–34.

62 For a firsthand report on American-style skyscrapers erected in Europe in the late 1950s and early 1960s, see Henry-Russell Hitchcock: "Notes of a Traveller (III): European Skyscrapers," *Zodiac*, 9, 1962, pp. 4–17.

63 Some suggestive if preliminary reflections on this issue are afforded in Alan Colquhoun's essay

"Regionalism and Technology," in: *Modernity and the Classical Tradition: Architectural Essays 1980–1987*, Cambridge, Mass.: MIT Press, 1989, pp. 207–11.

64 In this respect, SAS and Pan Am symbolically salute each other from the skylines of their respective cities. The two buildings also share the complicated site problems of adjacency to a central railroad station and below-grade tracks.

65 Including the Jespersen Building, also by Jacobsen, completed in 1955 prior to SAS. Interestingly, the curtain wall of the eight-story Jespersen resembles that of another S.O.M. design on Park Avenue in Manhattan, the acclaimed Pepsi-Cola Building. Pepsi-Cola, however, was built in 1956–1960 – thus Jacobsen's building actually precedes it! Hitchcock, who saw the SAS Building not long after its completion, was among the few critics to express a negative opinion. In his article in *Zodiac* (cited note 57), he faults the building for its siting, suggesting – ironically enough, given the far denser conditions in New York – that it would have been preferable to locate it in a less congested part of the city, or at least to have provided an open plaza at the base rather than a relatively solid and massive podium. He also considered the curtain wall of the tower too "dainty" in its dimensioning, and would have preferred a color that contrasted more with Copenhagen's grayness (p. 11).

66 By coincidence, the day after the conference that generated the present book the Copenhagen newspaper *Politiken* published a feature article on the phenomenon of "copytecture," taking the example of Lever House and the SAS Building as a precedent for a number of recent examples of the same phenomenon in Copenhagen. See Peter Mose: "Midt i kopitektur-tid," *Politiken*, November 3, 1996, pp. 14–15.

Part II

Perception

Chapter 7

Permeable Boundaries
Domesticity in Post-war New York

Gwendolyn Wright

American domesticity, if culturally located in the suburbs, takes on distinctive qualities in cities, nowhere more so than in New York. The quintessential urban characteristics of density, proximity, ambiguity, and diversity play havoc with the conventional suburban ideal of self-sufficient families, each one comfortable in a spacious dwelling which provides for every need. Domesticity in New York is necessarily more contingent and crowded, less clearly bounded by architecture or activities.

This is by no means to imply (as many suburbanites would contend) that the city cannot sustain, even nurture, deeply meaningful domestic lifeworlds. One could even argue that the pleasures, routines, and commitments universally associated with home (to use the English term[1]) in fact flourish in the absence of suburban obsessions about "normal" family life enshrined in detached single-family villas. Certainly the city supports a multitude of definitions for family, housed within all sorts of different residential settings, rather than insisting on one normalized incarnation of the two.

The experience of, and spaces for, domestic life of course vary historically in small yet significant ways, requiring us to situate them precisely. During the years just after World War II, suburbs grew at exponential rates across the United States, including the Tri-State area around New York, while federal slum clearance policies demolished whole districts of working class homes in large cities, condemning them as "blighted, substandard slums."[2] Despite these pressures many urban neighborhoods continued to thrive, nourishing a variety of domestic lives within a larger, overlapping framework of work and leisure, routines and adventures.

Like any myth, this golden age of the 1950s betrays a nostalgic longing: close-knit families in a safe, congenial neighborhood, each a distinctive piece within a vibrant mosaic of cosmopolitan complexity.[3] The sentimentality in such a portrait does not necessarily refute its link to historical reality; it can instead serve as a reminder of the many kinds of experience that remained on the periphery even outside of that ideal setting. In particular, inequalities and the unending threat of discontinuities (violence, eviction, illness or other crises) made home life constantly problematic, even precarious, for most poor minority residents of New York. This ceaseless pressure makes it all the more impressive that many black women, day by day, created and recreated domestic stability for their families.[4]

Across a wide range of circumstances, New York's post-World War II years thus highlight the paradoxical elements of urban domesticity: the process whereby playful inventiveness enlivens repetition, a sudden juxtaposition recasts routine habits, and the pleasant comfort of well-being can modulate restraints and restrictions. In this, as in all things, the city combines isolation with belonging, traditions (not one, but many) with modernity (again, not one, but many).

Literary and artistic representations of modernism rarely consider domestic environments, focusing instead on the solitary individual in public space: Baudelaire's "man of the crowd" or Benjamin's "refuse collector." Estranged or liberated, the *flâneur* inhabits an expansive anonymous realm; consciously or not he (almost always a masculine figure) rejects the *heimlich* qualities of the home, returning to its dull confinement only when exhausted.[5] Likewise Le Corbusier railed against the "sentimental hysteria" surrounding the "cult of the house." His heroes – businessmen, engineers or artists – came most alive in public settings for work or physical exercise; the dwelling provided only a "machine for living in."[6]

Yet isn't this image itself a caricature, a part taken for the whole of experience? Even in a modern city each individual must engage certain human memories and bonds within the structure of domestic life, if only for brief moments in time: the gendered cosmos that is reproduced (and resisted) in the respective duties of the home; the intimate space of a couple; the generational structure of early childhood dependence (often succeeded by the later ties of parenthood, an extended family, or old age); the roles that come to be expected within the social enclave of a building, a block, a neighborhood or other less spatially determined communities of interest.

Likewise, even as late as the 1950s, the traditional habitudes of class or ethnicity continued to affect the nature of domesticity for many urbanites, both in the home and in the world just outside its boundaries. Again, this is not to dispute modernity's destabilizing effect on such unifying bonds as class, culture or family, but rather to bring into question the tendency to take this effect as complete and totalizing – especially within the domestic sphere.

Television in its early years often portrayed just such an interpenetration of influences, most notably in ethnic working class enclaves. Early comedy shows like "The Honeymooners," "The Goldbergs," "I Love Lucy" or "Amos 'n' Andy" featured a range of distinctly urban personae, including children and old people, friends and strangers.[7] The action radiated out from one main room in an apartment – limited of course by the era's studio space and cumbersome technology – to encompass exchanges across open windows and hallway corridors as well as events outside the building. To be sure, walls and social decorum separated each unit from the others, yet daily life continually flowed over these boundaries in the form of visits, gossip, childcare, shared activities, and the loan of objects, money or other forms of assistance.

High culture, which followed a very different pattern of cosmopolitan inventiveness, remained similarly bounded by the residential neighborhood. New York witnessed an explosion of artistic and intellectual innovations in the late 1940s and 1950s which catapulted the city's status into that of a new world capital for painting, sculpture, dance, music, and literature, as well as scholarship and cultural entrepreneurship. The international reputation, while justified, can easily obscure the fact that most New Yorkers' lives, even for artists and intellectuals, still revolved principally around discrete locales, each of which blended the domains of public and private. In 1947, declaring that the fate of American art was being decided below 34th Street by "young people, few over forty, who

General store in Harlem. A lot of business was conducted on the
New York. Thousands of stores like the one above, spilled their g
the sidewalks to enlarge their display areas.

▲ **7.2** Molly Goldberg and her New York apartment house neighbors in the popular sitcom, "The Goldbergs," which premiered on television in 1949. Courtesy of New York Public Library.

◄ **7.1** Commercial and social life spilled out onto the Harlem sidewalks. Text by John Von Hartz, Dover Press, 1978. Andreas Feininger, *New York in the Forties.*

live in cold-water flats and exist from hand to mouth," Clement Greenberg captured the austerity and centrifugal force of the Abstract Expressionists' living arrangements; if anything, he suggested too capacious a geographical territory, extending so far above 14th Street.[8]

At least three such settings have been celebrated as the nuclei of creative vitality during this decade: Greenwich Village, the pleasantly disheveled habitat of Abstract Expressionist painters and Beat poets, living alongside older Italian families; the donnish neighborhood of Morningside Heights, extending into the Upper West Side, a heady enclave of intellectual intensity surrounding Columbia University, then at the crest of its world renown; and Harlem, the cauldron of black urban experience, vividly depicted in the paintings, novels, and poems of the generation that succeeded the Harlem Renaissance. (On the west side of town Harlem borders directly on the Upper West Side, surrounding Columbia's Morningside Heights, even if it does not officially begin until 125th Street.)

While they do not represent all of New York, the experiences and descriptions of these three sites crystallize more pervasive, if less clearly inscribed, trends throughout the city. What then was the place of domesticity in these urban settings? Several qualities stand out, each one a synthesis of architectonic form with quotidian experience.

An emphatic localism characterized even the most cosmopolitan groups. Each enclave remained self-consciously separate from the rest of the city, including the other nodes of creativity. New York artists, then as now, pride themselves on never going above 14th Street; Columbia faculty seldom venture below 110th Street or east of Amsterdam Avenue. Racial segregation as much as a shared cultural domain meant that black life on Manhattan converged in the area above 96th Street. Such parameters do not undermine

7.3 Jacob Lawrence's "Fulton and Nostrand," a 1958 portrait of a black neighborhood in Brooklyn, echoes the street life of Harlem. Private collection. Courtesy of Terry Dintenfas Gallery, Inc., New York.

modern urbanity, no more than urbanity subverts domesticity. After all, the Parisian *flâneur* had likewise set clear boundaries, beyond which the world seemed less intriguing.[9]

Outsiders were pariahs in each enclave, as outside neighborhoods were largely ignored and invisible. Separation reached its apotheosis in the segregated ghetto of Harlem. If the artistic and intellectual communities of white liberals actively spurned the racial segregation that colored America, their black compatriots were, at best, "cousins," causes, or a primitivist inspiration – a trope for intensity, even redemptive violence, in texts like Norman Mailer's "The White Negro."[10] Harlem represented an idea, for some good, for others bad, but few whites knew much, if anything, about the reality of its streets or housing.

Domestic space intersected and overlapped with public space in New York. Residents moved about freely within a quarter, whatever their age or gender, inhabiting a sizable realm between the private domain of the dwelling and the public expanse of the city. Urban domesticity seldom pretends to self-sufficiency; one usually goes elsewhere, often on a daily basis, to carry out a range of activities (laundry, social entertaining, child care, and schoolwork). Both adults and children spend much of their time outside the home, on front stoops or sidewalks, in corner shops, libraries, local bars or other informal meeting-places. The legendary appeal of three sites confirms this aura: the Cedar Tavern in Greenwich Village, the West End bar near Columbia, and the Apollo Ballroom in Harlem (whose weekly Amateur Nights launched many celebrated black singers).

In these porous circumstances home retained its essence: simultaneously a haven and a structure within the maelstrom of daily life. Yet the potency of its supposed sovereignty, so central to the mythic allure of suburban dwellings, was greatly diminished, not simply by the small size of urban apartments, but also by the enticing lure of life outside the dwelling.

This description should not be taken as a naive celebration of the urban village. Any neighborhood could become claustrophobic for those who wanted to challenge the limits of acceptable behavior and routine responses. Some surroundings engendered psychological torment, even physical danger. James Baldwin wrote of cramped Harlem dwellings where "no labor could ever make it clean."[11] Given that home extended beyond the walls of such apartments, one's efforts could become truly herculean. "To live in Harlem," wrote Ralph Ellison, "is to pass a labyrinthine existence among streets that explode monotonously skyward with the spires and crosses of churches and clutter under foot with garbage and decay."[12] In Ann Petry's novel, *The Street* (1946), the devastated area around Lenox Avenue and 116th Street slowly crushed its inhabitants by causing them to assimilate the harsh attributes of their surroundings.

Urban domesticity therefore requires the active interpretation of space and circumstances, followed by the improvised responses typically associated with city life. Even if the borders of the neighborhood and the home itself define safety and belonging, they still require continual assessment. Like the members of a family, local residents assimilate certain expectations and strategies: which places to avoid, what times are dangerous, how to judge possible difficulties as one enters a space. Such knowledge is usually imparted indirectly, without open discussion of risks and responses, and the actions are seldom fully self-conscious. Yet the process of sizing up a physical and social situation, then deciding how (or whether) to interact, does allow some degree of choice, even if it may be impossible to exert real control.

Other options have always existed in cities, of course. Some individuals insisted on mobility in the 1950s: both Columbia's Meyer Shapiro and the black novelist James Baldwin lived in the Village, while Alfred Kazin called his memoirs *A Walker in the City*, and Lionel Feininger's literally moving photographs of New York emphasized the various systems for redemptive transportation. Even within an urban routine it was possible to choose another path through the labyrinth, to change the venue for a task, to pick a different time of day, and thereby to transform the structure of a prosaic narrative.

Within the home and outside, urban domesticity thus encourages moments of improvisation and imagination. Daily life occurs in settings that may appear nondescript, even purposefully drab and ordinary; in fact, with closer scrutiny, they yield a richly textured and multi-faceted domain, resistant to easy classifications of public or private, new or old, tedious or enticing. This ambiguity, at once frustrating and liberating, extends from the city's sidewalks to its residential buildings. In the home as in the city streets, it is possible to transmute the banalities of life into game or art or solace.

This brings us to another, more circumscribed dimension of urban domesticity: the spaces within an urban apartment by and large transcend precise definitions. Rooms typically contain multiple uses and overlapping pathways; furnishings comprise an assortment of new and old, transcending any single imprimateur of stylistic vocabulary or semantic message.

Few apartment residents sought to replicate the sacred precincts of the postwar suburban dwelling: the living room and dining room, each with a complete set of furniture, whether of a historic revival theme or the recent fashion for "Danish modern;" a "master bedroom" for the conjugal couple; a separate bedroom for each child attesting to his or her unique individuality – defined largely through one's visible place in the collective consumer world; a slick modern kitchen, colorfully equipped with the latest appliances; the gleaming bathroom as a sanctuary to hygiene; and the new family room adjoining the backyard patio, designed for informal togetherness around the television set.

The ensemble of space and furnishings in an urban apartment instead suggested an ongoing process of urban bricolage. Even in new buildings social spaces had to serve family as well as guests, adapting to children's play and homework, household accounts and leisure-time projects. Bedrooms provided functional space for sleeping and a modicum of privacy. "Efficiency kitchens" and bathrooms were small and serviceable. Even wealthy urbanites resisted the fetishized "family room" of post-war American domesticity – in their city apartments, at least, if not in their country houses. Neither the parts nor the whole strained to achieve the suburban illusion of a perfect fit, in which the plan symbolized the harmonious, self-sufficient family, and thereby guaranteed its endurance.

A related phenomenon concerns the interpenetration of work and domesticity. Home did not provide the suburbs' promise of a reprieve, neither for those who had to take in piecework to earn money, nor for the professionals and writers who found here, at last, the chance to engage in "their own work."

The most imaginative alternative to conventional living arrangements came, not surprisingly, from downtown artists. Eager to find the most possible space for the least possible cost, they began to rent industrial lofts that could combine living with work space, and often performance space as well.[13] Owners were eager to comply, despite the illegality of such use, for they needed to recoup a profit when manufacturing left the city in the aftermath of the war. The loft aesthetic challenged the traditional imagery of home with a new form of domestic expression: a celebration of raw industrial materials, unencumbered space, and the imaginative reuse of urban debris. In their expansive empty volumes as in their purposefully unsystematized decor, these "live-work spaces" spurned the comfortable conventions of bourgeois domesticity.

Bodies too occupied the urban domestic realm in distinctive ways. The Beats resisted prescriptive gender roles as well as dress codes, revelling in open sexuality and homo-eroticism, as did many less rebellious intellectuals. Husband and wife did not necessarily seem a sacrosanct union since variations, even taboos, were openly tolerated: a couple could live together without marriage; affairs and prostitution were not necessarily hidden; homosexual life defined many bars, clubs, and parks.[14]

A city typically encompasses all cycles of the human body, including the infirmities of age and the dependence of childhood. If New York provided few special services for any single generation, a mixture of age groups inhabited every neighborhood and, until the 1950s, virtually every building. However, while New York experienced a baby boom, much like the rest of the country, the city's post-war housing stock made only minimal provision for families with children. By 1955 only a quarter of all new rental apartments in Manhattan accommodated children, while the number of single- and two-person households catapulted to an unprecedented majority.[15] In Stuyvesant Town (where the Metropolitan Life Insurance Company housed 24,000 middle-income residents) abundant space was indeed allocated for various outdoor activities in the complex, but the majority of apartments had only one bedroom.[16]

Statistics can usually be interpreted in more than one way, undermining the tendency to see any such polarity as natural. Did the shortage of adequate family housing in American cities fuel the suburban exodus, or was it simply the market's response to demographic trends? By choice or design, if the majority of families with children did not live in new residential buildings, they still made do quite well in older apartments. Yet since those who made policy – government officials, banks, developers, and architects – focused,

7.4 A group of New York painters on the "Tar Beach" roof of their live-work loft building downtown at Coenties Slip in 1957. *From left to right*: Delphine Seyrig, Robert Indiana, Duncan Youngerman, Jack Youngerman and Agnes Martin. Indiana, Kelly, Martin, Rosenquist, Youngerman at Coenties Slip. Exhibition catalog 1993 from the Pace Collection. Photo © Hans Namuth.

7.5 Manhattan House, built in 1950 by Skidmore, Owings & Merrill, epitomizes the new luxury apartment buildings of post-war New York. Courtesy of New York Public Library.

then as now, so overwhelmingly on the paradigm of recent buildings (their appearance, floor plans, financing, and services), the shift in new construction itself reinforced the national trends toward an urban-suburban division.

The split cuts in both ways, however. Perhaps the most vivid character of New York domesticity, especially in these three neighborhoods of predominantly older housing, was its contempt for middle-class conventions about home. Such disdain implicitly turned against the twin prototypes of post-war modern architecture: the open-plan suburban villa, extending into its lush garden, and the brave new urban world of sleek apartment towers-in-a-park. Throughout the 1950s, a majority of New Yorkers still rejected the proverbial "good life" of conspicuous innovation, whether it derived from the comfort-seeking consumerism of suburbia or the more refined elegance of the city's luxury apartments.[17] This attitude held sway despite the Museum of Modern Art's official endorsement of both models, epitomized in Mies van der Rohe's Lake Shore Apartments in Chicago (1948–1951) and Marcel Breuer's model suburban house, built for display in the museum's garden in 1949.[18]

Yet if older New Yorkers and the city's flourishing artistic world resisted these canonical models of domesticity, the market embraced them. When building resumed in 1950, a frenzy of new development favored modern luxury apartment towers over any other type of domestic architecture. New York's set-back towers and courtyard housing of the 1920s seemed as outmoded as the tenements, now being swept away as unhealthy, backward living environments. Most new construction was concentrated on the Upper East Side, north of 60th Street, the neighborhood of choice for the employees of fast-growing midtown corporate headquarters such as Lever House or the Seagram Building. Manhattan House (1950) by Skidmore, Owings & Merrill provides a paradigmatic example. One architectural magazine lauded its achievements: a strip of land ceded to the city widened the adjacent street into a barrier; a large mid-block slab further maximized distance from surrounding buildings; an "indoor-outdoor synthesis" with immense windows looked out onto a private greensward; and armchair balconies (derived from Danish modernism) expanded private living space for each unit.[19] This image of domesticity anticipated the insular gated communities which have come to define so much late twentieth-century domesticity, in cities as in suburbs.

Vociferous opposition erupted when large-scale modern housing such as this was proposed in other neighborhoods. By and large opposition did not signal aesthetic timidity or social antagonism, but rather a commitment to the urban lifeworld that still characterized much of New York. Downtown critics declaimed the middle-income residential complexes of Stuyvesant Town and Two Fifth Avenue. By the late 1950s Village residents successfully repelled Robert Moses' plans for a gigantic middle-income housing project and a new highway through Washington Square Park; Jane Jacobs led the defense of heterogeneous, unplanned street life as the very foundation of urban domesticity, which would soon become the basis for her influential book *The Death and Life of Great American Cities* (1961).

In a similar vein, speaking from both sides of 96th Street, blacks and whites alike condemned the dreary, repeated monoliths of recent public housing, most of which was concentrated in the black and Puerto Rican districts of East Harlem. Here too the critique turned not against modern architecture, but against the inability to differentiate between intention and reality: these grim enclaves of brick towers did not represent the elegant order of modern domestic life. James Baldwin lambasted the first "project," Metropolitan Life's Riverton of 1947 (necessary because of racial segregation policies at Stuyvesant Town). "Hideous, cheerless as a prison," he insisted angrily, this architecture conveyed a "hated . . . insult to the meanest intelligence, . . . [It is a sign of] the real attitude of the white world."[20]

So too, beginning in the early 1950s, residents of Morningside Heights assailed the university's grandiose post-war proposal for slum clearance and new apartment towers, charging that this would "change the character of the neighborhood."[21] Prominent faculty enjoyed spacious apartments facing Olmsted's Riverside Park; they did not wish to bear responsibility for gentrification, even less for their neighborhood becoming too conspicuously middle class.

In their quite different ways, many New Yorkers thus critiqued the prevailing post-war notions of domesticity in homogeneous suburban enclaves and autonomous urban

7.6 Riverton Houses of 1947, a segregated housing project for blacks in Harlem built by the Metropolitan Life Insurance Company. Courtesy of the MetLife Archives.

apartment towers. They did not self-consciously construct new paradigms – even the appeal of downtown artists' lofts derived principally from the immense space at such low rents – yet their lives, at home and on their streets, affirmed the possibility of alternatives.

While resonantly sensitive to spatial aesthetics and the poetic geography of environments, these other domesticities resisted any fixed architectural form. They derived instead from the continuous stimuli of experience and events juxtaposed with the polymorphous tactility of urban surroundings. One did not need to be a stranger to enjoy and engage in these pleasures.

The aura of this richly textured lifeworld still holds in many New York neighborhoods, but it is at risk of being packaged as an "authentic" historic context, to be imposed for preservation and new construction alike. The formula, by which a magical composite of things promises to fulfill social or personal desires, is not unlike that of suburban fetishization. The domestic life of New York, extending into the streets and sidewalks, does not reside in the architectural form of older neighborhoods – no more than it would be categorically impossible to experience its pleasures in modern buildings. Its essence lies instead in an ongoing process of adaptation and interaction, a playful responsiveness to what is lacking as well as what is there. This sensibility, so attenuated outside of cities, encourages adults and children alike to distill the vibrant possibilities within the ordinary, in the private realm of domesticity as in the public arena of the streets.

Notes

1   The German origins of home in the word *Heimat* suggest its range of meanings: the physical structure where one resides; a place in which one feels comfortable, free of stress (which can easily extend beyond the dwelling *per se*); the valued source from which the person (or the nation) originates; the human and cultural world associated with happiness and security. Of course, neither word should be allowed to mask the repressive demands, tedious routines, and even the threat of hidden violence that can also reside here.

2   At this time, only 10 percent of an area had to be classified as "blighted" for the government to subsidize slum clearance of the entire site, after which it would guarantee private redevelopment of the area for luxury apartments and office buildings. While American suburbs grew twice as

fast as central cities between 1940–1950, they grew forty times faster in the next decade, depleting every metropolis.

3   On New York in the 1950s see, *inter alias*, Alfred Kazin: *A Walker in the City*, New York, 1951; Chester Himes's *Pinktoes, A Novel*, New York, 1965; Edward Lewis Wallant: *The Pawnbroker*, New York, 1961; David Halberstam: *The Fifties*, New York, 1993; and Marshall Berman: *All That Is Solid Melts Into Air: The Experience of Modernity*, New York, 1982, as well as the photographs of Robert Frank, Lionel Feininger, and Fred McDarrah. The quintessential portrait of the city on the eve of this decade is, of course, E.B. White's poetic essay: *Here Is New York*, New York, 1949.

4   The need to internalize and continually recreate home was a recurring theme in Anna Deveare Smith's recent panel discussion at New York University, "Whatever Happened to Lorraine Hansberry: Where Sits Home in the Imagination of Black Women Artists?" on November 25, 1996.

5   Walter Benjamin, *Gesammelte Schriften*, Frankfurt-am-Main, 1983, vol. 5, p. 525. Freud's 1919 essay on the uncanny discussed the estrangement whereby something *heimlich* is transformed into its strange obverse, the *unheimlich* (literally "unhomely" or "haunted"), while philosophers as diverse as Lukács, Bachelard, and Heidegger linked modern life to an unsettled "transcendental homelessness." For an interesting discussion of this represssive tendency see Christopher Reed (ed.): *Not at Home: The Suppression of Domesticity in Modern Art and Architecture*, London, 1996 and Anthony Vidler, *The Architectural Uncanny: Essays in the Modern Unhomely*, Cambridge, 1992.

6   Le Corbusier: *Vers une architecture*, Paris, 1923, pp. 17, 222. Beatriz Colomina expands upon this theme, most notably in *Privacy and Publicity: Modern Architecture as Mass Media*, Cambridge, 1992.

7   All of these series predate later 1950s classics like "Ozzie and Harriet." However, the television version of "Amos 'n' Andy" featured a black middle-class family, now transported to a suburb, whereas the earlier radio version had featured white actors in broad "black-voice" caricatures of urban working-class blacks. See Karal Ann Marling, *As Seen on TV: The Visual Culture of Everyday Life in the 1950s*, Cambridge, 1994 and Gerald Jones: *Honey, I'm Home: Sitcoms Selling the American Dream*, New York, 1992.

8   Clement Greenberg: "The Present Prospects of American Painting and Sculpture," *Horizon* 16, October 1947, pp. 25, 29.

9   I would like to thank Sven Erik Larsen for reminding me of this important detail.

10 Daniel Bell made the comment about James Baldwin and Ralph Ellison as "cousins" of the *Partison Review* "family" in *The Winding Passage*, New York, 1980, p. 128, cited in Thomas Bender: *New York Intellect: A History of Intellectual Life in New York City, from 1750 to the Beginnings of Our Own Time*, New York, 1987, p. 254. Mailer praised blacks' ability to live consciously in the present, with jazz and hip street talk as "a pictorial language . . . imbued with the dialectic of small but intense change, . . . man, for it takes the immediate experiences of any passing man and magnifies the dynamic of his movements," *The White Negro*, San Francisco, 1957, section 3, published earlier that year in *Dissent*, as cited in Mona Lisa Saloy: "Black Beats and Black Issues," in: Lisa Philips (ed.): *Beat Culture and the New America: 1950–1965*, New York, 1996, p. 157.

11 James Baldwin, *Go Tell It on the Mountain*, New York, 1953; reprint New York, 1985, pp. 21–22.

12 Ralph Ellison: "Harlem in Nowhere" (1948), *Shadow and Act*, New York, 1964, pp. 295–96, cited in William Sharpe, "Living on the Edge: New York in Literature," in: Leonard Wallock (ed.): *New York: Culture Capital of the World, 1940–1965*, New York, 1988, p. 76.

13 For an overview of the phenomenon, extending into the colonization of Soho lofts by wealthy young professionals in the 1970s, see Sharon Zukin: *Loft Living: Culture and Capital in Urban Change*, Baltimore, 1982.

14 For an earlier stage of homosexual life in the city, see George Chauncey: *Gay New York: Gender, Urban Culture, and the Making of the Gay Male World, 1890–1940*, New York, 1994.

15 George Sternlieb: "New York's Housing: A Study in *Immobilisme*," *The Public Interest*, 16, Summer 1969, pp. 126–30.

16 The complex contained 8,759 apartments, most with three rooms (one bedroom), a majority of the rest as four-room units (two bedrooms), and only 400 five-room suites. (Arthur Simon, *Stuyvesant Town, U.S.A.: Pattern for Two Americas*, New York, 1970, pp. 26–27.)

17 Frederick Gutheim: *Houses for Family Living*, New York, 1948; Katherine Morrow Ford and Thomas H. Creighton: *The American House Today*, New York, 1951; Robert Woods Kennedy: *The House and the Art of Its Design*, New York: 1948; Russell Lynes: *The Domesticated Americans*, New York, 1957; Mark Jarzombek: "'Good-Life Modernism' and Beyond: The American House in the 1950s and 1960s: A Commentary," *Cornell Journal of Architecture*, 4, Fall 1990 pp. 76–93; and Gwendolyn Wright: *Building the Dream: A Social History of Housing in America*, New York, 1981; reprint, Cambridge, 1983, pp. 240–61.

18 Among the museum's publications that promoted these two residential icons, see Henry Russell Hitchcock and Philip Johnson: *Built in USA: Post-war Architecture*, New York, 1952; Peter Blake: "The House in the Museum Garden," *Bulletin of the Museum of Modern Art* (*BMMA*), 16, Spring 1949; Elizabeth Mock: "Tomorrow's Small House," *BMMA*, 12, Summer 1945; and Mock: *If You Want to Build a House*, New York, 1946.

19 "'Manhattan House' Replaces Old Carbarns," *Architectural Record*, 105, May 1949 pp. 106–07, 206.

20 James Baldwin: "[Nobody Knows My Name] Fifth Avenue Uptown: A Letter from Harlem," *Esquire*, July 1960, p. 63.

21 Daniel Bell and Virginia Held, "The Community Revolution," *The Public Interest*, 16, Summer 1969, pp. 171–72.

Chapter 8

The Machine in the City
Phenomenology and Everyday Life in New York

Grahame Shane

I INTRODUCTION

> The old man would wander through the streets of the neighborhood, advancing slowly,
> sometimes by the merest increments, pausing, moving on again, pausing once more, as
> though each step had to be weighed and measured before it could take its place amongst
> the sum total of steps.[1]

In *The City of Glass* the American novelist Paul Auster identifies two opposed readings of
the city. Initially the author's voice describes New York as a place of modernity, speed
and efficiency. Slowly this voice is eroded by contact with an opposing force. This second
voice imagines the city as a den of iniquity, a Babylon, in which redemption can only be
found by extreme acts of faith and self-mortification. Memory, timelessness and ritual are
more important than speed or efficiency for this voice, which infects its modern counterpart with fatal doubts. Each of the two main characters symbolizes a particular
lived-world and in Auster's novel contact between the two of them proves fatal to both
parties. In the end Auster evolves beyond this encounter into the fluid, hybrid interchanges
of the everyday life of the city. Towards the end of the novel a third voice emerges which
moves beyond both parties, merging into the everyday life of the city, including the electronic and print media.

Quinn, the modernist protagonist, first appears as the author of hard boiled detective stories. He lives in obscurity in the grid of the Upper West Side. His fictional detective
knows how to operate within the tough matrix of the City Machine with maximum efficiency. The detective's Bogart-like alienation was both a product of the machine and a
defense against it, a critical distancing which increased his operative capacity. For him
time was of the utmost importance, movement and speed were essential.

Auster tells the story of the writer Quinn's decision to become a detective himself.
His first case leads to an encounter with the older Mr. Stillman, a broken, ex-Columbia
University Professor. Research in the Public Library's newspaper archives reveals that
Stillman was tried in court for incarcerating his son for years after his wife's death. At the
start of the novel he has just been released from a state mental institution and the detective's job is to tail him from his arrival in Grand Central Station. Quinn's client is the
severely brain damaged son and his girlfriend, whose kiss haunts Quinn's mind
throughout the case and who, he felt, might prove his salvation. Auster writes of Quinn's
first attempts to shadow the slow, wandering pace of the old man:

> Moving in this manner was difficult for Quinn. He was used to walking briskly, and all this starting and stopping and shuffling began to be a strain. He was a hare in pursuit of a tortoise, and again and again he had to remind himself to hold back.[2]

Quinn's body resists the discipline imposed by the old man's scouring of the sidewalks of the neighborhood picking up shards. The difference in walking styles sums up a vast gulf which lay between them.

I would like briefly to explore the gap between the two contrasting world views of Auster's novel, which he weaves together with such skill. My aim in this exploration is to examine two mythical strands of New York imagery which Auster draws on. The first theme is the world of the mythical and symbolic city of pre-scientific knowledge with its magical, redemptive community. This urban village theme also has a long, shifting history linking back to the role of ritual and theater in the life of the city of faith. The second is the theme of the city as a super-modern machine. This theme also has a long history, especially in terms of the European interpretation of New York. Several layers of interpretation are bound up in this imagery, shifting over time as technology and communication systems changed.

Neither theme is adequate in itself and both are dependent on each other for their definition as a pair of opposites. This chapter will explore their interconnectedness as well as their differences. It will evaluate Auster's novel for clues as to how the two world views might more openly interpenetrate and interweave in the everyday life of the city in this age of staged, spectacular, mass communication images.

II THE PHENOMENOLOGY OF THE PRE-INDUSTRIAL CITY

In *The City of Glass* the modernist Quinn, playing detective, follows Stillman through the streets of Manhattan everyday. Finally Quinn realizes that the ex-professor was spelling out letters of the alphabet in his slow meanderings of the city streets. He was literally writing a letter a day, using the machine grid of the city as his framework. Auster illustrates Quinn's discovery with a small map of the Upper West Side and sample diagrams of Stillman's letters, as decoded against the grid of the city. Quinn works out that Stillman was slowly inscribing the words "Tower of Babel" upon the Upper West Side of Manhattan, a key phrase from the Bible, representing the phase before salvation arrived and Milton's paradise was regained.

While Quinn the modernist was busy efficiently recording the details of the case in his lined, detective's notebook, the ex-professor was walking the streets to spell out his message addressing the heavens above. Auster's Stillman represents a long tradition of belief that the city could address heaven and be redemptive. He did not believe in modern technology or science. He still lived in a "City of Faith" dreaming of a paradise regained after passing through a period of abjection. The ex-professor saw the city as a broken shard to be rendered whole by his redemptive skills in the invention of a new language which was essential for the re-entry into paradise. His message could only be read or

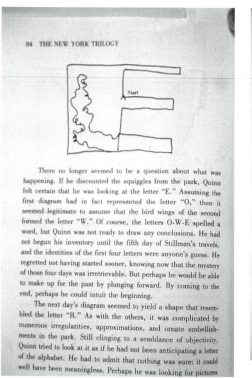

There no longer seemed to be a question about what was happening. If he discounted the squiggles from the park, Quinn felt certain that he was looking at the letter "E." Assuming the first diagram had in fact represented the letter "O," then it seemed legitimate to assume that the bird wings of the second formed the letter "W." Of course, the letters O-W-E spelled a word, but Quinn was not ready to draw any conclusions. He had not begun his inventory until the fifth day of Stillman's travels, and the identities of the first four letters were anyone's guess. He regretted not having started sooner, knowing now that the mystery of those four days was irretrievable. But perhaps he would be able to make up for the past by plunging forward. By coming to the end, perhaps he could intuit the beginning.

The next day's diagram seemed to yield a shape that resembled the letter "R." As with the others, it was complicated by numerous irregularities, approximations, and ornate embellishments in the park. Still clinging to a semblance of objectivity, Quinn tried to look at it as if he had not been anticipating a letter of the alphabet. He had to admit that nothing was sure: it could well have been meaningless. Perhaps he was looking for pictures

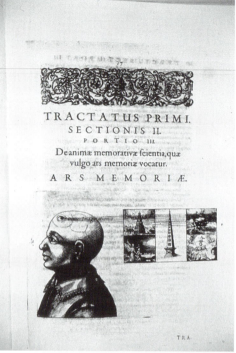

TRACTATUS PRIMI.
SECTIONIS II.
PORTIO III.
Deanimæ memorativæ scientia, quæ vulgo ars memoriæ vocatur.
ARS MEMORIÆ.

8.1 Detective Quinn's diagram of Professor Stillman's peregrinations in the Upper West Side Grid from Paul Auster, *The New York Trilogy; City of Glass*. Courtesy of Sun and Moon Press, Los Angeles.

8.2 The Village in the City; Memory and Navigation; the first page of the *Ars memoriae* showing Robert Fludd's memory theater system of 1619.

understood by someone positioned overhead, paying minute attention to the old man's actions everyday, held in position over Manhattan for a period of over two weeks.

Stillman, the antiquarian literary scholar, had his head still filled with the mythology of the Bible, Milton and the dream of a salvation. Joseph Rykwert in the *The Idea of a Town* (first published in 1957) describes the antiquity of this tradition, showing how the rational grid of ancient Roman colonial cities was embedded in multiple myths and rituals of purification (like the ploughing of the boundary of the city by white oxen, the lifting of the plough at the impure gates). In addition the augur's reading of slaughtered animal entrails helped site the town and the centrum mundi, a hole in the ground where settlers buried treasures from their previous lives, anchoring it to its site by these symbolic, memory fragments. Such mytho-poetic events were very much part of the pre-scientific, mythical world inhabited by Auster's second protagonist Stillman in *The City of Glass*.

Stillman's mytho-poetic and iconographic approach to the city tries to recoup the hidden knowledge of a pre-modern world view buried in magic, myth and pre-Cartesian science in an attempt to move beyond the scientific Machine City. Frances Yates's texts on *The Art of Memory* (1966), with their conception of the city as a theater in the mind's eye of the trained observer, gave a focus to phenomenological urban research. As in Stillman's case, the entire world could be interpreted as a kind of symbolic memory theater seen in the trained imagination. Yates describes how in the pre-modern, classical memory system knowledge was stored by attachment to iconic images, which were placed in a carefully constructed architectural sequence of rooms and niches. Statuary figures in the niches acted as mnemonic triggers for stored information. Yates argued that Shakespeare's Globe Theater (and Palladio's reconstructions of Roman theaters) were memory theaters in disguise. These privileged theatrical spaces had an enormous impact on the shaping of the pre-modern urban vision and overlapped with the introduction of modern perspectival constructions in the Renaissance.

This tradition of the world as a communal memory theater survived in Kevin Lynch's *Image of the City* (1960), which described the American city as a similar set of mnemonic enclaves, clusters of paths, nodes and landmarks (but from a pragmatic viewpoint). These visual elements formed a series of districts with edges and boundaries resulting in a city of villages. In his last book *Good City Form* (1984), Lynch outlined three different city systems using these enclave elements, recognizing first a "City of Faith," then the "City Machine" and finally the "Organic City" as equally unsatisfactory rivals. The "City of Faith" was the religious and feudal city, dominated by temple enclaves and religious iconography, built on the redemptive power of religious faith, imprinted in the city as a redemptive increment. As a Pragmatist, trained by Dewey, and a democratic architect, trained by F.L. Wright, Lynch rejected this faith-based model of the city, but beautifully described it in a series of diagrams and photographs.

The same ideal of the pre-industrial village was at the core of Jane Jacobs' *The Life and Death of Great American Cities* in the early 1960s. Jacobs gave voice to the small-scale appreciation of daily life of the city, on the streets of Greenwich Village. Christopher Alexander in his *A Pattern Language* of 1977 (written with Sara Ishikawa and Murray Silverstein and other team members) bases the fundamental patterns of his work on a theatrical, Shakespearean, life cycle of an idealized, small, urban village community. The built-form of the community was formed from small units which were combined by the builders to form and fit the community needs. The books highlighted these units in a lexicon of parts. The life cycle of the village was accommodated locally within these built elements, which in turn form part of a larger pattern of self-replicating, flexible, small urban units which aggregate to form the metropolis. This same theoretical reading of the city as a system of self-replicating urban villages, based on communal event spaces, shapes the intense activity of the village center in a new "Urban Forum" in the Kentish Town Project of Dalibor Veseley and Moshen Mostafavi studio designs of the 1970s.[3]

Phenomenologists, such as Christian Norberg Schulz in *Existence, Space and Architecture* (1971), continued this village lifeworld tradition in his own description of the city. Like Lynch, Norberg Schulz constructed a tripartite system, but in his diagram three separate "lived worlds" were linked in a feedback loop. Each world contained a private part of individual impressions, a public or social part of shared impressions and another section for the realm of objective or scientific information. Clearly the communal "lived world" of the town could be categorized in this way, segregating the scientific or modern business world from the areas of community. Here the pre-industrial village was

8.3 The Machine in the City and the Urban Village; Scale Contrasts. John Sloan, "The City from Greenwich Village," 1922, oil on canvas, 26″ × 33″. Courtesy of the National Gallery of Art.

an important model of community values. Norberg Schulz's favorite district in Manhattan was Greenwich Village, both for its scale and its differentiation from the Manhattan grid. He wrote of the streets as "a small universe" where the character of a town or district is presented in a condensed form for the visitor.[4]

It is not hard to imagine how a phenomenological reading of New York would stress all the various knowledge worlds and their interaction, beginning with the pre-modern history of the city, when it was a small Dutch village by the river. A village but also a world-theater, full of strange half-scientific magics, settings for strange rituals based on various exiled sects. The settlers' confrontation with the myths and rituals of the nomadic, native Americans would have been traumatic for both parties. The position of the Dutch traders and their settlement stockade on the tip of the long thin island was crucial, as were the differences between the various rivers, currents and wind flows running around the island. The climate was also important, with its strange mixture of Nordic winters and Mediterranean summers (the city is on the same latitude as Naples). This position created paradoxical combinations of brutal snow and intense heat, prompting a layered preoccupation with heating and cooling structures, shading, shuttering (with summer migrations for the wealthy to the Maine sea shore, the Hamptons or distant mountains). The hills and rivers that formed the topography of the island, the steep bluffs or easy slopes down to the shores, all shaped the early settlement patterns of the city, as did the vulnerability of marshes and flatlands to flooding and freak tides.

The theater of the city was thus conditioned by the proximity to water, the horizon, its insular position, climate and topography, machines and communities, all of which remained thinly veiled beneath the commissioner's mechanical grid. The theatrical urban chronicle, even in the age of the American Technological Sublime described below, always involved the view from the harbor. It was precisely this view which captivated Europeans on the great liners at the beginning of the twentieth century. Views to the water and wide horizon of the river or bay, framed by wharves and industry towards the rising or setting sun, were an essential part of the city's natural setting (until very recently these waterside edges were also the main work places of the vast majority of the population). Thus the first pre-modern city was linked to the port and the ship, to a trading culture which was accelerated in the nineteenth century by the advent of steam power, the railway and telegraph. The city still remained anchored to the port around the great basin of the harbor, while new flows of immigrants increased its size and settled in ethnic enclaves which would later form the basis for the classic ethnic ghettos.

New York's various squares acted as "Urban Forum" at different points in the city's history (Bowling Green, City Hall Park, Washington Square, Union Square, Madison Square, Times Square, etc.), while Broadway and Fifth Avenue formed armatures parallel with the Hudson. The poor were concentrated close to the river and the docks on the periphery of the island in the nineteenth century. The wealthy moved up and down along the carefully policed central spine along Fifth Avenue, leading to Central Park. As the city grew north, the great north–south avenues, wider and opening to the sky, formed the backbone of two linear cities on either side of Central Park, East Side and West Side, the latter weaving around the long spine of Broadway. This spine, along with Fifth Avenue and Wall Street, provides the three great ceremonial settings for civic rituals and pageantry, parades and pomp. Along the wider avenues taller structures and apartment buildings created the archetypal scale of the New York City canyon, forming great cliffs of dwellings making their edges against parks and river.

The regularity of the grid formed the framework, as in Auster's novel, for the inscription of events and shifting boundaries containing specific populations. Just as the grid was distorted by the topography and climate of the city, creating shade and shelter from the sun with trees, etc., so a culture of village life infects and influences the lived world within the Machine City. As the urban geographer Eric Homberger demonstrated in *The Historical Atlas of New York City* (1994) poverty, race and class, as well as wealth, move with waves of populations across the face of the city.

The shifting villages and their lifeworlds act as accelerators, blockages or delays, creating friction and resistance within the body of the Machine City grid. A history of villages and community enclaves would chronicle the history of successive waves of immigration into successive spatial enclaves, setting up the typical American, urban "melting pot." Several phases can be distinguished. The first phase would be the muddled and mixed immigrant areas around the old Dutch city and Lower East Side, before the establishment of the system of ethnic enclaves. The second phase would see the establishment of the classic ghetto, enforced by laws which confined all people of a particular group to a specific spatial location. This was the modernist city of ethnic neighborhoods, when Little Italy, Little Germany, the Jewish Ghetto, African-American Ghetto and Irish "quarters" were established. All strata of society were contained in these ghettos, from the middle class doctors and teachers to the poorest of the poor. This system was undermined by the third phase with the shift to the automobile city and the development of the suburbs, allowing the middle classes of all ghettos to escape (African-Americans were the last wave, only allowed out after civil rights legislation of the 1960s). Finally in the fourth post-modern phase two distinct trends can be seen in the development of these enclaves. In one, communities have thrived following Jane Jacobs' advocacy of urban villages, linking into the real estate cycles of gentrification, becoming Special Districts, Preservation Areas, even Business Improvement Areas. In the other trend the ghettos stripped of their middle class inhabitants have become "Hyperghettos," enclaves of intense poverty, drugs, disease and impoverished education, medical services and social services.[5]

The problem for Stillman's fundamentalist approach is that the everyday occurrences in the life of the individual and community in a technocratic age tend to escape their sacred village location. Stillman confined and tortured his son in order to try to force him into a mold which he believed would prepare him for the return of Christ. Almost too much attention was applied to the individual and details of life in a closed space. Stillman's lived world of redemptive theocracy was badly out of step with the daily reality of the city. As a result he was rejected by his son and he lived like a homeless person, shuffling about the streets. There every broken object was for him a sign of divine grace and intercession, while in return he spelt out his secret message on the grid of the city. His individual everyday life thus literally had a message, but was lived in the gutter removed from the rest of society. Similarly the redemptive communal rituals of the pre-scientific society have also often been replaced by new, highly mediated, secular events in the city, such as sports marathons, rock concerts or ethnic parades, which appeal to a much wider, hybrid community.

III THE CITY MACHINE AND THE AMERICAN TECHNOLOGICAL SUBLIME

Quinn, Auster's detective, inhabited a very different world from Stillman. He wrote Sublime, detective fantasies in the paranoid-critical tradition of the surrealists, creating an impossible utopia of speed and logical transparency set in a super-banal world. He was obsessed with the Technological Sublime. His writing described the operations of a man who knew how to read the signs and clues of the city in order to solve cases efficiently. When Quinn offered his services as a detective he attempted to make this fictional space into his real lived world, projecting himself into his construction of the city with tragic consequences. In this gesture he identified himself with the Sublime logic of the Machine City and its limitless aesthetic of boundless expansion, grids without end, knowledge without limits. The settings of his encounters with Stillman were impeccably chosen and deeply symbolic. He first researched the subject of his investigation in the newspaper archives of the New York Public Library. He first glimpsed his subject in the flesh on the ramps up from the platforms of Grand Central Station (causing a temporary blackout of consciousness). His first verbal contact with his subject takes place in the remedial landscape of Olmstead's Riverside Park.

The phenomenology of the Sublime has often been celebrated in architectural literature, since the naming of the category by Burke in the early 1750s. The desire to create, heterotopic, efficient worlds became an American passion, as identified by Leo Marx in *The Machine in the Garden* (1964) with a special technological twist. While this passion first found its outlet in the conquest of nature and the American continent, it produced its own internal logic and lived world. Marx illustrates how the machines enabled humans to construct an improved world for themselves both in the material world and in their literary or pictorial imaginations. Marx concentrates on the bucolic and rural applications of the machine to nature, emphasizing the new balance between man and nature made possible by the machine (pastoralism), but largely ignoring the great urban clusters.

David Nye in *The American Technological Sublime* (1994) drives home the inflexible technological logic which repressed all other worlds and applied this logic to cities, especially in the construction of bridges, highways and skyscrapers, with world's fairs as a testing ground. Nye emphasizes that the apparent rationalism of the City Machine and its triumphant technology concealed a variety of hidden worlds, desires and motivations. He spotlights the almost religious transcendental zeal which drove so many of the American technological innovators, including the builders of the skyscrapers. These structures were most magical and ethereal when illuminated at night, outlining the city in light (Koolhaas had previously made the connection to Coney Island's lighted towers and rides).

Nye points out the irrational passion which drove the American Technological Sublime. The most spectacular of the American technological marvels very often did not make economic sense. Nye shows that Woolworth acknowledged that his building, the tallest in the world at the time, could not make a profit. He justified it as the largest publicity billboard in the world for his chain of stores. Similarly Nye recounts that the Empire State Building was only 25 percent occupied on its completion and the Rockefeller Center is alleged to have been a major drain on the family's fortunes. The gigantic, vacant, twin towers of the World Trade Center had to be rescued on their completion by New York State in the late 1970s. The developers of the World Financial Center went bankrupt, despite all their subsidies and business acumen. These machines were driven by an aesthetic formula which required the pursuit of a sense of sublime power, the sense of overcoming nature on a gigantic scale, the sense of a subservient domain (as corporate executives looked down on the city from their high floors), reaching for the sky and dominating the city skyline.[6]

While Nye stresses the irrational passion which drove the Machine City, Lynch pointed to its narrow, scientific rationality which guaranteed its success in its own terms. In *Good City Form* Lynch diagrammed the Machine City as an open system designed like a computer chipboard, with separate, heterotopic cells containing specialized functions, connected by rapid channels of communication and transport. Lynch described the Machine City as a system of inter-related cells, connected by lines of flow, both mechanical (traffic) and informational. Lynch highlighted the hierarchical nature of the Machine City, which operated from the top down, with big dominating little. He noted its global and regional reach as a network. He attacked the autonomous life and logic of the self-replicating, mono-functional system, which only sought profit and acted independently of human desire and natural conditions. Lynch criticized the way in which the systems approach directed people as abstract flows in patterns totally unresponsive to local conditions and people's needs. In particular Lynch attacked the way in which this system could quickly abandon a cell in one area, say the inner city, and build another to replace it anywhere, perhaps the outer suburbs, perhaps South America or Asia.

Lynch's Machine City diagrams accurately portrayed the inner logic of Quinn's city, with its modern means of transportation and places of specialization, whether of production or consumption, knowledge or wealth, sickness, justice or education. After a period of domestic production, expensive machines were quickly grouped in factories to make places of great productivity and profit. These places of great efficiency were separated from the everyday life of the city, they were moved away from the city, sometimes surrounded by walls. The logic of Taylorized mass production, industrialization under monopoly capitalism and the increasing globalization of trade meant that the original Dutch village at the tip of Manhattan was quickly transformed into a forest of corporate skyscrapers by 1900. Moving away from the harbor, railways allowed factories and residential districts to migrate northwards on Manhattan or outwards to the outer boroughs. These factories and skyscrapers were "other" spaces, heterotopias of efficiency, where work and living were segregated. They were separated from the messy business of everyday living, away from the village or shanty town housing the workers and their families. Skyscrapers operated as mono-functional cells, segregating specialized uses, vertically about an elevator shaft. The old Dutch village core of New York, centered on Wall Street, came to represent the global symbol of capitalism and high finance. The old village center had become the skyscraper City Machine par excellence, the first modern downtown.[7]

The three-dimensional logic of this capitalist clustering in the City Machine was displayed in images of New York from the beginning of the twentieth century. The approach from the port was spectacular with the Standard Oil Building, the Cunard Building, the Equitable Insurance Building, the Singer Building and the Woolworth Building forming a spine along Broadway, while Wall Street towers loomed behind. Some of the most impressive downtown skyscrapers of the first wave belonged to the new media companies (like Hearst's group), forming a cliff-like phalanx along Newspaper Row facing City Hall across City Hall Park. In the 1920s Europeans continued to use the image of downtown New York seen from the sea or air to epitomize machine-age modernity. The spectacular image of the New York skyline, with the skyscrapers of the Wall Street area sprouting from the tip of Manhattan, epitomized the vertical dynamic of the unbridled capitalist city. This view was echoed in Paul Citroen's Dadaist, "metropolis" photomontage of 1923, which collaged many New York landmarks into what must surely be the first portrayal of the dense, clustered, global city in our collective unconscious. Even the Russian constructivist Kazimir Malevich collaged his "Project for a Supremacist Skyscraper for New York City" (1926) onto a similar view of Wall Street and downtown. The chaotic image of New York City became an especially German preoccupation, being repeated in Eric Mendelson's *Amerika* (1926) and in Ludwig Hilbersheimer's *Groszstadt Architecture* (1927). This same chaotic, vertical and sectional dynamic was used by Fritz Lang as the model for his set showing the life of the androids in his *Metropolis* (1926).[8]

Americans attempted to rationalize the three-dimensional logic of the Machine City from an early date, proposing various codes and height controls, like Louis Sullivan in Chicago in the 1890s. New York's 1916 Zoning Code recognized the downtown, Dutch village core as a special district where exceptional heights occurred, setting a precedent for many other village clusters to follow. Elsewhere the 1916 code linked building height to street width and a system of setbacks. The logic of the hyper-dense Machine City became a particularly New York preoccupation. King's futuristic, aerial view of New York of 1911, represented a city of unbelievable density as a multi-layered city of skyscrapers,

8.4 The Machine in the City; The vision of the multi-layered futurist city street and towers; "King's Dream of New York," 1911. Courtesy of Avory Architectural and Fine Arts Library, Columbia University, New York.

bridges, railways and airplanes. This first phase metropolitan vision was immensely popular with Europeans as well as Americans. This view of the hyper-dense city was disseminated throughout Europe and America on the cover of the *Scientific American* on July 26, 1913, entitled "The Elevated Sidewalk," showing an enormously complex section of a futuristic New York street. The vista led up from the subways and elevated railways to a dense cluster of skyscrapers, connected by bridges at various levels. This same preoccupation with the vertical, multi-layered, Machine City can be seen in Henard's contemporary sketches for future streets of Paris, in Sant'Elia's sketches of the Futurist City or heard in Marinetti's panegyrics to speed, the automobile or airplane. Reyner Banham argues that these images of speed and density were repressed, along with futurism, by later modernists. These later propagandists were intent on a radical formal purity and were disturbed by the eclectic skins, deep street canyons and chaotic layout of these early towers.[9] Hilbersheimer, for instance, wanted to rationalize and standardize the complex street section, which became the podium base for his long, slab blocks in a tree-less, three-dimensional, gridded street matrix.[10]

In New York the construction of Grand Central Station represented the embodiment of these first machine-age and futurist's dreams. This was a layered, machine-age hub inside the city, further accelerating the efficiency of the grid city. Here mass transportation systems were segregated on several levels according to distance and line, while street cars and subways ran along 42nd Street and automobiles by-passed the station on the elevated roadway on the axis of Park Avenue. The section of the station complex was also

8.5 The Machine in the City; Sectional Perspective of Grand Central Station at 42nd Street and Park Avenue. Reed & Stem and Warren & Wetmore, 1903–1913, used by *Scientific American* as a cover 1912. Courtesy of Avery Architectural and Fine Arts Library, Columbia University, New York.

published in *Scientific American* in 1912, which devoted its cover to this "Monumental Gateway to America's Greatest City." In combination with the development of skyscraper office towers and hotels around the station, the mass transportation interchange formed a super-efficient enclave and hub, a city-within-the-city. It was a multi-layered microcosm of the larger City Machine of mass consumption and production.[11]

The construction of Penn Station and Grand Central Station triggered an enormous shift in the operations of the City Machine, as a rail-based city region replaced the water-based city around the harbor basin. The new stations linked to a vast, regional and national hinterland. Before this time, many train journeys had begun with a ferry ride to the train terminals on the Jersey side of the Hudson. Industries like the garment industry moved uptown to be close to the stations. Clusters of skyscrapers developed about these transportation hubs, like the Chrysler Building (1930), beside Grand Central, and the Empire State Building (1927), beside Penn Station. Indeed the construction of these streamlined, art deco skyscrapers increased the identification of New York with the speed and efficiency of the City Machine. The early skyscrapers had emerged from the irregular plan of the old Dutch village settlement downtown; in midtown they were situated in the rational clarity of the 1811 Commissioners grid. Yet even here they clustered about hubs, forming small skyscraper villages. Rockefeller Center, constructed in the depths of the Great Depression, conformed to this same pattern, while also reinforcing the image of the city as an invincible machine, whose speed and efficiency might even defy market logic. This enormous complex engaged the grid of the city, but also arranged its towers in an asymmetrical manner around a pedestrianized central axis, its own internal high street, the Promenade, the equivalent of Wall Street in Downtown.

There was no reason why the logic of this hyper-dense City Machine of three dimensional village-like clusters should be confined to the twin poles of Downtown and Midtown. Initially the absence of bedrock for foundations had limited skyscraper locations, but later this technical restraint no longer applied. The bi-polar system of nodes and networks could easily be expanded to cover a region. Hugh Ferris's drawings of the 1930s showed enormous clusters of towers based on the Rockefeller model, with giant set-back, stepped formations from the 1916 zoning regulation, projected to form vast mountains of development at key nodes extending up the Manhattan grid. Ferris developed the idea of New York as the ultimate cluster of efficient, standardized, high-rise offices connected by powerful, mechanical, mass transportation systems in multi-layered street canyons of incredible density, as shown in the Regional Plan Associations illustrations of 1929.[12]

The expansion of the Machine City from a single node to a bi-polar system and then to a multi-centered regional system had been anticipated in Ebenezer Howard's *Garden Cities of Tomorrow* (1902) (Forest Hills Gardens had been begun on this model in 1907). In the 1929 Regional Plan Howard's polycentric, yet concentric models were distorted to fit the island of Manhattan, the direction of the coastline, Long Island and New Jersey. The rivers and bridges played a major role in aligning the network of surrounding towns asymmetrically in linear sectors up the coast on either side of the center. Under this plan the City Machine would spawn residential villages in a green belt around its periphery, connected by rail to the twin central business districts. Robert Moses' contemporary activities initiating the Parkway system followed the same hypothesis, but based on private cars. Post-war development, supported by Federal subsidies for housing, highways, etc., greatly accelerated this process, expanding the scale of the garden city enormously and draining the inner city. True to the recalibration of the Technological Sublime at a new regional scale in the 1950s, a Second Regional Plan based on the highways called for the shift of industry out of Manhattan to an inner ring of new working class suburbs, leaving the center clear for the spectacular construction of a new, global business center. The enormous, horizontal, post-modern wastelands in the New Jersey Wetlands and Hackensack Meadowlands have been the sad heritage of this policy, along with the vast container depot at Port Elizabeth, New Jersey, and airports like Kennedy and Newark, also set in fragile ecologies.[13]

As the Machine City was reconfigured as a multi-centered regional system, so the Central Business District was reconfigured to match its altered role. Following the logic of the Technological Sublime in the early 1960s, the City Planning Commission altered the Zoning Code to allow sleek towers to rise directly from the gridded ground plane of the city, without unnecessary or decorative setbacks. Unlike Le Corbusier's isolated towers in the "Ville Radieuse" which rose from a park, these towers were implanted in the city. Mies van der Rohe built the Seagram Tower as a single insertion on Park Avenue to demonstrate the modernist solution for isolating towers on a plaza at the end of city blocks. This model became the norm in the 1961 Zoning Ordinance, repeated ad nauseam across the midtown and at a gigantic scale in the downtown World Trade Center's twin towers. Here beneath the plaza lay buried an enormous underground shopping mall and commuter railway station, as well as vast car parks. The stark contrast between the modernist Penn Station and the Beaux Arts original makes the change in codes clear. Where the Beaux Arts Penn Station had a series of grand public spaces modeled on ancient roman bath houses, the new Penn Station had a private sports stadium whose dense mass above the center pushed the circulation of the station below ground. Here a system of functional, low passages created a subterranean maze, only loosely connected with the free-standing tower and stadium standing on the plaza at street level. It was little wonder that the demolition of the old Penn Station triggered so much resistance and, with the threat to Grand Central, the Historic Preservation movement.

The problem for the advocates of the Technological Sublime has always been the limitations of machines, the accommodation of everyday life and the necessity of "invisible labor." Quinn himself worked as an impoverished writer of detective stories in the decaying backwaters of the inner city on the Upper West Side. Even with the advent of computerization and robots, machines cannot do everything always as economically as humans. The result has been that the Technological Sublime often depends on hidden realms of workers kept in substandard conditions in order to support the technological fantasy of excess. In New York heterotopic containers, like Grand Central Station, the Empire State Building or even the New York Public Library, often have a hidden dark side. Rachel Bowlby in *Just Looking* (1985) examined the one such heterotopic typology. She studied the contradictory role of the department stores in the emancipation of women. Bowlby looked at the different lived worlds created for women by these temples of consumption. Using novels by Dreiser, Gissing and Zola, she showed how the male creation of these dream spaces to "liberate" female consumers was predicated upon the disciplined misery of many live-in servants and shop-girls. Nye writes in similar terms of the "invisible labor" necessary for the American Technological Sublime. The laborers imported from China who built the western end of the transcontinental railway were rarely photographed. He mentions the complaints of the work crews on the Empire State Building, whose steel erectors were often native Americans, subjected to fast track assembly line techniques to complete the building in 11 months.

In the American Technological Sublime the dark side and hidden spaces of the oppressed may be located many miles from the image space of the Machine City. Professor Stillman, for instance, is incarcerated in the distant suburbs, where Quinn never ventures. Thanks to modern communications and transportation systems, the dark underbelly may be elsewhere in the city, the country or even the world (as in the case of the Philippine sweat shop manufacturing Empire State Building T-shirts). Quinn himself falls through the cracks of the City Machine, despite his devotion to the Technological Sublime. Auster notes in the voice of an outside observer:

> How he managed to keep himself hidden during this period is a mystery. But it seems that no one discovered him or called his attention to the authorities. No doubt he learned early on the schedule of the garbage collectors and made sure to be out of the alley when they came. Likewise the building superintendent, who deposited trash each evening in the bin and the cans. Remarkable as it seems, no one ever noticed Quinn. It was as though he had melted into the walls of the city.[14]

Quinn ends up living naked, mostly in a fetal position, in an empty room of his ex-client's abandoned apartment, mysteriously being fed by an unseen stranger. Stillman, the ex-Columbia professor, throws himself from the Brooklyn Bridge, one of the key icons of Nye's *American Technological Sublime* after his conversations with Quinn.

IV PROFESSOR AUSTER'S IN-BETWEEN WORLD

The tragic fates of Auster's two protagonists in *The City of Glass* point to the impossibility of holding their two images of the city completely separate. Neither image is entirely satisfactory and each protagonist is infected by the other, producing deadly hybrids. Neither protagonist can in fact conform to their ideal. Quinn lives a totally marginal life, excluded from the wealth, power and prestige of the Machine City and its media. Stillman is completely oblivious of the rituals and rhythms of everyday life in the city, which form the basis of community, instead being obsessed with his fundamentalist faith. Both protagonists are seen as failures and they reverse roles in a curious inversion of lifeworld codes and belief systems in their deaths. Stillman uses the dynamic of the sublime technological object to violently end his life, Quinn retreats into a world of total self-absorption, stasis and internal peace isolated from the city.

Auster points to a third position which balances the interaction of these two lifeworlds and moves beyond them into the post-modern city. He implies that both the dream of the Machine City and the dream of the redemptive City of Faith taken to extreme provide an inadequate model for an effective lived world. Both have their advantages, both also include elements of each other. In *The City of Glass* there is a young Professor Auster, with a wife and young child, connected into the life of the Columbia University and the city, who is consulted by Quinn about Stillman at one point of the narrative. Later it is he who watches television and tells Quinn, by now disassociated from the Machine City, of Stillman's death, prompting further withdrawal. It is he who keeps in touch longest with Quinn, tracking him down, and it is he who at the end of the book is berated by the unknown narrator's voice for letting him fall through the net of the city.

Professor Auster represents a post-modern hybrid of Village and Machine City, information systems and regional media connections. He is simultaneously a father committed to family life (in the Village City life cycle) and public persona, a professional expert consulted by Quinn the modernist detective at the beginning of his quest (in the Machine City). He is able to operate in both realms and balance both realms, yet even he fails. While he is berated for his failure to catch Quinn in the city's safety net, it is clear that at that point he was the only person who might have cared for Quinn (other than the mysterious person who fed him). The hybrid figure of Professor Auster fails, but is a far more sympathetic failure from the point of view of the author's last voice. This ironic, self-referential creation, Professor Auster, who is so wise and kind, combines both a knowledge of the mytho-poetic City of Villages and the mytho-poetic realm of the Technological Sublime. He understands the symbolism of the city and also its reliance on communication systems to overcome distance. He sees that such systems involve their own form of myth making, as a way to overcome distance. The mythology of places, enshrined in the urban poetic of the skyscraper or the village, are both fictions created in this communication system to draw people to specific places for specific purposes. Professor Auster also understands that this is a dynamic system, constantly changing and shifting, reflecting the commodification of the city and its image as real estate in a far larger city-region.

Both village and skyscraper are framed by belief systems which intermingle in the lived reality of the post-modern city. Manfredo Tafuri in *Architecture and Utopia* (1976) recognizes the concept of the City Machine as a uniquely American "negative utopia," a neutral framing device of enormous creative power, a constant and unchanging reference point in the midst of rapid change. Tafuri identifies the basic 200 ft by 600 ft or 800 ft module of the New York grid plan, employed by both Stillman and Quinn, as deeply symbolic of the pragmatic, machine-age mentality of the Enlightenment land surveyors (who also subdivided the American continent into gridded lots). At the same time Tafuri wrote of "The Disenchanted Mountain," contrasting the disciplined regularity of the grid plan with the vertical flexibility and flamboyant styling of the skyscraper as an artifical "mountain" which had no other logic than display and irrational seduction.[15] It was in the same period, the mid-1970s, that Cooper and Eckstudt planned Battery Park City as a grid extension of New York, proposing to replicate the city's best features of rowhouse and apartment blocks on the landfill from the World Trade Center twin towers.

Rem Koolhaas' *Delirious New York* (1978) dramatically highlighted the hybrid nature of the post-modern city, while his descriptions enthusiastically carried on the tradition of the Technological Sublime. In this post-modern reading the image of the City Machine is acknowledged as a poetic fiction, the product of the author's "paranoid-critical" method derived from Salvador Dali and the surrealists. Koolhaas is interested in the irrational dreams and poetic desires that haunt and drive the Machine City. In his "fevered" imagination buildings become anthropomorphic, magic personalities. They take on a life independent of the city as images in a parallel mytho-poetic world of mediated hyper-reality. This imaginary world is beautifully illustrated by Madeline Vreisendorp's cover picture in which the Empire State Building and Chrysler Building are shown relaxing in bed, with a discarded Goodyear balloon between them on the sheets. Through the window of the apartment the other skyscrapers watch as an assembled community of magic tokens. For Koolhaas New York City was a sublime object, something totally out of the ordinary, superhuman and magical. Its scale, its complexity, its density and "Culture of Congestion" distinguishes it from all other cities. Mechanical efficiency was a given, but not the goal. The attraction was a hybrid aesthetic pleasure and a delight in urban efficiency and artificiality pushed to poetic excess. This is New York as the hyper-machine, the delirious phantasmagoria of the fourth-generation visiting European.

The problem for this mediated, hyper-real world of machine and village is that every part of life had to be brought to a pinnacle of perfection in a specialized enclave, an image space which is part advertising hype, part very human need. Everyday life had to be disassembled into a series of precise actions. Both the village and skyscraper become part commodity, part community, as communities are gentrified and skyscrapers abandoned and recycled (at one point in the mid-1990s 28 percent of the downtown office space was vacant). The result is that the Machine City and village hyper-real combination provides a miniature network of mini-spaces for services in highly specialized, heterotopic containers, each one separate from the other. Each provider of these services competed with each other and desperately tried to distinguish themselves from the rest, to establish a market niche. Robert A.M. Stern's post-modern portraits of New York were acutely tuned to these hybrid, in-between spaces in which the Sublime aesthetic was domesticated in a series of interior urban worlds. Stern and his co-authors document the interiors and exteriors of the many "Third Spaces" (neither private home nor entirely public arenas) which provided the super-seductive resting places for the bourgeois New Yorkers. These gentlemen's clubs, night clubs, dance halls, cafés, bars, restaurants, ladies tea rooms, newsstands, barber shops and beauty saloons provided a temporary resting place in the city. Here in a frenzy of activity or in comparative calm, the well-to-do citizen could contemplate the spectacle of the city with some detachment (parks and gardens functioned in a similar manner in the open air).[16]

This ambiguous reading of the City Machine and City of Villages also informed the self-reflexive exhibition of images of New York in the fall of 1996 at the Whitney. Here images of the efficiency of the sleek Machine City intermingled with the humanity of its inhabitants. In this "Third Space" washing on a clothes line might be displayed against the city's magnificent skyline of skyscrapers, as inhabitants had a cigarette on the rooftop in the summer heat. Entitled "New York; City of Ambition," at first sight the exhibition appeared to be dominated by machinist imagery. But the exhibition selection drew on the book *New York; the Painted City* of 1992 by Grace Gluek, a long-time art correspondent for the *New York Times*. While Gluek quotes the W.P.A. Guide on the "feverish energy" of everyday life in the city, her choice of images portrays New York as a dynamic machine, which relentlessly raises some on high and debases many others. Both sides of the coin are shown, high and low, the skyscraper machine and the elevated railways passing through the village.

8.6 The Machine/ Village confrontation; resistance to gentrification; James Romberger, "The Battle of ABC," 1991, drawing, 60″ × 50⅜″. Courtesy of the Metropolitan Museum of Art.

Gluek's selections show the interaction of human and machine, from George Ault in the 1920s, through Charles Sheiler and Georgia O'Keeffe in the 1930s, to Richard Estes, Leigh Behnke and Roger Winter in the 1980s. Oskar Kokoschka's Expressionistic dynamic breaks the hard-boiled mask of the Machine City while Jane Dickson's view from her window of a Times Square prostitute at the street corner suggests that all was not entirely well in the booming metropolis of the 1980s. Gluek ends with James Romberger's "The Battle of ABC" (1991) showing police and firemen fighting with squatters in the East Village.

As both masks fail, it is the very human everyday life of the city, its media and its memory theater which emerge as the glue which binds the hybrid city together as a third force. In fact New York is incredibly bad at dealing with the necessities of everyday life and this, as much as its legendary efficiency, is a crucial part of its character. The city works, despite its mythology of speed, to slow people down and to bring them together in spectacular assemblies, either as individuals face to face or as great masses. The city provides a multitude of slowing down functions in special enclaves attached to its clogged armatures of transportation and communication (where the pace is further slowed, even to a halt). Any New Yorker can tell horror stories of the subways or traffic jams in rush hour which make the "Culture of Congestion" a bad joke. Passengers at 72nd Street subway station are afraid of being pushed from the narrow, overcrowded platforms into the path of the arriving trains, yet massive new housing construction is proposed at exactly this point in the system. Radio stations regularly report long delays on the bridge and tunnel crossings, as well as enormous delays shifting through the highway system following accidents and road repairs. The pollution produced by automobiles in central cities is still very dangerous to health. Being a pedestrian on the city sidewalks is far more dangerous than flying on an airplane, even though the average speed of traffic in central New York is under 4 mph. The city is entirely unable to organize the sorting and recycling of its garbage and is still completely disconnected from the national rail freight system, forcing all goods to be transferred to highly polluting local delivery trucks.

We do inevitably operate in an everyday world of contradictory mythologies and perceptual–conceptual hybrids, which make nonsense of our analytical stereotypes. The memory theater of the city, for instance, has become immensely more complicated since regionalization and now globalization. Our isolated homes are now plugged into vast corporate and state memory banks of images and information, which may be disseminated in the propaganda model to our homes, or we may choose to burrow with our mice through the vast maze on the Net. In either case the result is the same, the city has a new conceptual dimension which further complicates the distribution and competition of aesthetic enclaves within the larger field. Our neighborhoods and machine icons now take on a more complicated hybrid nature as part machine-memory icon and part memory theater as lived world.

V CONCLUSION

Professor Auster's lesson is that we must of necessity now live hybrid lives, part everyday necessity, part phenomenological, part mechanical and media driven, the city thus forming a part of our multiple identities. The sublime dream of the modernist and the pheno-menological dream of the memory theater are both important parts of this city, but so too is the everyday life flow of the city with its inconsistencies, contradictions and messy relationships. We need to be open to every possibility, while recognizing the different frameworks which foster and support a variety of lifeworlds. We need to be able to move freely between these various lifeworlds and it is this liberty which in many ways defines urbanity. We are also still only gendered humans, with all the attendant weakness and strengths, love of myths and rituals, movies and books. The global city, not the village predicted by MacLuhan, has arrived weaving into our everyday life in countless ways. With it has come a strange, new hybrid perception of reality, in which both the mythic and the machine merge in a new lived reality of the sidewalks of New York. Meanwhile author Paul Auster's fourth, last, weak, disembodied voice reminds us not to forget our shared humanity and responsibility for others in the hybrid delirium of self-promotion, exploitation and hype of the post-modern city.

Notes

1   P. Auster: *The New York Trilogy; City of Glass*, New York: Penguin, 1987, p. 93.
2   Ibid., p. 93.
3   From studios at the Architectural Association, London, in the 1970s (recorded in *Architecture and Continuity* (1982)).
4   Christian Norberg Schulz in *Existence, Space and Architecture* (1971) cited Bergson, Husserl, Heidegger, for their insights into the limitations of science. Norberg-Schulz drew on Levi-Strauss, Piaget and Lynch for their understanding of "lived worlds," which have set horizons, built on lines of interest and inquiry, creating a tradition and body of knowledge. For Three Worlds diagram, see p. 38.
5   For Special Districts, BIDs and Historic Districts, see R. Babcock and U. Larsen: *Special Zoning Districts*, Cambridge, Mass., 1990 and for HyperGhettos see W.J. Wilson: *The Truely Disadvantaged*, Chicago, 1987 and Loic Wacquant: "The Ghetto, the State and the new Capitalist economy," in P. Kasinitz, (ed.): *Metropolis; Center and Symbol of Our Times*, New York, 1995, pp. 413–49."
6   For the opposite view, see Carol Willis' arguments in *Form Follows Finance* (1996).
7   For heterotopias, see M. Foucault: "Of Other Spaces; Utopias and Heterotopias" (1967) reprinted in J. Ockman, (ed.): *Architecture Culture 1943–1968: A Documentary Anthology*, New York, 1993. For Foucault's two types of heterotopias, see B. Gennochio: "Heterotopia and its Limits," in: *Transitions*, #41, 1993, pp. 33–41, and "Discourse, Discontinuity and Difference," in: S. Watson and S. Gibson: *Post-Modern Cities and Spaces*, Blackwell, 1995, pp. 35–46. See also E. Soja: *Post-modern Geographies* (1989), pp. 16–22.
8   See Dawn Ades: *Photomontage*, London, 1976, pp. 98–103.
9   Reyner Banham in *Theory of Design in the First Machine Age* (1962).
10   See Richard Pommer: "More Necropolis than Metropolis," in: *The Shadow of Mies; Ludwig Hilberseimer; Architect, Educator and Urban Planner*, pp. 16–53.
11   See Deborah Nevins (ed.): *Grand Central Terminal; City Within a City*, New York, 1982, p. 34.
12   See Hugh Ferris: *The Metropolis of Tomorrow*, New York, 1929.
13   The technological Sublime still has its defenders, Joel Garreau enthusiastically described the fruits of this growth into twenty-eight new urban, commercial clusters around New York as *Edge Cities* (1991). For Garreau the New York region had become the heart of an eastern seaboard megalopolis which stretched from Boston to Washington, requiring that the central area was again reconfigured with new towers as a regional and global entertainment center.
14   See *The City of Glass*, op. cit., p. 178.

15   Reprinted in *The American City; From the Civil War to the New Deal* (1979).
16   R.A.M. Stern and his team's more measured and sober *New York 1900* (1983), *New York 1930* (1987) and *New York 1960* (1995), by their volume and frequency, portray the mind-boggling speed and growth of a machine-age metropolis of skyscrapers that seemed to know no bounds.

Bibliography

Alexander, Christopher (with Ishikawa, Sara and Silverstein, Murray and other team members), *A Pattern Language*, Oxford University Press, 1977.

Auster, Paul, *The New York Trilogy; City of Glass*, Penguin: New York, 1987.

Bowlby, Rachel, *Just Looking*, 1985.

Gluek, Grace, *New York; The Painted City*, Layton, Utah, 1992.

Hilbersheimer, Ludwig, *Groszstadt Architecture*, Berlin, 1927.

Homberger, Eric, *The Historical Atlas of New York City*, 1994.

Howard, Ebenezer, *Garden Cities of Tomorrow*, London, 1902.

Jacobs, Jane, *The Life and Death of Great American Cities*, Penguin, 1960.

Koolhaas, Rem, *Delirious New York*, 1978.

Le Corbusier, *Ville Radieuse*, Paris, 1934.

Lynch, Kevin, *The Image of the City*, MIT Press, 1960.

Lynch, Kevin, *Good City Form*, MIT Press, 1984.

Marx, Leo, *The Machine in the Garden*, 1964.

Mendelson, Eric, *Amerika*, Berlin, 1926.

Nye, David, *The American Technological Sublime*, 1994.

Rykwert, Joseph, *The Idea of a Town*, MIT Press (first published in 1957).

Schulz, Christian Norberg, *Existence, Space and Architecture*, London, 1971.

Stern, R.A.M. and team members, *New York 1900* (1983), *New York 1930* (1987) *and New York 1960* (1995)

Tafuri, Manfredo, *Architecture and Utopia*, MIT Press, 1976.

Tafuri, Manfredo and Cuicci, Georgio, *The American City; From the Civil War to the New Deal*, 1979.

Veseley, Dalibor and Mostafavi, Moshen, *Architecture and Continuity*, London, 1982.

Yates, Frances, *The Art of Memory*, Chicago, 1966.

Chapter 9

Imaging New York
Representations and Perceptions of the City
Andrea Kahn

I "LOOKING DOWN FROM ABOVE": REPRESENTING THE URBAN

Representations are powerful formulations. They structure an understanding of urban life-worlds by organizing perceptions and everyday experiences of the city. By inscribing an idea of "the city" (which is only ever an idea), they impact materially and ideologically on notions of what the urban "is" and aspirations of what it could become. Whether considered in visual terms as modes of physical description (like the maps, plans, models and drawings of architects and urban designers) or non-visually, as the function of more abstract frameworks (like the economic and social policies, or municipal regulations of city planners) urban representations are a form of stabilization. They stall the mobile ground of urban territories, presenting "the city" as a rational construct and thereby making it available to analysis and critique. Acting as emulsifiers, projective imaging techniques as well as prescriptive regulatory constraints "discipline" a city's inherently unsettled and unsettling qualities through neat maneuvering that conflates many conflicted and contestatory views of the urban condition into one smooth image.

The challenges to perception presented by the city's diverse and often incommensurate orders are long-standing, as are the conventions of representation devised to overcome, or oversee, them. Historically, representations of the urban have tended to overlook the city's thickness by inscribing thin accounts that veil the physical density of the urban section, the temporal depth of historic layering, and the symbolic weight of collective memory. These rationalizing representations are linked to the persistence of a totalizing and resolute term – they reinforce a stable "concept" of city which can be traced back to the Renaissance, at least. Michel de Certeau refers to this tenacious notion as the "concept-city."[1] As he explains in *The Practice of Everyday Life*, it represents an attempt to overcome the contradictions and incommensurabilities arising from urban agglomeration. The "concept-city's" presumed legibility stands against the mobile opacities producing, and reproduced by, the practices of everyday life. As de Certeau notes "[t]he desire to see the city preceded the means of satisfying it. Medieval or Renaissance painters represented the city in a perspective that no eye had yet enjoyed."[2] Today, this tendency lives on in representations of the urban site that strive, again in the words of de Certeau, to "make the city readable by immobiliz[ing] its opaque mobility in a transparent text." Maps and diagrams (associated with design practices and physical planning) lift out and separate facets of the urban that cannot actually be easily disentangled; topography, transportation systems and urban densities; open space, building typologies and class distinctions; functional zoning, historic growth patterns and political districting – these are but a few of the many interrelated aspects of urban situations isolated through analytic and descriptive representation. Urban policies (used to monitor and spur urban development) reveal a similar process of distillation, in this case achieved by bracketing social, political and economic issues as discrete, rather than interdependent, aspects of urban problems. Rather than admitting to a multiplicity of logics, representations flatten the urban's multivalent, diffuse and contestatory spaces.

When architects, planners, developers and politicians continue to imagine – and image – urban sites as boundable, free of perplexing situations, their normative appraisals of the city, especially of what constitutes the "urban," are predicated on immutable ideals that when applied as measures to current urban configurations mask their multiple realities and in turn, depreciate their value. This is because even in the face of ever changing definitions of urban space, the myth of the knowable, ideal city continues to hold sway. The question that inhabits the space between the single, knowable "concept" city (and its closely allied stable images) and the more elusive and mobile ground of the lived city is whether one can imagine another model of urban representation that can enhance knowledges of the urban without repressing and dismissing its lived complexity.

To pursue this question I am going to draw on two representations of New York, each of which proposes a particular idea of the urban. Both bring up representation in the sense of "imaging" as well as in the sense of having the authority to "stand" or "speak" for the interests of others. The first is the Panorama of New York, a "city in miniature" dating from the early 1960s that provides an image of the city marked by the desire for the appearance of coherence. The second is the Business Improvement District (or BID), a specific legislative and financial mechanism currently reconfiguring large areas of New York. The BIDs project the city as a set of discrete enclaves with left-over spaces in between, yet despite its apparent fragmentation, this urban image is actually very homogeneous. A close examination of the Panorama and the BID allows a reassessment of the role of representation in maintaining the fiction of the city as a contained and controllable site. By picking these examples, the purpose is neither to set up a polarity (since none really exists), nor to discern a "truer image" (for which city image is "true"?); nor to determine whether one or the other more adequately captures experience and perception (since these also smooth over the urban's jarring adjacencies). The issue is not one of choosing between two versions of "concept-city." Quite the contrary. At stake is a more fundamental question regarding the very notion of a "knowable" city and how it shapes expectations of what the urban is, or might become.

II "OMISSION": THE PANORAMA

Even when they take the form of supposedly objective documents, visual representations of urban situations are always more than secondary descriptions of physical facts. The Panorama of New York (originally commissioned by the municipal builder, Robert Moses, for display at the New York City Pavilion of the 1964 World's Fair) is a "retro-

9.1 Robert Moses' Panorama of New York City, partial view of Manhattan and the Bronx.

spective" construction that attempts to capture an image of New York at a specific moment in history. Stalling the city in time and identifying it with the legal limits of its five boroughs, the Panorama's urban vision presumes the city to be a discrete "thing" available to comprehensive and finite documentation. As an artifact, the Panorama posits an attitude toward the urban site predicated on the idea of the city as a physically stable and isolated place uncomplicated by flows and linkages to broader political, social and temporal contexts.

The Panorama is a 1:100 scale model of the five boroughs of New York.[3] While remarkable, it is hardly unique. As early as 1915, an illuminated, 550 square foot model of New York City was shown at the San Francisco World's Fair. But a more influential precedent is found in the "Futurama," the most popular feature of the 1939 New York Fair, designed by Norman Bel Geddes for the General Motors Highways and Horizons building, and known by Moses to have been a huge success. The Panorama borrowed construction techniques from the Futurama, and its "simulated helicopter ride" is a direct reinterpretation of the earlier exhibit's narrated "carry-go-round." But, while the Bel Geddes' display was an imaginary vision created to transport visitors to the year 1960, dubbed in brochures as "the beautiful world of tomorrow," the Moses model was intended as an objective, up-to-date depiction of New York City.

Building this supposedly comprehensive urban view took 3 years. To insure that the finished product did not exceed a 1 percent margin of error (Moses' stipulation), existing specialized city maps showing individual structures were augmented by a set of aerial photographs, as well as by a specially commissioned set of five thousand oblique photographs portraying building elevations. These documents, in addition to a United States Geological Service topographic survey and maps of city-owned facilities, provided the base information needed to create the large three-dimensional model. The Panorama's base was molded to show topography at a slightly exaggerated scale. Highways, streets, blocks and parks were traced onto its many sections in preparation for the placement of buildings (830,000 structures included in 1964). Of these, 25,000 were custom-made, showing such landmarks as the Empire State, Columbia University, and City Hall; 100,000 were made by combining standardized elements, and the remainder were mass-produced, variously shaped, plastic units depicting the city's residential fabric (one- and two-family homes, as well as brownstones and tenements). Public buildings and city services were identified by tiny colored lights, and borrowing from Con-Ed's 1939 World's Fair Diarama "The City of Light," the whole exhibit was lit to give the impression of a changing dawn to dusk cycle. According to one contemporary description, the overall effect of the Panorama when viewed from the "helicopter ride" around its perimeter was "a spectacular presentation."[4]

A large part of that spectacle involved contextualizing the efforts of Robert Moses himself, since only with the construction of the Panorama were his many projects presented all together in one comprehensive view. The Panorama represents Moses' individual works as if they had been conceived as part of an integrated vision. Yet, at the same time, his urban interventions still stand out. The choice of construction materials highlights the *products* of Moses' career. While the majority of the Panorama's buildings are made of plastic and wood, its thirty-five bridges (many erected under Moses' direction of the Bridge and Tunnel Authority) are meticulously crafted in brass to show off their structure and design; lightly colored highways and parkways jump out at the viewer, underscoring Moses' work as a municipal roadbuilder; reflective green open spaces (which glow in the dark) present a glorified picture of Moses' role as City Parks Commissioner. Among its many idealizations, the Panorama registers an apparently continuous swath of open green space adjacent to high-speed roadways (so-called "parkways") through Brooklyn, the Bronx and Queens. In fact, most of the vividly painted areas that look so appealing as interconnected public spaces are actually dead zones inaccessible for recreational use.[5] Presenting an idealized image of urban development as viewed from "on high" (physically, from above, as well as ideologically, from the "aloof" position of a builder more interested in the abstract intentions than the real effects of his projects) the model creates a fictional cohesion out of what had actually been an extremely piecemeal and disruptive *process* of large-scale urban interventions overseen by Moses throughout his long career.

Unveiled in the opening days of the Fair, the Panorama was dubbed a "model city" by local journalists. While obviously referring to a "city in miniature," the Panorama is a "model city" in another sense as well. Before being named the World's Fair Corporation President (which essentially marked the beginning of the end of his 50-year career), Robert Moses held many positions in state and municipal government as an appointee rather than an elected official. In his various capacities he not only oversaw many large-scale construction projects, but was also directly involved in writing (and rewriting) the regulations and policies governing New York's public urban development process. For a time, he even had the all-embracing title of "City Construction Coordinator." As Patricia Phillips observes,

"Perhaps more than any other individual, Moses is responsible for the physical character of the 20th century of New York. The Panorama is an apt image of the scope of this powerful, often reviled, modern master builder."[6] In *Space, Time and Architecture*, Giedion praises Moses for having the "enthusiasm and energy of Hausmann," but the comparison is not quite fitting, since despite the scope of his interventions, Moses did not share Hausmann's overarching vision.[7] While partially guided in his choice of projects by proposals first outlined in the 1929 Regional Plan of New York, Moses was a master-builder who openly expressed his dislike for planners and master-plans.[8] In his capacity as head of various Public Authorities (quasi-private corporations chartered by state law that operate beyond the reach of public accountability) he worked on seven major New York City bridges, the majority of the area's expressways and regional parkways, large amounts of public housing and a vast number of parks, most conceived as discrete interventions without the guidance or framework offered by a larger urban plan.[9] The desire to present a "complete" picture of these endeavors using the Panorama is characteristic of Moses. That he would tolerate no more than a "1% margin of error" evidences this man's lifelong interest in gaining and maintaining control over projects (and people) as well as his disregard for the constant modulations and transformations that characterize the urban condition. Even his modelmaker, Raymond Lester, was aware of the dilemma when he told a reporter that to meet the requirement "we had to make a cut off date because there's always something being built or torn down."[10]

Returning to de Certeau, the supposedly objective Panorama can be understood as "a 'theoretical' (that is visual) simulacrum, in short a picture, whose condition of possibility is an oblivion and misunderstanding of practices."[11] What is obliterated in this "concept-city" exceeds the practices of everyday life as de Certeau would classify them. By blocking New York City's first Planning Commission's initiatives to develop long-term planning goals in the early 1940s, Moses is effectively responsible for the city's ongoing lack of any comprehensive planning policies. His Panorama must be seen as an endgame, a final and carefully orchestrated view constructed to represent as coherent a career actually built on a strange combination of a profound disdain for comprehensive approaches, and an equally profound will to exert total control. Missing is any record of the myriad political, bureaucratic and social conflicts sparked by so much of Moses' work. Representing the city as atemporal (caught in a moment in time), planar (as a surface to receive built form) and static (disconnected from regional and ecological systems), the Panorama exemplifies what de Certeau describes as the "totalizing stage of the map," where "elements of diverse order are brought together to form a 'tableau' of a state of geographical knowledge, push[ing] away into its prehistory or into its posterity ... the operations of which it is the result or the necessary condition."[12]

Instead of presenting the city's multiple layers and logics, or a registration of Moses' partial working process the Panorama provides "the appearance of optical coherence."[13] It obscures the always shifting horizons of urban experience and their articulation of interactive *scales* (whether local, metropolitan, regional, or global). By depicting New York City as an autonomous site (the model floats in a blackened display area, with no regional markers to fix it in relation to a larger context) the Panorama perpetuates the idea of the urban as a definable location, which can be physically delimited and "objectively" described. It also omits the depth of the urban *section*, where spatial and temporal layerings of urban perceptions are embedded. Because of its many oversights, the contradictory spaces characterizing urban agglomeration (not to mention the controversies which marked Moses' career) are nowhere to be seen in the Panorama's overview.

III EXCLUSION: THE BIDS

If Moses intended for the Panorama to picture a unified New York, Business Improvement Districts apparently suggest a very different kind of urban construction. A BID is a self-taxing enclave aimed at enhancing "business oriented areas." BIDs proliferated in the 1980s and 1990s, but their origins can be traced to the late 1960s when the urban design group of Mayor Lindsay's Planning Commission created "special district" zoning. This move, a substantive departure from existing uniform controls, was seen by city planners and urban designers as a means to recognize unique characteristics that distinguish one neighborhood from another. "Special districts" arose from the realization that zoning legislation could affect the design of cities by setting down design objectives specifically tailored to particular areas.[14] In the late 1970s, following the creation of "special districts," New York City introduced "Special Assessment Districts." These offered a method of financing and implementing projects that did not rely solely upon the police power of city government to enforce mandatory controls. SADs were an early attempt to relieve the financial burden on local governments for revitalization projects, and Business Improvement Districts (initiated in the early 1980s) are their more recent incarnation.

A crucial fact distinguishes "special districts" from Business Improvement Districts. While the former are zoning ordinances, the latter are private corporate entities. Technically, a BID is a legislative and financial mechanism that operates as a self-taxing enclave; it can only be formed by a majority of local property owners. However, this "majority" is determined by the total taxable value of land. A few owners of highly valued property therefore have proportionately more weight in the decision to form a BID than a larger number of owners holding lesser-valued properties. To create a district, this coalition must submit a plan to their local government detailing their district's boundaries, proposed improvements, budget, and method for determining assessment rates. Up to $60,000 in municipal public money is available to help finance the preparation of a BID plan. After a public review process, the BID proposal can be accepted by city government (which then effectively drops out of the picture, by providing no design or monitoring guidelines). Once approved, the district forms a non-profit corporation with board members drawn from local property-holders, and all property owners within its bounds (whether initially supportive of the plan or not) must subsequently pay assessments into BID coffers. These are collected by the municipality (in New York, the City Finance Department) and then returned to the corporation for local use. A number of legal constraints affect how the BID corporations function: their budgets cannot be greater than 20 percent of the general municipal taxes levied against property within BID bounds; their indebtedness cannot exceed 7 percent of the value of taxable real property in the district; funds can be used either for enhancements promoting a better business environment (street improvements, landscaping, signage, etc.), or for maintenance to augment, but not replace, public services like sanitation and security; finally, BIDs can't be disbanded as long as they are indebted.[15]

The city council of New York was authorized by the State government to create BIDs in 1982. In 1996 in a report by the Department of Business Services of the City of New York, thirty-seven districts were listed with budgets ranging from $67,000 (for a small BID in the Bronx), to almost $10 million (for the richest Manhattan BID, Grand Central Partnership). The third and fourth largest BIDs – 34th Street and Times Square – effectively create a mega-district with the Grand Central Partnership since they are all spatially adjacent. At one point, the three even shared one director, Dan Biederman, dubbed by the *New York Times* as "the Mayor of Mid-Town." Except for one Industrial BID in East Brooklyn, all New York's BIDs are commercially oriented. While their size, budget and improvement agendas vary widely, all BIDs are in the business of managing the public image of their own locally contained domains. Smaller districts in outlying boroughs provide limited services (street cleaning and private security, promotion for local retailers, holiday lighting, etc.). The largest and richest Manhattan districts go much further, funded by major bond issues, federal and local partnership grants, and corporate sponsors with a direct interest in upgrading local property values. Between 1992 and 1994, Grand Central Partnership and its affiliate, 34th Street Corporation, made bond offerings totaling $87 million. Probably the most publicized (and most controversial) New York BID, Grand Central Partnership, has over 50 million square feet of commercial floor space, more than in the entire downtowns of all but three other US cities.[16] It covers an area exceeding seventy blocks, and its CEO (whose salary is triple that of the New York's mayor) is an important player in local redevelopment initiatives, funding large-scale projects and providing levels of "public" service the city government can no longer afford.

In the late 1980s and early 1990s the reaction to BIDs by both city government and the New York press was overwhelmingly positive. It is important to note here that the *New York Times*, whose offices are located off Times Square, was (and remains) a major player in the Times Square/42nd Street BID. Many of its articles and editorials praised BIDs for their part in cleaning up city streets and reducing crime through private law enforcement, and even after a series of investigative reports in 1995 and 1996 on district problems, the paper still remains enthusiastic about their contributions to the city.[17] Until very recently, the risk of confusion between public and private responsibility, and the BIDs' lack of public accountability was noted by only a few critics. In 1992, the mayor of New York was quoted (in the *Times*) as saying (with a positive inflection) that BIDs "are filling in for government." City Hall's lack of concern regarding the question of account-ability is underscored by the fact that their first review of the privately run, self-taxing districts (prompted by external reports of shady dealings) occurred in November 1995, over a decade after they first appeared. The panel found a host of problems – misman-agement, excessive executive salaries, the hiring of illegal aliens paid below minimum wage to do menial jobs. The most serious scandals (both involving the Grand Central Partnership) included the misdirection of funds and the operation of questionable "social service" programs. The president of the Grand Central BID (Biederman) tried to divert funds from his district to start another BID across the Hudson River, in Newark, New Jersey (totally illegal according to State law); and it was reported on the front page of the

New York Times that previously homeless men, hired by the BID as "outreach workers" and street sweepers, used physical force to clear other homeless people from the area. As a result of their findings, the City Council called for stricter financial oversight by BID boards as well as by the City Department of Business. At the same time, a suit was brought against the Partnership claiming that its board failed to adequately represent the interests of local residential property owners, who were nonetheless levied assessments just like their commercial counterparts.[18]

In response to these developments, the growth of BIDs fell off somewhat during 1995. Nevertheless, the biggest corporations continued to visibly gain power by controlling their local and regional image through interventions in both the physical public realm (renovating streetscapes) and the virtual public realm (orchestrating media coverage of these "improvements" in newsletters, newspapers, and television). In the fall of 1996 (almost a full year after the first municipal review panel) and in response to Mayor Guiliani's relatively late realization that the largest BIDs were "in essence, creating public policy" yet operating without any system of checks and balances, the mayor's office suddenly reversed its earlier hands-off stance and called for placing limitations on district bond issues. At first an avid supporter of the BIDs' private investment initiatives as a way to rescue a financially strapped city government, Guiliani was apparently becoming wary of their powers to act as surrogate mini-governments (as well as fearful of the possibility of a BID default, which would place the city's municipal bond rating at risk). In September 1996, marking the change in the city's official position, the *New York Times* reported that "sentiment [in city council] appears to have turned against some of the groups."[19]

While City Hall's new-found concern is welcome, it still does not confront how BIDs image the city and how this image affects the urban experience. Mid-Manhattan BIDs in particular have initiated a wide range of "improvements" altering their area's character by erasing the city's visible and experiential diversity. The changes are primarily aesthetic, motivated first and foremost by an interest in evoking a high-end commercial image. Some are physical. They include repaving sidewalks, adding street lighting, providing new street furniture and introducing planters with pollution resistant trees. Designs for these streetscape elements are unremarkable, their most evident feature being the district's logo. In the Grand Central Partnership district, banks of newspaper dispenser-boxers are neatly lined up mid-block, painted the same green as the street lights – color-coded elements signaling the BID's presence and its agenda to "unify" the street. All the large midtown BIDs provide free design consultation services (promoted in the monthly newsletters for members) to help shopkeepers upgrade their storefronts in keeping with district guidelines that dictate signage lettering sizes, colors, and the extent of horizontal projection from building facades. There are bans on paper signs, temporary sidewalk advertising boards and fluorescent lighting, presumably because these are associated with lower-end (and therefore less desirable) commercial activities. Further legal restrictions exist in the form of riders to retail leases detailing streetfrontage design constraints. The result of all these graphic controls is a streetscape that bears a remarkable resemblance to the "internal streets" of suburban shopping malls – where similar rules about signage are used to generate a simulation of urban diversity within a highly systematized and regular building frame. BIDs also furnish private security forces to patrol their streets, and sanitation

9.2 Private security personnel, 5th Ave. BID.

services to supplement what the city provides. Private logo-sporting patrol officers and brightly uniformed street-cleaners are becoming a ubiquitous presence in many parts of Manhattan, human advertising for the "safe" and "clean" environment provided by the local business community.

BIDs are a forceful but skewed form of urban representation that overlooks the interests of anyone (or any group) that is not a major business or commercial property holder. Their improvements have a homogenizing effect – visually, at the level of everyday detail, economically, through particular types of commercial ventures, and socially, singling out limited groups of users. Though employing very different means from Moses in his Panorama, these corporations yield a similar result, suppressing the conflicted and contestatory aspects of the urban condition in the service of constructing a highly controlled and limited image of New York. By attracting higher-end retail and entertainment providers, the midtown BIDs are becoming increasingly geared toward a "public" made up of tourists and wealthy consumers, effectively excluding many of New York's other constituencies who once came to midtown for their entertainment and shopping needs. While a study in the early 1980s revealed that a majority of people who frequented the area now defined by the Times Square/42nd Street BID were from New York's outer boroughs (Queens, Brooklyn, the Bronx and Staten Island), today publicity for the Times Square Redevelopment Project (covered by the BID) heralds the arrival of mass numbers of tourists instead. Techniques for "revitalizing" the district include the renaming of streets ("42nd Street" becomes "The New 42nd Street"); removing adult-entertainment businesses (a thirty-two square block area around Times Square will be allowed to retain between six and ten porn shops, just about the "right" number, according to current BID president, Gretchen Dyskstra); introducing family entertainment providers like cyber-malls and tourist services; importing new "local" color in the form of cafés and restaurants associated with other parts of the city, like Little Italy or Greenwich Village; and keeping the entire area spick and span with an army of street sweepers in bright red jumpsuits. Thanks to Disney, the New 42nd Street Corporation, and a group of highly cooperative city and State officials, Times Square is being "transformed" from a "sewer" (so called by the prior State Governor Cuomo) and brought into "a whole new era" of wholesome family fun. That BIDs equate urban "safety" and "cleanliness" with superficial images of well swept streets peopled by happy consumers prompts serious questions about their role

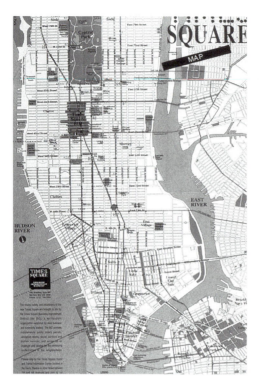

▲ **9.4** "The New 42nd Street."

◄ **9.3** "The vitality, safety and cleanliness of Times Square is brought to you by the Times Square BID.": Text accompanying a 1995 map showing the extent of the Times Square Business Improvement District.

in the city's future, since as a collection of exclusive enclaves they can only exacerbate the underlying causes of economic and social inequity found in the city today.

While BIDs have reduced the amount of garbage on the streets and the number of visible homeless (by displacing them into other neighborhoods with fewer street patrols), their corporate boards only represent commercial business interests; their "improvements" radically diminish New York's characteristic pedestrian-level diversity; their employees do not get labor protections.[20] As part of their campaign to "improve" the urban public realm by purging it of socially "noxious" uses, midtown BIDs have set up social service programs (to move the homeless off their streets); spearheaded campaigns to reduce the presence of sidewalk vendors (the sole source of inexpensive food in Midtown), and limited the type of goods for sale in newspaper stands (BID publicity brochures claim that the proliferation of products in the stands was turning them into "third world bazaars"). Limiting the location and number of vending-carts in their districts not only creates problems for licensed owners (who depend on selling in highly trafficked areas), it reduces the kinds of exchanges that can occur in the public realm and erases a strong sensory aspect – the smells of charcoal grills, roasting nuts, hot pretzels, steaming sauerkraut and hot dogs – from the experience of the street itself. BID mandated signage restrictions are another effective means of controlling the image of their domains, making it harder for businesses geared toward lower-end consumers to survive. Many of the cheaper family-run and fast-food restaurants around Grand Central have disappeared since the formation of the Partnership, as have off-price and discount retailers serving midtown's large constituency of pink- and blue-collar workers.

9.5 Typical New York City newsstand, dubbed by BID publicity as "a third world bazaar."

9.6 Newsstand designed and installed by the Grand Central Partnership.

9.7 Typical Eighth Avenue storefronts, around the corner from "The New 42nd Street."

9.8 New storefronts on 42nd Street.

The BID's most ambitious projects are even larger scale, involving renovations of prominent public spaces, which yield increased property values in the surrounding area. Bryant Park, the largest open space in Midtown located behind the New York Public Library, was refurbished in the early 1990s in a project funded by the Bryant Park Corporation. Newly designed landscaping, movable Parisian-style garden chairs placed around a central lawn, and permanent foccacia and cappuccino kiosks located at the park's edges are intended to conjure up images of grand "European" public parks. The BID also sited an expensive restaurant on park land, a concession that turns over a portion of its profits to cover ongoing park maintenance costs. Further moneys are provided by renting out the public park for private events, including the city's annual fashion shows. Eight blocks south, the 34th Street BID is funding the renovation and 10 years of annual maintenance for Herald and Greeley Squares (actually triangular islands) just outside of Macy's, one of the city's largest department stores. According to Peter Malkin, chairman of the 34th Street business group, "There is no justification to spend as much money as we are on a few thousand square feet of space, just to improve that space. We're trying to create a new image for the most highly traveled area of Manhattan."[21] Another similar public space project is the redesign for Pershing Square (across from Grand Central Station) to provide a weekday outdoor café, facilitated by the closing of a public street.

Sharing traits with the "concept-city" outlined by Michel de Certeau in *The Practice of Everyday Life*, the BIDs attempt to overcome the incommensurabilities and contradictions arising from urban agglomeration through their alterations to the city's public space.[22] Established by self-serving and powerful private interests, BIDs are partitioning New York City into market-controlled enclaves. As the city government pulls back and leaves urban development to these private corporations, what is being created is a city "in the image of the BID," effectively redefining the urban condition as a business venture, the street as a shopping mall, and the city resident as a high-end consumer. BIDs propose "*un espace propre*": an area sanitized through concerted removals of the undisciplined and unruly; a lively, trouble-free environment arranged by savvy marketers whose interests lie in "selling the city" to anyone with money to spare. Marking the conjunction of local and regional political agendas with global economic forces, BIDs adopt motivated design strategies to create their urban images. These significantly alter urban experience by constraining everyday practices and precluding uncontrolled events, reconstructing the public realm as an exclusive and fragmented field. In a strategic operation which tries to isolate and stabilize the urban, BIDs replace the city's characteristic diversity with an aestheticized simulacrum won through spatial, social and economic exclusions.

IV "THE OVERLOOKED": COMING UP FROM BELOW

Like Moses' Panorama, BIDs try to make the urban condition understandable by projecting it as limited and legible. The two urban representations are similar in their underlying desire to control the image of the city by masking the multiple realities of the urban lifeworld. They also share in being the result of powerful actors who exploit the complex interface between public authority and private market freedoms to achieve their ends. (Robert Moses was a publicly appointed figure who operated according to the rules of private corporate enterprise, while the BIDs are private corporations that function like public policy makers.) Separated by more than 30 years, the two are also historically related. Created in the waning moments of modernist master-planning, the Panorama marked the end of an era which would be followed by the rise of advocacy planning and community-based urban design, symbolized most notably by the publication of Jane Jacobs' famous critique of modern approaches to city planning, *The Death and Life of Great American Cities*. This change had a substantial influence on New York City's development practices and the regulations guiding them, leading to the introduction of localized "special district" zoning, a policy move away from comprehensive zoning that foreshadowed the formation of BIDs.

Jacobs brought the importance of everyday street life to the attention of urban planners, resisting Robert Moses and leading the community group that fought his late-career Manhattan Expressway Project (a proposed high speed artery that would have cut east–west across lower Manhattan through what is now known as SOHO). In the public arena of neighborhood activism and through her early writings, Jacobs decried the "sameness" of modern planning initiatives. In her first full length article on urban issues, "Downtown is for People" (published in a 1957 anthology and containing the seminal ideas for her subsequent book), she argued that the only way to accurately assess large-scale urban redevelopment projects was by walking the city streets where their failures became glaringly apparent.[23] Instead of "top-down" planning methods, she advocated attention to the local and human scale and called for looking closely at how people used the city in their everyday lives. For Jacobs, the way to a successful and vital urban environment was to be found through more densification and the enlivening of city streets "with variety and detail." Thirty years later, the BIDs have seemingly taken up Jacobs' call to attend to the streetscape, but the results are not what she forecast. Instead of a registration of the multiple (and often conflicted) lifeworlds of the city, BIDs are contributing to the creation of a uniform urban image. Coopted by real-estate market interests, Jacobs' earlier campaign for social and cultural diversity in the street has been transformed into a recipe for sameness.

Considered in broader terms, the Moses model and the BID expose the problematic endeavor of urban representation generally. At issue is a presumption of total legibility that both sustains the myth of the city as determinate, and constitutes an objective idea of the urban that excludes its partisan, disruptive and accidental facticity. Since any city is simultaneously a continuous spatial system and an aggregation of discrete parts, contrasting the Panorama's urban idea with that of BIDs sets up a moot distinction. One presents a totalizing image that masks a set of fragmented operations, while the other presents a fragmented image that conceals a singular and homogeneous agenda. While one is based on the rationalized models of modernist planning reinforced by the supposed fidelity and transparency of representational techniques, and the other reflects trends of late capitalist economics supported by media simulations, both remain, at base, uniform "representations of space," identifying "what is lived and what is perceived with what is conceived."[24] Each submits the indeterminacy of urban agglomeration to strategic controls; each images a "knowable city" by adopting a limited set of measures to approach and organize the (limitless) urban condition.

Since the constant production of urban space runs to such a surplus, cities necessarily resist forms of stabilizing registration. The "knowable city" is thus a strategic operative; it posits the city as static, universal and anonymous by refusing to contend with its vital, particularized and multivalent characters. It covers up the fact that cities can never really be fixed (either corrected, or held in place). In essence, the representational model of a "knowable city" erases the very conditions that make cities "urban," by reducing the incommensurate to one acceptable image. Is it possible to find a model for urban representation that acknowledges the city as an indeterminate and constantly shifting term? The challenge is important because it engages the gap between "concept-city" and "lived city" – or put another way – it initiates a way of working with (rather than against) the city as unstable ground. At issue is finding a way to deal with the unclear, conflicting and even irreconcilable realities of the city.[25]

The goal here is not to close the gap between "represented" and "real" city (since neither a "gap" nor a "city" exists) but to examine and occupy the territory between different representations – to recognize the existence of many cities in one city and acknowledge their roles in projecting the future of the urban as more than a simulacrum or entertainment experience. Drawing together divergent urban images is one way to enhance our understanding of "city" by working with and through conflicting measures without trying to resolve their differences. To return to my two New York stories: rather than assuming the Panorama and the BID as limited, unified, and mutually exclusive terms (which they are not, since their fragmentary and comprehensive images are codependent) one could instead think about their interrelations and interruptions, inconsistencies and consistencies, recognizing that any representation of the city is a function of many ineffable, contradictory and unaccountable processes. This approach to the urban as "indeterminate and undefinable" replaces the notion of the "knowable city" with something less established, perhaps best described as contingent, compounded, and compacted "urban knowledges" (plural). In essence, it tries to learn from the city's own protocols of layering, subduction, interruption, accretion (to name but a few), as well as its crafty and accidental densification and so doing, provides a way to work through, rather than gloss over, the myriad urban spaces which occupy a single physical place. Moving beyond totalizing depictions like those presented by the Panorama, and away from a fictionalized homogeneity, this "messy" model approaches the urban as a multivalent projection. It rejects the anti-urban drive evident in the BIDs to overdetermine situations, and replaces it with another ground upon which to build – one that conjoins incommensurate terms, more in keeping with the often contradictory, and strange adjacencies of the city itself.[26]

Notes

1   Michel de Certeau: *The Practice of Everyday Life*, Los Angeles: University of California Press, 1984, p. 94.
2   Michel de Certeau: *The Practice of Everyday Life*, p. 92.
3   Today, after a series of updates, the latest completed two years ago, the model is on permanent exhibit in the Queens Museum, at the site of the 1939 and 1964 World's Fairs, in Flushing Meadows Park.
4   Robotti Guide, 1964.

5   The issue of inaccessability presents itself in other civic projects as well. As Marshall Berman notes, "Robert Moses used physical design as a process of social screening." Long Island Parkway underpasses were deliberately constructed to a height that made it impossible for buses to pass through, thus insuring that poor inner-city residents who did not own private cars would not make it out to the "public beaches" Moses had supposedly designed for their use.

6   Patricia Phillips: *City Speculations*, Princeton Architectural Press, pending.

7   S. Giedion: *Space Time and Architecture*, Cambridge: Harvard University Press, 1969, p. 831.

8   Helen Liggett and David Perry: "Robert Moses at Work," in: Dennis Crow, (ed.), *Geography and Identity*, Washington: De Maissoneuve Press, 1996, p. 198.

9   "Some Thing for Everyone, Robert Moses and the Fair," in: Marc Miller, *Remembering the Future: The New York Worlds Fair From 1939 to 1964*, New York: Rizzoli, 1989.

10 Raymond Lester, quoted in *NYT*, April 26, 1964, "View from the Air."

11 Michel de Certeau: *The Practice of Everyday Life*, p. 93.

12 Michel de Certeau: *The Practice of Everyday Life*, p. 121.

13 Situationist Space, Thomas McDonough, October, p. 65, referring to Lefebvre, pp. 355–56.

14 Special districts allow for zoning regulations tailor made to particular sets of circumstances, in particular areas of the city, as opposed to comprehensive zoning, which has ordinances applicable to the entire metropolitan area.

15 Barbara Samel, BIDs, NYCOM Management Series, #19. June 1990.

16 These facts are from a public relations release of the Grand Central Partnership, on file at Avery Library, Columbia University.

17 "Making a BID to Improve a Bronx Neighborhood," *New York Times*, December 8, 1996, an overwhelmingly positive article about the formation of a new BID associated with a large hospital in the Bronx.

18 "City Apartment Owners Challenging Business District," T.J. Leuck, *New York Times*, November 29, 1995. This case was decided in April 1997; the plaintiffs lost in their demands for greater representation.

19 "Mayor Seeks Stricter Curbs on Business Improvement Districts," *New York Times*, September 5, 1996.

20 In early 1997, the Grand Central Partnership's sanitation workers finally unionized, but only after the National Labor Relations Board intervened to throw out prior election results on the grounds that BID management had illegally intimidated workers against unionization.

21 "The Greening of Herald and Greeley Squares (They'll Become Parks)," *New York Times*, November 30, 1996.

22 Michel de Certeau: "Walking in the City," in: *The Practice of Everyday Life*, Los Angeles: University of California Press, 1984.

23 Jane Jacobs: "Downtown is for People," in: W. Whyte (ed.): *The Exploding Metropolis*, New York: Time Inc., 1957, pp. 157–88.

24 Lefebvre: *Production of Space*, p. 33.

25 The following discussion draws from Theodor Bardmann: "Social Work: 'Profession Without Qualities,' Attempt to Link Social Work and Cybernetics," *Systems Research*, vol. 13, No. 3, 1966, pp. 205–14. All subsequent references are page numbers from this publication.

26 Urban representations are functions of power embedded in particular historical conditions. In the time elapsed since the original research and publication of this study, much has changed and will continue to change in New York City. The ongoing debates about BIDs (too lengthy to detail here, and just as impossible to arrest in time as the physical city depicted by Moses' Panorama) confirm that no urban representation – including essays such as this – can ever hope to stabilize the shifting dynamics of urban lifeworlds.

Chapter 10

Four Ways of Overlooking Copenhagen in Steen Eiler Rasmussen

Henrik Reeh

> A city shall not be the frame around
> a masquerade but around an everyday life
> that appears healthy and natural
> to the inhabitants.[1]

I INTRODUCTION: COPENHAGEN – "A HIDDEN MAIN THEME"

Inside the international community of architecture and urban studies, the name of Steen Eiler Rasmussen, prolific Danish architect and urban planner (1898–1990), is associated foremost with his books *London: The Unique City*,[2] *Towns and Buildings*,[3] in addition to *Experiencing Architecture*,[4] which received the A.I.A. International Architecture Book Award 1996 as "Classic Book of the Century." Nothing in these titles seems to indicate that Rasmussen's approach to Copenhagen, the city in which he was born and lived nearly all his life, should be of any particular importance. Yet, Copenhagen is somehow omnipresent in Rasmussen's writing, whether it be in an explicit or in a more subtle way.

As early as in Rasmussen's first book, *London*, from 1934, aspects of the British capital are compared to similar conditions in Copenhagen. Rasmussen even mentions the idea of making Danes "learn from London" as a major impetus behind his study: "I thought that Danes should be able to learn much ... I really wanted to get acquainted with these conditions that gave me so much to think about, in order, maybe later, to make it easier for others to learn from London."[5]

Throughout Rasmussen's written œuvre, Copenhagen is compared with aspects of foreign cities. Rasmussen's comparison of Copenhagen and Istanbul[6] by reference to similar strategic positions of these two cities may in this respect be less surprising than his observation of a certain Copenhagen touch in Athens; due not only to fresh drinking water but also to features of nineteenth-century urban architecture. In this regard, Athens appears as the "Copenhagen of the South."[7]

Such parallels between Copenhagen and other cities may in return generate new impressions of the Danish capital. Rasmussen notes how, coming home from a trip to the other Nordic capitals,

> one experiences one's own city with renewed senses, discovers some of what is particular to it, and that one may never have seen before ... Seen in this way I would say that Copenhagen is classical in its horizontal extension ... What a beneficially integral and quiet profile this city has.[8]

All the same, Rasmussen's approach to Copenhagen does not stop at the form of the city as seen at a distance. From the 1920s until the late 1980s Rasmussen's writing abounds with reflections on the fate of Copenhagen, in terms of urban planning and architectural analysis. Occasionally, Copenhagen is even considered as a perceptive environment involving vision as well as the other senses.

Retrospectively, in a book from 1969, based on Rasmussen's final lectures given at the Royal Danish Academy of Fine Arts, School of Architecture, in Copenhagen, Rasmussen explains that his international urban studies are a means of approaching the Danish capital. Thus the reader of *København – Et bysamfunds særpræg og udvikling gennem tiderne (Copenhagen: The Particularities and Development of an Urban Society Through The Ages)*, is informed that Rasmussen's in-depth study of Copenhagen is nothing but "the termination of a life-long series of lectures that may most often have dealt with towns and buildings in foreign countries but always have been aimed at Copenhagen, a hidden main theme behind the entire series."[9] Whether mentioned or not, Copenhagen is ultimately revealed as the common denominator of Rasmussen's life-long body of research.

Although Rasmussen's writing about Copenhagen certainly indicates both conditions and features of an "urban lifeworld," it should be noted from the very beginning that Rasmussen never employed the sociological and philosophical term "lifeworld" (let alone "urban lifeworld"). Nor should one consider his writings a deliberate attempt to gain direct access to this field of urban experience – a field that may after all be characterized epistemologically by a certain inaccessibility and, in turn, by its lack of representability.

Such philosophical issues hardly interested Rasmussen who was first of all a writer and teacher questioning urban planning and architectural praxis, and not a speculative and philosophical mind. Instead of pondering the epistemological difficulties of the concept "lifeworld," Rasmussen explored a variety of genres through which a *complex urban reality* appears, highly analogous to that of the urban lifeworld. Thus, the lifeworld of the city is circumscribed in concrete and vivid ways, which may to a certain extent be more appropriate than the more systematically intended and theoretically informed approaches.

Rasmussen's six decades of writing on the Danish capital generated a comprehensive series of diverse studies and essays. These texts provide a multi-layered representation of Copenhagen and, further, seem to negotiate and refine Rasmussen's own relationship to the Copenhagen lifeworld. In the present study, Rasmussen's approach to the urban lifeworld of Copenhagen is to be articulated along *four different meanings of the term "overlooking"*[10], each of which corresponds to a *particular point of view* and a *corresponding discourse or genre*.

First, as an *urban planner*, Rasmussen remains attached to ways of thinking which conceive the city as a totality by representing urban space *from above*. Having been appointed the first lecturer in urban planning ever at the Royal Danish Academy of Art, School of Architecture, in Copenhagen at the age of 26 (in 1924), Rasmussen never ceased promoting the idea of master planning for the entire region of Copenhagen. Yet, as this notion of master plan remained an unfulfilled project, Rasmussen's references to overlooking in this first sense of the word (implying a systematic *survey* of urban space and its problems) do not reflect concrete planning practices towards the socio-spatial totality. Instead, they express his own conviction that the decisive problems of contemporary Copenhagen were to be overcome through an appropriate planning scheme addressing the metropolitan region as a whole.

Second, as a *professor of urban and architectural history*, Rasmussen addresses spaces and monuments in a *horizontal perspective* – corresponding to that of a well-educated city dweller walking the streets of Copenhagen. This second level of analysis explores overlooking by focusing on the disregarded aspects of space. Desiring to situate urban-architectural elements in their social and spatial totality and, further, to single out overlooked contextual relations of time and space, Rasmussen develops a new representational drawing technique in which urban buildings – apart from being rendered in elevation and plan – are depicted as "doll houses" (as Rasmussen himself notes). In this manner Rasmussen brings aspects of urban architecture into visibility, which otherwise would remain neglected or ignored.

Third, as a culturally and ethically *engaged citizen-architect*, Rasmussen defies certain manifestations of economic and political power through urban space. This is especially the case in the 1970s and 1980s, when after retiring from his professorship, Rasmussen comes to the defense of a group of young people squatting in an abandoned military area in central Copenhagen; for the sake of new and experimental ways of living. Criticizing an inflexible political order, Rasmussen illustrates the term overlooking, first of all, in correspondence to *surveillance and control*.

Fourth, as an *essayist and autobiographical writer*, Rasmussen experiences the limits of a culture of vision. Thus he emphasizes the importance and contribution of the non-visual senses to an urban life that otherwise tends to exaggerate visuality and looking and conversely downplays the importance of multi-sensory impressions, i.e. perceptions generated through hearing, smelling, and touching. At this *fourth* level of analysis, Rasmussen addresses overlooking when the term – to be read as "over-looking" – designates a hegemony of vision which at times cedes to other sensory experiences.

In short, Rasmussen does more than illustrate overlooking as a term oscillating between the two meanings "surveying" and "omitting" (or neglecting to see); he transgresses the issue of seeing versus not seeing, and enters the realm of urban space as a field for political struggle and bodily experience. In so doing, Rasmussen explores two other significations of overlooking (now meaning surveillance and excessive vision) and consequently challenges the idea of a neutral and contemplative vision.

The ways in which Rasmussen's approach to Copenhagen – via the four modes of overlooking (to be summarized by the terms survey, neglect, surveillance, and excessive looking) – articulate various aspects of a particular urban lifeworld will now be examined.

II OVERLOOKING 1: IMAGINING COPENHAGEN AS A PLANNING TOTALITY

> In a small town people can overlook the local
> problems and eagerly take part in the negotiations

10.1 Photomontages of Manhattan, NYC, and the area around the Frederiksstaden, Copenhagen, by Steen Eiler Rasmussen. Courtesy of Una Canger and Ida Nielsen.

> regarding what is important to and wrong with the town.
> But Copenhagen has reached a size and degree of division
> which make it difficult for the ordinary citizen to comprehend.[11]

Throughout his life-long career in urban planning, Rasmussen was most often critical of the official urban policies concerning the Copenhagen region. At certain times he was opposed to particular planning initiatives that he considered destructive to architecture or urban quality as well as to human and natural values in the existing environment. In one of the few cases where Rasmussen treats Copenhagen and New York City in the same context, he deployed considerable rhetorical means in order to make his critical position unambiguous.

This juxtaposition of Copenhagen and New York City was published in a special supplement of the Danish newspaper *Politiken* (1978); a supplement written solely by Rasmussen, as one of his last attempts to raise the discussion of master planning in the Copenhagen region. Two aerial photographs of New York City and Copenhagen, with dotted white lines added, provide both a concrete and critically intended representation of the excessive scale implied by the urban planning principles proposed in 1975 as part of the so-called "Second Regional Plan."[12] Whereas the photograph of central Copenhagen corresponds to only a minor portion of the large transportation void alongside which future urban structures of greater Copenhagen were to be developed, the image of New York City's Manhattan – a city center which is "probably the biggest in the world"[13] – is employed because the width of the space represented is about the size of the central urban corridor imagined for the Copenhagen region.

Although no demolition inside central Copenhagen had been envisaged, Rasmussen, as a means for communicating his own hostility to the proposed planning principles, powerfully exploits the widespread fears of the 1960s and 1970s that an urban void could be traced through the historical districts of Copenhagen.[14] As one can see in the images, Rasmussen doubted that authentic urban life would be possible in future towns around Copenhagen if these were to be localized along a large transportation corridor and bordered on each side by considerable anti-noise zones and zones for central functions. In response, Copenhagen and New York City dimensions are invoked in favor of a city based on human interaction and proximity. Rasmussen's judgement is severe:

> Although I have some experience in decoding plans and have studied cities and urban plan-
> ning all over the world, I find it difficult to imagine the consequences of this grandiose plan
> or even to imagine this plan being realized. And in my conviction it would be a disaster if
> it was carried through on Zealand [i.e. the island where Copenhagen is located].[15]

No genuine comparison of New York City and Copenhagen is intended in the photomontage, since *the fate of the Copenhagen region is the sole focus*. Similarly, the following analysis will concentrate on Rasmussen's representations of Copenhagen, representations to be detected in his book publications rather than in his numerous and widespread articles published in newspapers and professional journals.[16]

If the photomontages of Copenhagen and New York City convey an image of Rasmussen as an opponent of urban planning, or even master planning, this is far from

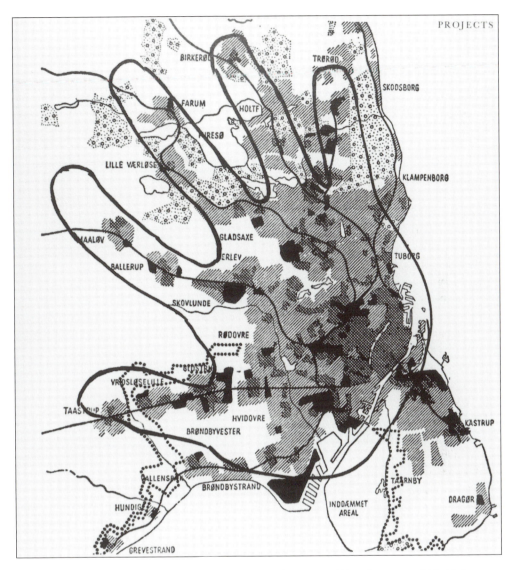

10.2 The "Fingerplan" – one of many versions . . . . Courtesy of Una Canger and Ida Nielsen.

being accurate. For half a century, Rasmussen incessantly argued that the problems of Copenhagen as a city ought to be considered and treated within the context of the metropolitan region in its entirety. As early as 1927, Rasmussen – at that time editor of the professional journal of Danish architects, *Architekten* – published a series of essays by international urban planners. Most of these addressed Copenhagen's various planning and traffic issues not at the level of the city, but at that of the region.[17]

During the time spanning the *enquête* of 1927 and the special *Politiken* supplement of 1978, Rasmussen wrote numerous articles and two full-length books concentrating specifically on Copenhagen.[18] The enduring ideological and political impact of this body of work upon laymen and professionals (rather than on politicians) was strengthened by Rasmussen's position as chairman of numerous planning commissions – dealing either with areas in central Copenhagen or with the region as a whole – from the 1940s onwards.

After all, Rasmussen's most profound and lasting contribution to the representational image of Copenhagen was the so-called "Fingerplan" of 1947, whose name and form remains enigmatically present not only among professional architects and planners but also in the minds of ordinary Danish citizens.

Many people recognize this image without necessarily knowing its origins. In fact, the "Fingerplan" began as a proposal by a semi-private area-planning commission started in 1945 under the direction of Rasmussen. Thanks to its extreme iconographic simplicity, the rhetorical power of this "Fingerplan," representing Copenhagen anthropomorphically as a hand with its transparent fingers stretching out to delicately touch the landscape (without totally covering it), has seldom been surpassed in the cartographic figurations of modern urban planning. The mental and graphic power of the hand image was so compelling even among the planners themselves, that the cartographic reality of Copenhagen had to be rearranged a bit in order to make the model fit![19]

Rasmussen explains the "Fingerplan" as the Danish adaptation of Britain's World War II planning ideas. But instead of recommending satellite cities as in Britain, the Danish planning commission – chaired by Rasmussen – stipulated that Copenhagen should grow organically toward its periphery, along five fingers of urbanized structures. Interstitial green areas – located between the fingers – were to be maintained in order to prevent the landscape from becoming dominated by built structures. Thus a dialog between green and grey components in the landscape of Greater Copenhagen would be established as close to the city center as possible.

According to Rasmussen's retrospective account, the success of the "Fingerplan" in post-war Denmark was due foremost to the political independency of the commission, composed mainly of experienced managers from various branches of public planning, and supported by a minor permanent staff of progressive architects and civil engineers.[20] As the commission had no political power[21] to impose its solutions, its investigations and conclusions were systematically discussed with the municipalities of the Copenhagen region. In this way, the very method of planning was based on *consultation* rather than ordination – a principle that may in hindsight be singled out as characteristic (if not constitutive[22]) of Danish urban planning. Although the "Fingerplan" itself never became a law, the basic distinction between *urban* and *rural* zones necessary for the application of its planning scheme – imposing a *qualitative difference* between the urban fingers and intermediate green spaces – was passed in 1949.

In fact, the term "urban lifeworld" is neither used nor taken into account as a field of particular value by the arguments underlying the "Fingerplan." However, the policy of maintaining green areas in the midst of a predominantly urban region expresses the conviction that natural surroundings and organic environments generate valuable human and aesthetic relations. The relevance of this supposition may be illustrated by the informal and intense human interactions taking place in the parks of central Copenhagen during the summertime – a kind of social and cultural life that may in turn be cited as the expression of a certain "Copenhagen lifeworld".

Despite the ideological and administrative success of the "Fingerplan," Rasmussen's writings during more than five decades lament repeatedly the political absence of a veritable master plan for the Copenhagen region: "One misses a vision of the totality, a master planning of Copenhagen." In 1950 Rasmussen pointed out the consequences of this lack of writing: "Instead one gets a multitude of dispersed particularities, determined by utmost different points of view." Thus Rasmussen deplores that the intellectual and administrative tools available, geared only for small-scale planning, remain incapable of solving the problems of Copenhagen as a city, whose influence extends far beyond the municipal borders.

Recurring in a variety of forms throughout the years, Rasmussen's dream of a master plan for the urban and suburban totality of Copenhagen determines many of his political moves and practical proposals. At one moment Rasmussen may insist on the necessity of more research on the historic quarters and on the development of traffic structures in and around the historic center of the city,[23] while at other times he writes open letters to some members of the government, suggesting that a commission be created with the task of preparing a new planning scheme for the Copenhagen region.[24] However different these interventions may be, the basic representation of Copenhagen as dependent upon its surroundings (and vice versa) remains common and fundamental to all of them.

A quotation from Rasmussen's *København* (1969) – the Copenhagen equivalent of his *London: The Unique City* (1934) – summarizes the general orientation of his argument:

> The misery, however, lies much deeper. As long as one cannot establish an organization of the capital that goes beyond the borders of the municipalities, one remains incapable of making plans for the central municipality. Urban planning is not a matter of solving separate problems but of creating a large cohesion . . . Copenhagen and all the municipalities around it are connected vessels – but unfortunately this is not the case at an administrative level. Today most Copenhageners live outside the borders of the Copenhagen municipality and don't feel themselves as members of a large urban society, the biggest and most important one in the country, . . . Everybody resides in some autonomous province, which has its own cash, its own accounts, its own restricted interests to defend, often conflicting with those of the neighbour municipalities. Everyone is locked up behind his own fatal line. There is no kind of common government, no plan for the totality, no expression of the community of interest that after all should unite the many municipalities.[25]

In Rasmussen's view, politicians never draw the necessary administrative and political conclusions of the connection between city and suburbs. The absence of general guidelines entails the incapability of taking precise decisions regarding the inner city of Copenhagen:

> When such a hesitation is reigning in particularities, it is a symptom of a lack of planning at the general level. One doesn't have the slightest idea of the role to be played by the inner city in the entire Copenhagen region. Until a global plan for the entire region of the capital exists, including what is outside the narrow Copenhagen municipality, one will miss both ends and means for solving all the particular problems.[26]

The *desire to overlook the urban totality* informs Rasmussen's vision of urbanism at levels involving the approach to nature, to issues of historic preservation, to traffic planning, etc. The same idea of a united metropolitan region seems to have been guiding Rasmussen in his analysis of Copenhagen and its various issues.

Rasmussen's idea of Greater Copenhagen as an urban totality justifies no particular power in place, since global planning schemes for the Copenhagen region have remained non-existent. Instead, Rasmussen's refutation of several actual planning policies reflects a critical and professional mind, not devoid of utopian thoughts.

In so far as Rasmussen addresses the systemic conditions allowing the urban life-world to develop, his plea in favor of an overall administrative and political framing of Copenhagen may in turn sustain the urban lifeworld. On the other hand, Rasmussen rejects the mentality corresponding to urban density, and thereby a certain kind of urban lifeworld:

> The very mentality of being cramped in created by the ramparts, still lives. In Denmark one thinks that it is not a real town if one doesn't have tall houses . . . The Copenhageners who had been locked up by the ramparts and suppressed by the rulers had become slave souls who now yielded to the yoke of land speculators.[27]

This mental situation – one variant of the urban lifeworld – is considered an expression of a historical reality from before the suspension of fortifications and demarcation lines: a reality that survived in the working class areas immediately outside the walled city, but seems to disappear in the suburbs.

Given this polemic against urban density, it is sometimes difficult to understand how Rasmussen himself is able to declare his love of Copenhagen: "But to me, Copenhagen is after all the best city, the city of all cities in the world in which I would prefer to live and die."[28] Yet one must remember, first, that Rasmussen's Copenhagen doesn't stop at the city border, and, second, the idea of surveying the urban totality from above, is but one approach to the city of Copenhagen. Loving a city may after all be the result of other view-points and perspectives than those of a global, regional analysis.

III OVERLOOKING 2: ORDERING THE OVERLOOKED IN URBAN ARCHITECTURE

Besides being a professor and a practician of urban planning, Rasmussen was an archi-tectural historian who understood urban space as an ever changing articulation of three-dimensional architecture and a multi-dimensional social life. The intensity of this profane relationship between space and society contributes to the fact that in everyday life, analytic contemplation of architecture is rarely practiced (except among architects). Even for architects it remains difficult to perceive and to decipher complex structures – such as all the buildings on a street and not only one single edifice – as an urban-spatial totality.[29]

In his book *Byer og Bygninger (Towns and Buildings)* (published in Danish, 1949), Rasmussen attempts to redress the situation by designating overlooked relationships in time and space – relationships that tend to be left out of consideration within the horizontal practices of city life. As if intending to overlook the overlooked, Rasmussen situates neglected architectural elements inside a spatial order to which he adds a functional and historical explanation. In this manner Rasmussen articulates the second meaning of overlooking. By now this term refers to *hidden and unremarked aspects of urban architecture*. To illuminate the overlooked aspects is the aim of Rasmussen's analyses.

Whereas the preface of *Towns and Buildings* argues in spatial terms for looking at buildings within a street context, in Section VII, in which a building in Copenhagen is addressed for the first time, Rasmussen makes *temporal and historical aspects* part of his explanation as well. Thus, his treatment of the urban mansion Charlottenborg serves to illustrate significant elements in his method of analysis and presentation.

As opposed to many histories of architecture, Charlottenborg, in Rasmussen's work, is not initially designated as a monument of a particular style, but as an architectural element of emblematic importance in the history of Copenhagen: "Charlottenborg at Kongens Nytorv [the New Square of the King] stands as a milestone in the history of Copenhagen," Rasmussen starts.[30] In fact, Charlottenborg represents "the beginning of a whole new city quarter outside the ramparts of the medieval town."[31] This particular building is introduced less in terms of style than it is as a result of an increasing congestion of population inside the walls of the medieval city – a congestion which had made the king expand the urban zone so that life would be easier, for the wealthy, at least.[32] It is true that, in Rasmussen's interpretation, changes of style from the very first sketches to the realized building make Charlottenborg appear as a transition between Renaissance and baroque. Yet Charlottenborg is first and foremost analyzed by Rasmussen as a mansion built by a relative of the king; for its cultural and historical significance.

As is implied by the height of the windows, rooms of more modest dimensions occur at the third floor, while the second floor with its tall ceilings is occupied by a central ceremonial hall (integrating a part of the third floor[33]) and a set of master bedrooms – the beds of which apparently provided the only warm place during the wintertime.[34]

This initial distribution of the interior space is so much the more significant to a Danish reader of *Towns and Buildings*, as Charlottenborg, today, is the main building of the Royal Academy of Art.[35] What used to be the ceremonial hall of Count Gyldenløve is still called the "Ceremonial hall of Charlottenborg" ("Charlottenborgs Festsal"). Throughout the twentieth century it has been the central lecture hall of the Academy of the Fine Arts, especially its School of Architecture. Rasmussen's analysis of Charlottenborg's spatialization of social relations in late seventeenth-century Copenhagen might indeed engender some kind of surprise and even self-reflection among present day Danish artists and architects. To a great extent, their knowledge of art and architecture has been transmitted to them inside this particular spatial framework which was not always (and may not always remain)[36] a public lecture hall.

All of a sudden, the Charlottenborg of the seventeenth century and that of the twentieth century fuse as an illustration of the ways in which both functions and significations of individual buildings are necessarily reinterpreted according to their changing uses. In this context, Rasmussen's tripartite pedagogical drawing (scaled 1 to 5,000 as are all of Rasmussen's drawings in *Towns and Buildings*) makes the building easier to read and

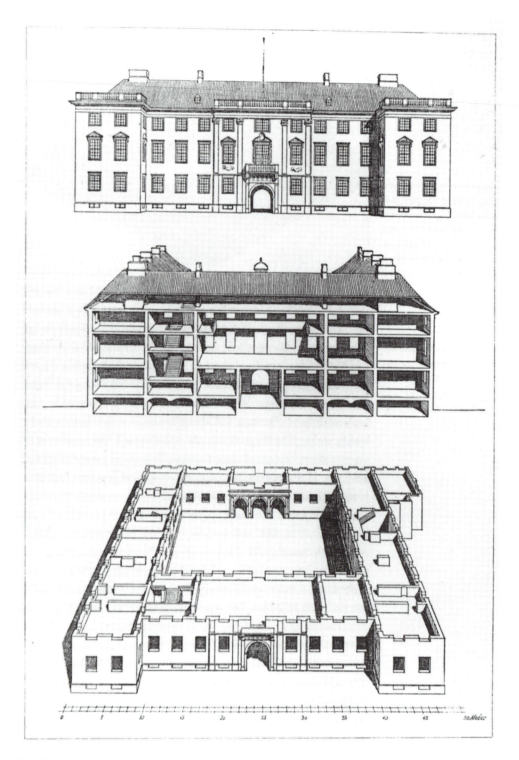

10.3 Rasmussen's triple drawing of Charlottenborg. Courtesy of Una Canger and Ida Nielsen.

nearly tactile, even for the non-architect. Rasmussen shows us Charlottenborg in the form of a "doll house,"[37] a doll house for the games of history. The changing functions of Charlottenborg itself and minor stylistic changes in the later royal palaces of Amalienborg and other buildings in the so-called Frederiksstaden outside the medieval city, do not prevent Rasmussen from acknowledging Charlottenborg's influence as a building *type* throughout several generations of Copenhagen's urban architecture.

Returning to the issue of "overlooking Copenhagen," one clearly notes the difference between the kinds of overlooked space and spatio-historical relationships that attract Rasmussen and those which were focused on by, say, the surrealists. Whereas surrealism discovers the outskirts of the city, Rasmussen's analysis of Charlottenborg focuses on overseen relations in the midst of monumental and official architecture. If neglected inter-relations are to be called to the fore in professional and civic architectural consciousness, Rasmussen seems to contend, these interrelations may at best be revealed inside a building of major importance in the history of urban society.[38]

IV OVERLOOKING 3: AGAINST POWER, IN FAVOR OF A "STRANGE REALITY"

> Here they don't beat up the director:
> they don't have time for it, and there is
> no director. This is not an institution but a
> huge hobby workshop. Look, this is how
> a fruitful environment comes into being.[39]

Whether it be a result of personal modesty or of an (implicit) desire to make individual experiences pervade a more general image of history, Rasmussen, in his major book on the history of urban problems in Copenhagen (*København*, from 1969), generally silences his own influence on Danish urban planning. It is no easy task to trace the ways in which Rasmussen's text justifies his own positions during his life as a planning consultant or urban planner, and, less significant, as an architect.[40] The (inevitable) aspect of justification becomes evident in Rasmussen's pages on the rebuilding of the Borgergade-Adelgade quarter in central Copenhagen. In all of *København*, this is one of the few occasions in which Rasmussen's own role is indicated.[41] Rasmussen was in fact the chairman of a four person commission in charge of counselling the city council of Copenhagen, as the project of the city itself had aroused critical remarks in 1941. With regards to Rasmussen's subsequent role in the elaboration of the "Fingerplan," not even his role as chairman of the Copenhagen Area Planning Commission (1945–58) is mentioned, whereas the role of Peter Bredsdorff, the director of the planning staff, is described at length.[42] This omission of Rasmussen's own involvement constitutes a methodological problem to the present day reader, who wishes to measure the concrete historical basis of the polemical tone that pervades Rasmussen's books on Copenhagen.

This being said about Rasmussen's historical outline of the development prior to 1970, one must recognize his self-critical courage in the heated political debate around the development of Christiania after 1970. Christiania is a former military area with barracks located at Christianshavn close to the city center of Copenhagen. Christiania had been illegally seized by squatters in 1971. Although Christiania had been accepted – and even recognized as a "social experiment" for three years by the Danish government – the experiment itself was severely criticized, especially by right wing politicians who wanted the "Free City of Christiania" ("Fristaden Christiania") to be closed down. Conversely, Christiania was defended by left wing groups and by a number of "cultural personalities"[43] and supported by a genuine mass movement capable, by the mid-1970s, of mobilizing tens of thousands of activists for political demonstrations in front of the Danish parliament building. Through his political commitment to the cause of Christiania (the very incarnation of anti-authoritarian youth), Rasmussen, now more than 75 years old, demonstrates that in social reality, overlooking may be perceived by citizens as an expression of political and ideological power (or at least of bureaucratic administration).

At first sight, Rasmussen's position may surprise. During his entire career as a professor and planner, Rasmussen had advocated the necessity of overlooking the Copenhagen region as a (somewhat utopian) means for overcoming those administrative and political divisions that prevented a premeditated and smooth development of a modern metropolis (and, implicitly, of the corresponding lifeworld). Having retired for reasons of age from any official position, Rasmussen now inverts the perspective by pointing out the doubtful human and political consequences of planning policies and power structures.

Rasmussen's position implies a striking element of self-critique, which becomes evident in a discussion with the Lord Mayor of Copenhagen. Replying to Rasmussen's critique of the Copenhagen municipality and its narrow-minded policy of constructing as many apartments as possible without taking into consideration the more general interests of the city and its inhabitants, the lord mayor polemically asks how Rasmussen can possibly reject municipal projects for apartments (instead of green areas) since, as an architect, Rasmussen himself has been in charge of constructing 2,000 apartments in a social housing project (Tingbjerg, situated at the periphery of the city of Copenhagen). Does Rasmussen really consider his own architecture "another heartless quarter of tenement houses"[44] the lord mayor asks in the Copenhagen daily *Politiken*?

This question may appear more rhetorical than substantial. But instead of eschewing discussion, Rasmussen faces the challenge and admits a certain disappointment with regards to Tingbjerg, an architecture and planning project, in which he invested so much energy and hope: "I shall not hide that this entire project has been my baby. I have dedicated years of my life to the realization of that program . . ."[45] Addressing the point raised by the lord mayor, Rasmussen asks himself: "But how about heartlessness?" And he answers:

> In fact, considering all you can say on both sides, there are indeed a lot of people having "landed" at Tingbjerg who really perceive it as a town of heartless tenement houses.[46]

Of course, Rasmussen's disappointment relates less to his own *architecture* than to the socially perceived *reality* of the Tingbjerg housing project. But this reality comprises the very *welfare institutions* that Rasmussen and his collaborators had conceived with the intention of improving the conditions for *living in the city*.[47] According to Rasmussen, these institutions are often judged bureaucratic and alien by the inhabitants of Tingbjerg. This negative feeling is experienced by the architect himself as he observes how bureaucratic rules neutralize the ideals behind adventure playgrounds, youth centers and other welfare institutions. Although Rasmussen never employs the conceptual dialectic "system versus lifeworld" (later to be developed by Jürgen Habermas[48]), the institutionalization of life in Tingbjerg appears to contain elements of what Habermas terms a colonization of the lifeworld. The intended strengthening of this lifeworld and its spontaneous, creative, and informal functioning appears to Rasmussen as having been an illusion.

This severe judgement of institutionalized life in the city may in part explain Rasmussen's fascination with the otherwise unplanned and unpredictable life among the squatters (with children and dogs) in "Fristaden Christiania." In Rasmussen's pamphlet on Christiania, this exceptional and peculiar place is interpreted in terms of a genuine and positive relationship between its inhabitants and its architecture.

In Rasmussen's opinion, the people in Christiania – "the Christianites" – make use of the former military buildings to the benefit of a certain freedom in life that remained inaccessible in Tingbjerg. Rasmussen phrases the contrast between Tingbjerg and Christiania in the following terms:

> From Tingbjerg in the one end of Copenhagen where everything is regulated and normalized and forced into the right forms in a fully heartless way, one can go by bus no. 8 to the other end of Copenhagen, to Christiania where everything is free, many would think *too* free.[49]

Rasmussen praises the ways in which the collectives working and the communes living in Christiania have saved the classical military buildings from their probable destruction by converting them into, among other things, a workshop for antique automobiles, a printer's shop, a jazz club, and a flea market. In Christiania, the activities similar to those which Rasmussen had hoped for at Tingbjerg developed spontaneously, without ever having been planned. Through participation in these activities, many social drop-outs seem to be given a new chance for social integration.[50]

In Rasmussen's defense of Christiania's particular lifeworld – against municipal and governmental interests (land for apartments and respect of social and moral order) – he confesses his own surprise at the Christiania experiment, which initially appeared chaotic but later proved to engender positive results. In Rasmussen's text, the surprise provoked by the encounter with Christiania's particular "lifeworld" is expressed in the double occurrence of the word "strange" – in Danish, "mærkelig" – within just a few sentences:

> For me, who has been occupied by the planning of dwellings and housing areas, Christiania has been a *strange* experience. Not in my wildest fantasy had I imagined that something could result from such a chaos. It has not simply been *strange*, but also elevating to see the positive capabilities of people – even of those who are the weakest – when you give them the possibilities (my italics).[51]

This mixture of positive surprise and relative inexplicability is condensed in the very word "strange," which also seems to involuntarily recur elsewhere in Rasmussen's descriptions of Christiania; for instance when he states that: "Christiania is not theory, politics or religion. Christiania is a physical reality, a strange [mærkelig] reality."[52]

These sentences indicate the degree to which Christiania has been an unexpected but strangely welcomed challenge to some of Rasmussen's own planning principles (if not to his reality principle in general), as well as a source of insight into certain repressive and non-liberal practices of "overlooking." Rasmussen's previous appeal to practices of overlooking (those referred to above as "Overlooking 1": establishing a survey facilitating coherent planning; or as "Overlooking 2": rendering visible and conscious spatial articulations and social dynamics) this recourse is not rendered superfluous. On the other hand, Rasmussen's approach to Christiania's anarchist and anti-hierarchical reality signals a radical shift in focus from a dream of an ordered and planned totality into that of an unexpected and much more spontaneous and creative way of conducting individual and communal life.

In the case of Christiania, Rasmussen adopts a position that is clearly opposed to the *overlooking powers of police and of politicians*. "The criminals in this game are those who created and still create the lawlessness that reigns in Copenhagen," he states.[53] The responsible politicians – and not the inhabitants of Christiania – are characterized as "criminals" because they intervene in the life of Christiania without any legal motif, let alone a master plan for the city of Copenhagen to guide the particular decisions for a unique area with unique buildings close to the center of the city:

> There is, to me, no doubt that Copenhagen by its lack of planning has created the lawless condition, and that the "Free City of Christiania," by taking the law into their own hands, saved the situation and preserved important buildings for posterity. *And now the lawless, the politicians of the city, will make the positive forces outlaw.*[54]

Thus, Rasmussen's early idea of overlooking the totality of Copenhagen via regional planning joins the new project of defending social and cultural experiments menaced by the actual overlooking powers of politicians – and the police.

Throughout the 1970s, Rasmussen continues to defend the inhabitants of Christiania against police harassment.[55] In the early 1980s Rasmussen even takes the defense of young squatters occupying old factories and vacant buildings in Copenhagen, against the repression exerted by police forces.[56] In this way, the distinguished elderly professor of urban planning seems to adopt a politically radical position – the aim of which is simply a defense of rights and principles constitutive of a liberal welfare society.

V OVERLOOKING 4: AGAINST EXCESSIVE VISION

> Foreigners visiting Copenhagen may find motifs
> for photographs and say that it is a beautiful city.
> Somebody who lives in the city doesn't see it
> in that way. For him it is life that counts.[57]

Rasmussen's attempts, first, to overlook and thereby establish a survey of the planning issues in the Copenhagen region and, second, to articulate aspects of what is usually overlooked in urban architecture, both expressed an *affirmative* approach to practices of overlooking (practices which in these cases didn't correspond to actual social realities, one might add) in so far as comprehensive insight and visual representation was the goal. Conversely, Rasmussen's position on the issue of Christiania (and Tingbjerg) clearly *rejected* the overlooking powers and, instead, promoted the values of an immediate – i.e. spontaneous and unmediated – social and creative everyday life. In short, Rasmussen *criticizes* overlooking practices in so far as they impoverish the complexity of the urban lifeworld. On the other hand, he *promotes* practices of overlooking on the condition that they improve the conditions of everyday life in and around the city.

Yet, if Rasmussen's position towards overlooking may imply elements of critique, little seems to indicate that Rasmussen goes as far as questioning the role of the *sense of sight* in modernity's division of labor between the senses. However, in some of his later writings, Rasmussen does in fact challenge the predominant role of vision in modernity and, conversely, emphasizes the idea of a city in which hearing and touching, tasting and smelling, all have essential roles to play. In this way, Rasmussen explores overlooking in its *fourth* possible meaning, in which overlooking designates excessive vision and thereby draws the attention to particular sensory experiences that respond to excessive looking by *transgressing the visual paradigm*. By staging urban perceptions going beyond the sense of sight, some of Rasmussen's writings on Copenhagen single out the contribution of non-visual senses to the urban lifeworld.

Multi-sensory perception is present less in Rasmussen's writings on planning and architecture than in some brief, mostly later, essays dealing with his Copenhagen childhood at the beginning of the twentieth century. Recalling the shops in his own neighbourhood of Østerbrogade,[58] in a vocabulary which is not only visual, but also *tactile* as well as *olfactory*, Rasmussen outlines a particular form of urban culture. This city of Rasmussen's childhood stands out in his memory as a universe of its own. This is a world of pure objectivity, devoid of smartness and design, a world from before the arrival of the shop designer.[59] In Rasmussen's own boyhood memories, accompanying his mother when shopping, a certain culture of the object comes to the fore. Rasmussen talks of this culture in terms of "elaborate style,"[60] for the simple reason that in this period "when one cultivated one's own specialty, when one purified the object[,] [o]ne didn't *talk* about culture. . . . One *had* it."[61] It was a city in which "every shop was a separate world of form, and material, and smell, conserved in memory as a complete work of art."[62]

Inside the memories of such non-designed and yet cultivated shop interiors, even one's sense of hearing is active, as in Rasmussen's mentioning of "dried cod that sounded like wood."[63] Sounds enter the otherwise very classical and elaborate writing of Rasmussen in a nearly onomatopoetic way, when he describes the sensory environment of a "buttershop with the big kegs of butter and flat, small, ribbed wooden spades, and clash and clash, and wrapping."[64] In these memories, the spaces of retail commerce are represented as stages of a complex sensoriality in which vision is but one aspect of the experience of the city, suddenly revealed as if experienced by a child.

Notwithstanding the sensory richness of these shops, Rasmussen, elsewhere, opposes behavior in the orderly *streets* to experiences on the *Common;* a wide surface of open land which at the beginning of the twentieth century was not yet a park.[65] Although the Eastern Common of Copenhagen was geographically located in the immediate environs of young Rasmussen's Østerbro, it was the symbol of another world, where multi-sensory experiences of a new and strange order became possible.

Where in the street, immobile and disciplined looking at shop windows was a dominant feature, the Common stands forth in memory as a place for non-mediated bodily sensations, such as running and being moved by the wind. Young boys of respectable families were not supposed to go to the Common on their own. So little Steen went there, not with his mother but with his older brother. In this manner, the common comes to represent a distinct landscape, radically different from that of the street. This difference is noted even in the way of experiencing the weather:

> There was this strange thing that when the wind was blowing in the streets – and it often did so, since there was always a whistle of air between the tall buildings – it was unpleasantly cold, although one was dressed in a coat for outdoors. But when the wind was blowing on the Common, then it was just something which was part of it.[66]

The presence of the wind in this extra-territorial landscape inside the city provides for other bodily practices such as flying a kite, which is described in Rasmussen's text (resembling a poem in prose) in the following terms:

> Then one could fly a kite and it was pleasant and one could run and let oneself be carried along by the wind. . . . In the street one could stand watching the shops and decide what one should desire. . . . But on the common one could move, sense the weather and the place and experience something.[67]

Rasmussen's mental identification with Copenhagen may at times have been hard to understand and believe in his urban planning discourse, which emphasized the physical and mental effects of former ramparts and present city borders, all of which were considered factors of enclosure.[68] But in Rasmussen's autobiographical texts, referring to personal experiences of life in the city, the affection for his native Copenhagen proves to be grounded in his own differentiated lifeworld, an everyday universe with strongly individual elements.

The exception that sets the general absence of non-visual perceptions from Rasmussen's urbanistic writing in relief is provided in an essay from 1929, "Paa Sangens Vinger" ("On the Wings of Singing").[69] In this essay Rasmussen analyzes the extraordinary vocal technique of a fishwife, who walks the "sterile streets"[70] of his neigborhood, crying or singing the names and the prices of her fish, in an acoustic environment that she alone could master. Rasmussen transcribed her singing into notes and, around 1930, accompanied Dagmar Hansen[71] to a studio in a Copenhagen department store to make a recording of her cries.[72]

Having listened just once to a recording[73] of Dagmar Hansen, one fully understands why Rasmussen considers her cries close to music. If Rasmussen tends to do so, he

10.4 Rasmussen's transcriptions of Dagmar Hansen's cries. Courtesy of G.E.C. Gads Forlag, Copenhagen.

prolongs a long tradition of architecture (dating back to Vitruvius, at least) in which music and architecture were understood as analogical, mediated by proportion. Yet it would be a simplification to conceive of urban sound and hearing in traditionally musical terms only.[74] In an essay – not on Copenhagen, but on Paris[75] – Rasmussen demonstrates that he is aware of the fact that the urban soundscape in its metropolitan amplitude is more diffuse (and in a certain way more overwhelming) than most music. The practice of listening in (and to) a metropolis such as Paris requires a particular attention to the basic sounds, always present like "a slightly boiling noise of the big city."[76] Sound proves to be part of the entire sensory cityscape and has profound consequences for visual as well as tactile and spatial perception of that environment.

In his essay on Paris, Rasmussen notes this importance of sound to the sensation and experience of urban space. No traditional musical order dominates the urban soundscape. Instead, sound serves to translate and amplify visual impressions. Rasmussen explains that it is: "nearly like hearing the undeterminable gleam that one sees in the sky above all the houses."[77] Furthermore, sound becomes *quasi-spatial* and even *spatial-tactile*:

> The noise stands between the tall houses. The foundations and the walls of the hotel are shaking. As one lies there in bed, one feels the nervous vibration of the big city.[78]

Encountering metropolitan intensity, Rasmussen recognizes the importance of sound to a multi-sensory perception of space. Where in the context of Copenhagen Rasmussen might very well have deplored such sounds as mere *noise* and interpreted the ever-present noise as the symptom of a city that had not yet fully overcome the historical ramparts around it, he seems to have enjoyed the condensed soundscape experienced whilst visiting Paris.

The difference between living in a city and visiting it affects the sensory approach to the urban space: "It doesn't matter that I lie in bed, awake, because I have no duties tomorrow, absolutely no duties! I have come here just in order to sense my Paris."[79] The visitor of a big city may experience essential characteristics of urban life, in so far as pure and disinterested (more or less) perception is the typical privilege of the traveler. The traveler is generally more conscious of, but also more tolerant of, the sensory aspects of urban life while traveling, whereas the average city dweller seldom renders explicit his or her urban sensory experiences but tends to take the city (and the perception of it) for granted.

However unhealthy it may appear from certain points of view, sensorial intensity will often be indispensable parts of the urban lifeworld to someone who is actually living in a big city. Yet, the fact that spatial and social density affects urban practices is often left aside by professional planners. Paying no particular attention to urban perception, planners consider their task in functional and intentionally objective terms, leaving perceptual and cultural issues in a subordinate position. Similarly, urban planners may hesitate to address the fascination of urban life. Addressing this polarity between the planner and the traveler, Rasmussen writes: "I am moved by all the trouble one has had from creating my Paris . . . without showing the slightest consideration for the many people who shall live here all their life, and in reality live very uncomfortably."[80]

However, in another essay – not on Copenhagen, but on New York City – Rasmussen observes how an amalgam of nuisances and inspirations makes up the paradoxical second-nature of the metropolitan lifeworld. Having recounted his own difficulties in understanding people's preference for the big city, Rasmussen goes on to convey his surprise as he learned that a friend, whom he expected to be living in idyllic Santa Barbara, had moved to filthy New York City:

> She was in noisy, busy, and polluted New York City which is sooty, where Santa Barbara is mediterranean blue and shining white, and [New York City] has an unbearably warm summer and a cold dank winter. She lived there with her husband next to Columbia University – and lived very well.[81]

Rasmussen explains, that for this woman New York City was the right place to live, in relation to her life as a scientist. Expert colleagues and associates are only provided by – in – the big city: "They existed in the enormous assortment of human beings, but not in the idyll of Santa Barbara,"[82] Rasmussen notes.

Comparing New York City with Cambridge, England, Rasmussen emphasizes the qualities of New York City, where the intellectual is less isolated from the world outside the university. Considered in a cultural and intellectual perspective (and no longer in hygienic or natural terms), the city suddenly appears in a completely different light:

> Looking around one cannot avoid realizing that our civilization is the fruit of the concentration of people in big societies. . . . The vast majority of cultural progresses have been engendered by metropolitan institutions, massive centers for research and education that *might* have existed outside the action radius of the big cities; but have done so only to an astonishingly minimal extent. Whereas many have claimed that one should fight the big city, I myself think that we cannot live without it. In fact, if it didn't exist, one would indeed have to invent it.[83]

Something like a paradigmatic change in Rasmussen's view of cities is under way in such passages in which he seems to distance himself from his own profession, from his practice as an urban planner who used to think principally in terms of survey, spatial articulations, administration, and politics. Where in his writings on Copenhagen Rasmussen repeatedly emphasized the qualities of a single-family house with a garden, he suddenly appears to subscribe to the existence of big cities (although they may not always be that clean and well organized). It certainly looks as if Rasmussen's exploration of multi-sensory urban life makes him sympathetic to the metropolis. Now, even New York City – however haunted by problems of climate, health, pollution, social and racial inequality, etc. – is appreciated as a place of an extraordinary cultural and social intensity.

VI CONCLUSION: HAS NEW YORK CITY BEEN OVERLOOKED?

Rasmussen's œuvre provides no elaborate comparison of Copenhagen and New York City, let alone of sensorial and social life in these two cities. Yet, New York City plays an important role in Rasmussen's understanding of cities.[84] The back cover of Rasmussen's essay volume *Dejlige stæder* (*Wonderful Cities*) seems to assign a nearly utopian significance to New York City. Considered in totality, the drawing and its two captions add an interesting comment to Rasmussen's experience of New York City.

A typical Rasmussen drawing of a composite cityscape along 78th Street eastbound is annotated in his own hand as follows: "The snow is about to melt. But the cars are still snowed up."[85] A typeset text, that may very well have been written by Rasmussen himself,

10.5 Drawing of New York City, by Steen Eiler Rasmussen. Courtesy of G.E.C. Gads Forlag, Copenhagen.

adds the decisive comment: "Steen Eiler Rasmussen put a drawing from New York City here as a consolation prize for those who think that there should have been even more beautiful cities [dejlige stæder] in this book."

New York City – beautiful? One cannot avoid thinking that by ranging New York City among the beautiful cities of the world, Rasmussen may silently and indirectly recognize that, in some strange way, the experience of such a big city like New York City has been overlooked in most of his own writing about Copenhagen during a lifetime.

Notes

1   Steen Eiler Rasmussen: *København 1950*, Copenhagen: Nyt Nordisk Forlag Arnold Busck, 1950, p. 11. All translations from Rasmussen's texts in Danish are mine.

2   Steen Eiler Rasmussen: *London, the Unique City*, Middlesex: Penguin Books, 1960 (abridged version of revised edition first published by Jonathan Cage, 1937). Original Danish edition, 1934.

3   Steen Eiler Rasmussen: *Towns and Buildings*, Cambridge, Mass.: Harvard University Press, 1951 (revised edition of the Danish original, 1949).

4   Steen Eiler Rasmussen: *Experiencing Architecture*, Cambridge, Mass.: The MIT Press, 1959 (Danish original, 1957).

5   Translated from Steen Eiler Rasmussen: *London*, Copenhagen: Gyldendal, 1934, p. 6.

6   Steen Eiler Rasmussen: *København – Et bysamfunds særpræg og udvikling gennem tiderne*, Copenhagen: G.E.C. Gads Forlag, 1969, p. 21.

7   "It is a stale joke to call Copenhagen the 'Athens of the North', but one could justifiably call modern Athens the Copenhagen of the South." Steen Eiler Rasmussen: *Dejlige stæder i Alverdens lande*, Copenhagen: G.E.C. Gads Forlag, 1964, p. 16. Certain Danish architects such as the brothers Christian and Theophilus Hansen did in fact design buildings for Athens by the mid-nineteenth century.

8   Steen Eiler Rasmussen: *Dejlige stæder i Alverdens lande* (*Wonderful Cities in Countries from All over the World*), Copenhagen: G.E.C. Gads Forlag, 1964, pp. 7–8. A comparison of Stockholm and Copenhagen opens Rasmussen's book on Copenhagen, op. cit., pp. 11–12, photos pp. 14–15.

9   Steen Eiler Rasmussen, *København*: op. cit., p. 11. *København – Et bysamfunds særpræg og udvikling gennem tiderne* is based on his final lectures as a professor at the Royal Danish Academy of Fine Arts, School of Architecture, in Copenhagen during the academic year of 1967–1968, whereas his 1934 book on London was based on a series of lectures from 1930.

10   I first developed the quadruple signification of overlooking in a series of reflections and suggestions for the exhibition of urban architecture and art which was to be entitled *Den oversete by – det sansede København*, or in English: "*Overlooking the City – Perceiving Copenhagen.*" Divided into four sections corresponding to the four meanings of overlooking, the exhibition was eventually shown at the 1300 square meter Charlottenborg Exhibition Hall in central Copenhagen from December 27, 1995 to February 4, 1996.

11   Steen Eiler Rasmussen: *København 1950*, Copenhagen: Nyt Nordisk Forlag Arnold Busck, 1950, pp. 5–6.

12   Cf. Arne Gaardmand: *Dansk byplanlægning 1938–1992*, Copenhagen: Arkitektens Forlag, 1993, pp. 209–10.

13   Steen Eiler Rasmussen: "Københavns udvikling," in: *Politiken* (daily), Copenhagen, September 19, 1978, section 3, p. 10.

14   This policy had been applied in Odense, a major Danish city, with serious damage to the city's own cohesion as the immediate and everlasting result. Cf. Gaardmand op. cit., pp. 62–63 and p. 241.

15   Steen Eiler Rasmussen: "Københavns udvikling," in: *Politiken* (daily), Copenhagen, September 19, 1978, section 3, p. 10.

16 Cf. Finn Slente: *Bibliografi over Steen Eiler Rasmussens forfatterskab* (*Bibliography of Steen Eiler Rasmussen's Writings*), Copenhagen: The Royal Danish Library and Strubes Forlag, 1973.

17 A summary of this *enquête* can be found in Steen Eiler Rasmussen: *København*, op. cit., pp. 253–54.

18 Apart from the title already mentioned: *København – Et bysamfunds særpræg og udvikling gennem tiderne* (*Copenhagen – the particularity and development of an urban society through the ages*, from 1969), Rasmussen also published *København 1950*, Copenhagen: Nyt Nordisk Forlag, 1950, a book of some 136 pages, dealing with the state of Copenhagen half-way through the twentieth century.

19 Cf. Arne Gaardmand: *Dansk byplanlægning 1938-1992*, Copenhagen: Arkitektens Forlag, 1993, p. 35. Variations can be noted between the different Fingerplans drawn from 1947 onwards.

20 The secretariat worked under the daily leadership of Peter Bredsdorff who was later to be appointed professor of urban planning at the Royal Academy, School of Architecture, in Copenhagen. For elaboration on Peter Bredsdorff's merits as an organizer and as an urban planner in Copenhagen, see Arne Gaardmand: *Dansk byplanlægning 1938–1992*, Copenhagen: Arkitektens Forlag, 1993, p. 75.

21 It depended on the Danish Laboratory of Urban Planning (Dansk Byplanlaboratorium).

22 Cf. Gaardmand, op. cit. Cf. "Byplanens politik og bykulturen," chapter XII, in: Henrik Reeh: *Den urbane dimension: Tretten variationer over den moderne bykultur* (*The Urban Dimension: Thirteen Variations on Modern Urban Culture*), Odense: Odense University Press, 2001. The book contains a 4200-word summary in English.

23 Steen Eiler Rasmussen: *København 1950*, Copenhagen: Nyt Nordisk Forlag Arnold Busck, 1950, p. 101.

24 Steen Eiler Rasmussen's 16-page supplement for the Copenhagen daily newspaper *Politiken* "Giv hovedstaden bedre vilkår" ("Improve the Conditions of the Capital"), published on September 19, 1978, concludes with an open letter to the Danish Minister of Environment. Rasmussen writes: "Therefore the Ministry of Environment should appoint a fast working commission for a comprehensive planning of Copenhagen, Frederiksberg [a separate municipality surrounded by the municipality of Copenhagen], the Harbour, and the properties of the State. An *extensive, expert commission* representing the many fields of interest to be satisfied by the necessary grand plan for the development of Copenhagen," p. 14.

25 Steen Eiler Rasmussen: *København – Et bysamfunds særpræg og udvikling gennem tiderne*, Copenhagen: G.E.C. Gads Forlag, 1969, pp. 281–82.

26 Ibid., p. 244.

27 Ibid., p. 106.

28 Ibid., p. 12.

29 Cf. the preface of Rasmussen's *Byer og Bygninger*, Copenhagen: Fremad, 1949, p. I.

30 Ibid., p. 65.

31 Ibid.

32 Ibid., pp. 67–68.

33 Ibid., p. 74.

34 Ibid., p. 69.

35 Steen Eiler Rasmussen published two essays on the history of the Royal Danish Academy of Fine Arts in a small volume entitled *Fra Akademiet paa Charlottenborg gennem to hundrede aar* (*From the Academy at Charlottenborg during two Centuries*), Copenhagen: Boghallen, 1953.

36 In the mid-1990s, the Royal Academy of Fine Arts, School of Architecture, in Copenhagen was relocated from Kongens Nytorv in the center of the city to previous naval buildings of Holmen on the other side of the city's harbor. Charlottenborg and its ceremonial hall are already the objects of a certain nostalgia among architects who dream back to the days when they were surrounded by civic architecture in the dense city center and not by the (extraordinary) military buildings of Holmen.

37 Steen Eiler Rasmussen: *Byer og Bygninger*, Copenhagen: Fremad, 1949, p. 3.

38 By addressing the radically changing uses of urban architecture, Rasmussen may also avoid playing what he considers to be the game of tourism. Already in *København 1950*, Rasmussen stresses the risk of being seduced by some picturesque building at a time when modern office space starts leaving the facades of the buildings as kitsch. This critique is reiterated in *København* (1969).

39 Steen Eiler Rasmussen: *Omkring Christiania*, Copenhagen: Gyldendal, 1976, p. 11.

40 *Københavnsegnens planlægning – Status 1950*, Copenhagen: Ejnar Munksgaard, 1951, published under the sole responsibility of Rasmussen (cf. pp. 7 and 71), constitutes the official presentation of the work of the "Fingerplan" commission.

41 Steen Eiler Rasmussen: *København – Et bysamfunds særpræg og udvikling gennem tiderne*, Copenhagen: G.E.C. Gads Forlag, 1969, p. 233.

42 Ibid., p. 262.

43 See list, for instance, in *Omkring Christiania*, p. 57, of Christiania's supporters among whom Rasmussen played a significant role. This role was based on his relatively old age and his reputation as a liberal (not left wing), and his position as a respected intellectual in society.

44 In Danish "lejekaserner," which is the equivalent of "Mietskasernen" in German. Cf. Steen Eiler Rasmussen: *Omkring Christiania*, Copenhagen: Gyldendal, 1976, p. 28.

45 Ibid., p. 29.

46 Ibid., pp. 31–32.

47 Cf. Steen Eiler Rasmussen: "Byer til at leve i" ("Cities for living") from Steen Eiler Rasmussen: *Ogsaa et sovemiddel*, Copenhagen: Gyldendal, 1975, pp. 60–69. This essay was written in 1963, i.e. at the period of the construction at Tingbjerg. The hope invested in social institutions for solving social problems in the modern city is present in such early essays by Rasmussen as "Fra Slumkvarter til Legeplads" ("From Slum Quarter to Playground,") in: Steen Eiler Rasmussen, *I Danmarks Have* (*In the Garden of Denmark*), Copenhagen: Gyldendal, 1941, pp. 58–74.

48 Cf. Jürgen Habermas: *Theorie des kommunikativen Handelns*, Frankfurt am Main: Suhrkamp Verlag, 1981.

49 Steen Eiler Rasmussen: *Omkring Christiania*, op. cit., p. 35.

50 Ibid., p. 38.

51 Ibid., p. 51.

52 Ibid., p. 7.

53 Ibid., p. 15.

54 Ibid., pp. 16–17.

55 Cf. Steen Eiler Rasmussen: *Forunderlige menneskesind* (*Whimsical Human Minds*), Copenhagen: Gyldendal, 1982, pp. 42–47.

56 Cf. Steen Eiler Rasmussen: *Forunderlige menneskesind*, Copenhagen: Gyldendal, 1982, pp. 26–38.

57 Steen Eiler Rasmussen: *København – Et bysamfunds særpræg og udvikling gennem tiderne*, Copenhagen: G.E.C. Gads Forlag, 1969, p. 277.

58 Steen Eiler Rasmussen: "Min barndoms butikker" ("The Shops of My Childhood"), in: *Humor vort bedste vaaben*, Copenhagen: Gyldendal, 1973, pp. 115–25.

59 Steen Eiler Rasmussen: "Min barndoms butikker," in: *Humor vort bedste vaaben* (*Humor, Our Best Weapon*), Copenhagen: Gyldendal, 1973, p. 115. The essay was originally published in *Politiken*, February 8, 1968.

60 Steen Eiler Rasmussen: "Min barndoms butikker," op. cit., pp. 115 and 125.

61 Steen Eiler Rasmussen: "Min barndoms butikker," op. cit., p. 125.

62 Steen Eiler Rasmussen: "Min barndoms butikker," op. cit., p. 115.

63 Steen Eiler Rasmussen: "Min barndoms butikker," op. cit., p. 118.

64 Steen Eiler Rasmussen: "Min barndoms butikker," op. cit., p. 125.

65 The scheme for the future "Park of Common" "Fælledparken," laid out between 1908 and 1911, is reproduced in Rasmussen's *København* op. cit., p. 207.

66 Steen Eiler Rasmussen: "Hovedstadens jorder" ("The Lands of the Capital"), in: *Sig det med*

blomster (*Say it with Flowers*), Copenhagen: Gyldendal, 1976, p. 104. The common is situated close to the street of Rasmussen's childhood shops, Østerbrogade in Østerbro, situated northeast of Østerport, the former East Gate of the city.

67   Steen Eiler Rasmussen; "Hovedstadens jorder," in: *Sig det med blomster*, Copenhagen: Gyldendal, 1976, pp. 104–05. Originally, this essay was published in the journal of cultural criticism, *Fælleden* (*The Common*), September 1975.

68   It is indeed a striking feature in Rasmussen's essays on Copenhagen from his professional years, that the non-visual senses or the urban lifeworld are of little importance. Such issues were relegated, at best, to works on general subjects such as *Experiencing Architecture*. Steen Eiler Rasmussen: *Om at opleve arkitektur*, Copenhagen: G.E.C. Gads Forlag, 1957, US translation: *Experiencing Architecture*, Cambridge, Mass.: The MIT Press, 1959.

69   According to a reprint of this essay in Steen Eiler Rasmussen's book *Teater*, from 1979, the text had been written in "London oktober 1929." Cf. Steen Eiler Rasmussen: *Teater*, Copenhagen: G.E.C. Gads Forlag, 1979, p. 16.

70   Steen Eiler Rasmussen: "Paa Sangens Vinger," in: *En Bog om noget andet* (*A Book about Something Else*), Copenhagen: Gyldendal, 1940, p. 49. This essay was first published as a newpaper article in *Nationaltidende*, November 10, 1929, morning edition, pp. 11–12.

71   Dagmar Hansen, 1871–1944.

72   The 1930 recording session is described much later in an essay entitled "Stormagasinets forunderlige verden" ("The Whimsical/Wonderful World of the Department Store"), in: Steen Eiler Rasmussen: *Humor vort bedste vaaben*, Copenhagen: Gyldendal, 1973, pp. 31–43, originally published in *Politiken*, December 14, 1969. The essay relates the encounter of the fishwife, fully dressed up in her best clothes, and the particular disciplined ambiance of a recording studio inside the Copenhagen department store Magasin du Nord. Under such studio conditions the fishwife proves incapable of singing her street cries and ends up doing the recording in the open department store.

73   The archives of the Danish National Radio (Danmarks Radio) contain a brief but instructive recording of Dagmar Hansen crying her street cries.

74   Cf. Henrik Reeh: *Den urbane dimension*, Chapter 3, "Rum, hørelse, storbylyd" ("Space, Hearing, Urban Sound") (concerning considerations of hearing in Simmel's *Sociologie* and Rasmussen's *Experiencing Architecture*).

75   Steen Eiler Rasmussen: "Mit Paris," in: *Humor vort bedste vaaben*, Copenhagen: Gyldendal, 1973.

76   Ibid., p. 61.

77   Ibid., p. 68.

78   Ibid., p. 62.

79   Ibid., p. 62.

80   Ibid., p. 59.

81   Cf. Steen Eiler Rasmussen: "Drømmen om de smaa samfund" ("The Dream of Small Societies"), in: *Sig det med blomster* op. cit., p. 88. This friend of Rasmussen's didn't explain her being in New York City by pointing directly to the sensory density of such a big city. The importance of the city is indirect, since the *intellectual* environment is cited as the decisive difference between Santa Barbara and New York City: "It was not enough to have a well equipped laboratory – because she might have had this in Santa Barbara . . . No. The decisive point was the professional climate inside the walls. . . . She must have congenial colleagues, with whom she could talk, must have easy access to securing good collaborators for the laboratory" (p. 89). This difference, however, is in large part due to the city surrounding the laboratory and the university.

82   Steen Eiler Rasmussen: "Drømmen om de smaa samfund," in: *Sig det med blomster*, op. cit., p. 89.

83   Ibid., p. 90.

84   Examples from New York City are connotated both negatively and positively in Rasmussen's writing. Pointing to New York City's Wall Street, Rasmussen rejects the city's trategy for urban

density in comparison to the localization of the Copenhagen stock exchanges (of Christian IV), which Rasmussen praises. Cf. Steen Eiler Rasmussen: *København*, op. cit., p. 271. Another negative reference to New York City is given by Rasmussen in his book *Teater* (*Theater*), in which a project for the extension of the Royal Theater in Copenhagen is refuted by means of a commentary on a new glossy theater in midtown Manhattan. (Ibid., pp. 118–22.) Dealing with problems of concrete planning, both of these observations hardly touch upon issues of urban life considered in social and cultural terms.

From the point of view of urban culture, New York City has a more positive role to play. In *Om at opleve arkitekture* (*Experiencing Architecture*) Rasmussen illustrates the perception of architecture from an automobile with an example from New York City. Cf. Steen Eiler Rasmussen: *Om at opleve arkitektur*, Copenhagen: G.E.C. Gads Forlag, 1957, p. 149. See also the magnificent photograph by Andreas Feininger, which figures at the very beginning of the book, providing a visual preface to Rasmussen's text. The image shows the New York City skyline in the background whereas the foreground is occupied by a cemetery in Queens. No easy access to the urban lifeworld seems to be available.

85 Steen Eiler Rasmussen: *Dejlige stæder i Alverdens lande*, Copenhagen: G.E.C. Gads Forlag, 1964, cover, p. 4.

Part III

Representation

The Ashcan Artists
Journalism, Art and Metropolitan Life[1]

Robert W. Snyder

At the dawn of the twentieth century in the city of New York, you might have seen them: Robert Henri, searching the faces of the passing strangers; Everett Shinn, laughing with the crowd at a vaudeville theater; George Bellows, sitting elbow to elbow with the fight fans at ringside; William Glackens, eyeing the strollers in Washington Square Park; George Luks, pondering the rhythms of immigrant life on the Lower East Side; and John Sloan, revelling in a streetcorner flirtation conducted by the lights of a movie marquee. The six were artists who collectively became known as the Ashcan School; they went to New York City to make art rooted in the defining social trends of their time and created a record of a gregarious, contradictory and hybrid moment in the history of urban life.

They were never a formal school and they painted much more than ashcans, the metal barrels that held incinerated garbage at the curbside. The "Ashcan" title was applied after their most productive years together in a humorous reference to their fascination with gritty street scenes.[2] Nevertheless, as the art historian Rebecca Zurier has demonstrated, their work offered a distinct urban vision that was animated by the people of New York, inspired by the city's commercial energy and fascinated by its mosaic of communities. The Ashcan artists depicted particular responses to sweeping social changes. Their work was distinctly sensitive to the wholes and parts of the city, to the local and the metropolitan. They left uncommon records of the common experience of learning to navigate a city of strangers.

The Ashcan artists had a great subject: New York City in the years 1897 to 1917, when the metropolis became an emblem of modernity. Unlike their contemporaries who celebrated the emerging towers of the Manhattan skyline, the Ashcan artists explored New York at street level and grasped the new social trends that changed the daily life of the city: immigration, advertising and mass communication, popular entertainment, the development of grand public spaces, the gap between rich and poor, and shifting gender roles.

Journalism, as Zurier's research shows, was a vital ingredient in the artists' success. The Ashcan painters brought to art the energy and big city vernacular of newspaper illustrations as they appeared in the late nineteenth century, just before photographs became the dominant element in visual journalism. Their literary counterparts were writers such as Mark Twain, Theodore Dreiser, Jack London, and Stephen Crane, who moved from journalism to writing novels and short stories in a spirit of realism.[3]

Eventually the Ashcan artists all left journalism, partly because illustrators' jobs dried up and partly because they found the work routines and formulaic visual representations of pictorial journalism too constraining. In some cases, to their detriment, they carried the limiting formulas of their journalism into their art, resulting in works with the feel of cartoons. But at their best their art was enriched by a journalist's sense of curiosity and a journalist's desire to connect with a broad public. Their ability to see as journalists – with an appreciation for the new, for social processes, for relationships of power, for urban narratives – helped them as artists.

The Ashcan painters transcended the conventional distinctions between fine art and popular art. They created paintings with brushwork inspired by Velazquez and Rembrandt and settings inspired by Manhattan streetlife. They were the artistic heirs of Walt Whitman, the newspaper reporter and editor who transmuted his metropolitan journalism to produce poetry that was grounded in his experience of New York City, democratic in its sensibility, and fascinated with New York's ordinary people.[4]

Like so many other New Yorkers, the Ashcan artists came from somewhere else. Bellows aside, five of the six laid the foundations of their careers in the Philadelphia of the 1890s. Henri studied at the acclaimed Pennsylvania Academy of Fine Arts, traveled and studied in Europe, and taught at Philadelphia's School of Design for Women. Sloan, Shinn, Glackens and Luks all worked as graphic artists at Philadelphia publications.[5]

Photoengraving, introduced in the 1880s, provided a fast and cheap way to reproduce drawings for news stories and advertisements. Photographs had not yet become the dominant visual element in the mass media, and sketches brought drama to the printed page. In Philadelphia, as in other big cities, modern illustrated journalism was taking shape at the dynamic intersection of urban growth, technological change and commercial culture. An increasing number of newspapers served a growing population of city people; their feature stories and illustrations brought readers to corners of the city that they could not know first hand. Improvements in printing and typesetting technology increased the speed of newspaper production. The cost of producing papers was increasingly born by advertisers, particularly the owners of department stores (the quintessential institutions of an emerging urban consumer culture) who wanted to see their wares displayed in elaborate illustrated advertisements.[6]

Philadelphia's three leading newspapers competed with illustrated Sunday supplements, bold headlines, lurid writing and dramatic drawings executed on location. Individuals with a flair for art but no wherewithal for academic training found jobs as graphic artists and newspaper illustrators. Offers of better pay then lured them to jump from paper to paper.[7]

A newspaper art department, as Shinn recalled, was without peer in its ability to inculcate powers of memory and rapid observation. A news artist assigned to cover a fire or traffic accident scribbled down rough details – the height of a burning building, the shape of a wrecked vehicle – and returned to the newspaper to transform the notes into a fully-fledged drawing. Glackens was especially admired for his ability to cover events without pencil or paper. With "one look on an assignment," Shinn noted, Glackens could take in enough information to return to the newsroom and create a perfectly accurate image.[8]

The artists learned to draw in a rapid, abbreviated and standardized style. It was fast to depict a building on fire by scribbling a cloud of smoke rather than drawing the structure behind it – and it was faster still to work from a memory, imagination or a second-hand description.[9] Newspaper illustrators practiced a visual version of the news-

11.1 Everett Shinn, "Fire on 24th Street," New York City, 1907. Courtesy of the Cheekwood Museum of Art, Nashville, Tennessee.

writing techniques noted by the reporter-turned-historian Robert Darnton, who observed that much of news writing involves fitting breaking stories into standard templates of news writing – in effect, "making cookies from an antique cookie cutter."[10]

A newspaper illustrator lived a harried life, with work routines that resembled an industrial assembly line. Seeking greater development for their talents, and an artistic community, Glackens, Shinn, Sloan and Luks began to take part-time classes at the Pennsylvania Academy of Fine Arts. Frustrated with a curriculum that emphasized drawing from plaster casts, Sloan and other part-timers, many of them newspapermen, left the Academy. They set up an informal class in life drawing, which they dubbed the Charcoal Club, and hired a trained artist as a critic. When the club disbanded he encouraged them to gather at his studio to sketch, drink and talk. The artist was Robert Henri, and out of these sessions came the nucleus of the Ashcan group.[11]

In thought and action, Henri bridged the classical and the popular. He was both a product of, and a rebel against, French academic training. He read widely – from the philosophical writings of Ralph Waldo Emerson to the muscular political tracts of Thomas Paine to the humanitarian novels of Zola and Tolstoy. Above all, he celebrated the life and work of Walt Whitman, the journalist turned poet who found the raw material for the poem "Leaves of Grass" in court reporting, Broadway rambles and editorial writing. "Walt Whitman," argued Henri, "seems to have found great things in the littlest things of life." Henri painted, and taught his students to paint, in the same spirit. "Walt

Whitman was such as I have proposed the real art student should be. His work is an auto-biography – not of haps and mishaps, but of his deepest thought, his life indeed."[12]

To Henri, art was an ennobled act of communication. "Painting is the expression of ideas in their permanent form," he wrote. "It is the giving of evidence. It is the study of our lives, our environment." He argued, "The true artist regards his work as a means of talking with men, of saying his say to himself and to others."[13]

Henri encouraged his students to turn their emotions and experiences directly into art, to paint quickly across an entire canvas rather than toil over any single section. He urged them to work the way news artists did: "Do it all in one sitting if you can. In one minute if you can. There is no virtue in delaying."[14]

Yet Henri wanted his students to produce something more than newspaper illustrations rendered in oil paint. He encouraged them to transcend the divisions between high art and popular art and create works that were rooted in the contemporary scene, like the news, but enduring in their quality, like traditional paintings.

Henri urged his students to seek inspiration from the Old Masters – to learn from Rembrandt's ability to capture "the real, intimate life of people," "the beautiful dignity always in Velasquez," the "majesty" of Titian. Henri also told his students to study graphic artists of the past. He recommended that they study the paintings of Winslow Homer, which he said made a viewer feel "the force of the sea."[15] In Henri's thinking, the artists' newspaper days and reportorial vision were the raw material for vigorous paintings that would be contemporary, distinct, and still worthy of comparison with great works of the past.

By the mid-1890s several of the group had begun to experiment with painting scenes on the streets of Philadelphia and abroad. But to make the most of Henri's challenge each of the artists, including Henri himself, would have to move to New York. Gotham was the capital of the newspaper and publishing industries, the center of the American art world, and the metropolis where all the driving forces of modern life – immigration, changing gender roles, an emerging entertainment industry and more – took shape on the city streets. Moreover, New York was a city capable of rewarding ambition – which was not in short supply among the artists who gathered around Henri. As Sloan wrote to Henri in 1898, "a good thing done in New York is heralded abroad – a good thing done in Philadelphia – is well-*done* in Philadelphia."[16]

New York City was a hub where culture originated or was imported from elsewhere, then transmitted back to the rest of the country and to the world. The artists were drawn to Manhattan because it was a magnet for talent, powered by the city's dual position as capital of both the nation's publishing industry and its art world.[17]

In the 1890s, New York eclipsed Boston and became the capital of American book publishing. Manhattan became the national headquarters for inexpensive, illustrated magazines pitched to a mass audience. New York newspapers grew in prominence, and their stories were syndicated throughout the country. News from New York – stories about the city's business deals, fashions, cultural affairs, politics, neighborhoods and everyday life – acquired a national readership. At the same time, an arts journalism scene appeared. By 1900 several art magazines were edited in New York. At least eight city newspapers employed their own art critics. The city's art scene was the focus of articles in dozens of national publications. For ambitious artists and illustrators, New York was a place to make a reputation.[18]

Luks and Glackens moved to Manhattan in 1896, Shinn in 1897. Sloan came for a few months the following summer but would not settle in New York permanently until 1904. The transplanted Philadelphians worked as sketch-reporters at New York's major newspapers. Although photographs were beginning to replace drawings, a boom in illustrated Sunday supplements and comics created many work opportunities for them. Luks, for example, drew hilarious scenes of tenement life for the pathbreaking Sunday newspaper comic, *The Yellow Kid*. The artists also found more flexible, lucrative and engaging work in the growing magazine market where Luks drew mordant cartoons for the monthly *The Verdict*.[19]

Unlike newspaper artists who had to grind out daily drawings, freelance illustrators had more control over their time. In New York, the artists could visit museums and galleries, meet professional critics, and gather to exchange opinions on art and politics. Sloan, for example, moved in Greenwich Village circles, where he attended the salon of Mabel Dodge, a favorite gathering place for radicals, bohemians and literary figures.[20]

In its scale, complexity, color and energy, New York was a great city for a journalist to cover. Daily life was the raw material of a multitude of pictures and stories. The Ashcan painters produced memorable art partly because, like their counterparts in the metropolitan press, they chronicled the creation of a New York that would define urban life in America for the rest of the century. In 1900, a list of the subjects of Ashcan paintings was very much like a list of story ideas for a great New York City newspaper.

Two massive currents shaped and reshaped the city, consolidation and diversification. Manhattan and adjacent territories were consolidated into a five-borough city in 1898, and soon afterwards New York acquired a mass transit system that knit four of the boroughs into one functioning unit. Banks, factories, the stock market, and corporate headquarters were concentrated in New York City, making its bankers, businessmen and financiers uniquely powerful nationally and internationally. Skyscrapers were built for the first time and the number of apartment houses grew dramatically, defining the character of the city's physical plan for the rest of the century.[21]

Diversification was strongest in realms of culture. The immigrants who thronged to the city were not only different from the city's natives, but also from each other. Despite efforts to "Americanize" them in schools and settlement houses, they made New York a city where no one ethnic group could readily claim to represent the majority. In the relations between men and women, consumer culture created more opportunities for leisure activities open to the mixing of both sexes which emphasized self-expression over self-control. The entry of women into the workforce gave them a measure of economic autonomy and new social roles. In many ways both subtle and dramatic, the rigidly defined gender roles of the nineteenth century were eroded.[22]

Despite their differences, the forces of consolidation and diversification could at times be complementary. The subways brought the city's boroughs together, yet they spurred the construction of neighborhoods where immigrants and their children perpetuated a polyglot ethnic geography. Vaudeville theater, whose roots lay in rowdy Bowery music halls, used a modern booking system of industrial proportions to make New York the capital of the entertainment industry; at the same time, its vibrant song, dance and comedy helped to shatter the restrained culture of American Victorianism. New York's mass circulation newspapers concentrated cultural power under one roof, yet they created cultural forms – such as feature stories – that introduced city dwellers to new ways of thinking and feeling.[23]

For natives and newcomers, as for men and women, identities were in a constant state of flux. The inhabitants of the city that O. Henry called "Bagdad-on-the-Subway" struggled to decipher the meaning of the crowds around them and tried to establish their own place in the urban fabric. For the Ashcan artists and their fellow New Yorkers, it was never easy to draw a firm line between the watchers and the watched.[24]

The Ashcan artists, in their questing spirit, tried to interpret and represent the dynamic social forces that made and remade New York City. It was a difficult task. American art offered few usable precedents, and European images of urban life did not always provide effective ways of envisioning the American scenes. In their efforts to depict New York life the artists sought inspiration from sources in both art history and popular imagery. Although their work covered the same grounds as newspapers, documentary photography and entertainment, they often found new ways of depicting their subjects and distinct ways of thinking about them.[25]

The artists often depicted moments or individual locations. The titles of Ashcan works frequently convey a specific address, activity, season, or personality. Their approach to the city – block-by-block, incident-by-incident – resembled the strategy of the guidebooks and magazine articles of the day. Ashcan images did not depict New York from the top down. Instead, they presented an endless succession of neighborhoods to discover and incidents to observe. Their street-level perspective, which was fascinated with the particular, helped them to transcend the binary categories of the sunshine and shadow books, the nineteenth-century guidebooks that depicted the city as a series of alternating tableaus of vice and virtue. With few exceptions, the Ashcan artists put people at the

11.2 Robert Henri, "Portrait of Willie Gee," 1904. Courtesy of The Newark Museum/Art Resource.

11.3 Everett Shinn,
"Footlight Flirtation,"
1912. Courtesy of
Arthur G. Altschul.

center of their drawings. As the historian Ian Gordon has observed, they sought to over-come the distance that separated their subjects, themselves and their audience – in effect, to redeem the promise of a democratic American life. At the same time, they recognized the obstacles to, and shortcomings of, that promise.[26]

Yet for all their shared general interests, each of the artists had his own enthusiasms and techniques. Henri was especially interested in portraits of individuals; his painting of an African-American youth, "Willie Gee," is classical in its technique yet reportorial in its realism. In an era of pervasive ethnic and racial stereotyping, when the stereotypes of African-Americans were the worst of all (and when Henri himself could say, with so many others, "always I find the race expressed in the individual"), "Portrait of Willie Gee" is remarkable for its warmth, clarity and individuality. Part of the credit should go to the boy himself, whose dignity and posture are striking, but part of the credit must also go to Henri, who was willing to abandon his own stereotypes when confronted by the reality of an individual.[27]

Shinn specialized in large-scale pastels that depicted theater, urban fashion and sensational news. His painting "Footlight Flirtation," which shows an actress trying to grab her restless audience with a glance that is both flirtatious and intense, draws on his own knowledge of the stage.[28]

Glackens' works, packed with activity, recall his magazine illustrations. Given the stereotypical quality of much illustrated journalism in this period, especially when dealing with racial and ethnic groups, some of his images have the feel of monotonous cartoon-ing. His drawings executed in the Jewish quarter on the Lower East Side frequently depict immigrants as ugly, frightening people. Still, his sketches of people on the street, done in the manner of preliminary drawings that a newspaper artist would work up into a full illustration, reveal an extraordinary sensitivity to posture, gesture, body shape and deportment.[29]

11.4 Wm. Glackens, "Sheet of Sketches." Courtesy of Smithsonian Institution, National Museum of American Art (Gift of Mr and Mrs Ira Glackens).

Sloan's pictures of immigrants and working class people are infused with a deep sense of humanity and an appreciation for the humor, dignity and high spirits to be found on the streets of New York. He was also influenced by both feminism and the revolt against Victorianism. Sloan transcended old categories of women as virtuous or fallen: his prostitutes were strong women, his factory girls sensual and self-sufficient. Many of Sloan's New York pictures, Zurier has noted, such as "Movies," which depicts a sidewalk flirtation outside a theater, suggest stories that begin when a man looks at a woman. "Women," writes Zurier, "play several roles at once in Sloan's art: beyond being objects of desire, they record the new independence of modern New Yorkers while also presenting a variation on old ideals of beauty in art."[30]

Sloan was an active member of the Socialist Party. Like Bellows, he made explicitly political drawings for the radical journal *The Masses*. Sloan, however, tried to keep polemical statements out of his paintings. Nevertheless, some of Sloan's paintings of city life show an awareness of class distinctions and hint at his affinities: "Gray and Brass" depicts rich people motoring through Central Park as the sort of dullards that Goya found in the Spanish royal family, while the working class subjects of "Scrubwomen, Astor Library" radiate strength and good humor.[31]

Unlike Sloan, Bellows was enough of a success as a painter, printmaker and teacher that he relied on journalistic illustration to make his living only briefly. By studying with Henri, however, he acquired the equivalent of a newspaper illustrator's penchant for rapid, vigorous execution of topical subject matter, and of exploring extremes of New York life. Bellows, as Robert Hughes has observed, had a journalist's instinct for a good story. He was fascinated by boxing, which was in the process of evolving from street

11.5 John Sloan, "Movies," 1913. Courtesy of Toledo Museum of Art, Toledo, Ohio.

11.6 George Bellows, "Both Members of this Club," 1909. Courtesy of Chester Dale Collection, National Gallery of Art, Washington DC.

brawling and semi-legal club fighting into a recognized professional sport. His paintings such as "Both Members of this Club" and "Stag at Sharkey's" explode with color and emotion. In both, the crowd is as much a part of the spectacle as the fighters themselves.[32]

The contrasts among the artists' works reveal the futility of trying to select one painter or painting as the perfect representative of the Ashcan School – they just had too many ways of seeing the city. Nevertheless, a painting by George Luks does suggest the kinds of limits and strengths that appear and reappear in the artist's work. Luks was best known for his renditions of the comic *Hogan's Alley*, which depicted the tenement adventures of the wise-cracking Mickey Dugan (known as the "Yellow Kid" because of the smock he wore) and a gang of friends. Luks was drawn to the immigrant Jewish quarter on the Lower East Side, and his painting "Hester Street" depicts a well-known street in the district. Most journalists of the period described the area as a transplanted piece of

11.7 George Luks, "Hester Street," 1905. Courtesy of Brooklyn Museum of Art, New York.

Eastern Europe, animated by the antique practices of an ancient religion. Luks saw something different. His painting shows a market scene populated by Jewish immigrants whose derbies, beards and prominent noses conform to the stereotype of the time.

At this point, however, Luks' sharp powers of observation made the painting a revealing social document. One man stands out: he is clean-shaven, wearing a light fedora, and smoking a cigarette. To the right of him is a woman in a shirtwaist blouse and fancy hat, her garb a contrast with that of an immigrant woman draped in a shawl, talking to a shopkeeper. In one scene, Luks grasped the process of acculturation, and its effect on dress and behavior. Luks, like any good illustrator, condensed a story into a single image. Although the stereotypes of popular culture are present in his painting, his sense of realism led him to depict a narrative of assimilation that was not always prominent in accounts of the neighborhood.[33]

Despite such achievements, the Ashcan artists most creative and productive years came to an end at the time of World War I. The city that the artists had known disappeared by the end of the century's second decade. Immigration from Europe declined during the war. During the 1920s, Federal quotas would severely limit immigration from Southern and Eastern Europe in an effort to maintain America's Anglo-Saxon purity. The great waves of immigration that had transformed the city were over. In subsequent decades, the Italian and Jewish immigrants and their descendants would settle into the city so completely that by the 1970s, they would be thought of as its establishment, with the Statue of Liberty as their Plymouth Rock and the dumbbell tenement as their log cabin.[34]

African-Americans from the South became the city's source of cheap labor. They moved into Harlem, a neighborhood which developers hoped would become a middle class suburb but which was opened to blacks of all social classes when overbuilding created vast vacancies in the Harlem real estate market. In the 1920s, Harlem became the New York neighborhood that attracted the mixture of seekers of exoticism and earnest reformers who had once flocked to the Lower East Side.[35]

The war also transformed the era's spirit of radicalism. Super-patriots in and out of government equated dissent with treason. The Federal government banned from the mails the radical magazine *The Masses*, which had featured work by Sloan and Bellows. The repression of the war years spilled over into the Red Scare of 1919. The questioning spirit which animated New York and some of the artists' best work was driven underground.

Pictorial journalism moved away from the era that had shaped the Ashcan artists. The photograph, and not the artists' sketch, became the defining visual element in newspapers. While tabloid newspapers of the 1920s maintained the fascination with ordinary people that had inspired so much Ashcan art, they also embraced a culture of celebrity that was very far from the Ashcan ethos. Bellows and Sloan, for example, painted their share of rich people, but they always put them in a social context that explained something about them. Many tabloid photographs, on the other hand, pushed pictorial journalism toward creating pictures of people who were famous simply for being famous.[36]

By the closing years of the second decade of the twentieth century, much of what was shocking and new to the Ashcan artists when they arrived in New York was a familiar part of urban life – and less likely to inspire their highest artistic abilities. The gas-lit city of five-story tenements was becoming a place of electric light and skyscrapers – a setting better suited to the scenes of urban anonymity made famous by Edward Hopper.[37]

Ironically for the Ashcan artists, who saw themselves as painters of modern life, the main currents in American art turned toward the abstract. The realism of the Ashcan group came to seem very far from "modern" art. Nevertheless, as Virginia Mecklenburg has observed, the Ashcan artists influenced the topical Hopper, the vigorous and ribald Reginald Marsh, and others who would try to make art out of life in New York City. Documentary photographers of the 1930s also owed much to the Ashcan artists, who if nothing else established a foundation for urban art that was of its own time and place.[38]

11.8 John Sloan, "Pigeons," 1910. Courtesy of Museum of Fine Arts, Boston.

Perhaps their greatest influence, as *Washington Post* critic Paul Richard pointed out, was on Hollywood: Bellows' urban panoramas and Glackens' Madison Square anticipate the bustling downtown of "Miracle on 34th Street;" Sloan's "Pigeons" could have inspired the rooftop scene of "On the Waterfront;" Sloan's "Hair Dresser's Window" is revisited in "Man With the Golden Arm;" Bellows' "Paddy Flannigan" anticipates Jimmy Cagney and the Dead End Kids. Ashcan art went full circle: rooted in journalism and developed to its fullest through artistic training under Henri, its power and perspective circled back to invigorate popular cinema – and appropriately so. American movies – like Broadway musicals, modern dance and Tin Pan Alley – have always blended high and low in the kind of proportions that invigorated Ashcan art.[39]

In the years since the early twentieth century the Ashcan artists' works ceased to be records of contemporary events and became historical artifacts in their own right; they acquired, for many viewers, a patina of nostalgia that obscures the turbulence of turn-of-the-century New York City. At the same time, journalism and New York City changed. It seems unlikely that either will again offer the same kind of inspiration that invigorated Henri and his colleagues. The big-city daily newspaper is no longer a cutting-edge medium. The fascination with immigrants and the working class that fuelled so much turn-of-the-century journalism and Ashcan art is missing from the media of our own time. In search of affluent readers many newspapers have all but erased working class people from their pages and replaced them with either celebrities or an implausibly large middle class. American television once showed its viewers people and places that were different; today it thrives by explaining Americans to themselves in the most inward-looking terms. And New York City is not the same metropolis that the Ashcan artists knew: the flight to the suburbs, the shadow of crime, the privatization of public space, economic dislocation, and the stubborn persistence of bigotry have all challenged the optimism of their vision of urban life. The city, for most Americans, is no longer the new frontier that beckoned to the Ashcan artists.

Still, the lives and work of the Ashcan painters carry important lessons for the present. One of the hardest to appreciate, in the twenty-first century, is their desire to put themselves on the streets of the city, to regularly and enthusiastically try to make sense of the relationship between themselves and the strangers they encountered. At their best, the Ashcan artists learned from people who were different from themselves. A century after they set out to make art out of the street life of New York, it is a lesson worth remembering.[40]

Notes

1   This chapter is derived from material that appeared in a different form in Rebecca Zurier, Robert W. Snyder and Virginia M. Mecklenburg: *Metropolitan Lives: The Ashcan Artists and their New York*, Smithsonian/Norton, 1995. For a more detailed analysis of the artists' relationship to journalism and other forms of visual culture, see Rebecca Zurier's forthcoming book, derived from her dissertation "Picturing the City: New York in the Press and the Art of the Ashcan School, 1897–1917," Yale, 1988.

The material presented here benefited from comments and questions at "The Urban Life World" conference at the University of Copenhagen, November 1–3, 1996. Outside the conference, Jennifer Kelley, Rebecca Zurier, Ian Gordon, and Clara Hemphill all offered insightful suggestions. Kathleen Collins provided helpful editorial assistance during final revision of the essay.

2   On the origins of the term "Ashcan School", see: Elizabeth Milroy: *Painters of a New Century: The Eight and American Art*, ex. cat., Milwaukee: Milwaukee Art Museum, 1991; and Robert Hunter: "The Rewards and Disappointments of the Ashcan School", in: Lowery Stokes Sims: *Stuart Davis: American Painter*, ex. cat., New York: Metropolitan Museum of Art, 1992, pp. 35–41.

3   See Shelley Fisher Fishkin: *From Fact to Fiction*, New York: Oxford, 1985.

4   See Paul Zweig and Walt Whitman: *The Making of the Poet*, New York: Basic Books, Inc., 1984 and Steven H. Jaffe, "Whitman and the New Journalism," *Seaport*, Spring 1992, pp. 27–31.

5   Will Jenkins: "Illustration of the Daily Press in America," *International Studio*, 16, June 1902, p. 255.

6   Wm. David Sloan, James G. Stovall (eds), and James D. Startt (assoc. ed.): *The Media in America: A History*, Worthington, Ohio: Publishing Horizons, Inc., 1989, pp. 218–23, 235–36.

7   Jenkins: "Illustration of the Daily Press in America," p. 225.

8   Quotations are from Everett Shinn: "Life on the Press," in: "Artists of the Philadelphia Press," *Philadelphia Museum of Art Bulletin*, 41, November 1945, pp. 9–12 *passim*.

9   John Sloan, quoted in "Artists of the Philadelphia Press," n.p.; see also Shinn, "Life on the Press" and the photograph of Shinn in the newsroom (Archives of American Art, Smithsonian Institution), reprinted in *City Life Illustrated, 1890–1940: Sloan, Glackens, Luks, Shinn – Their Friends and Followers*, ex. cat., Wilmington: Delaware Art Museum, 1980, p. 15.

10   Robert Darnton: "Writing News and Telling Stories," *Daedalus*, 104, Spring 1975, pp. 188–93.

11   Rebecca Zurier: "The Making of Six New York Artists," in Rebecca Zurier, Robert W. Snyder, and Virginia M. Mecklenburg: *Metropolitan Lives: The Ashcan Artists and their New York*, Smithsonian/Norton, 1995, pp. 61–62.

12   For a discussion of Henri see Zurier: "The Making of Six New York Artists," pp. 62–64. Also Robert Henri: *The Art Spirit*, New York: Icon, 1984 reprint, pp. 84, 142.

13   Henri: *The Art Spirit*, pp. 116, 117.

14   Henri: *The Art Spirit*, p. 26.

15   Henri: *The Art Spirit*, pp. 110, 171, 269, 118.

16   Sloan letter to Robert Henri, October 1898, in Bernard Perlamn (ed.): *Revolutionaries of Realism: The Letters of John Sloan and Robert Henri*, Princeton: Princeton University Press, 1997, p. 32.

17   Zurier: "The Making of Six New York Artists," p. 64.

18   Zurier: "The Making of Six New York Artists," pp. 64–65; also John Tebbel and Mary Ellen Zuckerman: *The Magazine in America: 1741–1990*, New York: Oxford University Press, 1991, p. 58.

19   Zurier: "The Making of Six New York Artists," pp. 65–66.

20   Zurier: "The Making of Six New York Artists," pp. 65–66.

21   Robert W. Snyder: "City in Transition," in: *Metropolitan Lives*, pp. 29–30.

22   Snyder: "City in Transition," p. 30.

23   Snyder: "City in Transition," p. 30.

24   Snyder: "City in Transition," p. 31.

25   Snyder and Zurier: "Picturing the City," in: *Metropolitan Lives*, p. 85.

26   Snyder and Zurier: "Picturing the City," p. 85; Christine Stansell: "What Are You Looking At?" *London Review of Books*, October 3, 1996, p. 25; Zurier: "The Making of Six New York Artists," p. 69; Ian Gordon: "All that Jazz: New York, Modernism and Advertising", *Australasian Journal of American Studies*, 16, July 1997.

27   Snyder and Zurier: "Picturing the City," pp. 129–30; Robert Henri: "Portrait of Willie Gee"; Henri: *The Art Spirit*, p. 143.

28   Zurier: "The Making of Six New York Artists," pp. 70–71; also Snyder and Zurier: "Picturing the City," p. 163; Everett Shinn's "Footlight Flirtation."

29   Zurier: "The Making of Six New York Artists," pp. 73–75; William Glackens' "Far from the Fresh Air Farm"; Glackens' "A Football Game," pp. 24, 132, 140.

30   Zurier: "The Making of Six New York Artists," p. 78.

31   Snyder: "City in Transition," p. 45; Snyder and Zurier: "Picturing the City," pp. 112, 175; Zurier: "The Making of Six New York Artists," pp. 79–81; John Sloan's "Scrubwomen, Astor Library"; Sloan's "Gray and Brass."

32   Snyder and Zurier: "Picturing the City," p. 163; Stansell and Robert Hughes: "The Epic of the City," *Time*, February 19, 1996, p. 63.

33   Snyder and Zurier: "Introduction," pp. 26–27; George Luks' "Hester Street."

34   Snyder: "City in Transition," pp. 54–56.

35   Snyder: "City in Transition," p. 54.

36   Karin E. Becker: "Photojournalism in the Tabloid Press," in: Peter Dahlgren and Colin Spanks (eds): *Journalism and Popular Culture*, London: Sage, 1993, pp. 140–42. Jeffrey Toobin's comments on the circular nature of fame in the late twentieth century have informed my thinking on these points.

37   Stansell: "What Are You Looking At?," p. 25.

38   Virginia M. Mecklenburg: "Manufacturing Rebellion: The Ashcan Artists and the Press," in: *Metropolitan Lives*, pp. 212–13.

39   Paul Richard: *Washington Post*, "Guts! Guts! Life! Life!," November 24, 1995, D7.

40   For ideas on public life and culture, see: Dana Brand: *The Spectator and the City in Nineteenth-Century American Literature*, New York: Cambridge University Press, 1991, pp. 194–95.

Chapter 12

Imagined Urbanity
Novelistic Representations of Copenhagen

Peter Madsen

> "Let me flit out in the world!," I begged with tears in my eyes.
>
> H.C. Andersen

Hans Christian Andersen and Søren Kierkegaard are both of world renown – and both lived in a city that was confined to a narrow space limited by age-old fortifications. Copenhagen had not yet experienced the abolishment of the ramparts and the expansion of the city that would turn it into a modern metropolis. They reacted in very different manners to the narrow surroundings. Kierkegaard went to Berlin several times, but apart from that his sphere was restricted to Copenhagen, except for occasional visits to Northern Zealand and a trip to Jutland. Andersen was – on the contrary – immensely curious about the world. He traveled again and again, to Sweden, Switzerland, Germany, to Italy, Spain and Portugal, to England, to Greece, and the near Orient.[1] His first novel is in a romantic mode, an ironic play with literary trends and conventions elaborately entitled *Journey on Foot from Holmen's Canal to the Eastern Point of Amager in the Years 1828 and 1829*,[2] not much of a journey, it turns out: a few hours before and after midnight, most of it fantasies and literary allusions. On New Year's Eve the lonely author contemplates the snow-covered roofs around him from his tiny room. Satan invokes the sinful idea: to become an author. Since all the poetic roads are already taken, he chooses prosaic Amager "as playground for my young impetuous blood" (8). His experience is in this book confined to Copenhagen and Amager even if his attempts to use a borrowed pair of hundred-league boots tentatively bring one of his feet to Germany, Austria, and the North Sea, only to be withdrawn for various reasons. His journey in time is more elaborate, though. Reflecting on the picture of his own era from the point of view of the future he is carried 300 years ahead: an opera poster has the year 2129 and a door leads to "a new theater that showed all the theater-effects of the Nineteenth Century in an immense kaleidoscope" (21), retrospectively. He eventually reaches a winding step leading to "a panorama as beautiful as fantasy can conjure up" (23) that provides a view of the city of the future: "Everything down there had changed beyond recognition. Nearly all the streets were straight and regular; every building seemed like a palace. The city had expanded considerably; the Peblinge Lake was inside the ramparts [the actual location of the lake was outside the ramparts], surrounded by allées for promenades . . . The harbor abounded with foreign ships and gave me an intimation of Denmark's bloom." Above his head he senses "an immense corpus spewing black clouds of smoke passing like a lightening. I soon realized that it was an air-steamer invented at that time" (23).

Andersen's sense of time and space is expansive. His fantasy is in tune with technological innovations and he is operating within a visual regime defined by inventions of his own time that create an inclusive vision: panorama and kaleidoscope. Even the ramparts, the enclosure of the city, are displaced outwards. Historically speaking, Andersen was writing during a period marked by the effects of state bankruptcy in the aftermath of England's defeat of the Danish navy in 1807. The blooming of the harbor as a vision of the future may recall the previous so-called *époque florissante* towards the end of the eighteenth century.

I PUBLIC SPHERE, *FLÂNERIE*, AND DISTRACTIONS – SØREN KIERKEGAARD'S *THE SEDUCER'S DIARY*

> . . . you went secretly, as a stranger, in the midst of all those many people . . .
>
> Søren Kierkegaard

If Andersen's vision was expansive, Kierkegaard's was not. It was confined to the narrow world of Copenhagen within the ramparts and most especially to intimate interiors. But to him even small-town Copenhagen was marked by features that were typical of "a capital and royal-residence city": "the noise and traffic in the streets . . . the meeting and parting, the haste and hurry in which the most diverse matters equally assert themselves . . . the noisy community in which everyone contributes his share to the general racket." In the "social poscimur [we are summoned] of the capital" "it is so easy to go along, where at any moment one can get rid of oneself, at any hour find a seat in an omnibus, everywhere encompassed by diversions."[3] Besides speed and noise the crucial feature has to do with the position of the individual: it is easy to lose oneself, to become just another serial part in the "Omnibus" (which should be taken not merely literally, but also symbolically), each single moment represents an opportunity, but in particular an opportunity for diversion or distraction ("*Afledning*": leading away or in a new direction). Kierkegaard's view of urban conditions is also eloquently demonstrated in his description of Rome in one of the writings in his own name (*Three Upbuilding Discourses* from 1843 – i.e. the same year he published *Either-Or* and *The Seducer's Diary*):

> In the world's capital, in proud Rome, where all the splendor and glory of the world were concentrated, where everything was procured whereby human sagacity and rapaciousness tempt the moment in the anxiety of despair, everything to astonish the sensate person, where everyday witnessed something extraordinary, something horrible, and the next day had forgotten it upon seeing something even more extraordinary – in far-famed Rome, where everyone who in any way believed himself able to capture public attention hastened as to his rightful stage, prepared everything in advance for his reception so that he, although intoxicated with self-confidence, might shrewdly avail himself of the scantily allotted and begrudged propitious moment – there lived the Apostle Paul as a prisoner . . .[4]

Øieblikket, the instant, as opposed to duration and eternity, the extraordinary as opposed to the ordinary, sensuality as opposed to spirituality, masses as opposed to the

12.1 Drawing by J.P. Lund of a street in Copenhagen, about 1860, showing the character of the streets at the time of Andersen and Kierkegaard. Courtesy of Copenhagen City Museum.

Admiralgade set fra Holmens Canal.

individual and the religious community (Paul's letter to Ephesus is the occasion for Kierkegaard's discourse): "the lustful and inquisitive mob" opposed to "the most lonely, most abandoned" in "tumultuous Rome where nothing could withstand the unbridled power of time which swallowed everything as quickly as it made its appearance, which consigned everything to forgetfulness without leaving a trace" (81). Johannes, the seducer, is precisely involved in the sensuous pursuit of exciting instants, the pleasure of the extraordinary moment without future consequences, the aestheticizing attitude that engenders anxiety, *dread*. That is one side of the modern mode criticized by Kierkegaard. The other side is the public sphere, the masses that follow what is interesting for the moment. Both, the aestheticizing individual and the masses attached to the public sphere, are devoured by time since they avoid the relation to eternity that is potentially invoked by the anxiety engendered by the way in which they handle the kind of freedom that is the condition of subjectivity in modernity. Paul was "the most lonely, the most abandoned," but he represented Jesus Christ – "while everything around him was rushing on in futility, for him the conviction stood firm." And so did Kierkegaard, who was no less lonely.

In *The Seducer's Diary* he depicted one possible attitude to modern subjectivity, the aesthetic attitude, the distanced empathic relation to the fascinating young woman, the fantasy of manipulation. In his works Kierkegaard made, in a way, an attempt to do something similar, but with a view toward provoking in his readers a subjective insight that should eventually lead to the road to God. Although he detested the public sphere as a medium for the formation of public opinion and for the crystallization of common interests, i.e. as a medium for democracy, he tried to use the public sphere through his publications in the same way as he imagined acting as a kind of Socratic Jesus by talking to people in the street. It was a small town, and to some extent people in the street and the reading public overlapped. In a sense, Kierkegaard was thus a small town philosopher and writer. In this setting the absolute opposite to the bustling crowd was to him a kind of negative print of the public sphere. In one of his *Christian Discourses*[5] he addresses the community on a Friday:

> Openly before everyone's eyes and yet secretly, the single individual came to church today . . . No one except God knew his way; it did not occur to any passerby that you were going to God's house . . . You did not expect, as on a holy day, that the passerby would be going the same way and with the same thoughts; and therefore you went secretly, as a stranger, in the midst of all those many people. You did not . . . formally greet people as on a festival day. No, the person passing by simply did not exist for you; with downcast eyes, you secretly fled, so to speak, to this place.

The crowd is present here as "all those many people" who pass by, but the ideal individual is anonymously on his way to a community that is defined by matters beyond the public sphere. Nothing could be farther from "A," whose papers in Kierkegaard's play with pseudonyms is published in the first volume of *Either-Or*.[6] The protagonist of *The Seducer's Diary*, Johannes, represents an aesthetic attitude and thus a specific aspect of Kierkegaard's philosophical-religious vision. But taken as a novel, *The Seducer's Diary* is also an early demonstration of a particular way of living in a city. Johannes is a kind of *flâneur* with what borders on an exclusive interest in young women – his eyes are certainly not downcast, he is not in the street on his way to God's house, he is out on the streets looking for girls.

The novel is about his relationship with Cordelia, how he meets her by chance in the street, how he manages to gain access to her home, how he becomes engaged to her, manages to make her break the engagement in the name of freedom, and how he finally manages – as it is implied – to get her to bed, only to leave her immediately. This story is told by a few letters from Cordelia to Johannes, and first and foremost by his diary and letters to her. But the diary is interspersed with descriptions of, and reflections on, other chance encounters. The women are – with one exception – unknown to him, but he will always be able to get information about them and arrange meetings with them: "in two hours I will know who you are – why else do you think the police keep census records?" (323). This quite peculiar admixture of strangeness and familiarity corresponds in a sense to the size of Copenhagen at that time. "That beautiful season will soon be here when one can buy up in the public streets and lanes the small claims that cost dearly enough during the social life in the winter season, for a young girl can forget much, but not a situation" (326). On the one hand, anonymity as an urban condition, on the other hand a community that does not preclude the establishment of personal relations to whomever you want. Whether this actually corresponds to real conditions in Copenhagen at that time is not as important as the kind of public sphere that is implied, since Johannes' position in a sense corresponds to Kierkegaard's own as a writer. His publications are anonymous, but they are written with a view toward readers he imagines knowing. Johannes' sidelong glances at a young lady correspond in this sense to Kierkegaard's hints to his readers, Johannes the seducer and Kierkegaard the educator possess the same double position: anonymous and personal. Kierkegaard would walk in the street and talk to the man in the street.

Johannes' *flânerie* is similar, although his intention is obviously not: "Be careful; such a glance from below is more dangerous than one that is *gerade aus* [direct]! It is like fencing; and what weapon is as sharp, as penetrating, as gleaming in its movement and thereby as illusive as the eye?" (318). A contemporary of Kierkegaard gave the following account of the effect of the philosopher's own eye:

> With just a glance at a passerby he could irresistibly "establish a rapport" with him, as he expressed it. The person who received the look became either attracted or repelled, embarrassed, uncertain, or exasperated. I have walked the whole length of a street with him while he explained how it was possible to carry out psychological studies by establishing such rapport with the passerby. And while he expanded on the theory he realized it in practice with nearly everyone we met. On the same occasion he surprised me by the ease with which he stroke up conversations with so many people. In a few remarks he took up the tread from an earlier conversation and carried it a step further, to a point where it could be continued again at another opportunity.[7]

Johannes gets the first glimpse of Cordelia during a walk on the ramparts (306), that afford a view of not only the city but also the surroundings: "The sun had lost its vigour; only a recollection of it was preserved in a soft glimmering that spread over the landscape. Nature breathed more freely. The lake was still, smooth as a mirror. The pleasant, friendly buildings of Blegdam were reflected on the water, which further out was as dark as metal . . . Although I had been prepared for this for a long time, it was impossible for me to control a certain restlessness, a rising and falling like that of the lark as it rises and falls in its song over the nearby fields" (331).

"Surroundings and setting do have a great influence upon a person and are part of that which makes a firm and deep impression on the memory or, more correctly, on the whole soul" (389), Johannes writes – and correspondingly the settings for the various "situations" are described in detail. In particular the interiors, as Adorno underlines in his book on Kierkegaard.[8] Johannes' encounters with women take place in the street, in shops, at an exhibition and in similar public spaces. He is moving around in the inner city, in particular in the most fashionable part:

> What do I see? A public display of fancy articles. My beautiful stranger, it may be shocking on my part, but I am following the bright path . . . She has forgotten what happened [i.e. his glance a few moments earlier: "At precisely the crucial moment a sidelong glance falls on its object. You blush; your bosom is too full to unburden itself in a single breath" (315).] – ah, yes, when one is seventeen years old, when one goes shopping in this happy age, when every single large or little object picked up gives unspeakable delight, then one readily forgets. As yet she has not seen me; I am standing at the other side of the counter, far off by myself. There is a mirror on the opposite wall; she is not contemplating it, but the mirror is contemplating her. How faithfully it has caught her image . . . (315)

Sidelong glances, mirror-images: the young woman is constantly under observation from his spying position, just like people in the street can be observed from the interior in the gossip mirror or window street mirror, the "reflection-mirror" as Johannes has it (354). The behavior of the seducer has a criminalistic touch (his reference to the police census records is appropriate), the private eye of the *flâneur* picks up bits of information, but just as important are his reflections on the state of the girl's mind. His attitude is empathic, but for his own purpose.

The imagined insight into the mind of others at a distance is a distinctly urban attitude. It is played out in a variety of concrete situations in Johannes' diary. Baudelaire has depicted a similar attitude in the Parisian context in his prose poem "Crowds": ". . . enjoying a crowd is an art . . . The poet enjoys the incomparable privilege of being able to be himself or some one else, as he chooses . . . What men call love is a very small, restricted, feeble thing compared with this ineffable orgy, this divine prostitution of the soul giving itself entire, all its poetry and all its charity, to the unexpected as it comes along, to the stranger as he passes."[9] There is no Parisian crowd in Copenhagen, and Johannes has specific reasons for his exercises in empathy, but in both cases the chance encounter, the unexpected, the relation to a stranger, and the specific psychic attitude that allows the poet and the flâneur to share the experience of others with joy all call our attention to urban conditions.[10]

II EXCITEMENTS AND DISILLUSIONS – HERMAN BANG'S *STUCCO*

> This atmosphere of gas, transpiration, scents, breath and fumes of wine may kill you, but you are alive in it.
>
> Herman Bang

It is a commonplace that the novel is intimately related to urban experience in the sense that in many of the great novels, the subject matter is life in big cities. But what is the relation between urban experience and narrative structure? The unity of the *Bildungsroman* is provided by the life of the protagonist. The two major nineteenth-century French examples of novelists of the metropolis, i.e. Balzac and Zola, do depict individual lives, but a characteristic feature of their systems of novels, *La Comédie Humaine* and *Les Rougon-Macquart*, is the intertwining of a multiplicity of individual lives that form a pattern corresponding to the complexity of urban life. Whereas one individual life, or rather a part of it, can provide the skeleton for one of the novels of the cycle, the entire texture of each novel is interrelated in multiple ways with the rest of the novels in the series and thus with a multitude of destinies.

"It is only the books that end: Life goes on," says the protagonist in Herman Bang's *Stucco* from 1887[11] (557). How, then, to end the books, when the death of the protagonist, the final integration in society or similar major stages in the destiny of a protagonist do not seem to correspond to the form of experience in the big city? There is obviously not one single answer to this question (which is one formulation of the question about the very structure of the urban novel). But it does provide a foreground for the relation between the individual and the city, a decisive feature of life, of course, as well as of novels based on urban experience. For more than one young man from the provinces, the big city becomes his destiny in a sense that was not foreseen when he arrived with all his aspirations or illusions: the life of Lucien de Rupembré is not unique, neither in novels nor in real life.

It is significant that the titles of so many novels from *Don Quixote* and onwards are so often identical with the names of the protagonists. So much more significant are the titles when this is not the case. By introducing *"Broken Illusions"* already in the name of his novel, Balzac pointed to the typical character of Lucien's destiny as a life historical experience. The general character of a title like *L'Assommoir* or the mythical-historical title of *Germinal*, does – in Zola's case – introduce not only the general social destiny, but also a layer of symbolic identifications. In the Danish novelist Herman Bang's œuvre we find a variety of titles, from the name of the protagonist *"Tine,"* through the historical-psychological *"Håbløse Slægter"* (*"Generations Without Hope"*) to his novel about Copenhagen: *Stucco*. Even if there may be a series of other examples, no other novel readily comes to mind (except perhaps Gladkov's *Cement*) which is named after a building material – not a protagonist, not a family, not a psychological experience, not a historical reference, not a mythic layer, but sheer matter. Albeit matter that is appropriate as representation of crucial themes. It does first of all (as a metaphor) represent fragility, as well as a combination of splendid appearance and simple essence. Furthermore it is (metonymically) related to the specific historical period, the *"Gründerzeit"* and the historicist building boom in Copenhagen in the last decades of the nineteenth century (the novel was written in 1886–1887). Finally this, so to speak, static ambiguity is doubled by the titles of the two parts of the novel: "Shower of Gold" and "Shower of Ashes." This dynamic transformation from gold to ashes, in fact, corresponds to what turns out to be one of the main symbols in the novel: the fireworks in Tivoli, the amusement park. What appears to be solid building, the decorative stucco, turns out to correspond to a brief moment of ecstasy, followed by the disappointing experience of finding the sooted tube, i.e. what is left of that splendid moment of fireworks. To the condensation represented by the fireworks corresponds the condensation of a larger historical period into a brief narrative: "It is an attempt to give a development that really was stretched over a decade, in the frame of the events of two years," Bang wrote, in a sketch for an unpublished postscript.[12] This development is as much the development of the city as the development of the lives of the many characters in the novel.

In a sense Herman Bang made this intertwining of personal and urban life the explicit theme of *Stucco*. In the retrospective summary of his life before he became a student, Herluf Berg (the protagonist, if there is any) remembers: "Now he began to live – together with the new Copenhagen" (366), and when he is about to become the director of a new entertainment establishment, "The Victoria-Theater," he has this moment of self-definition: "All of his talent, he did realize it now, had only been his life together [*samliv*] with this city . . ." (341).

Clear as this may seem, it is rather a disguised statement of a question, since the meaning of "this city" is not at all obvious. To say that the "life together" is about the relation between the individual and the collective would be, if not untrue (a major feature of crucial chapters is in fact the installation of an anonymous agent: the group, "they" [*man*], etc.), then imprecise, since "the collective" as a concept refers to other individuals,

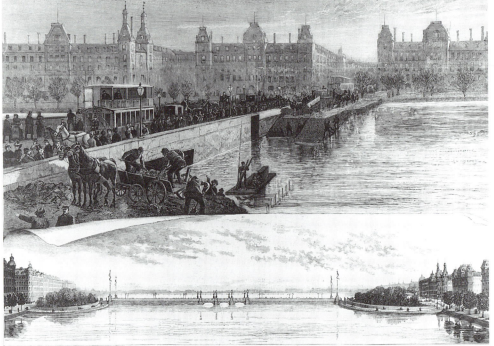

Den ny Peblingebro: Arbejder ved Opfyldningen. Prof. Dahlerups Plan.

12.2 Paris in Copenhagen. The very popular *Illustreret Tidende* (*Illustrated Journal*) presented this depiction of the works on the widening of a bridge across one of the lakes outside the old Copenhagen. Mass traffic demanded more space. Below is the architect's drawing of the planned bridge. To the right is the area outside the abolished ramparts. To the left the beginning of the working class area Nørrebro. The design of the buildings on the inner side of the lake, in particular the roofs, obviously represents an attempt to bring an air of Paris to Copenhagen. This is the new Copenhagen that was built in the last decades of the nineteenth century (vol. XXVI, no. 23, 1884–1885, p. 301). Courtesy of Royal Library, Copenhagen.

not to such specific elements in the novel as the Victoria-Theater, Tivoli, the newspaper ("Bladet") or the Central Bank. The life of the protagonist, or rather a certain period of his life, is intertwined not only with the lives of a substantial number of other characters, but even more importantly with the "life" of decisive *institutions* – the "life of the city" means the "life" of both characters and institutions. *Stucco* is a "collective novel" (like novels by Balzac or Zola), but not only that, it is a novel about characters and institutions that determine their lives.

The relations between individuals and institutions are of various kinds, since the institutions belong to the public sphere as well as to the economic sphere. The public sphere includes the interaction between public opinion and what is aptly called public relations. The economic sphere includes the interactions between the business of entertainment and the economics of the bank world. And this is where the overall structure of the novel is based in the story of an entertainment institution – the Victoria-

Theater. The rise and fall of that project is what forms the novel just as much as the life of Herluf Berg during the corresponding period.

The Russian avant-garde writer Sergei Tretjakov was looking for a novel that should take a thing as protagonist instead of a person. That would turn it into a materialist novel, he argued. Tretjakov would probably have appreciated Hans Christian Andersen's stories about "The Collars" (*Flipperne*), "The Rags" (*Laserne*), and "The Darning Needle" (*Stoppenaalen*), or indeed Herman Bang's *feuilleton* (essay) about the life of female dresses entitled "In the Boutique" (*I Modesalonen*), where he is referring to Andersen's stories and, in fact, following up not only on Andersen, but also on Kierkegaard's description of the galanterie-boutique:

> How the mirrors are tempting! Women to ruin themselves and men to destroy them . . . How they are lying there craving and dreaming, all the wonderful dresses. They have fever in the blood, they are longing for gas jets and light, for the heat of the dining rooms and the rejoicings of the dancing salons. They have forebodings, they are trembling, full of hope . . . Their life was an entire fairy tale, like the darning needle's, the collars', the rags'. Although the best was yet to come, they knew it: they had not yet seen the wondrous.[13]

In *Stucco* the protagonist is not a thing but rather a social institution and the plot might be defined as the dynamics of the interrelationships between this institution and other institutions, like the Central Bank. If *Stucco* is seen from this angle, the main structure is a *social* structure, and neither a personal nor a material one. The stucco turns out not to be sheer matter, but rather a historical-social substance, in a manner of speaking.

There is a geography of the urban novel implied here: certain itineraries, certain locations, etc., imply a specific "mapping" of Copenhagen. There are the female actors from "Nørregade" (i.e. "Folketeatret") and from "Kongens Nytorv" (i.e. The Royal Theater), and first and foremost, there is the Casino on Amaliegade, the Victoria-Theater, and Tivoli – the main locations of the entertainment industry. What is added is mainly the newspaper ('Bladet') and the Central Bank.

In another sense, the novel is all about "new Copenhagen," since its main sphere are the areas of expansion (the former ramparts and moats, and the area outside the old city, e.g. Farimagsgade). It is thus significant in this light that the room where Herluf Berg is living when he becomes a student is located right on the border between the old city and the new areas. There is a historic dynamic involved: the dynamics of building, its gains and losses. The geography of the novel is intimately conjoined with the historical dimension.[14]

But this is all a reconstruction of the novel on the level of realistic – although condensed – representation of institutions and social relations. On the *thematic* level the Victoria-Theater is a "symbol" of, or metaphor for, on the one hand, national development, and on the other, the psychological condition of a generation. The story of the theater corresponds to a national economic development, the fluctuations of boom and slump, a fact that introduces yet another dimension of the narrative, i.e. its integration of individual events in the larger framework of the historical movement. But this is ambiguous, since an entirely different aspect of the national history, i.e. the loss of

Southern Jutland after the war with Germany in 1864, the "wound fever from Dybbøl," is evoked.

This ambiguous historical frame (simultaneously the fluctuations of the market and the national war history as frames of interpretation) is then related to ideas concerning the psychological condition of the generation of Herluf Berg and the generation that fought at Dybbøl. The male members of Herluf's generation are not going to be fathers, many of them are not able to love. This depiction of a psychological attitude is, of course, the immediate theme of the novel: the energy, the psychic investment is, in the case of Herluf and others, thrown into the ecstasies of the entertainment industry. And this is seen as a sign of the times, just as is the Victoria-Theater.

Here one further organizing structure is important, probably the basic theme: *the opposition between the ecstatic and the burnt-out*, the fireworks being one incarnation of the thematic opposition. But of crucial importance for the construction of the novel is the economics of bills of exchange, and further: forged bills. *Time* is here the basic question: the question of the time of payment. This is the economic question that relates the institution of economics to the institution of entertainment, and this is the temporal structure that is underlying *the thematics of enjoyment and despair*. The Victoria-Theater thus summarizes an entire cluster of themes. It is built on swampy soil (and dry-rot is growing fast in the building) and is no less swampy from the economic point of view – but for a while it does engender ecstatic joy.

The time of payment, the abrupt interruption of ecstatic enjoyment, is thus a fundamental theme in *Stucco*.

Narrative in the urban mode, then, turns out – in Bang's case – to be structured according to a variety of principles, among them, of course, fragments of the life of the characters, but with the "life of the city" in the forefront. For a long time *Stucco* was considered a failure as a novel. It was only to the extent that urban experience came to the forefront of critical attention that the book came to gain recognition as an advanced piece of modern writing.

III MODERNITY'S REALM OF SHADES – HENRIK PONTOPPIDAN'S *THE REIGN OF THE DEAD*

> . . . some subterranean tormenting place, where millions of shadows restlessly are in a wild rush in pursuit of illusory happiness . . .
>
> Henrik Pontoppidan

Henrik Pontoppidan was the most important Danish novelist of his time. His major work, *Lykke-Per* (1898–1904),[15] was already in his own time established as a European classic (it was one of Georg Lukács' examples in his treatment of the "novel of disillusion" in *Theory of the Novel*). In 1917 he received the Nobel Prize for literature, two years after he had published the last volume of another major novel, *The Reign of the Dead* (1912–1915).[16] Here the disillusioned author offers a fierce critique of modernity and of attitudes and ideas in which he himself – at an earlier stage – had taken part, particularly left-liberal, so-called "radical" ideas in the tradition emanating from the great literary critic Georg Brandes. The novel is not so much about Copenhagen as a city as it is about the urban culture centered in Copenhagen. Modernity is prominently represented by New York and by an Italian tourist center, but it is in Copenhagen that its symptoms are spelled out. Like *Stucco* this is a novel with a multitude of characters depicted in their relations to cultural and political institutions and to economic activities (although two characters are in the forefront); an entire era is depicted from the point of view of disillusion.

The novel operates within a symbolic geography that distributes historical and ethical themes among various locations in Denmark. In opposition to Copenhagen is a manor house in Jutland where a kind of renewal of feudal values crystallizes towards the end of the novel under the auspices of its owner, Dihmer. In between these poles, a manor house in Funen (the second largest island, located between Jutland and Zealand, where Copenhagen is situated on the eastern coast) represents a kind of battleground. In the end it is taken over by a coffee wholesaler from Copenhagen named Søholm: old values are thus repressed, but to the same extent they are simultaneously reinforced in Jutland, where Dihmer, who is a former radical politician, withdraws into a kind of feudal-agrarian utopia. He has lost all faith in the modern world: "I am firmly convinced that we are approaching a world catastrophe. What is called civilized society has during a century worked like a madman on ruining itself" (ED: 129). As a landowner he has learned to understand himself as "a peasant and a son of a peasant" (128 – the disregard of class differences in the countryside establishes an undifferentiated "land" in opposition to the city) and he is taking this change of mind as a homecoming: "There was an evening in New York when I was sick of longing for the feeling of my own ground under my feet." This opposition between New York's pavement and Jutland's ground indicates the thematic field of tension within which Copenhagen is invested with historical and symbolic significance.

Dihmer's new insight has a political dimension, too: "No. You cannot produce human happiness on a machine. The entire solemn apparatus with parliament and government has become ridiculous to my mind" (128). Dihmer (and Pontoppidan) inscribes himself in the broad anti-democratic tendencies of his time.

The features of modernity are more visible on the international scene, especially in America, i.e. the US, but the destruction of Denmark has its center in Copenhagen. That is where parliament and government are located; that is where the cult of science takes place.

Dihmer has realized that he is living in a "Realm of Shades"; he is someone capable of realizing that modernity is a realm of shades, the reign of the dead, Hell (cf. TJ: 153). He summarizes his experience gathered during a long journey abroad: "I have often in both Europe and America had a feeling of being at some subterranean tormenting place, where millions of shadows restlessly are in a wild rush in pursuit of illusory happiness" (ED: 129).

It is the modern world, modernity, that is the reign of the dead. Pontoppidan wrote the novel in accordance with this vision. The depiction of its characters is often grotesque. A characteristic figure is Zaun, a managing director presented as a metropolitan intellectual who is mainly interested in newspapers and political maneuvering. He is introduced as "a short man of Jewish origin with a black beard" (TJ: 101), his golden *pince-nez* "mounted on his oriental facial projection [*Ansigtsfremspring*]" (106), and he is moving "with curiosity peering from all his features" (107). Dihmer seems to remember his "voice and its strange guttural sounds, his passionately wrinkled skin of the forehead, the way in which he every moment nervously fastened the pince-nez with his whole hand, and finally his newspaper gluttony, his simian attention to everything ephemeral taking place in the world" (110) – the simian aspect, of course, not only refers to curiosity, but also the combination of strange guttural sounds, the wrinkled forehead and the use of the whole hand.

This piece of vintage, standard anti-Semitism is not only creditable to Dihmer. The author is deeply involved. But it could be argued that the satire is directed against metropolitan culture as such.

America is the main symbol of international influence that is, on several levels, putrefying Denmark and is represented intellectually by Zaun. But on a wider global scale, international capitalism is even more important. It is represented by the wholesale dealer Søholm: "It was initially his cheap coffee that established his name and gave him notoriety as a local commercial genius of the American mold. But apart from that, he traded in anything that gave a chance to swindle, from pins to South African gold mines and their human lots" (ED: 43).

The press is the most obvious representative of urbanity. Its readers have turned into an audience, just like the former *listeners* to political speeches became an audience (ED: 183). This audience is (according to Dihmer) the great harlot, like the Babylonian Harlot in St. John's *Revelations*. Modernity, metropolis, and press are one and the same. The press has not escaped destructive American impulses: "American 'nigger' journalism" is introduced, and a new religious movement has "following transatlantic patterns . . . taken advantage of the service of advertising and fun of the fair in the fight for Faith . . ., introduced devotional events with transparencies, prayer meetings with teas, processions in the streets and the entire American Catholicism" (ED: 192).

The depiction of the press proceeds on several levels. One revolves around artistic life in Copenhagen. The character who represents cultural journalism is a drunk, a failed poet and prone to bribing. The art world is dependent on the press, and the gentlemen of the press are described as "the usual happy fraternity of worn out talents, literary pimps, and baying sleuthhounds hunting news, who from the surface of the metropolis meet in the newspapers' reporter rooms like waste water in a cesspool" (F: 108).

The development of the press is increasingly dominated by economic considerations rather than political attitudes; it has become "large scale industry" (TS: 61–62). But the changing character of political life also has its impact. Politicians no longer address listeners, but rather a public. This is a crucial change. Listeners are individuals gathering to take in and reflect on a political occasion. A public is rather a mass phenomenon that is prone to follow trends and moods.

Among the people involved in the press is Mads Vestrup, a vicar from Jutland who has been a victim of his unruly sexual impulses and whose mind is permeated by religious imagination. Arriving in Copenhagen, he does not recognize the city he studied in. Only in the inner city, the old medieval area of Copenhagen, does he find "reminiscences of the former, provincial Copenhagen, he was familiar with." This opposition between the inner city as the site of old values and the new areas as sinful is a general theme in the novel.

His first impression is the new Central Station: "With his carpet bag in one hand and umbrella in the other hand he followed the stream up the stairs and into the hall, where the white sea of light made him open his eyes wide. Shyly he contemplated the sumptuously decorated room, thinking by himself that it was probably larger and costlier than any church in the country" (TS: 4–5). The system of transportation that unites the country and links it with foreign countries is thus elevated above God's houses. It is precisely the relations to foreign countries that are – according to this novel – destroying Denmark. This is where tyranny stems from. The city has changed, fundamentally:

> But he stopped again at the first corner of the "Passage," suddenly disheartened by the huge, noisy traffic. Was this really Copenhagen? He had certainly heard that the city during the last years had changed a lot and become a metropolis. But the crowds of people on the sidewalks, the long rows of trams moving with the pace of trains and belching forth sulfurous blue sparks from the wheels, the swarm of driving machines flying like giant beetles with blood-red eyes, this pandemonium of horns and peal of bells like in a market place – was this really Copenhagen? The illumination reached even over the roofs. "Whisky is a drink for gentlemen" was written with ruby fire-letters over a six-story building at the opposite side of the street. "Dancing in Elysium till 2 a.m." was written somewhere else over the sky by an invisible hand. And suddenly a spark flashed out of the dark over the inner city and the entire eastern sky was in flames. "Søholm's coffee is best" was proclaimed, with immense letters. (TS: 5–6)

"But this is Hell!" he mumbles to himself – and a pimp approaches him.

The new Copenhagen as a sink of iniquity is thematized elsewhere in the novel. Now it is on Vesterbro with the "lively boulevard turmoil" (TS: 97) that the entertainment institutions are concentrated. This is where the most prominent female character in the novel meets her future fiancé, as she dines with a cousin: "They had attended a stupid Viennese comic opera which every night at this time occasioned a Copenhagen migration prompted by an impudent episode when one of the actresses slowly undressed in front of the audience down to her trousers, whereafter they too were stripped off during the rapid fall of the curtain – everything being followed by *douce* music and changing colours from a spotlight in the wings" (TS: 101). At the restaurant where they are dining after the spectacle, "all kinds of peculiar women entered from the street with their escorts" (104). By the story line as well as through the symbolic-historical character of the settings, the new Copenhagen is linked to all sorts of impure spirits (*alskens urene ånder*), as St. John has it. This modern Sodom is peopled by publicans and sinners, as indicated by the title of the third and middle volume of the novel.

Nor does the depiction of political life reinforce confidence in modern Copenhagen. In "Publicans and Sinners" the political combatants are introduced in a depiction of a debate in the parliament building (located at that time on Bredgade, in the eighteenth-century annexation area of Copenhagen known as the Frederiksstad):

The fog covering the city was now so dense that the globes of the incandescent lights were hanging in the air as smoking lamps. The Town Hall Square was drowning in the dimness. The lighted dial of the tower clock seemed to float in the air like a pale moon. On Strøget ["The Stroll"], in the narrow streets where the big shops created an artificial day, there was a crush on the sidewalks. It was one of those evening hours, when the stream is inwards, towards the theaters, the concert halls and evening parties. The stout omnibus-horses were steaming. Automobiles went honking by with dressed up and happy people. And the Town Hall clocks' solemn hymnal tone floated up and down in the air.

On the King's New Square you met darkness again. The lights of the cars were mirrored in the wet pavement. They were all hurrying to the theatre, where the lighted loggia was teeming like a beehive entrance. It was an opera evening – and the darling of the nation, the tenor robusto, would be singing one of his star roles. (19–20)

In this nebulous realm, this *Niflheim*, this *Reign of the Dead*, where people are like insects and solemn hymnal tones are met by the laughter of dressed up people and the horns of their cars, politics emerges as "a tall, stout, barefaced figure" (20), who turns out to be the prime minister, in conversation with another man: "They were walking slowly, in quiet conversation, and when someone came closer on the same sidewalk, they lowered

12.3 Valencia, a major entertainment establishment on Vesterbro, 1927. Among the earlier names was Folies-Bergères. At this point jazz was the preferred music. Courtesy of Copenhagen City Museum.

their voices even more or were silent until they were alone again" (20). Political conversation does not seem to be fit for the ears of outsiders; politics and conspiracy seem to merge.

Inside the parliament, the public's seats are full. Political conflicts have an audience: "you flocked there for an entertainment event, hoping to witness a dramatic scene" (21). Political debate is thus associated with theater or opera, and prominent politicians with the popular *tenor robusto*. What ought to have been politically committed *listeners* in the public's seats turns out to be (or rather, are described as) a *public* craving sensations and entertainment. The newly elected members of parliament "had difficulties forgetting that they were acting with the curtain up. Again and again they had to steal a glance at the gallery of the listeners, and particularly the box reserved for the ladies" (23).

The political scene is dominated by "speculators and political adventurers." In sum, politics is depicted as intrigues, personal power brokering, and manipulation of moods – not only in the parliament hall, but just as importantly through the press – and the press is dominated by commercial or religious principles. It is the audience that is the primary reference point for the political scene, and not political questions or principles.

Despite the multifaceted critique of metropolitan Copenhagen, and most especially its press, *The Reign of the Dead* is paradoxically a clear manifestation of an urban mood or state of mind that is widespread among intellectuals and in the press. Skepticism is at stake here, i.e. there is a kind of critique that does not spare anybody, turns in all directions, but does not adhere to any alternative. It knows better, but it does not know anything in particular. It promenades as being principled, but is more interested in persons and their peculiarities than in principles and political perspectives. It takes itself as being autonomous, but does not present any alternative position. It has great difficulties in taking political deliberation as a serious process.

This is the kind of position Pontoppidan prepares for his readers. An anti-urbanism that is deeply rooted in urban attitudes.

IV SOUL, IDEA, AND *DÉROUTE* – TOM KRISTENSEN'S *HAVOC*

> . . . he felt restless and conscious of the quickening pulse brought on by night air and broad sidewalks.
>
> Tom Kristensen

In novels that take place in Copenhagen, the mapping of the city is significant. Andersen is reaching beyond the city in time and space, Kierkegaard's *flâneur* is taking his rounds in the inner city in search of young ladies, hoping to attract their attention by his sudden glances. Herman Bang's protagonist is living on the border of the old and the new city, his world being defined first by a newspaper and a bank, second by entertainment institutions ranging from Tivoli to a new theater, and third by private spaces just outside the old city: only the bank and the newspaper are located in the old city. In Pontoppidan's novel the simultaneously realistic and mythic mode embraces sites of the press and of politics within the borders of the old city, the inner city with its traditional bourgeois life, and the dubious tendencies outside the old fortifications: the entertainment district close to the Central Station has a crucial role to play as hellish opposition not only to decent old bourgeois life in the inner city, but also to aristocratic life in the countryside.

In Tom Kristensen's novel *Havoc* from 1930, Copenhagen is defined almost exclusively by the new areas.[17] The world of his protagonist is the world of the twentieth century. There are two points of gravitation. One is his work place, *The Daily*, the model being *Politiken*, the newspaper that was created in the 1880s as a forum for left-liberal ideas, but is now – according to the novel – prone to opportunistically catering to public whims; the question of sustaining radical ideas is one of the main themes of the novel. In this sense it follows up on the disillusions of Pontoppidan's novel. The paper has moved from the inner city to the new Town Hall Square, i.e. outside old Copenhagen. The other point of gravitation is the apartment of the protagonist and his wife, located on Istedgade, i.e. one of the new streets outside the old center in an area that is close to entertainment institutions and prostitution. The thematics of Pontoppidan's novel are not far away in this respect, either.

There are a few excursions to other areas of the city. Most importantly to the court-house in the old center, or more specifically to the detention hall: the protagonist gets arrested and ends up in detention among drunkards. This is a moment of *déroute*: the anarchistic intellectual is confined by authorities. Similarly he does, at some point (after having experienced a kind of symbolic burial in the ramparts of Christianshavn), walk by the police headquarters (a newly erected building close to the harbor that looks like a fortress). The inner city is thus defined exclusively as the site of centralized power.

Outside the inner city is the sphere of entertainment, of the press, of ideological encounters. In Herman Bang's novel, the bank was a crucial factor that determined the narrative. In Kristensen's novel, economics has become an intellectual theme. This represents a significant development: Bang's genuine insights into the ways of the world are here superseded by grandiose themes, in intellectual debates such as Catholicism versus communism, ideologies without much influence in a political situation that was in so many ways defined by social-democratic, left-liberal and diverse conservative attitudes.

The protagonist of Kristensen's novel is not only experiencing a *déroute* in relation to his private life (his wife leaves him with their child), he is also neglecting his job as a literary critic. Significantly, the *déroute* is taking place not only in his own neighborhood, but also, and especially, right next door to the newspaper. The two worlds of the newspaper and of the *Bar des artistes* next door are thus interconnected. But this theme is subservient to the theme that has to do with the political-ideological situation. Kristensen is, in fact, depicting the horizon of his protagonist as though the choice were between Catholicism and communism. The basic theme is the opposition between *déroute*, personal disintegration, and *some* kind of idea. The motto does not leave much hope in personal integrity; something else has to rescue the individual: "Beware of the soul and cultivate it not, since it resembles a vice." "Communism" is thus integrated in the novel as a remedy for intellectuals.

The city is a world that appeals to vices. Its fascinating aspects are dangerous. In that sense, Kristensen's novel is surprisingly close to the Christian coloring of Pontoppidan's novel. But in another sense, it is entirely different: it takes part in the fascination of the new city, even if this is regarded as risky. This novel has a real protagonist. It is his point of view that defines the perception of Copenhagen and the development of the narrative. In this respect it is different from both *Stucco* and *The Reign of the Dead*. The relation between form and experience is different in *Havoc*. This novel is about the way in which a personal crisis is intertwined with urban conditions. How mood and situation merge. How the pulse of the city, the pulse of jazz and the pulse of the protagonist interfere. It is also about an intellectual crisis, but it is first and foremost about the way in which this crisis is lived out in, and formed by, the urban setting. The protagonist's final, but presumably temporary, withdrawal to Berlin as a secretary for a radical professor of economics has no affinity with the withdrawal to feudal conditions in *The Reign of the Dead*.

Havoc is a visual novel. This is what the city looks like from the point of view of the protagonist sitting is his office at *Dagbladet*, "The Daily":

> But through the windows, which the evening rain had stippled with long dotted lines, came the flickering lights from the wet square below. They cast a reflection on the ceiling, a restless, animated shimmering like that of an aurora borealis, a blending of the soft glow from the streetcars' colored lamps and the sharp beams of automobile headlights. The windowpanes emitted a dark luster mixed with a hint of light to the raindrops, and silhouetted against their smooth surface, in reverse, were the letters that spelled DAGBLADET. (33–34)

"Dark luster" emanates from the windows of the newspaper, the vision is expressionistic. The space outside is no less dark: "the street lay dark and empty" (49) and the Town Hall Square "at night always seemed prodigiously big, with barren stretches where the streetcars rode in the daytime, and murky darkness around the sunken 'clamshell' amphitheater in front of the Town Hall. Between Strøget and Vesterbrogade a line of people made their way over the pavement in single file, as if crossing a frozen lake" (49). Associations to Dante – like in Eliot's *Waste Land* – cannot be discounted here. The setting is appropriate for an encounter with a prostitute: "She was not very tall and quite plump. Big shoulders. Her face was heavily powdered. But even at their distance from the arc lamps, which imparted an icy glare to the streetcar tracks, they could make out the dark shadows under her eyes. Her rouged lips had the effect of a heavy black streak" (50). By daylight, the scenery is different: "the street seemed endless. The forenoon sun glistened on a myriad of windowpanes as if they were raindrops, and out near Enghaveplads the gray and yellow building facades rose like distant hills until they were dissolved in a shimmering haze" (56). This is the kind of description that has made the novel famous as a novel about the new Copenhagen. This street is in one of the areas built in the late nineteenth century dominated by rather modest apartment buildings. The description catches the repetitive patterns but turns it into an impressionistic vision. A rendering of an afternoon is no less striking: "A little later they were strolling diagonally across Vesterbro Passage and past the obelisk of the Freedom Statue, which shone with a dull luster the color of old chocolate. The sun hung in a glowing afternoon haze above Vesterbro's rooftops, and even though Jastrau and Steffensen had their backs to it, they were dazzled by the flickering

12.4 Vesterbrogade, the entertainment district on a rainy night, 1927. Photo by Tage Christensen.

light from the automobile windshields and bicycle handlebars – a constant stream of glistening glass and nickel that blinded them . . ." (94).

During an election night the city offers not only a visual but also an auditive accumulation of impressions:

> A cold wind was blowing, and Jastrau pulled his coat collar up around his ears. But he felt restless and conscious of the quickening pulse brought on by night air and broad sidewalks. Glowing red and gaseous blue neon tubes flashed like signatures written with a single fiery stroke: Scala. Blue electric light bulbs flickered mysteriously like carriage lanterns half-hidden by foliage: Marble Garden. Names in yellow lights. An electric news bulletin coursed swiftly across the top of a building, a veil of mist dragging along behind each letter. Ahead of and behind him megaphones from the several newspaper offices bellowed the election results out over the streets so that the air seemed filled with voices (65).

City and soul merge: "the quickening pulse brought on by night air and broad sidewalks." This urban mood is far from the correspondence between the song of the lark and Johannes' mood as described by Kierkegaard. A similar correspondence is described in an evening scene, although the perception here is determined by a state of mind just as much as the other way around:

> Getting out into the street always put life in him. The cool night air and the traffic acted as stimuli. But his heart was still beating violently . . . the traffic gave him a momentary relief.

A line of people, trooping like a flock of geese, made their way along Istedgade over to the railroad station, following the same path as always . . . He half ran, half walked, with the ridiculous gait of a harassed schoolmaster who is late for a class . . . Vesterbrogade served to take his mind off his troubles. Theatre-goers hurrying into taxis. Glimpses of people in evening dress, bare necks with furs and flashing gems, white shirt fronts, high hats . . . It must be nearly midnight. People in a hurry. Several young men shouting. A poor wretch out at the edge of the sidewalk, cowering and miserable. Women who walked slowly through the crowd, taking a zigzag course and discreetly blocking the passage of an occasional man. A lingering appraising glance. Silk-clad legs in sleek profile against the dark building fronts . . . The streetcar tracks were so coated with gasoline that they glistened like lacquer when the beams of the automobile headlights swept over them. Yes, all this served as a stimulant. The red Scala sign was glowing. The blue lights of the Stadil shone discreetly. And high against the midnight sky squinted the veiled yellow eyes of the Town Hall clock. (116)

Tom Kristensen started out as a poet, and the poet's approach is quite clear in this juxtaposition of visual fragments. Occasionally the depiction of the city includes a contextualization of the immediate impressions, as in this summary of Jastrau's knowledge of the behavior of citizens at various points of the day, as he walks away from the court-house and his visit to the detention hall:

But this morning it seemed as if something were wrong with the buildings. They were not really where they belonged. And yet, he knew them well, knew them as they appeared at virtually every hour of the day. At six o'clock in the morning when the Town Hall Square lay flooded with light before the entrance to dark Frederiksberggade, at twelve when the sun was directly over the street and bareheaded office workers ran across to a café during the lunch period and hatless shop girls dashed out to do their own shopping, at four when the strollers along Vesterbro had the glare of the sun full in their faces or beating down comfortably against their backs, at six when the light was more subdued and the swarm of cyclists was at its thickest, all on their way home to the suburbs, and then at evening and at night when it was as if Jastrau could read the hour by the tempo of the crowd and the brightness of the lights. But at eight o'clock in the morning – the hour it was now – every-thing seemed foreign to him. He was not familiar with things as they appeared in the forenoon light; the shadows fell differently. The office workers came cycling into town . . . He looked at their faces, fresh from a good night's sleep but still expressionless. One cyclist after another rode by him. They gave the impression of wooden figures or gray shadows on a film, not yet filled with blood. (156)

At a crucial point, when Jastrau is on his way to the newspaper in order to quit his job, the impression of the city changes: "Whistling happily and yet feeling sad, yes sad, he walked across the Town Hall Square. All the buildings looked lovely and transfigured. How beautiful they were. The red color of bricks, the Town Hall, the Palace Hotel, the Bristol. The red chestnuts. He felt as much at home there as he did in a living room – his own living room. He felt pleasantly at ease, like a familiar figure who cut across the square every day – a Copenhagener. There goes Jastrau, damn it" (265). Well-known or unknown, Kristensen's readers were more at home in Copenhagen by turning the last page of his novel.

Havoc is not only about existential questions, the risks involved in the cult of the soul, debates about ideas, or a novel about the author's age, the "jazz-age," with a certain pulse and pace, it is also about Copenhagen, about the new Copenhagen, that was constructed before the eyes of Herman Bang, about the new center around the Town Hall Square and about the new areas beyond the abolished fortifications. Light is crucial here (and darkness), the changes of light from the sun and its reflections, the new kind of light from electric advertising signs. Pontoppidan's vicar from Jutland was not in doubt: "This is Hell," was his reaction to the scenery Kristensen depicted a few decades later. To Kristensen's protagonist, the Christian sphere of association is consciously a problem. It is not absent. Nor is it accepted. It colors some of the descriptions of the city (and they are all seen through the eyes of the protagonist), but in the end the reader is left with a multifaceted vision of the city. He has taken another step forward in being initiated as a twentieth-century Copenhagener.

Notes

1   Cf. Elias Bredsdorff: *Hans Christian Andersen. The Story of his Life and Work, 1805–75*, London, 1993.
2   *Spaziergang in der Sylvesternacht 1828/29*, aus dem Dänischen von Anni Carlsson, Frankfurt am Main: Insel-Verlag, 1988. The book does not seem to have been translated into English. References are to the Danish version in *Fodreise*, Copenhagen: Borgen, 1986.
3   From "Guilty?/Not Guilty?," in: *Stages on Life's Way*, translated by H.V. and E.N. Hong, Princeton, NJ: Princeton University Press, 1988, pp. 276–77.
4   *Eighteen Upbuilding Discourses*, translated by H.V. and E.N. Hong, Princeton, NJ: Princeton University Press, 1990, p. 80; Jørgen Bonde Jensen has pointed to this text in his essay on *The Seducer's Diary* in his contribution to Marianne Barlyng and Søren Schou (eds): *Københavnerromaner*, Borgen: Valby, 1996.
5   Translated by H.V. and E.N. Hong, Princeton, NJ: Princeton University Press, 1997, pp. 269–70.
6   *Either/or*, edited and translated with introduction and notes by Howard V. Hong and Edna H. Hong, Princeton, NJ: Princeton University Press, 1987.
7   Hans Brøchner in Bruce H. Kirmmse (ed.): *Encounters with Kierkegaard. A Life Seen by His Contemporaries*, Princeton, NJ: Princeton University Press, 1998, p. 229.
8   *Kierkegaard. Konstruktion des Ästhetischen*, Frankfurt am Main: Suhrkamp, 1979.
9   Charles Baudelaire: *Paris Spleen*, translated from the French by Louise Varèse, New Directions: New York 1970, p. 20.
10   After the completion of this chapter, Martin Zerlang directed my attention to Georg Pattison's newly published book *'Poor Paris!' Kierkegaard's Critique of the Spectacular City*, Kierkegaard Studies, Monograph Series 2, Berlin, New York: Walter de Gruyter, 1999.
11   German translation in *Werke in drei Bänden*, hrsg. von Heinz Entner, Carl Hanser: Munich, 1982. What follows is in part based on my essay "Tidens smerte og storbyens atmosfære. Journalisten Herman Bang og hans roman *Stuk*," reprinted in: Olav Harsløf (ed.): *Omkring Stuk*, Copenhagen: Hans Eitzel, 1977. References are to *Værker i Mindeudgave*, Bd. 3, Copenhagen: Gyldendal, 1912.
12   *Omkring Stuk*, p. 24.
13   Herman Bang: *Københavnske Skildringer*, Copenhagen, 1954, pp. 20, 22.
14   On novels and geography, cf. Franco Moretti: *Atlas of the European Novel 1800–1900*, London: Verso, 1998.

15   Translated into numerous languages, recent German version: *Hans im Glück*, mit einem Essay von Winfried Menninghaus, Frankfurt am Main: Insel, 1981.

16   *De Dødes Rige*. In German: *Totenreich*, translated by M. Mann, Leipzig, 1920. The following is based on my essay "Den store Stad – Storby, modernitet og skepticisme i Henrik Pontoppidans *De Dødes Rige*," in: *Københavnerromaner*. Quotations are translated from the first edition, in five volumes; initials refer to the titles of each volume.

17   *Hærværk*, translated into English by Carl Malmberg: *Havoc*, University of Wisconsin Press, 1968.

Chapter 13

Urban Life as Entertainment
New York and Copenhagen in the Mid-nineteenth Century
Martin Zerlang

I THE CITY AS A UTOPIA

In March 1630, on board the *Arbella* and heading for New England, Governor John Winthrop delivered a sermon in which he told his fellow Puritans that "we must consider that we shall be a city upon a hill." Utopia is almost always envisioned as a city, and, from a certain point of view, all cities, whether as old as Copenhagen or as new as New York, may be interpreted as parcels of Utopia. At first glance a comparison between Copenhagen and New York may seem far-fetched, but starting from this shared utopian dimension it is possible to point out some important similarities underlying their obvious differences. In the mid-nineteenth century they shared a particularly entertaining and non-puritan version of this urban utopia and an entrepreneurial Dane, Georg Carstensen, became a key figure in the development of both cities, in Copenhagen as the founder of the Tivoli Gardens (1843) and in New York as one of the two architects behind the Crystal Palace of "the Great Exhibition" of 1853. In the following, I shall explore some of the forms and functions of urban entertainment in Copenhagen and New York around 1850. But first, a few general remarks on the idea of the city as a utopia.

In his book, *The Rebellion of the Masses*, the Spanish philosopher José Ortega y Gasset claims that the history of cities starts with the epoch-making demarcation of an empty space: the Agora, the Forum, the city square. Whereas the farmer encloses his property in order to keep out other people, the founder of a city encloses a city square in order to invite strangers to exchange commodities and opinions. The farmer protects this particular piece of land, with its particular possibilities for agricultural products, in contrast to the urbanite whose main objective is communication and circulation. The rural space is defined by its material potential, whereas the urban space is defined by its social potential. The empty space mentioned by Ortega y Gasset is a plot in the spatial sense of the word – but a plot that might turn into a plot in the narrative sense of the word. All cities, therefore, owe their origins to utopian expectations.

In the utopian tradition, America and the American cities have played an important part. Thomas More refers to America in his *Utopia*, written in 1517, only 25 years after the Great Discovery; Francis Bacon refers to America in his *Nova Atlantis* (1627) and Campanella refers to America in his *Sun State* (1623). Utopian fantasies of Eldorado were a motivating force behind some of the expeditions of the Spanish conquistadores. In Thomas More's *Utopia* the geometrical order of the fifty-four, all quite identical cities, demonstrates the very same superiority of the utopian mind over topographical reality as the grid-iron structure now characterizing the division of America into states and the division of American cities into blocks. The conquest of America was a conquest of space, and space was conquered in both directions, horizontally under the slogan "Go West," and vertically under the slogan "The Sky's the Limit."

II GEORG CARSTENSEN, THE TIVOLI GARDENS, AND THE NEW YORK CRYSTAL PALACE

An example of the utopian atmosphere during the expansive and explosive urbanization of nineteenth-century America is to be found in one of the two known musical compositions by Georg Carstensen, whose fame is based on his founding of the Tivoli Gardens. His *Go-Ahead-American-Forward-Galop* is a dynamic piece of music containing a description of a ship entering New York, a quotation from "Yankee Doodle Dandy" plus a revolver shot (according to the anecdote, the musicians needed to obtain permission to

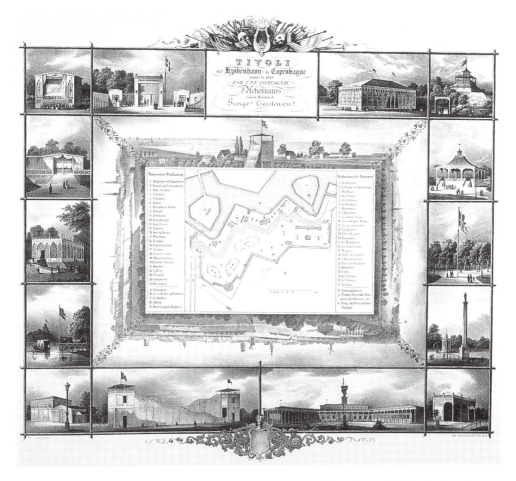

13.1 Tivoli, map and buildings. Courtesy of Kunstakademiet, Samlingen af Arkitekturtegninger, Copenhagen.

bear arms when they played this tune). As suggested by the composition, Carstensen was fascinated by "the American way of life," and as a seminal figure in the urban histories of both New York and Copenhagen he is an obvious choice for a comparison between the great urban expectations of these cities in the mid-nineteenth century.

The board of the first World's Fair, held in New York in 1853, gave its approval for the plans for an exhibition building submitted by Georg Carstensen and the German-American architect and artist Charles Gildemeister, and as stated in an article in *New-York Daily Times* on the opening day, July 14, 1853, this Carstensen, who had only "recently arrived here," was "the designer of the Tivoli and Casino of Copenhagen, the principal public grounds of that city."

The Tivoli Gardens from 1843 and the New York Crystal Palace from 1853 both served as harbingers of modernity and cradles for the sophisticated lifestyles of the modern city. These were places where the citizens could learn to adjust to the new terms of urbanized and industrialized life; places where people could test out the possibilities of new technologies, and places where they could get familiar with the city as a "world of strangers." Now, it may be difficult to understand how difficult and even terrifying they could be, the first experiences in the city, where people would have to offer themselves to public scrutiny, attune themselves to strangers, overcome the fears of agoraphobia and claustrophobia, survive the embarrassment that reflected "the unstable, altered context of honor, shame, and reputation in the market economy" (Kasson, 1990: 114) and even to learn bodily management in public, how to walk in a crowd and how to discipline the eyes. In the processes of civilization and mental urbanization the importance of such establishments as the Tivoli Gardens and the World's Fairs cannot be underestimated.

III THE TIVOLI GARDENS

In Denmark in the middle of the nineteenth century, a highly influential rural and petit-bourgeois utopia could be formulated in sentences such as: "the country where few have too much and even fewer too little," and "to remain at the earth is best for everybody." At the time Carstensen introduced modern ways of living in Copenhagen in the 1830s, this was a city characterized by repression and self-repression, a royal residence where, as late as 1808, the king personally held the keys to the city when its gates were locked at night. Almost one-third of its population – which grew from 100,000 to 150,000 between the years 1800 and 1850 – was in the service of the king – as subjects of the court, officials, soldiers or servants. In short, Copenhagen presented an environment for social experimentation that was markedly different from New York's skyscraping ambitions. In caricatures the prototypical Dane was portrayed as "Mr. Sørensen," who would draw his night-cap over his head whenever troubles came close. It was a culture of inhibitions rather than a culture of exhibitions.

The walls around Copenhagen became a straitjacket in the context of the city's expansion, an expansion that took form as a compression. The pressure was particularly intense at the gate of the western wall. A report from 1842 stated that everyone would understand that a change was necessary when seeing:

the flood of people – thousands and thousands – fluctuating over the bridges at Vesterport [the West Gate], while the mighty omnibuses and mail coaches and the multitude of smaller means of transport were making their way through the living crowd, which would nervously press up against the sides in order not to be crushed under the wheels or trampled down by the hoofs of the horses, and when seeing people gather outside the vaulted gate – rumbling from the noise of the carriages – in order to catch the right moment when they can rush into the open space behind an incoming carriage and how they then – tumbling and bustling with the threatening horses' trot behind – precipitate through the dark room dragging along crying children or breathless old people . . .

In the 1840s the physical as well as the mental straitjacket was about to burst, and the first "explosion" took place at Vesterport, when the opening of the Tivoli Gardens was celebrated with fireworks and a grand illumination. As the very first, Georg Carstensen obtained the right to establish an amusement park on the fortifications at Vesterport, which had surrounded and "defined" Copenhagen for centuries. By definition, Vesterport and the Tivoli Gardens were situated at the periphery of the old city, and experience shows that the dynamic center of urban development is always placed at the periphery – until this periphery becomes the new center. Today this is the area where we find not only the Tivoli Gardens but also the City Hall Square, the main artery for Copenhagen's flow of traffic, the Central Railway Station and the monuments of modernist architecture in Copenhagen.

Even though the opening of Tivoli also represents the very first opening of the medieval system of walls and moats surrounding Copenhagen, Tivoli itself was planned and realized as an old-fashioned city with an Oriental gate, with high walls and with an

13.2 Bazaar in Tivoli. Courtesy of Kunstakademiet, Samlingen af Arkitekturtegninger, Copenhagen.

intricate system of streets and squares. This construction of old-fashioned cities-within-the-city became characteristic of the new Copenhagen, but Tivoli was the first of these cities in miniature, and it was the only one with its own newspaper. On July 20, 1844 the readers could enjoy this description of Tivoli as a model city:

> At the north-eastern side of Zealand, close by the capital of Denmark, you find the little town of Tivoli, established in the fourth year of Christian VIII's regime, situated along the coastline of Kallebodstrand. It is a beautiful and regular town with many admirable gardens and interesting public buildings. The town is surrounded by walls and moats and it has a wide view to Amager and Frederiksberg, and here you can comfortably see what time it is on the tower-watches of Copenhagen.

Among the buildings of Tivoli one must mention the Tivoli bazaar, the Tivoli Concert Hall, the two Divan-restaurants, the two tea pavilions and the two buffets. All of these spectacular buildings – like the Alhambra founded by Carstensen in 1857 – were erected in an oriental style, which was not influenced by any undue measure of respect for the differences between Moorish, Turkish and Chinese styles. Thus, the so-called Chinese tower from around the turn of the century is really a Japanese tower.

Again and again, *Tivoliavis* (the Tivoli newspaper) published articles which – humorously – described Tivoli in terms of a social and political experiment, as an example of modern progress. In an article entitled "Geographical Information," it is stated that "politically this city already takes up a leading position," in fact a position so eminent that "all arch-politicians have more respect for Tivoli than for Russia," and in another article entitled "The Telegraph of Tivoli" it is claimed that "One may well go back in time as far as one wants, and in vain one will seek a country or a state where civilization has progressed as fast, where such a forceful, internal life of State has developed with so quick a pace as in the Summer-Tivoli of Copenhagen."

A prerequisite for any political culture, of course, was a public culture, an ability to act and interact in public, a demolition of the mental ramparts protecting the parochial spirit of pre-modern Copenhagen. In 1842, the year before the opening of Tivoli, a certain Niels Volkersen, who would later make a career as the first Pierrot in Tivoli's pantomimes, wrote an article on the almost agoraphobic dislike of public life among his fellow Copenhageners:

> Yes, it sometimes looks ridiculous to see how people behave at public places. Just make a visit to Kehlet's coffee-house. Is it not as if most of the guests are paralyzed with an excessive fear of prostituting themselves and making scandals? You'll see how most of the guests enjoy their refreshments with an earnestness, a reserve bordering on anxiety, as if they were treading the path of vice, as if they were doing something wrong, as if they were suffering from bad conscience, or at least as if they wished to make done undone.

A couple of decades later, another commentator – J. Plenge – wrote a book entitled *Nogle Træk af Livet i København for en Menneskealder siden* (*Some features of life in Copenhagen thirty years ago*) and he put the difference between pre-modern and modern

Copenhagen very succinctly: "In the old days everybody had the feeling of being at home, even when they were visiting other people; now people feel as if they are out, even when they are at home" (84). It is very likely that this break-up of the familiar world is one of the main reasons why Danish culture became enveloped in Oriental garments in the nineteenth century. The foreign Orient became a reflection of the experience of alienation in the familiar world now undergoing all sorts of changes. In the Tivoli newspaper from 1844 there was a description of how visitors to the garden, from the early morning on, could amuse themselves and at the same time muse on their new identity in Oriental luxury:

> You don't have to be embarrassed. The hospitable divans will welcome you with open arms and at your command your favorite drink shall be placed before you, hot and steamy. But no! You prefer to enjoy your drink in open air; the Mohammedan drink, Mocha coffee, must be imbibed in true Mohammedan style as you smoke your tobacco pipe in great draughts.

Tivoli functioned as a laboratory for the future of Copenhagen. Here people would learn to adjust to the new terms of a modern, industrialized and urbanized society, to familiarize themselves with new technologies like steam engines, trains and photography and to become members of a new mass culture. If mixed company had formerly been a term of abuse, people would now enter establishments such as the Tivoli Gardens for the sheer joy of mixing with the crowds on the public street. Even if uptight Victorianism reigned in the private sphere, the public amusement parks would constitute a sphere of humanity and good humor.

IV NEW YORK CRYSTAL PALACE

In the first half of the nineteenth century, New York was a most unattractive place to visit. The Commissioners' Plan of 1811 had divided most of Manhattan north of Washington Square into a gridiron which has been described as a biased aid to speculation, with no public monuments, with no architectural refinement and with only four small parks and three large open spaces set aside for public use – a parade ground, a market, and a reservoir. In 1831, Alexis de Tocqueville visited the city, which by then, with a population of more than 200,000 citizens, was the largest and busiest city of the United States, and he wrote to a friend:

> To a Frenchman the aspect of the city is bizarre and not very agreeable. One sees neither dome, nor bell tower, nor great edifice, with the result that one has the constant impression of being in a suburb. In its center the city is built of brick, which gives it a most monotonous appearance. The houses have neither cornices, nor balustrades, nor *portes-cochères*. The streets are badly paved, but sidewalks for pedestrians are to be found in all of them. (Rybczynski: 98)

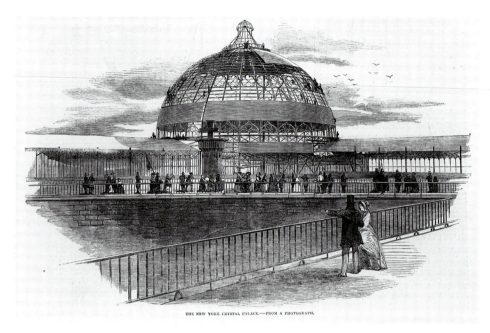

THE NEW YORK CRYSTAL PALACE.—FROM A PHOTOGRAPH.

13.3 New York Crystal Palace, *Illustrated London News* 6.8.1853. Courtesy of New York Public Library.

In 1853, on July 14, however, a monumental building with a dome was erected on the "Reservoir Square," situated at the northern extremity of the city, bounded by 42nd Street. This was the New York Crystal Palace, and the opening of this dazzling parallel to the Crystal Palace of London marked the transformation of New York into the metropolis of America. President Franklin Pierce was welcomed by a cheering crowd as if he were a king making his "entrée," and one of the speakers at this great event, Mr. Guthrie, who was Secretary of the Treasury, sketched out the remarkable history of New York:

> Though I have been a public speaker for nearly forty years, I never was abashed till now. What can one from the banks of the Ohio, from a comparatively new State, offer this assembly in commemoration of the Industry of all Nations; in the commendation of the Arts of Peace; the toleration of religious and political sentiments; the extension of Commerce; the extension of Agriculture; the extension of Manufactures; the extension of Arts and Sciences? I have nothing to say, but to offer you the example of my countrymen in the arts of Agriculture. They have felled the forests, and made cultivated fields to spring up. They have added State after State to this glorious Union, until we now number thirty-one. They have built city after city. Seventy years ago, the city where we now stand was about a mile and a half in length, and a mile in breadth, with 21,000 inhabitants. Now it is more than five miles in length, and two miles wide. Then it was built of wooden houses, from one to two stories high. Now it is a City of Princely palaces, from four to six stories high, of solid and costly structure, and contains a population of over 600,000. And this is the City that has given an example of industry to all the nations of the earth.
>
> *New York Daily Times*, 7.17.1853

INAUGURATION OF THE NEW YORK CRYSTAL PALACE.—PLATFORM IN THE NORTH NAVE.—FROM A DAGUERREOTYPE.—(SEE PRECEDING PAGE.)

13.4 New York Crystal Palace Inauguration, *Illustrated London News* 13.8.1853. Courtesy of New York Public Library.

Reporting on the arrival and reception of President Pierce, the *New-York Daily Times* noted that "the whole city was alive with the interest and excitement which the event occasioned" (7.15.1853). Joseph Paxton's Crystal Palace at the first World Exhibition in London in 1851 had triggered Manhattan's ambition for acquiring a Crystal Palace that was even more spectacular than the original. Paxton himself submitted an entry, but his design did not fit the site. According to the conditions of the competition for the new palace, it should be as different from the London Crystal Palace as possible, so that it would be "endowed with the charm of novelty and originality," and Carstensen and Gildemeister satisfied this requirement for difference by choosing the so-called "Venetian" style for their Crystal Palace. An article in the *New-York Daily Times* gave an extensive description of the building:

> The main features of the building are as follows. It is, with the exception of the floor, entirely constructed of iron and glass. The general idea of the edifice is a Greek Cross, surmounted by a dome at the intersection. Each diameter of the cross is 365 feet 5 inches long. There are three similar entrances . . . each is 47 feet wide, and that on Sixth Avenue is approached by a flight of 8 steps.

The dome, with a diameter of 100 feet and a height to the crowning arch of 123 feet supported by 24 columns, was the great architectural feature of the building and had a striking effect. On the opening day, the *New-York Daily Times* wrote that "it is impossible for any thinking man to stand today beneath the great dome, and not feel deeply penetrated with a conviction of the grandeur and utility of the undertaking." The dome aroused feelings of sublimity which were connected with the grandeur of the United States. The observer in the *New-York Daily Times* noted that the magnitude of the proportions alone were:

> calculated to excite feelings of profound awe in the spectator's mind; and when we see added the gorgeous but subdued chromatic decoration with which the interior is ornamented, and the innumerable works of art and industry with which it is already partially filled, we may well be proud of an erection which is destined to confer honor on the American name.

In his speech at the opening, President Franklin Pierce emphasized this nationalistic aspect of the world's fair:

> Sir, if you had achieved no other good, but that which you have in bringing together in this metropolis citizens from all parts of the Union, you would have fulfilled, perhaps, one of the most important of missions – that of strengthening and perpetuating that blessed Union.

A couple of days later, on July 17, the *New-York Daily Times* published a sermon by a certain Reverend Chapin on "the moral significance of the Crystal Palace," an elaborate and eloquent "reading" of this piece of architecture as a text on "moral progress": "The Crystal Palace, whose doors have just been opened, exhibits the results of sweat and muscle; of patient, plodding, superintended toil; and does honor to these. But it illustrates something greater than these. It represents *Ideas.*"

If all man-made objects tell about man as "Inventor" or "Artist" or "Discoverer" or even "Civilizer," then the Crystal Palace as "a mirror of our present civilization," according to Reverend Chapin, "not only illustrates the Providential dignity of Labor, but the power of *ideas . . . great* progress, peace and unity."

The uplifting effect of the palace could also be experienced in the literal sense of the word, as the Dutch architect and writer Rem Koolhaas quotes from a contemporary description: "Its slender ribs seem inadequate to sustain its vast size and it presents the appearance of a balloon expanded and impatient for a flight into the far-off sky . . ." (23).

In a little illustrated book on their building, Carstensen and Gildemeister stated that "architecture is the art-form, which frames the social necessities of mankind," but the quotation suggests that this architecture of exhibition led to a suspension of all inhibitions. The dizzying weightlessness was not only physiological, but also psychological, moral, maybe even political.

A line can be drawn from this weightlessness to the "delirium" in amusement parks like Coney Island that has been diagnosed by Koolhaas in *Delirious New York*. In his comment on the "Trip to the Moon" he mentions that in Coney Island's Luna Park "the whole structure of mutually reinforcing realities on earth – its laws, expectations, inhibitions – is suspended to create a moral weightlessness that complements the literal weightlessness that has been generated on the trip to the Moon" (39). In his novel, *Ragtime*, E.L. Doctorow describes a scene where Freud and Jung explore the "Tunnel of Love" in Luna Park. This was the place where anything goes – or even floats.

Edward Tilyou, son of the founder of Steeplechase Park in Coney Island, said that the amusement parks provided "a gigantic laboratory of human nature" (Kasson, 1978: 59), and as an example of the giddy sense of irresponsibility he mentioned what in Danish we call "the merry kitchen," a booth with imitation china dishes and a sign: "If you can't break up your own home, break up ours!" (Kasson, 1978: 59).

Another well-known characterization of modern experience is "that all that is solid melts into air," and the creation of a glass-building certainly appeared to replace solid building materials with fragile, almost immaterial materials. From Rationalism, Victorian culture had inherited the idea of *architecture parlante*, of buildings as carriers of legible meaning, and the rhetoric of the Crystal Palaces in London and New York was a praise of modernity: it was not exclusive in the manner of a feudal castle, but inclusive or even inviting; it was not obscure, dependent on a caste of interpreters, but open and transparent; instead of referring to the barbarian need for fortification, it referred to the modern ideal of comfortable living; one might even claim that the message of the crystal or the glass was that all boundaries, including the fundamental boundary between exterior and interior, had been dissolved. The *Illustrated News* proclaimed: "New materials suggest new methods, and this will ultimately, in keeping with the spirit of the times, lead to a new style," and in the *New-York Daily Times*' report on the opening of the Crystal Palace, the author enthused over this utopian prospect of a man-made transparency, where darkness would no longer reign:

> Thus waned the day in the interior of the Crystal Palace. A day hallowed in American history . . . A day pregnant with promise to our industrial world. And though the sun that

BURNING OF THE NEW YORK CRYSTAL PALACE,
on Tuesday Oct. 5ᵗʰ 1858.
DURING IT'S OCCUPATION FOR THE ANNUAL FAIR OF THE AMERICAN INSTITUTE.

13.5 Crystal Palace burning, Eno Collection. Courtesy of New York Public Library.

glittered through the Palace panes soon sank below the West, and though the cold, blue night speedily fell on the dome warmed with the noon day heat, that sun of American industrial splendor which rose to-day shall never set, but shine like the arctic luminary, ever above the horizon.

Opponents of the Great Exhibition in London had feared that the dissolute crowds would present a danger to the fragile glass-houses, but it turned out that the clean and well-lighted Crystal Palace was attended by thousands of well-behaved visitors. Obviously, the excesses of destruction in the "merry kitchens" functioned as safety-valves of a kind for people who had learned the lesson of proper public conduct in the modern city. The attractions in the amusement parks certainly challenged prevailing notions of public conduct, but they also contributed in solidifying new norms and standards.

The architecture of Crystal Palace was indeed an architecture of luxury but it was nonetheless edifying as a sermon in glass and iron. The dome of Carstensen's and Gildemeister's Crystal Palace in Venetian style was an architectonic quotation from the great dome of the Cathedral of Saint Mark in Venice, but it also derived its effect and impact from its association with the "pleasure domes" of panorama buildings, circus buildings and other temples of modernity. In his *Philosophical Enquiry into the Origin of our Ideas of the Sublime and Beautiful*, Edmund Burke asked "why a *rotund* has such a noble effect" (68), and his answer was, that the "artificial infinity" due to the combination of "succession and uniformity" explains the sublime effect of rotundas (and domes). As an artificially produced "infinity," the experience of the dome comes closer to what I would prefer to call spectacular rather than sublime, but in any event the dome is one of the two key-tools – the other being the tower – which makes it possible to create an artificial world, where experience can be reproduced and almost any sensation fabricated. The dome and the tower – or the globe and the needle as Rem Koolhaas puts it – are devices that alienate the earth's surface from nature and turn it into a magic carpet, a synthetic reality that compensates for any "Reality Shortage" (62) in the metropolis.

V THE ILIAD OF THE NINETEENTH CENTURY

The *New York Illustrated News* reporter was exalted by the sublime spectacle of the Crystal Palace, and in his eulogy he declared that "the Crystal Palace may be termed the Iliad of the Nineteenth Century, and its Homer was the American people" (Kasson, 1990: 147). Walt Whitman must have been among the most frequent visitors to the great exhibition: "I went a long time (nearly a year) – days and nights – especially the latter – as it was finely lighted, and had a very large and copious exhibition gallery of paintings (shown best at night, I tho't) . . .," and to Whitman just as to the news reporter the exhibition was an epic experience which could only be adequately represented in an epic form. Whitman's free-verse catalog, his series of unrhymed lines of varying length, each listing or naming some single, concrete, complete image of a person or thing or place may – as Miles Orvell observed – be conceived of as "a form that stands classical epic poetry on its head, making what used to be an extended pause in the action into the main substance and structure of the poem" (3).

Whitman characterized the Crystal Palace as "an original, esthetic, perfectly proportioned American edifice – one of the few that put modern times not beneath old times, but on equality with the best of them," and in his usual prophetic style he declared that "iron and glass are going to enter more largely into the composition of buildings," and as to his own "rules of composition" the Crystal Palace served as a model: "Rules of Composition – A perfectly transparent, plate-glassy style, *artless*, with no ornaments." The all-encompassing flexibility of the exhibition hall with "fabrics and products and handiwork from the workers of all nations" mirrored his own expansive verse-"catalogs" praising all the things and objects of the New World.

In 1871, at the fortieth annual Exhibition of the American Institute, Whitman read his "Song of the Exhibition," where he invites the "Muse" to migrate from Greece and Ionia and to replace "those immensely overpaid accounts, that matter of Troy and Achilles' wrath, and Aeneas', Odysseus' wanderings" with "a better, fresher, busier sphere," those exhibition halls where: "all that forwards perfect human life be started, / Tried, taught, advanced, visibly exhibited," that is to say: halls such as the Crystal Palace:

> Around a palace, loftier, fairer, ampler than any yet,
> Earth's modern wonder, history's seven outstripping,
> High rising tier on tier with glass and iron facades,

Gladdening the sun and sky, enhued in cheerfulest hues,
Bronze, lilac, robin's-egg, marine and crimson,
Over whose golden roof shall flaunt, beneath thy banner Freedom,
The banners of the States and flags of every land,
A brood of lofty, fair, but lesser palaces shall cluster.

VI THE MOST MODERN FRAGMENTS OF THE WORLD

The epic dimensions of the exterior of Crystal Palace were reflected by the objects exhibited within its doors, and most awe-inspiring was the Danish contribution, a group of statues by the world famous neoclassicist sculptor Bertel Thorvaldsen. According to the *New-York Daily Times* this group of statues – which attracted "more admiration than almost any other portion of the Exhibition" – was a key to the educative, civilizing and "polishing" effect of it all, making it more than just an immense show-case "ministering solely to the eye" (22.7.1853).

> It is curious to notice the effect it produces upon those who examine it. The refined and cultivated visitors who have come miles to behold it, as well as the rough, unpolished laborers, who chance to pass near it, seem alike impressed with its beautiful significance. Many who look upon the group almost involuntarily uncover their heads, as they would in entering a sacred edifice, and stand silently gazing upon it, or quietly conversing in respect to its meaning. The contrast between this and other portions of the buildings is very striking, even to a casual observer. (7.20.1853)

Thus, just as Georg Carstensen, Bertel Thorvaldsen may be considered a mediating figure in this comparison between Copenhagen and New York, and if we can rely on the rhetoric of the newspapers of that time, the most characteristic aspect of the new "culture of spectacles" was the uplifting effect on the mentality of the urban dwellers of the new urban landscapes. In *Delirious New York*, Rem Koolhaas explicitly mentions Carstensen's New York Crystal Palace as the cradle of modern Manhattan, relating it to the amusement parks on Coney Island from the last decades of the nineteenth century, which he characterizes as "incubator(s) for Manhattan's incipient themes and infant mythology" (30), for "the most modern fragment of the world" (42).

Just as Tivoli was a laboratory for the future of Copenhagen, the Luna Park, the Steeplechase Park and the Dreamland on Coney Island represented "a gigantic laboratory of human nature" (Kasson, 1978: 59), to quote the son of one the pioneers at Coney Island. It was "a marvelous realm of transformation" (Kasson, 50), where the cultural melting-pot assumed a most literal form in the "Barrel of Fun" (Kasson 1978: 60), where patrons would be rolled off their feet and where strangers would be brought into sudden, intimate contact. Here the prototypical urban experiences were transformed by the carnival spirit of the mechanized rides. And the monotonous or monumental architecture of responsibility was replaced by an architecture of pleasure, cultivating the oriental, the gothic, the eclectic.

A BEAUTIFUL REPRESENTATION OF THE NEW YORK CRYSTAL PALACE.

13.6 New York Crystal Palace, Eno Collection. Courtesy of New York Public Library.

As already mentioned, showbiz orientalism was also the trademark of Tivoli, which may be interpreted as a realization of the fantasies of the romantic poets. Georg Brandes, the intellectual leader of the Modern Break-Through in Denmark, once wrote that Aladdin, who was the protagonist of the masterpiece of Danish Romanticism, Adam Oehlenschläger's *Aladdin or the Wonderful Lamp*, could be compared to "a gigantic lighthouse statue illuminating the entrance to a harbour." This description inevitably calls to mind the gigantic Goddess of Freedom illuminating the entrance to the New York harbor. In the context of our attempts here to compare New York and Copenhagen, however, it is most striking that, in fact, America does not become an important utopian reference in Denmark until the turn of the century. Even though the cosmopolitan Carstensen had already in the 1830s lived and worked in America, he staged Tivoli as an Oriental, and not an American utopia. In 1872–74, Robert Watt, one of Carstensen's successors as director of Tivoli, wrote *Hinsides Atlanterhavet: Skildringer fra Amerika*, a book in three volumes, which included a description of his promenades in New York, but although he was fascinated with the size, the density and the never-ending variation of life in New York, he did not make any thematic use of America for creating attractions inside Tivoli. He offered an enthusiastic description of Broadway – at least twice as wide as Strandvejen, the most fashionable street of the Copenhageners, and lined with houses more impressive than most of the Danish mansions and palaces – but he never created a mini-New York in Tivoli.

The main difference between the shape of Copenhagen and the shape of New York – or between Tivoli and Coney Island – was that the development of the New Copenhagen was governed by the image of the old city, a city encircled by a wall, whereas the sky became the only limit to the development of New York – as manifested in the famous skyline of Manhattan. Just by being placed on the "bastion," on the ramparts surrounding Copenhagen, Tivoli heralded a new era, but it also heralded an era where the new and even exotic was mediated by traditional images of the city.

Rem Koolhaas argues that the urbanistic experiments on Coney Island – between 1900 and 1910 – would eventually lead to the construction of the skyscraper, which combines three distinctly urbanistic breakthroughs: the reproduction of the world, the annexation of the tower, and the block alone. A whole world, or at least a whole city, is contained within the skyscraper, where each of the artificial levels can be treated "as if the others did not exist" (85), like a "stack of privacies" (85). The skyscraper thus becomes the consummation of the hypothetical "first city" imagined by José Ortega y Gasset, because its "indeterminacy means that a particular site can no longer be matched with any single predetermined purpose" (85). If, however, the Chinese tower of the Tivoli Gardens, the dome of the New York Crystal Palace and the projected skyscraper of Coney Island are all interpreted as instances of the urban utopia, one is left with one question for further reflection: What happens to the political life envisioned by Ortega y Gasset?

Bibliography

Allwood, John: *The Great Exhibitions,* London: Studio Vista, 1977.
Boye, Ib: *Georg Carstensen,* Copenhagen: Fiskers Forlag, 1988.
Carstensen, Georg and Charles Gildemeister: *New York Crystal Palace. Illustrated Description of the Building,* New York: Riker, Thorne, & Co. Publishers, 129 Fulton Street, 1854.
Coleman, Earle: "The Exhibition in the Palace. A Bibliographical Essay," in: *Bulletin of the New York Public Library,* vol. 64, no. 9, 1960.
Giedion, Siegfried: *Space, Time, and Architecture. The Growth of a New Tradition,* Cambridge, Mass.: Harvard University Press, 1974.
Hirschfeld, Charles: "America on Exhibition: The New York Crystal Palace," in: *American Quarterly* 9, 1957.
Kasson, John F.: *Amusing the Million. Coney Island at the Turn of the Century,* New York: Hill & Wang, 1978.
Kasson, John F.: *Civilizing the Machine. Technology and Republican Values in America. 1776–1900,* 1976.
Kasson, John F.: *Rudeness and Civility. Manners in Nineteenth-Century Urban America,* New York: Hill and Wang, 1990.
Koch, Søren: *New York Crystal Palace. En beretning,* Rapport nr. 200 fra Instituttet for Husbygning, Lyngby: Den polytekniske læreanstalt, Danmarks Tekniske Højskole, 1990.
Koolhaas, Rem: *Delirious New York,* New York: The Monacelli Press, 1994.
Landon, Philip: "Great Exhibitions: Representations of the Crystal Palace in Mayhew, Dickens, and Dostoyevsky," in: *Nineteenth Century Contexts. An Interdisciplinary Journal,* vol. 20, no. 1, 1997.
Linvald, Steffen: *Rådhuspladsen i fortid og nutid,* Copenhagen: G.E.C. Gads Forlag, 1950.
New-York Daily Times, 1853.
New York Illustrated News, 1853.
Ortega y Gasset, José: *The Revolt of the Masses,* New York: Norton, 1957.
Orvell, Miles: *The Real Thing. Imitation and Authenticity in American Culture 1880–1940,* Chapel Hill and London: The University of North Carolina Press, 1989.
Plenge, J.: *Nogle Træk af Livet i Kjøbenhavn for en Menneskealder siden,* Copenhagen, 1873.

Rybczynski, Witold: *City Life. Urban Expectations in a New World*, New York: Scribner, 1995.

Steen, Ivan D. "America's First World Fair: The Exhibition of the Industry of All Nations at New York's Crystal Palace, 1853–54," *New York Historical Society Quarterly*, vol. 47, no. 3, 1963.

Tivoliavis, 1843–46.

Watt, Robert: *Hinsides Atlanterhavet: Skildringer fra Amerika*, Copenhagen, 1872–74.

Whitman, Walt: *Prose Works*, vol. 2, edited by Floyd Stovall, New York: New York University Press, 1964.

Whitman, Walt: *The Collected Writing of Walt Whitman. Leaves of Grass. Comprehensive Reader's Edition*, New York: New York University Press, 1965.

Zerlang, Martin: "Orientalism and Modernity: Tivoli in Copenhagen," in: *Nineteenth-Century Contexts. An Interdisciplinary Journal*, vol. 20, no. 1, 1997.

Zerlang, Martin: "Aesthetics and the emergence of the modern city: on the sublime and the spectacular," forthcoming in Ragni Linnet (ed.): *Aesthetic Theory*.

Chapter 14

The Double Erasure of Times Square

M. Christine Boyer

> Things must be twice-told in order to be safely redeemed from time and decay.[1]

By the late 1990s, Manhattan shows signs of suffering from a series of Disneyfications and Theme Park simulations. Times Square/42nd Street, for example, the meeting of two triangles that form an "X" at 42nd Street, was once was the popular entertainment district of vaudeville and the Broadway theater. This rowdy playground has been the central public place where New Yorkers have celebrated New Year's Eve since the early twentieth century. Frequented by thousands of daily commuters who arrive via its labyrinthian subway system, Times Square/42nd Street is intimately linked to the entire metropolitan region. It has been, as its name designates, the location of great newspaper and radio headquarters. But at this very moment in time, Times Square/42nd Street has been rendered by Disney and turned into a wax museum with the likes of Madame Tussaud. It is regulated by guidelines that call for a requisite number of Lutses (Light Units in Times Square) and controlled by urban designers who have planned its spontaneous unplannedness. Times Square/42nd Street has become Disney's "New York Land." Patrolled by private policemen, its garbage picked up by private collectors, and its signage refurbished by private allocations – under the general guidelines set down by its Business Investment District (BID) – it is as clean and pure as a whistle.

How has this happened to such an iconic place of popular culture? Will Times Square/42nd Street survive, will its competitive chaos and tough-guy allure be able to hold out against the latest onslaught of improvement schemes? Or has a grand mistake been made – and this dysfunction junction mauled by disimprovement policies amending its authentic nature instead of its corruption? Has Times Square/42nd Street become another *non-place* instantly recognizable from the images that circulate on television and cinema screens but a space that is never experienced directly?[2] Is it in danger of extinction or disappearance – reduced to an *any-space-whatever*? Gilles Deleuze claims that "*any-space-whatever* is not an abstract universal, in all times, in all places. It is a perfectly singular space [like Times Square/42nd Street] which has merely lost its homogeneity, that is, the principle of its metric relations or the connections of its own parts, so that the linkages can be made in an infinite number of ways. It is a space of virtual conjunction, grasped as pure locus of the possible."[3] Indeed, Times Square/42nd Street appears to be a postmodern "any-space-whatever" – a heterotopic space juxtaposing in a single real place several types of spaces. This open-ended disjunctive set of sites co-exists simultaneously as a retro-theater district, a media center, a Disneyland, a suburban-style shopping mall, an advertising zone, a corporate office park, a movie but also a song, a novel, a play,

14.1 Times Square/42nd Street, looking west along the south side of the street from Broadway crossing. Summer 1999. Photograph: M.C. Boyer.

a street, and a way of life, a place where prostitutes, pimps, hucksters, or teenagers rub shoulders with out-of-town conventioneers, theater audiences, corporate executive secretaries, tourists, and families. Can it also be a center for the visual arts, a place of emerging electronic industries, a truly plugged-in space connected to the rest of the world?

In his review of Döblin's novel *Berlin Alexanderplatz*, Walter Benjamin asked what is Alexanderplatz in Berlin and why is the subtitle, "The story of Franz Biberkopf"? Benjamin considered this montage-work to be a virtual monument to Berlin, an open-ended narrative form based on documentary evidence, a realm in which the reader dwells and forgets everything beside and outside of the place. Alexanderplatz – like Times Square/42nd Street – ruled over the existence of the hero, a cruel and absolute ruler. Benjamin recounts:

> It is the place where the wildest changes have been taking place for the past two years, where excavators and jackhammers work without interruption, the ground shaking from their blows and from the columns of busses and subways, where the guts of the metropolis, the backyards . . . are open more deeply than elsewhere, and where neighborhoods from the 1890s have been preserved more silently than elsewhere, in the untouched labyrinths . . . where the secretaries . . . are crammed in a tenement house, and . . . where the prostitutes go their old ways at night . . . And then, its sociological counterpart: the thieves . . . whose ranks are swelled by the unemployed . . . The Alexanderplatz rules over his existence. A cruel ruler if you like. An absolute one.[1]

Bernard Tschumi responded to this cruel ruler by claiming in *Manhattan Transcripts* (1983) that 42nd Street was a typical New York Street in which a dozen different worlds coexisted along its stretch from the East River to the Hudson, from the Chrysler Building to the cheap whorehouses, from Bryant Park to the derelict piers. "Each border [thresholds of the separate zones that exist on the street] becomes a space with the events that it contains, with the movements that transgress it. 'He gets out of jail; they make love, she kills him; she is free.'"[5] "So when he got out of jail, he thought he could pass safely from one to the next . . . but then he met her. To him, she was an enigma – bold, shy, wanton and childlike in turn. From the moment he saw her he was a man possessed – by a woman who was beautiful to look at, but lethal to love . . . THE STREET."[6] And so the challenge is raised: if the post-modern city or Times Square/42nd Street is the allegorical *femme fatale*, can it be liberated and set free from the lethal and dominating order intent on killing the place? Or is there another reading of contemporary urban space?

As a media center, Times Square has been at a crossroad since 1961 when the *New York Times* sold its 24-story triangular Times Square Tower, originally built in 1904. Even "the Great White Way," the razzle-dazzle electronic wizardry of great neon signs that have turned the night lights of Times Square into a midtown Coney Island since the mid-1920s, has been tampered with by requiring that neon signage now adorn every new structure. "Lutses" have been turned loose in the Square – defined by a 1987 ordinance that mandates the amount of illuminated signage and the degree of brilliance that new buildings *must* carry. The first "luts" appeared on the giant juke box exterior of the

14.2 Lutses (Light Units in Times Square). Northwest corner of Seventh Avenue and 42nd Street, October 1996. Photograph: M.C. Boyer.

Holiday Inn Crowned Plaza Hotel at Broadway and 48th Street in 1989. The city wants these new signs to be as flashy as possible, and advertising is clearly allowed, hoping to cover over the fact that Times Square has become a dull and dark canyon of over-large skyscraper office towers, the unintended result of zoning bonuses that operated in the territory around the square from 1982 until 1987.

Artkraft Strauss Sign Corporation has kept the competitive glow of Times Square alive since the first animated ball dropped on the square in 1908. They have even been responsible for the famous Camel ad which belched rings of smoke into the square, the moving-headline "zipper" around the Times Square Tower created in 1928, and even the Fuji Film panel on 43rd Street. Artkraft has put up about 99 percent of the signage in the square or more than 200 miles of neon. It has designed the new fast paced triple zipper on the Morgan Stanley Building on Broadway between 47th and 48th Streets that tells the spectator the latest financial data and stock quotes.[7] There is plenty of new signage to be seen in the Square: 8 O'Clock's steaming coffee mug, Calvin Klein's computer colored vinyl billboard, 55 tons of fiber optics on the scrolling ticker of the Coca-Cola sign, the Sony Jumbotron TV. In fact Times Square is now so bright at night that not only can you see its glow from lower Manhattan looking up seventh or eighth Avenue, but a new ball was required for New Year's Eve in 1995 because the old one no longer stood out in the blaze of lights.[8] But a cry has been heard on the Internet that this traditional media center is losing its vitality and will never survive the electronic media revolution.[9] It is feared that Times Square/42nd Street as a cultural pulse-point is doomed to become a ghetto for quaint neon signage and saccharine musicals like *Cats* or *Beauty and the Beast* for the operative word on the square is nostalgia – or staged chaos – not reconceptualizing the future.

Instead of retro signage, Times Square needs a dozen fast past flex-face billboards that change every 30 seconds. And it should become an incubator space for the new electronic arts rather than the proposed format of yet more shopping and having fun.

All of these so-called improvements have taken place under the watchful eyes of the self-proclaimed "three witches" who keep an eye on "the gestalt of Times Square": that brew of the "electric, vital, colorful and sort of in your face, a certain aesthetic chaos." Cora Cahan is president of the New 42nd Street, a non-profit organization responsible for restoring the eight outmoded theaters on the block between seventh and eighth Avenues; Rebecca Robertson, is head of the 42nd Street Development Project, the state agency in charge of redevelopment along 42nd Street; and Gretchen Dykstra is president of the Times Square BID established in 1992 that has $6 million in annual assessments to spend.[10] But will all of this improvement activity salvage the trashy, glitzy, raffish quality of the underbelly of life that once defined Times Square? Or is that desire only blatant nostalgia, what Gretchen Dykstra calls "romanticizing the gutter"?

As the 1933 musical movie proclaimed *42nd Street* (1933) was a "naughty, bawdy, gaudy, sporty" place already well in decline when it lent its iconic title to the film opening at the Stand Theater, five blocks away.[11] Even so, 42nd Street was still the most imaginary yet glamorous street in the world, it was the hub of the entire theater world for thousands who dreamed of becoming an actor or dancer. "That little thoroughfare" in "the heart of old New York," invites the spectator to "come and meet those dancing feet" and as the heroine begins her tap routine, the chorus line – in one of Busby Berkeley's great production numbers – turns it back and mounts the stairs enabling the spectators to see the placades that form an animated image of the New York skyline. While the buildings sway, the chorus line begins to exit along the prone body of the Empire State Building. The movie had that lean, hungry, underlit look of gangster films of the same era – a "hard-boiled Musical" as Hollywood called it – for it had a social message that spoke to the times.[12]

The spectacle of *42nd Street*, the act of putting on a play, or a show within a show, is largely about securing a job in the theater. In fact, the movie was called " . . . the Times Square of the assembly line."[13] The narrative of the play points out that " . . . the machine could not pause to brook over the destinies of the human beings that are caught up in its motion. Machines are impersonal things not given to introspect and retrospect. All that driving force was pounding relentless toward one goal – a successful premier on Forty-Second Street."[14] The film parodies Siegfried Kracauer's comments on the Tiller Girls, in "The Mass Ornament" (1927):

> Not only were they [the girls] American products; at the same time they demonstrated the greatness of American production . . . When they formed an undulating snake, they radiantly illustrated the virtues of the conveyor belt; when they tapped their feet in fast tempo, it sounded like *business, business*; when they kicked their legs high with mathematical precision, they joyously affirmed the progress of rationalization; and when they kept repeating the same movements without ever interrupting their routine, one envisioned an uninterrupted chain of autos gliding from the factories of the world, and believed that the blessings of prosperity had no end.[15]

The movie captured the ethos of the Depression years. Its opening coincided with the inauguration of Franklin D. Roosevelt as President, and opportunistically, Warner Brothers advertised the film with the slogan "Inaugurating a New Deal in Entertainment."[16] Upon taking office, Roosevelt said: "If I have read the temper of our people correctly, we now realize as we have never realized before our interdependence . . . If we are to go forward, we must move as a trained and loyal army willing to sacrifice for the good of a common discipline."[17] Cooperation was the new deal and Peggy Sawyer, the heroine of the movie, embodies this new sense: she works hard, resists temptation and gets her break but she does so as a cog in a vast machine, cooperatively following orders.

Commenting on Americanism and Fordism in the 1920s and 1930s, Gramsci noted that "American industrialists are concerned to maintain the continuity of the physical and muscular-nervous efficiency of the worker. It is in their interests to have a stable skilled labor force, a permanently well-adjusted complex, because the human complex (the collective worker) of an enterprise is also a machine which cannot, without considerable loss, be taken to pieces too often and renewed with single new parts."[18] The New Deal in Entertainment, was a lullaby on Broadway, a dreamworld of escape, from the repetitions and fragmentations of the conveyor belt and the assembly line. Sergei Eisenstein noted the same mechanism of escape in the animated cartoons of Disney in the 1930s, labeling them compensation for the suffering and the unfortunate whose lives were graphed by the cent and the dollar and divided up into squares:

14.3 Disney Store, southwest corner of 42nd Street and Seventh Avenue, October 1997, Photograph: M.C. Boyer.

Grey squares of city blocks, Grey prison cells of city streets, Grey faces of endless street crowds. The grey, empty eyes of those who are forever at the mercy of a pitiless procession of laws, not of their own making, laws that divide up the soul, feelings, thought, just as the carcasses of pigs are dismembered by the conveyor belts of Chicago slaughter houses, and the separate pieces of cars are assembled into mechanical organisms by Ford's conveyor belts.[19]

But now as the global economy shifts and turns, information or data-processing has replaced the production of goods, the computer stands in for the machine, and leisure time not work time is on the rise. Thus Americanism has turned into consumerism transforming the landscape of cities into new imagescapes for the display of commodities. While leisure time has been utilized to stitch the worker into a commodified network of pleasurable and innocent entertainments. Long ago, Walter Benjamin noted that architecture was always consumed by the collectivity in a state of distraction; all acts of forgetting take the form of distractions never allowing the essence of a thing to penetrate perception. Thus it should be no surprise that Times Square/42nd Street is the latest urban territory to be shaped by global capitalism or that it substitutes signs of the real for the real.[20] Distracted, we forget what role architecture in the city once might have held.

Why should we be critical of the new imagescape of Times Square intended to be televised more than experienced? Walter Benjamin warned us that:

Criticism is a matter of correct distancing. It was at home in a world where perspectives and prospects counted and where it was still possible to take a standpoint. Now things press too closely on human society. The "unclouded," "innocent" eye has become a lie, perhaps the whole naive mode of expression sheer incompetence. Today the most real, the mercantile gaze into the heart of things is the advertisement . . . For the man in the street, however, it is money that . . . brings him into perceived contact with things. And the paid critic, manipulating paintings in the dealer's exhibition room, knows more important if not better things about them than the art lover viewing them in the showroom window . . . What, in the end, makes advertisements so superior to criticism? Not what the moving read neon sign says – but the fiery pool reflecting it in the asphalt.[21]

Benjamin reveals in this quotation the cynical impact of the power of money on the culture industry – notice the seller's superior relationship to art over the contemplative aesthetic view – but there is hope expressed as well, for literary critics must learn to use the involuntary effects of advertising, its simultaneous diversions and subversions. Their verbal images must act on the reader's mind, they must mimic the advertising sign and become tactile projections. The tempo of modern life – or so Benjamin warned – no longer facilitated the old contemplative style of rhetorical convincing but required a new form of picture-writing taken from advertising.[22]

Advertising was a peculiarly American event, and Le Corbusier upon visiting America in the 1930s surmised its origin lay in the great size of the country – its millions of citizens stretched over vast open spaces had constantly to be informed that this or that existed. Yet advertising was banal and without plastic quality,

... the traffic lights cause vertigo; in the streets and along highways immense, shining, and as it were cellophaned, posters – young men and young women of the pure American type, exuberantly healthy, their cheeks provided with useful reflections – fruits shining and also cellophaned, with all their reflections; boxes of various products, bottles, cars, always cellophaned and supplied with reflections . . . M. Ingres, raising his finger, said to his students: "Gentlemen, reflections are unworthy of great art."[23]

But the lights of Broadway were seductive even to the purism advocated by Le Corbusier. So he wrote:

> . . . I cannot pass by the luminous advertising on Broadway. Everyone has heard about that incandescent path cutting diagonally across Manhattan in which the mob of idlers and patrons of motion pictures, burlesque shows and theaters moves. Electricity reigns, but it is dynamic here, exploding, moving, sparkling, with lights turning white, blue, red, green, yellow. The things behind it are disappointing. These close-range constellations, this Milky Way in which you are carried along, lead to objects of enjoyment which are often mediocre. So much the worst for advertising! There remains a nocturnal festival characteristic of modern times. I remember that the light filled our hearts, and that the intense, powerful color excited us and gave us pleasure. And on Broadway, divided by feelings of melancholy and lively gaiety, I wander along in a hopeless search for an intelligent burlesque show in which the nude white bodies of beautiful women will spring up in witty flashes under the paradisiac illumination of the spotlights.[24]

Far from pitting desire against rationality, the compelling advertising image against the purities of high art – opposing forces that lead nowhere – Walter Benjamin noted instead that "The commodity . . . celebrates its incarnation in the whore."[25] She is both cunning saleswoman and item for sale and sets up a burning desire that can never be quenched. She is the one who leads the stroller of city streets astray by enticing him to step over the threshold of lust into oblivion. "In the large cities, . . . the places where one stands on the threshold to nothingness are countless, and the whores are the Lares of this culture of nothingness, as it were, and stand in the entrances to tenement houses and on the more softly resounding asphalt of the [squares] *perrons*."[26] And so the destabilizing forces of desire must be eradicated from contemporary Times Square if it is to be transfigured into a pleasurable, innocent, or enchanted but never seductive locale – a place that will incorporate and use productively the very play with advertising signs that simultaneously threaten its existence with disruptive impropriety.

Since the decline of legitimate theater along 42nd Street or "The Deuce" as the block of 42nd Street braced by Times Square and Eighth Avenue is called, Times Square/42nd Street has seen the spread of pornography and a sordid undercurrent of crime and prostitution take over its terrain. It should be pointed out, however, that the last legitimate stage production on 42nd Street closed in 1937 and most of that street's theaters became movie houses shortly after the Brandt Organization bought them in 1933. Of the thirteen fabled theaters that once adorned 42nd Street – all built between 1899 and 1920 – there are only five survivors. Beginning in 1982 when John Portman's fifty story Marriott

Marquis Hotel was built, the city has waged a war to "clean up" the area. But Times Square has always had its burlesque shows, its B-rated movies, its fleapit paradises and it has also had other improvement crusaders, vice squads, and prohibitions – so why do its improvers continue to tell tall tales of the decline, danger and sordidness of Times Square and its need for redevelopment? Why erase this popular good time place from the city's collective memory?

No other American place stands out as a monument to raucous commercial enterprise more than does Times Square. After two decades of debate, this famous space has been placed in a state of suspension and only time will tell whether it has been weakened beyond repair, or been given a new lease on life. Will the city be strong enough to override these disimprovements and invade its sanitized domain? Even though the city promised the developers of the four major towers known as Times Square Center – designed several times by Philip Johnson and John Burgee in the early 1980s – unbelievably large tax abatements in return for their land costs, abatements that may have extended as long as 50 years,[27] in 1992 it was decided to postpone the controversial project until the twenty-first century when the real estate market is expected to have regained its strength. Meantime, the public and architects have been given time to rethink the importance of Times Square as the crossroads where consumers and producers of popular culture inevitably meet.

Of course it is still an open debate whether 42nd Street – or "The Deuce" – was either as seamy, honky-tonk and full of sleazy characters or as grim and eerie a reminder of its old vaudeville glitter and theatrical bustle as some accounts insist. Rebecca Robertson believes "that 42nd Street is a street that means New York to a lot of people, but for many years what 42nd Street has meant is six to seven crimes a day . . . It's meant child prostitution. It sometimes seems to me the people who sentimentalize it are up in their houses in northern Connecticut."[28] Even many of the legitimate businesses, the development corporation claims, were no better than stash houses for drug dealers or manufacturers of false identification cards. 42nd Street was seen as a cancer holding back Times Square's recovery and as long as dozens of private owners controlled the street, Robertson contended, there was no chance for revitalization.[29] The *New York Times*' architectural critic Herbert Muschamp pointed out that

> the goal of the $20 million plan [of 42nd Street, Now! was] . . . not so much to overhaul the street physically as to reconstruct people's perception of it . . . A lot of time, money and public relations have gone into constructing the image of 42nd Street as a squalid corridor of horrors that can only be redeemed by ripping it apart. The image is not unconnected to reality. The decay, crime, drugs, pornography and prostitution are real, and no one thinks that these are civic assets. Still, even in its most blighted state the street continued to draw people who came to enjoy the bright lights, crowds and budget movie tickets. And it has never been clear that real estate development is the ideal deterrent to squalor or crime.[30]

We could claim that New York City real estate values and the midtown zoning district that operated between 1982 and 1987 and allowed taller and bulkier skyscrapers from Time Square to Columbus Circle along the Broadway spine killed Times Square and turned it into a corporate office park. Or we could mention the competition with the Wall Street area in lower Manhattan that favored Times Square as a new office park because it lies near the city's most densely populated mass transit hub and is in close proximity to commuter rail lines at Grand Central Station and Penn Station. And of course there has been the city's economic development policies that have pushed family-style entertainment for the masses as a tourist incentive and demanded that the gutter sordidness and notorious vice zone of Times Square be erased by reallocating sex to safety zones on the periphery of the city. Since this law went into effect in November of 1996, Times Square and its architecture of ludic pleasures has been considerably diminished. It will keep, for the sake of nostalgia, six to ten of its original porn shops – but more than ten evidently would tip the scales and produce sordid secondary effects such as crime, drugs, and declining real estate values.

I NARRATING THE STORY OF DISAPPEARANCE

Real estate values alone do not explain why the void exists in Times Square that enables its improvers to tell tall tales about crime, prostitution, drugs, and illicit businesses. Perhaps, instead, the role this public space has held in the popular memory of the city needs to be examined, for it will be found that a double gap has occurred in the city's memory devices – one in the late 1940s and another in contemporary times – facilitating the telling of twice-told stories. These gaps enable a distinction to be made between realistic representation and simulated effects. And this distinction, in turn, engenders a twice-told story that lingers nostalgically over the memory of Times Square trying to keep it from change and destruction.

Deleuze argues that "*any-space-whatevers*" began to proliferate after World War II – they were demolished or reconstructed towns, places of undifferentiated tissue or under-utilized and fallow lands such as docklands, warehouses or dumps.[31] Represented in film, these "*any-space-whatevers*" became spiritual spaces: an amorphous set that eliminated that which happened and acted in it, a non-totalizable space full of shadows and deep black holes.[32] They were pessimistic sites, offering no promise of comfort or retreat. Times Square as a vortex of negation and indeterminacy was a quintessential post-war "*any-space-whatever*."

In post-war America, when the first memory gap occurred and the first story was told, central places such as Times Square were beginning to be threatened with disappearance. Seldom experienced directly these places were retreating into abstraction. As a result, Times Square, along with other important places of the city, were reduced to representational images that could stand in for places no longer explored by pedestrians nor remembered from the details of direct encounters. This was a way of memorializing their loss, without committing them to nostalgic re-enactments. A certain degree of command and control over these unknown terrains could be effected, however, by narrating a series of technical facts and enumerating their characteristics. The detective story and the police narrative are devices that offer an illusion of reality in narrated form. They can be used to focus on, underline, point out and remember parts of the city that have been covered over by mysterious events. Edward Dimendberg argues in "Film Noir and Urban Space" that the dominant visual trope of the genre of detective films known as *film noir* is the material deformation and visual dematerialization of a city that once held a physical center or series of urban spaces that were known to the pedestrian through numerous strolls and routines, or through representational stereotypes such as gridded street patterns, skyscraper skylines, public parks and landmarks. Abandoned for the suburbs, fragmented by urban renewal, and tormented by the automobile, the post-war American city was a place of discomfort and disorientation, a space that was increasingly unknown to the spectator. The dark city of *film noir* not only played on this experience of loss and anxiety, but offered a set of mapping procedures, synoptic views and other communicating devices, that presented an imaginary centered and legible city and thereby enabled the spectator to "cognitively map" or gain command and control over a place that was no longer experienced directly.[33]

Kevin Lynch used the term "cognitive map" in *The Image of the City* (1960) to explore how mental images not only affected a spectator's sense of identity, well-being and belonging to a particular city but also made the city memorable or imageable.[34] A good city form would have readable or identifiable nodes, paths, edges, districts and landmarks. Such readable symbols formed a "cognitive map" orienting spectators in space and time. Fredric Jameson argues that this cognitive framework enables a spectator to project an imaginary image of the total city even where it might be broken in parts. The spectator is able subsequently to gain a sense of place and to construct a composed ensemble that can be retained in memory, and used to map and remap the city along flexible and changing trajectories.[35] But this was the problem in post-war cities: the relationship between the spectator's perception of the physical structure of the city had been shattered and a "cognitive map" could no longer be based on direct experience. Some other device had to mediate between the two and render the city readable. A "cognitive map" could be produced, for example, by the realistic images of cities depicted in films and photographs.

The semi-documentary *The Naked City* (Jules Dassein, director 1948) provides an excellent example of such mediating devices that "cognitively map" the city. Not only is this the first crime film to utilize location shooting but it develops a keen sense of verisimilitude by starring the streets and landmarks of Manhattan as its main feature attraction. The cameraman, Daniels, learned from Erich von Stroheim that "reality lays itself bare like a suspect confessing under the relentless examination of the commissioner of police."[36] And so this narrated story attempts to represent the city as it is, naked and objective as possible, a city of steel and stone, of buildings and pavements, and in this manner tries to save at least the memory of it from eradication and disappearance.[37] Moreover the film employs voice-over narration in an unusual manner: by borrowing the authority that documentaries try to assume, the voice-over both enhances the story's factual base and ennobles its realistic narration of the methodology of crime detection.[38] Voice-over narration was used to illustrate the case history of police work and to tie together the 107 different locations filmed in the streets and buildings of New York City.[39] It maps out a city that once might have been well known by the audience – or that used to mean something to the everyday life of the spectator – but now required a guide to link together its landmarks and places.[40] The *American Cinematographer* noted that "several buildings of the city were photographed for the last time, having since been demolished to make room for the United Nations Buildings." Interiors were shot in the Roxy Theater, offices of the Mirror Newspapers, Stillman's Gym – none of which survived beyond 1947. In addition, the Third Avenue "L" at 59th Street was gone as was Livingston's Dress Shop on 57th Street.[41] From the movie's beginning, then, the spectator is presented with a bird's eye view of the city, stretched out below and waiting for inspection – not unlike "a patient etherised on a table."[42] This is a truthful story, the Naked City whose facts will be exposed, whose crimes will be revealed. And it is voice-over narration, a streetwise voice, that takes this information – raw data, overheard conversations, telephone messages – and composes it into an invisible labyrinth that must be penetrated by the detective. "[Voice-over] is the oral map-making of [the detective's] journey through the labyrinth."[43]

There are several layers to the voice-over narration of *The Naked City* that help to establish a "cognitive map" for the spectator and to remind the audience that there are "eight million stories in the Naked City and this is just one of them."[44] The narrator/director Mark Hellinger is above all a storyteller who maps out the space of New York while simultaneously directing the flow of narration. His voice-over remarks on the next move, the next action, synchronizing this storytelling with the visual narrative. At the bottom, the voice-over informs the viewer of police routines and offers background information on the characters. It enables the spectator to dip in and out of "representative" New Yorker's minds as they go about their daily routines. Voice-over commentary, for example, accompanies the opening series of early morning banal shots – recounting that "A city has many faces – It's one o'clock in the morning now – And this is the face of New York City – when it's asleep on a hot summer night"[45] – while the shots such as a deserted Wall Street, a cat digging into a garbage pan, a tugboat on the Hudson towing two barges are reminiscent of the exploratory techniques of the Lumière Brothers' "Actualities" of the 1890s.[46] Then the narrator omnisciently withdraws to a higher contemplative level – gazing back upon the city – from where he weaves together the montage of images and storylines as the camera constantly shifts its visual and narrative focus.[47] Hellinger tells the young detective Halloran who is staring out of a large window that looks out over the city, "[t]here's the layout, Jim. The man who killed Jean Dexter is somewhere down there. Can't blame him for hiding can you?"[48] It is up to this detective to make the connections that solve the mystery just as he slowly blocks out one street after another street on his sectional map of lower Manhattan searching step by patient step for the killer's address. The framing of the city as a closed system, the solving of a crime as the spectator visually progresses alongside the detective through the streets of the city, become important elements of the mise-en-scène.

Voice-over narration holds the same role that the film's many images of telephone exchanges and communication devices direct. The telephone is one of the many invisible networks that tie the city together, that move the story line along. Police telephone switchboards, police radio operators, the detective's office phone, the young detective's home phone, the phone in the subway booth, the older detective's bedroom phone, the drug store phone booth are all represented in the film. Closing in on the chase, the Police Headquarters radio operator speaks into the microphone: "Emergency . . . All squad cars on the East Side of 14th Street to the Williamsburg Bridge, from 1st Street to 5th Avenue, proceed immediately to Rivington Street between Essex and Delancey. Block off and surround both sides of the street. Institute immediate house-to-house search for . . . two men – Detective James Halloran and William Garza. Halloran is twenty-eight years old."[49] The film thus actually maps out sections of the city for the spectator, sections that were threatened with urban renewal and blocks that would never survive the bulldozer's rout. The closing shots on the Williamsburg Bridge are among the best in the film – as the murderer finds himself trapped at the top of the structure, the camera moves out from this dangerous and precarious site to provide a sweeping panoramic view of the city below – revealing in this manner a city indifferent to the life and death concerns of its many inhabitants.[50]

In 1960, Parker Tyler made the following assessment of *The Naked City*: ". . . it is Manhattan Island and its streets and landmarks that are starred. The social body is thus, through architectural symbol, laid bare (naked) as a neutral fact neither, so to speak, good nor bad, but something which, like the human organism itself, may catch a disease – the criminal – and this disease may elude its detectors . . . The fact is that the vastly complex structure of a great city, in one sense, is a supreme obstacle to the police detectives at the same time that it provides tiny clues as important as certain obscure physical symptoms are to the trained eye of a doctor . . ."[51] It was the scriptwriter Malvin Wald's task to break down the essential information of how crooks operate and how police detectives track them down so that these procedures become intelligble to the spectator, just as it was the camerman's work to establish shots that follow the detective as he walks through the city, that capture him mapping out block after block on his map. These shots plus skyline panoramas and views out over the city, in addition to the invisible lines of telecommuni-cation, "cognitively map" the city for the spectator in an attempt to offer a synoptic view that spatial fragmentation – both the reality of the post-war American city and the filmic process of montage – increasingly rendered impossible.

To explore another manner in which the title of "The Naked City" and even the process of mapping have been replayed, it should be noted that the title for Hellinger's movie was taken from a 1945 book of photographs entitled "Naked City" by Weegee, the sensational crime photographer. Before the title adorned a Hollywood movie and its subsequent television series, it was Weegee who turned the prying eye of his camera on the bizarre and disorderly life of New York. He recorded the spectacle of its streets: the cruel and violent life of murders, fires and accidents and the compelling scenes of loneli-ness, homelessness, and poverty.[52] His sensational snapshot of a car accident (1945), published in *Naked City*, captures a policeman's futile gesture towards a paper-covered corpse while a movie marquee just above him ironically announces the "Joy of Living." The quickness of this image and its jarring juxtapositions inhibit the auratic potential of photography which otherwise would have endowed it with a timeless quality. Instead, this street photography sets up a virtual monument to the death of the city, the withdrawal of life, money and people from communities that were being "killed" by the bulldozer or being racked by a demeaning capitalist society. The dark photographs of *Naked City* map this death, this twilight of the life of a great city and the blackness that smothers it and cannot be erased.

By the summer of 1957, the MIBI ("Mouvement Internationale pour un Bauhaus Imaginiste," one of the precursors of the Situationist International) had reappropriated the title for a map of Paris created by Guy Debord.[53] This map, like its predecessors, under-scored a developing crisis in both the construction and perception of contemporary urban form. By now a well-known image, the map consisted of nineteen cut-outs from a pocket guide to Paris that were printed in black ink with red directional arrows linking each section. The cut-outs depicted what Guy Debord defined as a "unity of atmosphere" – a special place such as the Luxembourg Gardens, Les Halles, the Ledoux Rotunda, or the Gare de Lyon – often a wasteland or an old district left behind in the wake of modern-ization which contained unusual attractions for strollers and enabled unknown encounters to occur. The arrows, on the other hand, illustrated tendencies of orientation for a stroller who might cross the area devoid of specific intentions. This was an experimental "map" representing a system of playful spontaneity enabling sensitive participants to experience the city's many marvels, to recode and repossess its terrain. Some "unities" such as Les Halles, the central market district of Paris, were *plaques tournantes* – simulating a rail-road turntable or a place for trafficking. Railroads can only run on well-laid tracks and so too the pedestrian in the space of contemporary cities was held captive under the constraints of capitalism. The arrows thus symbolized the random turns of direction a pedestrian might take through "different atmospheres of Paris, or of a city, in disregard to the normal connections that ordinarily govern his conduct."[54]

Thus the map of "The Naked City" becomes a heterotopic narrative of open possibi-lities where each follower must choose different paths through the city and overcome the obstacles the city presents. As the film entitled *The Naked City* strips Manhattan bare, enabling its streets and landmarks to become the stars of the film, so the sectional cut-outs are the stars of Paris. If the city of New York offered only tiny clues to be used to over-come the obstacles it presented against its many unsolved crimes, then Paris too yielded only tiny clues to a future narration of new possibilities. And if the film inverted the synoptic view of mapping the city, only adding to its fragmented reality and its threatened dismemberment, then so too Debord's map fragments the experience and perception of the pedestrian who drifts from one selected "unity of atmosphere" to another without knowing either how these juxtapositions are connected or how they might present an illu-sion of the city as a totality. The map's self-reflective intention is to actualize – and thus to make the spectator aware of – the artifice of spatial construction, of the city planners' arbitrary creation of spatial districts, and their imposition of a false unity on the face of the city. By foregrounding the experience of pedestrians and their attempts to recode the city through arbitrary promenades through the city, Debord's map simultaneously outlines the spatial contradictions that capitalism produces, its false appearances and creations, its erasures and disappearances.[55]

Yet another attempt to provide the spectator with a "cognitive map" of the trou-bled terrain of the post-war American city can be found in Stanley Kubrick's 1955 film *Killer's Kiss*. Here again New York City is the site of extensive location filming. Dimendberg points out that Kubrick's cinematic settings such as Times Square and Penn Station are nostalgic landmarks reminding the spectator of an earlier time before the auto-mobile dominated pedestrian spaces such as Times Square and made the railway station redundant as the major gateway to the city. Unknown to the film director, however, Penn Station, which frames the narrative with opening and closing shots, would be destroyed eight years later, and thus it stands not only as a reminder of the industrial city, but it forecasts the ruination that the modernist city will spread.[56] The film opens with a scene that shows Davy Gordon, a boxer on the run from his grueling existence, standing in the brightly lit and spacious station, where he begins his narrative flashback. This scene thus assures the spectator that the story will have a happy ending, and that Davy and his girlfriend Gloria will escape the snares of the city and disappear into the west.[57] Awkwardly told, this happy ending appears to be only a weak palliative, hardly assuaging the spectator's fear that the center of the city and its well-known landmarks were threatened and about to be lost.

But Penn Station and Times Square are also transient spaces that generate psychophysical correspondences. It appears that Kubrick intended to juxtapose these chaotic public places against intensely private worlds of lonely rooms and lonely existences. Vincent Rapallo, the owner of the shabby dance hall Pleasureland where faceless people in somnambulent movements seek some kind of solace and company, fends off his own loneliness and despair by trying to control the lives of others.[57] The spectator sees shots of Davy in his dressing room preparing for a boxing match, which he has little hope of winning, intercut with scenes of Gloria preparing for yet another bout of encounters on the dance floor where she serves as a hostess. And as Vincent and Gloria watch Davy's match on television, Vincent begins to maul and manipulate Gloria, setting up a parallel between personal and public blows and the assaults of modern existence. These voyeuristic and sexual probes are then doubled yet again as Davy is viewed in his lonely apartment talking on the telephone while simultaneously trying to view Gloria undressing through her window across the courtyard. Davy is frustrated in his attempt and only able to glimpse the scene in its mirrored reflection since the cord of his telephone will not allow him to reach his own window and gain a full view. Kubrick has established a mirrored doubling between the hero Davy and the protagonist Vincent that will cause them to fight it out to the death in a storeroom of dismembered and chaotically arranged dolls and mannequins.[59]

Since the modern city imposes on the dweller an excess of nervous stimulation, it requires the development of both perceptual and behavioral defenses against the blows and shocks of modern existence. That is why Kubrick highlights the numerous blows to the body that Davy the boxer and Gloria the dance hostess receive. These experiences are stressed and redoubled by the montage sequence of shots that cuts between Davy routing his opponent in a boxing match and Gloria being violently seduced by Vincent. Montage sequences also capture the overload of visual stimulation and the perpetual motion that transient spaces present. After the opening scenes at Penn Station, for example, *Killer's Kiss* examines a series of images: a portrait in boxing gloves, a flyer advertising the match, a poster on a wet pavement stepped on by a pedestrian, a flyer on a lamp post against the empty background of Times Square.[60]

Throughout the film, Times Square represents a landscape of centrality that causes events to emerge either in memory as a site of traditional rituals or in expectation of the deserted center it would soon become. Times Square is the major setting of the story and all connections between Davy and Gloria seem to crisscross through this site.[61] Even though Times Square is generally filmed in motion, a source of continual flux and anxiety, yet it is also the neutral background onto which experiences of shock are projected after Gloria's encounter with her protagonist or Davy's reception of boxing blows. It is a landscape that intends to reconcile the characters and the spectators to the alienating experience of the metropolis.[62] "In an age of suburbanization [Dimendberg argues], the experience of the urban center cannot escape an ambivalent oscillation between attraction and repulsion. And as the physical face of the city slowly loses its traditional landmarks, the psychophysical correspondence we experience in cinema allow us to redeem the urban environment from a non-existence that is increasingly real, rather than virtual."[63]

II NARRATING A TWICE-TOLD STORY ABOUT TIMES SQUARE

As expressed above, the first told story relied on a taste for realistic representation that grew out of a failure of memory effected by the disappearing or increasingly invisible city. But now a distinction must be drawn between these 1940s and 1950s realistic representations of urban space and our contemporary representations that display a taste for simulation, for delight in wax museums, theme parks, retro-architectural splendors, and the suspension of disbelief that "planning can create the appearance of the unplanned" in the redevelopment of Times Square.[64] In other words the contemporary production of spaces such as Times Square is a twice-told story that depends on a second memory gap and creates a different effect. We are no longer searching for photographic realism, for mapping techniques, for documentary rendering of a city that is beginning to disappear from our lived experience and collective memory. Now the technical apparatus that can produce the illusionary reappearance of Times Square or "The Great White Way" is foregrounded enabling the masterful display of this artistry with all of its theatricality, pretenses and tricks to become the show. This re-enchanted world depends on the power to simulate and distorts the proclaimed purity and objectivity of representative realism.

In order to explore this twice-told story, let me turn to the late nineteenth century when simulation as a means of popular entertainment achieved its full height. Taking Paris's famous wax museum, the Musée Grévin, as an example, we find that as soon as it opened in 1882 it became an immediate success attracting half a million visitors yearly. Modeled in part on Madame Tussaud's London wax museum, it was founded, however, by journalist Arthur Meyer and newspaper caricaturist Alfred Grévin. They intended this museum to mimic the newspaper, offering a random juxtaposition of tableaux similar to the manner in which newspaper columns presented their readers with a series of unconnected stories and they changed these tableaux often according to popular taste.[65] The organizers promised their displays would "represent the principal current events with scrupulous fidelity and striking precision . . . [It was to be] a living museum."[66] In order to heighten the realistic representation of well-known accounts they utilized authentic accessories such as Victor Hugo holding his real pen, or the death of Marat in his actual tub.[67] The museum offered the spectator the novelty of visualizing in exacting detail familiar newspaper stories, famous people and events, at a time when photographs were not easily reproducible and had yet to accompany newspaper reports. These views required, furthermore, that spectators willingly acknowledge the link between known facts or events and their representation. But in addition, these simulations enabled visitors to inhabit multiple perspectives and to experience the surprise of being able to see the scene from several points of view or to see things that one might not ordinarily view. For example, in 1889 the museum presented a tableau of the Eiffel Tower before it had been officially opened as a dress rehearsal for the marvelous views it would one day offer. Viewers saw not only Gustav Eiffel and several Exposition officials inspecting the Tower in mid-construction, but they witnessed workers who had stopped to watch the dignitaries, and they saw a panoramic view of Paris as it would eventually become familiar from the second level of the Tower. Three sights were cleverly combined into one special view.[68]

These three-dimensional tableaux vivants, along with panoramas, dioramas, magic lantern shows, photographs and stereoscopic views, offered the nineteenth-century spectator a new kind of visual realism utilizing the most advanced technical means.[69] Not only did they faithfully represent all the details, texture and look of actual events or things, but they were "mirror[s] with a memory" reflecting events and objects from the past but projecting them onto the present.[70] Furthermore, they relied on technical means or an apparatus of vision to organize, manage and produce their effects, be it the dissolves of a magic lantern show or the three-dimensional illusions of a stereoscope. It was not just representational realism but mechanical or instrumental realism that enthralled spectators in the late nineteenth century. They flocked to theatrical spectacles which were produced by mechanical means and thrilled at scenographic appearances being magically transformed by machines and devices. This was one way that Victorian society could become accustomed to living with machines and mechanical processes. Technical accomplishments became the spectacle itself for at that time "to represent, to know, to transform become not only mutually reinforcing but united activities, three forms of appropriation of the material world which both produce and assimilate the modern experience of command and control."[71] Modern realism enabled the world to be described in factual form, uncompromised by theory, values or magical events and it enabled sight to be produced by the same industrial techniques that produced the objects of sight. Paradoxically, however, once the world had been deprived of wonder through its instruments of realistic vision, once occult and supernatural effects had been destroyed through too much understanding, the nineteenth century then re-enchanted this view in theatrical events, visual spectacles and quasi-magical shows. It simulated the enchantment of inexplicable processes and magical effects, hiding the apparatus of display and highlighting the technical artifice of re-creation. No matter how great the factual details of realism were, there was always a pressure to move from mere representation and factual understanding to simulation and the demonstration not explication of how effective illusions and wonders were produced. On the other side of rational and instrumental control over material reality lay the willing suspension of disbelief and the pleasurable immersion in fantastical simulated worlds.[72]

Consequently, even though dioramas, panoramas and even wax museums had been popular entertainments in the late eighteenth century, they nevertheless experienced a revival at the end of the nineteenth century (1860–1910). As witnessed above in the popular displays that the Musée Grévin presented, that era revealed an unquenchable taste for the spectacle. Now, however, pleasure resided not just in seeing the world duplicated in realistic exactitude, an act demonstrating that one could appropriate that world, master it, map, project or reconstruct it – but pleasure arose as well from the ability to simulate that world and this entailed an apparatus or technician to create such special effects and to reveal an instrumentalist's control over physical reality. Wonder had been transformed from acknowledging the perfection of draughtsmanship or a particular scenographer's theatrical skills, as was admitted in front of a spectacular panorama, to the instrumental ability of mechanical techniques to produce an appearance of reality, a complete illusion where the spectator lost the sense of being in a constructed world. For example, the stereoscope – first displayed to the world at the Great Exhibition of 1851 – created the illusion of three-dimensional depth, "enabling" the viewer to move into the surface of an image, look around its objects, and feel their solidity. The stereoscope and all the other nineteenth-century spectacles of illusion cheated the senses by removing the marks of their construction.[73]

So it might be said of contemporary Times Square whose simulated arrangements have produced an ontological confusion in which the original story has been forgotten and no longer needs to be told. Simulation plays on this shifting of ground and is enhanced when an unstable relation exists between representation and experience. Times Square, by now, is known only through its representations, its sign systems, its iconic cinematic presence. While pleasure derives from experiencing the illusion of "The Great White Way" by simulating its Lutses (Light Units in Times Square), by planning its unplannedness, by foregrounding the apparatus that produces these manipulated representations. Since the need for realistic representation that provides a "cognitive map" of unknown terrain has declined, the pressure for simulation as a twice-told story increases. Now the narration of stories resides in the combinatorial replay embedded in the codes of a computer memory, in the technical apparatus of simulation, in the regulatory controls of urban design. These devices have become this era's mirrors with a memory.

Consequently, Times Square as a quintessential public space of an American city has been transformed into a simulated theme park for commercial entertainment. Once Robert A.M. Stern was put in charge of the interim plan for "42nd Street Now!," giving the project a decidedly razzle-dazzle orientation, it was hoped that architects would remember that the real star of the show was Times Square – "our most democratic good-time place."[74] "For this Crossroads of the World has long been a symbolic intersection between art and communication. Here, advertising attains the dimension of a cultural monument, while theater sustains intermittent hope that art should aspire to broad popular appeal."[75] It appears, however, that the guiding light behind the 42nd Street revitalization plan is Robert Venturi's 1966 proclamation that "Main Street is almost alright." New Yorkers will be given an opportunity to "Learn from 42nd Street" as they once "Learned from Las Vegas," for the double coding of the new plan – paradoxically based on a principle of unplanning – is a set of design guidelines that extrapolates from the realism of the street's popular and commercial features and returns this to privileged spectators who subsequently can relish the commercial illusion in a sanitized and theatricalized zone. Each of the thirty-four refurbished structures that line the street between Broadway and Eighth

14.4 42nd Street Now! rendering, Executive Summary 1993. 42nd Street at Seventh Avenue. Courtesy of Robert A.M. Stern Architects, New York.

14.5 42nd Street Now! rendering, Executive Summary 1993. 42nd Street at Eighth Avenue. Courtesy of Robert A.M. Stern Architects, New York.

Avenue must now be wrapped and layered with spectacular signage, some animated and some lighted, but all legible from a distance and displaying outstanding visual impact. A chart of coordinated colors has been developed, diversity in styles, scales, and materials encouraged, and a melange of restaurant and retail types expected.[76]

> In short the plan is devised to reinforce the street's existing characteristics. The layered accretion of forms over the past century. The mix of styles and scales. The lack of visual coordination . . . Above all, the street will be unified by the prominence given to signs: video

screens, painted billboards, theater marquees, faded murals from the past, LED strips holograms – an uninterrupted commercial interruption.[77]

This play with popular forms drawn from America's image-saturated commercial landscape, helps to destabilize the position that architecture once held in the city, for architecture no longer determines a city's unique visual identity but is reduced to nostalgia stereotypes. Drawing from a ubiquitous series of already determined and ordinary advertisements, signs and billboards, and even relying on the potential drawing card of Mickey Mouse and Donald Duck, Times Square has been incorporated into a larger sense of assembled space, where all of its simultaneity and immediacy can evaporate into astonishing imagescapes. Here, as the earlier commercial entertainments of the diorama, panorama, and lantern slide shows demonstrated, spectators thrill at the re-creation of the real, wondering at the technical procedures which convincingly transport them into an experience that may never have existed in reality. But now, in contemporary times, designers bring all of their information processing abilities into play in order to demonstrate the technical and organizational power of planning regulations and design controls that can turn the material form of the city into such an effective illusion. Like any successful magic show, spectators are doubly thrilled when the illusion is produced by invisible means, when the prosaic world can be re-enchanted and disbelief suspended albeit for a moment.

Notes

1   Guide Fink: "From Showing to Telling: Off-screen narration in the American cinema," *Littérature d'Amérique* 3, 2, Spring, 1982, p. 23. Quoted by Sarah Kozloff: *Invisible Storytellers: Voice-Over Narration in American Fiction Film*, Berkeley: University of California Press, 1988, p. 21.

2   Marc Augé: *Non-Places: introduction to an anthropology of supermodernity*, translated by John Howe, London and New York: Verson Press, 1995.

3   Gilles Deleuze, *Cinema I The Movement-Images*, translated by Hugh Tomlinson and Barbara Habberjam, Minneapolis: University of Minnesota Press, 1986, p. 109. Deleuze states that any-space-whatever is Paul Augé's term: [Cinema I: 109] [or Pascal Augé [Cinema I: 122]].

4   Walter Benjamin: "Crisis of the Novel: On Döblin's *Berlin Alexanderplatz*," *Critical Texts*, 7, 1, 1990, pp. 12–17 (quote p. 15).

5   Bernard Tschumi: *The Manhattan Transcripts*, London: Academy Editions 1994, original 1983, p. 8.

6   Tschumi: *The Manhattan Transcripts*, 24.

7   *New York Times*, December 31, 1995: Section 13, 7.

8   A new Times Square subway entrance is currently being constructed at the southeast corner of 42nd Street and Seventh Avenue: it will be "a glitzy exterior of glass and bright lights and colored discs and strips." *New York Times*, December 10, 1995: Section 13, 6. And the high-tech flashing-neon visual frenzy that is Times Square is being used as a model for a new fence, a 164-foot long artwork displaying thirty-five bright orange faces, forged in coiled steel, that will adorn Times Square from 45th–46th Street and is the work of Monica Banks. *New York Times*, December 27, 1995: B3.

9   Dale Hrabi: "Will the 'New' Times Square be New Enough?" dhrabi@aol.com

10   Bruce Weber: "In Times Square, Keepers of the Glitz," *New York Times*, June 25, 1996: B1, B6.

11   J. Hoberman: *42nd Street*, London: British Film Institute, 1993 p. 9.

12   Quoted in Hoberman: *42nd Street*, p. 19.

13   Hoberman: *42nd Street*, p. 9.

14   Rocco Fumento: "Introduction," in: *42nd Street*, Madison: University of Wisconsin Press, 1980, p. 12.

15   Siegfried Kraxauer: "The Mass Ornament" (1927). Quoted by Hoberman: *42nd Street*, p. 34.

16   Fumento: *42nd Street*, p. 21.

17   Hoberman: *42nd Street*, p. 69.

18   Quoted by Jonathan L. Beller: "City of Television," *Polygraph*, 8, 1996, pp. 133–51.

19   Jay Leyda (ed.): *Eisenstein on Disney*, translated by Alan Upchurch, London: A Methuen Paperback, 1988, p. 3.

20   As the president of New York City Economic Development Commission put it, "good glitz" or "showboating" has never hurt Times Square and so he heralded the opening of a Virgin Megastore in Times Square in the spring of 1996, containing the largest record, movie, book and multimedia store on earth (located on Broadway between 45th and 46th Streets). Thomas J. Lueck: "Times Square Heralds Megastore," *New York Times*, April 24, 1996: B2.

21   Walter Benjamin: *Reflections*, translated by Edmund Jephcott, New York: Schocken Books, 1978, pp. 85–86.

22   Rainer Rochlitz: *The Disenchantment of Art: The Philosophy of Walter Benjamin*, translated by Jane Marie Todd, New York: The Guilford Press, 1996, p. 118.

23   Le Corbusier: *When the Cathedrals Were White*, translated by Francis E. Hyslop, Jr., New York: McGraw-Hill Book Company, 1947, p. 101.

24   Le Corbusier: *When the Cathedrals Were White*, p. 102.

25   Quoted in Sigrid Weigel: "'The Female-Has-Been' and the 'First-born Males of his Work:' From Gender Images to Dialectical Images in Benjamin's Writings," *New Formations*, 20, Summer 1993, p. 31.

26   Quoted in Weigel: "The Female-Has-Been"; pp. 30–31.

27   Thomas J. Lueck: "Financing for Times Square Leads to Harsher Criticism," *New York Times*, July 28, 1994: B3.

28   James Bennet: "Taking the Deuce," *New York Times*, August 9, 1992: 44.

29   David Dunlop: "Times Square Plan is on Hold, But Meter is Still Running," *New York Times*, August 9, 1992: 44.

30   Herbert Muschamp: "42nd Street Plan: Be Bold or Begone!" *New York Times*, September 19, 1993: Section 2: 33.

31   Gilles Deleuze: *Cinema 2 The Time-Image*, translated by Hugh Tomlinson and Barbara Habberjam, Minneapolis: University of Minnesota Press, 1986, p. xi.

32   Gilles Deleuze: *Cinema 1 The Movement-Images*, p. 111.

33   Edward Dimendberg: "Film Noir and Urban Space," unpublished Ph.D. Dissertation, University of California, Santa Cruz, 1992.

34   Kevin Lynch: *The Image of the City*, Cambridge: MIT Press, 1960.

35   Fredric Jameson: *Postmodernism, or, The Cultural Logic of Late Capitalism*, Durham: Duke University Press, 1991, pp. 51–52, 415–17.

36   Carl Richardson: *Autopsy: An Element of Realism in Film Noir*, Metuchen, NJ & London: The Scarecrow Press, Inc., 1992, p. 94.

37   Carl Richardson: *Autopsy*, p. 108.

38   Voice-over enables the audience to hear someone narrating a story although that speaker is never seen on the screen. The voice comes from another time and space than that of the film and thus as an overlay it can comment and draw together parts of the story. Kozloff: *Invisible Storytellers*, pp. 2–3, 82.

39   Added during post-production, voice-over allows the inclusion of important exteriors, or scenes shot in the noisy streets of New York, but then shown without such background interference. Kozloff, *Invisible Storytellers*, p. 22.

40   The producer and voice-over narrator Mark Hellinger wanted to capture the excitement of a big city like New York. Thus in an entirely innovative gesture, he billed the city itself as the

major feature of a Hollywood film turning the island of Manhattan into a film studio rather than displaying Hollywood's usual painted backdrops or back lot street sets. Malvin Wald, "Afterword: The Anatomy of a Hit," in: Malvin Wald and Albert Maltz, *The Naked City: A Screenplay*, Carbondale and Edwardsville: Southern Illinois University Press, 1949, pp. 137, 144.

41 Carl Richardson: *Autopsy*, p. 90.
42 Carl Richardson: *Autopsy*, p. 88.
43 Nicholas Christopher: *Somewhere in the Night: Film Noir and the American City*, New York: The Free Press, 1997, p. 9.
44 Wald, "Afterword," p. 140.
45 Wald and Maltz: *The Naked City*, pp. 3–9.
46 Carl Richardson: *Autopsy*.
47 Sarah Kozloff recounts "by the film's end, we have a very clear sense of the narrator's person-ality – his self-aggrandizement, his cynicism, his sentimentality, his devotion to The City and its inhabitants. This narrator combines both authority and the voice of one man, part lecturer, part tour-guide, part barside raconteur." Kozloff, *Invisible Storytellers*, pp. 86–96; quotation: p. 96.
48 Wald and Maltz: *The Naked City*, p. 31.
49 Wald and Maltz: *The Naked City*, pp. 126–27.
50 Carl Richardson: *Autopsy*.
51 Parker Tyler, in: *The Three Faces of the Film* (1960). Quoted by Wald, "Afterword," p. 148.
52 Hellinger bought the rights to the title for a thousand dollars. Wald, "Afterword," p. 144.
53 Thomas McDonough: "Situationist Space," *October* 67, Winter, 1994, pp. 56–77 and Simon Sadler: "The Situationist City," unpublished manuscript, 1995, pp. 84–96.
54 McDonough: "Situationist Space."
55 McDonough: "Situationist Space," p. 75.
56 Edward Dimendberg: "Film Noir and Urban Space," p. 143.
57 Thomas Allen Nelson: *Kubrick: Inside a Film Artist's Maze*, Bloomington: Indiana University Press, 1982, p. 23.
58 Nelson: *Kubrick*, p. 24.
59 Nelson: *Kubrick*, pp. 24–25, 28.
60 Dimendberg: "Film Noir and Urban Space," pp. 140–62.
61 Dimendberg: "Film Noir and Urban Space," pp. 150–51.
62 Dimendberg: "Film Noir and Urban Space," pp. 154, 160.
63 Dimendberg: "Film Noir and Urban Space," p. 162.
64 This latter is the intention specified in the planning report for Times Square, produced by Robert A.M. Stern and M. & Co.: "42nd Street Now! A Plan for the Interim Development of 42nd Street," *Executive Summary*, New York: 42nd Street Development Project, Inc., New York State Urban Development Corporation, New York City Economic Development Corporation, 1993.
65 Vanessa R. Schwartz: "Cinematic Spectatorship before the Apparatus," in: Linda Williams (ed.): *Viewing Positions: Ways of Seeing Film*, New Brunswick, New Jersey: Rutgers University Press, 1994, pp. 94–105.
66 Quoted by Schwartz: "Cinematic Spectatorship before the Apparatus," p. 94.
67 Schwartz: "Cinematic Spectatorship before the Apparatus," p. 95.
68 Schwartz: "Cinematic Spectatorship before the Apparatus," pp. 97–98.
69 The following account that draws a distinction between representation and simulation follows closely the work of Don Slater: "Photography and Modern Vision: The spectacle of 'natural magic,'" in Chris Jenks (ed.): *Visual Culture*, London and New York: Routledge, 1995, pp. 218–37.
70 This is how Oliver Wendall Holmes described the daguerreotype in 1859. Quoted by Slater: "Photography and Modern Vision," p. 218.
71 Slater: "Photography and Modern Vision," p. 222.
72 Slater: "Photography and Modern Vision," pp. 218–37.
73 Slater: "Photography and Modern Vision," pp. 218–37.

74 Stern and M. & Co.: "42nd Street Now!", p. 2.
75 Herbert Muschamp: "The Alchemy Needed to Rethink Times Square," *New York Times*, August 30, 1992: Section 2: 24.
76 Stern and M. & Co.: "42nd Street Now!"
77 Herbert Muschamp: "42nd Street Plan," p. 33.

Chapter 15

The Musical (Theater) as Equipment for Urban Living

Michael Eigtved

Popular musical theater is directly – and historically – connected with the modern city. The shows reflect the urban reality of modern Western cities. The musical can be traced back to the middle of the nineteenth century, but it was not recognizable as a genre until the first years of the twentieth century. It is therefore the modern urban society of the twentieth century and its salient characteristics – big cities, mass media, density, flow and fragmentation – that constitutes the rock bottom of musicals. What is suggested in the following essay is that musical theater can function not only as a way to reflect a specific society and its changes but also as a way to deal with these.

A preliminary look at the genre already makes the connection to urban life obvious. The very titles of the shows like *Street Scene*, *Chicago*, *West Side Story*, *42nd Street* and *On the Town* indicate clearly in what sphere the action takes place. The sound of urban popular musical expression, like ragtime, jazz or rock, rings in the ear – not to mention the fact that Broadway and West End in the respective hearts of New York and London are the mysterious and glamorous epicenters of the genre.

From the outset, the musical was a cross-fertilization of mass entertainment and popular musical drama. With equal measures of influence, operettas like *La Vie Parisienne* by Jacques Offenbach and American vaudeville, with its entertainers and circus acts, stand at the roots of the genre. They shared one characteristic in common: they were both directed towards the mass audience of the modern metropolises, whether we are talking about Paris or the big cities on the American West Coast. In very different ways they reflected the same problem: the difficulties raised in living inside the big city.

The form in which musicals are constructed reflects their connection with the intensity of life in the city. The show is established through a series of steadily changing feature episodes consisting of various elements. Normally these are brief independent scenes – a song, a dance, a piece of dialog – or large production numbers and ensemble intersections. A musical is a montage of fragments that ultimately establishes a storyline. The essential formal characteristic of musicals is, then, the large number of changes. In contradistinction to the more steady naturalistic drama, musicals, on account of this, bear a mimetic relationship to the characteristics of the city. The continuous emotional and physical stimulation, perhaps the most salient features of life in the city, are thus incorporated in the show. The constant shocks of noise, the changing lights and the speedy pace of the city are given an aesthetic form of representation in the musical.

This continuous transformation of the text, the scenery, the music and the lights is also part of the inner meaning of the show, reflecting the characters' psychological or emotional changes. The staging, the choreography and the lighting are all integral parts of the show.

15.1 *42nd Street*: The familiar metropolitan soundscape with hundreds of hard heels hitting the pavement was organized and made into an aesthetic experience by the tap-dancing Broadway chorus line. In the 1933 film *42nd Street* the entertainment district of New York itself played the leading role. Courtesy of Warner Bros and Vitaphone.

I THE CLASSIC BROADWAY MUSICAL

The musical theater has always been a very sensible barometer of its age. An example to illustrate this point is found in the history of the creation of Bernstein's *West Side Story*. When work on the show began in 1949, it was to be called "East Side Story" and the plot was to evolve around conflicts between Jews and Catholics. But before it ever got onto stage, this problem was overtaken by another more urgent one. The mass influx to New York of immigrants coming from South America and from Puerto Rico was what people were concerned with in the mid-1950s, so the scenario of the show was changed to the slums of the West Side and the musical inspiration to South American rhythms. The basic story though continued to follow the line of Shakespeare's *Romeo and Juliet*, and cultural integration remained the show's crucial issue.

Up until 1968, a Broadway musical was thematically built on a love story, always between two equal persons and with just one genuine obstacle for the fulfillment of the romance: the two of them frequently came from different social and cultural backgrounds.

The overall fictional frame was positioned around getting these two to overcome that problem and find each other in the end. The stories thus reflected a problem common to the large immigrant population layers of the big cities in the United States: the problem of adjusting to life in the new cultural environment without totally losing their own identity. Integration was the underlying theme. But every character on stage was rooted in a society, be it that of Puerto Ricans, chorus girls or gamblers, and nobody stood alone as an outsider.

The first show that is recognized as being a modern musical is *Show Boat*, from 1927, and from the outset, urbanization was the crucial issue. A young girl, Magnolia, leaves the safe but hard life on her parent's sailing theater on the Mississippi in order to settle down in 1880s Chicago with her gambler husband. The lures and treats of life in urban surroundings, contrasted with the simpler, hard-working rural existence led, for instance, by the pier-worker, Joe, become a main theme in the show. And the book by Oscar Hammerstein II, in its discussion of nature as opposed to culture, anticipates aspects of the librettist's subsequent collaboration with composer Richard Rodgers.

In *Show Boat*, which has also been labeled the last American operetta, the realities of urban life finally become all too unpleasant and almost 30 years later, we see Magnolia returning to the boat's smaller society. But her daughter, now a grown-up woman, has become a famous Broadway singer. It seems that it takes at least one generation after moving from the countryside to become comfortable with urban life, that's one way to read this story.

What came into being with *Show Boat* was the integrated musical. Songs were now specifically composed for the exact spot in the show where they were to be played. Not like the earlier shows, where songs were fitted into the story but did not necessarily have any direct relation to the plot. The book and the lines now had to be skillfully written to make the shift from speech to singing appear "natural."

This – the most significant feature of the musical genre – was refined over the years, attaining its zenith with the Rodgers & Hammerstein era (1943–1959). Here, integration was the key word, not just in the technical sense but also thematically. In the Rodgers & Hammerstein shows, a celebration of American values and beliefs was combined with the earlier mentioned stories about the two citizens' needs to merge into a new cultural environment. Often, the action did not actually take place in urban settings, but the expanding cities were never far away – like in *Oklahoma*, which is a celebration of the conquering of the West. Here the cowboy must adapt in order to succeed in his romance with the farmer girl. He must give up his right to move freely and in the end (along with all the farmers and the town folks) salute the new railway line bringing civilization (read: urbanization) to the territory. The shift from wilderness to civilization is acted out rapidly in a little less than 3 hours.

Another example of the main characteristic mentioned above is Leonard Bernstein's *On the Town*; here, with a more directly urban experience but also with a time limit. In *On the Town* three sailors have 24 hours to see New York and experience life in the big city. Like actors in a living Baedecker, the three men continue to move from scene to scene, browsing through the city's infinite possibilities. The show, interestingly enough, opened in 1940, just as New York was becoming filled with Europeans fleeing Nazi Germany.

The visualization of urbanity and urban experiences in the classic Broadway musical has assumed a number of forms, but it has always been the guiding factor of the shows.

II MUSIC IN MUSICALS

Each song in a musical is just one among many played throughout the evening. A fundamental condition of music in musicals is that which applies to shop windows. It needs to display, to some degree, what people expect to see there, but at the same time it has to stand out, so that it captures the attention of the audience. Essentially, the music has to be catchy, to differentiate itself somehow from the constant stream of musical stimulation that modern man experiences.

The musical's roots in popular entertainment like vaudeville and the music hall are essential to understanding the genre's development. By the turn of the century, vaudeville and music hall were the main showcases for new songs, dances and musical trends. Song pluggers and famous entertainers supplied the audience with songs that were directly connected with life in the metropolis. New inventions, new means of transportation, new fashions and new fancies were what inspired the writers and composers. Songs were a news medium as well as a way to come to terms with life. Ragtime music was the way popular music reacted to modern reality, postulating precisely the same point as modern philosophy: life had become fragmented and time and place were no longer unquestionable.

As the genre came into being, the musical outlines were heavily refined. The composer Jerome Kern led the way and set the standards in *Show Boat*, using musical references from a wide range of genres. The backbone of the score was, for the first time, black American popular music, like blues and ragtime, but the elaborate operetta form supplied the framework. Thus, the sound of the show was clearly popular, but due to the heritage from European classical music, the musical statements could be widened. An example of this is the way Kern musically shows the connection between the steady values of nature and the more light-hearted beliefs of the entertainment business. The musical theme in the up-beat opening number "Cotton Blossom" (which is the name of the boat) sung by the entire ensemble, is an inversion of the theme from the slow blues-inspired ballad "Ol' Man River," sung by the old black man, Joe.

Over the years, a Broadway style evolved, drawing on both the vaudeville legacy and the various emerging new styles, preferably jazz, swing and blues. The operetta element disappeared and was replaced by plurality in terms of genres and references. The music gradually took on two major functions.

First, as a way to look into the character who was singing. Songs would appear when tension or action in a scene had built up to a point where speech could no longer release it. It became part of the musical's conventions, willingly accepted by the audience, that a person would burst into song at a given time – provided it had been properly prepared. Thus the shift from one level to another, from realistic speech to the symbolic level of singing or dancing, was rendered "natural." And this allowed the audience to glance into the love life or speculate about the characters on stage.

Second, the music acted as an auditive setting, pointing the audience's attention towards the time and place of the action. The stylized car horn honks in *On the Town* left no doubt about its setting in the middle of a contemporary city's traffic jam. Through its choice of genre, style and form, the music also pointed the audience towards the person who was singing: the ballad, for instance, functioning in much the manner of an auditive "close-up."

In the classic Broadway musical, the music was meant to support the story and not to present itself as an independent piece of art. The task for the composer was to write music that mirrored both the contemporary cultural environment and at the same time had the distinctive mark of the historical period or location in which the action took place. Writing music for the theater indeed demanded a far-reaching talent.

III STAGE SETTING

In the early years of the Broadway musical, the stage settings were quite inventive. The large-scale revues like *The Ziegfeld Follies* and *The George White Scandals* had set a Broadway standard for lavish shows, which was reflected in the big production numbers of the contemporary musicals. In the classic period (from around 1930–1960), though, the dominant picture was that of an admixture of traditional stage settings and stage design ideas stemming from the early modernist avant-garde.

Until the late 1950s, traditional painted backdrops were still in use. But not like the naturalistic illusionary "in a forest" sceneries. Rather, the backdrops were like the shows themselves, blotting-papers for their own specific time, and they always used the visual images of the city for their inspiration. The German director Max Rheinhardt's somewhat paradoxical concept of "stylized realism" combined with collage and assemblage techniques constituted the predominant feature. Backdrops drawn with the particular aesthetics of the billboard or built up as a collage of newspaper headlines could be seen.

Slowly, the old fashioned set pieces were replaced by three-dimensional scenery, changing the stage setting from a montage of flat pictures to a sculpture or architectural environment constructed by fragments of reality – fragments from the interior of the city: streets, stairs, doors, sidewalks, neon lights, etc.

In Leonard Bernstein's *West Side Story* (1957) "The Rumble," the big fight between the two groups of juvenile delinquents, The Sharks and The Jets, takes place under a highway bridge. There is a stunning resemblance to the vaults of a cathedral, as the audience only sees the bottom part of the bridge (and thus must imagine the rest). This cathedral is produced by the concrete constructions in the urban wasteland and the audience's imagination. A perfect setting for the archetypal ethnic – and religious – conflict.

The use of stylized realism is connected to the narrative structure in the musicals of this period. The classic Broadway musical operates through idealizations, through types. The show's storylines are enacted through everyday persons, representatives of certain social or ethnic groups – types, that is to say, rather than specific individuals. The characters on stage visualize and act out abstract, but commonly shared problems, not individual fates. The stylized stage setting was thus devised to support this general feature.

15.2 *West Side Story*: Trapped under a concrete bridge in New York's waste land, juvenile groups Jets and Sharks fight a bitter battle over territory. *West Side Story* from 1957 was the first Broadway show to put forward a dystopic depiction of life amongst urban ethnic minorities. Photo: Fred Fehl. Courtesy of the New York Public Library.

A backdrop, when employed, rarely illuded a specific location, it merely produced perspective, so that characters on stage were presented as a sort of bas-relief. And as is the case on the reliefs, the persons become types which are known and read on the basis of their attributes. The way modern man navigates through the crowds of the city, reading it "in passing," also applies to the understanding of the action on stage.

A final feature deserves to be mentioned: in the musical, the crowd, or even the mass is in itself a part of the show. In musicals, the masses are on stage in the form of the large ensembles which are an inseparable part of the show. They are staged as the societies from which the leading characters originate and they are always, physically, a part of the show, be they chorus girls, Salvation Army soldiers, gamblers or just plain ordinary people in the street. The crowd is the human backdrop for the action, and the happy ending in the classic Broadway musical always takes place during some sort of social event – a parade, a ball, a convention – uniting the crowd in the auditorium with the crowd on stage.

IV THE BREAKAWAY FROM BROADWAY

Up until around 1970 the undisputed center for the musical genre was Broadway, in New York City. It was here the genre arose and it was here that it was developed. The musical genre came into being as a way for people to relate to the processes of urbanization. It is thus important to note that the genre – in its classic form – lost influence by the beginning of the 1960s. The classic Broadway musical was apparently no longer capable of expressing the issues that concerned its audience. A new wave of musicals of British origin – set off in Swingin' London, took over on Broadway. Shows that sprung from the vital center of pop culture, with its fashion, pop music and trendy behavior. Where the urban setting formed the backdrop for young, self-conscious people exploring new ways of living.

During the cold war period, ticket prices for the big Broadway shows increased.[1] The previous status of theater as a media for everybody, a democratic art form, was altered. At the same time, the suburbanization gradually altered the character of New York. The change in the composition of the audience meant that the shows, on the one hand, lived up to the audience's conservative expectations, but on the other hand, they no longer reflected its life conditions. The result was lots of revivals and lots of nostalgic new shows. But the genre's original justification, and that which made it so appealing, namely its capacity for providing a way of understanding contemporary urban conditions, was no longer being fulfilled.

This is bound up with the way modern cities and the Western world in general were so radically changing during this period. The basic urban characteristics – the density, the speed, the loneliness, the cultural clashes, etc. – were unchanged to some extent, but the way people experienced them was going through changes. The notion of being deeply socially rooted, and anchored in class, culture and tradition was rapidly deteriorating.

In popular culture, this had already started in the beginning of the 1950s, having been touched upon by the rootless rebel characters in movies and rock music. But what had previously been limited to a minority of juvenile delinquents was beginning to look like a common condition. This was something which rock music and pop culture were designed to deal with. Here, one could be part of a community evolving around the music and the ideas and at the same time celebrate the newly won freedom – or the loneliness – depending on the viewpoint.

After 1968, the shows changed radically. When rock music burst upon the scene with the "tribal love show" *Hair*, thus arriving in the theaters, tragic, lonely heroes and rebellions populated the stages. It was the heroic fight for life or for society that constituted the story in the new wave of musicals like *Jesus Christ Superstar*, *Chess* and *Les Miserables*, etc. The outsider became the new hero and the essential story of the shows was to illustrate loneliness in the midst of the crowd, a theme which mainly, in the theater, had up until then been dealt with in modernist drama.

The emergence of rock music, and with it the rock musical, as new possibilities, became part of what constituted the popular musical theater. From being a drama in an urban environment where the modern city fashioned the setting that determined the life forms, and where the characters were nonetheless deeply rooted in a particular social context, the shows now became a visualization of the urban experience itself. A loud, fast, frustrated and often tragic drama, depicting an individual's fight for – or against – a community. It became urbanity as theater. And thus the musical genre again reflected the urban reality outside the theater.

V FUNCTIONALITY

The guiding assumption in the following is that popular musical theater (as described so far) also possesses a functionality. To support this view, one can turn to the American literary critic Kenneth Burke. He states, in an essay entitled "Literature as Equipment for Living" (which has partly lent its title to the present essay) that literature has a function. It is through an analysis of proverbs that Burke arrives at this conclusion. He maintains that proverbs are literature. And that they are not merely text but also have a function: revenge, comfort, fame, etc. And most importantly: they deal with situations that recur so often that we need "a name for them." Burke says:

> Social structures give rise to "type" situations, subtle subdivisions of the relationships involved in competitive and cooperative acts. Many proverbs seek to chart, in more or less homey and picturesque ways, these "type" situations.[2]

Proverbs can therefore be situated in categories that enhance their active nature (that is to say, as comforting, revenging, etc.). Burke's idea is that proverbs, and thus also literature in a broader sense, are strategies for handling situations. Because certain situations are recurrent in a given social structure, people develop names for them – and strategies to deal with them.

This idea can be broadened to embrace cultural production as such. And the products of popular culture, in particular, carry this element. Especially when they use modes of storytelling that have the quality of the proverbs. As has been suggested, the plot of a musical can always be reduced to a set of binary oppositions that are solved or reconciled in the course of the show; in classic Broadway theater, through the eventual happy ending and in the newer shows, frequently through the death or disappearance of the hero. Popular culture is, in this sense, also a tool with which we organize possibilities and point toward solutions.

In urban relations, the big problem is that beside a number of recurrent situations, there is a constant flow of new ones. This is perhaps the most fundamental condition and also the most urgent problem of life in the modern city. The renewal of the language, for instance, is bound up with the fact that new ways of reacting to new situations are also engendered through the emergence of new words. New expressions, slang or street jargon constitute articulations of new situations. Burke's point can be applied to a cultural field: New forms arise as responses to new situations.

The American historian Albert F. McLean points to this in his book *The American Vaudeville as Ritual*. His studies of the development of the American variety show have led him to the conclusion that it arose out of a need to have new ways to respond to urban realities.

> ... urbanization came as a distinct trauma within the American experience ... Vaudeville
> was one means – a primary one – by which the disruptive experience of migration and
> acclimatization was objectified and accepted.[3]

For the thousands of immigrants that came to America at the beginning of the twentieth
century – for instance, those who came from rural Europe – the shocking encounter with
the city was impossible to overcome with the use of their own native rituals and stories.

But in the modern variety show, with its fast and literally sensational numbers, the
vast number of new situations from everyday life in the city could be exemplified and
handled. The juggler's control over reality or the escape artist's way of slipping out of the
ropes were two very symbolic expressions. The escape routine can be seen as the strategic
symbolization of a recurring situation, the reflection of a pattern of experience which was
so recurrent and so very representative that a name for it was needed.

In a pure form, this sociological approach would mainly target its interest on the
strategies – on the name – not on how they actually appear. It would be possible to say
something about how cultural expressions function as tools but not much about the
aesthetics of the expression. Burke says:

> Art forms like "tragedy" or "comedy" or "satire" would be treated as equipments for
> living, that size up situations in various ways and in keeping with corresponding various
> attitudes.[4]

In this context, the analysis of the popular musical theater will thus say something about
what strategies are being used to deal with life in the big city.

It is important to stress at this point that a purely sociological approach like this one
does not tell the whole story. The lure of the theater is certainly also the spectacle, the
staging and the sound. But as a very important indicator of a function of the popular
musical theater, this notion of a strategy might prove to be very helpful.

VI SOCIOLOGY

A refining of the sociological approach and an application of the same directly to popular
theater are necessary. The theater sociologist J.S.R. Goodlad operates in his book *The
Sociology of Popular Drama* with a very brief definition of culture as the reaction to, and
handling of, its environment by groups of people. This continues the line traced from
Burke's "sociology of function" and furthermore stresses the importance of looking at
culture in two aspects: with an expressive element and an instrumental element. That is
tantamount to asking, on the one hand, how the group shows its understanding of the
environment and on the other hand, how it attempts to control and handle these
environments. In practice, though, Goodlad admits, is it very difficult to distinguish these
two.

The question that must be asked, then, is whether popular theater is a mirror of the
society or a model for the behavior of its members. A place to start this investigation,

according to Goodlad, is a survey of which unsolved conflicts are recurring, analogous to those "type" situations alluded to by Burke. And they are obviously recurring because they are not solved through the process. Not at first, anyway. This will tell something about whether the process is expressive or instrumental.

What can be established is, according to Goodlad, that:

> . . . popular drama deals with the areas of social living in which members of a community find it most difficult to comply with the moral requirements necessary for the survival of the prevailing social structure.[5]

It is the most urgent problems in a given time that are treated: the meaning and handling of those parts of life which the members of a society have most doubts about. It is thus not clear whether or not it is expressive or instrumental. Perhaps it is exactly the tension between the way a conflict is presented and how the audience meets it that is interesting. What is possible in the scope of this view is to say something about the construction as a whole; over a given period of time, to discern how, and how often, a certain problem is recurring in the theater. And how the actual way of expressing this is changing.

Popular musical theater is, in this view, not a place where the audience escapes realities or the society that surrounds them. It is rather, in Goodlad's words, a questioning of the fact that:

> They are not escaping from their social obligations, but escaping into an understanding of society, which is necessary to them for their participation in society.[6]

VII THE CHANGING OF CHARACTERS

As stated in the beginning of this chapter, the classic Broadway musical showed people deeply rooted in a social and cultural context, people who had their backgrounds contrasted in the meeting with the modern metropolis. And the point was to give this meeting, this situation, a "name." This constituted equipment – for urban living – useful for the way this life was to be led in the first half of the century.

But as Robert Toll points out in his book *The Entertainment Machine*, Broadway totally lost its momentum towards the end of the 1960s.[7] The changes loosely sketched out at the beginning of this paper now became so urgent that they pushed the difficulties of integration into the background. New problems were now in need of a strategy.

Toll mentions two possible reasons for the stagnation on Broadway: first, the producers were largely dependent on an audience with expense accounts, a strategy which did not really encourage any innovation. And second, the new rock music and the rise of a youth culture with its inherent ideology had a great impact on these matters.

The traditional Broadway music style that emerged out of a cross-fertilization between the theaters, Tin Pan Alley and Hollywood was no longer the central creative force in popular music. The music people heard outside the theaters and the things that these songs dealt with did not look or sound like what took place inside. Musical theater did not reflect the society outside its realm anymore – and could no longer be employed for dealing with its various aspects.

However, the new wave of rock musicals from London could. Here, the pluralistic eclecticism of pop culture was staged. And most important: they gave a name to the new situation. It was the tragic heroic myth that was underlying the show. The happy ending disappeared, and so did the obvious utopia. But a discussion of control also began, not only about control over our own lives but also about control that is forced upon us in various forms; and in the shows, very often in the form of mass-media influence. A typical example is the Lloyd Webber show *Evita*. More than anything, it was control over masses and the media that was being staged. And how, through a clever use of public speeches, she made the people follow her.

In a way, it was the story about how a radiant personality became the dominator of the crowd. It was a reflection on and discussion about a new social character, specifically related to modern mass society and enhanced by the mass-media explosion.

David Riesman gave a name to this in his book *The Lonely Crowd*. To Riesman, character is:

> . . . more or less permanent socially and historically conditioned organization of an individual's drives and satisfactions – the kind of "set" with which he approaches the world and people . . . "Social character" is that part of "character" which is shared among significant social groups and which, . . . is the product of the experience of these groups. The notion of social character permits us to speak . . . of the character of classes, groups, regions and nations.[8]

In other words, character is comprised of the strategies a person uses to handle things. But it is also constituted by those common features which are necessary to secure what Riesman (with a concept drawn from Eric Fromm) calls the conformity.

It is the change in these two features that is crucial for the change of social character in modern society.

The early industrialization was significant in that there constantly arose new (unknown) situations which the codification of the former traditional society was not equipped to predict. Consequently, the personal choice was very important, to a greater degree than choices which in traditional societies were governed through strict social organization. Most importantly: these choices were made by a rigid but yet highly individualized character. A firm character. People directed by inner goals, implanted from early childhood – the inner-directed character. Exactly the kind of people that were on stage in the pre-1968 musicals.

But in the move towards consumer society, where the number of people working in production is decreasing and where work hours are shorter, there is an increase of material abundance and leisure. In this society, the stamina and enterprise of the inner-directed people are not requisite to the same extent. Now it is not so much the material environment as it is other people who constitute the "problem."

People intermingle more and more, and in this process they become more sensitive to each other. At the same time, the few surviving traditions are watered down even more.

The new middle class of bureaucrats and white-collar workers are well educated. They read and they have money to spend. This is followed by an increased consumption of words and pictures, mainly through the mass media. A new "type" arises, according to Riesman: other-directed people.

What they have in common is that it is their contemporaries who are governing entities, either those one actually knows or those with whom people are indirectly connected through cultural expressions or the media. This direction is internalized in so far as the dependence on it is implanted from early childhood. And, of course, the goal toward which other-directed people seek is not stable. Only the process of fighting towards a goal and the process of being very attuned to the signals from others remain unchanged through life.

Riesman's suggestions for a new social character do find a resonance in the major changes in the musical theater – and vice versa. The new wave of musicals, which draw heavily on inspiration from mass-media, pop and youth culture and its concerns, clearly reflects a type of character which corresponds with Riesman's description. What is staged is (more or less obviously) a drama between members of the Lonely Crowd. And for the audience, this drama represents a possibility to direct themselves. The musical, then, from 1968 and up until the present time has been adjusting itself to remain an adequate reflection of life, or, as it were, an adequate equipment for living.

VIII LOGOS AND URBAN SETTING

One single sign marks this development very clearly. And it is actually something that points back to the physical, urban reality itself. The major shift in the musical theater also became visible in the marketing of the shows. It meant a change from the poster as the most important visual feature to the use of the logo, a manifestation of the mass stenography of modern marketing.

Looking back some 40–50 years, big musical shows were represented by posters and heralded themselves with the names of the stars in neon lights on the theater marquee. The poster would often be a drawing depicting the main characters in a situation from the show. The image would directly reflect the time and context in which the show was set. Even the letters spelling out the title would be printed in a typography which said something about time and place. It was on the posters, as in the shows, that the cultural and social context was communicated.

With the coming of the rock musical, more massive marketing techniques were applied to the musical theater. *Evita*, from 1978, was the first to have a logo. Lights shining as a halo (or radio waves from an antenna) radiating from a silhouette of Eva Peron herself and beneath this, the title of the show. Over the next few years, the use of a simple sign, depicting the main character, combined with the title, in a characteristic writing style, became institutionalized. From the publicity surrounding *Cats*, in 1981, the air-raid marketing, with logos bombing the city on buses, subways and billboards became the normal way of presenting a show.

A closer look at the *Cats* logo reveals that the eyes of the cat are the shadows of two dancers. From this time on, the use of a drawing, not of a situation from the show, but rather a symbolic representation of the underlying idea, became common. The logo became a metaphor, interpreting the story of the show.

When put together, the image and the text tell a story. The logo from *Les Miserables* tells us that in this show there will be small girls (with frightened eyes) from past times, fighting with waving flags for France. The girl is the main subject – not France, the society or the revolution. Looking at the logo from *Miss Saigon*, it depicts a beautiful Asian girl, disappearing in the slipstream of an American helicopter. Both logos tell us about a single individual who is in trouble. The frightened look on the French girl's face together with the shabby flag certainly does not suggest harmony or happiness. Neither does the Asian woman, for she is evaporating into thin air. And helicopters and the word "Saigon" indicate the tragedy of war.

To conclude, what has been suggested is that the central functional tasks of the popular musical theater, to present strategies and to name situations, are present once again. The post-1968 shows depict lonely, tragic characters searching for a meaning in a fragmented and ever-changing world, and this is present even outside the theater.

It is a convention in the popular musical theater that the plot, as in a crime novel, is always presented in the first scene. The individual and the community to which he or she stands in opposition are displayed in the first scene following the overture.

But with the logo as an integrated part of the presentation of the show, the story already begins out in the city. Act 1, scene 1 is acted out in the streets. Urban realities still provide the fuel and constitute the setting.

Notes

1   Gerald Bordman: *American Musical Theater – a Chronicle*, New York, 1992, pp. 642–44.
2   Kenneth Burke's essay is in the book *The Philosophy of Literary Form*, Berkeley: University of California Press, 1973, the quotation: p. 294.
3   Albert F. McLean: *American Vaudeville as Ritual*, University of Kentucky, 1964, p. 3.
4   Burke, p. 304.
5   J.S.R. Goodlad: *The Sociology of Popular Drama*, London: Heinemann: 1971, p. 9.
6   Goodlad, p. 178.
7   Robert Toll: *The Entertainment Machine*, New York: Oxford University Press, 1982, pp. 152 ff.
8   David Riesman: *The Lonely Crowd*, Yale University Press, 1989 (1961), p. 4.

Chapter 16

Jenny Holzer and Barbara Kruger at Times Square

Anne Ring Petersen

When the New York artist Jenny Holzer first infiltrated the city and the visual field of urbanites, it was with banal sayings like "Abuse of Power Should Come As No Surprise," "Money Creates Taste," and "People Are Nuts If They Think They Control Their Lives." It was not the art audience she wanted to reach with her posters and subsequently with texts displayed on electronic signboards but, on the contrary, the disinterested people of everyday existence. Holzer wanted people to stop short while they were walking capriciously through the streets of Manhattan or elbowing their way through the crowds at Times Square. With her so-called *Truisms* Holzer wished to catch people's attention while they were waiting for the last train or at the moment they were grabbing their luggage in the transit zone of the airport to rush out into the metropolis. Some of *The Truisms* sounded like slogans from an ultra-conservative politician or doomsday prophecies in ad-man's phrases, others like well-worn folksy proverbs or the critical, sardonic statements of revolutionary minorities. On the face of it, Holzer's *Truisms* seemed all the more puzzling because the mutually independent sentences were always reproduced in clusters, so that a polyphony of different voices would emerge, a polyphony that excluded the possibility of tracing the messages back to a single author. Moreover, the mutual differences or downright incompatibility of the statements undermined the notion that speech is a medium for truth. As the American philosopher and art critic Arthur C. Danto has pointed out, Holzer's fusion of text and image raises issues concerning truth and falsity in ways that are pertinent to the field of rhetoric and poetry rather than to the field of illusionism in the visual arts.[1]

An area in which rhetoric and its means of persuasion and balancing truth against falsity are applied daily is precisely the urban textual landscape of advertisements and posters in which Holzer has inserted her texts. Although her work must be considered in terms of verbal language, speech acts and graphic layout, she has not chosen the book page as the locus for her art. It is her preference for non-verbal surfaces and her way of treating them as pictorial surfaces on which color effects and rhythmic compositions can be created that makes Holzer a visual artist. Whether her words are carved into polished memorial benches, reproduced on plain stickers or broadcast from electronic displays, she has deliberately chosen surfaces that have been used for specific purposes in Western culture and have acquired a distinct set of connotations with use – connotations that obviously add significant layers of meanings to Holzer's texts.[2]

Like Barbara Kruger – another New York-based artist with whom Holzer has frequently been compared[3] – Jenny Holzer is among the artists who has continued and renewed the avant-garde tradition of what was once a heretical assimilation of elements from the entertainment industry and popular culture into the system of fine arts. Both of these artists have asserted their interest in the urban lifeworld as a framework of significations by literally breaking out of the white cubes of the museums and galleries and into the babel of signs and signifiers that are meandering through the streets. They are, thus, running the risk of having their works drowned out by the visual noise of the city or simply disappearing, unnoticed, in the frenzied circulation of signs typical of the public spaces of the metropolis. Since 1981, Kruger has been conducting guerrilla warfare against the conventional patterns of thought which advertising builds up and reinforces by virtue of its power to confirm. As her ironic feminist photomontage *Untitled. (I Am Your Reservoir of Poses)* (1983) illustrates, Kruger has attempted to sharpen people's consciousness about the techniques of manipulation applied toward making inroads into the private sphere of the addressee at a subliminal level. By means of a subversive appropriation of advertising methods, its catchy slogans, striking images, and stereotyped role models, she has tried to lay bare advertising's psychological mechanisms. Kruger is well known for her eye-catching layouts, rooted in Russian constructivism. She usually combines a black-and-white montage of photos from old photographic annuals with bold-face phrases printed in white letters on red bands that intersect the picture plane. Her layout quickly became an immediately recognizable mode of pictorial composition, a kind of extended "signature," primarily due to the fact that Kruger reiterated this design to mark out her territory, and did so with a consistency analogous to that of a multi-national company which prints its patented logo on everything it produces.

The following reflections on artists' interventions in the public urban space take as their point of departure a small body of works by Holzer and Kruger that was shown in the early 1980s on the giant Spectacolor Board, mounted on the facade of the Times Building which faces Times Square. The choice of such an unorthodox site for the display of art raises questions about what it is that makes Times Square – and the outdoor city space as such – an attractive place for temporary installations of art, and about *how* the works are actually perceived by the spectators in these turbulent surroundings. In 1982 Holzer wrote selected *Truisms* in the flashing lights of LED notation on the Spectacolor Board, and in 1985–1986 her words appeared again on the Times Square signboard, this time with a selection of texts from *The Survival Series*. To my knowledge, Barbara Kruger has only used the Spectacolor Board once, when she displayed the purely verbal work, *I'm Not Trying To Sell You Anything*, in 1983. The first sentence displayed on the screen – identical with the title of the work – was in the nature of an anti-commercial, whereas the rest of the text was written as a coherent speech containing a pacifistic and rather commonplace message about the connection between warfare and male sexuality.[4] The displays were arranged as part of the project *Message to The Public* which the Public Art Fund sponsored throughout a 10-year period. The Public Art Fund bought time for the artists on the Spectacolor Board. Every month, a new artist would present a 30-second sequence of pictures in color. Fifty times each day, it was sandwiched in between the ordinary advertisements as interruptions with the result that the sequences were seen daily by a full cross-section of urban society.[5]

In the 1980s, Holzer and Kruger developed a new kind of self-conscious and critical public speech that blended the sectarian legacy of concept art with the strategies of mass

16.1 Jenny Holzer: *Truisms*, 1977–79. Spectacular signboard. Installation: Times Square, New York, 1982. *Message to the Public*, sponsored by the Public Art Fund, Inc. Courtesy of Jenny Holzer and Cheim & Read Gallery. Copyright © Jenny Holzer.

communication and which was easily adapted to being communicated to the surging crowds of Times Square. As Arthur C. Danto has remarked with reference to Holzer's works, the projects for Times Square appeared to be "a symbolic condensation" of the American national culture, "up-to-the-minute in technology, populist in format, moralistic in tone." Danto briefly adds that the verbal messages in lights were also "transformative in spiritual intent"[6] – I shall return to this potential for transformation later. Inasmuch as the works were literally displayed in the heart of the city their messages were, in a way, channeled directly out into the urban environment. Conversely, the visuality and connotations of the surrounding commercial and social cityscape would also inevitably interfere with the reception of the works. A primary concern of this essay is this interplay of, on the one hand, the artists' ambitions to utilize the techniques of the mass media in a critical way, and, on the other hand, the capacity of the veritable universe of signs at Times Square to erase the signifiers of the individual signs and assimilate them in one great collective signifier. This interference also poses the question of the integrity of art, in so far as the dialectical relationship between the site-specific work and its environment affects the very status and function of the work of art.

I SITE-SPECIFICITY AND THE MODALITIES OF PERCEPTION

An important aspect of Kruger's and Holzer's rethinking of the relations between art and the public sphere is their choice of site. They have often exhibited their works in the busy and motley environment of streets and squares swarming with potential spectators, but they have seldom had such a large audience as when they occupied the Spectacolor Board. Situated high up on Times Tower, it spoke like a visual megaphone to the estimated 1.5 million people that cross Times Square every day.[7] A significant quality of the works that the artists have designed for display outside the art institutions is their deliberate adaptation to the urban perception. Holzer and Kruger compose their works for outdoor spaces in such a way that they comply with what the art critic Brian O'Doherty once called "the vernacular glance" – the quick and habitual urban scan that almost unconsciously registers and sorts out the city's overwhelming multitude of visual information. According to Brian O'Doherty, who introduced the term in a discussion of Robert Rauschenberg's silk-screen paintings:

> The vernacular glance is what carries us through the city every day – a mode of almost unconscious or at least divided attention. Since we are usually moving, it tags the unexpected and quickly makes it the familiar, filing surplus information into safe categories. Casually self-interested, it accepts the miraculous as routine. Its self-interest becomes so habitual that it is almost disinterested. This is the opposite of the pastoral nineteenth-century "walk," where habitual curiosity provoked wonder, but found nothing but ugliness in the city. The vernacular glance doesn't recognize categories of the beautiful and ugly. It just deals with what's there. Easily surfeited, cynical about big occasions, the vernacular glance develops a taste for anything, often notices or creates the momentarily humorous, but doesn't follow it up. Nor does it pause to remark on unusual juxtapositions, because the unusual is what it is geared to recognize, without thinking about it . . . The vernacular glance sees the world as a supermarket. A rather animal faculty, it is pithy, shrewd and abrupt, like slang. Its directions are multiple . . . Its disorder needs no order because it doesn't require thinking about or "solution" . . . It is superficial in the best sense.[8]

An accommodation to the vernacular glance must necessarily take place if art is to become operative in the jungle of posters, billboards, electric advertisements, and shop signs that compete for people's attention on the basis of an ad-man's version of Darwin's tenet – only the most *efficient* will survive. As Marjorie Perloff has pointed out, "In the billboard culture of the late twentieth century, the 'successful' text is one that combines high-speed communication with maximum information."[9] Jenny Holzer's and Barbara Kruger's works at Times Square played on the perceptual mode of the vernacular glance, but only in order to cajole the spectator into adopting two alternative but differentiated modes of perception. The vernacular glance itself would not get the message because, as Brian O'Doherty remarks, it neither follows an occasion up, nor pauses to remark on the unusual. Just as it takes two individual acts of focusing to see both of the Gestalts in a puzzle picture, two distinct gazes were needed for perceiving the two clearly distinguishable visual and semantic orders of the works at Times Square. Which one of these was being perceived was dependent on the focusing. The two orders could not be perceived simultaneously, but it was possible to see both by change of focusing. Thus, any spectator had the possibility of oscillating between the two alternatives, picking up both of them, as when scrutinizing a puzzle picture.

One possibility was that the beholder could focus on the verbal message on the Spectacolor Board. This would presuppose a perceptual isolation of the text from its environment. The casual pedestrian would then become a reader who made more or less persistent attempts to decode and interpret the text. However, it remains an open and unsolvable question whether the works were really able to uphold their subversive intent under the powerful pressure from the context of advertising and popular entertainment. When one is compelled to cast doubt on the trenchancy of the works this is due to the fact that the impact of the individual signifiers at Times Square tends to fade out and give way to the general impression of the square as a spectacle. The situationist spokesman Guy Debord has characterized the society of late capitalism as "the society of the spectacle," that is, as a society in which the phantasmagorias of commodity fetishism and their theatrical and pictorial seduction of the consumer have become so predominant that they have attained the total occupation of social life. As Debord proclaimed, "The spectacle is not a collection of images, but a social relation among people, *mediated* by images."[10]

The fact that Holzer's and Kruger's works tend to merge into the landscape of luminous signs is, of course, owing to their preference for an identical material – electric light – and a prevalent medium of the street – the computerized signboard. The other, alternative mode of perception thus comes into being when the spectator looks at Times Square with a defocused gaze and gives in to the overpowering impact of the brilliantly colored blaze of light. In this case, the electronic signboard at Times Tower is not perceived as an isolated phenomenon, but is experienced as a constituent part of the overall psychological and aesthetic impression produced by the kinetic constellations of city lights.

The utilization of the Spectacolor Board for the display of art raises a general question: Why do artists like Holzer and Kruger implant their art in the city space at all? Why don't they prefer the spaces of the art institutions, which provide peace for contemplation and reflection? By inserting their works in the circuit of the mass media and the public space of the streets, Holzer and Kruger expose how art and the artist's work are interlaced with the city, not only as a physical fabric but also as a social and mental space, a lifeworld pervaded by commercialism and political interests as well as the mediated reality of information technology and mass media.[11] Obviously, it is not only the genre of so-called integrated art to which their works belong that is contextualized in this way. In a sense, all art, wherever it is exhibited, is embedded in these societal contexts. Still, the siting of the work of art makes a crucial difference in the way it is relating to them. Inside the exhibition spaces of museums and galleries, the institution is always there as a symbolic frame of primary importance and as a physical, architectural environment. One of its functions is to establish a kind of perceptual filter that places art at a certain distance from the outside world and screens it off from the various contexts to which it refers. In the case of works that have been moved out of the museums and galleries into the public spaces of the city, the institutional filter is not visibly there. Consequently, integrated art tends to engage the spectator in reading the site – its history, its functions, its topographical specifics, and its psychological resonance – no less than it engages the spectator in deciphering the work of art itself. There will inevitably be a seepage of the world into the work and the spectator's interpretation of it. This applies to all site-specific works no matter whether they are placed in the outdoor spaces of the public squares and streets or are installed in an indoor public space presently or formerly functioning as part of the city's everyday routine. This does not mean that the urban art projects are liberated from the discourses of the institution of Art. Although they represent an escape from the institutionalized exhibition spaces and the marketplace of the galleries they do not disengage themselves from institutionalization as such. Their realization is dependent on the conceptual parameters as well as the organizational, economical, distributional and informational structures of the art world. An unmistakable symptom of this condition can be detected in the accusations of elitism and "insiderism" advanced by the rather reactionary standpoint taken up by the critic James Gardener:

> There are two audiences for this art, the actual audience and the real audience. The latter watches the former, though the former doesn't realize it is being watched . . . [The latter] learns about Holzer's piece through magazines, books and word of mouth. Thus whenever Holzer flashes her words at Candlestick Park, or Piccadilly Circus, or Times Square, the art world experiences a frisson of excitement at the thought of all those people who have not the remotest idea what is going on; all those people who do not go to art galleries, who do not read Artforum, who are not in on the joke.[12]

A difficult navigation between Scylla and Charybdis is required of artists operating in the public space attempting to reach a broad and heterogeneous audience. On the one hand, the elitist imprint of advanced art must not be too pronounced, because then they risk stepping into the trap of vanguard hermetism or narcissism. On the other hand, the artistic nature of the projects, their otherness in form and intent and their resistance to adapt to the discourses of the environment must all be distinctly articulated. If not, the artists will then, as the art critic Hal Foster has pointed out, be stepping into the trap of turning art into a collaborator of what it had set out to examine and expose – in Holzer's and Kruger's case, the media spectacle. Drawing on Roland Barthes' *Mythologies* in which the dominant culture is seen to operate through appropriation, Hal Foster sees the paradoxical fusion of ideology critique and deconstruction inherent in appropriation art[13] such as that of Kruger and Holzer as a kind of "counter-appropriation." According to Barthes, the predominant culture abstracts specific signifiers of social groups into general signifiers that are then consumed as cultural myths. By appropriating the mythical sign, breaking it apart, and finally re-inscribing it in a critical montage the artist can circulate it as an artificial, subversive myth.[14] However, this strategic reversal of the production of signification poses a problem for artists and audiences alike – polemically summed up by Hal Foster:

> [W]hen does montage recode, let alone redeem, the splintering of the commodity-sign, and when does it exacerbate it? When does appropriation double the mythical sign critically, and when does it replicate it, even reinforce it cynically? Is it ever purely the one or the other?[15]

The various works by Jenny Holzer in the Times Square district are a case in point. In 1980 she participated in a loosely curated exhibition named the *Times Square Show*. It had been initiated by a semi-organized group of about fifty young artists known as Colab. It was housed in a ramshackle four-story structure on the corner of Seventh Avenue and 41st Street – a former bus depot and massage parlor turned into a kind of art fun-house for the month of June. Despite the deliberately improvised and trashy look of the exhibition it was professionally advertised – a *Times Square Show*-advertisement by June Dickson ran for free during the entire month on the Times Tower's electronic bill-board.[16] By and large, the participants used imagery that anyone familiar with the streets of New York would recognize. The art critic Jeffrey Deitch's eyewitness report is telling: "Such phenomena as media-hyped, sex-starved mass murderers, idiotic television plots, and useless plastic consumer goods figured prominently in the imagery. Found objects . . . were displayed right alongside the 'real' art, with no attempt at differentiation."[17] This accessibility of the imagery and deliberate blurring of the border between art and the urban environment were important conceptual components of the project. In the early 1980s – the historical backdrop of the *Times Square Show* and Holzer's display of *Truisms* on the Spectacolor Board – the district was troubled by the crime and prostitution appur-tenant to the spread of drugs and pornography since the 1960s.[18] Thus, as Deitch observed, the socio-political circumstances made it unnecessary to be excessively critical in order to communicate a critical message: "[M]uch of the art was politically charged. At the same time, most of the artists were smart enough to understand that the Times Square population scarcely needs to be harangued about the social inequities that it already knows too well."[19]

While the *Times Square Show* was based on a prevailing assumption among leftist artists, namely that the site of artistic transformation and political subversion is *elsewhere* than the institutional center, that is, in the field of the social or cultural other,[20] the *42nd Street Art Project* of 1993 offered no such field of subcultural otherness. The *42nd Street Art Project* was shown on West 42nd Street between Broadway and Eighth Avenue. It was a joint venture initiated by Creative Time – an established non-profit arts organization – a noted design firm (M. & Co), the 42nd Street Development Project, and The New 42nd Street, Inc. – a non-profit organization established to restore the thoroughfare's theaters to their past glory – and the exhibition starred Jenny Holzer as a prominent participant of international renown. According to the art critic, Roberta Smith, the aphorisms of Holzer's *Truisms* and *Survival Series* on the marquees of old movie houses had "never looked better nor seemed more pertinent" as they played well against the local store signs and created "almost imperceptible fissures and contradictions in the fabric of the street."[21] Nevertheless, as Christine Boyer explains in her contribution to this anthology, the Times Square area of the mid-1990s is radically different from that of the early 1980s. In 1982 the city waged a war to "clean up" the area, a clean-up operation that has been going on ever since. The imposition of improvement schemes has gradually been erasing the unique character of this iconic place, turning Times Square and 42nd Street into a nostalgic simu-lation of its own legendary past. Thus, the professionalized art enterprise of 1993 did not confer the same kind of street credibility on the participants as the previous subcultural manifestation in the rundown multi-story building around the corner. On the contrary,

16.2 Jenny Holzer: Texts from *Truisms*, 1977–79, and *Survival Series*, 1985–86, on theatre marquees. *The 42nd Street Art Project*, 1993. Photo: Maggie Hopp. Courtesy of Creative Time.

the collaboration with a development project vested with the authority to exercise a regulatory control of urban development in the area shifted the artists' position from the de-centered position of criticism to the centered position of complicity. Hal Foster's comment on the *42nd Street Art Project* therefore hits the nail on the head. He concludes that although the show included individual contributions of subversive intent, the art was "deployed to improve the image of a notorious piece of real estate slated for redevelopment."[22] Well aware of the symbolic potential of "ethnographic" site-specific art for animating lost cultural spaces and proposing "historical countermemories," Hal Foster nonetheless emphasizes the risk that artists can lose their integrity when participating in sponsored projects aiming at reshaping people's perception of a locality with a problematic or waning identity:

> [S]ite-specific work can be exploited to make these nonspaces seem specific again, to redress them as grounded places, not abstract spaces, in historical and/or cultural terms. Killed as culture the local and the everyday can be revived as simulacrum, . . . and site-specific work can be drawn into this zombification of the local and the everyday, this Disney version of the site-specific. Tabooed in postmodernist art, values like authenticity, originality, and singularity can return as properties of sites that artists are asked to define or to embellish. There is nothing wrong with this return per se, but sponsors may regard these properties precisely as sited values to develop.[23]

II DAZZLE AND DANGER

The fact that artistic interventions in the public urban space are much too easily turned into subtle vehicles for city policies or commercial interests suggests that Jenny Holzer and Barbara Kruger must have had other, more compelling motives for wanting to display their works at Times Square than the political ones. Thus, another question arises: How did Holzer and Kruger actually regard the setting that Times Square provided for their art?

The origin of *The Truisms* reveals how closely Holzer's art is connected to the Times Square area. In the very first poster editions of 1977–1979, *The Truisms* were listed very matter-of-factly in alphabetic order. As to the origin of this work, the explanation that is most frequently repeated in interviews and articles[24] is that it stems from Holzer's idea of making her personal *Reader's Digest* version of Western and Eastern thought on the basis of an indigestible reading list from the Whitney Museum Independent Student Program which she joined in 1977.[25] There is also, however, another source of inspiration: the poster. It is mentioned in several comments on *The Truisms*, but only as an explanation to why Holzer decided to distribute her street talk by means of posters, pasted up in dense clusters all over Manhattan, whereas the more comprehensive implications of her recollection of the discovery of the poster medium have almost passed unheeded into oblivion, until now. Holzer's own explanation reads as follows:

> I got the idea partly from someone – I assume it was a man – who went around plastering Times Square with posters that warned other men to stay away from the vice in the area, warning them that they would get leprosy and tuberculosis if they crossed this imaginary circle that he'd supposedly put around it. I was amazed at how the word "leprosy" on a poster could stop you short, and at how effective these posters were. He was tireless. They were absolutely everywhere . . . I would see that other people were amazed by them, too.[26]

A comparison of the leprosy poster with the previously mentioned *Truism* poster reveals that Holzer assimilated more than just the medium. The text was printed in bold, authoritative letters on a bare white surface, just like *The Truisms*. Moreover, the anonymous author of the warning against prostitutes and bums as carriers of disease also phrased his message in short sentences, which tended to fall apart in isolated statements. Nevertheless, the most significant common feature has nothing to do with bold layout and laconic speech, which are means of expression that Holzer undoubtedly could have learned anywhere in the streets of New York.[27] The crucial similarity consists in the feeling of danger and fear that pervades some of Holzer's most pithy texts, not only among the *Truisms*. Whoever was the real author of the poster, the idea must have suggested itself to the passers-by who read it that the initial letters of the signature – N.Y. – should be interpreted as the ordinary abbreviation for New York. The poster could thus be interpreted as "the voice of the city" – as a warning from the city against itself as the city of vice; against New York as a contemporary correlate to the legendary whore, the city of Babylon.

Barbara Kruger's opinion on the Times Square area differs somewhat from that of Jenny Holzer. In an unpublished critique of the dramatic makeover of the area around the square in the late 1980s, Kruger characterized New York as the epitome of transience, restlessness and shock stimulation, in the middle of which Times Square lights up like "a high-voltaged spectacle" that sparkles like "a fabulous diamond in a great setting."[28]

> A city like New York can be seen as a dense cluster of civilization: a rampant bundle of comings and goings veneered with the tumultuous urgency of people busy living and dying. Amidst all this, Times Square has existed as a kind of brazenly pumped-up light show, . . . Times Square was, and could again be, this kind of gargantuan yet contained spectacle that perpetually flirts with our senses of wonderment and pleasure.[29]

The fabulous dazzle as well as the undertow of danger in the area, that is, the confrontation with the city as a frightening abyss, thus attracted the two artists and motivated them to use the computerized display on Times Tower – the former headquarters of the *New York Times* which gave its name to the square in 1904, confident that it would develop into a junction of media headquarters with metropolitan public life, rather than the gaudy entertainment center it soon became.[30] Since the mid-1920s, the square has been the pivot of one of the most important entertainment districts of New York as well as a symbol of American showbusiness as such, always most dazzling at night, wrapped in the multi-colored nimbuses of neon advertisements. Accordingly, Times Square has not only been associated with news and entertainment. It was – and still is – a spectacular showcase for an aggressive, electric "commercial aesthetics" pushing it to the visual forefront of American urban life where it deeply affected the way people experienced reality. Apart from the promotion of products and companies, the purpose of this commercial aesthetics was to produce a pecuniary climate and to stimulate a spirit of acquisition. At the same time, it possessed the potential for conveying a sense of wonder and awe.[31] The phantasmagoric quality of Times Square is due to this commercial aesthetics. In the evening, the substance of the framing buildings seems to dissolve as the cacophonous profusion of electric signs, ostensibly suspended in the air, displaces darkness. As the architectural historian Ada Louise Huxtable has rightly pointed out, Times Square is a "non-architecture of place" with a very powerful "image of place."[32] Here, the dynamics of the city is intensified as the traffic and crowds make the ground move, while the signs transform the static lines of architecture into kinetic, electrified set pieces. As a rule, Holzer's and Kruger's application of the signboard is intended to provoke a shock, but a shock that differs from "the shock of the New" associated with modernism. The shock effect of their works has nothing to do with the fetishism of novelty value that modernism shared with advertising. The shock effect has to do with the inner tensions of the work, as Holzer has suggested in an explanation of why she prefers to use electronic signboards:

> Because signs are so flashy, when you put them in a public situation you might have thousands of people watching . . . So I was interested in *the efficiency of signs* as well as in the kind of *shock value* the signs have when programmed with my peculiar material. These signs are used for advertising and they are used in banks. I thought it would be interesting to put *different subjects*, kind of *a skewed content*, in this format, this ordinary machine.[33]

Holzer and Kruger are not interested in the shock occasioned by the encounter with radical innovation. Rather, they intend to fixate a tension between extremes. They aim at a shock of antagonisms, or as Walter Benjamin would say, "dialectics at a standstill."[34] In the quoted passage, Holzer comments on the shock released by the opposition between people's *anticipation* of the information to be gleaned from electronic signs and the *actual encounter* with the artist's distorted and misplaced message. Although it represents an aesthetic formalization of shock experience, the "shock value" of her signs is intended to release a type of response that is normally provoked, not by the contemplation of art, but on the contrary, by the encounter with the rapidly changing lifeworld of the big, industrialized city. As a shock reaction of the kind Holzer is talking about is not an aesthetic response *per se*, the shock factor makes the distinction between art and reality grow dim, or to put it even more succinctly: it makes aesthetic experience converge on urban sensibility.[35]

One of the crucial points of Walter Benjamin's essay *"The Work of Art in the Age of Mechanical Reproduction"*[36] was that the Dada collage, photography and especially film were able to rouse spectators from habitual trains of thoughts and deep-rooted stimulus-response patterns by means of shock stimulation. As to the works by Holzer and Kruger in the public space, the shock aesthetics is ideally intended to create the effect Benjamin assumed that the artistic utilization of the techniques of mechanical reproduction would have, that is, to provoke a sudden flash of enlightenment, a momentary and critical awakening from the social, cultural and commercial phantasmagorias. Holzer's and Kruger's use of shock stimulation is closely linked to their sophisticated manipulation with modes of perception. In what follows, I'll resume the subject of the two gazes, beginning with the focused, reading gaze. The artists themselves conferred priority on this mode of perception since they intended to transform people's horizon of consciousness.

III ENLIGHTENING *DÉTOURNEMENT*

The Austrian-American philosopher and sociologist Alfred Schütz has analyzed the way in which the members of a society rely on and relate to patterns of interpretation – a horizon which is transmitted to the individual in the process of socialization and is taken for granted. The theories of Schütz's phenomenological sociology are developed from the phenomenology of Edmund Husserl. His theory of relevancies elaborates not so much Husserl's concept of the lifeworld as his concept of the natural attitude. In this naive attitude concerning our mundane life, the world and the typicality of its contents are accepted as unquestionably given until a situation occurs that situates it in question. According to Alfred Schütz, the individual approaches any situation with expectancies based on the assumption that the structure of the world is constant, and the validity of his or her experience of living within the world is analogous.[37] In his article "Some Structures of the Life-World" Schütz discusses the process of cognition and the modification of the horizon that occurs when the individual is confronted with structures that *diverge* from expectancies, and which he or she cannot comprehend by referring to his or her "actual stock of knowledge."[38] Schütz makes a distinction between several types of relevancy for the subjective consciousness that a phenomenon can acquire. These distinctions are useful conceptual instruments for explicating the way in which Holzer's and Kruger's works, especially those at the Spectacolor Board, were "transformative in spiritual intent," as Danto observed.

Schütz introduces the term "*motivational relevancy*" to designate the interests and the orientation that determine which elements of both the world's ontological structures and individual foreknowledge guide the perceptions, interpretations and acts of a particular person. Schütz characterizes this form of relevancy as "motivational" because it is experienced as subjective, and the individual's understanding of a given situation or perception is determined by subjective motives. Since the individual's stock of knowledge is also culturally and socially conditioned the subjective sphere of interest will inevitably be determined by the collective horizon as well. Or, as Schütz writes, "[by] what within . . . our culture is accepted as unquestionable, what can become questionable and what *appears* as worthy of questioning."[39] The subject's foreknowledge will not always suffice for new situations. Using Schütz's terminology, it means that the part of the horizon which is insufficient is no longer given as unquestionable, but acquires "*thematic relevancy*." It becomes an object of intensified attention.[40] "What had been accepted as unquestionably given then becomes a problem, a theoretical, practical or emotional problem, which must be formulated, analyzed and solved."[41]

This, I submit, is precisely what happens when one unexpectedly encounters Jenny Holzer's or Barbara Kruger's texts in the commercialized textual and pictorial babel of Times Square. When discovering a disconcerting statement like "Private Property Created Crime" in the place where one would have anticipated an advertisement for a multinational company. Or, when disturbed by a desperate scream like "Protect Me From What I Want" in the heart of an area that has been created especially for satisfying any desire. By restructuring the content of the media, these statements create an ambivalent tension on the site. As Schütz puts it, "the situation proves to be one which cannot be referred by synthesis of recognition to a previous situation typically alike, similar, etc. because it is radically new."[42] At the beginning of the 1980s it had become a well-worn artistic gambit to subject the effluvia of the spectacle to a situationist *détournement*, that is, a kind of diversion, deflection or hijacking, suitable for undermining the power structures of the spectacle by confronting it with its own ideology in reverse.[43] But in the commercial context of Times Square, it must have seemed all the more strange and surprising.[44]

When a phenomenon acquires thematic relevancy it is subjected to interpretation, discussion, and appropriation. This process involves the reference to specific aspects of the subject's horizon with respect to the actual theme. Accordingly, this takes on a third kind of relevancy – which Schütz designates as "*interpretational relevancy*." Interpretational relevancy occurs when the subject tries to comprehend a strange phenomenon or an atypical situation by bringing in a knowledge of the typicality of familiar objects and events. This act of comparison may lead to a transformation or expansion of the subject's schemata of expression and interpretation as "the thematic-problematic" is transformed into a knowledge that "henceforth will be possessed as unquestioned."[45] Holzer and Kruger aimed at initiating a transformative process of this kind, and this ambition was expressed most poignantly with Kruger's opening statement, "I Am *Not* Trying to Sell

You Anything." By using the technique of *détournement*, Holzer and Kruger staged situations that forced the spectator to revise his or her habitual horizon, paving the way – ideally – for a more critical outlook.

IV SUBLIME ILLUMINATION

As mentioned above, besides appealing to the focused, isolating gaze the works on the Spectacolor Board also made their appeal to a defocused, inclusive gaze. The prime reason was hardly the distracting and stunning chaos of the environment. The fact that the spectator could easily be cajoled into the second, contemplative mode of perception must rather be ascribed to the luminosity of the signboard and the surrounding signscape. This is substantiated by the fact that the lights of "The Great White Way" have continued to spellbind all kinds of people. It has been a source of inspiration for artists long before the *Message to The Public* project. One of the most impressive representations was painted between 1920 and 1922, by the Italian-American painter Joseph Stella. In *The White Way*, from the series *New York Interpreted (The Voice of the City)*, Joseph Stella has condensed the impression of Broadway into an abstract image of energy – pure light and rhythm. Stella's interpretation of the dynamic visuality of the electrified cityscape anticipates Holzer's and Kruger's intervention of the same. Even though Stella translated the dazzle and movement of the lights onto a canvas, whereas Holzer and Kruger utilized electric light – directly – as a raw material, their works converge on the same psychological and aesthetic response to the illuminated metropolis.

In his book *American Technological Sublime* the historian David E. Nye compares the experience of "The Great White Way" from within Times Square to the experience encompassed in Kant's concept of the dynamic sublime in his *Critique of Judgement*.[46] The dynamic sublime concerns the contemplation of overpowering and terrifying natural forces, by a subject who is safe from immediate danger. Nye argues that the sublime, in what he considers its updated, artificial and urbanized variant – "the technological sublime" – is at the core of the awe and wonder, frequently tinged with an element of terror, which Americans have felt when confronted with tremendous architectural and technological achievements such as gargantuan bridges, towering skyscrapers, and spectacularly illuminated cityscapes. Nye points out that in an increasingly de-sacralized world, the technological sublime represents "a way to reinvest the . . . works of men with transcendent significance."[47]

At night the city is reshaped by artificial light. The architecture seems to melt into air, and illumination turns the babel of signs with competing messages into a text without meaningful words, rewriting the city as a sublime landscape. Nye concludes that, "The electrified landscape's meaning lay precisely in the fact that it seemed to go beyond any known codification, . . . it had become a vibrating, indeterminate text that tantalized the eyes and yielded to no definitive reading."[48] Thus, there are two answers to the question of why the artists may have wanted to display their art at Times Square: as the inclusion of Alfred Schütz's theory on transformations in the subject's horizon was intended to clarify, Jenny Holzer and Barbara Kruger had sociological aims. Their projects were

16.3 Joseph Stella: *The White Way I* from *The Voice of the City of New York Interpreted*, 1920–22. Oil and tempera on canvas. Collection of The Newark Museum, Felix Fuld Bequest Fund. Photo: Armen. Courtesy of The Newark Museum/Art Resource, New York.

designed to reshape people's horizon so as to sharpen their awareness of the urban life-world as a framework of significations. The Spectacolor Board offered an opportunity to communicate messages that were both subversive and transformative to a mass audience. However, as Holzer's participation in various art projects in the Times Square area has demonstrated, interventions in the urban fabric make it difficult for artists to maintain their aesthetic and/or critical integrity inasmuch as infiltration cuts both ways. While the artists are infiltrating the public's discourses in order to shake up its meanings and values, their work may in turn become the indirect vehicles of the very same values that they have set out to expose. The *42nd Street Art Project* is a case in point. As the comparison with Joseph Stella's painting *The White Way* suggests, the concept of the sublime pervades Holzer's and Kruger's use of light as material. By inserting their works in what Kruger has called "the high-voltaged spectacle" of Times Square, the works on the Spectacolor Board would become an integrated part of the illuminated cityscape and, thus, a manifestation of the sublime. By this strategy of intervention, the art would not only be transformed into a more efficient means of critical mass communication. It would also appear to go *beyond* codification, exercising an impact on the spectator that transcended the words, the messages, and the question of truth and falsity.

Notes

1 Arthur C. Danto: "Jenny Holzer," in: *The Nation*, February 12, 1990, pp. 213–15.
2 Arthur C. Danto, op. cit., p. 214.
3 For instance, in Hal Foster's article on the two artists: "Subversive Signs," in: *Art in America*, vol. 70, March 1982, pp. 88–92.
4 In the course of time, the electronic signboard has become one of Holzer's favorite media, and today her name is chiefly connected with the application of LED displays. It has become her "signature medium" as Michael Auping has observed. (Michael Auping: "Reading Holzer or Speaking in Tongues," in: Karen Lee Spaulding (ed.), *The Venice Installation*, Buffalo: The Buffalo Fine Arts Academy, 1990, p. 25.) Conversely, Kruger's project for the Spectacolor Board remains exceptional for her *œuvre*. The texts of the individual displays, all written in majuscules, read as follows: "I'm not trying to sell you anything./I just want you to think about what you see when you watch the news on T.V./Wars happen when the men who lead the nations of the world get their egos bruised./One guy says he's the strongest because he has the biggest weapon./His Rival says, 'No, mine is bigger and I won't reduce its size/because then I will be less powerful./And the more powerful I am, the richer I will become.'/These arguments will blow us to bits./We are all being held hostage by a bunch of greedy guys who are worried about/the size of their weapons: worried about their manhood./So I guess the T.V. news is really the hottest sex show going/and a lot cheaper than paying out five bucks a shot at the movie around the corner." Quoted from Kate Linker, *Love for Sale. The Words and Pictures of Barbara Kruger*, New York: Harry N. Abrams Inc., 1990, p. 27.
5 Virginia Maksymowich: "Through the Back Door: Alternative Approaches to Public Art," in: W.J.T. Mitchell, *Art and the Public Sphere*, Chicago and London: The University of Chicago Press, 1992, pp. 147–57; p. 154. Like the works it once displayed, the Spectacolor Board is now history. It has been replaced by more advanced technology, *namely* a SONY Jumbotron screen for video-based commercials. According to Hal Foster, Holzer displayed nine Truisms in a 40-second sequence March 15 to 30, 1982. Hal Foster 1982, op. cit., p. 92. Only six of these are known to me from photographs documenting the work, partly illustrated in Hal Foster's article and partly the catalog: *Jenny Holzer*, Basel: Kunsthalle Basel; Villeurbanne: Nouveau Musée,

1984. They read as follows: "Money Creates Taste," "Often You Should Act Sexless," "Private Property Created Crime," "Torture Is Barbaric," "Fathers Often Use Too Much Force" and "Expiring For Love Is Beautiful But Stupid."

6   Arthur C. Danto, op. cit., p. 213.

7   Virginia Maksymowich, op. cit., p. 154.

8   Brian O'Doherty: "Rauschenberg and the Vernacular Glance," in: *Art in America*, vol. 61, September–October 1973, pp. 82–87; p. 84. Also see Øystein Hjort: "Kunst, kitsch, Überkitsch," in: *Kritik*, no. 88, Copenhagen 1989, pp. 86–103; p. 96.

9   Marjorie Perloff: *Radical Artifice. Writing Poetry in the Age of Media*, Chicago and London: The University of Chicago Press, 1991, p. 93.

10   Italics added. Guy Debord: *La Société du Spectacle* (1967), par. 4. The English translation is quoted from Martin Jay's introduction to Guy Debord's concept of the spectacle in: *Downcast Eyes. The Denigration of Vision in Twentieth-Century French Thought*, Berkeley, Los Angeles, London: University of California Press, 1993, p. 427. For a distinction between the concept of the spectacle and the concept of the sublime, see: Martin Zerlang, *The City Spectacular of the Nineteenth Century*, paper 9, Urbanity & Aesthetics, Copenhagen, 1995. In his book *The Object of Performance. The American Avant-Garde since 1970*, Chicago and London: The University of Chicago Press, 1989, p. 199, Henry M. Sayre briefly mentions Guy Debord's concept of the society of the spectacle in connection with works by Holzer and Kruger displayed in outdoor urban spaces, but without amplifying the point.

11   As Marjorie Perloff has stressed, "even as the 'great divide' between 'high' and 'low' breaks down, the discourses of art and the mass media are not merely exchangeable; rather, theirs is a relationship of enormous variation and complexity." According to Perloff, poetry – and, one could add, the arts in general – has been "shaped by the electronic culture that has produced it. There is today no landscape uncontaminated by sound bytes or computer blips, no mountain peak or lonely valley beyond the reach of the cellular phone and the microcassette player." Marjorie Perloff, op. cit., p. xiii.

12   The problem with James Gardener's approach to Holzer's art is that he takes the spectator's realization of the conceptual framework of her art – the discovery of her messages *as* being Art – as being the whole point of her work, thus denying the content of the texts and the impact of this content on the audience/passers-by any significance whatsoever. James Gardener: *Culture or Trash: A Provocative View of Contemporary Painting, Sculpture, and Other Costly Commodities*, quoted from an excerpt, occasioned by the publication of the book, in: *The New York Times*, Arts Section, January 9, 1994, p. 34.

13   Hal Foster: *The Return of the Real*, Cambridge, Mass.: The MIT Press, 1996, pp. 118–19.

14   Hal Foster 1996, op. cit., pp. 92–93.

15   Hal Foster 1996, op. cit., p. 93. Marjorie Perloff has also expressed doubts as to whether the artists' deconstruction of the discourses of the advertising industry is subject to its own simplifications. She specifically mentions Barbara Kruger's work in which "the alleged deconstruction often seems just as stereotypical as its object." Marjorie Perloff, op. cit., p. 130. Although Perloff's critique of Kruger is just as simplifying as the artist's work appears to her, her conclusion arrives at this point: "Indeed, what the more stringent aesthetic of the 1990s has come to recognize is that, given the advertising industry's own self-consciousness, its ability to undo its own existing clichés . . . art discourse must work, not just to reverse the 'commercial' stereotype, but to undo its own presuppositions about the stereotype in question." Ibid., p. 133.

16   For further details on the event, see Jeffrey Deitch's thorough "Report from Times Square," in: *Art in America*, no. 7, September 1980, pp. 58–63. All data on the exhibition is taken from Deitch's review. My discussion of the development and implications of Holzer's siting of her works is an offshoot of a fruitful discussion during the conference "The Urban Lifeworld" and the points of view and information put forward by Christine Boyer, Richard Plunz, Gwendolyn

Wright, and Andrea Kahn among others. No information on exactly which works Holzer contributed to the *Times Square Show* has been obtainable, but an installation view of the show's so-called "Souvenir Shop" reproduced in Deitch's article reveals that printed sheets of paper with some of her longer texts – possibly from the series *Inflammatory Essays* (1979–1982) or *The Living Series* (1980–1982) – were included in the show.

17   Jeffrey Deitch, op. cit., pp. 60–61.

18   Ada Louise Huxtable: "Re-inventing Times Square: 1900," in: William R. Taylor (ed.): *Inventing Times Square. Commerce and Culture at the Crossroads of the World*, New York: Sage Russell Foundation, 1991, pp. 356–70.

19   Jeffrey Deitch, op. cit., p. 60.

20   For a discussion of the leftist assumptions concerning "the other" so prevalent in contemporary art, see, Hal Foster 1996, op. cit., pp. 173ff.

21   Roberta Smith: "A 24-Hour-a-Day Show, on Gaudy, Bawdy 42d Street," in: *The New York Times*, July 30, 1993, p. C26. According to Roberta Smith's review, the following texts were displayed: "Go Where People Sleep and See If They're Safe," "Raise Boys and Girls the Same," "What Urge Will Save Us Now That Sex Won't" and "Boredom Makes You Do Crazy Things." The brochure about the *42nd Street Art Project*, published by Creative Time, Inc., New York 1993, includes several illustrations of theater marquees with texts by Jenny Holzer: "A Man Can't Know What It's Like To Be A Mother," "Slobby Thinking Gets Worse Over Time," "You Are Trapped On The Earth So You Will Explode," "It Is In Your Self-Interest To Find A Way To Be Very Tender," "Murder Has Its Sexual Side," " Hiding Your Motives Is Despicable," and "Categorizing Fear Is Calming."

22   Hal Foster 1996, op. cit., note 41, pp. 281–82. The information brochure about the *42nd Street Art Project* actually emphasizes that this was indeed the purpose. The introduction states that, "The redevelopment of Times Square and 42nd Street aims to restore some of the prosperity and luster of the days when the area had more theater inside the buildings than out. To inaugurate part of the effort, several parties came together and asked over twenty artists to create works for spaces left vacant by the process of rebuilding . . . 42nd Street can be a symbol of the decadence of our culture. But in its fearsomeness and danger, can we also find hope? We can change the order of things, we can redevelop – and artists, with wit, wisdom and passion, can help us do it." For more details on the city- and state-aided redevelopment plans, see: Ada Louise Huxtable, op. cit., pp. 361–62.

23   Hal Foster 1996, op. cit., p. 197.

24   Michael Auping: *Jenny Holzer*, New York: Universe, 1992, p. 26.

25   In an interview, Holzer has explained the origin of *The Truisms* as follows: "[The reading list] included numberless books, all of which were heavies, so just the prospect of wading through them was enough to make me do Jenny Holzer's *Reader's Digest* version of Western and Eastern thought. I loved all these great thoughts on Western culture, but figured I was reasonably bright and reasonably well educated, and if I couldn't plow through it, certainly a lot of other people couldn't either. I realized the stuff was important and profound, so I thought maybe I could translate these things into a language that was accessible. The result was the 'Truisms'." Jenny Holzer, in Bruce Ferguson: "Wordsmith. An Interview with Jenny Holzer," in: *Art in America*, no. 12, December 1986, pp. 109–15, 153; p. 111.

26   Jenny Holzer, in: Bruce Ferguson, op. cit., p. 111. The poster is illustrated in ibid., p. 18.

27   Jenny Holzer's characterization of downtown Manhattan in the late 1970s as a "postering society" indicates that she had familiarized herself with the possibilities and the efficiency of the poster as a means of communication adapted to the urban environment. Holzer quoted in: Michael Auping, op. cit., p. 78.

28   Barbara Kruger: "An 'Unsightly' Site," in: Barbara Kruger: *Remote Control. Power, Cultures, and the World of Appearances*, Cambridge, Mass.: The MIT Press, 1993, pp. 16–19, 17–18.

29   Barbara Kruger, op. cit., pp. 16–17.

30   William R. Taylor: "Introduction" to: William R. Taylor (ed.): *Inventing Times Square. Commerce and Culture at the Crossroads of the World*, New York: Sage Russell Foundation, 1991, p. xii.

31   William Leach: "Commercial Aesthetics. Introductory Essay," in: William R. Taylor (ed.): *Inventing Times Square. Commerce and Culture at the Crossroads of the World*, New York: Sage Russell Foundation, 1991, pp. 234–42; p. 234, p. 238. According to O.J. Gude, one of the pioneers of electric advertising, the illuminated signboard produces such a hypnotic effect on people that it virtually forces its messages upon them so that, ". . . everybody must read them, and absorb them, and absorb the advertiser's lesson willingly or unwillingly." O.J. Gude: "Art and Advertising Joined by Electricity," in: *Signs of the Times*, November 1912, p. 3. Quoted from: William Leach, ibid., p. 236. As to the content of the signs, there is hardly anything as apt for stopping people as the unexpected confrontation with existential issues. Holzer has emphasized this in an interview, "If you want to reach a general audience, it's not art issues that are going to compel them to stop on their way to lunch, it has to be life issues." Jenny Holzer, quoted from: Michael Auping, op. cit., p. 16. As an example, she actually refers to the anonymous warning against leprosy mentioned above: "It wasn't art as far as I know, but I was impressed with the idea that, if a text says something out of the ordinary, people take notice." Jenny Holzer quoted from: ibid., p. 21.

32   Ada Louise Huxtable, op. cit., pp. 358–59.

33   Italics added. Jenny Holzer quoted from Jeanne Siegel: "Jenny Holzer's Language Games," in: *Arts Magazine*, December 1986, pp. 64–68; p. 65.

34   Walter Benjamin elaborates his concept of "eine Dialektik im Stillstand" in his analysis of the dialectical structure of the baroque allegory in his dissertation *Ursprung des deutschen Trauerspiels*, in: Walter Benjamin: *Gesammelte Schriften*, Rolf Tiedemann and Hermann Schweppenhäuser (eds), Frankfurt am Main: Suhrkamp Verlag, 1974, vol. I.1. Particularly apt in the context of visual aesthetics is Dorthe Jørgensen's designation of this Benjaminian concept as referring to the experience of a perceptual doubleness or dichotomy of closeness/ distance, dream/reality, transitoriness/eternity, materiality/abstraction, destruction/redemption, phenomenon/idea. Dorthe Jørgensen, *Nær og fjern – spor af en erfaringsontologi hos Walter Benjamin*, Århus: Modtryk, 1990, p. 7.

35   In the essay *Über einige Motive bei Baudelaire* (1939) Walter Benjamin mentions the affinity of shock aesthetics with the perception of urban reality. He defines the shock effects of photography and especially film, which destroy the aura, as an aesthetic formalization of perceptions in the form of shocks, i.e. of an urban perception, threatened by the sensory overload of rapidly changing impressions. Walter Benjamin: "Über einige Motive bei Baudelaire," in: *Gesammelte Schriften*, Rolf Tiedemann and Hermann Schweppenhäuser (eds), Frankfurt am Main: Suhrkamp Verlag, 1974, vol. I.2, pp. 630–31. In the article "At tage ved lære af Times Square. Nogle betragtninger over forholdet mellem storbyen og samtidskunsten," in: *Kultur & Klasse*, no. 82, vol. 24, no. 2, 1996, pp. 87–115, I have analyzed the shock of illumination that Holzer's *Truisms* are ideally intended to release with reference to Walter Benjamin's concepts of distraction and concentration.

36   Walter Benjamin: "Das Kunstwerk im Zeitalter seiner technischen Reproduzierbarkeit" (2nd edition), in: Walter Benjamin, *Gesammelte Schriften*, Rolf Tiedemann and Hermann Schweppenhäuser (ed.), Frankfurt am Main: Suhrkamp Verlag, 1974, vol. I.2, pp. 471–508.

37   Alfred Schütz: "Some Structures of the Life-World," in: Thomas Luckmann (ed.), *Phenomenology and Sociology. Selected Readings*, New York: Penguin Books, 1978, pp. 257–74; pp. 257–58. See also Peter Madsen's introductory essay, "The Urban Lifeworld. Approaches to the Analysis of Urban Experience."

38   Alfred Schütz, op. cit., p. 264. In an introduction to Alfred Schütz, Aron Gurwitsch has stressed the importance of this concept, "With his notion of 'stock of knowledge at hand' Schütz . . . made an important contribution toward *further elucidating our specific familiarity with the world of*

daily experience, a familiarity that Husserl distinguished from scientific knowledge, especially in the modern sense. That the world of common sense is taken for granted – not only its existence, but *also the way in which it is interpreted* – is a consequence and another expression of un-questioned acceptance of the 'stock of knowledge at hand' " (italics added). Aron Gurwitsch: "Introduction," in: Alfred Schütz: *Collected Papers. III: Studies in Phenomenological Philosophy*, I. Schütz (ed.), The Hague: Martinus Nijhoff, 1966, p. xviii.

39   Alfred Schütz, op. cit., p. 260.

40   Albert Schütz. op. cit., p. 265.

41   Alfred Schütz, op. cit., p. 258.

42   Alfred Schütz, op. cit., p. 265.

43   Martin Jay, op. cit., p. 424.

44   The expectation that it might still be possible, within the field of advertising, to provoke a kind of mental shock that vanguard art no longer seemed capable of initiating may very well have been a contributory cause of the artists' intervention of the urban commercial textscape.

45   Alfred Schütz, op. cit., p. 268.

46   Immanuel Kant: *Kritik der Urteilskraft*, Zweites Buch. "Analytik des Erhabenen," § 24 and § 28, in: Immanuel Kant: *Werke in sechs Bände*, Wilhelm Wieschedel (ed.), vol. V, Darmstadt: Wissenschaftliche Buchgesellschaft, 1983.

47   That the artifact in question is a result of consumer capitalism, as in the case of Times Square, does not diminish its power to evoke a notion of the sublime. David E. Nye: *American Technological Sublime*, Cambridge, Mass.: The MIT Press, 1994, p. xiii.

48   David E. Nye, op. cit., p. 196.

Index